Lena Nogossek-Raithel
Dis/ability in Mark

Beihefte zur Zeitschrift für die neutestamentliche Wissenschaft

Edited by
Knut Backhaus, Matthias Konradt, Judith Lieu,
Laura Nasrallah, Jens Schröter, and Gregory E. Sterling

Volume 263

Lena Nogossek-Raithel

Dis/ability in Mark

Representations of Body and Healing in the Gospel Narrative

DE GRUYTER

Dissertationsschrift, Humboldt-Universität zu Berlin (Theologische Fakultät), 2022.

ISBN 978-3-11-221525-8
e-ISBN (PDF) 978-3-11-118333-6
e-ISBN (EPUB) 978-3-11-118483-8
ISSN 0171-6441

Library of Congress Control Number: 2023940085

Bibliographic information published by the Deutsche Nationalbibliothek
The Deutsche Nationalbibliothek lists this publication in the Deutsche Nationalbibliografie; detailed bibliographic data are available on the internet at http://dnb.dnb.de.

© 2025 Walter de Gruyter GmbH, Berlin/Boston
This volume is text- and page-identical with the hardback published in 2023.
Printing and binding: CPI books GmbH, Leck

www.degruyter.com

Acknowledgments

This book is a revised version of the dissertation titled "Dis/ability in the Markan Healing Narratives," which was accepted by Humboldt-Universität zu Berlin in the winter semester of 2021/22, and successfully defended in the summer semester of 2022. Some passages have been slightly adapted in terms of language and content for this publication. As the following section is written from the heart, it is presented in my native language, German.

Die Arbeit wurde finanziell und ideell vom Evangelischen Studienwerk Villigst gefördert. Großer Dank gebührt den engagierten, ermutigenden und wertschätzenden Menschen um die Villigster Treppe herum, die vor allem die erste Phase der Promotionszeit mit Spiel und Spaß bereichert haben.

Ich danke Prof. Dr. Jens Schröter, der diese Arbeit neugierig und hilfsbereit von den ersten Ideenskizzen an begleitet hat. Er hatte immer eine offene Tür für meine Fragen und Probleme und hat mit sachlicher Kritik und fachkundiger Weitsicht geholfen, Schwerpunkte zu setzen und Kapitel abzurunden. Nicht zuletzt seinem Zuspruch – insbesondere auf den letzten Metern – habe ich es zu verdanken, dass diese Arbeit schlussendlich so zustande kam. Sein Forschungskolloquium bot zudem Raum und Zeit für erste gewagte Thesen, kritische Diskussionen sowie praktische und motivierende Hinweise. Für die Gestaltung dieses Schutzraums und die Offenheit gebührt insbesondere und stellvertretend für die wechselnden Teilnehmer*innen PD Dr. Christine Jacobi und Dr. Konrad Schwarz großer Dank, ebenso wie Prof. Dr. Joseph Verheyden, Prof. Dr. Tobias Nicklas und Prof. Dr. Christine Gerber, welche die Arbeit in größeren Forschungsrunden mit neuen Perspektiven und frischen Ideen weiter brachten.

Ich danke Prof. Dr. Philip van der Eijk und seiner montäglichen Runde an versierten Philolog*innen und Expert*innen für antike Kultur für die kritischen Nachfragen und hilfsbereite Expertise, die mir immer wieder aufs Neue die Vielfältigkeit antiker Texte nahegebracht hat. Seine und ihre Hinweise haben an vielen Stellen für die nötige Präzision und Abgrenzung gesorgt.

Ich danke dem Verlag de Gruyter und den Herausgeber*innen der Reihe BWNT für die Aufnahme meiner Arbeit und Alice Meroz und Dr. Katrin Hudey für die stets hilfsbereite und freundliche Betreuung des Manuskripts.

Ich danke den Menschen, die in den vergangenen Jahren das Leben um die drei Schreibtische mitgestaltet haben, an denen diese Arbeit entstand: Frau Graffmann und Herrn Bomba an der Augustana Hochschule in Neuendettelsau für die „bibliographische Betreuung" am Anfang und Ende der Arbeitszeit; meinen Freund*innen für immer ausreichend Ablenkung und Anteilnahme auf die unterschiedlichsten Weisen, insbesondere den Pandas, Erdmuth und Lydia für all die bewegenden Worte; meinen Geschwistern Tine und David und ihren Familien für sprachliche und technische Hilfe, sowie Zusammenhalt und Zuspruch.

Ich danke meinen Schwiegereltern Peter und Ute Raithel für den ruhigen Hor(s)t, den sie ihren Enkelkindern und auch mir in trubeligen Diss-Zeiten bereitet haben.

Ich danke meinen Eltern Marianne und Paul Nogossek für die Freiheit, kritisch zu sein und nichts zu müssen, die immer interessierte Frage nach „der Arbeit" und die maßgeschneiderte Unterstützung von Kinderbetreuung, über In-Design bis Zur-Verteidigung-Fahren. Meiner Mutter danke ich für das Lesen-Lehren und ihre „Matrizen", meinem Vater danke ich für das „dumdi-dumdi-dumdi-dum".

Ich danke meinem Mann Jan Raithel dafür, dass er nicht müde wurde, mit mir Freiräume zu schaffen und diese bestmöglich zu gestalten. Er hat mich auf vielfältige Weise unterstützt – vor allem im abenteuerlichen ersten Trimester im letzten „Trimester".

Ich danke meinen Kindern, die alles aus allernächster Nähe miterlebt haben, ohne sich dafür entschieden zu haben. Ihnen ist diese Arbeit gewidmet. Ihr seid das Beste überhaupt. Ihr!

Lena Nogossek-Raithel
Nürnberg, im Juli 2023

Contents

Abbreviations —— IX

1 Introduction —— 1
1.1 Prelude —— 1
1.2 Dis/ability Studies —— 1
1.3 Dis/ability History —— 3
1.4 Dis/ability and Biblical Studies —— 5
1.5 Healing Narratives —— 9
1.6 Dis/ability in Mark's Healing Narratives —— 11
1.7 Scope of This Study —— 13
1.8 Terminological Considerations —— 14
1.9 Brief Summary and Outline —— 15

2 The Markan Summaric Accounts as Showcases for Markan Dis/ability —— 20
2.1 Mark 1:32–34 —— 21
2.2 Mark 1:39 —— 28
A In Focus: Markan Images of Sickness and Possession —— 30
2.3 Mark 3:7–12 —— 33
2.4 Mark 6:5 and 6:13 —— 38
2.5 Mark 6:53–56 —— 42
2.6 Summaric Accounts as Showcases of Dis/ability and Literary and Theological Benchmarks —— 46

3 Mark 1: Jesus in a Dis/abled World —— 51
3.1 Mark 1:21–28: Antagonistic Authority and Identity —— 52
B In Focus: Mark's Jesus and Opposing Forces (with Consideration of 3:20–35) —— 57
3.2 Mark 1:29–31: The Continuous Change of the Mother-in-Law —— 70
3.3 Mark 1:40–45: The Tangible Healing of a Skin-Sensitive Man —— 81
C In Focus: Mark's Healing Touches —— 90
D In Focus: Silencing in Mark's Healing Narratives —— 101
E In Focus: Healing Spaces in Mark—Synagogues, Houses, and In-Betweens —— 104
3.4 Conclusion and Interpretation of Dis/ability in Mark 1 —— 106

4 Mark 2:1–3:6: A Plot in Motion —— 109
4.1 Mark 2:1–12: The Forgiven (Im-)Mobile Man —— 110
F In Focus: Markan Healing and Forgiveness (with Consideration of 9:42–48) —— 121
4.2 Mark 3:1–6: A Withered Hand and Petrified Hearts —— 128
4.3 Conclusion and Interpretation of Dis/ability in Mark 2:1–3:6 —— 144

5 Mark 5: The Physical Protagonist between Pathologization and *Pistis* —— 146
5.1 Mark 5:1–20: Possessive Spirits —— 146
5.2 Mark 5:21–43: Intercalated Healings of Two Daughters —— 159
G In Focus: Mark's Relational Pistis —— 176
H In Focus: Mark's Holistic Salvation —— 179
I In Focus: The Markan Jesus' Dynamic Identity —— 181
5.3 Conclusion and Interpretation of Dis/ability in Mark 5 —— 185

6 Mark 7:24–37: Transitional Dis/ability —— 188
6.1 Mark 7:24–30: Syrophoenician Negotiations —— 188
6.2 Mark 7:31–37: Intelligible Communication —— 195
6.3 Conclusion and Interpretation of Dis/ability in Mark 7 —— 212

7 Mark 8–10: Beyond Dis/ability —— 214
7.1 Introductions: Sensory and Spiritual Comprehension —— 216
7.2 Images of Dis/ability —— 223
7.3 The Healings —— 242
7.4 Conclusion and Interpretation of Dis/ability in Mark 8–10 —— 252

8 Conclusion: This Is (Not) the End … —— 256
8.1 Mark as a Gospel of Dis/ability and Relational *Pistis* —— 256
8.2 The Physical Protagonist and His Dynamic Identity —— 260
8.3 Beyond Binaries: Holistic Salvation —— 262
8.4 Future Prospects —— 266

Bibliography —— 269

Index —— 315

Index of Biblical and Ancient Sources —— 319

Abbreviations

Unless noted below, abbreviations follow The SBL Handbook of Style for Biblical Studies and Related Disciplines, 2nd ed. (Atlanta, GA: SBL Press, 2014). References to Mishnah, Talmud, and Related Literature follow the Guidelines of the Encyclopedia of the Bible and Its Reception (Berlin/ Boston, MA: de Gruyter, 2009–).

Acts Pet.	Acts of Peter
Acts Thom.	Acts of Thomas
Add Est	Additions to Esther
Aelian, *Nat. an.*	Aelian, De natura animalium
Aelian, *Var. hist.*	Aelian, Varia historia
Aeschylus, *Prom.*	Aeschylus, Prometheus vinctus
Aesop, *Fab.*	Aesop, Fabulae
Aëtius, *Tetrabibl.*	Aëtius of Amida, Tetrabiblos
Alexander Aphrodisias, *Feb.*	Alexander of Aphrodisias, De febris
Alexander Med., *Lumbr.*	Alexander Trallianus Med., Epistula de lumbricis
Amm.	Ammianus Marcellinus, Res gestae
Anth. Gr.	Anthologia Graeca
AP	Anonymus Parisinus, De morbis acutis et chroniis
Appian, *Bell. civ.*	Appian, Bella civilia
Apuleius, *Apol.*	Apuleius, Apologia (Pro se de magia)
Apuleius, *Flor.*	Apuleius, Florida
Aretaeus, *Sign. acut.*	Aretaeus, De causis et signis acutorum morborum
Aretaeus, *Sign. diut.*	Aretaeus, De causis et signis diuturnorum morborum
Aristides, *Or.*	Aelius Aristides, Orationes
Aristophanes, *Pax*	Aristophanes, Pax
Aristophanes, *Thesm.*	Aristophanes, Thesmophoriazusae
Aristotle, *Eth. Nic.*	Aristoteles, Ethica nicomachea
Aristotle, *Hist. An.*	Aristotle, Historia animalium
Aristotle, *Ins.*	Aristotle, De Insomniis
Aristotle, *Metaph.*	Aristotle, Metaphysica
Arrian, *Epict. diss.*	Arrian, Epicteti dissertationes
Artemidorus, *Onir.*	Artemidorus Daldianus, Onirocritica
Athenaeus, *Deipn.*	Athenaeus, Deipnosophistae
Caelius, *Acut.*	Caelius Aurelianus, Celeres passiones
Caelius, *Chron.*	Caelius Aurelianus, Tardae passiones
Caesar, *Bell. civ.*	Caesar, Bellum civile
Celsus, *Med.*	Aulus Cornelius Celsus, De medicina
CH, *Acut.*	Corpus Hippocraticum, De ratione victus in morbis acutis
CH, *Aer.*	Corpus Hippocraticum, De aere, aquis, locis
CH, *Aff.*	Corpus Hippocraticum, De affectionibus
CH, *Alim.*	Corpus Hippocraticum, De alimento
CH, *Aph.*	Corpus Hippocraticum, Aphorismata
CH, *Arte*	Corpus Hippocraticum, De arte

CH, *Artic.*	Corpus Hippocraticum, De articulis reponendis
CH, *Cap. vuln.*	Corpus Hippocraticum, De capitis vulneribus
CH, *Carn.*	Coprus Hippocraticum, De carnibus
CH, *Coac.*	Corpus Hippocraticum, Praenotiones coacae
CH, *EDMHI*	Corpus Hippocraticum, Letter to Hippocrates by Democritus
CH, *Epid.*	Corpus Hippocraticum, Epidemiae
CH, *Flat.*	Corpus Hippocraticum, De flatibus
CH, *Fract.*	Corpus Hippocraticum, De fracturis
CH, *Genit.*	Corpus Hippocraticum, Genitalia
CH, *Hum.*	Corpus Hippocraticum, De humoribus
CH, *Iudic.*	Corpus Hippocraticum, De iudicationibus
CH, *Loc. hom.*	Corpus Hippocraticum, De locis in homine
CH, *Mochl.*	Corpus Hippocraticum, Mochlichon
CH, *Morb.*	Corpus Hippocraticum, De morbis
CH, *Morb. mul.*	Corpus Hippocraticum, De morbis mulierum
CH, *Morb. sacr.*	Corpus Hippocraticum, De morbo sacro
CH, *Mul.*	Corpus Hippocraticum, De mulierum affectibus
CH, *Nat. hom.*	Corpus Hippocraticum, De natura hominis
CH, *Prog.*	Corpus Hippocraticum, Prognostica
CH, *Prorrh.*	Corpus Hippocraticum, Prorrhetica
CH, *Superf.*	Corpus Hippocraticum, De superfetatione
CH, *Vet. med.*	Corpus Hippocraticum, De vetere medicina
CH, *Vict.*	Corpus Hippocraticum, De victu
CH, *Virg.*	Corpus Hippocraticum, De virginum morbis
CH, *Visu*	Corpus Hippocraticum, De visu
Cicero, *Div.*	Cicero, De divinatione
Cicero, *Leg.*	Cicero, De legibus
Clement of Alexandria, *Paed.*	Clement of Alexandria, Paedagogus
Clement of Alexandria, *Strom.*	Clement of Alexandria, Stromateis
Diodorus, *Bib. hist.*	Diodorus Siculus, Bibliotheca historica
Dioscorides, *Mat. Med.*	Dioscorides Pedanius, De materia medica
Epictetus, *Ditr.*	Epictetus, Ditribai (Dissertationes)
Eup.	Eupolemus
Euripides, *Suppl.*	Euripides, Supplices
Eusebius, *Hier*	Eusebius, Against Hierocles
Galen, *Alim. fac.*	Galen, De alimentorum facultatibus
Galen, *Ars med.*	Galen, Ars medica
Galen, *Caus. puls.*	Galen, De causis pulsuum
Galen, *Comm. CH Aph.*	Galen, Hippocratis aphorismi et Galeni in eos commentarii
Galen, *Comm. CH Epid.*	Galen, Commentarii in Hippocratis Epidemiarum
Galen, *Comp. Med.*	Galen, De compositione medicamentorum
Galen, *Cur. rat. sect.*	Galen, De curandi ratione per venae sectionem
Galen, *Def. Med.*	Galen, Definitiones medicae
Galen, *Die. Decr.*	Galen, De diebus decretoriis

Galen, *Diff. Febr.*	Galen, De differentiis febrium
Galen, *Diff. Morb.*	Galen, De differentiis morborum
Galen, *Fac. nat.*	Galen, De facultatibus naturalibus
Galen, *Glauc. meth. med.*	Galen, Ad Glauconem de medendi methodo
Galen, *Loc. aff.*	Galen, De locis affectis
Galen, *Marc.*	Galen, De Marcore
Galen, *Meth. med.*	Galen, Methodi medendi
Galen, *Morb. Caus.*	Galen, De morborum causis
Galen, *Puer. epil.*	Galen, Puero epileptico consilium
Galen, *San. tu.*	Galen, De sanitate tuenda
Galen, *Simpl. med. temp.*	Galen, De simplicium medicamentorum temperamentis et facultatibus
Galen, *Subf. empir.*	Galen, De subfiguratio(ne) empirica
Galen, *Usu part.*	Galen, De usu partium
Galen, *Ven. sect. Er.*	Galen, De venae sectione adversus Erasistratum
Galen, *Vict. Att.*	Galen, De victu attenuante
Gos. Naz.	Gospel of the Nazarenes
Gos. Thom.	Gospel of Thomas
Herodotus, *Hist.*	Herodotus, Historiae
Hesiod, *Op.*	Hesiod, Opera et dies
Homer, *Il.*	Homer, Ilias
Homer, *Od.*	Homer, Odyssea
Iamblichus, *Bab.*	Iamblichus, Babyloniaca
Iamblichus, *Vita Pyth.*	Iamblichus of Chalcis, De vita Pythagorica
Isidore, *Ethym.*	Isidore of Sevilla, Etymologiae
JosAs	Joseph and Aseneth
Josephus, *A.J.*	Josephus, Antiquitates Iudaicae
Josephus, *B.J.*	Josephus, Bellum Iudaicum
Josephus, *C. Ap.*	Josephus, Contra Apionem
Josephus, *Vita*	Josephus, Vita
LAB	Liber antiquitatum biblicarum (Pseudo-Philo)
Lactantius, *Opif.*	Lactantius, De opificio Dei
Lucian, *Abdic.*	Lucian, Abdicatus
Lucian, *Alex.*	Lucian, Alexander (Pseudomantis)
Lucian, *Merc. cond.*	Lucian, De mercede conductis
Lucian, *Peregr.*	Lucian, De morte Peregrini
Lucian, *Philops.*	Lucian, Philopseudes
Lucian, *Tim.*	Lucian, Timon
Lucian, *Tox.*	Lucian, Toxaris
Maximus Tyrius, *Diss.*	Maximus of Tyre, Dissertationes
Meletius Med., *Nat. hom.*	Meletius Med., De natura hominis
Nonnus, *Dion.*	Nonnus of Panopolis, Dionysiaca
Origen, *Cels.*	Origen, Contra Celsum
Ovid, *Met.*	Ovid, Metamorphoses
Paulus Aegineta	Paul of Aegineta, Epitomes iatrikes biblia hepta
Pausanias, *Descr.*	Pausanias, Graeciae descriptio

Philo, *Abr.*	Philo of Alexandria, De Abrahamo
Philo, *Agr.*	Philo of Alexandria, De agricultura
Philo, *Cher.*	Philo of Alexandria, De cherubim
Philo, *Conf.*	Philo of Alexandria, De confusione linguarum
Philo, *Decal.*	Philo of Alexandria, De decalogo
Philo, *Deus*	Philo of Alexandria, Quod Deus sit immutabilis
Philo, *Ebr.*	Philo of Alexandria, De ebrietate
Philo, *Flacc.*	Philo of Alexandria, In Flaccum
Philo, *Fug.*	Philo of Alexandria, De fuga et inventione
Philo, *Gig.*	Philo of Alexandria, De gigantibus
Philo, *Ios.*	Philo of Alexandria, De Iosepho
Philo, *Leg.*	Philo of Alexandria, Legum allegoriae
Philo, *Legat.*	Philo of Alexandria, Legatio ad Gaium
Philo, *Migr.*	Philo of Alexandria, De migratione Abrahami
Philo, *Mos.*	Philo of Alexandria, De vita Mosis
Philo, *Opif.*	Philo of Alexandria, De opificio mundi
Philo, *Plant.*	Philo of Alexandria, De plantatione
Philo, *Post.*	Philo of Alexandria, De posteritate Caini
Philo, *Praem.*	Philo of Alexandria, De praemiis et poenis
Philo, *Sacr.*	Philo of Alexandria, De sacrificiis Abelis et Caini
Philo, *Sobr.*	Philo of Alexandria, De sobrietate
Philo, *Somn.*	Philo of Alexandria, De somniis 1, 2
Philo, *Spec.*	Philo of Alexandria, De specialibus legibus
Philodemus, *Rhet.*	Philodemus of Gadara, Volumina rhetorica
Philostratus, *Her.*	Flavius Philostratus, Heroicus
Philostratus, *Vit. Apoll.*	Flavius Philostratus, Vita Apollonii
Pindar, *Nem.*	Pindar, Nemeonikai
Plato, *Apol.*	Plato, Apologia
Plato, *Leg.*	Plato, Leges
Plato, *Men.*	Plato, Menon
Plato, *Phaedr.*	Plato, Phaedrus
Plato, *Resp.*	Plato, Respublica
Plato, *Symp.*	Plato, Symposium
Plato, *Theaet.*	Plato, Theaetetus
Plato, *Tim.*	Plato, Timaeus
Pliny the Elder, *Nat.*	Pliny the Elder, Naturalis historia
Pliny the Younger, *Ep.*	Pliny the Younger, Epistulae
Pliny the Younger, *Pan.*	Pliny the Younger, Panegyricus
Plutarch, *Adul. amic.*	Plutarch, Quomodo adulator ab amico internoscatur
Plutarch, *Alex.*	Plutarch, Alexander
Plutarch, *Alex. fort.*	Plutarch, De Alexandri magni fortuna aut virtute
Plutarch, *An. corp.*	Plutarch, Animine an corporis affectiones sint peiores
Plutarch, *Exil.*	Plutarch, De exilo
Plutarch, *Fort.*	Plutarch, De fortuna
Plutarch, *Mar.*	Plutarch, Marius
Plutarch, *Marc.*	Plutarch, Marcellus

Plutarch, *Mor.*	Plutarch, Moralia
Plutarch, *Quest. conv.*	Plutarch, Questionum convivialum
Plutarch, *Sera*	Plutarch, De sera numinis vindicta
Plutarch, *Sull.*	Plutarch, Sulla
Plutarch, *Tim.*	Plutarch, Timoleon
Plutarch, *Tu. san.*	Plutarch, De tuenda sanitate praecepta
Polybius, *Hist.*	Polybius, Historiae
Pr Azar	Prayer of Azariah (AddDan)
Procopius, *Bell.*	Procopius, De bellis
Ps. Aristotle, *Probl.*	Pseudo Aristotle, Problemata
Pss. Sol.	Psalms of Solomon
Ptolemy, *Tetrabibl.*	Claudius Ptolemy, Tetrabiblos
Quintilian, *Inst.*	Quintilian, Institutio oratoria
Seneca the Elder, *Contr.*	Seneca (the Elder), Controversiae
Seneca the Younger, *Apol.*	Seneca (the Younger), Apolocyntosis
Seneca the Younger, *Ben.*	Seneca (the Younger), De beneficiis
Seneca the Younger, *Ep.*	Seneca (the Younger), Epistulae morales
SHA	Scriptores Historiae Augustae
Sib.	Sibylline Oracles
Sophocles, *Ant.*	Sophocles, Antigone
Sophocles, *Oed. tyr.*	Sophocles, Oedipus tyrannus
Soranus, *Gyn.*	Soranus of Ephesus, Gynaecia
Strabo, *Geogr.*	Strabo, Geographica
Suetonius, *Galb.*	Suetonius, Galba
Suetonius, *Vesp.*	Suetonius, Vespasian
T.Ab.	Testament of Abraham
T.Ash.	Testament of Asher
T.Benj.	Testament of Benjamin
T.Dan	Testament of Dan
T.Jud.	Testament of Judah
T.Levi	Testament of Levi
T.Mos.	Testament of Moses
T.Naph.	Testament of Naphtali
T.Reu.	Testament of Reuben
T.Sim.	Testament of Simeon
T.Sol.	Testament of Solomon
Tacitus, *Ann.*	Tacitus, Annales
Tacitus, *Hist.*	Tacitus, Historiae
Theophilius, *Autol.*	Theophilius, Ad Autolycum
Thuc.	Thucydides, Historiae
Vettius, *Anth.*	Vettius Valens, Anthologiae
Xenophon, *Cyr.*	Xenophon, Cyropaedia
Xenophon, *Mem.*	Xenophon, Memorabilia

XIV — Abbreviations

	1QS	Rule of the Community (Serek haYaḥad)
1Q33	1QM	War Scroll (Milḥamah)
	CD	Cairo Genzia copy of the Damaskus Document
1Q20	1QapGen[ar]	(Aramaic) Genesis Apocryphon
11Q11	11QapocrPs[a]	Apocryphal Psalms[a]
1Q28[a]	1QS[a]	Rule of the Congregation (appendix a to 1QS)
4Q265	4QMiscellaneous Rules	Miscellaneous Rules
4Q266	4QD[a]	Damascus Document[a]
4Q269	4QD[d]	Damascus Document[d]
4Q270	4QD[e]	Damascus Document[e]
4Q272	4QD[g]	Damascus Document[g]
4Q274	4QTohorot A	Tohorot A
4Q394	4QMMT[a]	Miqṣat Ma'aśe Ha-Torah[a]
4Q396	4QMMT[c]	Miqṣat Ma'aśe Ha-Torah[c]
4Q444	4QIncantation	Incantation
4Q510	4QShir[a]	Shirot[a] or Songs of the Sage[a]
4Q511	4QShir[b]	Shirot[b] or Songs of the Sage[b]
4Q560	4QExorcism[ar]	Magical Booklet
8Q5	8QHymn	Hymn
11Q5	11QPs[a]	Psalms Scroll[a]
11Q19	11QT[a]	Temple Scroll[a]

1 Introduction

1.1 Prelude

> Mark hinges Jesus's claim to authority almost exclusively on the healing miracles in the beginning of his gospel. Mark is completely dependent on disabled characters to get his overarching message across. Without any deaf, blind, lame, leprous, and possessed people to heal, Jesus's special character, in fact, his divinity, is not revealed at all. Disability is the crutch the narrative needs in order to show that God is great.[1]

Surprisingly, there are no comprehensive studies that investigate the characterization, function, and occurrence of these Markan "crutches." Rather, ignorant, discriminative, anachronistic, or simply fragmentary interpretations dominate the exegetical landscape in regard to an analysis of the Markan display of "deviating bodies."[2] The following study aims to change that.

1.2 Dis/ability Studies

Since the 1970s, disability studies have been concerned with the construction and discursivity of bodies and disability.[3] Emerging from the Anglo-Saxon political disability movements, the now transdisciplinary and internationalized academic discipline considers disability a historically and socially specific and changing phenomenon. Critical and cultural disability studies, particularly, approach disability as an analytical category.[4] As such, it is not a self-evident property of the individual

---

[1] Solevåg 2018. 52.
[2] This terminology refers in the following to the *biblical* descriptions of physical difference according to an implied norm on textual basis. The *historical* and *narrative* evaluation of these bodies and physical states will be regarded in each chapter. Thereby, a modern equalization of this term is neither intended nor implied (see below).
[3] Cf., e.g., Albrecht; Seelman; Bury in Albrecht; Seelman; Bury (ed.) 2001; Goodley 2011.
[4] Each approach has its own objectives and methodologies: The *medical model* diagnoses and pathologizes the physical and biological "natural facts" of the individual body according to a modern, predominantly Western medical framework and promotes medical intervention. The *social model* focuses on the social reactions, implications, and limitations in response to "unacceptable" bodies and the undercurrent cultural patterns of interpretation and evaluation. While the prior is criticized for its disregard of social structures (i.e., exclusion, marginalization, and "disablement"), the latter differs between impairment (as embodied difference, often a structural or functional physical, cognitive or sensory disruption of an individual) and disability (as the structural discrimination and limitation by society in response to physical deviance); cf. Dederich 2007. 57. In addition,

body but a product "of symbolic orders, bodily practices and social institutions"[5] and moreover an integral mode of the discourses through which it emerges.[6] This perspective opens the investigation of body evaluation, "normalization," classification, expectation, and regulation to its overarching cultural, historical, and social (transformational) patterns, where not only the "deviating" body and its societal "disabling" are of interest but also the highly variable normalizing body scheme in itself. By addressing the discursive practices of pathologization, labeling, and interpretation and their contingent social and cultural categorizations and assignments (*what* is "impaired, disabled, normal..."), the taxonomies, structures, and conventions are also called into question (*how* and *why* this is labeled "impaired, disabled, normal...").[7]

Thereof, the term *dis/ability* with its forward slash evokes the question of the interdependent and contrasting differentiation: what is the culturally prescribed norm from which this body deviates, and to which cultural taxonomies and evaluations does it relate (i.e., certain aesthetics, abilities, functionality, expectations, and personal or societal well-being)? Moreover, the term's formal distortion connotes and challenges the ways and means of the cultural productivity, transformation, mediation, intentionality, and institutionalization behind these constructions.[8] It provokes one to ask, "Why are certain differences subsumed under the label 'disabled' and others considered as 'normal' manifestations of human diversity? Why do societies see the need to categorize people as 'normal' and 'deviant'? Why and how is disability negatively valued? In which ways is 'otherness' or 'alterity' (re-)produced in history, society and culture?"[9]

Hence, this perspective calls for an investigation of the mutual interweaving of —among many other areas—medical, social, political, and religious aspects within

---

specializing models enforce complementing nuances, such as the *relational model* that emphasizes the universal vulnerable condition of humanity which demands societal support or the *religious/ moral model* with particular attention to the etiologic, economic, and social interconnections between disability and religious institutions or ethical and moral evaluation of bodily difference. These models are not mutually exclusive. See generally Solevåg 2018. 4–6, and comprehensively Altman in Albrecht; Seelman; Bury (ed.) 2001; Thomas in Weisser; Renggli (ed.) 2004; Shakespeare in Davis (ed.) 2006; Dederich 2007; Meekosha; Shuttleworth 2009; Goodley 2011; Schneider; Waldschmidt in Moebius (ed.) 2012; Goodley 2014; Devlieger et al. 2016; Waldschmidt 2018.
5 Waldschmidt 2018. 75.
6 Cf. Schipper 2006. 20.
7 Regarding a variety of perspectives, including ancient and current issues, see van der Eijk; Ganten; Marek 2021.
8 Cf. Waldschmidt 2018. 76.
9 Ibid. 74. Cf. moreover, Waldschmidt in Bösl; Klein; Waldschmidt (ed.) 2010. 20.

one framework, a socio-historically constructed and contingent sociology of knowledge.[10]

1.3 Dis/ability History

Although built on a modern philosophical framework, dis/ability becomes an interesting analytical category for historical studies, similar to race or gender, precisely because it questions, not presupposes, cultural paradigms of physical differentiation.[11] Hence, any historical—in this case, ancient and literary—source can be reviewed according to the images of physical deviance it deploys: which physical characteristics, properties, and behaviors are labeled as deviant? How are these "tropes"[12] evaluated and against which normalizing backdrop? Which conventions, attitudes, and/or symbols are attached to them, and how, and maybe even why, are these bodies shaped this way? Are there cultural discourses attached to these representations of dis/ability, and how does the source partake in them?[13]

Dis/ability is not defined in contrast to disease, sickness, and impairment but primarily serves as an umbrella term for any kind of physical deviance described. By its broadness, vagueness, artificiality, and formal distortion, it is not only applicable to the range of labels used in Greek, Hebrew, and Latin but encompasses a variety of classifications[14] and reassesses contrasting ideals of physical norm(s) explicated by the relevant source. Thereby, this definition eludes modern premises (such as the sharp distinction of, e.g., scientific medicine; religious and folk practices of healing; biological, philosophical, or physiognomic notions of embodiment,

---

10 Cf. Thomas in Weisser; Renggli (ed.) 2004; Waldschmidt in Bösl; Klein; Waldschmidt (ed.) 2010; Moss; Schipper (ed.) 2011; Grue 2017.
11 Cf., e.g., Bösl 2009; Bösl; Klein; Waldschmidt 2010; Nolte et al. 2017. Cf. esp. Klein in Bösl; Klein; Waldschmidt (ed.) 2010; Bösl in Bösl; Klein; Waldschmidt (ed.) 2010; Waldschmidt in Bösl; Klein; Waldschmidt (ed.) 2010.
12 Cf. Garland-Thomson in Davis (ed.) 2010 [2002]. 354.
13 Cf. Solevåg 2018. 9–10.
14 Cf. Rose 2003. 2, who states a lack of a comparable category altogether in ancient Greece; or Vlahogiannis in Montserrat (ed.) 1998. 16–17, who defines those with "appearance and socially ascribed abnormalities, such as polydactylism, left-handedness, old age, obesity, impotence, and even those who are socially ill-positioned, such as beggars, the poor, the homeless, the ugly and the diseased" as dis/abled, cf. also Samama in Laes (ed.) 2017. Thereof Solevåg 2018. 13, concludes, along with Garland 1995. 5; Kelley in Avalos; Melcher; Schipper (ed.) 2007. 33–35, that "disability overlaps with deformity [...] as physical abnormalities and bodily malfunction are not always kept apart," and Laes in Laes (ed.) 2017. 4, proposes the relative term "infirmity" for premodern society. The relevant taxonomies at play in the biblical accounts are regarded in close analysis of the Markan accounts in the following. For the Hebrew Bible, see, e.g., Raphael 2008. 14–15.

all of which did not exist as such in antiquity). Moreover, this open paradigm allows a primary unrestricted investigation of phenomena frequently separated due to presupposed modern classifications of, for example, etiologies (as in the case of demon possession) or physical localizations and groupings (as in the case of cognitive dis/abilities or sensory impairments).

Hence, (modern) categorical and institutional boundaries of dis/ability are opened for a review of different (historical) descriptions of corporeality, which, moreover, is applicable to intersectional perspectives such as gender studies;[15] monster, crip, and stigma theory;[16] analyses of political and religious rhetoric;[17] and social location and family status[18] with particular aspects such as age[19] or ethnicity.[20]

However, the "lived experience" of those dis/abled remains elusive and only indirectly traceable due to a lack of firsthand sources.[21] Neither its reconstruction nor a retrospective diagnosis and/or modern medical approach is helpful with regard to the ancient understanding of dis/ability.[22] Nonetheless, the texts can indicate "possible scenarios as well as discursive openings in the narratives themselves."[23]

Furthermore, this cultural approach can be refined by findings from historical research on medical history[24] and anthropological discourses,[25] as well as by other studies on disability in relatable cultures or text corpora of antiquity.[26]

---

[15] See, e.g., Hester 2005; Vander Stichele; Penner 2009; Kartzow; Moxnes 2010; Garland-Thomson in Davis (ed.) 2010 [2002]; Carter 2015; Henning 2015; Solevåg in Laes (ed.) 2017; Belser 2018; Solevåg in Lehtipuu; Petersen (ed.) 2020; Nogossek-Raithel in El Maaroufi; Strube; Williger (ed.) 2020.
[16] See, e.g., McRuer 2006; Gevaert; Laes in Laes; Goodey; Rose (ed.) 2013; Solevåg 2016.
[17] See, e.g., Jochum-Bortfeld 2008; Belser; Morrison 2011; Carter in Moss; Schipper (ed.) 2011; Harrocks in Taylor (ed.) 2014; Solevåg in Nicolet; Kartzow (ed.) 2021.
[18] See, e.g., Harrill in Collins; Mitchell (ed.) 2001; Stewart in Moss; Schipper (ed.) 2011; Moss; Baden 2015; Bengtsson 2016; Valentine 2018.
[19] See, e.g., Barclay 2007; Laes 2008; Solevåg in Laes; Vuolanto (ed.) 2017.
[20] See, e.g., Schüssler Fiorenza in Nasrallah; Schüssler Fiorenza (ed.) 2009; Wainwright in Alkier; Weissenrieder (ed.) 2013.
[21] Cf. Lawrence 2013. 2; Solevåg 2018. 11–12; Laes in Laes (ed.) 2017. 3, different to Marx-Wolf; Upson-Saia 2015. 270–272.
[22] Regarding biblical topics, see Short 1953; Levin 1988; Muhammed 2013; and generally, Graumann in Laes; Goodey; Rose (ed.) 2013; Leven in Horstmanshoff; Stol; Tilburg (ed.) 2004.
[23] Solevåg 2018. 12.
[24] These medical findings, however, must be regarded as part of a social health care system and not an exclusive analytical category as proposed by the medical model. See, e.g., Krug 1993; van der Eijk; Horstmanshoff; Schrijvers 1995; Edelstein; Edelstein 1998; Nutton 2004; van der Eijk 2005a; Golder 2007; van der Eijk in Jackson (ed.) 2011; Brockmann 2013; Kudlick in Rembis; Kudlick; Nielsen (ed.) 2018.

1.4 Dis/ability and Biblical Studies

With dis/ability studies and dis/ability history developing into established fields in humanities and cultural studies, dis/ability also grew to a more frequently applied approach in biblical studies fueled by theological studies on embodiment, especially in the past twenty years.[27] While its social and political roots lead to an important critical turn in religious and ethical practices and experiences of Christian communities and ministries,[28] the literary and historical focus on the biblical texts in particular provoke controversy with regard to different approaches:[29] while some scholars try to "redeem" difficult and dis/ability invective passages and shift any stigmatizing results to the interpretation and reception history of the texts,[30] others outright reject the biblical texts in question and, in a post-scripturalist modification of this approach, opt to disregard ancient texts for any kind of normative meaning-making.[31] A *primary* step before shifting the focus to a modern interpretation in one or the other direction offers an open historical approach without determined advocacy or ecclesiological and theological application. Although criticized for its break with the inherent political and social roots of dis/ability studies,[32] a historical analysis of biblical representations of dis/ability is of utmost relevance[33] for a precise understanding "of how these texts both reflect and reinforce ancient cultural ideas about identity and social organization"[34] that

---

[25] See, e.g., Weissenrieder 2003; Thommen 2007; Weissenrieder in Alkier; Weissenrieder (ed.) 2013; Tieleman 2014; Garrison 2014; Weissenrieder; Dolle 2019; and with particular focus on early Christianity, Avalos 1999; Pilch 1999; Wainwright 2006.

[26] See, e.g., Garland 1995; Edwards 1996; Edwards in Mitchell; Snyder (ed.) 1997a; Edwards in Davis (ed.) 1997b; Abrams 1998; Stiker 1999; Rose 2003; Laes 2008; Laes 2011; Laes; Goodey; Rose 2013; Harris 2013; MacFarlane in Garrison (ed.) 2014; Holmes in Garrison (ed.) 2014; Laes 2017; Belser 2018.

[27] Cf., e.g., Eiesland 1994; Martin 1995; Moltmann-Wendel 1995; Isherwood; Stuart 1998; Creamer 2009; Kamionkowski; Kim 2010; Garner 2011.

[28] Cf. prominently for German scholarship Bach 2006, and in response Grünstäudl 2011. See also, e.g., Colston 1978; Anderson; Foley 1994; Eiesland; Saliers 1998; Hull 2001; McCloughry; Morris 2002; Krahe 2002; Betcher 2007; Reinders 2008; Eurich 2008; Liedke 2009; Mohr 2011; Kellenberger 2011; Brock; Swinton 2012; Reinders 2014; Neumann 2017.

[29] Cf. the outlines of a brief history of research in Avalos 2007b; Moss; Schipper (ed.) 2011. Cf. also Avalos; Melcher; Schipper in Avalos; Melcher; Schipper (ed.) 2007; Schumm; Stoltzfus in Schumm; Stoltzfus (ed.) 2011; Schipper; Junior in McKenzie; Kaltner (ed.) 2013.

[30] Cf. esp. Wynn 2007; Yong 2007; Yong 2011.

[31] Cf. Wilhelm 1998, and the discussion in Avalos; Melcher; Schipper in Avalos; Melcher; Schipper (ed.) 2007. 5. Cf. also Raphael 2008. 21–26; Laes in Laes (ed.) 2017. 8; Solevåg 2018. 24.

[32] Cf. Goodley 2011. 2.

[33] Contra Avalos 2007b. 100, who doubts its relevance.

[34] Moss; Schipper (ed.) 2011. 6. Cf. also Schipper; Junior in McKenzie; Kaltner (ed.) 2013. 33.

henceforth in their Christian interpretation "normate"³⁵ physical experience. Without an unbiased and distinct attempt to regard the basic meaning of these images, biblical texts can neither be rejected (for what?) nor redeemed (from what?). A historical analysis of the texts forms the hermeneutical basis of their following (re)appropriation, (re)evaluation, and (re)interpretation and their sociopolitical power in the spirit of dis/ability studies.

In addition to scholarly dispute over these successive, not diverging approaches, the intersection of dis/ability and biblical studies brought forth several detailed historical and narrative investigations. The first substantial monographs show a predominant interest in texts from the Hebrew Bible,³⁶ as do the successive edited essay collections³⁷ that were primarily inspired by the 2004-founding of the Society of Biblical Literature section "Healthcare and Disability in the Ancient World" (formerly "Biblical Scholarship and Disability Consultation"). Prominent for German scholarship is the series "Behinderung – Theologie – Kirche," with mainly practical theological and sociopolitical impulses yet also exegetical collections³⁸ and entries.³⁹

In recent years, the number of dis/ability studies with reference to early Christian texts has increased, including more extensive monographs on biblical topics embedded in the medical and philosophical context of the ancient Mediterranean world.⁴⁰ A novelty is the 2017 published commentary "The Bible and Disability,"⁴¹ which supplies a short yet, in its treatment of each canonized book, comprehensive survey of the Bible's portrayal of disability as part of the interdisciplinary series

---

35 As coined by Garland-Thomson 1997. 8, "normate" designates "the constructed identity of those who, by way of the bodily configurations and cultural capital they assume, can step into a position of authority and wield the power it grants them."
36 Cf., e.g., Marx 1992; Abrams 1998; Olyan 1998; Schipper 2006; Olyan 2008; Raphael 2008; Schipper 2011; Avrahami 2012; Ben Zvi; Edelman 2014; Schipper 2015. See also the short synopsis of several of the mentioned monographies in Melcher in Melcher; Parsons; Yong (ed.) 2017. Regarding the Dead Sea Scrolls, see in particular Shemesh 1997; Dorman 2007; Wassen in McCready; Reinhartz (ed.) 2008; Dorman in Ben Zvi; Edelman (ed.) 2014, and fundamentally, Holden 1991.
37 Cf. Avalos; Melcher; Schipper 2007; Moss; Schipper 2011; Grünstäudl; Schiefer Ferrari 2012, also Schumm; Stoltzfus 2011; Moss; Baden 2015. For early studies on dis/ability in the NT and early Christianity outside the mentioned edited volumes, see, e.g., Avalos 1999; Parsons 2006; Moss 2010; Moss 2011a; Brock 2011.
38 Cf. Grünstäudl; Schiefer Ferrari 2012.
39 Cf. Kliesch in Eurich; Lob-Hüdepohl (ed.) 2011; Oeming in Eurich; Lob-Hüdepohl (ed.) 2011.
40 Cf., e.g., Betcher in Alkier; Weissenrieder (ed.) 2013; Henning 2015; Solevåg 2016; Clark-Soles 2016; Bengtsson 2016; Valentine 2018. Cf. for monographs with concrete reference to dis/ability studies: Lawrence 2013; Lawrence 2018; Gosbell 2018; Solevåg 2018; also Hartsock 2008, and the unpublished thesis of Just 1997.
41 Cf. Melcher; Parsons; Yong 2017.

"Studies in Religion, Theology, and Disability" (2011). Therein, the gospel texts have primarily received an overview on distinct passages and topics: The prominent monograph, "Sense and Stigma in the Gospels: Depictions of Sensory-Disabled Characters" (2013) by Louise Lawrence, reviews images of sensory impairment in the gospels from the perspective of dis/ability studies and cultural anthropology, enriched with ethnographic insights "to offer new and cathartic interpretations which reconfigure the profiles of these flat and often silent characters in fresh and innovative ways."[42] Conducted with great care for historical accuracy, the dialogue with modern theories of comparative cultural and religious studies is indeed inspiring and proves the focus on sensory impairment is not an anachronistic but a productive framework for biblical scholarship. However, the author's focus on the "stigmatizing" history of interpretation and rather detached presentation of various gospel texts could be refined by an assessment of the actual (problematic) rhetoric, composition, and function of the biblical passages themselves. In a previous article, she had already proven that such a concentrated analysis of sensual perception for a defined literary text particularly beyond the scope of the so-called healing narratives is worthwhile.[43]

In a similar vein of a rather broad investigation interested in an exemplified intersectional perspective, the 2018 publication of Anna Rebecca Solevåg's "Negotiating the Disabled Body" also includes selected passages from noncanonized texts and addresses various images of dis/ability. Again, the consultation with interdisciplinary theories proves a constructive and encouraging inspiration for more comprehensive historical research of the actual literary sources. In the same year, Louise A. Gosbell published her investigation "Physical and Sensory Disability in the Gospels of the New Testament," again on selected passages from three literary works. Importantly, her New Testament survey follows a substantial historical review of "the Landscape of Disability" of the Greco-Roman World, the Hebrew Bible, and Second Temple Judaism and emphasizes the cultural context crucial for dis/ability research of any given historical source, yet it could be more closely related to the relevant passages in the following chapters.

Another inspiring overview, this time of the gospel of Matthew and Mark as individual literary compositions, has been provided by Candida R. Moss as part of the aforementioned 2017 commentary "The Bible and Disability." In eighteen concise pages, she compiles important topics of the Markan text that can and should be related to a study of dis/ability in this gospel text. Also bound to the

---

42 Lawrence 2013. 9.
43 Cf. Lawrence 2011.

scope of the publication, she is only able to offer interesting vantage points for further studies that widen the view beyond the so-called healing narratives.

Taking these prominent publications on New Testament texts into account, this study draws on their inspiring, pioneering investigations with its own concentrated and therefore limited scope on the representations of dis/ability in the Markan healing narratives[44] in the hope to be complemented by further studies.

While the concrete methodologies of each cited study differ according to text and topic, a frequently applied framework is that of literary and narrative criticism. As a medium of discourse, literature, with its narrative representations[45] of bodies, is also embedded and partakes in the discursive processes of classifications and meaning-making in historical and cultural contexts.[46] Prominently, Mitchell and Snyder have formulated the thesis that disability always serves as a *"narrative prosthesis* [...], as a crutch upon which literary narratives lean for their representational power, disruptive potentiality, and analytical insights."[47] As with any image of deviance, its evaluation then also depends on (literary) conventions and its specific functions for the text as characters evoke suspense, tragedy, certain emotions, even moral reasoning or symbolize abstract conflicts and problems due to their "abnormal" features.[48] Therefore, not only are the cultural settings of any representation of dis/ability and its literary medium relevant but also its narratological context.[49] The latter then leads to literary and narrative approaches[50] as established for the gospels in the early 1980s, predominantly for the Markan text by Werner H. Kelber, David Rhoads and Donald M. Mitchie, Robert

---

[44] For the sake of convenience, the following continues to designate passages of the gospel text that depict the physical transformation of a dis/abled character invoked by Jesus or his disciples as "healing narratives" with the cultural contingency of the transformed physical state implied.
[45] The term reflects that these literary texts do not witness to an objective experience of historical characters with dis/abilities or an actual physical body but a literary image that however contains and transports cultural knowledge about physical deviance. Cf. Dederich in Dederich (ed.) 2007. 112–114; Bösl in Bösl; Klein; Waldschmidt (ed.) 2010. 34.
[46] For a comprehensive summary, see, e.g., Dederich in Dederich (ed.) 2007.
[47] Mitchell; Snyder 2001. 49; and Mitchell; Snyder in Davis (ed.) 2013.
[48] For recent studies on characterization in ancient literature, see, e.g., Grethlein; Rengakos 2009; Temmerman; Emde Boas 2018.
[49] Cf. comprehensively Nünning in Reitz; Rieuwerts (ed.) 2000.
[50] Since approaches with focus on the literary and narrative context of the gospels developed into a vast international and interdisciplinary field, the following avoids labeling them solely as "narrative criticism," "reader-response criticism," or "(cognitive) narratology," et al. Cf. in summary Nünning; Nünning in Nünning; Nünning (ed.) 2002; Heinen; Sommer 2009; Pier in Huber; Schmid (ed.) 2017. Regarding biblical studies, cf. Powell in Iverson; Skinner (ed.) 2011, who offers a helpful systematization according to three not exclusive strands of scholarship, namely "author-oriented," "text-oriented," and "reader-oriented" approaches.

Tannehill, Jack Dean Kingsbury, and Ernest Best,[51] with increasing interest in the portrayal of characters, literary dramaturgy, and patterns of plot of each intentional composition. Various studies with distinct and diverse interests and refined hermeneutical and methodological outsets followed in recent years.[52]

Based on the outlined hermeneutical framework and its history, the following section addresses Markan healing narratives against the backdrop of biblical dis/ability studies and with the methods applied by literary and narrative approaches to the biblical texts.

1.5 Healing Narratives

The healing narratives as presented by the gospel texts of the New Testament offer an additional dimension to this hermeneutical approach as they not only emphatically depict characters with physical deviances but narrate their transformation to another in the texts positively valued physical state. The interrelation to a contrasting "normal" body is not only an implicit theme by the deployment of dis/abilities but the actual topic of these passages. Hence, an analysis of dis/ability in these texts seems particularly accessible and can furthermore explore whether the Markan passages presuppose a binary body scheme or transpire further "other" physical conditions within their literary function and sociocultural context. Moreover, since this dis/ability transformation is on a story level performed by a mainly physically active Jesus, his corporality plays an additional role, as do the bodies of other characters described with physical traits, if only as another contrast foil for the marking of "bodily difference"[53]: Is there an implied "default normal state of human experience from which disability deviates,"[54] a non-disability or able-

---

51 Cf., e.g., Kelber 1979; Tannehill 1979; Rhoads; Michie 1982; Rhoads 1982; Kingsbury 1983; Best 1983; Kingsbury 1989; Klauck in Klauck (ed.) 1989, also pioneering Wilder 1964; Beardslee 1970; Hahn 1985, and for other Gospel texts Culpepper 1983; Kingsbury 1986; Tannehill 1986, 1990. Cf. in review the second and third edition's introduction of Rhoads; Dewey; Michie 2012, and Rhoads 2004; also Resseguie 2005; Iverson; Skinner 2011. Cf. in summary for German and American scholarship, Dormeyer 2005. 82–134. See also Breytenbach in Becker; Runesson (ed.) 2011. 20–21, for a survey of monographs from 2000–2009.
52 Cf., e.g., Tolbert 1989; Fowler 1991; Malbon 1991; Heil 1992; Camery-Hoggatt 1992; Broadhead 1993; Davidsen 1993; Juel 1994; Müller 1995; Klauck 1997; Iersel 1998; Naluparayil 2000; Malbon 2000; Horsley 2001; Bolt 2003; Oko 2004; Bourquin 2005; Danove 2005; Rose 2007; Pramann 2008; Jochum-Bortfeld 2008; Stewart 2009; Malbon 2009; Bosenius 2014; Kiffiak 2017; Rüggemeier 2017; Seifert 2019.
53 Melcher in Melcher; Parsons; Yong (ed.) 2017. 9.
54 Schipper 2011. 19.

bodiedness that relates to creation, eschatology, physical integrity, or maybe the healing body of Jesus? Jesus is not only the mediator between the "categories," linking etiology with therapy but, as the protagonist, connects the narratives that serve his characterization. In the gospels, these characters and their stories are mainly employed to show and sustain Jesus as a powerful healing character. More than that, by adhering to the method outlined above, representations of deviating bodies serve each narrative's specific function within the gospel's storyline and its theological claims, which change from narrative to narrative.[55]

Of course, other gospel passages might also shed light on the overarching classifications of dis/ability represented (i.e., the suffering and marked body of the crucified Jesus), but for a primary concentrated look, the healing narratives offer the most forthright material that may serve as groundwork for further investigations.

Apart from the outlined research from the perspective of dis/ability studies, there are numerous exegetical expositions of "classical biblical scholarship" that deal in detail with the healings narrated in the New Testament. Among the fundamental works are Hendrik van der Loos' "Miracles of Jesus" and Bernd Kollmann's "Jesus und die Christen als Wundertäter," as well as "Neutestamentliche Wundergeschichten."[56] These comprehensive and insightful studies outline important problems such as the relationship of New Testament narratives to Hellenistic and Jewish medical, religious, and/or cultic (healing) traditions. However, individual healing narratives, gospel texts and their composition, and the plurality of ancient body concepts are beyond the purview of their investigations. In addition, care must be applied with regard to their rather anachronistic and modern demarcations of, for instance, scientific medicine, magic cults, and mystery religions, as well as various "miracle" conceptions.[57] Larry P. Hogan, Werner Kahl, Howard Clark Kee, and John J. Pilch, among others, attempt to sharpen the perspective.[58] With very concentrated studies, they differentiate significant problems and modern coalescences of narrated dis/abilities and healing methods: Pilch's phenomenological and terminological distinction among "sickness" (as a generic term for physiological impairments), "disease" (for the description of the biological, pathological dimension), and "illness" (to designate the social and individual implications) and Kahl's narratological description of a healing story as a movement from a lack (of health) to its overcoming through the action of an active subject were groundbreaking.[59] Moreover, with regard to the function of the gospel's heal-

---

55 Cf. Solevåg 2018. 155.
56 Cf. van der Loos 1965; Kollmann 1996; Kollmann 2007.
57 Cf. the overview of research history in Zimmermann 2013. 7–14.
58 Cf. Kee 1986; Hogan 1992; Kahl 1994; Pilch 1999; Kahl 2011.
59 Cf. Kahl 1994; Pilch 1999; Kahl 2011.

ing narratives and their depiction of "sickness," von Bendemann analyzes the body's "salutogenic" conceptualization by the powerfully demonstrated transformation that implies a variable normalizing and interrelated body scheme.[60] Furthermore, there are specific studies on individual texts or dis/abilities, such as Annette Weissenrieder's work on Lukan conceptions of illness and Michael Wohlers' thesis on epilepsy.[61]

A concentrated analysis of dis/ability in the healing narratives of one gospel text can complement these either very broad or very focused investigations by regarding the paradigms behind the dis/abled and healing bodies, which are narratively as well as culturally interrelated and mutually dependent.

1.6 Dis/ability in Mark's Healing Narratives

With regard to the scant and detailed, yet fragmentary investigations of New Testament texts, the Gospel of Mark offers an intriguing starting point for a comprehensive analysis of representations of dis/ability in one stylistic, linguistic, and narrative corpus due to its age, brevity, and composition: As the oldest of the Synoptic gospels available, it offers a unique approach to the plot as the prior work.[62] Secondly, due to its dense composition without genealogy, the characterization of Jesus relies on the comparatively frequent feature of healing narratives, especially in the programmatic beginning of the gospel text.[63] As such, the importance of Markan healing narratives (and other accounts on powerful deeds) of Jesus was critically regarded around the 1970s as redaction criticism began to unravel the unique and independent theological style and textual and literary composition of Mark,[64] advanced by the increasing international—at first structuralist—linguistic and narratological approaches (see above). This, however, also led to a negative evaluation of these narratives as intentionally integrated but only employed and redacted as minor and ancillary accounts regarding Jesus' teachings

---

60 Cf. von Bendemann in Pichler; Heil (ed.) 2007; von Bendemann in Kollmann; Zimmermann (ed.) 2014. 253.
61 Cf. Wohlers 1999a; Weissenrieder 2003.
62 However, at times the following refers to the Lukan or Matthean versions as comparative, epistemic sources for cultural knowledge of the body.
63 Cf. Zimmermann 2013. 193; Solevåg 2018. 50.
64 Drawing on the (also problematic) premises of Wrede 1963 [1901], pursued by, e. g., Sjöberg 1955; Marxsen 1959 [1956]; Schweizer 1964; Schweizer 1989 [1967], in discussion with, e. g., Roloff 1969; Pesch 1976; Pesch 1980. With regard to the style and motifs of the narrative units, also form critical examinations were of relevance, cf., e. g., Bultmann 1921; Dibelius 1933; Theissen 1974. 57–83; Berger (ed.) 1984a. 1212–1218; Berger 1984b. 305–310.

and the Markan *theologia crucis*, particularly due to the motifs of silencing and secrecy.[65] While it is difficult to negate the revelatory and climactic function of Jesus' passion and resurrection for the plot, the following investigates and proves the utmost relevance and paradigmatic position of depictions of physical dis/ability for a) the Markan composition, b) the characterization of the Markan Jesus, and c) the summary of his message.

Thirdly, as also explicitly expressed by the gospel text itself (1:34), Mark's gospel features very diverse representations of corporeality (only characters labeled with "demon possession" and "blindness" occur more than once) that mutually effect the portrayal of Jesus' healing body with a variety of techniques.[66] Hence, the characterization of Mark's healing Jesus is not regarded on its own but in interplay with the representations of his diverse dis/abled interlocutors. While there is an abundance of publications that treat the Gospel of Mark and its narratives of physical transformation—however, again, in either very broad or specific regards,[67] often with particular theological, Christological, soteriological, or ethical interests,[68] and focus on Jesus the physician, the "θεῖος ἀνήρ,"[69] the savior, and Christ,[70] the bearer of a healing δύναμις[71]—the protagonists' physicality rarely receives attention.[72]

---

[65] Cf., e.g., Schulz 1967. 64–79; Weeden 1971; Schenke 1974; Schulz 1976. 219–223, and in revision Schenke 2005. 121–129. For a summary of these positions and their arguments, cf. Dschulnigg 1984, regarding Schenke, 514–522; Weeden, 541; Schulz, 459–461, moreover, Best 1983. 55–65; Weiser 1993. 60–65; Dschulnigg 2007. 39–40, also Kertelge 1970.
[66] In the interplay of the summaric passages and the individual narratives, a crucial subject of Dis/ability Studies is also addressed: while people are depicted in the summaric accounts "through their common association with incapacity and aberrancy," their "enormously varied bodily experiences and capacities" are clarified in the individual narratives. Their shared "political and communal identity" (Mitchell; Snyder 1997. 7) is addressed, but contextualized by the individual, detailed descriptions of dis/ability and Jesus' situational, intimate, personal, physical healings. Moreover, the dis/abled characters are at times named, assigned social locations, encountered in specific and plot-relevant situations. Cf. also van der Loos 1965. 305–336.
[67] Cf., e.g., Kertelge 1970; Schenke 1974; Koch 1975; Söding 1985; Blackburn 1991; Broadhead 1992a; Dwyer 1996; Dormeyer 1999; Fink 2000; Suk 2002; van Oyen in Labahn; Lietaert Peerbolte (ed.) 2006; Eibisch 2009; von Bendemann 2010; Becker 2010; Cotter 2010; Schmidt 2010; Kahl 2011.
[68] Cf., e.g., Koch 1975; Söding 1985; Broadhead 1992a; Eibisch 2009; Schmidt 2010; Kahl 2011.
[69] Cf. fundamentally and comprehensively, du Toit 1997.
[70] Cf., e.g., Blackburn 1991; Dormeyer 1999; Fink 2000; von Bendemann 2010; Cotter 2010.
[71] Cf., e.g., Pesch 1970.
[72] Cf. Zimmermann 2013. 15–18. Cf. however, Tiwald in Grünstäudl; Schiefer Ferrari (ed.) 2012.

1.7 Scope of This Study

Complementing, not contrasting, historical methods, this study deploys a synchronic approach to the text presented as the gospel's final form for a concentrated analysis of dis/ability as a *literary* device.[73] By reading the text as an episodic narrative,[74] the structure of this study follows that of the gospel text to review the representations of dis/ability within their literary setting, narrative function, and episodic composition. Following the enumeration of chapters as given in NA28 is due to pragmatic reasons of referencing yet does not bear historical value; neither do the arrangement and assemblage of all relevant passages in six chapters (see below). Based on a high regard for the Markan narrative flow with its transitions, twists, turns, and overlapping and proleptic features, the structure of this study is attributable to the plot's intentional progression and composition with certain focus points to which each section serves specific functions that are intrinsically connected to its featured images of dis/ability. An exception forms the collective treatment of the so-called summaric reports in chapter 2: Due to their stylistic distinctiveness as selective, generalizing, and summaric presentations of healing, they are analyzed as a collection of interpretative tendencies that already indicate the gospel's function, mapping, and accentuation of dis/ability and thereby hint at its classifications of deviating physicality. In this chapter as well as each subsequent one, each passage is introduced by a survey of its narrative context, literary composition, and plot integration with a focus on the most relevant literary features for an analysis of dis/ability. A comprehensive and extensive narratological investigation, however, is beyond the scope of this study and might distract from the analytical category of dis/ability at hand.

Subsequently, the terms labeling the deviant bodies and their described clinical picture, symptoms, behavior, and any further characterization receive detailed attention, as do the applied physical healing and possible further contrasting bodies in recourse to ancient determinations and descriptions of physicality. Since different forms of epistemic texts can convey and recall the same cultural knowledge, relevant references include treatises that can be assigned to ancient medicine as well as Old and Intertestamental early Jewish and Christian writings (including LXX, Qumran, rabbinic writings) and cultic and biographical texts of Greco-Roman antiquity that reveal somewhat historically and culturally contiguous con-

---

[73] As such this investigation mainly draws on commentaries with narrative and literary focus, such as, e.g., Lührmann 1987; Hooker 1991; Iersel 1998; Moloney 2002; Focant 2012, however, also relies on analyses and interpretations of more comprehensive approaches such as, e.g., Marcus 2000; Collins 2007; Marcus 2009.

[74] Cf. Breytenbach in Breytenbach (ed.) 2021 [1985].

ceptual frameworks of dis/ability.⁷⁵ Their genre-specific features can then be helpful in answering questions about the intention and institution of knowledge production, as well as in examining certain formulations and the literary strategy of the texts.

If necessary, further investigations were conducted regarding discourses and conceptions drawn upon (i.e., coherent literary features like the Markan settings for healing or overarching narrative and cultural paradigms such as the concept behind πίστις language). They are placed where they appeared to be of particular relevance for the analysis at hand. Due to their transversal importance, however, they are numbered with capital letters and headed "In Focus" to display and highlight their comprehensive content. Moreover, intersectional perspectives are briefly touched upon when evoked by the source, yet an expressive analysis warrants a comprehensive literary survey.

Each pericope is then conclusively analyzed according to the textual representations of dis/ability deployed, its cultural undercurrents, and literary inventions. In synopsis with other deviating bodies of the gospel section and in dialogue with the increasingly defined analysis of the overall use and function of dis/ability for the Markan plot, each chapter presents an interpretative conclusion. Those are then evaluated at the end of the study.

1.8 Terminological Considerations

The designation "the Gospel of Mark" refers, for the sake of convenience, to the narrative according to Mark, a *chiffre* for the composer(s) of the currently available story text with whatever exact genre(s) implied.⁷⁶

Based on the hermeneutical framework of dis/ability studies, the term *dis/ability* as established, refers to the textual representation of deviating bodies in interrelation to an "other,"⁷⁷ an implied norm from which it deviates, surrounding other physical characters but also the healing body of Jesus. This term allows an unhindered, open investigation of otherwise a priori and thereof anachronistically distinguished phenomena, as, e.g., of sickness and demon possession. For analytical purposes, it may include what is otherwise classed as impairments, diseases, demonic phenomena, and/or social "disablements."

---

75 See also Hengel; Schwemer 2007. 193–243, esp. 216–224.
76 Cf. Rhoads; Dewey; Michie 2012. xi–8; Breytenbach in Breytenbach (ed.) 2021 [1985].
77 Cf. Waldschmidt 2018. 74.

The term "healing" denotes a physical transformation of this condition, hence also includes the treatment of demonic ailments. Whether this transformation implies a removal of physical and social, even spiritual, limitations; an integrity according to certain aesthetic or functionality standards; a societal or individual well-being; and/or a creational and/or eschatological normality is discussed. Hence, "healing" and "health" denote, for lack of a better word, open, maybe even polyphone signifiers for physical condition(s) beyond the presented deviances.

Moreover, despite these analytical (re)definitions, the following analysis only applies People First Language[78] if the ancient text allows for an unaltered and historically and literary accurate evaluation of the language used. It is expected that modern applications of these biblical texts refrain from any reproduction of stigmatizing notions precisely because of the attempted thorough cultural contextualization.

For clarity of the hermeneutical framework, the study refrains from employing complex and ambiguous terms from narratological research. "Plot" and "story" refer to the presented text as well as its developments, events, and characters.

1.9 Brief Summary and Outline

1.9.1 The Markan Summaric Accounts as Showcases for Markan Dis/ability

The first chapter focuses on the so-called summaric accounts of Jesus' healing activity as they provide an overview of the Markan treatment of dis/ability (1:32–34, 39; 3:7–12, 6:5, 13, 53–56). Scattered over the course of the first six Markan chapters, their stylistic purpose lies in the summarizing and generalizing, yet also specific highlighting and heightening, of individual accounts to supply cohesion and spur the narrative on. The accounts deploy general images of dis/ability with emphasis on generic labels of suffering, weakness, and torments to depict a vast and unrelenting need for Jesus' healing. Thereby, they reveal the Markan distinction and narrative functions of sickness and possessions. More so, they pick up specific motifs of dis/ability as presented in individual accounts and bundle narrative and theological threads together by marking embodied *pistis* and salvation (σῴζω) and embodied yet transmittable power as compositional threads. As benchmarks in the gospel text, the deviating bodies also witness to the plot's progression as Jesus' popularity, along with his geographically expansive and public healing min-

---

78 Cf. Goodley 2011. 12–13.

istry and mission scheme, is programmatically staged yet reaches its personal and spatial limits and is transferred to his disciples. Jesus is characterized as an accessible, tangible, itinerate healer, who by his opposition to harmful, evil entities reveals his divine identity.

1.9.2 Mark 1: Jesus in a Dis/abled World

This chapter starts at the beginning as dis/abled characters introduce Jesus as a powerful healer in Mark 1:23–28, 1:30–31, and 1:40–45. A possession with an unclean spirit, a febrile, and a skin condition—quite general, relatable dis/abilities with ranges of possible symptoms and severities—are briefly narrated and pinned to concrete characters, locations, and/or personal situations. All are connected to a continuous tension about the revelation of Jesus' divine identity and authority as depicted in knowing demons and commands to silence, mysterious ἐξουσία, and efficacious healing touches within the setting of a cosmic dualism. The healings attest to Jesus' appointment, accompany the beginning of his proclamation, and nuance the initial characterization of his disciples and opponents. Accordingly, this chapter incorporates an introduction on the Markan conception of demonology (including Mark 3:20–35; 16:9) and on the diverse locations of Jesus' healing ministry (public, domestic, and sacred spaces). Jesus is established as a popular, benevolent, tangible healer with a characteristic curative touch, who faces humanity with a general susceptibility to dis/abling influences.

1.9.3 Mark 2:1–3:6: A Plot in Motion

This chapter analyzes the two healing narratives of Mark 2:1–12 and 3:1–6 within the context of the five concentrically structured confrontations between Jesus and his opponents in Mark 2:1–3:6. The (partial) mobility impairments of a man who cannot walk and a man with a withered hand are contrasted by an immobile and judgmental opposition, active *pistis*-practicing carriers, and a versatile and authoritative Jesus in teaching and action. Amidst Jesus' unchallenged popularity of the framing passages—exemplified by images of dis/ability (1:40–45; 3:7–12)—both narratives aim with the entire gospel section at a vivid illustration of the ensuing conflict with Jesus' malevolent and skeptical opponents. As the plot is put in motion, the audience is confronted by several ways to respond to Jesus and his message according to the various character groups and their embodied reactions. Moreover, the two healing narratives amplify the characterization of Jesus when not only his ἐξουσία is further unraveled, but his authority to partake in the divine prerogative to forgive sin and his interpretative power of Sabbath and law regulations are demonstrated by the dis/abled characters. By this theological contextualization and illustration, which is discussed further in consideration of the word of autoamputation of Mark 9:42–48, Jesus' ministry is broadened to an eschatological horizon, as are the dis/abled bodies: their transformation alludes to eschatological potential as they rise forgiven and are restored according to a primordial creation-ideal and eschatological expectations.

1.9.4 Mark 5: The Physical Protagonist between Pathologization and *Pistis*

Mark 5 depicts Jesus' continuous broadened reach with three healing accounts around the Sea of Galilee. There Jesus liberates a violent man from his tormenting and socially marginalizing demonic force, a *pistis*-practicing woman from her continuous blood flow, and a young girl from her early death bed. All three depict the human susceptibility and submission to dis/abling, mundane forces and social pathologization, which Jesus addresses both in his physically communicated, intimate, and astounding healings. All three transformed bodies, thereafter, reveal a healed existence, which transpires eschatological nuances. Moreover, all three narratives depict various but never conclusive approaches and reactions toward Jesus, which engages the audience of the gospel to participate in the responding process. By its own elaborate discourses of dis/ability, this section challenges characterizations of deviating bodies with ambiguous allusions to representations of dis/ability, including the peculiar depiction of the impressively tangible but highly elusive protagonist. Right in succession to the previous controversy about Jesus' identity and authority and as an answer to the τίς ἄρα οὗτός ἐστιν of 4:41, the three healing accounts deploy three hopeless and severe images of dis/ability that vividly illustrate Jesus' embodied cosmic sovereignty over mundane forces and his intrinsic curative force. Furthermore, this chapter, with its three healing narratives, unfolds an interplay of relational πίστις causing holistic *salvation* hinging on an understanding of Jesus' *dynamic* identity in preparation of the following plot.

1.9.5 Mark 7: Transitional Dis/ability

As the locational shifts and final summaric statement (6:53–56) already suggest, Mark 7 depicts the transition of Jesus' message and mission to new places and foreign people, to a new storyline and its theological nuances. Both deviating bodies of this section embody this: Firstly, Jesus argues in Mark 7:24–30 with a Syrophoenician woman about her cultural identity and participation in his ministry over the remote healing of her possessed daughter. As in Mark 5, the child's body forms a contextual frame for the message to the petitioning parent and gospel audience, nevertheless embodying central aspects of the narrative, here, by its image of demonic possession, questions of intrusion, exclusion, and integration. Secondly, Jesus heals a man with an inability to hear and difficulty speaking, in a very sensually narrated account with focus on an extraordinary sequence of Jesus' healing actions (7:31–37). The intimacy, intense physicality, and ambiguously charged substances and methods not only illustrate the man's dis/ability in participating in verbal communication but define Jesus' corporality as divinely legitimized and his healing ability as astonishingly conspicuous and noteworthy. This peaks in the final eulogistic declaration of this chapter with creational and eschatological connotations (Gen 1:31^{LXX}; Isa 35:5–6^{LXX}), which confirm the implicit allusions of previous chapters to a physical norm beyond an everyday binary of health and sickness that seems to be characteristic for Jesus' transitional ministry and proleptic message. This is taken up in Mark's final three healing narratives and a sensory rhetoric regarding the comprehension and perception of Jesus and the gospel. As such, the formerly intestable man of Mark 7:31–37 heralds Jesus' astonishing, uncontainable, and increasingly obvious divine healing ability and identity with unhindered spiritual cognition and clear spiritual communication.

1.9.6 Mark 8–10: Beyond Dis/ability

The final three healing accounts of the gospel depict three sensuous healing narratives: two healings of blindness (8:22–26; 10:46–52) frame the liberation of a boy possessed by an impure, deafening, and muting violent spirit (9:14–29). While the latter focuses on a display of Jesus' embodied exorcistic authority and divine legitimacy connected to the omnipotence of *pistis* practice, the flanking narratives illustrate a spectrum of (in)sight into the identity of Jesus. This reflects the development of the plot in the pursuit of the two blind characters as Jesus is sought out as a renowned, benevolent, personal healer yet recognized to have a historical, cosmic, and maybe messianic heritage. Moreover, in the same way Jesus communicates his embodied healing force by the sensuous attention these images of dis/ability require, the texts themselves focus on a sensuous, engaging *narration* of the tactile, visionary, and auditory cures to lead the audience likewise to an experience of the embodied healing power of Jesus. This is contrasted by this section's predictions of his physical suffering and dematerialization yet underscored by a performative passion prediction, exemplary and encouraging depictions of *pistis*-practicing characters, and impressive allusions to divine omnipotence and prayer. In this ambiguity of symbolic dis/ability and embodied healing, these images of dis/ability furthermore transcend any strict binary of sickness and health as they witness to a spectrum of dis/ability, continue the gospel's allusions to a healed existence beyond such bifurcation, and reflect a polyphonic normativity in the bodies presented.

2 The Markan Summaric Accounts as Showcases for Markan Dis/ability

In addition to individual narratives, the Gospel of Mark features summarizing passages dealing with physically deviating characters and their healing[1] in a collective and conclusive manner. In Mark 1:32–34; 1:39; 3:7–12; 6:5; 6:13, and 6:53–56 Jesus' healing ministry is briefly depicted by describing general and universal physical transformations. While Mark 1:32–34, 3:7–12, and 6:53–56 are longer, compact literary units or separable parts within those, 1:39, 6:5, and 6:13, are only short notes that are firmly connected to the surrounding verses. These passages have been previously analyzed for their traditional, redactional, and editorial value with strong emphasis on their framing function for the individual Markan narratives regarding the chronological and geographical composition of the storyline[2] as they are not essentially connected to the surrounding pericopes and/or mainly feature generalizing information. By their redundant style and frequent use of the imperfect tense, they underline the iterative, continuous, and "customary" character of the events depicted.[3] They condense Jesus' healing to a comprehensive ministry. Moreover, in their specific context, they expand geographically and temporally and at times also with regard to narratological and theological motifs.[4] Hence, they are important for the depiction of the growing significance, range, and chronology of Jesus' ministry, especially since all of these accounts are found within the first six chapters of the gospel, set in Galilee and steadily broadening to the Decapolis and Syrophoenician coastal areas. More importantly, however, they also offer important digests on the conceptions and classifications of (deviating) physicality

---

[1] As explicated above, the term "healing" designates any kind of physical transformation of characters that are explicitly described with deviating features, including those that experience demonic possession.

[2] Not only the term "summaric account" is used very differently in scholarly research, also the deciding criteria, featured stylistic devices, and regarded passages diverge, cf. Becker 2010. Esp. 465. Schmidt 1919. Esp. 66, 105, 107, 160, explains the Markan "Sammelberichte" as general, mainly traditional statements taken up by the evangelist to interweave the storyline in an enigmatic and magnifying way, filling in the fragmentary chronological and topographical frame of the life of Jesus. Dodd in Dodd (ed.) 1953. 6–8; Dodd 1970. 46–52, finds that some summaric passages give—when strung together—the outline of the onset of Jesus' ministry functioning as connectives that probably "belonged to a form of the primitive *kerygma*," cf. similarly, Perrin 1974. Cf. also Egger 1976; Hedrick 1984, and more recently, Hultgren 2002, who includes the Gospel of Luke and Matthew in his analysis. Commentating literature then mainly follows these more extensive studies.

[3] Cf. Schmidt 1919. 60; Egger 1976. 11, 27–38.

[4] For the latter cf. esp. Becker 2010.

in the Gospel of Mark. As this is the focus of the following analysis, it remains—at this point—vague on certain "transversal" motifs of Markan healing narratives (e.g., concrete parameters of demonic dis/ability, directions and implications of curative touches, and the interplay of *pistis* practice and *salvific* healing) that are explicated and concretized in the more detailed accounts but also utilized by the summaric passages.

2.1 Mark 1:32–34

The first summaric account is the shortest of the three separable sequences in the Gospel of Mark. It is set in the beginning of Jesus' programmatic healing ministry after two individual healing narratives have been told (see ch. 3). In five short sentences connected with καί, all (πᾶς) those suffering (κακῶς ἔχοντες) and demonized (δαιμονιζόμενοι) are brought to Jesus, who cures them (θεραπεύω) and publicly casts out their demons (ἐκβάλλω). The scene is set in the first sentence by a *genitivus absolutus:* The day drew to an end, and the sun has set (aorist), and while they are continuously bringing the suffering and possessed to Jesus (imperfect), the whole city had already gathered in front of the door (pluperfect).[5] With regard to the verses before, the emphasis lies on the end of the Sabbath (cf. 1:21), when carrying or bringing the afflicted to Jesus is licit according to certain Jewish regulations.[6] Due to the lack of statements concerning a change of day and scenery, the place of action remains Capernaum (1:21), and Jesus' activity occurs in front of a house door, possibly that of Simon Peter.[7] The temporal and geographical statements connect this account to the verses and scenes before and frame the introductory description of the gathering crowd (vv. 32, 33) before Jesus cures and exorcises, foregrounded in the aorist (v. 34; see fig. 1). Finally, the imperfect in the last

---

[5] The use of πρός in this context has given rise to discussions on the exact location of Jesus' healing in relation to the door (cf. 2:2; 11:4; further Acts 3:2), cf. Dschulnigg 1984. 145. For aspects of the tenses, see Breytenbach in Breytenbach (ed.) 2021a [2019]. 192–193.
[6] Cf. Lev 23:32; Neh 13:19; Luke 23:54; John 19:31–42; *bShab* 34b. Cf. also, e.g., Taylor 1957. 181; Neirynck 1972. 46; Egger 1976. 68; Marcus 2000. 196–197; Collins 2007. 175. For Jesus' Sabbath healings cf. ch. 4. Regarding the Markan style of these "dual time expressions," cf. Neirynck 1972. 14–15, 46; Marcus 2000. 196.
[7] Cf., e.g., Taylor 1957. 180–181; Lane 1974. 78; Collins 2007. 175; Dschulnigg 2007. 84–85; Gnilka 2010. 86. For a symbolic interpretation of the place see Marguerat 2008. 284. Cf. also E. In Focus: Healing Spaces in Mark.

sentence highlights, as an ongoing action in the background, that Jesus did not allow the demons to speak, for they already knew him (pluperfect).[8]

Excursus: Tenses in the Gospel of Mark

The Gospel according to Mark is a historical narrative mainly told in the aorist that spurs the plot forward. Present, imperfect, and perfect are applied to enhance this storyline with specific aspects shaping the significance of actions and events in its "back- and foreground"[9] and by their alternation influence the pace of the narration.[10] The aspects of the verbs reflect the viewpoint of the author toward the narrated event. The present tense is used to record actions in closer proximity to the main storyline as dramatic interruptions and significant details for the scene,[11] similarly to the perfect tense that even enhances this effect ("frontground"). Then the imperfect is used to depict more remote, often parallel actions and give explanatory information in various nuances.[12]

While each narrative is in the following individually analyzed according to the most important features of its alternating tenses and their nuanced meanings, several common and distinctive features of their interplay in the healing narratives have proven noteworthy:

a) Mainly, the imperfect is used against the aorist to set the scene. Either in form of (cor-)relative statements (cf., e.g., 3:8; 5:40b; 6:55; 7:25, 36) or as parallel (at times ongoing) background information at the beginning of sections/ new scenes (e.g., 1:21–22; 2:2; 3:2; 5:3–4, 24, 40a; 7:24; 9:15; 10:46),[13] even intensified as periphrastic conjunctions (e.g., 2:6; 5:5, 11). Hence, the imperfect often introduces dis/abled characters with ongoing suffering and difficult, crowded circumstances for their healing as part of the setting.

b) While the processes of healings are mainly narrated in the aorist with its focus on completed actions carrying the narrative, the imperfect at times records the continuous effect of the physical transformation as *additional*, hence emphasizing details of the already stated successful treatment (cf., e.g., 1:31; 5:41–42; 7:34–35; 8:25; 10:52; similarly 5:13),[14] and permanent deliverance is underscored by the perfect tense (e.g., 5:34 and 10:52; 7:29–30).

---

[8] Cf. Breytenbach in Breytenbach (ed.) 2021a [2019]. 193, who translates "because they had already recognized him."

[9] As Decker in Porter; Pitts (ed.) 2013. 351, n. 12, points out, there is no uniform terminology for these functions. To clarify, in the following the storyline in the aorist is the point of reference supplemented by "background" information in the imperfect and prominent statements to "foreground" the storyline in the present. This metaphorical terminology proves to be useful to grasp the relative interplay of events narrated. Cf. esp. Campbell 2007.

[10] Cf. Porter 1989; Fanning 1990, and their discussion in Carson; Porter 1993. Cf. furthermore, Campbell 2008, and for the following esp. Decker in Porter; Pitts (ed.) 2013; Breytenbach in Breytenbach (ed.) 2021a [2019]; Breytenbach 2021, who prove Mark's careful and deliberate use of tenses. See also Emden 1953/54. 40–47; Doudna 1961.

[11] Cf., e.g., 1:30, 2:3–4.

[12] This is along its basic functions termed, i.e., iterative (e.g., 4:37; 5:18), progressive (e.g., 5:24; 6:20), conative (e.g., 6:48; 9:48 et al.), et al.

[13] Cf. Decker in Porter; Pitts (ed.) 2013. 357.

[14] Cf. Emden 1953/54. 148; Decker in Porter; Pitts (ed.) 2013. 358.

c) Furthermore, the rush to participate in Jesus' effective healing is narrated as a continuous, even habitual reaction of those seeking his help in the imperfect tense (cf., e.g., 1:32, 45; 6:56; 9:15). While this is mainly due to the summaric character of the passages giving general background information, other reactions are also depicted "imperfected" (e.g., 5:20; 7:37) as are the ongoing curative treatments and exorcising deeds (e.g., 6:5–6; also of the disciples, 6:13).

d) Regarding two summaric passages, it is striking that commands to silence are recorded in the imperfect against the main storyline of healing in the aorist (cf. 1:34 and 3:[10], 11–12). Hence, the threat that the knowledgeable unclean spirits pose is depicted as an ongoing struggle in the background (at least at this point of the plot), which fits the demonological conceptions of the Markan gospel (see B. In Focus: Mark's Jesus and Opposing Forces).

e) Moreover, in many instances, direct speech is introduced either in the present tense, mainly regarding Jesus' words, or in the imperfect tense. In the first case,[15] the audience is drawn into the narrative as active listeners, with high emphasis on the following words.[16] Thus, it does not come as a surprise that in all these narratives, the healings support surrounding *arguments* (i.e., Jesus' will to heal, power to forgive sins, stance on the Sabbath, etc.; see below). Secondly, introductions to direct speech in the imperfect[17] occur with several terms and functions,[18] so only a faint pattern can be established: Mainly, these verbs introduce speech that serves an explanatory function (often with γάρ, cf., e.g., 5:8, 28; cf. also 3:21, 30) and/or signal the following utterance to be a part or summary of a longer ongoing speech or "imperfective" process.[19] The occurrence with the plural ἔλεγον reflects a statement of a group that the narrator pushes to the background to generalize it and create a distance for the audience from the voiced opinion.[20]

In the case of ἐπηρώτα/ἐπηρώτων, the terms are in their nature incomplete until answered, which could explain their use in the imperfect, followed by an answer or responsive action in the aorist or present tense (λέγει in 5:9; εἶπεν in 9:28; however, ἔλεγεν in 8:24).[21] This also fits the occurrence not of an interrogative verb but ἔλεγεν (imperfect) followed by ἀπεκρίθη (aorist) and λέγει (present) in 7:27–28.[22] Hence, at times the imperfect introduces utterances similar to open questions that the narrator plans to subsequently answer with rhetoric effect by the verbal aspects used.[23] In all three cases (Mark 5:8–9; 8:23–24; 9:28–29), the specific quality of the dis/ability and its respective healing is discussed: the quantity and quality of the

---

[15] Cf. λέγει in 1:41, 44; 2:5, 8, 10; 3:3, 4, 5; 5:[9], 19; 36, 39, 41; 7:34; 9:19; yet also significantly of the Syrophoenician woman in 7:28 and of Jaïrus [παρακαλεῖ] in 5:23.

[16] Cf. Breytenbach in Breytenbach (ed.) 2021a [2019]. 214–215.

[17] Cf. references to indirect speech in, e.g., 2:1; 3:9; 5:29, 30, 43; 6:55, 56; 8:22.

[18] Cf. ἐπηρώτα/ἐπηρώτων in, e.g., 5:9; 8:23; 9:28; ἔκραζεν/ἔκραζον in 3:11; 10:48; ἔλεγεν/ἔλεγον in, e.g., 5:8, 28, 30, 31; 7:27; 8:24; 9:24.

[19] Cf. 3:11; 10:48b; 5:30–31, as background for the woman's reaction (v. 33), and 9:24 for healing on the basis of πίστις practice (v. 25); cf. also, e.g., 1:21; 7:26; 2:2; 5:10, 18; 10:48a in similar function but without direct speech and just a reference to spoken words. Cf. Decker in Porter; Pitts (ed.) 2013. 355; Breytenbach in Breytenbach (ed.) 2021a [2019]. 215.

[20] Cf. Decker in Porter; Pitts (ed.) 2013. 354–355; Breytenbach in Breytenbach (ed.) 2021a [2019]. 210–213, 215.

[21] Cf., e.g., 5:31; with reference to Jesus' healing deeds also 2:16, 24; 3:21, and 9:16, 21 (14:60) in aorist marking plot-enhancing questions. For more examples see Breytenbach in Breytenbach (ed.) 2021a [2019]. 209.

[22] Cf. also indirect speech: παρεκάλει in 5:10, 18; 6:56.

[23] Cf. Breytenbach in Breytenbach (ed.) 2021a [2019]. 209–210.

possessive demons as necessary information for the following exorcism, the only partially restored eyesight, and the effective treatment of "this kind" of spirit (τοῦτο τὸ γένος). All serve as valid arguments for the narrator to construct his individual punchline (see below).

As established, the analysis of the alternation of tenses in Markan healing narratives hints at significant characteristics of the Markan representations of dis/ability: First and foremost, it reveals an ongoing setting of dis/ability which the popular Jesus decisively and powerfully heals with lasting effect. As particularly severe cases, challenging circumstances, and demonstrative outcomes are emphatically recorded, the continuous battle with the knowledgeable demons develops into a major storyline. Moreover, the interplay of the tenses underscores important arguments of the gospel narrative, similar to the employed images of dis/ability.

The composition of Mark 1:32–34 visualizes the parallel structure of the crowd's action and Jesus' reaction. It emphasizes Jesus' growing popularity and his distinct treatment of the described dis/abilities.

The first verses witness to the growing popularity of Jesus at the very beginning of his public ministry: *all* those "suffering" and "possessed" are brought to Jesus; *the whole city* comes together at the door. These hyperbolic adjectives explain that Jesus' reputation for being a mighty healer has spread, and expectations run high in the entire town. The crowd remains amorphous and unidentified, framed by fixed temporal (v. 32a) and geographical (v. 33b) statements. Jesus' healing is displayed to be universally available. Furthermore, the imperfect impersonal plural ἔφερον suggests a continuous rush of sufferers;[24] the tenses in v. 33 (ἦν [...] ἐπισυνηγμένη) describe a growing crowd. A constant, heavy stream of a vague mass of people is drawn to Jesus and his healing ability. Jesus indeed treats *many* (πολλοί), as the chiastic structure in v. 34 accentuates: πολλοὺς κακῶς ἔχοντας – δαιμόνια πολλά. The use of the adjectives in this passage should be understood inclusively,[25] due to the form and function of the emphatic summaric accounts, as well as the context of the passage (see below) and in accordance with the equivalent interpretation of the Semitic *rabbîm*:[26] Jesus heals many, not only a few.[27]

---

24 Cf. Hooker 1991. 71.
25 Cf., e.g., Lagrange 1935. 11; Jeremias, πολλοί. 541; Lohmeyer 1967. 41; Lane 1974. 79; Hooker 1991. 71; Dormeyer in Zimmermann (ed.) 2013. 195. For an exclusive interpretation alluding to a "realistic" interpretation of Jesus' growing popularity and ministry, cf., e.g., Pesch 1976. 134; Grundmann 1980. 64; Becker 2010. 455; Gnilka 2010. 87. Cf. also the interpretation of an overwhelmed and "weak" Jesus in Lamarche 1996. 81–82.
26 For an extensive analysis, cf. Marcus 2000. 197.
27 Cf. Boring 2006. 67; Focant 2012. 74. Interestingly, in Matt 8:16 many are brought and "all" are healed (πᾶς), in Luke 4:40 "all" are brought and Jesus lays hands on "everyone" (ἕκαστος).

Tab. 1: Composition of Mark 1:32–34 according to content and structure.

Action of Crowd	Reaction of Jesus
[32] Ὀψίας δὲ γενομένης, ὅτε ἔδυ ὁ ἥλιος,	
ἔφερον πρὸς αὐτὸν	[34]καὶ ἐθεράπευσεν
πάντας τοὺς κακῶς ἔχοντας	πολλοὺς κακῶς ἔχοντας
	ποικίλαις νόσοις
καὶ	καὶ
τοὺς δαιμονιζομένους	δαιμόνια πολλὰ
	ἐξέβαλεν καὶ
[33]καὶ ἦν ὅλη ἡ πόλις ἐπισυνηγμένη	οὐκ ἤφιεν λαλεῖν τὰ δαιμόνια,
	ὅτι ᾔδεισαν αὐτόν.
πρὸς τὴν θύραν.	

The account closes with a suspenseful punchline: Although Jesus' popularity and reputation were highlighted, and he reacts as the crowd expected of him, he wants the demon's understanding of him hidden (οὐκ ἤφιεν λαλεῖν ... ὅτι ᾔδεισαν αὐτόν). This tension of disclosure and privacy of Jesus' identity with regard to his healing ministry is carried through the entire gospel on several levels, stretching from the author's and audience's knowledge to the notions of the narratives' characters and the opinions of disciples and demons, prophets and Pharisees.

2.1.1 Labels of Dis/ability: κακῶς ἔχοντες, νόσος, θεραπεύω, and δαιμόνιον, δαιμονίζομαι, ἐκβάλλω

This account witnesses to a complementary structure of ailments and cures. The terminology describing the dis/abled characters which are brought to Jesus (v. 32) is reiterated again reflectively (only with slight variation and exemplification) in the narration of their healing (v. 34). This makes a direct comparison and straightforward correlation of the descriptions possible (see fig. 1 for an illustration of the opposition): The ailing people (κακῶς ἔχοντες) suffering from many different sicknesses (νόσος) are being cured (θεραπεύω), while the demons (δαιμόνιον) of the possessed (δαιμονίζομαι) are cast out (ἐκβάλλω). The parallel sentence structure, buttressed by the double πολύς, implies that each καὶ (vv. 32, 34) must be understood enumeratively and paratactically: those suffering from sicknesses and those possessed are listed as two different groups, requiring different therapies. However, both are brought to Jesus. The Markan common use of φέρω, here with the dis/abled characters as the objects,[28] can refer to people being carried or being led. Accordingly, this wide spectrum of autonomy and some sort of social integration alludes to rather vague images of dis/ability.

This is also reflected by the expression of the unusual adverbial composition κακῶς ἔχοντες, which is found four times in the Gospel of Mark (1:32, 34; 2:17; 6:55),[29] always in context of physical deviance. While it is used very broadly in 1:32, the reason for the suffering is explained in 1:34: ποικίλοι νόσοι, another general description that is singular in the Gospel of Mark.[30] In 2:17, it is contrasted with ἰσχύω in an aphorism-like saying of Jesus, where both opposing depictions are utilized in a figurative sense in the context of the dictum. However, it describes the need of the attention of an ἰατρός, which connotes an immediate physical interpretation. Furthermore, in 6:55, those who are suffering are also being carried around (περιφέρω). Hence, in the Gospel of Mark, κακῶς ἔχω describes a very general physical weakness that is reliant on the strength of others and some sort of curative treatment.[31] The latter is expressed with the term θεραπεύω, which in this context alludes to its basic meaning of "care taking" (of something, e.g., land and people), maybe even more specifically of "treating medically" as it is in Mark only applied to physical ailments.[32] Aside from one exception, the label only occurs in the summaric accounts (cf. 1:34; 3:2, 10; 6:5, 13), which confirm the broadness and universality of the healings described: many afflictions are being "treated," often by physical touch (cf. 3:10; 6:5). This is in accordance with its use in literature on medical concerns and the LXX,[33] although it occurs in both cases much less frequently in comparison to the similar and also general ἰάομαι

---

[28] Cf. 2:3; 7:31–37; 8:22; 9:17, 19, 20; [7:32]; 8:22; [11:2, 7], although this use is quite unusual for the NT.
[29] Cf. also Matt 4:24.
[30] In the NT it is only found in summaries of healings, mainly in the Synoptics and once in Acts. Often it is used in a direct opposition to possession (e.g., Matt 10:1; Luke 6:18; 7:21; 9:1; Acts 19:12), yet also in listings of several more detailed ailments (e.g., Matt 4:24; Luke 7:21), and in connection to other general vocabulary describing physical weakness (e.g., μαλακία in Matt 4:23; 9:35; 10:1; βάσανος in Matt 4:24; ἀσθένεια in Matt 8:17; Luke 4:40; μάστιξ in Luke 7:21).
[31] Elliott 1993. 99–101, explains this phrasing as a variation of the more common phrases in classical Greek κακῶς πράσσοντας and κακῶς πάσχοντας with the Markan tendency to use ἔχω. Cf. also Lattke, κακῶς. 590–591.
[32] Cf., e.g., BDAG, s.v; Beyer, θεραπεύω. 128–129; Grimm, θεραπεύω. 355; LN, s.v 23.139, 35.19; LSJ, s.v; Montanari, s.v; Rupprecht, θεραπεύω. 1203, and below.
[33] For the prior cf., e.g., CH, *Aph.* 6.38; *Vet. med.* 9; Xenophon, *Cyr.* 3.2.12; cf. esp. Asklepeian use: IG IV21, no.121,20 and IG IV² 1, 122, 26, and Wells 1998. 31–39. For the latter cf., e.g., Tob 12:3 but 6:9; 1Esdr 1:4; Jdt 11:17, and Wells 1998. 103–119.

(cf. only 5:29).[34] Here, as well embedded in its wide range of meaning, it carries the nuance of a course of treatment or an active service of (medical) attention, which is in line with its use in Mark 3:2 with an association of work according to the controversial Sabbath context (cf. ch. 4). Furthermore, an effective aspect is expressed with the aorist in almost every occurrence (1:34; 3:10; 6:5), which marks the success of Jesus' attention, while the only imperfect in 6:13 alludes to the ongoing commission of the disciples. While the general nature of the form and terminology of the accounts makes it difficult to determine a concrete meaning regarding the physical treatment, in Mark's gospel, the verb θεραπεύω is used to describe an active and successful healing ministry that is always associated with Jesus' teaching in crowded places (see esp. 6:1–6).[35] Similarly, Jesus' treatment of those possessed is also connected to his teaching, as he expels their demons, here distinctly described, with ἐκβάλλω.[36] In the gospel, this first occurrence of many is mainly used within the context of healing those tormented by δαιμόνια (Mark 1:34, 39; 3:15, 22–23; 6:13; 7:26; 9:18, 28, 38; cf. 16:9, 17) and πνεύματα ἀκάθαρτα (9:18), a phenomenon Mark interchangeably describes with these two labels.[37] The prepositional terminology reflects the notion that the demon dwells inside the host. The forcefulness of the verb connotes a superior authority to effect the vacating of the movable entity from its susceptible yet permeable host. Both are common features of the succeeding exorcism accounts (see below). The lexeme often occurs together with descriptions of Jesus' and his disciples' preaching activity, here displayed by the strong temporal and geographical connection to Jesus' teaching in Capernaum (διδάσκω; cf. the following analysis of Mark 1:39).

---

34 Cf. the thorough analysis in ibid. 31–39, 103–119, 222–229. Nevertheless, her conclusion, that θεραπεύω refers to human service in contrast to divine healing termed ἰάομαι (God of the LXX; Asclepius; Hygieia), is in light of the analysis of very few sources not a comprehensive observation unequivocally applicable to the gospels, hence does not necessarily characterize Jesus as "a son of God, rather than God in human form," ibid. 227. Cf. also Wainwright in Alkier; Weissenrieder (ed.) 2013. 58.
35 Cf. Wells 1998. 138, 154, 228–229, yet again with slightly disproportionate conclusions from scarce evidence. See also Wainwright in Alkier; Weissenrieder (ed.) 2013. 58.
36 See ch. 3.1. Cf. the Gospel of Matthew and Luke, where θεραπεύω is also used when Jesus "treats" demonic possession and particular ailments, such as blindness and paralysis (cf., e.g., Matt 4:24; 12:22; 17:16; Luke 6:18; 8:2; furthermore, John 5:10; Grimm, θεραπεύω. 355). The medical nuance of θεραπεύω in the Gospel of Luke has been thoroughly analyzed by, e.g., Ramsay 1908. 16–17; Harnack; Wilkinson 1911. 15–16.
37 Cf. esp. 3:15 and 6:7, 13; 5:2, 8, 13 and 5:15, 16, 18; 7:25–26; furthermore, Matt 10:1; 12:43; Luke 4:33 and 4:35; 8:27, 33 and 8:29; 9:1; 9:39, 42; 11:24. See p. 56, n. 26.

2.1.2 Contextualization and Function

With regard to its immediate context, two motifs in Mark 1:32–34 stand out: firstly, the parallel description of sickness[38] and possession (πολύς) as two distinct phenomena separated with a paratactic καί and differed in treatment and, secondly, the motif of silenced knowledgeable spirits. The latter reprises and connects this account with the previous exorcism of the πνεῦμα ἀκάθαρτον (1:21–28): the demons have recognized Jesus (1:34), as the unclean spirit knew who he is (οἶδα σε τίς εἶ in 1:24); both are silenced by Jesus.[39] Therefore, by invoking this motif of the exorcism narrative and its close connection to the preceding account (as indicated by the geographical and temporal statements in 1:29–31), the summaric report appears to summarize these earlier events anaphorically, but in a broader and more abstract manner, using hyperbolic language and terminology.[40] Then its inherent universality merges Jesus' healing deeds to a comprehensive ministry:[41] the two differentiated groups, those weak *and* those demon possessed, are being brought to Jesus to be healed,[42] and the silencing of demons becomes a common and characteristic, in the imperfect, even ongoing feature of Jesus' encounters with the spirits (cf., e.g., 3:7–12)[43] as does the correlation of Jesus' healing and teaching (cf. esp. 1:39).

After this primary summary of Jesus' increasing popularity, Jesus goes out and seeks privacy to pray but is found by his disciples and recalls his mission to preach (κηρύσσω; 1:35–38).

2.2 Mark 1:39

The following short summaric statement narrates the fulfillment of his proposal: Jesus travels throughout Galilee, in the synagogues of the neighboring towns around Capernaum (κωμόπολις, 1:38), preaching and exorcising *the* demons, not many or few. He continues with his ministry in synagogues by widening his reach.

---

[38] Accordingly, this denotes any kind of physical affliction apart from possession.
[39] Cf. Egger 1976. 65.
[40] Cf. Marcus 2000. 197; Becker 2010. 453.
[41] Cf. Becker 2010. 460.
[42] Cf. φέρω, 1:32; 2:3; 6:55; 7:32; 8:22; 9:17, 19, 20; θεραπεύω, 1:34; 3:2, 10; 6:5; 6:13, and ἐκβάλλω, 1:34, 39; 6:13; 7:26; cf. 3:15, 22–23; 9:18, 28; 5:8; also 16:9, 17.
[43] Cf. ch. 3, D. In Focus: Silencing in Mark's Healing Narratives.

By separating the historic presence from the initial aorist indicative the structure of the verse clearly shows that the emphasis of the passage lies on κηρύσσω and ἐκβάλλω.[44]

Tab. 2: Composition of Mark 1:39.

1:39 καὶ ἦλθεν
κηρύσσων
εἰς τὰς συναγωγὰς αὐτῶν
εἰς ὅλην τὴν Γαλιλαίαν καὶ
τὰ δαιμόνια ἐκβάλλων.

This account concentrates in its short, precise structure on the question of the relation between Jesus' teaching and his healing ministry that was already alluded to in Mark 1:21–28. This strong association here is termed δαιμόνιον ἐκβάλλω – κηρύσσω as in two other instances in the Gospel of Mark: in 3:14–15, Jesus commissions his disciples to perform these two actions[45] and 6:12–13 witnesses to their success.[46]

2.2.1 Labels of Dis/ability: δαιμόνια, ἐκβάλλω

The demonological language from 1:34 is directly reprised—the demons (δαιμόνια) are being thrown out (ἐκβάλλω) by Jesus. Building on the distinctive treatment of demonic afflictions of Mark 1:32–34, this verse here and Jesus' missionary statement in Mark 6:7 only witness to preaching and the expulsion of demons without any mention of curative treatments of sicknesses whatsoever. This could signify an inclusive meaning, which would align with Mark 6:13 where the disciples also explicitly cure other dis/abilities (see below). On the other hand, Mark 1:39, with its repetitive initial καί conjunctions in each verse, could *also* be interpreted as a prelude to the subsequent healing narrative of the man suffering from *lepra*, suggesting that exorcism and curative treatments are different but both integral components of Jesus' mission, as previously explained in Mark 1:32–34. In its ambiguity, this verse is paradigmatic for the Markan conception of a) a distinct treatment of

---

44 Cf. 1:14; 1:39; 4:1; 5:21–22; 6:1; also 2:18, and Kiffiak 2017. 137, n. 384.
45 In all three Synoptics the commissioning is expressed in present infinitives and therefor marks a "habitual action by the disciples," see Mark 3:14–15; cf. Wells 1998. 209.
46 Cf. also the secondary 16:15–18.

demonic and other afflictions in the depiction of their pathology and healing, which are, nevertheless, b) both in the liberative act significant aspects of Jesus' mission, yet c) characteristically different as the image of possession carries collateral nuances that serve an additional narrative function:

A In Focus: Markan Images of Sickness and Possession

For once, the described symptoms of demon possession depict a distinct clinical picture, namely that of disparate embodiment expressed by locative terminology and socially transgressive and (auto-)aggressive behavior. This is true even if the account of Mark 9:14–29 witnesses to additional symptoms yet never casts doubt on the etiology (see 7.2.2).

Secondly, the etiology *and* therapy of demon possession always distinctly reflect a fusion, respectively, separation of spirit and host (see ch. 3).[47] While it was common in ancient times to attribute (unexplainable) afflictions to divine or numinous entities, the Markan text never, not even implicitly, discusses alternative etiologies, leaving open the possibility that sicknesses could be attributed to demonic influence. However, the narrative distinction between sickness and demon possession, and the distinction between curing and exorcising, suggests that the text refrains from making a general attribution of sickness to demonic influence, yet without ruling it out entirely.[48]

Nevertheless and thirdly, Mark 1:39, with its focus on preaching and exorcising, even if ambiguous in its placement, suggests that the establishing of Jesus' superiority over demons has an additional function. This is confirmed by Mark 3:7–10, which only witnesses to Jesus' curative treatment without a reference to exorcisms. Although Jesus also encounters spiritual entities, only their silencing is narrated. Just like the image of dis/ability in itself, Markan possession embodies two narrative functions regarding host and spirit: for once to witness to Jesus' all-encompassing healing powers as he frees the host from the affliction and, secondly, to illustrate his intrinsic opposition and divine superiority over the knowledgeable spirits. In that, Mark 1:32–34 is paradigmatic: both, the sick and possessed, are healed, and additionally the demons are silenced. The threat of the knowledgeable demons is conveyed as a permanent struggle in the background (see B. In Focus: Mark's Jesus and Opposing Forces) as Jesus' commanding them to silence

---

[47] See 3.4 on why the Markan "departure" of *fever* and *lepra* is different.
[48] Cf. Martin 2004. 37–38, 53–54, 271–72, n. 14, on the Hippocratic discussions on the "scientific" or supernatural etiology of the so-called "Sacred Disease," Celsus' reception of divine physical punishment in Classical texts, and the conceptions of "Neoplatonism" regarding disease, body, and divine/demonic powers.

is narrated in the imperfect (their knowledge in pluperfect; cf. 1:34 and 3:[10], 11–12). This aligns with Mark 1:39, where Jesus' divine authority is intrinsically connected to his preaching of the εὐαγγέλιον and opposes the harmful spiritual realm—their expulsion is a given (see below). Successively, the demoniacs in Mark 1:21–28 and 5:1–20 do not encounter Jesus with the wish to be healed like those with other ailments (by themselves or via petitioners; Bartimaeus in Mark 10:46–52 is even asked what he wants, see ch. 7), but react violently and overpowered to Jesus' sheer presence. This adds another, cosmic dimension to his unavoidable superior authority, narratively unraveling identity, and explicated liberative mission. The account of the exorcism from afar, although initiated by a pleading mother in Mark 7:24–30, emphasizes this by her argument (see ch. 6.1), as does the narrative of the possessed boy with his increasingly confiding father in Mark 9:14–29 (see G. In Focus: Mark's Relational *Pistis*).

Due to these textual indications, a demarcation between sickness and possession is not an anachronistically imposed bifurcation—at least for the Gospel of Mark.[49] As established, ancient discourses also discuss, and not mutually exclusively, spiritual influences as etiology for ailments. For the Gospel of Mark, however, the clear distinction between the two phenomena serves first and foremost a narrative function: liberation from both underscores Jesus' abilities as a powerful healer; moreover, his superiority in light of an antagonistic yet intriguing force serves a more nuanced depiction of his divine identity, authority, and mission (see ch. 3.1.2; cf. paradigmatic Mark 1:32–34).

2.2.2 Contextualization and Function

Mark 1:39 functions as an important connective point for its immediate context yet also coins a motif that spins a significant thread throughout the gospel narrative.

In the first instance, the last phrase of this account links it closely with identical key terms in the first summaric passage in 1:32–34, extending Jesus' exorcism ministry. At the same time, this passage relates Jesus' explanation of his ministry's goals from Mark 1:14–15 directly to its successful opening in 1:38–39: Jesus is introduced as the successor of John the Baptist (cf. Mark 1:4, 7), having come to *preach* (κηρύσσω) the εὐαγγέλιον of God, namely, that the βασιλεία τοῦ θεοῦ is near, and his listeners should "repent" (μετανοέω) and practice *pistis* with regard to this εὐαγγέλιον. In straight continuation, Jesus repeats his mission statement in Mark 1:38, broadening his reach to the neighboring towns (κωμόπολις) where he is

---

49 Cf., e.g., on the Gospel of Luke, Machiela in Notley; Garcia (ed.) 2015.

going to *preach* (κηρύσσω), because this is what he came to do (γάρ ἐξῆλθον). The summaric note in question follows right after this proposition as its fulfillment, adding *exorcising* (ἐκβάλλω). Therefore, Mark 1:39 can be seen as another moment in the impressive introduction of Jesus' ministry in Galilee, which reaches its climax in 1:45, where Jesus' proclamation becomes the proclamation *of* Jesus. Henceforth, the gospel's elaborative mission mandate evolves with the key terms δαιμόνιον ἐκβάλλω – κηρύσσω that Mark 1:39 coins: In 3:14–15, Jesus commissions his disciples to *preach* and gives them authority (ἐξουσία) to *cast out* demons, which they do successfully, as 6:12–13 reports summarically (see below). Interestingly, κηρύσσω is also used to describe how the healed or their witnesses tell of what Jesus has done to and for them: In Mark 1:40–45 and 5:1–20, κηρύσσω terms the proclamation of the men freed from λέπρα and unclean spirits, and in Mark 7:31–37, the witnesses of the healing of a man with sensory impairment proclaim widely (see chs. 3, 5, and 6). In almost all these instances, the public proclamation is suppressed by Jesus (cf. 1:44; 7:36; but: 5:19–20), just as in 5:43 and 8:26, and similar to his orders silencing the demons and unclean spirits (1:24–25, 34; 3:10–12), a motif regarded in greater detail in chapter 3, D. In Focus: Silencing in Mark's Healing Narratives. However, the *proclamation* of Jesus' message is, after the final healing in Mark 10:46–52, taken up as a separate thread and developed into a grand "evangelization scheme," without explicit mention of his healing ministry (cf. Mark 13:10 and 14:9).

While the twist on messenger and message is explicated in Mark 1:45, it is only in Mark 1:14 and here (1:38–39) that Jesus is the proclaiming subject, not John the Baptist (1:4, 7), the disciples (3:14; 6:12), or those witnessing his healing (5:20; 7:36; cf. also 13:10; 14:9). Then, this account is the only one binding these two threads together: the preaching Jesus and, by succession of the terminology, the preached Jesus.

Henceforth, Jesus' preaching is, although differently termed, intrinsically linked to his healing ministry: First and foremost, his teaching (διδάσκω)[50] and healing are explicitly woven together into a narrative on his astonishing ἐξουσία when primarily in Mark 1:21–27 Jesus expels the unclean spirit in a synagogue, which makes this place of teaching the vantage point of his ministry (see ch. 3.1). Precisely this combination of wise words and powerful deeds is reprised in the astonishment of synagogue attendees in Nazareth in Mark 6:2 (see below;

---

[50] For the Markan text it is futile to distinguish between preaching (κηρύσσω) and teaching (διδάσκω) as both are used interchangeably (cf. esp. Mark 1:21 with 1:39 and 6:12) or implicate one another (cf. esp. 1:14–15 and the content of his teaching in 4:1–20; 8:31; 9:31; 12:14). Cf. France in France; Wenham (ed.) 1980; Broadhead 1992a. 69; Marcus 2000. 1871.

cf. 6:6). Furthermore, Jesus is called διδάσκαλος in 5:35 and 9:17, ῥαββουνί in 10:51, and he is told to λαλέω αὐτοῖς τὸν λόγον in 2:1.[51]

Hence, Mark 1:39 is a key peg for the first chapter of Mark's gospel by drawing together vv. 14–15, 21–28 with 34 and 38, condensing Jesus' mighty deeds and astonishing teachings. This is spun further by explicitly connecting them to the key term κηρύσσω, which henceforth links the (com)mission of preaching the εὐαγγέλιον (3:14–15; 6:12–13; [13:10 and 14:9]; cf. also the secondary 16:15–18) and witnessing of encounters with Jesus (1:40–45; 5:1–20; 7:31–37) to the liberation from physical afflictions. This then ascribes to him legitimization and authority. Furthermore, by accounting for this and the Markan explanation on Jesus' opposition toward the demonic forces (see ch. 3), it can be firmly established that dispelling demons is as a key proposition of Jesus and his ministry along with preaching μετάνοια and teaching the βασιλεία τοῦ θεοῦ or, vice versa, confirming it by the silenced, banished, overall inferior demons.

2.3 Mark 3:7–12

Mark 3:7–12 is set after a sequence of controversial teachings and healings in Mark 2:1–3:6 (see ch. 3). Directly succeeding the decision of Jesus' opponents to kill him, this summaric account initiates a new onset as it opens with a change of location: Jesus and his disciples are followed by a large crowd "to the sea" (Sea of Galilee; θάλασσα). The geographical circle is enlarged from this point by the description of the various precisely named places of the people drawing to Jesus. His degree of popularity is heightened, and the knowledge of his deeds stretches in almost every cardinal direction, to the south (Judea, Jerusalem, Idumaea), to the east (Transjordan), and to the north (Tyre, Sidon, Syro-Phoenicia), "progressively distant from the Jewish world to the pagan world [...] beyond the borders of Israel."[52] Once again after Mark 1:32–34, Jesus' prominence and reputation are the main statements of this account.

---

51 All these specific descriptions are regarded in their specific context in each relevant chapter.
52 Cf. Focant 2012. 127. For a short summary of the religious backgrounds of these places see Marcus 2000. 260. While it seems possible, that these places reflect the locations of Christian "churches" at the time the text was written/edited (Marxsen 1959 [1956]. 39), they mainly illustrate geographically Jesus' rise to popularity (Malbon 1991. 20) and the universality (Egger 1969. 480–481) and extent (Schille 1957. 155) of his ministry and mission.

Tab. 3: Composition of Mark 3:7–12 according to content and structure.

Action of Jesus and His Disciples	Reaction of the Crowd
⁷καὶ ὁ Ἰησοῦς μετὰ τῶν μαθητῶν αὐτοῦ	καὶ πολὺ πλῆθος
	ἀπὸ τῆς Γαλιλαίας
ἀνεχώρησεν	ἠκολούθησεν,
πρὸς τὴν θάλασσαν,	καὶ ἀπὸ τῆς Ἰουδαίας
	⁸καὶ ἀπὸ Ἱεροσολύμων
	καὶ ἀπὸ τῆς Ἰδουμαίας
	καὶ πέραν τοῦ Ἰορδάνου
	καὶ περὶ Τύρον
	καὶ Σιδῶνα
	πλῆθος πολὺ ἀκούοντες
	ὅσα ἐποίει
	ἦλθον πρὸς αὐτόν.
⁹καὶ εἶπεν τοῖς μαθηταῖς αὐτοῦ	
ἵνα πλοιάριον προσκαρτερῇ αὐτῷ	ὥστε ἐπιπίπτειν αὐτῷ
	ἵνα αὐτοῦ ἅψωνται
	ὅσοι εἶχον μάστιγας.
διὰ τὸν ὄχλον ἵνα μὴ θλίβωσιν αὐτόν	
¹⁰πολλοὺς γὰρ ἐθεράπευσεν,	¹¹καὶ τὰ πνεύματα τὰ ἀκάθαρτα,
	ὅταν αὐτὸν ἐθεώρουν,
	προσέπιπτον αὐτῷ καὶ
	ἔκραζον
	λέγοντες
	ὅτι σὺ εἶ ὁ υἱὸς τοῦ θεοῦ.
¹²καὶ πολλὰ ἐπετίμα αὐτοῖς	
ἵνα μὴ αὐτὸν φανερὸν ποιήσωσιν.	

The structure of this passage clearly displays the opposition of the two groups and their re-/action to another: Jesus and his disciples are opposing the pressing crowd. The passage already starts with Jesus and his disciples withdrawing (ἀναχωρέω), a verb that requires a preceding action or previously named place to retreat from and connotes the wish for privacy, for a refuge from the conflict in the preceding verses. Perhaps it even foreshadows the following pushing throng. Additionally, having only the Sea of Galilee to their back, this location resembles a trap with the crowd cornering Jesus and his disciples from all directions. Jesus even asks his disciples to have a boat close at hand (προσκαρτερέω) as a refuge and escape. The eagerness of the people and their physical pursuit of Jesus are described vividly with highly active vocabulary characterizing the crowd's action potential (ἀκολουθέω, ἀκούω, ἔρχομαι, θλίβω, ἐπιπίπτω). The only other time in the New Testament that the phrase the "pressing crowd" (θλίβω) is found is in Mark 5:24, 31 (συνθλίβω), where it stresses the publicity and sensation of Jesus healing the daughter of Jaïrus and the woman with the issue of blood (see ch. 5.2). Since Jesus cured (θεραπεύω) *many* (πολλοί), an even greater tumult of people with μάστιγες is encouraged to fall upon him (ἐπιπίπτω) and reach out to touch him (ἅπτομαι). Again, the focus lies entirely on his reputation and popularity, his healing being the reason (γάρ) for an even greater, more threatening tumult.

Through all of this, great emphasis is placed on the description of the serious magnitude of the surrounding crowd through the impressive, chiastic description πολὺ πλῆθος – πλῆθος πολὺ. Furthermore, the two groups, Jesus and his disciples facing the tumultuous throng, are opposed syntactically, as figure 2 shows: while the latter press and harass Jesus, he confides to his following disciples about the need for more distance from the crowd. The μαθηταί – πλῆθος/ὄχλος association is not uncommon in the Gospel of Mark.[53] In this account, it paints a dualistic, suspenseful scene: Jesus with his disciples at the lake on the one side, the pressing, "perilous"[54] crowd coming from all directions on the other side. Jesus does not face the crowd on his own; his entourage is always with him. However, he also interacts with both by helping and healing some and confiding in and seeking help from the others.

The scene closes with Jesus in conflict with unclean spirits, who also react tumultuously with falling and screaming. Jesus strongly rebukes (πολύς; ἐπιτιμάω) the πνεύματα ἀκάθαρτα to not make him known. An actual exorcism is not mentioned explicitly; rather, this section is entirely narrated in the imperfect to depict the conflict in rather broad strokes as continuous background information.[55]

---

[53] Cf. 6:45; 7:17; 8:1, 6, 34; 9:14; 10:46; moreover, Dschulnigg 1984. 180.
[54] Focant 2012. 128.
[55] See *Excursus: Tenses*, p. 22–24; cf. also Mark 6:53–56 and Breytenbach in Breytenbach (ed.) 2021a [2019]. 188–189.

2.3.1 Labels of Dis/ability: ἔχω μάστιξ, ἅπτομαι and πνεύματα ἀκάθαρτα, ἐπιτιμάω

The images of dis/ability are first mentioned in vv. 10–12. Under the premise (γάρ) that Jesus already cured (θεραπεύω) many, the following verses serve as an explanation for his ever-growing reputation and popularity.

Hanging on to this prior condition, those with μάστιγες are reaching out to *also* be healed (v. 10). The term μάστιξ is found four times in the New Testament, three of those in the Gospel of Mark (Mark 3:10; 5:29, 34; Luke 7:21), always denoting a form of physical ailment, literally meaning "whip/lash."[56] In Mark 5, it classifies the sickness of the woman with the issue of blood, an ailment associated with im/purity, which it also references in other passages of ancient Jewish literature. However, μάστιγες also describe striking punishments of the gods and thereby insinuate a divine etiology without regarding specific symptoms.[57] Another possible and quite general nuance to a sickness referred to as μάστιξ simply poses its literal meaning: It describes a sickness "scourging" or "attacking" the body, unspecific in its etiology. In Luke, Jesus heals those suffering from νόσοι, μάστιγες, and evil spirits (πνεύματα πονήρα), suggesting a differentiation of the mentioned ailments or a line of reductions: there are ailments in general, and μάστιγες—perhaps caused by god(s) or impurity—and πνεύματα πονήρα in particular. While the Lukan conception of dis/ability is a question of its own, the Markan understanding behind this ambiguous term is more closely regarded in the more detailed context of Mark 5:25–34 (see ch. 5.2). For the summaric account it first and foremost paints a vivid picture: "those who have been attacked and lashed by disease [...] in their turn attack Jesus in their eagerness to be healed."[58] Severe suffering and helplessness are characteristic of their dis/abilities.

The therapy applied by Jesus, causing this tumult in the first place, is termed θεραπεύω (v. 10, see above), which, as established, witnesses to an active course of (medical) treatment. However, the patients also try actively to be healed, and those who are plagued throw themselves onto Jesus in order to touch him (ἅπτομαι). While Jesus' curative touch has already been narrated in the gospel text (1:31; 1:41), this implication of his body transferring healing when being touched serves as an illustration of his popularity at this point of the narrative. However, in successive accounts, it becomes a motif of Jesus' intrinsic healing ability (see below, respectively in ch. 3 and 5). It is noteworthy to again point to the general and im-

---

[56] Cf., e.g., Balz; Schneider, *μάστιξ*. 975; BDAG, *s.v.*; LN, *s.v.* 19.9, 23.153; LSJ, *s.v.*; Montanari, *s.v.*; Schneider, *μάστιξ*. 524; Spicq, 2.539–542.
[57] Cf., e.g., Homer, *Il.* 12.37; 13.812; Aeschylus, *Prom.* 682; also BDAG, *s.v.*; LSJ, *s.v.*; Montanari, *s.v.*
[58] Marcus 2000. 258.

precise meaning of θεραπεύω and its exclusive use in summaric contexts in Mark (Mark 1:34; 3:2, 10; 6:5; 6:13).

The clinical picture of demon possession (in Mark, interchangeably described with δαίμων/δαιμόνιον; see for the following also ch. 3.1.2)[59] is further illustrated: Bodily functions, such as seeing (θεωρέω), moving (προσπίπτω), and speaking (κράξω, λέγω), are taken over by the spiritual entity (v. 11). Their knowledge about Jesus also seems to exceed that of most other literary characters; they call Jesus out to be ὁ υἱὸς τοῦ θεοῦ just like the divine voice in 1:11 and later in 9:7 (cf. also 5:7). Although the behavior of those "plagued" and those with "unclean spirits" is both virulently physical, there are distinct differences: while the wish to be freed from μάστιγες is expressed by pressing Jesus and by pouncing onto him (ἐπιπίπτω) to touch (ἅπτομαι) the renowned healer, the latter fall down before him (προσπίπτω; cf. 5:33; 7:25) screaming (κράξω), seemingly struck by his divine identity, as the title indicates. Jesus reacts not with an exorcism, as previously witnessed, but by emphatically (πολλὰ) commanding (ἐπιτιμάω) the spirits to be silent regarding their communicated knowledge in direct speech. The extent of the lexeme's meaning is here, without an explicit exorcism, tied to its hierarchal and authoritative connotation of silencing. Considering its previous and impressive use in the account of Mark 1:21–28, the effective subordination of the entities is reprised, even if the sequence lacks a conclusive statement, and is taken up again in subsequent narratives (cf., e.g., 9:25, furthermore, 4:39; 8:33). The imperfect here, as in the order to silence in 1:34, reflects the permanence in the conflict with the spirits, which furthermore sets their rebuke apart from healing encounters; Jesus' primary concern here is the demon's unwarranted proclamation. The inferior spirits are continuously silenced from witnessing Jesus' superiority and authority.

2.3.2 Contextualization and Function

Mark 3:7–12 is a true melting pot of common Markan motifs featured in preceding and subsequent accounts of healings, all connected to portray Jesus' popularity and widespread fame. Semantically, the general term θεραπεύω connects this account with the summaric passages in 1:32–34 and 6:5, 13 (see above and below) but also with the directly preceding conflict about the curative treatment on the Sabbath (vv. 1–6; see ch. 4). Moreover, the description of those "plagued" seeking Jesus' cura-

---

[59] Cf. esp. 3:15 and 6:7, 13; 5:2, 8, 13 and 5:15, 16, 18; 7:25–26; furthermore, Matt 10:1; 12:43; Luke 4:33 and 4:35; 8:27, 33 and 8:29; 9:1; 9:39, 42; 11:24. For a more detailed survey on the terminology of evil forces in the NT see, e.g., Sorensen 2002. 121–122; Wahlen 2004. 177. In the LXX, δαίμων/δαιμόνιον translates "Hebrew terms for demonic entities," cf. Sorensen, *Demons, Demonology III. NT.* 540.

tive touch foreshadows the passage of the woman scourged with an issue of blood, who taps his healing power (cf. esp. 5:27–34). The motif of Jesus' reputation to heal by *being* touched (3:10), as it is empathically reprised again (cf. 5:27, 28, 30, 31; 6:56), is regarded closely in chapter 3, C. In Focus: Mark's Healing Touches. Furthermore, the motif of title-brawling unclean spirits that are being rebuked by Jesus to be silent about their extraordinary knowledge about his identity is taken up again throughout the gospel narrative,[60] as is the fact that those asking for help are frequently prostrating before Jesus[61] while the crowd is pressing onto him (5:24).

2.4 Mark 6:5 and 6:13

The final summaric accounts are embedded in Mark 6, which accounts for a narrative shift as it initiates questions about the limits of Jesus' ministry that continue to be posed as the passion narrative is prepared. In that, the summaric notes in Mark 6:5 and 6:13 oppose one another. While 6:5 focuses on the deeds that *Jesus is not able* to do in *Nazareth*, 6:13 speaks of his *disciples* and the mighty deeds they are *able to do elsewhere* after being commissioned (vv. 7–11). This is enforced by the same images of dis/ability in the second half of each verse, only to point to the differences in success and, chiastically, in therapy. Mark 6:5–6 states Jesus' actions as ongoing reactions toward the perpetual rejection in his hometown in the imperfect (cf. vv. 2–3, also in the imperfect); the few healings are told as completed actions in the aorist.[62] Mark 6:13, on the other hand, witnesses to the ongoing deeds of the disciples in the imperfect.

Tab. 4: Comparison and composition of Mark 6:5 and 6:13 according to content and structure.

Jesus' Actions at "Home"—6:5	Disciples' Actions Elsewhere—6:13
καὶ οὐκ ἐδύνατο ἐκεῖ ποιῆσαι οὐδεμίαν δύναμιν,	
	καὶ δαιμόνια πολλὰ
	ἐξέβαλλον,
εἰ μὴ	καὶ ἤλειφον ἐλαίῳ

---

60 Cf. 1:21–28; 1:32–34; 5:1–20; 9:14–29; see also D. In Focus: Silencing in Mark's Healing Narratives.
61 Cf. 5:33 and 7:25; 5:6, 22; also 1:40.
62 Cf. Breytenbach in Breytenbach (ed.) 2021a [2019]. 204–205.

Tab. 4: Comparison and composition of Mark 6:5 and 6:13 according to content and structure. *(Continued)*

Jesus' Actions at "Home"—6:5	Disciples' Actions Elsewhere—6:13
ὀλίγοις ἀρρώστοις	πολλοὺς ἀρρώστους
ἐπιθεὶς τὰς χεῖρας	
ἐθεράπευσεν.	καὶ ἐθεράπευον.

2.4.1 Labels of Dis/ability: (οἱ) ἄρρωστοι and θεραπεύω

In both accounts, (οἱ) ἄρρωστοι is used to characterize the people being cured (θεραπεύω) by Jesus (v. 5; cf. Matt 14:14) or his disciples (v. 13).[63] While the lexeme is generally ambiguous in its meaning, in Mark 6:5 and 6:13, ἄρρωστοι seems to refer to a physical, sickly weakness that needs to be cured. Both accounts emphatically close by stating a general curative treatment (θεραπεύω; see above, Mark 1:34; 3:2, 10; 6:5; 6:13) administered by touch: In Mark 6:5, Jesus heals by actively laying both of his hands (ἐπιτίθημι τὰς χεῖρας) *on* the not necessarily specific part of the weak body, illustrating his curative treatment beyond the previous explicated general ἅπτω by the help-seekers (cf. Mark 3:7–12; furthermore, 6:56). Mark 6:13, on the other hand, mentions the casting out of demons and the anointment with oil of those physically weak. As established, ἐκβάλλω δαιμόνια – κηρύσσω form a customary Markan compilation (see above; cf. Mark 1:39 and 3:14–15),[64] linking the exorcism closely to the preaching of Jesus and his disciples. The anointment with oil for healing is only referenced in the New Testament in this passage and in Jas 5:14–15 (with the addition of healing ἐν τῷ ὀνόματι τοῦ κυρίου) and it may have a symbolic function or be related to its use in ancient medicine as a cleansing

---

[63] Besides these occurrences within the context of healing narratives, ἄρρωστοι is also found in 1Cor 11:30 where Paul describes the "sick and weak" in the church regarding unworthy conduct when receiving the Eucharist. Since Pauline language and literary purpose differ widely from the Markan style and context, it is only pointed out, that the following κοιμῶνται, a Pauline euphemism for the process of somatic dying, suggests Paul is talking literally about the physical realm of weakness with both lexemes, ἀσθενεῖς and ἄρρωστοι. Additionally, the references to πολλοί and ἱκανοί suggest a synonymy and only stylistic variation of the many, being gradually different from the few κοιμῶνται. Cf. comprehensively for the NT accounts, Balz; Schneider, *ἄρρωστος.* 380; Zmijewski, *ἀσθενής and cogn.* 408–413; Stählin, *ἀσθενής and cogn.* 488–492; Bauer, s.v. 229–230.

[64] See also secondary 16:15–18.

and soothing emollient.⁶⁵ Additionally, it could have religious and ritual significance that complements its natural pharmacological properties.⁶⁶ Due to the lack of any other information in the Markan text, nothing concrete can be put on record.

2.4.2 Contextualization and Function

Mark 6:1–6 emphasizes and questions the relation of mighty deeds and *pistis* (δύναμις, v. 5 and ἀπιστία, v. 6), an issue introduced in Mark 2:1–12, established in Mark 5:21–43, and addressed again in Mark 9:14–29, and is here implemented as an interconnection of the two elaborate accounts in Mark 5 and 9 (see in ch. 5, G. In Focus: Mark's Relational Pistis, H. In Focus: Mark's Holistic Salvation, and I. In Focus: The Markan Jesus' Dynamic Identity). The positive reaction and response to Jesus from previous summaric reports is reversed: although the people in his hometown of Nazareth are astonished (ἐκπλήσσω; v. 2) about Jesus' teaching and mighty deeds, he experiences skepticism (cf. the questions about his identity in v. 3), anger (σκανδαλίζω; v. 3), dishonor (ἄτιμος; v. 4), and ἀπιστία (v. 6). There are no pressing crowds, not many but only a few (ὀλίγος) are cured (5b) because Jesus is simply *not able* (δύναμαι) to do more (5a). This (for Hellenistic Greek, not uncommon) double negative (not able, any deed) and double statement (except)⁶⁷ reaches the effect that "5b modifies the rigour of 5a by stating an exception,"⁶⁸ which by the following verse seems to hinge on *pistis:* is Jesus not being able to unleash his full healing power in this setting of *a-pistia* and his healing ability only reaches a few ἄρρωστοι,⁶⁹ those probably practicing *pistis*,⁷⁰ as insinuated by the opposi-

---

65 Cf., e.g., Isa 1:6; Luke 10:34; Josephus, *B.J.* 1.657; *A.J.* 17.171–172. For a thorough summary of the ancient conceptions of anointment for healing, see Kranemann, *Krankenöl.* 915–920; Taylor 1957. 306; Schlier, *ἀλείφω*; van der Loos 1965. 311–312. Kollmann 1996. 319, even presumes Christian healers had acquired common ancient pharmacological-medical proficiencies which might be reflected in these occurrences yet is difficult to prove.
66 Cf. esp. col. 915 and col. 918 in Kranemann, *Krankenöl.* Cf. also Nutton, *Medizin.* 1110. Regarding the notion of oil as a powerful remedy against demonical forces, cf., e.g., *QohR* 1:8 (9a); *T.Sol.* 18:34; Ḥarba de-Moše A 3, 14.21.41, and Kranemann, *Krankenöl.* 919. Lührmann 1987. 112, argues against an exorcistic connotation of oil in this context with regard to its ancient *medical* use that is also reprised in Luke 10:34. However, a concrete distinction between the two forms remains to be presented.
67 Cf. Collins 2007. 292, who sees here the same sentence structure as in v. 4: a negative followed by an exception.
68 Taylor 1957. 301.
69 Cf. Lane 1974. 204; Ernst 1981. 170.
70 Cf., e.g., Grundmann 1980. 158.

tion of πολλοί (vv. 2–3), who question and resent Jesus, and ὀλίγοι (v. 5), who get healed? Moreover, the first group is not only skeptical about Jesus' teaching but wonder about αἱ δυνάμεις διὰ τῶν χειρῶν αὐτοῦ γινόμεναι, which links v. 2 strongly to v. 5 (cf. also the connection of 1:21–28 to 6:2): his preaching and ability to perform δυνάμεις is questioned, the latter apparently rightfully. The reference to his hands in context of the gospel's preference to depict tangible healing connects Jesus' healing ability again strongly to his own corporeality (see ch. 5 on the concept of δύναμις/δυνάμεις, πίστις, curative touches, and ἐξουσία).[71] This confirms the connection established in Mark 2:5 and 5:34 of commended *pistis*-practicing characters and their healing. Here, Mark 6:5 not only bundles the already established motifs of Jesus' astonishing, highly efficacious, and usually well-received curative touch but sets them in an intriguing spotlight by questioning Jesus' healing ability that is transmittable by touch and commission and seems inevitably connected to πίστις.[72] Nevertheless, this summaric note stays vague on the concrete parameters of *pistis* practice and receiving of healing.

In correlation with Mark 6:13, it is striking that although Jesus' healing ability seems somewhat physically incorporated and connected to *pistis*, it is also transferrable to his disciples (v. 13). In Mark 6:7–12, Jesus is sending out his followers with the authority over impure spirits,[73] not, however, to heal, which they nevertheless do successfully. Accordingly, this passage suggests an inclusive conception, i.e., that authority over unclean spirits also includes the ability to heal. Although vv. 12–13 describe the actions of the disciples almost in a chronological order with the exorcising and anointing paratactically, the final θεραπεύω without any pronoun does not necessarily refer to the previously mentioned ἄρρωστοι but can encompass both actions or add a third: first they go out (aorist participle), and then they preach μετάνοια (aorist) while (imperfect) casting out demons, anointing the ἄρρωστοι, *and* curing.[74] However, the chiastic structure of δαιμόνια πολλά and πολλοὶ ἄρρωστοι insinuates an independence of each group and concurrence of casting out and anointing, which has been similarly witnessed in other Markan accounts (see above, A. In Focus: Markan Images of Sickness and Possession).

---

71 The connection of *pistis*, preaching, and healing by laying on of hands as established in 6:1–6 is heightened and expanded in the secondary 16:16–18.
72 Cf. Mark 2:1–12 (cf. v. 5); 5:25–34 and 5:21–24, 35–43 (cf. vv. 34 and 36) and 9:14–29 (vv. 23 and 24).
73 Cf. ἐξουσίαν τῶν πνευμάτων τῶν ἀκαθάρτων; cf. Mark 3:14–15.
74 Since the object changes from *the people* being taught repentance, to *the many demons*, to *the many ἄρρωστοι*, it is unlikely that the progression is meant causal: only after the people repented, the disciples could cast out their demons and anoint and heal them as they were weak after the "exorcism."

Furthermore, the fact that θεραπεύω is used exclusively to refer to physical weakness (cf. 1:34, 3:2, 10, 6:5, and 6:13) and is even contrasted with the treatment of demonic possession (cf. 1:32–34) suggests that it is used climactically to describe the effect of the anointment on the ἄρρωστοι. Without this, the account of the disciples' success would only have an implied or unfinished result, unlikely for an account on the success of the disciples. Furthermore, and strictly speaking, Jesus also did not give the disciples the commission to preach μετάνοια in v. 7, yet it seems to be the main activity in v. 12 against the backdrop of their healing activity.[75] This is supported by the function of this verse in its broader context: In succession of Mark 3:14–15, these passages focus on the transference of Jesus' ministry to his disciples with the main responsibility to teach the εὐαγγέλιον. As this is intrinsically connected to an opposition and superiority over harmful spiritual entities, their expulsion is a given. Physical healing of those seeking help, however, seems to be a *pistis*-related "byproduct." Hence, following Mark 6:5, v. 13 serves as a contextual focus and contentual crux for the gospel narrative.

2.5 Mark 6:53–56

Thereafter, the gospel text continues its narrative plotting by witnessing to the death of John the Baptist and focusing once again on Jesus' travels, popularity, and mighty deeds around the Sea of Galilee. Fittingly, this summaric account starts with a long exposition on the location. Jesus and his disciples land with the boat in Gennesaret, which probably means the region in the west of the lake between Capernaum and Tiberias, north of Magdala, southwest of Bethsaida. Jesus is immediately (εὐθύς) recognized, causing a continuous (imperfect) wild movement of people following him, with those sick on stretchers. The entire area is taken up with the frenzied search for Jesus and his healing power; as the space broadens (villages, towns, hamlets), so does the temporal character of the actions. The finally narrated healing is comprised in one short sentence in the aorist at the end of the long exposition over two and a half verses, spiked with repetitive relative clauses.[76] Jesus' popularity and publicity reach a peak: not only are Jesus' whereabouts known and people are able to follow him there, but the healings happen in the town squares—the centers of social life as much as of political and economic

---

75 Cf. Kollmann 1996. 319; Kranemann, *Krankenöl*. 920.
76 Cf. Koch 1975. 191.

power. The general relative clauses ὅπου ἤκουον in v. 55 and ὅπου ἂν and ὅσοι ἂν in v. 56 support the universality of Jesus' reach.[77]

Tab. 5: Composition of Mark 6:53–56 according to content and structure.

Action of Jesus	Reaction of Crowd
6:53 καὶ διαπεράσαντες ἐπὶ τὴν γῆν ἦλθον εἰς Γεννησαρὲτ	
καὶ προσωρμίσθησαν.	
54 καὶ ἐξελθόντων αὐτῶν ἐκ τοῦ πλοίου	εὐθὺς ἐπιγνόντες αὐτὸν
	55περιέδραμον ὅλην τὴν χώραν ἐκείνην
	καὶ
	ἤρξαντο ἐπὶ τοῖς κραβάττοις
	τοὺς κακῶς ἔχοντας
	περιφέρειν
56 καὶ ὅπου ἂν εἰσεπορεύετο εἰς κώμας ἢ εἰς πόλεις ἢ εἰς ἀγρούς,	ὅπου ἤκουον ὅτι ἐστίν.
	ἐν ταῖς ἀγοραῖς ἐτίθεσαν
	τοὺς ἀσθενοῦντας
	καὶ παρεκάλουν αὐτὸν
	ἵνα κἂν τοῦ κρασπέδου τοῦ ἱματίου αὐτοῦ ἅψωνται·
	καὶ ὅσοι
	ἂν ἥψαντο αὐτοῦ
	ἐσῴζοντο.

This final summaric account heightens Jesus' reputation, his widely stretched popularity, and the explicit publicity of his actions to an even greater extent by not concentrating on one geographical reference for the healing encounter alone; rather, Jesus himself is depicted as a moving point of reference. The crowds in the whole area Γεννησαρὲτ are drawing to him, wherever he is (περιτρέχειν and περιφέρειν). Furthermore, as the opposition "action of Jesus" and "reaction of

---

[77] Cf. Egger 1976. 135.

crowd" exemplifies, Jesus is portrayed as a *passive* point of reference, only characterized by his travels as a moving target of the crowd. Neither demonic spirits nor Jesus' teachings are mentioned. He does not even participate actively in the effective "healing" (σῴζω, ch. 5); he is simply *being* touched (see fig. 4).

2.5.1 Labels of Dis/ability: κακῶς ἔχοντες, ἀσθενεῖς, σῴζω

The deviating bodies are again generally described as κακῶς ἔχοντες (Mark 1:32–34; see above) and are brought to Jesus (this time περιφέρω) on their stretchers. Unlike in Mark 1:32–34, κακῶς ἔχοντες here is not further differentiated by an explicative connection to a medical condition (cf. 1:34, ποικίλοι νόσοι). However, the lexeme κράβαττος, which means "multipurpose bed, stretcher of the poor,"[78] depicts limited mobility. The term is used four times in the healing narrative of the παραλυτικός (Mark 2:4, 9, 11, 12; see ch. 4.1), while Mark 4:21 and 7:4, 30 describe the κλίνη as more of a common bedding. Besides its generality, κακῶς ἔχοντες expresses in this context ailments associated with corporal immobility.

Furthermore, the ἀσθενεῖς (see above) are brought to the marketplace. Regarding healing narratives, the lexeme and its cognates are only used here.[79] In the broadest sense, it can be translated as weakness or frailty in a physical, economical, mental, or spiritual sense.[80] In correspondence with the description of necessary stretchers and the plea for Jesus' renowned (curative) touch (cf. ἐπιγινώσκω, v. 54), the physical aspect lies in the foreground of the general human frailty associated with this term. The image of continuously rushing, tumultuous crowds with also immobile and weak petitioners trying to touch one single moving target, conveys that the popularity of Jesus has reached an impracticable extent.[81]

While the plea (παρακαλέω) for a healing touch (ἐπιτίθημι τὰς χεῖρας and ἅπτομαι) is also mentioned in Mark 5:23; 7:32, and 8:22 (cf. 5:10, 18), the request there is for being touched *by* Jesus. As in Mark 3:7, here again the physical nearness

---

78 Donahue; Harrington 2002. 217. Cf., e.g., Luke 5:19; Acts 5:15. Cf. also LN, s.v. 6.107.
79 There is only one other occurrence: in Mark 14:38, ἀσθενής is used to describe the incapability of the disciples to resist temptation; there are no occurrences of ἀσθένεια or ἀσθένημα.
80 Cf. in its comprehensive use, e.g., Plato, *Leg.* 854a; 1Pet 3:7; 1Cor 2:3; 2Cor 10:10; regarding economic factors, e.g., Herodotus, *Hist.* 2.47; Aristophanes, *Pax* 636; spiritual and mental capacities, e.g., Aristotle, *Eth. Nic.* 19/1150b; Thuc. 2.61.2; Epictetus, *Ditr.* 1.8.8, and regarding physical conditions, e.g., Herodotus, *Hist.* 4.135; Josephus, *B.J.* 1.76; *A.J.* 15.359; John 5:5; Acts 28:9; Luke 10:9. Cf. also, e.g., BDAG, s.v.; Coenen; Haacker, *Krankheit/Heilung.* 1197; Heckel, ἀσθένεια. 1200; Link, ἀσθένεια. 1199; LN, s.v. 22.2, 23.126, 23.143, 25.269, 74.23; LSJ, s.v.; Montanari, s.v.; Stählin, ἀσθενής *and cogn.* 488–489; Zmijewski, ἀσθενής *and cogn.* 408–413.
81 Cf. Marcus 2000. 436–437.

to Jesus seems to be, as v. 56 specifies, a necessary requirement and prior condition to be healed and mainly serves to illustrate Jesus' popularity and the trust in his intrinsic healing ability.

Contrary to all the other summaric accounts, where θεραπεύω is the complementary term to the general descriptions of ailments and physical frailty (cf. esp., κακῶς ἔχοντες – θεραπεύω in Mark 1:32–34), this passage depicts the nonspecifically weak as being "saved" (σῴζω) after touching Jesus. The range of meaning of this term, from physical to spiritual or even eschatological restoration,[82] in contrast to the physically curative θεραπεύω, suggests an interpretation beyond a mere physical transformation. This fits the occurrence in other passages of the gospel, where, however, it is always attributed to specific clinical pictures. A simple explanation regarding the anaphoric composition of the summaric accounts is only a feeble argument in light of the climactic position of the term in the account's punchline: *all* are effectively "saved" (aorist). Due to its stylistic prominence also regarding the account's conclusive character at this position of Mark's gospel (see below), the use of σῴζω here in this universal and general setting rather suggests that the term insinuates a notion beyond a binary re-storation to any kind of "not weakened." While the common summaric terms for human physical suffering are reprised, the motif of Jesus' literally *tangible* and passive healing power is heightened and emphasized not just by the necessary approach but by the effect, which suggests more than a physical cure (see ch. 5, H. In Focus: Mark's Holistic Salvation).

2.5.2 Contextualization and Function

The depicted corporal helplessness and immobility overcome by the physical abilities and helpfulness of hopeful others, who bring those who are weak on pallets to Jesus, links this account to Mark 1:32–34 and 2:1–12 and the subsequent 7:31–37, 8:22–26, and 9:14–29.

Furthermore, the motifs of actively hoping for healing and reaching out *toward* Jesus connect this passage to Mark 3:7–12 and 5:25–34 and express an embodiment of the knowledge of and trust in Jesus' healing power (see C. In Focus: Mark's Healing Touches). While in Mark 3:7–12, the sick touch Jesus, and in 5:25–34, the woman with the issue of blood touches his ἱμάτιον, it is here his κράσπεδον believed to be the healing counterpart. Jesus' power expands gradually

---

[82] Cf., e.g., BDAG, s.v.; Foerster, σῴζω. 990; LSJ, s.v.; LN, s.v. 21.18, 21.27, 23.136; Montanari, s.v.; Radl, σῴζω; Schneider, σῴζω; Spicq, 1.629–643. See also Wells 1998. 180–181.

to the "fringes" of his physical existence. This is underscored by the use of the singular to refer to the traditionally four Jewish ritual fringes (Deut 22:12; Num 15:38–39; cf. Matt 23:5), which, if not generally understood as the "seam" of his garment, indicates an additional hyperbolic nuance that even the touch of *one* of the fringes might be enough for healing.[83] Nevertheless, their "salvation" is recounted to be affected after touching him, not his garment or its fringes (v. 56).

Moreover, the strong connection to Mark 5:25–34 is exhibited in the common topic of the "automating" and "autonomy" of Jesus' power and its surprising holistic effect (cf. [κἄν] ἅπτομαι – ἱμάτιον – σῴζομαι), which is heightened here regarding the sheer quantity and universality of those seeking the tangible healer.

2.6 Summaric Accounts as Showcases of Dis/ability and Literary and Theological Benchmarks

The images of dis/ability in the Markan summaric accounts are characterized by generality in their overall terminology and specificity in their references to certain individual healing accounts. The summaric passages highlight, heighten, generalize, and universalize the individual accounts, and/or, vice versa, the individual healing narratives color in the rough sketches that the summaric reports drew. The dense summaric accounts depict action as general background information for the longer and slowly narrated healings of particular characters. By that, they not only hint at several significant parameters of the Markan conceptions of dis/ability but bundle narratively and theologically crucial threads of the storyline together.

2.6.1 Showcases of Dis/ability

The accounts are all characterized by a similar use of general vocabulary and numeral adjectives, which underline the unrelenting and vast healing activity and its universality (even in 6:5, by contrast). The general terminological designations of those suffering as κακῶς ἔχοντες, ἄρρωστοι, and ἀσθενοῦντες (1:32–34; 6:5, 13; 6:53–56) link the passages closely to each other and emphasize their comprehensiveness by the general yet imprecise images of dis/ability that nevertheless highlight a form of physical weakness and dependence. The physical deviance that the summaric accounts portray focuses on this suffering and indicates non-desirable

---

[83] Cf. Acts 5:15–16; 19:11–12; also *bMen* 43b–44a.

social implications. To the audience, the vastness of help-seekers must have been easy to imagine due to the general images applied yet probably lacked a specific identification. Only twice, this vague picture is filled in a little by the extensions that the help-seekers are suffering from ποικίλοι νόσοι (1:32–34) and μάστιγες (3:7–12). However, as established, both terms are ambiguous in meaning, emphasizing even more the universal conception of dis/ability depicted. A common symptom most of the weak share is that they suffer from an—yet again uncertain—ambiguous impaired mobility and are socially integrated: they are brought or carried by others to Jesus (φέρω). Their eagerness to be healed is, however, physically expressed (ἐπιπίπτω, 3:7–12; [παρακαλέω] ἅπτομαι, 3:7–12; 6:53–56). Similarly ambiguous and general is the description of Jesus' applied therapies. Mostly he simply cures those suffering (θεραπεύω; 1:32–34; 3:7–12; 6:5, 13) by laying his hands on them (ἐπιτίθημι τὰς χεῖρας; 6:5) or by being touched (ἅπτομαι him/his ἱμάτιον; 3:7–12; 6:53–56) while remaining vague on the explicit notions behind the transmittability of healing power, its transference to the disciples, and their use of oil (see C. In Focus: Mark's Healing Touches).

Furthermore and distinctly, some of Jesus' patients are described to have δαιμόνια (1:32–34, 39; 6:13) and πνεύματα ἀκάθαρτα (3:7–12) and are characterized by a body-possessing symptomatology: they make the body of the patient react physically toward Jesus (προσπίπτω and κράζω in 3:7–12) and possess preternatural knowledge about his identity (1:32–34; 3:7–12). This is mirrored when they are thrown out of their hosts' body (ἐκβάλλω, 1:32–34, 39; 6:13). Here, it is important to distinguish between the suffering possessed and opposing possessing characters: while Jesus frees from tormenting sicknesses and spirits, both are brought to him in Mark 1:32–34 (see also 9:14–29). The latter additionally pose an intrinsic opposition to Jesus, which is why their defeat is linked to the proclamation of his message (κηρύσσω, 1:39; 6:13; διδάσκω, 6:[2]5) and conveyed in the ongoing struggle to keep them silent about their understanding of Jesus' identity (1:32–34; 3:7–12; see above *Excursus: Tenses*, p. 22–24). While curative and exorcistic treatments both equally depict Jesus as a powerful healer (cf. also the foreign exorcist in Mark 9:38–40), his conflict with the demons reveals the Markan cosmology (see B. In Focus: Mark's Jesus and Opposing Forces).

The images of dis/ability they all cohesively deploy witness to a deviance regarding a physical weakness, social dependence, suffering from unpredictable and severe torments, and an eager wish for healing. Hence, the desired norm behind their healing transpires a personal yet also social, perhaps even societal wellbeing as they are often brought by others, however this is motivated. Since the short accounts do not depict the healed patients or their body and life after the encounter with Jesus, nothing certain can be put on record except that their physical suffering is transformed. In Mark 6:53–56, this is expressed with a term that alludes to a transformation beyond a mere physical well-being (σῴζω).

Differently and overall distinct, however, is the healing of those possessed with demonic spirits as they are seemingly encountered on the way. With a disregard of their wish to be healed, the spirits are commanded to leave as they oppose Jesus and his message. This suggests some sort of human susceptibility to the spiritual realm, which is physically expressed as their possessed bodies witness to this opposition by deviating behavior and preternatural knowledge. The Markan text thereby establishes a desired behavior in consonance with Jesus' presence.

Besides the imprecise description and labels of the pathological states and their cures, the passages feature terms, motifs, and concepts that reprise and foreshadow the individual healing narratives. In their universal style, they witness to specific common threads that interweave their vagueness with concrete references. In that way, the summaric accounts hold the entire gospel narrative together, supply cohesion and progression, and condense and heighten its message.

The physically deviating character groups, however amorphous and general, are characterized by suffering; they are weakened and tormented, and they witness to a wish to be transformed or—in the case of demon possession—to a cosmological necessity to be freed in Jesus' presence. In addition, the vastness of requested healing in the many places Jesus travels insinuates that physical deviance is more likely the rule than the exception.

By employing images of dis/ability, the longer summaric passages develop the themes of Jesus' popularity, publicity, and need for privacy during his ministry in Galilee, which are relentlessly described and condensed to spur the narrative on. This also accounts for the shortness of the gospel. Jesus is characterized as a popular and effective healer with an intrinsic liberative force. Moreover, the grounds for Jesus' mission scheme are laid out and developed in the short summaric notes by a connection to his healing activity, which is disclosed by strong images of embodied *pistis* and embodied, yet transmittable, power.

2.6.2 Popularity, Publicity, and Privacy in the Summaric Reports (1:32–34; 3:7–12; 6:53–56)

The rush for Jesus' healing is at times narrated in the imperfect tense to convey a continuous action that grows to an even habitual extent (cf. 1:32; 6:56), as are the healing actions of Jesus and his disciples (cf. 6:5–6, 13).

Three main literary factors can be observed: To start, a) the publicity of the healing places is heightened, and b) the geographical provenance of the crowding patients as a result broadened from one to the other. This can be seen in the opposing sequences of action and reaction of Jesus (and his disciples) with the crowd in each passage. In Mark 1:32–34, Jesus heals all (πᾶς) while ὅλη ἡ πόλις watches πρὸς τὴν θύραν; in 3:7–12, he is followed by πολὺ πλῆθος from various regions and heals πολύς (θεραπεύω) at the Lake of Galilee (θάλασσα); in 6:53–56, healing takes place wherever he travels (κῶμαι, πόλεις, ἀγροί, ἐν ταῖς ἀγοραῖς) in the entire area (ὅλη ἡ χώρα); the crowd is not even limited to enumerative adjectives but an amorphous force. Lastly, the action potential shifts gradually in each account from Jesus to the crowd seeking his help: In 1:32–34, Jesus is actively healing and exorcising, ordering the demons to not make him known, and the crowd and those suffering are gathering where he is. In 3:7–12, they express their wish for healing more actively and forcefully, Jesus' (healing) activity is slightly reduced, and the motif of him seeking privacy introduced. Finally, in 6:53–56, his actions are limited to his traveling while the crowd follows him flushed and frantic; even the healing is initiated by the sick themselves. The summaric accounts serve first and foremost as illustrations of Jesus' mutually dependent, continuously heightened, and autonomously advancing popularity and publicity as a result of his healing activity. As such, the summaric reports reflect the geographical outline of the first parts of the gospel from its starting point in Capernaum and the surrounding towns (1:32–34, 39), to the travels around the Sea of Galilee with its wide range of influence (3:7–12; 6:53–56), to Nazareth with an extended outreach (6:5, 13). By the general and constant confrontation with suffering and torments, Jesus is characterized as a mighty and powerful healer yet almost reticent and secretive about his abilities as his urge for privacy indicates c): He asks the demons to remain silent about his supreme identity proven by his ability to cast them out (1:32–34; 3:7–12; cf. also Mark 5:7), he seeks solitude under favor of his trusted disciples who oppose the growing crowds (3:7–12) and always travel (6:53–56) with him, and he unsuccessfully withdraws or expresses the wish to do so, preferably by boat (3:7–12; 6:53–56). The motif of seeking privacy is motivated by and increases concurrently with his popularity. The summaric accounts efficiently and intensely unfold Jesus' healing ability, the growing need for it, and its resulting powerful reputation as the tension of popularity, publicity, and privacy builds.

2.6.3 Jesus' Proclaiming and Proclaiming Jesus—Embodied *Pistis* and Healing: Short Summaric Notes as Markan Benchmarks (1:39; 6:5, 13)

The short notes describing Jesus' healing ability in the Gospel of Mark have first been viewed as torn-out statements from the surrounding passage before being regarded in their immediate context. This has resulted in a concentrated look at the themes condensed in one sentence before relating it to a broader literary field. Already in 1:39, the collocation of exorcised demons and the teaching of Jesus is made, followed by its combination in Jesus' commission of his disciples (3:14–15) and their stated success (6:12–13; cf. also secondary 16:15–18). This can be explained by the intrinsic and ongoing struggle against the demonic realm, which Jesus' presence and that of his message pose (see B. In Focus: Mark's Jesus and Opposing Forces).

Moreover, the connection of embodied *pistis* and healing by touch is spun from Mark 5:21–24, 35–43 and condensed to a theme in the summaric note 6:5 (cf. the secondary 16:15–18). While in the first instance, the girl is saved (σῴζω) after Jesus touches her, those weak in 6:5 are cured (θεραπεύω). In both cases, the vital issues are expressed physically: healing comes from the corporal connection with Jesus and those actively practicing *pistis* (cf. also ἅπτομαι in 3:7–12; 6:53–56; e.g., Jaïrus continues with Jesus to his house; Jesus is hindered by ἀπιστία) with the underlying notion of (divine) physicality and its stylistic and theological objective left to explore (see ch. 5.2).

The summaric notes prove to be benchmarks in the development of Jesus' mission scheme and characterize him as its initiator and "enabler," a physical carrier and distributor of his power to teach, cure, and exorcise (δύναμις; ἐξουσία) as he is met with embodied *pistis* (but 6:5). Furthermore, the summaric notes support the longer summaric passages and their motif of reputation and privacy (κηρύσσω and its undermining). Picking up and spinning these threads reveals the objective and compositional net spun in the gospel as it displays Jesus not only as a powerful healer with his continuously unraveling identity but as a controversial teacher, itinerate preacher, and systematic missionary.

3 Mark 1: Jesus in a Dis/abled World

The Gospel of Mark starts with an introductory sequence on the characterization of its protagonist. The short yet expressive heading[1] and the following verses that are often—however, not unproblematically—termed prologue[2] concentrate on Jesus' identity and his inauguration: with reference to Isaiah, Jesus' divine sonship is impressively but briefly narrated through the proclamation of his forerunner, John the Baptist; through the extraordinary baptism; and through Jesus' successful resistance to Satan's temptation in the desert. The audience is teased by this high-profile introduction charged with importance yet polyvalent in its concrete application. This is underscored when Jesus' message of reorientation and the *basileia* are simply alluded to, without greater detail as to what this εὐαγγέλιον precisely entails (1:14–15). With the call of Jesus' first disciples (1:16–20), the audience perceives a first concrete manifestation of the announced change. The strong focus on proclamation (κηρύσσω) and on the student-teacher relationship prepares the immediately following initiation of his teaching and healing ministry as the audience is invited to engage in the narrative and follow the proclaimed (1:7) and proclaiming protagonist Jesus (1:14–15, 38–39) into the synagogue of Capernaum.[3] While this beginning constitutes mainly characterizations of Jesus by other voices,[4] and the short encounters of baptism, temptation, proclamation, and discipleship-calling stay vague on concrete characteristics, the following section witnesses in greater detail to the protagonist on account of his behavior.[5] Here, within one day, two individual healing narratives and two summaric passages reveal Jesus' extending ministry and explicate his growing popularity. In a third, more detailed healing narrative, a few key features of Jesus and his mission are highlighted: his benevolent and powerful healing, conveyed through curative touches and intrinsically interwoven with this authoritative teaching, as well as his identity as someone who opposes the demonic realm, yet remains intriguingly ambiguous in its references to "Jesus of Nazareth" and "the Holy One of God" (1:9, 24).

---

1 Cf., e.g., Arnold 1977; Pokorný in Schnackenburg; Ernst; Wanke (ed.) 1977; Dormeyer 1987; Croy 2001.
2 Cf., e.g., Feneberg 1974; Boring 1990; Hankey 1995; Klauck 1997, and critically, Becker 2009.
3 Cf. esp. 1:4, 7, 14–15, 38–39, moreover, 3:14; 6:12; 13:10; 14:9; and in succession 1:45; 5:20, and 7:36. As established, διδάσκω and κηρύσσω are regarded as inseparable actions of Jesus' ministry, cf. esp. Mark 1:21 with 1:39 and 6:12, or 1:14–15, and its content in 4:1–20; 8:31; 9:31; 12:14. Cf. Marcus 2000. 1871; Broadhead 1992a. 69; France in France; Wenham (ed.) 1980.
4 Cf. 1:1; 1:2–3, 11; 1:7–8.
5 Cf. Rüggemeier 2021. 325–326.

3.1 Mark 1:21–28: Antagonistic Authority and Identity

3.1.1 Introduction to the Narrative

The hourglass-shaped "spatiotemporal framework" of Mark 1:21–39 is introduced as the scene narrows down from the broader context of Galilee (v. 16) to the time centered around the Sabbath in Capernaum.[6] Here, the following two accounts of healing are set. Then, after allusions to Jesus' fame spreading (v. 28) and a generalizing summaric account (v. 34), the reach of Jesus' ministry is broadened again to all of Galilee (v. 39).

As the scene is closing in on the setting, the narrator starts the account in the historical present, drawing the audience immediately into the following section of events. The scene is set by the place (the synagogue),[7] the time (the Sabbath), and verbs in the imperfect tense, which also introduce a few characters as part of the narrative's inventory: Jesus is teaching with ἐξουσία to the astonishment of those present; among them is a man with an unclean spirit.[8] The plural of the present εἰσπορεύονται (v. 21; cf. v. 29) provides continuity to the macro-context by referring to Jesus' previously called disciples, who are not explicitly named here. Only Jesus is recorded to enter the synagogue.

Against this setting, the first aorist in v. 23b functions as a dramatic debut for the subsequent events in the aorist: the man cried out (ἀνέκραξεν). What follows can be separated into three sequences along its speech acts (a. 1:23b–24; b. 1:25–26; and c. 1:27)[9] before reaching the conclusive v. 28:

a) The man asks Jesus a suspicious and hostile double question, which places him with his unclean spirit in opposition to Jesus: τί ἡμῖν καὶ σοί, Ἰησοῦ Ναζαρηνέ; ἦλθες ἀπολέσαι ἡμᾶς; As these questions remain unanswered, the audience is engaged to form an opinion.[10] The plural of his speech breaks with expected sociolinguistic patterns and casts doubt on the identity of the speaker: does it refer to the man and the spirit, suggest a multitude of spirits, or reflect a generalized notion of spiritual opposition? While "their" first address, Ἰησοῦ Ναζαρηνέ, con-

---

[6] Cf. Focant 2012. 64–65.
[7] On meanings and functions of places or gatherings termed συναγωγή, see, e.g., Runesson; Binder; Olsson 2010; Eberhart et al. 2020, and E. In Focus: Healing Spaces in Mark.
[8] The call to discipleship alludes to his teaching. This is the first of many passages establishing the Markan Jesus as a powerful teacher, cf. also 2:13, 4:1; 12:35; and his designation as διδάσκαλος in 4:38; 9:17, 38; 10:17, 20, 35; 12:14, 19, 32, also 5:35 and 14:14.
[9] Cf. Focant 2012. 64.
[10] Cf. Rüggemeier 2021. 335, and generally on the function of these Markan questions of identity, Oko 2004.

firms the audience's knowledge about Jesus' biographical identity (cf. Mark 1:9; cf. also 10:47; 14:67; 16:6), the title ὁ ἅγιος τοῦ θεοῦ in their concluding remark is singular in Mark and ambiguous in its contextual placement.[11] Generally speaking, it refers to those in close communicative proximity to God who are aligned with his will.[12] Here, it first and foremost reveals the opposition of the holy Jesus from Nazareth to the startling number of knowledgeable unclean foes, who verbalize their fear of being destroyed (ἀπόλλυμι) by Jesus.

b) The next section confirms their apprehension to be justified when Jesus rebukes (ἐπιτιμάω) the spiritual entity and commands its silence and exit out of the man. With reiterating emphasis, the unclean spirit follows the order, tearing the man and screaming loudly (see below). This separation of an enduring fusion of spirit and host is termed "exorcism" in the following.[13]

c) The perspective shifts to the witnesses of the dramatic dispute. They (ἅπαντες) verbalize their amazement (θαμβέω) by arguing (συζητέω) over the spectacle that encompasses Jesus' new and powerful teaching explicated in v. 22 (there: ἐκπλήσσω) and his mastery over unclean spirits[14] (cf. 1:39, 3:14–15, 6:12–13).[15]

Neither man nor spirit(s) is mentioned again. Rather, the concluding verse broadens the point of view: reports of Jesus spread throughout Galilee, a motif that is spun further in Mark 2:12 and 7:37 and is explicated in the summaric accounts (see ch. 2). The pericope closes with this emotional and widespread reaction toward Jesus and his teaching and exorcising, while the spiritual entities' comment on his identity is not further interpreted—yet.

---

11 Cf. Botner 2017a.
12 With regard to the HB/OT the title alludes to YHWH, the "Holy One" of Israel (cf. Isa 1:4; 5:19, 24; 10:17, 20; 40:25; 41:14, 16, 20; 43:3, 14–15; Ps 70:22; 77:41; 88:19^{LXX}); Moses (Wis 11:1); a pious person (Ps 16:10); Aaron (Ps 105:16^{LXX}); Israel (Deut 7:6); Elisha (2Kgs 4:9); cf. also Ps 15:10^{LXX} and Luke 1:35; Acts 3:14; 4:27, 30; 1John 2:20; Rev 3:7; moreover, Luke 4:34; John 6:69. See 3.1.2 and D. In Focus: Silencing in Mark's Healing Narratives; cf. also Collins; Collins 2008. Esp. 123–126.
13 This is underscored by the fact that there does not seem to be a common exorcistic practice technically termed yet. Rather, the etymological roots (ἐξ-) ὁρκίζω refer broadly to swearing oaths and adjurations of spirits, gods, and humans and only around the beginning of the second century develop into a more common concept of demonic expulsion. Cf. Böcher 1970. 161–168; Sorensen 2002. 132–133.
14 Again, this is put in plural, here however rather meant generalizing.
15 Cf. Strecker in Zimmermann (ed.) 2013. 206; Kiffiak 2017. 133.

3.1.2 Images of Dis/ability

The man is described as ἄνθρωπος ἐν πνεύματι ἀκαθάρτῳ, and his transformation is depicted by the separation of the two, when the spirit "exits out of the man" (ἐξέρχομαι ἐξ). The use of the preposition ἐν does not necessarily envisage only a locative relationship between the man and spirit but can also refer to a description of a certain condition or state or be translated with an instrumental nuance.[16] In any case, the prepositional descriptions imply that the man seems to experience a form of continuous physical penetrability that encompasses his entire being. This disparate corporeality is furthermore alluded to by the character's speech acts: For once, the man's initial outburst in volume and force implies socially deviating behavior that, paired with the grammar (the unexpected plural)[17] and the knowledgeable content, suggests that the man is not in (absolute) control of his speech apparatus. Furthermore, symptomatic of this somewhat fused state of being seems to be a vociferous and corporeal opposition toward Jesus: his presence and teaching in the synagogue seem to trigger the offensive outcry of the man-spirit, and Jesus' powerful and hostile command causes the violent physical reaction of tearing and screaming.

All of this depicts the man as a *physically* deviating character: the root of his socially inappropriate behavior, auto-violence, and corporeal opposition is explained by the embodied fusion of man and spirit, ἄνθρωπος ἐν πνεύματι ἀκαθάρτῳ. These symptoms are classed in the following as dis/abling effects.

3.1.2.1 Pneumatic Impurity

The meanings behind the terms πνεῦμα and its Hebrew equivalent, rûaḥ, are widespread. In biblical literature, it can basically refer to a fundamental, immanent power, energy, or force, associated with air and wind in a meteorological sense, physiological breath, and a (divine) inspirational force.[18] Similarly, in ancient medical and philosophical literature, πνεῦμα designates a versatile and complex notion of a life-force, fluid, and/or substance assigned to physiological processes such as breath, sleep, body temperature, moisture balance, and motion, even leading to diverse sicknesses when not available in adequate amount or quality. It can be located in veins, the brain, the heart, or nerves or influence the body from the outside,

---

[16] Cf. Mark 5:2 and 5:26; 1:7–8; Luke 22:49; also Mark 7:25 and 9:17, where the children *have* [ἔχω] a spirit. Cf. Doudna 1961. 24–25; Bazzana in Verheyden; Kloppenborg (ed.) 2018. 19–22.
[17] Cf. Marcus 2000. 192, different to Wahlen 2004. 91.
[18] Regarding the following, see for current analyses of individual ancient authors, sources, and the versatile ideas of pneuma, Lewis; Leith; Coughlin 2020. For short overviews, see Bieder, πνεῦμα; Kamlah, πνεῦμα; Kremer, πνεῦμα; Oser-Grote, *Pneuma*; Sjöberg, πνεῦμα. For a summary and relevant sources regarding NT and LXX, see Weissenrieder; Dolle 2019. 565–666, esp. 565–575; and with specific focus on NT exorcisms, Weissenrieder 2003. 26, 59–61, 259–260, 277–278.

as it also may refer to environmental factors. While the sources with their aims and undercurrent notions are diverse and complex, it can be established that the term πνεῦμα reflects connotations regarding transparent materiality and a certain "communicable" quality as it is depicted as an influential and inspirational force on physical, physiological, and psychological processes. By that, the term proves to be highly adaptable to diverse cosmological and ethical concepts. Taking this into account, the following engages in a focused analysis of Mark's understanding of pneumatic impurity.

In the Synoptics, πνεῦμα mainly occurs with a qualifier, ranging from the in the New Testament most common πνεῦμα ἅγιον, the holy spirit of God,[19] to a spirit within a human associated with perception,[20] to (most frequently in Mark) the mention of spirits with dis/abling effects on humans.[21] In Mark, the last is mainly attributed with the adjective ἀκάθαρτος.[22] In one narrative (cf. 9:25), it is additionally composed with ἄλαλος (Mark 9:17, referenced by the father of the boy; see ch. 7.2.2) and then complemented by κωφός (9:25b, designated by Jesus) and used without any qualifier (9:20, spoken by the narrator).[23] Interestingly, pneumatic impurity in Mark's gospel is but two exceptions only recorded by the narrator (1:23, 26; 3:11, 30; 5:2, 13; 6:7; 7:25; 9:25a), while in 1:27, the *witnesses* of Jesus' first exorcism reflect upon his power by using this term, and in 5:8, *Jesus* addresses the demonic entity as such. Hence, the reference to impurity might reflect a) the (Jewish) notions regarding the origin and realm of such hostile entities (see below), in addition to b) the (social) life-encompassing implications attributed to their effect similar to other states of impurity (see 3.3), and/or c) the opposing spheres of the holy and impure, which Mark alludes to in his concept of demonology (see below). After Mark 9, there is no further mention of dis/abling spirits. The notion of πνεῦμα as a material, natural, or environmental (life-)force is not explicitly attested in the Gospel of Mark, nor is the concept of spirits of the dead.[24]

Similarly and in Mark equally often, the term δαίμων/δαιμόνιον describes numinous substances with dis/abling impact on humans (in Mark exclusively with the

---

19 Cf. Mark 1:8, 10, 12; 3:29; 12:36; 13:11.
20 Cf. Mark 2:8; 8:12 (of Jesus); 14:38.
21 Cf. Mark 1:23, 26, 27; 3:11, 30; 5:2, 8, 13; 6:7; 7:25; 9:17, 25, also Wahlen 2004. 17–18, also 172.
22 Cf. Mark 1:23, 26; 3:30; 5:2, 8; 7:25; 9:25; Matt 12:43; Luke 8:29; 9:42; 11:24; in plural: Matt 10:1; Mark 1:27; 3:11; 5:13; 6:7; Luke 4:33; 6:18; Acts 5:16; 8:7.
23 Moreover, the Synoptics and Acts feature combinations with πονηρός (Acts 19:15–16), πύθων (Acts 16:16), πνεῦμα δαιμονίου ἀκαθάρτου (Luke 4:33), and πνεῦμα ἔχουσα ἀσθενείας (Luke 13:11).
24 Cf. Weissenrieder 2003. 26, 59–61, 259–260, 277–278; moreover, Bieder, *πνεῦμα*. 376; 370–373; Kamlah, *πνεῦμα*. 702–704; Kremer, *πνεῦμα*. 281; Sjöberg, *πνεῦμα*. 373; Sorensen, *Demons, Demonology III. NT.* 540; Oser-Grote, *Pneuma.* 717–718.

diminutive; concretized four times with δαιμονιζόμενος).²⁵ In the Synoptics, both terms denote entities hostile to humans with tormenting effect, exhibiting their influence by forcing those afflicted to socially deviating and (self-)destructive behavior and speech (1:23–24; 5:6–10, esp. v. 5; 9:22) with debilitated sensual capacities (e.g., 9:17; cf. Luke 11:14). In Mark's gospel, both terms are used interchangeably.²⁶ The gospel writings insinuate the notion that these spirits wield power over humans by entering them and taking control of their behavior and speech,²⁷ causing these symptoms for as long as they stay (Mark 5:3–5; 9:18–22).

> The idea of numinous entities termed δαίμων/δαιμόνιον that influence human life is also widespread and complex in Greek tradition yet semantically highly ambiguous, ranging in meaning from gods and subordinate or protective deities, to an "unknown superhuman factor," to forces that "overtake man" (i.e., fortune, death, destiny), to the "divinely related element in man";²⁸ Homer designates with the term δαίμων, among other things, the highest authority, Gods, or an unknown divine force, respectively—as many poets—a good or heavy burdened destiny;²⁹ Hesiod traces δαίμονες back to "deified" souls of heroes guarding humanity;³⁰ Plato expands the tasks of the adorable but subordinated God's demons, who are responsible for humans' εὐδαιμονία/ δυσδαίμων as well as their fate and death and are regarded as entirely trustworthy intermediary messengers.³¹
>
> Furthermore, δαίμων can designate the cause of an inexplicable occurrence or the event itself.³² Demons can be intermediary figures between the gods and humans as they guide cosmic proceedings and, with their power, influence human fate positively (i.e., as "sources of support, counsel, and inspiration"³³) or negatively (as tormenting and destructive forces), rea-

---

25 Cf. Mark 1:34, 39; 3:15, 22; 6:13; 7:26, 29, 30; 9:38; 16:9, 17; δαιμονιζόμενος: Mark 1:32; 5:15, 16, 18; δαίμων only in Matt 8:31. On the specific use of δαιμονιζόμενος in Mark 5, see 5.1.
26 This can also be explained as a stylistic variation regarding the implied Jewish *and* Greek audience, cf. Pesch 1976. 134, n. 3; Wahlen 2004. 106; Collins 2007. 176; Gnilka 2010. 87, n. 6. Cf. esp. Mark 3:15 and 6:7, 13; 5:2, 8, 13 and 5:15, 16, 18; 7:25–26; furthermore, Matt 10:1; 12:43; Luke 4:33 and 4:35; 8:27, 33 and 8:29; 9:1; 9:39, 42; 11:24. For a more detailed survey on the terminology of evil forces in the NT, see, e.g., Sorensen 2002. 121–122; Wahlen 2004. 177. Interestingly, in the LXX, δαίμων/δαιμόνιον translates "various Hebrew terms for demonic entities," cf. Sorensen, *Demons, Demonology III. NT.* 540.
27 Cf. Sorensen 2002. 118–124.
28 Foerster, *δαίμων.* 2–3, English translation taken from TDNT. Cf., e.g., Plato, *Apol.* 27d, 28e; *Tim.* 90c; *Phaedr.* 107d; Philo, *Somn.* 1.141; *Gig.* 6; 16–18; Josephus, *B.J.* 7.185, *A.J.* 13.317; 16.210; furthermore, Brenk (ed.) 1986. 2068–2145; Johnston, *Dämonen V. Griechenland und Rom.* Esp. 263–264; Frey-Anthes 2007. 2–3; Poplutz in Zimmermann (ed.) 2013. 97–98.
29 Cf., e.g., Homer, *Il.* 1.222; 3.413–418, 420; 5.438–41; 15.418; 467; 19.188; *Od.* 3.27; 5.396. Moreover, Brenk (ed.) 1986. 2074–2081, esp. 2081; Leven, *Dämonen.* 206; Poplutz in Zimmermann (ed.) 2013. 97.
30 Cf., e.g., Hesiod, *Op.* 122–126; furthermore, Leven, *Dämonen.* 206.
31 Cf. Plato, *Apol.* 27c–d, 28e; *Tim.* 40d–e; 90c; *Leg.* 717a; *Phaedr.* 107d.; *Symp.* 202d–e; *Resp.* 382E.
32 Cf. Philostratus, *Vit. Apoll.* 4.44 and the explications in Poplutz in Zimmermann (ed.) 2013. 97.
33 Moss in Melcher; Parsons; Yong (ed.) 2018. 287.

son enough to try to manage them by certain rituals or incantation.³⁴ This qualitative ambivalence can also be seen in the problematic and highly speculative etymological explanation of the term δαίμων: In connection to δαίομαι, it connotes the idea of "dividing" corpses or "distributing" fate, or, rooted in δάω, it conveys the notion of knowledgeable instruction.³⁵ The latter connection can be traced to the idea that the possessed speak the will of gods as they are depicted as mediums of numinous voices.³⁶ While they are often characterized as incapable of falsehood, there are also texts that witness to their deceitful nature.³⁷ The New Testament accounts only for evil intermediaries that correspond in their knowledge with divine messengers (e.g., ἄγγελος).³⁸

While in the Synoptics, demons are neither described as tempting forces, unlike Satan (Mark 1:13; 8:33; Matt 4; Luke 4; 13:16; 22:3), nor explicitly attributed to divine punishment, they are depicted with superhuman strength and knowledge. These "traditional traits" are important for the Markan gospel as demonic spirits are employed when depicting severely tormented characters by their extraordinary force (cf. Mark 5:1–20 and 9:14–29) and when "precognitive or supernatural knowledge"³⁹ about Jesus is shared via their hosts. Since the man's demonic deviance seems to reflect a distinct cosmological view and is deployed as a marker of such, the following examines the Markan notions behind the alluded forces, as displayed in Mark 3:20–35, to grasp the concrete extent and function of the man's deviating physicality.

B In Focus: Mark's Jesus and Opposing Forces (with Consideration of 3:20–35)

At this early point of the gospel storyline, there are only a few indications given regarding the Markan conception of demonology: Jesus is already known to the audience as endowed with πνεῦμα from heavenly realms (1:10–12), pronounced to immerse with holy πνεῦμα (1:8), and as having overcome the tempting σατανᾶς in the desert while being served by angels (1:12–13). When the hostile, unclean πνεῦμα now addresses Jesus with ὁ ἅγιος τοῦ θεοῦ, his opposing stance unfolds beyond the pericope's dynamic. While the witnesses of the exorcism openly ques-

---

34 Cf. Böcher 1970. 161–168.
35 Cf., e.g., Foerster, *δαίμων* 2; Frey-Anthes 2007. 2; Strecker in Frey; Oberhänsli-Widmer (ed.) 2012. 129–130; Poplutz in Zimmermann (ed.) 2013. 96–97.
36 Cf., e.g., Aristides, *Or.* 45.11. Plato, *Men.* 99c–d.
37 Cf., e.g., Homer, *Od.* 3.166; 2.134; 16.64; 18.256; 19.512; Philostratus, *Vit. Apoll.* 3.38.1; 4.20.
38 Cf. Böcher, *δαίμων* 656; Sorensen, *Demons, Demonology III. NT*; Riley, *Demon*; Reese, *Demons New Testament*. See moreover, Smith 2008; Oegema in Lange; Lichtenberger; Römheld (ed.) 2003.
39 Cf. Moss in Melcher; Parsons; Yong (ed.) 2018. 288.

tion the source of Jesus' ἐξουσία and by what authority the spirits obey him (1:27; cf. also 1:34, 39; 3:15), the audience gets a faint idea by the aforementioned opposition.

This *dualism* of opposing hierarchies of power fits that of intertestamental Jewish writings[40] that, contrary to early Greek literature, witness to only *one* divine hierarchy reliant on appeasement practices. Against this backdrop, an exorcism as depicted in the gospel narrative describes a separation of opposing forces by confrontation and domination.[41]

> The dense literary network of conceptions, developments, and differentiations on demonology from the Egyptian and Mesopotamian background to its influence in the Hebrew Bible/Old Testament; the books Tobit and 1 Henoch; writings from Qumran, Philo, and Josephus; and rabbinic literature, not to mention archeological and papyrological findings, can hardly be put in a nutshell.[42] Hence, only a few observations are made here bearing in mind the differences of the texts discussed in the following due to genre, time, historical, and regional dynamics.
>
> While in pre-exilic sources the thought of forces of chaos and danger, who set out to destroy or deceive humans but serve or are controlled by YHWH, predominates,[43] an increasing differentiation toward a more cosmological dualism with demons as negative antagonists can be seen, probably due to the influence of Zoroastrian thoughts.[44] A prominent example of this is the increasingly broad reception of the Fall-of-the-Angels-tradition, drawing on Gen 6:1–4 and developed in, e.g., *1En.* 6–11 and Jubilees.[45] Both describe how fallen angels or their descendants of human women seduce humans as evil spirits on earth to a life of impurity and lawlessness[46] (especially with regard to sexual conduct, circumcision, Sabbath observance, food regulations) and to worship them and/or their idols.[47] Furthermore, they cause sickness, pain, and death.[48] The connection to impurity is explained by their "unclean" procreation;

---

40 Rooted in Zoorastrian notions and mirrored esp. in Jewish apocalyptic literature according to Riley, *Demon.*
41 Cf. Sorensen 2002. Esp. 131–136.
42 In greater detail on individual writings/aspects, see, e.g., Lange; Lichtenberger; Römheld 2003; Wahlen 2004. 24–68; Frey-Anthes 2007. For broader surveys, see, e.g., Böcher, *Dämonen*; Maier, *Geister (Dämonen) B.I.c. Israel*; Wanke, *Dämonen (böse Geister) II. Altes Testament*; Kuemmerlin-McLean, *Demons. Old Testament.*
43 Cf., e.g., Isa 37:7; Amos 3:6; 1Sam 16:14–23; 2Sam 24:15–16; 1Kgs 22:20–22; Job 2:1–7; 3:8.
44 Cf. Sorensen 2002. 25–28, 37–40, 118–119, who qualifies this argument also with iconographic evidence.
45 Cf. Auffarth; Stuckenbruck 2003.
46 Cf., e.g., *1En.* 6–11; 15:3–12; 18:13–16; 19:1–2; 86–88; Jub 5:1–10; 7:21; 10:1–11; furthermore, *T.Reu.* 5:5–7; *T.Naph.* 3:5; Philo, *Gig.* 6; 18; *T.Sim.* 4:9; *T.Benj.* 5:2.
47 Cf., e.g., Tob 3:7–8; 8:1–3; *T.Reu.* 2:8–9; 3:3; 1QM 7.5–6; Jub 1:9–11; 2:18–22; 15:25–28; 22:16–17.
48 Cf., e.g., Jub 10:11–12; 11:5; 10:1–2; 49:2; Wis 1:14.

their affiliation to the holiness-opposing, "impure" sphere of the devil; or their profane actions.[49]

Interestingly, the Priestly literature with its strong influence on the gospel's conceptions of purity (cf. 3.2) is vague on the matter of "impure" spirits.[50] Besides, the terminology in the Hebrew Bible reflects neither a precise nor consistent "typology"[51] of hostile entities.

Successively, there is an increasing focus on the protection of the "religious integrity of Israel"[52] by local and ethnological demarcation. For example, Zech 13:2^{LXX} describes God's plan to banish images of idols, false prophets, and a πνεῦμα ἀκάθαρτον from the land, a phrase ambiguous in referring to an "internal human disposition" or "some divine malevolent force … perhaps associated with the idols"[53] mentioned before. Henceforth, a (hierarchic) demonology is differentiated[54] and often contextualized with im-/purity, an ethical impetus,[55] and/or a cosmological dualism, and/or an eschatological focus.[56] Often, counteractive practices, cleansings, and exorcisms are described that presuppose a physical possession with social consequences.[57] In rabbinic literature, demons are attributed with preferences concerning

---

[49] Cf. also 1Macc 1:48 Codex Sinaiticus; *T.Benj.* 5:2; 1QS 4.22; 4Q444 1–4i+5,8; 11Q5 19.15; *LAB* 53.5; *T.Sol.* 3:7 and later *BerR* 20. Cf. Wahlen 2004. 24–59, esp. 170–171. On purification and exorcism in PesRK 4.7, cf. Avemarie 1996. 205, 159–160.

[50] Cf. Milgrom 2004. 9, and scattered remarks to the contrary in, e.g., Lev 16:8, 10, 26; Num 5:11–31, according to Thiessen 2020. 123–125, who furthermore points out the distinct point-of-view represented in Priestly literature. Cf. also Avemarie in Bieringer; et al. (ed.) 2010. 277–278.

[51] Cf. the often ambiguous descriptions alluding to such forces in connection to the terms *śēʿîrîm* in Lev 17:7; 2Kgs 23:8; Isa 13:21; 34:14; *šēdîm* in Deut 32:17 and Ps 106:37; and proper names in, e.g., Isa 34:14; Lev 16:8, 10, 26; Deut 32:24; Job 5:7; Num 22:22–35; Zech 3:1. Cf. Schmitt, Demons, Demonology II. HB/OT. 537–538.

[52] Strecker in Zimmermann (ed.) 2013. 208.

[53] Thiessen 2020. 126.

[54] Cf., e.g., the reception of the angel-myth with a differentiation and hierarchization of different demons with names and identification with diseases in writings from Qumran (e.g., 4Q560 frg. 1 1.4) and the description of Satan as ruler over an army of demons in *Jub* 10:8; Job 1:6–12.

[55] Cf., e.g., purity and piety in Tob 3:8–14; the ethical dualism in connection with the demonic realm in, e.g., *T.Levi* 19:1; *T.Naph.* 2:6; 3:1; *T.Sim.* 5:3. Cf. moreover, Reed 2022.

[56] Cf., e.g., the eschatological conflict in 1QM 8; or apocalyptic notions of ending suffering and sickness with the defeat of Satan in, e.g., *T.Levi* 18:10–14; *T.Dan* 5:10–12; *T.Mos.* 10:1; *2Bar.* 73:1–3.

[57] Cf. prayer, curses, psalms in, e.g., 4Q560; 4Q444; 4Q510–511; 11Q11; 11Q5 19.1–18; *LAB* 60; Josephus, *A.J.* 8.44–47; substances such as plants and animals in, e.g., Josephus, *B.J.* 7.180–185; Tob 6:7, 16–17; 8:2–3. While Josephus witnesses to an ethical impetus regarding the visitations of good guardian spirits and evil, harmful, avenging spirits of the dead, mainly connected to war and bloodguiltiness (cf., e.g., *B.J.* 1.521; 7.180–185; *A.J.* 13.317; 16.76, 210; cf. also Philo, *Gig.* 6; 16–18; *Somn.* 1.141), he is dedicated to explications on the therapy of demonic effects with regard to narratives about David, Salomon, and Eleazar (cf., e.g., *A.J.* 6.166–169, 211–214; 8.42–49). Cf. Brenk (ed.) 1986. 2098–2107; Deines in Lange; Lichtenberger; Römheld (ed.) 2003. 50; Wahlen 2004. esp. 37–54; Bohak, Demons, Demonology V. Judaism A. and B.

specific times and places and the ability to procreate; furthermore, preventative measures are broached.[58]

Traces of such a Jewish antagonism of a sphere opposed to the sacred, associated with temptation, impurity, and disease, can also be found in the Gospel of Mark. While the gospels do not account for an origin of the evil spirits, Mark alludes to similar characteristics connected with the motif of "Satan"[59] and in Jesus' conflicts with demons. This is clearly expounded in Mark 3:20–35:[60] while the frame of the Markan intercalation (3:20–21, 22–30, 31–35) focuses on Jesus' relatives' rejection of his ministry, the sandwiched material explains his authority regarding his exorcisms. At first, the text witnesses to the response of Jesus' relatives[61] towards his popularity (v. 20) that is, from the beginning of the gospel, intrinsically connected to his healing ministry (see ch. 2, esp. 1:32–34; 3:10–11). They call him due to his doing "out of his mind" (ἐξίστημι),[62] hence want to restrain him. This explains their search for Jesus in vv. 31–35, where he finally rejects his mother and brothers as a consequence of their statement.[63] Against the backdrop of the rather common rhetoric that labels a misunderstood yet divinely inspired person with the "dis/ability invective" stigma of mental disorder, the Markan intercalation reveals that its conception of pneumatic possession is similarly intertwined with the symptoms of cognitive "incapacities".[64] While modern concepts of "mental disorders" mainly rely on a demarcation of body and mind, which is not necessarily a given in ancient anthropology,[65] the symptoms of those possessed by demons are described

---

[58] Cf., e.g., amulets, oaths, certain or good behavior, Tora observance etc. in, e.g., bHul 105b; bPes 111a; bNid 17a; bShevu 15b; bBer 5a and 9b; bMeg 3a; bPes 109b/bRH 11b. On the etiology cf. PRE 7 and 34; mAv 5:6 and BerR 7:5; mShab 2:5; mEr 4:1; bEr 18b and BerR 20:20; for characteristics and further differentiation according to name and preferences cf., e.g., bHag 16a; bGit 68a; bPes 110a–111b; bShab 151b; bMeil 17b; bEr 43a; bBer 6a; bQid 29b; in connection to illness and suffering cf., e.g., bPes 112b and bAZ 12b; bGit 67b. Cf. van der Loos 1965. 346; Bohak, Demons, Demonology V. Judaism A. and B; Wahlen 2004. 55–59.
[59] Cf. Shively in Skinner; Hauge (ed.) 2014. 137–138.
[60] Cf. also, e.g., Luke 10:18; furthermore, John 8:44; 12:31; 14:30; 16:11; 1Joh 3:8.
[61] On οἱ παρ' αὐτοῦ, cf., e.g., Bosenius 2014. 284, n. 45.
[62] Cf. Thumiger in Harris (ed.) 2013. 77–78, on the term in early Greek literature regarding mental soundness.
[63] On the rhetoric and stylistic context of metaphoric elements in argumentative texts, see Breytenbach in Breytenbach (ed.) 2021b [2019].
[64] Cf. Plato, Phaedr. 249c-d; Philo, Ebr. 145–146; also Collins 2007. 227; Solevåg 2018. 95–116. Esp. 102–107; moreover, Weissenrieder 2003. 305–314; Mainwaring 2014; Lawrence 2018.
[65] Cf. van der Eijk 2005a. 26–27; Solevåg 2018. 98–99.

similarly to those suffering from a physical imbalance affecting the mind,[66] termed, e.g., παράνοια, ἄγνοια, μανία, μαίνομαι, ἄφρων, and ἐξίσταμαι.[67] This can not only be witnessed by the combined accusation in Mark 3:20–30 but also in the vivid descriptions of the spirit-ridden men in 1:27–28 and 5:1–20 and tormented boy in 9:14–29.

In the following sandwiched section, Jesus' supposed cognitive *dis-* and witnessed spiritual *ability* is explicitly linked with the condition of possession, when his authority to cast out demons is discussed yet again by the scribes (cf. 1:21–28, 39; cf. esp. 1:27). In their initial provocation (v. 22), the accusers claim that Jesus is only able to cast out demons since he is possessed himself by the ruler of the demons (by Beelzebul, Βεελζεβοὺλ ἔχει), working as a "double agent for the demonic,"[68] not as an advocate for the *basileia* of God (1:14–15).[69] In his metaphorical (ἐν παραβολαῖς ἔλεγεν) retort, Jesus addresses this two-sided accusation in two parts (vv. 23–26) before finally disclosing his manner of exorcising (v. 27) and severely warning his counterparts to refrain from blaspheming against the holy spirit (vv. 28–29).

While the name Beelzebul (*Baal-zabub*) is not common in early Jewish literature, the Testament of Solomon mentions him to be the archon, the ruler of demons,[70] or σατανᾶς in the otherwise strikingly coherent Markan terminology.[71] Undisputed is the fact that Jesus powerfully exorcised; only the source of his authority is questioned.[72] Hence, Jesus uses the unchallenged condition for his refute: with kingdom and household imagery, he paints an analogous picture reliant on the fact that "Satan cannot cast out Satan" (v. 23) without causing internal division and dissension followed by the collapse of kingdom and household, of "dominion" and "community" of Satan's realm.[73] Then Jesus answers the implicit questions

---

66 Cf., e.g., Jouanna in Harris (ed.) 2013. 98–103; Goodey; Rose in Laes; Goodey; Rose (ed.) 2013. 17–19; van der Eijk in Harris (ed.) 2013. 310–312; Thumiger in Laes (ed.) 2017. 267–270.
67 See Thumiger in Harris (ed.) 2013.
68 Thiessen 2020. 142.
69 Cf. Matt 9:32–34; 12:22–29, Luke 11:15, 21–22; John 7:20; 8:48–52; 10:20; also *Gos. Thom.* 35 and Eusebius, *Hier.* 26; Origen, *Cels.* 1.6.
70 Cf. *T.Sol.* 2:8; 3:1–6; 4:2; 6:1–2, 9–10; 9:8; 16:3–5; 2Kgs 1:1–17; furthermore, Josephus, *A.J.* 9.19 and later Acts of Pilate; Cf. Collins 2007. 229–231; Breytenbach in Breytenbach (ed.) 2021b [2019]. 225.
71 Cf. Mark 1:12–13; 3:23, 26; 4:15; 8:33. For occurrences without a title in the sense of a (proper) name cf., e.g., 1Chr 21:1; Jub 10:11; 23:29 (cf. *T.Mos.* 10:1); *T.Reu.* 4:11; *T.Dan* 4:7; 6:1; *T.Ash.* 1:8–9. Cf. Bazzana in Verheyden; Kloppenborg (ed.) 2018. 7–14, for a detailed etymology of the two titles and their maybe not so reliable agreement.
72 Regarding possible severe implications, cf. Lev 20:27; CD 12.2–3; *mSan* 7:7; and Collins 2007. 228–229.
73 Cf. Breytenbach in Breytenbach (ed.) 2021b [2019]. 226–227.

about the source of his authority himself with another figurative statement: he can successfully exorcise demons because "the strong man" has been "bound first" so his house can be plundered.[74] Against the backdrop of his previous argument, it becomes clear "the house is not divided among itself, it is robbed"[75] by an external, stronger force.[76] Because Jesus is able to bind Satan (i.e., the strong one), he can cast out demons, an ability he furthermore connects with the source of his authority, the holy spirit, who is severely taunted by the scribe's "sinful" accusation (vv. 28–29).[77]

Within the gospel storyline, the terms ἰσχυρός, σατανᾶς, and πνεῦμα ἅγιον refer back to the beginning of the gospel narrative to the prelude of Jesus' first exorcism (1:21–28), where he is characterized as stronger (than John; 1:7), bestowed and associated with *holy* pneuma (1:8, 10, 12; cf. 3:28–30, not an *unclean* spirit), and most importantly able to resist the temptation of his adversary (1:12–13).[78] Moreover, the following impressive exorcism in Mark 5:1–20 alludes to similar imagery when no one is able or strong enough to bind the Gerasene demoniac (5:3, οὐκέτι οὐδεὶς ἐδύνατο αὐτὸν δῆσαι; 5:4, καὶ οὐδεὶς ἴσχυεν αὐτὸν δαμάσαι; cf. 3:23–27), who Jesus successfully frees from the possession of tormenting spirits (cf. 3:30 and 5:2).[79]

Mark 3:27 then confirms what the prior exorcisms already alluded to, a hierarchical understanding of the spiritual world: ἀλλ' οὐ δύναται οὐδεὶς εἰς τὴν οἰκίαν τοῦ ἰσχυροῦ εἰσελθὼν τὰ σκεύη αὐτοῦ διαρπάσαι, ἐὰν μὴ πρῶτον τὸν ἰσχυρὸν δήσῃ, καὶ τότε τὴν οἰκίαν αὐτοῦ διαρπάσει—Satan and his subordinated demons

---

[74] For an in-depth study on the spatial parameters this image entails, see Bosenius in Oyen (ed.) 2019. For an interesting corrrelation of houshold goods (σκεύη) with the human body, i.e., the "physcial vessel" for evil spirits in early Christian texts, see Bazzana in Verheyden; Kloppenborg (ed.) 2018. 16–17.

[75] Breytenbach in Breytenbach (ed.) 2021b [2019]. 228. Cf. Isa 49:24^{LXX}; Pss. Sol. 5:3, moreover, Hooker 1991. 116.

[76] Cf. the excellent analysis of Shively 2012. Esp. 59–83.

[77] On the stylistic and rhetoric structure and context, see Breytenbach in Breytenbach (ed.) 2021b [2019].

[78] Cf. Collins 2007. 64–65, 233–234, on referential texts from the HB/OT describing similar "strong" warriors, e.g., 1Sam 16:18; Judg 6:12; Ps 24:8; 1Macc 2:66, according to which Mark 1:7–8 possibly "could well have had connotations of the Davidic messiah as God's agent in the eschatological battle." Cf. also πνεῦμα ἰσχύος in Isa 11:1–2^{LXX}.

[79] Cf. Shively in Skinner; Hauge (ed.) 2014. 139, moreover, 147–148. On the thesis that v. 27 functions (also) as a metaphorical oblique prolepsis regarding Jesus' "binding" in Mark 15:1 (cf. also 14:46), see Bosenius in Oyen (ed.) 2019. Cf. also the "binding" of Asael by Rapahel in *1En.* 10:4–8 and allusions to Greek "binding" spells aimed at control over spirits in Bazzana in Verheyden; Kloppenborg (ed.) 2018. 16.

are countered by the divinely pneumatic Jesus via his exorcisms[80] and those in his name.[81] The Markan Jesus is their ultimate threat when they fear "being destroyed" (1:24), "bound" (3:27), "plundered" (3:27), or "tormented" (5:7) by him. The imagery of government and kinship within a Greco-Roman context implies hierarchy, sovereignty, and unity.[82] If understood as two analogous and opposing realms, the scribes' blasphemous (v. 29) accusation and miscomprehension of Jesus align *them* with Satan, the ruler of impure spirits, who is furthermore characterized not only as tempter and torturer but antagonist of Jesus' ministry in general (cf. 4:15 hindering the growth of ὁ λόγος and 8:33 as opposition to τὰ τοῦ θεοῦ).[83] However, the cosmic struggle[84] has already been decided, and Jesus is, throughout the gospel (from his baptism, the temptation,[85] and most importantly in his successful exorcisms), characterized as the superior, "stronger" one (cf. esp. the verbal statements of the demons).[86]

Furthermore, two inferences can be drawn from the intercalation in Mark 3:21–30 regarding the Markan concept of demonic dis/ability: Firstly, the cosmic frame serves to extend the narrative space and "elevates" the exorcism narratives "from the earthly immediacy of individual possession" to a significant step in Jesus' ministry, i.e., the cosmic conflict.[87]

Secondly, the images used here invert those ascribed to be symptomatic of the possessed: it is now not those who are bound to and by their demons or, in consequence, by society but the hostile entities and their master who are restrained; it is not only the possessed experiencing an internalized pneumatic force, but, analogously, also Jesus as the authority bestowed upon him is depicted as a pneumatic presence within him (cf. esp. Mark 5:1–20);[88] and it is not only those usurped by a destructive demon regarded as cognitively deranged and socially transgres-

---

[80] Cf. Mark 1:21–28; 5:1–20; 7:24–30; 9:14–29; cf. also 1:32–34, 39; 3:11–12.
[81] Cf. Mark 3:14–15; 6:6–13; 16:17, cf. also the disciples in 9:18, 28; the undesignated man in 9:38–41.
[82] Cf. Shively in Skinner; Hauge (ed.) 2014. 138.
[83] Cf. also the allusions in the testing of Jesus' human opponents in 8:11; 10:2; 12:15 with 1:13, also 14:38; the calming of the storm in 4:35–41 and the cleansing of the temple in 11:15–19 with his first teaching and exorcism in 1:21–28, moreover, 3:12, 9:25. For a more detailed analysis on these motifs, cf. Shively in Skinner; Hauge (ed.) 2014. Esp. 145–147.
[84] Cf. Malbon 2009. 80, cf. 80–83; Shively 2012. 81–82.
[85] Although not explicitly resolved, the audience knows he is guided by the holy spirit and served by the angels.
[86] Cf. Rüggemeier 2017. 246.
[87] Cf. Sorensen 2002. 141; Williams in Broadhead (ed.) 2018. 115–117.
[88] Cf. Sorensen 2002. 142; Söding in Lange; Lichtenberger; Römheld (ed.) 2003. 528–531.

sive but also the protagonist with the preternatural knowledge and divine appointment par excellence.

From this transpires a general susceptibility of human bodies to spiritual forces that, however, is in its evaluation dependent on the influencing force. The symptomatic deviance is "normalized" with a similar depiction of the protagonist, yet its demonic source is pathologized. Being restrained, pneumatically influenced, and regarded as socially transgressive and deranged is only a problem when it is caused by a demonic, not holy, force.

All the above is enforced by the increasingly demonstrative exorcism narratives following Mark 3:21–30, where Jesus banishes and destroys a legion of demons (5:1–20), casts a spirit out from the distance (7:24–30), and overcomes a particularly obstinate demon (9:14–29) before the cosmic conflict is taken over by the passion narrative.[89]

3.1.2.2 Demonic Dis/ability

While Mark does not seem interested in imparting a detailed demonology, it becomes clear that it is only in the human body that the hostile realm comes to speak. Satan remains silent, and it is only in the interplay of demon and physicality that the opposing forces interact with Jesus.[90]

This is, firstly, depicted with locative terminology[91] that reflects a fused corporality of host and spirit and spatial connotations regarding competing spheres.[92] Secondly, the cosmic power struggle is first and foremost depicted in violent terms and visualized by the demoniacs' deviance as socially non-conformative and physically destructive and dangerous behavior.[93] It is precisely this conduct that functions as behavioral, symptomatic pattern for the "possessed,"[94] transpiring a norm of adapted and conformed, non-disruptive behavior. In the comparatively short account of Mark 1:21–28, this behavior is reflected in the hostile and loud verbal outbursts in the beginning and the fierce and frenzied reaction

---

[89] Cf. Mittmann-Richert in Lange; Lichtenberger; Römheld (ed.) 2003. 489, who even relates the three demonic proclamations of insight to the three proclamations of suffering as the latter finally reveal Jesus' "conclusive" identity. Cf. also ibid. 494.
[90] Cf. also but on a different note Mark 8:31–33.
[91] Cf. Sorensen 2002. 133.
[92] Cf. ἐξέρχομαι in 1:25–28; 5:8, 13; 7:29–30; ἐκβάλλω in 1:34, 39; 3:15, 22; 6:13; 7:26; 9:18, 28; 9:38; 16:9, 17; [cf. also 1:12]; πέμπτω in 5:12, and ἀποστέλλω in 5:10 or δέω in 3:27.
[93] Cf. φιμόω in 1:23–28; ἀπόλλυμι 1:24; βασανίζομαι in 5:7; ἐπιτιμάω in 9:14–29; regarding authority: οὐκ ἀφίημι "by no means permit" in 1:34; [ἔχειν] ἐξουσίαν "to have authority" in 1:27.
[94] Cf. Strecker in Stegemann; Malina; Theissen (ed.) 2002. 58, 60, on the interpretation of possession and exorcism as "performance." See also 5.1.

of the physical tearing and screaming before exiting the body. The violent sound effect of the fused body's encounter with Jesus is described with ἀνακράζω (v. 24) and φωνέω (v. 26). The prior becomes a common term for Markan descriptions of demonic dominion of their host's speech apparatus (3:11; 5:5, 7; 9:26), the latter is emphasized with φωνὴ μεγάλη. The violent convulsion of the man's body is explicitly attributed to the spirit (σπαράσσω; v. 26). The sudden body movement also occurs with great emphasis in the account of the spirit-possessed boy in Mark 9:20, 26, where the destructive and uncontrollable tearing and force of the demon on the host's body is abundantly visualized yet emphasized with precisely this lexeme (by position and intensity markers; see ch. 7.2.2). In both instances, it denotes the last involuntary physical utilization of the spirit before leaving the host with a loud shout. Spirit and host are clearly separated. In all this, the host is portrayed as involuntarily possessed and inculpable for their state.

Thirdly, the knowledge of the demons, as a group of characters,[95] is characterized as reliable and extraordinary in contrast to other characters in the narrative yet in line with the knowledge of the audience. This is already established in Mark 1:24, where the spirit's verbal speech act not only reiterates correct common knowledge explicitly provided early on by the narrator (i.e., that the protagonist is "Jesus, from Nazareth," cf. 1:9; also 6:1–3; 16:6) but also witnesses to his implicit relationship to the heavenly realms alluded to by the description of his baptism in vv. 10–11.[96] This characterization by the voice of the demon is provided with great confidence (οἶδά σε τίς εἶ), answered by Jesus' prompt command for silence, and repeated and underscored in the summaric statement in 1:34.[97] The same pattern occurs in 3:11–12, where the imperfect, as in Mark 1:34, reveals Jesus' *permanent* struggle with the communicative entities, whose knowledge is emphatically recorded in direct speech (cf. also Mark 5:7; not, however, in Mark 7:24–30 and 9:14–29).[98] This knowledge is contrasted by the disbelieving and oblivious spectators of the healings.

Fourthly and most importantly, the symptomatic connection of non-normative and extraordinary behavior and speech with pneumatic possession serves explanatory[99] and rhetoric functions.[100] Like any ailment, symptoms of an unsound mind

---

[95] Cf. Rüggemeier 2017. 241–242.
[96] In line with YHWH, the "Holy One" of Israel, cf. Isa 1:4; 5:19, 24; 10:17, 20; 40:25; 41:14, 16, 20; 43:3, 14–15; Ps 70:22; 77:41; 88:19^{LXX}. Cf. also Ps 15:10^{LXX}; 2Kgs 4:9.
[97] Cf. Rüggemeier 2017. 242.
[98] Cf. ch. 2 and the *Excursus: Tenses in the Gospel of Mark*, p. 22–24. Cf. Rüggemeier 2017. 242.
[99] Cf. Stamatu, *Geisteskrankheit*. 334; Bennett 1978.
[100] Cf. Sorensen 2002. 154, who rightfully summarizes, that "sometimes the language of demonic possession in ethical contexts is employed for rhetorical effect as a metaphor of the outsider. In

could be attributed to a divine or demonic influence or taken as indication for possession,[101] yet the label of being possessed could likewise be used to pathologize deviating behavior and to delegitimize and marginalize, especially due to the fine line between inspirational or pathological "insanity" and the identity-encompassing quality of a fused or possessed body (cf. esp. Mark 3:21–30).

However, as established, the Gospel of Mark distinctly distinguishes between the clinical picture and necessary treatments of sickness and possession (see ch. 2). Since the text does not allude to other etiologies, it neither excludes nor witnesses to a general attribution of sicknesses to demonic influence. Rather, while exhibiting distinct clinical pictures, both phenomena are used to reflect Jesus' powerful healing ability in the context of his preaching, while his superiority over the demons, embodied in the exorcisms, is employed to integrate his authority and ministry in a cosmic hierarchy and narrative (cf. paradigmatic Mark 1:32–34). While sociopolitical[102] and psychological[103] interpretations of demonic dis/ability often fittingly describe implications of such disparate corporeality, its narrative function with distinct regard of its etiology must be valued.

3.1.3 The Healing

In Mark 1:21–28, the unclean spirit leaves the man, after Jesus' silencing and expelling command, with a final outburst. As established, the physical reaction (v. 26) to Jesus' order is symptomatic of a demon's indwelling yet emphasized here by its particularly violent shaking of the man (the separation is already reflected in the grammatical identification of subject and object) and its demonic death rattle (φωνέω with φωνῇ μεγάλῃ). Then the spirit leaves the man.

3.1.3.1 Order to Silence

Before issuing his expelling order, however, Jesus commands the spirit to silence. The order of the two speech acts and the fact that the silencing is used as an antidote to the symptomatic demonic verbal skirmish constitute it as part of the heal-

---

such cases the intellect becomes in a figurative sense 'possessed' by a spirit that misleads one into doctrinal aberrancies or intellectual disagreement," which frequently occurs in later Christian polemics.

101 Cf. Kelley in Avalos; Melcher; Schipper (ed.) 2007; Kelley in Schipper; Moss (ed.) 2011. Cf., e.g., Deut 32:24; Hab 3:5; Ps 78:50; 91:5; Job 5:7.
102 In combination with psychological ideas, cf. Crossan 1996. 122; Theissen 2007. 243. Cf. also Guijarro in Stegemann; Malina; Theissen (ed.) 2002.
103 Cf. comprehensively, e.g., Davies 1995. 81–89, 93–104; Theissen 2007. 241–246.

ing, even if only as a prelude. For the narrative, the function is clear: by silencing the demon, Jesus first and foremost forbids the demonic force the further use of the host's speech apparatus *pars pro toto* and thereby initiates the audible effect of his powerful command and following release. Moreover, the subsequent generalizations of Jesus' mighty healing and exorcising in Mark 1:32–34 and 3:10–12 portray a secondary function of the command rooted in the *content* of the demonic verbal outburst, namely, to prohibit the proclamation of Jesus' identity by the spiritual forces. Furthermore, considering the subsequently narrated commission of the disciples to heal and exorcise likewise but without explicit silencing (3:14–15), the very intense rebukes to proclaim Jesus' identity shift the focus entirely from the liberating act to the elusive actor Jesus.[104]

As established, the Markan demonic forces do proclaim correct and reliable information by their intermediary and preternatural nature, which is confirmed by information given by the extradiegetic narrator. Hence, their silencing by Jesus is puzzling for the audience. This first and foremost increases the importance of their esoteric knowledge in contrast to the rather clueless witnesses of the exorcisms in the story world (cf. Mark 1:11) and spurs the plot on with unspoken questions: why are they not let in on who Jesus is, and is there maybe even more to him than what the audience already knows? Secondly, it further illustrates Jesus' power since all the demons comply even though his increasing popularity is proof of the rather futile endeavor to keep his identity and mighty deeds hidden.

Due to the fact that in the encounters with demons in Mark 5:1–20, 7:24–30, and 9:14–29 no such command is explicitly issued, it seems to be of narrative value for the beginning of the gospel and not an essential part of the Markan exorcisms. It is striking that demons are not silenced anymore after Jesus himself revealed his authoritative position with regard to the demonic realm in Mark 3:20–35 (see above, B. In Focus: Mark's Jesus and Opposing Forces). Furthermore, subsequent healing narratives report orders to silence by Jesus issued to those healed or witnessing his mighty deeds (Mark 1:44; 5:43; 7:36; 8:30; 9:9), which is analyzed more closely at the end of this chapter in view of the narrative arc of the gospel (see D. In Focus: Silencing in Mark's Healing Narratives).

For the pericope here at the beginning of Mark, the command to silence issued to the demoniac initiates a) the successful parting of the vociferous force from its usurped host and establishes b) a notion of intrigue and mystery concerning the plot's unraveling of Jesus' identity.[105]

---

[104] Cf. Koch in Oyen (ed.) 2019. 583–585.
[105] Cf. ibid. 583–584, 587–593.

3.1.3.2 Embodied Authority

After the silencing, the source of the man's ailment is healed by Jesus' final speech act. Only the term ἐπιτιμάω can account for Jesus' exorcising technique here. While it is difficult to prove that this term reflects an exorcistic formula, the connection to the Hebrew term גער as eschatological binding of the evil sphere seems at least partially connoted by the Markan usage (cf. esp. 3:12 and 9:25, furthermore, 4:39; 8:33).[106] Firstly, however, it reflects an order with hierarchal authority, even "strong disapproval," maybe in the sense of "condemnation" or "punishment."[107] This fits the tone of Jesus' exorcistic imperatives in the subsequent Markan exorcisms. The spirits are expelled in direct speech with short and very firm statements (cf. 5:8; 9:25). Verse 27 repeats this term in the astonished response of the crowd, who explicitly connect Jesus' strict command with his effective authority, and verifies the success as neither host nor demon is mentioned again. Hence, the verb stresses Jesus' legitimately severe subordination of the demon:[108] his previously explicitly doubted authority is evidenced by the immediate obedience of the demon (cf. also 1:34; 9:26);[109] no further dialogues, expressions, or concessional pleas (cf. Mark 5:1–20), nor plays on names and hierarchies, are recounted. The demon leaves exactly as Jesus had ordered, as the repetition of the verbal command emphasizes. His exorcising "technique" is none; Jesus' mere authoritative presence that already triggered the demon (maybe linked to his teaching), caused the verbal outburst, and was reason for the silencing finally ends the possession. This is also reflected in the following Markan exorcisms to which only few motifs are added.[110] All accounts but Mark 7:24–30 are publicly and ostentatiously staged; all prove his word is enough.[111]

---

[106] Cf., e.g., Ps 18:6; 104:7; 2Sam 22:16; 1Q20 20.28; 1QM 14.9–11; also Barton 1922; Kee 1968. 232–246; Wells 1998. 145–146.
[107] Cf. 4:39, 8:33; also 6:27, 39; 8:30–33; 10:13, 48. Cf., e.g., BDAG, s.v; Giesen, ἐπιτιμάω; LN, s.v 33.419, 33.331; LSJ, s.v; Montanari, s.v.
[108] Cf. 1:25; 3:12, and Wells 1998. 145–146.
[109] Cf. Williams in Broadhead (ed.) 2018. 110.
[110] Cf. exorcistic practices such as name inquiry in 5:9; "epipompe" in 5:13; prohibition to return in 9:25 etc. Cf. comprehensively, Böcher 1970. Esp. 168–176; Twelftree 1993. 13–52; Cotter 1999. 83–89.
[111] Cf. Strecker in Stegemann; Malina; Theissen (ed.) 2002. 61.

3.1.4 Interpretation

The narrated dis/ability functions as an example par excellence for a narrative prosthesis as employed for plot development and characterization. While many other images of dis/ability are subsequently used with the same effect, none other than a demoniac could have exemplified the contrast of Jesus' divine identity, authority, and new teaching to a) the establishment and those present and b) the opposing, hostile, torturing realm of evil. The narrative leaves the audience tense about the character's reaction toward the continuous unraveling of Jesus' identity, here reflected in the spirit's extradiegetic "disclosure" and the crowd's surprised and rumoring amazement.[112] With regard to the emotional and verbal response of the crowd towards Jesus' ministry, this initial report is paradigmatic (cf., e.g., 2:12; 5:20; 6:2–3; 7:37; cf. also 6:14–15) and—also due to the generality of the anonymous characters in a public setting—a foil for comparison against which other reactions can be measured (cf., e.g., 1:45 and 7:36; 3:6; 5:14–17; 6:5; of individuals cf. 1:31; 5:20; 10:52).[113] The account not only sets the bar for the following depiction of Jesus' rising popularity (cf. v. 28) but also for the following constant contesting of his authority, which is even linked to possession and cognitive deviance. This is already signaled by Jesus' contrast to the setting here in Mark 1:21–28: in the Synagogue on the Sabbath, Jesus, who lacks any "institutional" legitimization (cf., e.g., 11:27–28),[114] teaches a "new" (not temporal but qualitative),[115] astonishing message that is reported without content and is witnessed together with the outburst of the spirit (maybe to the content of the teaching) and its hierarchal expulsion by command only: τί ἐστιν τοῦτο;—a question the audience also faces in light of the verbal recognition of the unclean spirit and its silencing.[116]

---

112 Cf. Kiffiak 2017. 134, also Hooker 1991. 65; Culpepper 2007. 56–57; Focant 2012. 67.
113 Cf. Kiffiak 2017. 134–135.
114 Focant 2012. 66, 68–69.
115 Cf. ibid. 67. Moreover, e.g., BDAG, s.v.; Behm, καινός; LN, s.v. 67.115; 58.71, 28.33; LSJ, s.v.; Montanari, s.v.
116 Cf. Focant 2012. 65.

3.2 Mark 1:29–31: The Continuous Change of the Mother-in-Law

3.2.1 Introduction to the Narrative

The second healing narrative in the Gospel of Mark is the pericope on the healing of Simon's mother-in-law in Mark 1:29–31. It is a very concise narrative, entirely written in the third person, with only a short, encapsulated dialogue (v. 30).[117]

The pericope starts with εὐθύς, which separates the narrative from the previous venture of Jesus (the exorcism in the Synagogue they now leave) yet ties both stories together to one day (the Sabbath) and town (Capernaum), enhanced by the use of the connecting participle (ἐξελθόντες).[118] An undefined group leaves the synagogue; it is only specified that it comprises Jesus, the two brothers Simon and Andrew, and James and John as they enter the house of the siblings.[119] These four named characters are known to Mark's audience as the first called disciples (cf. 1:16–20) and are present as witnesses and followers of Jesus throughout the gospel narrative. In the house, the successive action in aorist is interrupted and emphasized with a historical present when Jesus is told (λέγουσιν) that Simon's mother-in-law is struck down with a *fever*, which is narrated in the imperfect as background information. She is not named, unlike the four other male characters in these two verses, and as is common for ancient texts. She is defined by her relationship to a male relative, here her son-in-law Simon.[120] This also reflects the aim of historical identification and testimony strategy as the disciples are important figures in the history of Jesus and recurring characters in the gospel narrative.[121] Their naming gives the narrative a higher degree of authenticity and legiti-

---

[117] Cf. Collins 2007. 174.
[118] On Capernaum as a church community site for legitimizing purposes (Mark 9:33), see, e.g., Lau in Zimmermann (ed.) 2013. 216; on its historic roots, see Pesch 1968a. 272–274; Collins 1993. 18; moreover, see E. In Focus: Healing Spaces in Mark.
[119] See Klauck 1981. 15–20, for an analysis of the terminological determinations and socio-cultural definitions of οἰκία and οἶκος and Lau in Zimmermann (ed.) 2013. 216.
[120] The reasons for the historically rather unusual compilation of a mother-in-law and two brothers in one household probably lies in the biographical, catechetical, and/or memorial function of the narrative, cf. Fander 1989. 21. On comparisons with the customs of widows, see Mahr in Zimmermann (ed.) 2013. 538–539. See, moreover, Gundry 1993. 89; Trainor 2001. 93–94; Gnilka 2010. 85. See Krause in Levine; Blickenstaff (ed.) 2001. 48, n. 31, for more general literature on the position of women in family and society in Greco-Roman antiquity.
[121] On family and kinship in the NT world, see Malina 1993. 134–160; D'Angelo in Kraemer; D'Angelo (ed.) 1999; Freyne in Navarro Puerto; Perroni (ed.) 2012; Pellegrini in Navarro Puerto; Perroni (ed.) 2012.

macy.¹²² Untitled characters, such as the mother-in-law, then offer a negative or positive model for identification for the audience and are characterized solely by their family ties (mothers-in-law, daughters, sisters). Neither is Jesus explicitly named, only referred to with personal pronouns (αὐτῷ, v. 30), participles, and as a subject in the predicate (v. 31), which is grammatically common and not at all surprising for such a short narrative. However, staging him and the mother-in-law in the circle of named witnesses puts focus on their (physical) communication:¹²³ immediately after receiving the notice of her sickness, Jesus approaches her, takes her hand, and raises her up. The *fever* leaves her body, freeing her to serve the group. The sequence is again narrated in a succession of completed actions in aorist with the outcome in progressive imperfect.

3.2.2 Images of Dis/ability

Within these two short verses lies a strong emphasis on the mother-in-law's passivity and lack of power. Firstly, she is lying down, within the social context of her time probably "robbed of status and dignity, unable to offer hospitality."¹²⁴ Secondly, she relies entirely on others to represent her: "they" have to inform Jesus about her sickness. Whether or not this is interpreted as an act of intersession,¹²⁵ an indirect request for healing,¹²⁶ or an excuse for her conduct,¹²⁷ Jesus has to come close to her for an encounter. The used tenses underscore this even more as she is dramatically introduced with her condition in v. 30 in the historical present, while two imperfects narrate her dis/ability (v. 30) and transformation as frames for the healing (v. 31): she is lying down struck with *fever* (κατέκειτο) before she is raised and serving (διηκόνει) the group.¹²⁸ While the standard translation of

---

122 On the matter of gender and named characters, see Nogossek-Raithel in El Maaroufi; Strube; Williger (ed.) 2020.
123 The same applies to the narrative of the daughter of Jaïrus from the moment when the five named male characters and the nameless mother enter the girl's room and are only identified by their relationship to Jesus or the daughter (5:40): παραλαμβάνει τὸν πατέρα τοῦ καὶ παιδίου μητέρα καὶ τοὺς μετ' αὐτοῦ. See 5.2.
124 Boring 2006. 66.
125 Cf., e.g., Focant 2012. 72.
126 Cf., e.g., Taylor 1957. 178; Collins 2007. 174.
127 Cf., e.g., Boring 2006. 66.
128 A posture known for the sick (cf. Mark 1:30; 2:4, 15; 14:3; cf. Luke 5:25; John 5:3, 6; Acts 9:33; 28:8) and the dining (cf. Mark 2:15; 14:3; Luke 5:29; 7:37; 1Cor 8:10).

διακονέω means "to wait tables,"¹²⁹ the imperfect tense suggests a continuous, durative action that either points to a meaning beyond the meal preparation for her guests or simply emphasizes the change from a durative passive lying in sickness to continuous active serving. Due to its use in the gospel, this lexeme and its interpretation have been widely discussed.¹³⁰ Here, within the specific narrative context,¹³¹ the first-century mother-in-law with guests in her household serves them after being healed from her sickness. The message is clear: Simon's mother-in-law complies to her domestic duties and is able to offer the required hospitality.¹³² Her transformation is powerfully demonstrated.¹³³

3.2.2.1 Febrile Phenomena

In general, ancient treaties define *fever* (Gk. πυρετός; Lat. *febris*) as an abnormal increase of the body's temperature,¹³⁴ as its etymology connotes fire.¹³⁵ This, however, has to be strictly regarded as a qualitative evaluation in the context of ancient philosophical and anthropological conceptions of physical temperature differen-

---

129 Cf., e.g., BDAG, *s.v*; Beyer, διακονέω; Bietenhard; Heß, διακονέω. 46.13; LN, *s.v*; LSJ, *s.v*; Montanari, *s.v*.
130 Cf. also διακονέω in 1:13, where the angels serve Jesus when he is fasting for forty days in the desert; in 10:45, where Jesus describes the life of the Son of Man and his final offering as an act of service; in 15:41, where the women watching Jesus die on the cross are introduced with reference to their service while following Jesus in Galilee. Under the premise of some form of consistency of translation, the four occurrences might imply a distinct Christian discipleship term, cf., e.g., Fander 1989. 28, 32–34; Tolbert in Newsom; Ringe (ed.) 1992. 267; Schottroff 1994. 300, 313; Miller 2004. 23; Hentschel 2007. 200–202.
131 Following Krause in Levine; Blickenstaff (ed.) 2001. Esp. 41–42, 44; Smit 2003. 4–6, as they rightfully criticize this simple correlation of the verb in all four contexts and the imposed emphasis on the "utopian moment" of the text. Cf. also Schüssler Fiorenza 1983. 320–321; Tolbert in Newsom; Ringe (ed.) 1992. 267; Schottroff 1993. 80–118. Regarding the "overtone of Christian ministry," see Schenke 2005. 74; Boring 2006. 66; Dschulnigg 2007. 83–84, and for interpretations regarding so-called "F-voice" terminology, see, e.g., Kraemer; D'Angelo 1999. 139; Smit 2003, and methodologically, Brenner; Dijk-Hemmes 1993. Esp. 1–13. Moreover, on narrative representations of femininity in Mark, see, e.g., Corley 1993. 241; Krause in Levine; Blickenstaff (ed.) 2001. 49–52; Navarro Puerto in Navarro Puerto; Perroni (ed.) 2012. 157; also Dewey in Schüssler Fiorenza; Matthews; Brock (ed.) 1993. 470–509, esp. 508.
132 Cf. Schweizer 1989 [1967]. 53; Boring 2006. 65–67.
133 Cf. Pesch 1968a. 184; Hooker 1991. 70; Dschulnigg 2007. 83; Lau in Zimmermann (ed.) 2013.
134 Cf., e.g., CH, *Vict.* 2.66; Caelius, *Acut.* 2.100; Galen, *Morb. caus.* 2 K 7.4; *Caus. puls.* 4.7 K 9.165; Alexander Aphrodisias, *Febr.* (with appreciation to Philip van der Eijk for the discussion of his unpublished paper "Alexander of Aphrodisias on fevers" in the HU colloquium, 2021). Cf. also Gundert, *Fieber.* 299; Horn, *Fieber.* 879.
135 Cf. Miller 2004. 20; Gnilka 2010. 84, associates *bYom* 21b.

ces, not an instrumental-quantitative measurement of physical warmth.[136] The ancient qualification of physical warmth only advanced to a more systematic concept of *fever* as a sickness when the philosophic notion of fire/heat as an element and life force was connected with the humoral pathological knowledge of early Hippocratic medicine.[137] Hence, *fever* was not regarded as an illness with a "fixed norm," and it is often just listed as a symptom of other severe, mainly acute sicknesses caused by bile, phlegm, or "filling."[138]

In addition, causes from the physical-natural-environmental realm were discussed, such as winds and climate; changes of air, water, fire, and earth; dietary misconceptions; and physical presuppositions such as splenic conditions and cold, hot, damp surroundings.[139] Furthermore, there are Greco-Roman texts attributing astrological or divine inferences as causes of an observable increase of physical heat.[140] Even Asclepius supposedly charged and manipulated people with *fever*; so do Pluto, Hecate, Demeter, Persephone, the furies, the fates, and underworld gods. Some of these powers were invoked in "magical-religious" (curse) texts to bring *fever* on an adversary, and many statues of heroes and gods suggest they were worshiped and appealed to in this matter, as do stories of itinerate healers.[141] The threat and uncontrollability of febrile conditions is furthermore embodied in the Roman goddess *Febris*, a personified divine *fever*.[142] However, healing by divine intervention does not necessarily presuppose a divine etiology of the ailment. In comparison, *fever* was not often mentioned in narratives about (divine)

---

136 Cf. von Bendemann in Kollmann; Zimmermann (ed.) 2014. 232: "Es zeigt sich der Konstruktions-Charakter jeglicher Rede von einer 'Temperatur' des Menschen bzw. seiner 'Wärme', 'Hitzigkeit' [...] Diese enge Osmose von elementarer Weltdeutung und Heilkunde auf der Basis einer Korrespondenz von mikro- und makrokosmischen Vorgängen hält sich sowohl in der klassischen und hellenistisch-römischen Philosophie als auch in der späteren hellenistisch-römischen Medizin durch."
137 Cf. the precise and accurate analysis in ibid. 261, in great detail: 240–243.
138 Ibid. 243. Cf. also CH, *Acut.* 5; 20. L 2.232; *Aff.* 7; 9; 10; 11 L 6.214–220; 18 L 6.226–227; *Morb.* 1.23 L 6.188; 4.49 L 7.578–579; *Nat. hom.* 15 L 6.66; but CH, *Flat.* 6 L 6 96–97; and Lau in Zimmermann (ed.) 2013. 216; Nutton, *Fieber.* 511; Gundert, *Fieber.* 299; different to Mahr in Zimmermann (ed.) 2013. 537; Riede, *Fieber.* 1:360.
139 Cf., e. g., Ps. Aristotle, *Probl.* 1.22/859b; Plato, *Tim.* 86a; Clement of Alexandria, *Strom.* 8.9; Plutarch, *Tu. san.* 123a, *An. corp.* 502a. Athenaeus, *Deipn.* 3.18 ed. Kaibel. Cf. Cook 1997. 188–189; Mahr in Zimmermann (ed.) 2013. 537.
140 Cf., e. g., Homer, *Il.* 22.30–32; Vettius, *Anth.* 1.1; 2.41; 5.8; Nonnus, *Dion.* 5.276.
141 Cf., e. g., Pliny, *Nat.* 28.41–42; Lucian, *Philops.* 18–20, 25; P.Oxy. 1381.95–96, 113–121, 160–162; also Dittenberger 1917. 1239–1240; Kropp 1930–31. 2.69 (229–230), 2.71 (234); Horn, *Fieber.* 884, 889–890; Burke (ed.) 1996. 2266–2271; Cook 1997. 194; Edelstein; Edelstein 1998. 1.238–239, commentary 2.168.
142 Cf. Burke (ed.) 1996. 2266–2271; Nutton, *Fieber.* 511; Lau in Zimmermann (ed.) 2013. 217.

punishment and healing, which could allude to its ambiguity and volatile course[143] that are also reflected in the variety of possible origins and reasons.

Usually, febrile sicknesses were diagnosed by touch and observation and determined according to the distribution and location of heat within the body, its periodicity, and accompanying symptoms.[144] The Hippocratic treatises mainly discuss individual cases with detailed regard to the chronological progress of the illness and its discernable symptoms and circumstances (e.g., time, place, and climate; gender, age, physical, and character constitution of the patient; accompanying symptoms, e.g., sweat, nose bleeding, cough, etc.). The severity ranges from a self-healing seasonal overheating for a limited time to a life-threatening course, with advice for according healing methods.[145] Later, more systematic approaches to fluctuating physical temperatures advanced, e.g., Celsus in *De Medicina* and most prominently Galen, who, e.g., differentiated symptomatic *fever* and distinct clinical pictures among "ephemeral," "putrid" (categorized according to the rhythm of attacks into various forms of quotidian, tertian, and quartan *fever*), and "hectic *fevers*."[146]

A cure for the described febrile illnesses promised therapies aimed at the rebalance of liquids such as very common purging and bleeding or a strict dietary regime and increasing physical care, observation, and cooling.[147] Generally speaking, *fevers* are by the frequency of their mention a very common sickness yet difficult to specifically determine, unpredictable and at times fatal conditions.[148]

In the Hebrew Bible/Old Testament, febrile phenomena often occur in the context of divine intervention.[149] The term קדחת (*qaddaḥat*) in Lev 26:16 (LXX: ἴκτερος) and Deut 28:22 (LXX: πυρετός) refers to a punishment sent by God to those

---

[143] Cf. Horn, *Fieber.* 886–887; von Bendemann in Kollmann; Zimmermann (ed.) 2014. 251.
[144] Cf. Gundert, *Fieber.* 300; Nutton, *Fieber.* 510–511.
[145] Cf., e.g., CH, *Epid.* 6.14 L 5.247; Galen, *Diff. Febr.* 1 K 7.275; Alexander Aphrodisias, *Feb.* 18 and 17 (1.93 1); also Celsus, *Med.* 3.3–17; Mahr in Zimmermann (ed.) 2013. 537; von Bendemann in Kollmann; Zimmermann (ed.) 2014. 243.
[146] von Bendemann in Kollmann; Zimmermann (ed.) 2014. 244–248. See also Wittern 1989. Cf. *Meth. med.* 10.2 K 10.666–667; *Diff. Febr.* K 7.273–277.
[147] Cf. Nutton, *Fieber.* 511; Mahr in Zimmermann (ed.) 2013. 537.
[148] Cf. *vulgare maxime morbus*, in Celsus, *Med.* 3 1.2–3; Anth. Gr., Epigrammata sepulcralia (ed. Beckby) Epigram 588; Appian, *Bell. civ.* 1.12.105; Arrian, *Epict. diss.* 3.26.2; Lucian, *Peregr.* 44; Pausanias, *Descr.* 8.11.11; Plutarch, *Mar.* 17.11; Posidonius Fragment 200 (ed. Theiler); Procopius, *Bell.* 7.19.33; also Nutton, *Fieber.* 511; Cook 1997. 193–194, n. 41; Lau in Zimmermann (ed.) 2013. 216; von Bendemann in Kollmann; Zimmermann (ed.) 2014. 253.
[149] Cf. von Bendemann in Kollmann; Zimmermann (ed.) 2014. 234–235, on a short survey of Hebrew and Aramaic terms connoting (physical) heat. Differently but with allusions to febrile states, cf. 4Macc 3:17 with the hapaxlegomenon φλεγμονή that occurs often in context with feverish conditions, together with διαπυρόω in v. 15.

disregarding the commandments of his covenant.¹⁵⁰ Just like the Greek term πυρετός, its Semitic roots connote "fire," and it is often listed with other torments.¹⁵¹ In Deut 28:22, the third-person plural even suggests the *fever* to be a personal entity.¹⁵² Within the anthropological understandings of (ancient) Judaism,¹⁵³ later rabbinic writings address physical heat in the context of other discussions regarding life-threatening phenomena with seemingly no fixed unitary concept. It is contextualized with dietetic and climatological reasons and only later alludes to a more structured conceptualization with yet very individual opinions.¹⁵⁴

Flavius Josephus witnesses to two descriptions of feverish sicknesses, that of Alexander Jannäus, who suffers from a quartana (τετραταίαις), and that of Herod, who experiences πυρετός and other symptoms.¹⁵⁵ The medical terminology in these passages might only reflect at this time more common knowledge of the disease; however, a connection between the prominence of the patients and their access to medical practitioners behind their precise diagnosis also seems plausible.¹⁵⁶ An advanced pyretological knowledge is also reflected in Philo's writings.¹⁵⁷

The New Testament accounts for three healings of febrile illnesses. Besides the healing of the mother-in-law here (and Matt 8:14–15/Luke 4:38–39), John 4:46–54 witnesses to the healing of the son of a royal official from a severe sickness connected with *fever* by Jesus' commanding word; and Acts 28:7–8 tells of Publius' father, who is healed by Paul's prayer and laying on of hands from πυρετός and "dysentery." In contrast to the latter two accounts, the *fever* of the mother-in-law is the only characterization of and reason for her bedridden state together with the description of her healing. Hence, the Markan texts seems to depict a distinct illness, not a symptom (among others). However, the text gives no further information on the degree and severity of her illness, nor on its proposed etiology.¹⁵⁸ While it is

---

150 Cf. Philo commenting on Deut 28:22 in *Praem.* 143.
151 Cf., e.g., Lev 26:16; Deut 28:22; Num 11:1–3, and Kitz, *Fever I. HB/OT.* 1194.
152 Cf. ibid. 1195.
153 Cf. von Bendemann in Kollmann; Zimmermann (ed.) 2014. 233, cf. 261.
154 Cf. *bYom* 29a; *yShab* 1,4b [29–35]; *bShab* 66b, 67a; *bGit* 67b; *bBer* 32a; and von Bendemann in Kollmann; Zimmermann (ed.) 2014. 236–238.
155 Cf. Josephus, *B.J.* 1.103–106, 1.656; *A.J.* 13.398.
156 Cf. von Bendemann in Kollmann; Zimmermann (ed.) 2014. 236.
157 Cf. Philo, *Opif.* 124–125; *Praem.* 143 with regard to Deut 28; *Sobr.* 45, and von Bendemann in Kollmann; Zimmermann (ed.) 2014. 236.
158 Cf. Taylor 1957. 179. To von Bendemann in Kollmann; Zimmermann (ed.) 2014. 254–257, it is nevertheless clear that this ailment connotes a medical knowledge and diagnosis.

true that the Gospel of Mark knows of medical physicians (2:17; 5:26), who are prominently described as necessary for diagnosing (and treating) *fever*,¹⁵⁹ the text avoids pushing this interpretation: for one, contrary to Mark 5:26, no indication is given that the mother-in-law was treated by expensive yet failing doctors. Her social status, with which she is explicitly introduced, does not allude to such affluence (which is certainly the case in John 4:46–54 and Acts 28:7–8), even if she was of prominence to the early church.¹⁶⁰ Neither does the setting of the house explicitly allude to a house consultation but serves a different function within the gospel narrative (see E. In Focus: Healing Spaces in Mark), here in particular to imply kinship and intimacy, as well as to refer to a concrete reference point in early Christian history. Moreover, the mother-in-law's physical state is explained to Jesus *after* their entering, even if the primary reason is not outlined. Lastly, a specific medical connotation remains inaccessible due to the lack of additional symptoms, especially regarding the fact that many women are witnessed to suffer from febrile conditions yet always related to issues regarding a "female" φύσις, such as pregnancy.¹⁶¹

3.2.2.2 Physical Release

The healing from her illness is expressed by the distance of heat and body: the *fever* lets go of her; it leaves her (ἀφῆκεν αὐτὴν ὁ πυρετός, v. 31). This terminology is in line with Hippocratic phrasing,¹⁶² and there is no indication of an exclusive demonic explanation, even if it alludes to the *fever* as a body-grasping entity similar to impure spirits or demons (cf. 1:26).¹⁶³ The Markan text gives no reason to assume a distinct demonic etiology or exorcistic treatment, which is otherwise

---

159 Cf., e.g., Plato, *Theaet.* 178c; and Cook 1997. 187; von Bendemann in Kollmann; Zimmermann (ed.) 2014. 253, calls the awareness of medical competence with regard to πυρετός ancient "common sense," 254–255.
160 Cf. von Bendemann in Kollmann; Zimmermann (ed.) 2014. 253–254 and 257, n. 50.
161 Hence there is no indication of understanding *fever* as a physiologically distinct female ailment in the account of Simon's mother-in-law, cf. Weissenrieder; Dolle 2019. 365. Without excluding the existence of fluid and inter* gender in ancient texts—see for the NT, e.g., Matt 19:12; Acts 8:26–40—"female" designates the grammatical male-female dualism of the ancient texts. From an intersectional perspective, the question arises if male and female impaired bodies are represented differently and if so, how and why. On gendered disability in the Gospel of Mark, see, e.g., Nogossek-Raithel in El Maaroufi; Strube; Williger (ed.) 2020.
162 Cf. CH, *Epid.* 5.1.20; 7.1.51; *Progn.* 17.2; *Cap. vuln.* 20.10; *Iudic.* 11.4. Cf. von Bendemann in Kollmann; Zimmermann (ed.) 2014. 256.
163 Cf. Collins 2007. 174.

clearly described as such in the Gospel of Mark.[164] While it is true that "magical" remedies, such as cantations, amulets, and magic bowls, are accounted for against febrile illnesses, especially in the Jewish tradition and more frequently in early Judaism and Christianity,[165] a magical treatment does not always presuppose a demonical etiology.[166] In the Gospel of Mark, neither the described ailment nor the healing rule out a demonic explanation, but neither supports it either.

To conclude, the febrile condition of the mother-in-law cannot be specifically diagnosed due to the lack of more detailed characteristics of her physical state. This adds to the ambiguous and complex nature of πυρετός and its variety of possible severities, etiologies, diagnoses, and therapies; it is a very general and therefore relatable sickness. This is underscored by the frequent and common occurrence of *fever* in ancient texts, from an accompanying, rather ordinary symptom that one can recover from to vivid descriptions of its volatile course and life threat. The body of the mother-in-law is passive and weak, she is dependent on communicative and physical representation. The *fever* affects her entire being, and while it seems easy to detect by touch, it is even more difficult to interpret.

3.2.3 The Healing

After hearing of her condition, Jesus immediately overcomes the secluded passivity of the mother-in-law in a sequence of completed actions in aorist by actively coming up to her (προσελθών). Whether this means he enters the room, approaches

---

164 It remains speculative whether this is due to the author's/editors' criticism of magical explanations and approaches of sickness and health, as in later centuries. See Cook 1997. 198–206, on the early Christian interpretation of *fever* as demonic and Christian critique of "magic." Cf. the similarly ambiguous account in Luke 4:38–39. Cf. Taylor 1957. 179; Horn, *Fieber.* 893; Mahr in Zimmermann (ed.) 2013; Schenk, πυρετός. 484. Also, Pesch 1968b. 172–174, and Pesch 1976. 130; furthermore, Böcher 1972. 81–83; Fuchs 1981/2. 56–57; Gnilka 2010. 84; Horn, *Fieber.* 892; Weiß, πυρέσσω, πυρετός. 957–958, esp. n. 10.
165 Specifically, the healing of Simon's mother-in-law is referred to in several Christian amulets aimed at the healing of women with diseases, sometimes also of fever, and in a Byzantine prayer where the healing of the fever of a woman named Mary is asked for. Cf., e.g., *T.Sol.* 7:5–7; P.Oxy 8.924.2–3; *bShab* 66b–67a; *bGit* 70a; *bNed* 41a; furthermore, Pliny, *Nat.* 28.41–42; 2.16; Philostratus, *Vit. Apoll.* 4.10, and, e.g., Kropp 1930–31. 2.62–63 (2.16); 2.200–207 (2.48); 2.215–216 (2.58); 2.241 (73); 3.204–206; Preisendanz 1931. P18 (2.227); Naveh; Shaked 1987. 44–49 (2), 83–85 (9); and Horn, *Fieber.* 906; Cook 1997. 197–198, 201–202, 207; Mahr in Zimmermann (ed.) 2013. 539–540; Allison, *Fever II. NT.* 1195.
166 Cf. Külken 1985. 12, 15–18, 98–101; Naveh; Shaked 1993. 35, cf. also 36–37, 50–57, 60–66; Cook 1997. 196, n. 50.

her,[167] or "pulls the woman towards him"[168] is incidental. Jesus overcomes the physical distance and heals her by raising her and taking her hand (ἤγειρεν αὐτὴν κρατήσας τῆς χειρός). Although it is debatable whether κρατήσας is to be understood concurrent or antecedent,[169] it seems more natural to grab someone's hand and then help them get up.[170] In any case, ἤγειρεν, an indicative between two participles, is emphasized and highlights the woman's change from passivity to activity. Jesus initiates; she cooperates.[171] Neither action is explicitly witnessed in the very few ancient accounts regarding healings of febrile conditions.[172]

3.2.3.1 Forceful Hands

In the Gospel of Mark, κρατέω usually signifies "to seize"[173] (cf. the arrest of John the Baptist in 6:17 and of Jesus in 14:1, 44, 46, 49). Interestingly, the meaning of seizing a *hand* can only be accounted for Mark 1:31, 5:41, and 9:27,[174] the narratives of the healing of Simon's mother-in-law, Jaïrus' daughter, and of the deaf-mute boy, always together with ἤγειρεν (imperatively in 5:41, cf. 2:9, 11; 3:3; 10:49), in Mark 5:42 and 9:27, additionally with the lexeme ἀνίστημι marking the effect. In their frequent combination, they reflect a characteristic feature of the Markan Jesus' way of healing.[175]

Both "inanimated" children and the bed-struck and *fever*-ridden woman are helped up from their lying position—the deaf-mute boy after the spirit had left him—by taking their hand. The forceful connotation behind the verb "implies some form of resistance,"[176] at least in the sense that their physical state requires

---

167 Cf. Taylor 1957. 179; Mahr in Zimmermann (ed.) 2013. 537.
168 Miller 2004. 20.
169 Cf. Taylor 1957. 179.
170 Cf. Focant 2012. 72.
171 Cf. Trainor 2001. 92.
172 Famously, Chanina ben Dosa heals a boy, the son of Rabbi Gamaliel, of a "fever" from afar by prayer. Here too, no cause of the *fever* is given, yet it leaves the body autonomously, cf. *bBer* 34b; Kahl 1994. 170–171; Cook 1997. 186. Also, Hadrian's *fever* is healed by the touch of a blind man, SHA, Vita Hadriani 25.3–4; 24.9; cf. Gundry 1993. 90; Horn, *Fieber.* 880–887; Kollmann 1996. 142–144, 223; Lau in Zimmermann (ed.) 2013. 216. Cf. also, Pliny, *Nat.* 7.166; Philostratus, *Her.* 15.10–16.6.
173 Cf. 1:31; 3:21; 5:41; 6:17; 7:3, 4, 8; 9:10, 27; 12:12; 14:1, 44, 46, 49, 51. Cf., e.g., BDAG, *s.v.*; Braumann, κράτος; LN, *s.v.* 18.6, 37.16, 37.110, 13.34, 68.29; LSJ, *s.v.*; Montanari, *s.v.*; von der Osten-Sacken, κρατέω.
174 Cf. also the parallel accounts in Matt 9:25 and Luke 8:54.
175 To Pesch 1968a. 183—with reference to Mark 2:9, 11, 12; 5:41, 42; 9:27; cf. also 3:3; 10:49—the whole act of raising and seizing is a fixed "topos," the touching of the bodies even gives it a "schematic" connotation. Cf. Wagenvoort, *Contactus.* 416–418; Bultmann 1967. 237–238; Grundmann 1980. 63.
176 Wells 1998. 200, n. 690.

sudden force (i.e., in all three cases, a form of severe powerlessness and faint). An interpretation along the lines of a cosmic, demonic battle on the grounds of the dis/abled bears no further indication (see each chapter on the employed images of dis/ability).

Moreover, the terminology underscores the intentional immediacy of Jesus' actions; that is especially relevant in the case of Jaïrus' daughter, whose healing narrative depicts a race against time (see ch. 5.2). The fact that her father requested Jesus to lay his hands on her (5:23, ἐπιθῇς τὰς χεῖρας αὐτῇ) does not necessarily equate hand seizing with laying on of hands (see C. In Focus: Mark's Healing Touches);[177] it could also imply that the state of the daughter had worsened, and a more drastic action was required. In any case, the physical connection between Jesus' hands and the patient seems most relevant. Jesus' deliberate actions together with ἤγειρεν (and ἀνίστημι) convey a drastic change.

3.2.3.2 Radical Transformation

In the Gospel of Mark, ἤγειρεν is often found in the context of healing narratives (cf. 1:31; 2:9, 11; 3:3; 5:41; 10:49), or with regard to resurrections from the dead (of Jesus: 14:28, [16:6]; of others: 6:14, 16; 12:26), it carries the ambiguous meaning "raise up" and "rise from the dead."[178]

With synonymous use, ἐγείρω and ἀνίστημι frequently occur in (extra) biblical texts, with more or less similar applications as they signify the transition from one physical position to another, mostly in form of a (self-) elevation from a sitting or lying position (here, each with a transitive and intransitive meaning): the change from dream and (nightly) sleep in an awake state, the rise from one's place of the night;[179] from a weak, passive, absent state of mind to an excited, active, also official appearance or embarking on a journey; changing from a lying, sitting, passive position into an elevated, erected, active status (items as well); and in the context of the New Testament, especially the raising of the sick[180] and resurrection of the dead[181] that is often imperatively used in the sense of "Up!/Come on!" as it is also addressed to those without any ailments and those alive.[182]

---

177 Cf. Böcher 1972. 82.
178 Cf. BDAG, s.v.; Klaiber, ἐγείρω; Kremer, ἐγείρω; LN, s.v. 17.10, 17.9, 23.77, 13.83, 23.94, 13.65, 23.140; LSJ, s.v.; Montanari, s.v.; Oepke, ἐγείρω.
179 Cf. ἐγείρω in Mark 4:27, 38; ἀνίστημι in Mark 1:35; 16:9; furthermore, Luke 11:7–8; 22:46.
180 Cf. Acts 3:7, also Acts 9:40–41; but: Acts 9:34 (without a helping hand).
181 Cf. for ἀνίστημι: Mark 8:31; 9:9–10, 31; 10:34; 12:23, 25; for ἐγείρω: Mark 6:14, 16; 12:26; 14:28; 16:6, 14. Cf. esp. Matt 10:8.
182 Cf. Mark 2:14 (ἀνίστημι); 14:42 (ἐγείρω); in healing contexts cf. also Mark 2:9, 11(parr.); 3:3(par.); 10:49. Cf. comprehensively Oepke, ἐγείρω. 333–336; Oepke, ἀνίστημι/ἐξανίστημι. 368–372; Kremer,

Hence, the two verbs describe the transition from an (un)intended physical state of rest and passivity into an active state, which can be caused by one's own will and/or external impact.

In the case of Mark 1:31; 2:9, 11–12; 5:41–42, and 9:25, 27, the standing-up serves as a demonstration of the physical transformation. Apart from the boy in Mark 9, each elevation is followed by a description of subsequent physical actions (διακονέω in 1:31; αἴρω τὸν κράβαττον and ἐξέρχομαι in 2:11; περιπατέω in 5:42).

In Mark 5:41–42 and 9:27, the ambiguity of the physical states of both children is reflected when the semantically ambiguous verbs ἐγείρω *and* ἀνίστημι describe the overcoming of putative death (claimed by surrounding characters) and the first active movement of the healed children. The terminology used fits both conditions, those discussed by the witnesses and those explained by Jesus and the narrator. With regard to their later use in the gospel plot in the passion predictions and passion narrative, as often with Mark's ambiguous use of polysemes (cf., e.g., πίστις and σῴζω, see ch. 5.2.3), "there is every reason to think here of a discreet announcement of a symbolic theme whose harmonies will be developed in what follows."[183] As such, this is regarded more closely in ch. 7 on Mark 8–10. Here, foremost, the terminology serves to display the drastic physical healing from radical passivity.

3.2.4 Interpretation

The shortness of the narrative, some linguistic and redactional theories, and the seeming lack of a Christological punchline led many commentators to conclude that this was a personal memory of Simon Peter connected with the foundation of the church in Capernaum and the "calling" of the mother-in-law.[184] Only κατάκειμαι and διακονέω are set in the imperfect tense, only here the woman is the subject. She changed from being the permanently passive object to the permanently active subject of the narrative, with connotations of the used lexemes foreshadowing another meaning regarding the passion narrative and an eschatological horizon. Her dis/ability connotes a norm of functionality within social expectations

---

ἀνάστασις and cogn. 210–221; Kremer, ἐγείρω. 899–902; Kuhn, ἀνάστασις and cogn. 211–212; LSJ, s.v. 144, 469; Klaiber, ἐγείρω.
183 Focant 2012. 72.
184 Cf., e.g., Fander 1989. 26; Hooker 1991. 70. See esp. Schille 1957. 137–139; Schille 1966. 64–73; Schille 1967. 26–27, who argues that many healing narratives with specific statements of place legitimate churches located there and when set in a certain region, justify the mission program in this area.

by its ambiguous descriptions; however, what also transpires is a form of subversion as her independent, risen, serving existence might elude strict everyday parameters.[185] Her sickness, common yet ambiguous in its etiology, severity, and course, displays her as a relatable patient when Jesus overcomes the physical distance, and she is forcefully and intentionally pulled out of her passivity, and the *fever* is separated from her. This image of dis/ability in particular serves the programmatic start of the narrative, the initial characterization of Jesus, and alludes to a significant and intriguing change when being transformed by Jesus.

Oddly enough, there is no reaction of the witnesses recounted. Only as the gospel narrative unfolds, various responses of those witnessing Jesus' mighty deeds are pictured for the audience, which by contrast underlines this section's pragmatic, initial, and for now basic portrayal.[186] However, the section closes as the narrated day ends with a summaric report that accounts of a crowd that comes together at the door (of the house?) and receives healing and deliverance from demons. Jesus' popularity and publicity are emphasized (see 2.6.2) and connected to the previous exorcism in the synagogue and perhaps to rumors about the private healing of the mother-in-law.[187]

3.3 Mark 1:40–45: The Tangible Healing of a Skin-Sensitive Man

3.3.1 Introduction to the Narrative

The final narrative in this section is placed between two more abundantly described stays in Capernaum, suggesting Jesus was traveling in that area and is—by the lack of a more concrete placement—encountered in a geographically marginal place.[188] The account is neither pinned to a certain time (i.e., the Sabbath) nor person (i.e., Simon) and hence appears general[189] yet by characteristic motifs as succession of the start of Jesus' ministry in Galilee.[190]

The exemplary yet immediate aspect is also reflected in the used tenses as Mark highlights key passages in the historical present, namely the introductions

---

185 Cf. διακονέω in 1:13; 10:45; 15:41, and ἐγείρω in 14:28, [16:6], and 6:14, 16; 12:26.
186 Cf. Lau in Zimmermann (ed.) 2013. 215; Kiffiak 2017. 136.
187 Cf. Fander 1989. 32.
188 Cf. 1:39; also Rüggemeier 2017. 435.
189 Cf. Boring 2006. 70.
190 Cf., e.g., the crowd and Jesus in 1:33, 45; commands to silence in 1:34, 44; tactile treatments in 1:31, 41, and authoritative speech acts in 1:34, 43.

of the man's and Jesus' speech acts (vv. 40, 41, 44), thereby drawing the audience in while dressing the main storyline in aorist, which moves the plot forward.[191] Finally, introduced with the literally ingressive ἤρξατο (v. 45), he "zooms out" by moving the ongoing background actions in view via the imperfect.[192]

The narrative is very clearly structured and narrowed down in two opposing sequences of very physical action and reaction: in v. 40, the *leper* "comes – begs – kneels – says"; subsequently, Jesus in v. 41 "has compassion/is angry – stretches out hand – touches – assures he is willing." Then v. 42 states the healing followed by Jesus commanding the man to request priestly confirmation (vv. 43–44, namely by inspection [δείκνυμι] and purification offering according to Mosaic law), yet also warns him sternly to remain silent. The account ends by illustrating Jesus' heightened popularity that now hinders him from his mission (v. 45). The entire narrative focuses on the two characters,[193] who are from v. 40b on "referred to only by pronouns, with subject and direct object," solely and ambiguously "distinguished by context,"[194] which is also due to various text-critical problems.[195]

3.3.2 Images of Dis/ability

3.3.2.1 Scaly Skin

The man's character-absorbing dis/ability is designated with the term λέπρα. He *is* a "leper" (v. 40) and only in his cleansing separated from his sickness (ἀπῆλθεν ἀπ' αὐτοῦ ἡ λέπρα, v. 42). In the New Testament, λέπρα and its cognates occur only in the gospels: λεπρός ("scaly, rough, harsh [...] scaly, mangy"[196]) is found nine times; λέπρα, a "collective term for all kinds of skin diseases,"[197] four times. Besides the occurrences in this narrative and its parallel accounts (Matt 8:2–4; Luke 5:12–16), healing of *leprous* diseases is featured in Luke 17:11–19, in the report of Jesus' deeds to disciples of John the Baptist (Matt 11:5; Luke 7:22), in a reference to Naaman's healing by Elisha (Luke 4:27), and in the disciples' commissioning (only) in

---

191 Cf. Müller in Zimmermann (ed.) 2013. 221, 225.
192 Cf. Breytenbach in Breytenbach (ed.) 2021a [2019]. 188. On Mark's use of ἄρχω, see Turner in Elliott (ed.) 1993. 93–95; Decker 2014. 43.
193 Cf. Müller in Zimmermann (ed.) 2013. 222.
194 Boring 2006. 70.
195 Cf., e.g., Collins 2007. 177; Haelewyck 2013; Lisboa 2015; Rüggemeier 2017. 435
196 Cf., e.g., BDAG, s.v.; Montanari, s.v.; LSJ, s.v.; Michaelis, *λέπρα, λεπρός*.
197 Iersel 1998. 143. Cf. for the following, e.g., Köcher in Wolf (ed.) 1986; Preuss 1989; Baumgarten 1990; Qimron 1991; Manchester in Gourevitch; Grmek (ed.) 1992; Poorthuis; Schwartz 2000; Roberts; Lewis; Manchester 2002; Monot 2005; Nicklas in Nicklas; Kruger; Kraus (ed.) 2009.

Matt 10:8. Additionally, the narrative of Jesus' anointment takes place in the house of Simon "the *leper*" (Mark 14:3; Matt 26:6), although it remains unclear whether Simon has or had the disease or if his designation has other reasons; subsequently, he is not mentioned again.

In every instance, as here, καθαρίζω or καθαρισμός (1:40–42, 44) are used almost exclusively to denominate the reinstatement of *pure* physicality.[198] Matthew 10:8 even insinuates that the cleansing of λέπρα is a classification of its own when listed among healing the sick, waking the dead, and expelling demons.[199] Here, the references to ἱερεύς and Mosaic law (1:44) explicitly set the ailment within the broad context of Jewish purity regulations.

In both detailed accounts of Jesus' cleansing from λέπρα (Mark 1:40–44par. and Luke 17:11–19), he commands a ritualized restoration by sending those healed to show themselves to priestly authority and, in the case of Mark 1:44, offer a sacrifice. None of the New Testament accounts give precise details or a clear diagnosis besides the denominating label.[200] The clinical pictures associated with the term λέπρα and its Hebrew equivalent צרעת were only later (probably in the ninth century) identified with Hansen's disease, the modern "lepra" that was mainly distinctly termed ἐλέφας/ἐλεφαντίασις.[201]

In the Hebrew Bible/Old Testament, skin diseases designated with λέπρα/צרעת occur in several contexts and generically describe a (unidentified) form of scabies, often connected to social exclusion, with visible symptoms (e.g., flaky or white "as snow," patchy)[202] that show a similarity to psoriasis and can range from acute to

---

[198] Only Luke 17:15 uses additionally ἰάομαι.
[199] Wohlers in Maser; Schlarb (ed.) 1999b. 302, attributes this to the fact, that skin disease in the gospels is religiously and not medically assessed.
[200] Cf. thoroughly and with particular regard to ancient medical concepts and the Lukan text, Weissenrieder 2003. 129–225; Weissenrieder in Alkier; Weissenrieder (ed.) 2013.
[201] Its symptoms include deformations and mutilations of the body as a consequence of an infection with *Mycobacterium leprae*. To avoid confusion, both are designated in the following by their Greek terms. Cf., e.g., Celsus, *Med.* 3.25.1–2; Oribasius, *Collectionum Medicarum Reliquiae* 45.27.1; cf. also Galen, who employs ἐλεφαντίασις broadly: *Glauc. meth. med.* 11.142; *Simpl. med. temp.* 9.1; regarding social implications, cf. Aretaeus, *Sign. acut.* 4.13.19; Caelius Aurelianus, *Chron.* 4; Herodotus, *Hist.* 1.138; and comprehensively, e.g., Hulse 1975. 87–89; Wilkinson 1978; Browne in Hastings (ed.) 1989; Kaplan 1993. 507; Wohlers in Maser; Schlarb (ed.) 1999b. 297; Lieber in Conrad; Wujastyk (ed.) 2000. 101–104; Kazen 2002. 98–99; Hieke, *Leper, Leprosy A. ANE and HB/OT.* For a detailed survey on literary and paleopathologic findings on leprosy and ἐλέφας/ἐλεφαντίασις, see Thiessen 2020. 43–49. For an identification of λέπρα with *sbḥ* in Egyptian papyri, see Møller-Christensen in Brothwell; Sandison (ed.) 1967.
[202] Cf., e.g., Exod 4:6; Num 12:10; 2Kgs 5:27; Lev 13:2, 10, 19, 24 and 42 in contrast to vv. 12–13; cf. also Philo, *Deus* 127; *Plant.* 111; Lev 13:18–23, 24–28, 29–37, who describes yellow coloring, at times inflamed. Cf. Hulse 1975. 92–93, 95, 97–99.

symptomatic.²⁰³ The characteristic feature is a visible change on the surface of the skin when related to humans.²⁰⁴

Bearing in mind the variety of authors, times, genres, and corpora, a common concept of λέπρα/צרעת from Hebrew scripture and its translations is impossible to obtain, and the following highly simplified notions do not reflect a development but rather a collection of simultaneous concepts.²⁰⁵ There are, however, two rough currents that can be distinguished:²⁰⁶

Some writings attribute the etiology of λέπρα/צרעת to divine intervention or punishment,²⁰⁷ at times—especially in the wider reception history of these verses—even as a direct consequence of sin.²⁰⁸ Others, such as Lev 13–14, place λέπρα together with (mostly) natural, unavoidable, and vital physical matters such as genital discharges, childbirth, and corpse contact in context of cultic purity regulations that explain "certain incidents that recommend urgently refraining from partaking in the cult, at least temporarily."²⁰⁹ In these texts, there is no command of supplication, penance/sacrifice before healing, or a healing intermediary mentioned (unlike in Num 12; 2Kgs 5).²¹⁰ A successful treatment entails a priestly diagnosis and simply time to wait (isolated) for it to pass.²¹¹ Neither sin as the

---

203 On the one hand, a swift (seven-day) recovery is promised, cf. Josephus, *A.J.* 3.261–264; *C. Ap.* 1.281–282; *LAB* 13.3; Philo, *Spec.* 1.118, on the other hand seven to fourteen days of observation suggest a more permanent condition; Lev 13:11 and 2Kgs 15:5–7/2Chr 26:19–21 imply an unwavering suffering. Cf. Hulse 1975. 92, 95.
204 Also, textiles, leathers, and houses could be infested with a kind of fungal growth termed λέπρα/צרעת, cf. Lev 13:47–59; 14:37–54. Cf., e.g., Meier 1989. For a "typology" of צרעת, see, e.g., Staubli 1996. 114–119; Stewart in Melcher; Parsons; Yong (ed.) 2018.
205 Cf. Baden; Moss 2011. 653.
206 See ibid., where the authors convincingly attribute them to Priestly and non-Priestly texts.
207 Cf., e.g., Exod 4:6–7; Num 12:9–12; 2Sam 3:29; 2Kgs 5:27; 15:5; and 2Chr 26:19–23. Schinkel 2003, plausibly puts forward an interpretation of Miriam's צרעת not as punishment but authentication mark for Moses (cf. Exod 4:6–7).
208 Cf., e.g., Milgrom 1991. 823; Maccoby 1999. 131; and e.g., *WayR* 17:3; *bAr* 16a; *tNeg* 6:7; 4Q270 frg. 2 2.12; 4Q272 frg. 1, 1.1; 1Q28ᵃ 2.3–4; 1QM 7.4–5; Josephus, *C. Ap.* 1.280–285; *B.J.* 5.227; *A.J.* 3.261–264.
209 Hieke, *Leper, Leprosy A. ANE and HB/OT*. 146. Skin diseases, like issues of blood (cf. Mark 5:25–34), are classified in the context of Lev–Deut as the temporary טומאה, that don't hinder normal everyday life, in contrast to visible bodily conditions (מומים) which could disqualify priests from sanctuary service. Cf. Stewart in Moss; Schipper (ed.) 2011. 74; Stewart in Melcher; Parsons; Yong (ed.) 2018. 57–58.
210 For details on the nature of prescribed sacrifice in Lev 14:12, see Baden; Moss 2011. 648–650.
211 Priests exclusively observe, inspect, and determine suspicious symptoms (e.g., infestation of scalp and discoloration of hair, cf. Lev 13:4, 10); declare, but not treat or heal im-/purity; witness to highly ritualized necessary social and spatial isolation, as well as purification rites. Cf. Hieke,

cause nor forgiveness as the remedy is referred to. The allusions to death and corpses found in many of the texts mainly relate to social consequences of the purity regulations and, more importantly, to similar physiological features with corpses,[212] yet do *not* imply a deadly disease, respectively a resurrection when being healed.[213] Rather, healing is conceptualized with "cleansing" but also designated with a physical transformation.[214]

The complexity of the undercurrent concepts of these texts cannot be stressed enough. Not only due to the mentioned textual variety but also regarding the different bodies to which these descriptions are applied: They recognize idealized and unblemished bodies in contact with the sanctuary, regulations for ritual body modification (e.g., circumcision, hair removal), legal guidelines for religious and social regulations, "observations of nature and natural body processes,"[215] and/or biographical characterizations of narrative role models (e.g., Moses or Miriam),[216] all with a variety of inherent sources and intended functions.

In all caution, what can be concluded from this very rough overview of the Hebrew Bible/Old Testament witnesses is, by its undesirability, the stigmatizing effect that a scaly skin disease has on the affected, whether it arises from notions of ritual unavailability or divine punishment, fear of (ritual) infection, "aesthetic objection," or disgust.[217] By inversion, the implied norm refers to a however intended non-stigmatization.

The difficulty in unraveling a distinct clinical picture of the disease(s) termed λέπρα is also reflected in writings of Greco-Roman heritage: while the Corpus Hip-

---

Leper, Leprosy A. ANE and HB/OT. 146–147. The focus of the isolation seems to lie on a prevention of the disease spreading, cf. Kazen 2002. 108.

212 For example, the illness of Miriam in Num 12 is compared to a stillborn child due to the similarity of the clinical picture, not necessarily with regard to its severity (cf. Hulse 1975. 93), and Elishas' healing of Namaan is (erroneously) matched with a resurrection, although *bSan* 47a only compares the "clinical pictures." Cf. Webb 2006. 188. Cf., e.g., Num 5:2–3; 12:12; Job 18:3; Lev 14:4–7; Num 19:1–13, and Josephus, *A.J.* 3.264, moreover, 4Q269 frg.7 4–7; 4Q272 frg. 1, 1.1–5; 4Q266 frg. 6, 1.10, and the differentiation of "dead" and "living" skin and hairs, cf. Thiessen 2020. 52. Cf. moreover, Hulse 1975. 93; Lieber in Conrad; Wujastyk (ed.) 2000. 107–111, and Milgrom 1991. 817–820; Hieke 2014. 474–475.
213 Cf. Kollmann 1996. 224; Kollmann in Zimmermann (ed.) 2013. 89.
214 Cf., e.g., רפא/ἰάομαι in Lev 13:18, 37; 14:3, 48 (of houses); Num 12:13.
215 Stewart in Melcher; Parsons; Yong (ed.) 2018. 86.
216 Cf. ibid. 62–63, 83, where he stresses the differences between (different) priests, their families, lay Israelites of different ages; and points out the function of "chief characters" of the biblical narratives.
217 Regarding "loose scales, which might have been thought akin to discharges," cf. Hulse 1975. 92–94, quote from 103. See on the association and emotional language of disgust in contexts of impurity, e.g., Kazen 2011; Feder 2013; Kazen 2014; Kazen in Spencer (ed.) 2017.

pocraticum relates the term to a wide range of conditions—from skin secretion to a severe illness with additional symptoms—Philo describes it as a variable disease with different forms, and Galen distinguishes among six forms of λέπρα and exceptionally separates it from ἐλεφαντίασις. Unsurprisingly, the plural is often used.[218]

Generally, the severity ranged from a useful and nonpathological cleansing, to an aesthetical blemish, to a harmless and curable change of skin, and a symptom of more severe, even deadly diseases.[219] As skin was considered a permeable, porous structure and an important therapeutic surface via which liquids were balanced from the out- and inside, λέπρα in the sense of a change of this structure could be regarded as such a therapeutic process or symptom for a more serious imbalance on the inside. This rebalance is at times also termed καθαίρω/ καθαρίζω.[220] Furthermore, environmental factors were perceived to be the means of such dermatological conditions, e. g., dry and hot climate or temperatures or (lack of) moistness of certain winds.[221] If regarded as a pathological occurrence, recovery was hoped to be found in rebalancing methods or treatment with pharmacological and organic substances (such as vinegar, plants, saliva).[222] Here, the skin condition implies an imbalanced holistic concept of the body.

3.3.2.2 Social Stigmatization?
While stigmatizing notions can be traced more or less throughout the reviewed texts, it remains dubitable whether and to what extent this had concrete and strict social implementations—especially in the context of purity regulations to which the Markan text alludes (cf. priests, Mosaic law)—in Second Temple Judaism.[223]

---

218 Cf. CH, *Aph.* 3.20; *Epid.* 2.1.7; 6.3.23; *Prorrh.* 2.43; Philo, *Post.* 47; also *Somn.* 1.202; Galen, *Intro. Med.* K 14.7.674–797: ἐλεφαντίασις, λεοντίασις, ὀφίασις, λέπρα, ἀλωπεκία, λώβη. Cf. also Hulse 1975. 88; Weissenrieder 2003. 141; Thompson, *Leper, Leprosy III. GRA*.
219 Cf., e. g., Galen, *Alim. fac.* 3.2; *Diff. Febr.* 1.4; CH, *Aff.* 35; *Alim. fac.* 20; *Morb.* 1.3; also CH, *Aph.* 3.20; *Epid.* 5.9; and *Prorrh.* 2.43. Cf. Leven, *Lepra.* 565; Wohlers in Maser; Schlarb (ed.) 1999b. 295–296.
220 Cf., e. g., the dispersion of superfluous bodily liquids via pores through heat, bloodletting, scarification, etc., if the body does not heal itself by peeling of skin, blisters and ulcers, discoloration, etc. Cf. CH, *Hum.* 20.4; *Epid.* 6; *Morb.* 1.15; 1.20.36; 2.2; and Wohlers in Maser; Schlarb (ed.) 1999b. 298; Weissenrieder 2003. 214–221, also 144–146, 151–152; Weissenrieder in Alkier; Weissenrieder (ed.) 2013. 74–78, 85. Cf. moreover, Duden 1987. 144; Benthien 1998; Benthien 2001. 49–56; Helm, *Hautkrankheiten.* 382; Michaelis, λέπρα, λεπρός; Hauck, καθαρός *and cogn. D. NT.* 427–428; Meyer, καθαρός *and cogn. C. Judentum.* 421–422.
221 Cf. esp. CH, *Aer.* 3 and 4; moreover, Weissenrieder in Alkier; Weissenrieder (ed.) 2013. 79.
222 Cf. CH, *Epid.* 2.5.23; 5.9; Pliny, *Nat.* 24.120.186 and 28.7.
223 Cf. also Job 28:24–25; *WayR* 15.

With regard to Leviticus, Josephus confirms concepts of ritual defilement by physical contact, stigmatizing appearances, housing areas outside of towns and villages for those with λέπρα, and their ritual purification and readmission. Nevertheless it is unclear if he only references Leviticus, an idealization of Mosaic times, or contemporary practices.[224] Qumranic texts, with their own emphasis on im-/purity, also confirm isolated housing in cities for those infected, stipulations regarding their religious participation, and very detailed purification rites, even if not invariable.[225] Rabbinic literature furthermore confirms the notion of a feared form of contagious contact, which is also reflected in neighboring cultures, as a Babylonian inscription suggests.[226] While the earlier sources rather focus on a diagnosis of impurity, the later evidence an increasingly moral punchline and at the same time an increasing leniency, also with regard to geographical distance to Jerusalem.[227] Detailed diagnostic descriptions are, for instance, found in the (later) Mishnaic tractate *Nega'im*, which encompasses a visual evaluation of "blemishes," *leprous* skin (*mNeg* 1:1–2; cf. also *mNeg* 1–2; 4–8), a specification of the clinical picture (white hair, quick flesh, spreading; 3:3),[228] "detailing the cases of leprous skin, boils or burns, scalls, baldness, garments, and houses"[229] (3:3; 9–13; cf. *tNeg* 7:3), and means for cleansing (*mNeg* 14).[230] Ritual defilement and social distancing were addressed and advised but mainly only under various circumstances, for example, with regard to non-Jews and resident aliens (*mNeg* 3:1), covering cultic participation in synagogues and dealing with sexual intercourse (*mNeg* 13:12 and 14:2),[231] and concerning *walled* cities (*mKel* 1:7) or the time of Jubilee observance (*bAr* 29a).[232] In addition, tractates from the Tosefta show a less stringent approach, as do later rabbinic texts that focus more on a connection to sin and de-

---

[224] Kazen 2002. 133, 113–114, argues that the latter is the case due to non-biblical details such as the mention of spring water for purification. Cf. Luke 17:12; Josephus, *C. Ap.* 1.280–285; *B.J.* 5.227; *A.J.* 3.261–264; cf. also Wohlers in Maser; Schlarb (ed.) 1999b. 298–299; Maccoby 1999. 143–144.
[225] Cf., e.g., 4Q274 frg. 1, 1.1–4; 11Q19 45.17–18; 46:16–18; 48:14–15; 1Q28ª; 1QM; 4Q394 3–10; 4QMMT B65–75. Cf. on the demonic etiology of *lepra* also 4Q266 frg. 6, 1; 4Q272 frg. 1, 1.1–2. Cf. Harrington 1993. 79, 81; Kazen 2002. 109–111; Berthelot 2006; Feder 2012; Thompson, *Leper, Leprosy III. GRA*; Cizek, *Leper, Leprosy IV. Judaism*; Thiessen 2020. 52–53.
[226] Cf. Grundmann 1980. 71; Milgrom 1991. 805; Cizek, *Leper, Leprosy IV. Judaism*, and on white skin conditions, Kinnier Wilson in Brothwell; Sandison (ed.) 1967.
[227] Cf. Kazmierski 1992. 44; Harrington 1993. 198–213; Kazen 2002. 110.
[228] Cf. the later development of *tNeg* 1:4.
[229] Cizek, *Leper, Leprosy IV. Judaism*. 150.
[230] Cf., e.g., Maccoby 1999. 141–148.
[231] Cf. Kazen 2002. 110.
[232] Cf. Maccoby 1999. 146–147; different to Kazen 2002. 110, n. 111.

scriptions of prominent cases.²³³ Simultaneously, they contain strong notions that reflect an infection to objects by contact, winds, and breath as transmitters and strict prescriptions to distance.²³⁴ Famously, the reconstructed Papyrus Egerton 2 (ca. 200 CE; from Egypt)²³⁵ witnesses to a man who developed *lepra* and is healed by Jesus. Compared to the Synoptic accounts, it is noteworthy that there is no mention of a healing touch, but instead a lengthy explanation is provided regarding how the man became ill, specifically through contact with other *lepers*.²³⁶ Additionally, the notion of sin as reason for the disease is referenced, although the description of the man's infectious behavior in itself is evaluated as unintentional.

It becomes clear that the observed texts reflect a struggle with the interpretation of Hebrew Bible/Old Testament regulations and represent a concern with *lepra* as a serious form of impurity and fear of contamination by sharing social space. This must have led to some sort of social stigmatization and ostracism of those infected even if concrete consequences are regarded more leniently and implemented differently here and there in Second Temple Judaism.²³⁷ This might be reflected in the Markan setting with no concrete placement, crowds, or witnesses mentioned.

3.3.3 The Healing

Three times the healing is described as καθαρίζω, a term designating to "cleanse, purify, pronounce clean in connection with λέπρα: eliminate, heal."²³⁸ It is found in a variety of texts, among them also sources on Jewish purity regulations that, however, do not use it exclusively to designate a transformation of λέπρα/צרעת. In New Testament healing narratives, it is only used for petitioners with *lepra* (Mark 1:40–45par.; Luke 17:11–19; Matt 10:8).²³⁹ Here, it is specifically described as an im-

---

233 Cf., e.g., *tNeg* 1:4; 2:7; 5:1; 6:1; *mNeg* 4:11–5:1, 9:2; 11:2; *bMQ* 7a–8a; *bYom* 11b–12a; *bSan* 107a–b; *ShemR* 11:6; *WayR* 16:1; 17:3; *BemR* 7:5; *bAr* 16a; *BerR* 20:4; 41:2; *ShemR* 1:34; 1; *PRE* 48; *bMeg* 12b; and Cizek, *Leper, Leprosy IV. Judaism*. 151.
234 Cf. *mZab* 5:6; *mNeg* 13:8; cf. Lev 14:33–57, esp. v. 36; *WayR* 16:3; 11Q19 46.16–18; 4Q274 frg. 1, 1.1–4; cf. Harrington 1993. 181–213, esp. 188; different to Wright 1987. 210. Cf. also Kazen 2002. 113.
235 Cf. Zelyck 2019. Esp. 126–141; also Mayeda 1946; Neirynck (ed.) 1991; Kazen 2002. 123–124, 122; Kollmann in Zimmermann (ed.) 2013. 89; Nicklas in Zimmermann (ed.) 2013.
236 This is unusual for rabbinic thinking where impurity not *lepra* can be contracted by touch, cf. *mKel* 1:1–4; *mNeg* 13:11.
237 Cf., e.g., Kazen 2002. 116–118; Thiessen 2020. 52–54.
238 Cf., e.g., BDAG, s.v.; LN, s.v. 79.49, 53.28, 23.137, also 79.48, 53.29 and 53.28; LSJ, s.v.; Montanari, s.v.
239 The only other occurrences in the Synoptics designate cleansing of dishes in a metaphoric saying on purity (Matt 23:25–26/Luke 11:39); cf. also the use of καθαρός.

mediate and abstract separation of patient and skin ailment (v. 42, ἀπῆλθεν ἀπ' αὐτοῦ ἡ λέπρα),²⁴⁰ which is a rather unusual depiction in light of the concept of a timely observation of symptomatic changes of the skin found in the Levitical texts (cf. Lev 13:16). This cleansing is affected by an emotional Jesus, his healing touch with his stretched-out hand (with two verbs: ἐκτείνας τὴν χεῖρα αὐτοῦ ἥψατο, v. 41)²⁴¹ and an oral formula: θέλω, καθαρίσθητι. Jesus responds physically, verbally, and emotionally to the man.

3.3.3.1 Physical Response

In the case of the manual healing of the *leprous* man, the matter of touching an impure person stands to question, especially regarding the ritual grammar of the Levitical laws to which it alludes. Strictly speaking, Jesus' touch was probably "not in line with the prevailing legal interpretation,"²⁴² yet the sources reflect notions from Second Temple Judaism with enough room for maneuver and a more liberal interpretation (see above, 3.3.2).

Moreover, manual healing is developed into a characteristic feature of the Markan Jesus, and the narrative neither here nor elsewhere (e.g., 5:25–34; 5:21–24, 35–43; cf. even 5:1–20) pushes an interpretation toward infringement, infiltration, or subversion of purity regulations by the motif of his healing touch. The focus lies entirely on Jesus' healing power transmitted, not laws or regulations disregarded (see esp. 5.2 on the woman with the issue of blood whose touch falls in a not precisely regulated gray area).²⁴³ However, Jesus' touch then functions as a visible first confirmation of reinstated purity.²⁴⁴

This is underscored by the fact that no other narrative speaks of healing of *lepra* by manual contact, even if, for that matter only, very few other accounts actually do witness to effectuated healings of λέπρα/צרעת or similar phenomena.²⁴⁵

---

240 Cf. Collins 2007. 179.
241 Cf. Focant 2012. 80.
242 Kazen 2002. 127, cf. also 109–117, and Thiessen 2020. 62.
243 Cf. Kazen 2002. 106. Neither does the gospel depict Jesus to be indifferent but teach and discuss Jewish (purity) laws nuanced, cf. 3:1–6; 7:1–23; 12:28–34.
244 Terming Jesus' healing power infectious, inversive, or dynamic *purity* (cf. with great impact Berger 1988. 240: "offensive Reinheit") runs the risk of blurring the concept of purity, as "purity is not a *force* but a *state* of being [... denoting the absence of impurity, not the actual presence of something]" (Thiessen 2020. 6, n. 18). It is to the point however, that Jesus' emanating power, "turns uncleanness into cleanness and thus reverts the contaminative impact that is characteristic of levitical impurity" (Avemarie in Bieringer; et al. [ed.] 2010. 276) and by the Markan depiction "behaves contagiously, in the way impurity used to do" (Holmén in Holmén; Porter [ed.] 2011. 2723).
245 Cf. the lack of such in Cotter 1999.

Proving the notion of a mild and easily curable disease, yet incumbent on divine aid, Galen reports an unknown disease to turn into λέπρα when treated by Asclepius, which was cured within days by administration of medication:

> Another wealthy man, this one not a native but from the interior of Thrace, came, because a dream had driven him, to Pergamum. Then a dream appeared to him, the god [Asclepius] prescribing that he should drink every day of the drug produced from the vipers and should anoint the body from the outside. The disease after a few days turned into leprosy [εἰς λέπραν]; and this disease, in turn, was cured [ἐθεραπεύθη] by the drugs [...?] which the god commanded.[246]

Similar phenomena attended to in Epidauran healing sites include growths and rashes but not explicitly λέπρα.[247] Moreover, the Hebrew Bible/Old Testament narratives in Exod 4:6–7, Num 12:4–6, and 2Kgs 5:8–14 all report healing after a ritual advised by YHWH or prophets, such as Elisha, was followed (e.g., seven-day confinement, washing).[248]

Hence, Jesus with his healing touch displays divine participation, shared with not only severe cases but also those considered suffering from more ordinary and temporary afflictions. The protagonist bridges, by the very nature of his tangible communication and his physical attention on the skin—the source of impurity and suffering—any implied social distance.

C In Focus: Mark's Healing Touches

As demonstrated in the analysis of the summaric accounts (see ch. 2), Jesus' tactile cures are characteristic of the Markan Jesus. This is exemplified in the programmatic introduction of Jesus' ministry in Mark 1:31, where he powerfully seizes and raises the mother-in-law, and in 1:41, where he effectively heals a man with a skin condition through touch. Since the subsequent narratives also put particular emphasis on hands communicating healing, the following joint consideration of those passages investigates the underlying conceptions. Terminologically, healing touches are described in Mark with the lexemes ἐπιτίθημι χεῖρά(ς) (ἐπί),[249] ἅπτω,[250] and the already analyzed κρατέω[251] of hands (see 3.2.3.1). Interestingly, not only does the healer treat the petitioners manually, but they are depicted to

---

[246] Galen, *Subf. empir.* 10, translation by Edelstein; Edelstein 1998. 1.250.
[247] Cf., e.g., ibid. 1.226, 1.234. Cf. also, Webb 2006. 184–185.
[248] Priests were only consulted for a confirmation of the cure, cf. Lev 14:2–32; *mNeg* 3:1. No healing is reported of the "leprous" in 2Kgs 5:27, 7:3, 15:5/2Chr 26:20–21.
[249] Mark 5:23; 6:5; 7:32; 8:23, 25.
[250] Mark 1:41; 8:22; and 3:10; 5:27–28, 30–31; 6:56.
[251] Mark 1:31; 5:41; and 9:27.

reach out and get healed by touching Jesus with their hands. Both phenomena are regarded separately in the following.

a) Jesus' Healing Touch
As the requests of Jaïrus and of those bringing the sensory-impaired man to Jesus insinuate, "laying-on-of hands," ἐπιτίθημι χεῖρά(ς) (ἐπί), is made out to be a known healing method of the Markan Jesus (Mark 5:23; 7:31), which is underscored in Mark 8:22–23 as the protagonist answers the request for a healing "touch," ἅπτω, with his "laying-on-of-hands." While Jaïrus' daughter is healed by Jesus seizing her hand and calling her to rise, and the communicatively impaired man is touched in a series of detailed curative steps, Mark 6:5 and then 8:23, 25 *explicitly* refer to Jesus' efficacious "laying-on-of-hands." In the latter example, Jesus uses his hands twice ("again," v. 25) after initially being only partially effective. This denotes a characteristic healing "technique" that is almost habitual or customary, as also reflected in the summary note in 6:5. In addition to imparting healing,[252] the gesture, as used in the New Testament, conveys a transmission of the holy spirit or blessings in the sense of an initiation, ordination, or commission.[253]

This echoes a manual movement from the Hebrew Bible/Old Testament together with or corroborating a verbal prayer (*sāmak yādô*; LXX ἐπιτίθεναι τὰς χεῖρας).[254] More commonly, the laying-on of one or two hands occurs with regard to animal offerings as "(1) transference of sin; (2) substitution of the sinner or inclusive substitution as identification of the offerer with the animal; (3) a gesture of ownership."[255] The notions of transference by manual contact also regard authority and legal testimony.[256] In the Hebrew Bible/Old Testament, there is, however, just one mention of healing in connection to a tactile gesture, which moreover lacks an actual skin connection as implied in the "laying-on" and is only alluded to, not efficaciously displayed. It is, furthermore, contrasted with a bath in the river Jordan (cf. 4Kgdms 5:11^{LXX}).[257] Hence, the (stretched-out) hand is used as a

---

252 Cf. also Mark 16:18; Luke 4:40; 13:13; Acts 9:12; 28:8; cf. also Matt 19:13, 15; Acts 5:12, 15; 3:7; 9:17, 41; 19:11.
253 Cf. Acts 8:17–19; 19:6; cf. also 2Tim 1:6; Heb 6:2. Cf. for the following and extended analysis of the motif in the HB/OT and NT, e.g., Parrat 1969; Irwin 2008. In the gospels it is never used in the nominal form as in Acts 8:18; 1Tim 4:14; 2Tim 1:6; Heb 6:2. See also the frequently and critically referred to Flusser 1957. Cf. to this effect, e.g., Dupont-Sommer 1960; Kirchenschläger 1976; Fitzmyer 2004; Machiela in Notley; Garcia (ed.) 2015.
254 Cf. Gen 48:14, 17–18; also Lev 9:22.
255 Körting, *Hands, Laying on of I. HB/OT.* 202. Cf. Lev 16:21; Lev 1:4; 3:2; 8; 13; 4:4, 24, 29, 33; see also Exod 29:10, 15, 19; Lev 4:15; 8:14, 18, 22; 2Chr 29:23.
256 Cf. Lev 24:14; Num 8:10; 27:18, 23; also Deut 17:7; 34:9.
257 Cf. Flusser 1957.

symbol and instrument for the power and will of God that can also be transferred to human hands (e.g., Moses').[258] The "right hand of God" becomes a topos for YHWH's strength, provision, and grace for the narrative and identity of the people of Israel. Just as characteristic and powerful is the divine finger, especially regarding creation, law, and healing.[259] Tactile communication of authority is moreover prevalent in Mesopotamian and Roman law.[260]

In Second Temple Judaism, the scriptural notions of laid-on hands in the context of offerings, law, and blessings are echoed, also with emphasis on God's protective hands.[261]

Interestingly, in 1QapGen^{ar}, Abram officiates an exorcism on behalf of the Pharaoh by prayer and laying his hands on the ruler's head (1Q20 20.28–29; cf. Gen 12:17).

Similarly, in Hellenistic traditions, the motif of the divine hand conveys a healing, blessing, and protecting notion that rarely is transferred to human healers.[262] However, sources around the Asclepius cult bear witness that not only touches of the hand but also painful kicks and (un-)gentle oral contact of gods and holy animals heal the sick, mainly during incubation.[263]

Furthermore, the laying-on-of-hands is a common medical gesture, and a physician's hands were regarded as an important instrument.[264] This, however, pertains more to the diagnostic process (such as reading the pulse, temperature, thresholds of pain and observing swellings, moisture, texture) than the curative process. Although there are a few tactile techniques mentioned that aid in the cure, they aim at physical manipulation rather than simple sensation (such as probing, palpation, taping for sound, administering ointments and bandages, etc.).[265] It seems that "the request for Jesus' touch implies belief that his touch transmits healing power," with his hands as a "symbol of intention and activity,

---

[258] Cf., e.g., Exod 4:4; 7:19; 8:1; 9:22–23, 14:16, 21, 26–27; Cf. also Grundmann, δύναμαι/δύναμις. 292–293; Fuchs, ἐκτείνω. 460.
[259] Cf., e.g., Exod 8:15, 19; 15:6, 13; 31:18; 32:11; Deut 4:34; 6:21; 9:10, 26, 29; 26.8; Isa 45:12; 51:16; Ps 8:4, 7; 138:7; Job 12:9; 26:13.
[260] Cf. Hibbitts 1992. 2.53–2.58.
[261] Cf. Josephus, *A.J.* 9.268; and 2Chr 29:23; also *Spec.* 1.202–4, 11Q19 26.10–13; Lev 16:20–22; 24:14; Sus 34; Josephus, *A.J.* 16.365; and Deut 21:18–21; Exod 21:17; Lev 20:9; *Jub.* 25.14; 26.22–24; *JosAs* 21.6–7; *Sib.* 3.795; *1En.* 67.2; and Körting, *Hands, Laying on of I.* HB/OT.
[262] Cf. Homer, *Il.* 9.420, 301; Tacitus, *Hist.* 4.81; Suetonius, *Vesp.* 7; furthermore, Weinreich 1909. 45–48; Herzog 1931. No. 31; Wagenvoort, *Contactus.* 404–421; Lohse, χείρ and cogn. 413–424.
[263] Cf. Herzog 1931. No. 3, 17, 26, 31, 38, 41, 43, 45; moreover, Oepke, ἰάομαι. 209.
[264] Cf., e.g., Sol. frg. 12,61f.; Seneca the Younger, *Ben.* 4.16.2; CH, *Epid.* 4.43; moreover, Weinreich 1909. 1–44; Gross 1985. 322, 329–330, 350, 373–375; 377–379; 386–387.
[265] Cf. Kosak in Petridou; Thumiger (ed.) 2015.

power and authority."²⁶⁶ While the main feature of Jesus' treatment is the establishment of a physical connection between his hands and the patient, the cured dis/ability seems to determine different kinds of tactile treatment.²⁶⁷ As established, Jesus deliberately and immediately *seizes* severely passive hands to pull the dis/abled characters drastically back into active life (see above, 3.2.3 on κρατέω τῆς χειρός, together with ἤγειρεν and ἀνίστημι; Mark 1:31; 5:41; 9:27).

Then, in Mark 1:41, the healing touch is initiated and therefore emphasized with the explicit mention of the extension of the hand (ἐκτείνω τὴν χεῖρα).²⁶⁸ The space between the *leprous* man and Jesus is bridged by this motion, conquering the social seclusion connected with the man's impairment. The emphasized manner of healing is furthermore underscored by the described dis/ability, a pathological change of the surface of the most sensitive organ, the skin.

Moreover, Jesus touches the man in 7:31–37 in the process of healing, alongside a variety of other actions. Here, he establishes contact with the dis/abled organs by putting his fingers in the man's ears and touching his tongue. The explicit mention of the fingers and not of the hands is singular for healing narratives in the Synoptic Gospels²⁶⁹ and has first and foremost a solely pragmatic function: Jesus puts his fingers in (εἰς) the ears of the deaf man. Quantity, size, and intensity are the determining factors of the movement (cf. 7:33; 8:25).

Jesus' healing touch varies according to the dis/ability to convey a) a drastic and deliberate measure when he seizes hands to curatively raise bedridden patients, b) his programmatic and holistic approach when he touches a literally and socially stigmatized and skin-sensitive man, and c) his proficient and sensitive care when he lightly puts his hands or fingers on the dis/abled sensory organs according to their number and measurements.

b. Jesus' Being Touched
The concept of Jesus' "curing-ἅπτω" shifts and takes on another dimension when *petitioners* are recounted for establishing contact and no concrete body parts are mentioned (not only due to the brevity of the [summaric] notes 3:10; 6:56; cf. esp. 5:27–28, 30–31). Especially the narrative of the woman with the issue of

---

266 Collins 2007. 393.
267 Cf. Böcher 1970. 171–173; von Bendemann in Härle; Preul (ed.) 2005. 62.
268 On a different note, the man with the withered hand in Mark 3:5 stretched out his hand in display of its transformation.
269 The only exception might be the reference to God's finger through which Jesus by his own account exorcises demons (Luke 11:20; but Matt 12:28). However, there is no clear connection to be made between these two occurrences. Cf. von Bendemann in Härle; Preul (ed.) 2005. 62–62.

blood with the emphasized four-time mention of ἅπτω (5:27, 28, 30, 31)[270] and a detailed description of the very physical healing process offers a possible explanation of the underlying concept:[271] when the woman touches Jesus' garment, he emanates δύναμις that is physically tangible for Jesus (ἐπιγνοὺς ἐν ἑαυτῷ) and for the woman, who immediately perceives in her body the accomplished healing. There is a "chronological and causal connection between the contact and the emission of the power."[272] Hence, Jesus inquires, after he felt δύναμις leave his body, who in the pushing throng has touched him; something must have distinguished the woman from the others and therefore qualified her to receive this curative force (see 5.2.3). Jesus' garment becomes a material medium of his δύναμις as it issues suddenly and seemingly unintentionally out of him (ἐξ αὐτοῦ δύναμιν ἐξελθοῦσαν), he appears as a clueless, passive carrier of this independent, immanent force.[273]

Similarly, narratives such as 2Kgs 13:20–21 and Exod 17:11–12,[274] 1Kgs 17:17–24 and 2Kgs 4:18–37 account for bodies (and bones) and personal items of prophets emanating effective power, although it is not healings that are recounted but raisings of the dead.[275] Sacred objects are further recounted to communicate holiness by touch.[276] Moreover, in narratives of Greco-Roman heritage, healing occurs due to transmitting objects and/or an additional medical practice/ritual (e.g., a blind man is healed by touching a sacred statue, and thereafter his eyes; Ammianus Marcellinus describes the healing effect of the physical contact of magical marble for stomachaches; and a blind woman is cured after she kissed Hadrian's knee and washed her face in temple water).[277]

Besides Jesus' healings, those of the apostles reflect similar notions, especially Acts 5:12–16 and 19:11–12 (cf. Acts 6:6),[278] while accounts of medical touches mainly describe diagnostic processes and are seldomly initiated by the patient.[279]

---

[270] Esp. because ἅπτομαι in v. 27 is the first indicative to break the long line of participles of the woman's introduction.
[271] Cf. also Metternich 2000. 212; furthermore, Behm 1968; Wagenvoort, Contactus. 416.
[272] Kahl in Zimmermann (ed.) 2013. 283.
[273] See 5.2.3 for a detailed analysis on this specific healing process and its underlying concepts of (restored) physicality, δύναμις, and πίστις.
[274] Cf. Gundry 1993. 280; Marcus 2000. 359.
[275] Cf. bBer 5b; Josephus, A.J. 8.353–54; furthermore, Gundry 1993. 280; Marcus 2000. 359; Boring 2006. 160.
[276] Cf., e.g., Exod 29:37; 30:29; Lev 6:10–11, 27.
[277] Cf. IG 14.966; Amm. 29.2.28; SHA, Vita Hadr. 25.1–4; Pliny, Pan. 22.3; Plutarch, Sull. 35.4; Iamblichus, Vita Pyth. 91–92. Cf. Weinreich 1909. 63–66, 175–178; Blackburn 1991. 114; Kazen 2002. 105.
[278] Cf. van der Horst 1976/77; van der Horst in Zimmermann (ed.) 2017.
[279] Cf. Weinreich 1909. 63–66; Müri 2001. 9–33.

c. Conclusion

Possibly, physical touch by and touch of Jesus share an inherent concept of transmission of power, blessing, authority, and/or δύναμις. As established, this then also includes differently termed tactile cures administered by Jesus that are only differentiated according to their specific function. Jesus' hands are not the exclusive instruments for healing; rather, his entire healing body manifests itself by its δύναμις as a spatial and sensually experienceable body. Healing by touch (actively and passively) is a characteristic feature of the Markan portrayal of Jesus' healing. Nevertheless, Jesus is also described to heal without touch. In Mark 2:1–20 and 3:1–6, his verbal command suffices to heal (partial) paralysis, similarly to the healing of blind Bartimaeus in Mark 10:46–52. Furthermore, his exorcisms operate entirely without tactile connections due to the different etiology and narrative function (see chs. 3.1; 5.1; 7.3.2).

As established, there are only a few witnesses to similar notions that relate more to a general concept of (divine) authoritative power imparted with healing by physical contact with the patient. The depiction of Jesus healing by touching *and* by being touched reflects this concept of transmittable δύναμις.

Moreover, touching addresses a holistic sensual experience as the multifunctional skin wraps around the entire body, and not only hands can function as the communicating body parts. Touching is reciprocal in its nature and by that mediates a sensation of participation, spatiality, materiality, and corporality for all involved.[280] Touching is being touched. In its complexity and dependence on shared space, the physical connection can be nuanced according to its quality, impact, intent, and social context, the last exposing its hierarchal component that highly depends on cultural norms. In a healing context, the patient's harmed and vulnerable physicality is exposed in hope of helping hands charged with expertise and curative powers.[281]

3.3.3.2 Verbal Response

Returning to the healing of the skin-sensitive man, Jesus calls the man after his touch to "be (made) clean/pure."[282] The translation of the aorist passive imperative lies in the ambiguity of *pronouncing* the man clean or *cleansing* him (i.e., removing the source of his impurity so that he can be pronounced clean). In other words, καθαρίζω can refer to the cure from the skin disease and/or the declaration of re-

---

[280] Cf. Benthien 1998; Benthien 2001.
[281] Cf. Kosak in Petridou; Thumiger (ed.) 2015. 257.
[282] In the following "pure" and "clean" and their cognates are used interchangeably.

instated purity.²⁸³ The Greek simply cannot express the nuanced meanings of the Hebrew *binyanim* of טהר here, namely the Pi'el ("be pronounced im/pure" [after observation]) and Qal ("be pure or purifying").²⁸⁴ In the context of λέπρα, the LXX always translates καθαρίζω to denote a (priestly) confirmation of "being clean" *after* healing and purification;²⁸⁵ the actual curative process is termed differently.²⁸⁶ Hence, a translation of the New Testament text in the sense of "cleansing/making pure," while in the realms of possible meanings, would diverge from its semantic use in the LXX and the ritual tradition it refers to here where healing and purification are separated.²⁸⁷ However, since the Markan text clearly states the curative process (v. 42), and Jesus asks the man to obtain a priestly declaration (v. 44), it is unlikely that the text describes a granted wish for *only* the declaration of purity, even if that would relieve the audience from wondering about Jesus' questionable touch of impurity—the man would have already been healed when encountering Jesus. By following the direction of the Markan text and translating καθαρίζω in Mark 1:40–44 as "making clean" (i.e., healing through Jesus' efficacious touch and word; vv. 41–42), the text accurately reflects the progression of purification described in Leviticus, which involves healing first and then declaration. Although this process is witnessed as immediate in Mark, rather than a longer-observed process, it still aligns with the Levitical progression. This also explains its explicit absence in summaric accounts as subsumed under "healing," even if it remains unclear why this is then not reflected with more general terminology, as used in the LXX.²⁸⁸

The narrator's directly following confirming statement of the pure state in v. 42, introduced with εὐθύς, marks Jesus' expression as performative. Furthermore, his actions in v. 41, especially regarding his emotional response (see below), make a *passivum divinum* (cf. vv. 41 and 42) unlikely. He is clearly established as the wanting-to-heal actor.²⁸⁹ The passive does, however, enforce a notion of a concealed cause or source of Jesus' healing ability while emphasizing his effective

---

283 Cf. Kazen 2002. 102; Kazen in Bieringer; Pollefeyt; Tomson (ed.) 2010. 282.
284 Cf., e.g., Lev 13:6, 17, 34.
285 Cf. Lev 13:6, 13, 17, 23, 28, 34, 37, 59; 14:4, 7, 8, 11, 14, 17, 18, 19, 25, 28, 29, 31, 48. See for the following Avemarie in Bieringer; et al. (ed.) 2010. 260–261; Hasselmann 2023. 289–290.
286 Cf., e.g., Lev 14:3^{LXX}: καὶ ἰδοὺ ἴαται ἡ ἀφὴ τῆς λέπρας ἀπὸ τοῦ λεπροῦ; Lev 13:37b^{LXX}: ὑγίακεν τὸ θραῦσμα· καθαρός ἐστιν, καὶ καθαριεῖ αὐτὸν ὁ ἱερεύς.; Lev 13:18; 14:48.
287 Cf. more detailed Hasselmann 2023. 289–293.
288 Cf., e.g., Lev 14:3^{LXX}; 13:37b^{LXX}.
289 Cf. Pascut 2012. esp. 314, n. 3 and 322–323; furthermore, Focant 2012. 80, different to Marcus 2000. 206, 209; Müller in Zimmermann (ed.) 2013. 222.

actions and performative words, a (from now on) recurring motif of Markan healing narratives.²⁹⁰

Therefore, while καθαρίζω in vv. 41 and 42 refers to the process of "making clean," the initial request in v. 41 and concluding command in v. 44 make use of the ambiguity of the term: the man most likely does not only wish to be physically cleansed but is desperate to be healed *and* declared an integral part of society again. Jesus puts this in prospect by his concluding request for priestly confirmation and sacrifice according to Mosaic law.²⁹¹ The Markan Jesus then does not subvert the priestly prerogative but corroborates it (cf. *mNeg* 3:1). While Jesus cleanses the man physically by healing the "impurity-creating condition," the ritual and thereby social cleansing is yet to be obtained by observing "the regulations of Leviticus 14 in removing the remaining ritual impurity."²⁹² However, the narrative remains silent on the actual completion: the focus lies entirely on the powerful act of removing *lepra*; the rest seems to be only a formality. Jesus' concise and imperative answer puts emphasis on *his* healing will (see below) and power, which effect the following physical cleansing: καὶ ἐκαθαρίσθη (v. 42).

3.3.3.3 Emotional Response

Jesus' physical and verbal response is embedded in descriptions of an emotionally charged Jesus.²⁹³ Foremost, he is said to be "moved with pity/compassion" or "an intense and active anger"²⁹⁴ at the man's request (v. 41), which forms the motivational basis for his healing touch and performative utterance (v. 41). Moreover, ἐμβριμάομαι and ἐκβάλλω are both used *after* the healing and therefore do not reflect a "trace of a thaumaturgic technique or an indication of the pneumatic excitement of the healer"²⁹⁵ when Jesus sends the man to receive priestly confirmation. Rather, the rare lexeme ἐμβριμάομαι that only occurs again in Mark 14:5²⁹⁶ signifies an agitated breathing and reflects a severe and stern warning, scolding, or rebuke that puts emphasis on the following instruction to remain silent and follow the purity regulations.²⁹⁷ This harshness in tone is underscored by the use of ἐκβάλλω. Common in exorcistic contexts, it gave rise to a demonic explanation of

---

290 See also 2:5; 3:5; 5:29; 6:56; 7:34–35; and ch. 4.1.3.
291 Cf. Kazen 2002. 102, n. 66, different to Cave 1978/79. 246.
292 Thiessen 2020. 63. Cf. Hooker 1991. 80; Williams 1994. 97; Collins 2007. 179.
293 For extensive research on emotions in the gospels and early Christianity, see, e.g., Elliott 2005; Gemünden 2009; Kuhn 2009; Barton 2011; Voorwinde 2011; Inselmann 2012.
294 Harris 2001. 401–402, cf. 50–70.
295 Collins 2007. 179. Cf. Bonner 1927; Theissen 1983. 57–58.
296 Cf. also Matt 9:30; John 11:33, 38.
297 Cf., e.g., LSJ, *s.v*; LN, *s.v.* 33.320, 33.421, 25.56; Wells 1998. 193; BDAG, *s.v*; Montanari, *s.v.*

the man's ailment,[298] although the first Markan use of the lexeme designates the holy spirit's driving Jesus into the wilderness (1:12) and 5:40, 9:47, 11:15, and 12:8 denote a stern, even violent action of spatial separation outside of demonic contexts. This spatial context is strange to the focal text due to the lack of a concrete spatially constructed environment with some sort of borders in the literal sense; Jesus and the man meet "in open social space."[299] This makes a meaning in the sense of "cause to leave" or "send away" more likely yet exceptional, maybe with a very stern, fierce, and forceful connotation (cf. Luke 10:2; Matt 9:38).[300] Jesus is strict with the man *after* the healing is performed yet possibly also prior, as the reading of ὀργισθείς instead of σπλαγχνισθείς suggests[301] Jesus' anger would correspond well with the following harshness in his tone when sending the man away.[302] In any case, both of the narrator-authenticated emotions depict a passionate and caring healer.

> The term σπλαγχνίζομαι is used to describe Jesus in three other contexts in the Gospel of Mark, where he actively helps those who approach him with their needs (cf. Mark 6:34; 8:2; and 9:22).[303] This suggests that Jesus is a compassionate healer, despite the harshness of his tone in the following passages.[304] On the contrary, he is not described as particularly angry at petitioners, although 3:5 (μετ' ὀργῆς), 8:12 (ἀναστενάζω), and 10:14 (ἀγανακτέω) depict an aggravated Jesus in the face of opposing understandings of his ministry. However, with regard to relational and personal aspects of anger,[305] its reflection prior to and after the healing, and the entire setting of the scene, it is quite plausible that Jesus' "value-

---

[298] Cf. 1:34, 39; 3:15, 22–23; 6:13; 7:26; 9:18, 28, 38; 16:9; 16:17.
[299] Müller in Zimmermann (ed.) 2013. 223; and Spencer 2014. 123.
[300] Cf., e.g., Annen, ἐκβάλλω; LN, s.v. 15.220, 15.44, 15.68, 15.174, 53.102, 13.68; LSJ, s.v.; Montanari, s.v.; moreover, Kazen 2002. 104.
[301] While the reading of ὀργισθείς appears in D, some old Latin witnesses, and Ephrem's Commentary on the Diatessaron, the *lectio facilior* σπλαγχνισθείς is featured in most of the other witnesses, including B, A, and ℵ. For a detailed discussion, see Baarda 2012; Lisboa 2015; Johnson 2017. Parallel accounts omit an emotional motivation all together, cf. Matt 8:1–4; Luke 5:12–16. There are many attempts to explain the two versions by copying errors and/or language confusions, cf., e.g., Lohmeyer 1967. 44–45; Metzger 1994. 65; Williams 2012. 2–4; Stählin, ὀργή E. 428–430, different to Ehrman 2006. 126–129.
[302] A change from having gut-felt compassion to being angry is not as easy to explain as it would be vice versa (*lectio lenior*). See Voelz 2013. 178; furthermore, Collins 2007. 178, n. 121.
[303] Cf. also Matt 20:34, 9:36; 14:14; Luke 7:1; Wells 1998. 193. As Eisen in Eisen; Mader (ed.) 2020. esp. 434, rightly and significantly points out: twice the omniscient narrator qualifies Jesus as "compassionate" to the audience, once Jesus acknowledges it himself in direct speech to his disciples, and lastly it is publicly witnessed to a large crowd when he successfully helps the pleading father in the story-world.
[304] Cf. also the complex and emotionally-charged discussion for Jesus' help in Mark 7:24–30. Moreover, Matt 9:36; 14:14; 15:32 and 20:34, and Luke 7:13.
[305] Cf. Spencer 2014. 115–117.

laden" reaction responds to an offense "critically significant to his core identity and reputation"³⁰⁶ in the initial and direct approach of the *leper* in v. 41.³⁰⁷ As established, neither the man's approach nor Jesus' responsive touch likely conforms to contemporary purity regulations yet are not portrayed to explicitly infringe them, which rules out that the Markan Jesus was furiously offended by or compensates apologetically for the man's (putative) law-opposing actions.³⁰⁸ Rather, the text suggests that the offensive presumption lies not in the fact that or how the man approaches Jesus, but in his subjunctive questioning Jesus' willingness to heal: ὅτι ἐὰν θέλῃς. His healing ability and will, which are established as key prospects of his concept of self and mission (cf. 1:23–28, 30–31, 32–34), are "publicly diminished,"³⁰⁹ to which he answers by his immediate curative touch and his reprimanding word: θέλω. This concurs with other emotionally charged encounters, crucial for the plot, that show the complex relationship between the divine Jesus' and human "will" (θέλω) regarding Jesus' mission and passion³¹⁰ and an aggravated Jesus when facing misunderstanding of or opposition to his ministry.³¹¹

Mark displays Jesus as indignant toward the man throughout the narrative: it is the motivational reason for (not in spite of) his healing, and after it, his firm rejection reinforces his programmatic characterization to be a "willful," benevolent healer.³¹² Then his anger is in its rhetorical effect not so different from the variant σπλαγχνίζομαι: both characterize Jesus as a passionate man, caring to his guts about his (divinely appointed) mission to heal the world, which causes his height-

---

306 Ibid. 117–118.
307 It is unlikely Jesus' response reflects anger about the interruption of his preaching ministry which is intrinsically linked with healing, as discussed by, e.g., Taylor 1957. 189, or that he anticipates the man's future disobedience to his command to silence (different to, e.g., Lane 1974. 87; Voorwinde 2011. 74, cf. 72–74) since it is a common motif never employed to reflect anger or friction with the immediate and unchallenged healing. Also, Jesus is only characterized as intuitive to *present* inner thoughts, cf. 2:8; 3:5; Spencer 2014. 120–121. Moreover, the Markan Jesus' healing is displayed with clear verbal commands (e.g., 1:21–26; 5:8–9) and not in accordance with "a Hellenistic miracle worker who snorts and growls as a result of the divine spirit at work within him," Boring 2006. 71 (for Jesus' sigh in 7:34, see 6.2.3). The continuous reprehension after the healing towards the man neither suggests Jesus' rejection to be directed at the domain of evil as the origin of sickness nor against a rigid purity system that promotes exclusion (cf., e.g., Taylor 1957. 189; Moloney 2002. 58, n. 56), Jesus asks for a priestly confirmation. His gestures make the reading that the *man* "put out his hand in a passion of rage and touched him [Jesus]..." implausible, Lake 1923. 197–198.
308 Cf. Rawlinson 1925. 22.
309 Spencer 2014. 122. Cf. also Iersel 1998. 142.
310 Cf. 10:35–45, 46–52; 14:32–36; 15:6–15; cf. also 6:14–29; and Spencer 2014. 124–128.
311 Cf. 3:4–5; 8:12; 10:14; on a similar note also 9:19, see 7.1.2; and cf. Ehrman 2006. 138; Spencer 2014. 123.
312 Cf. Spencer 2014. 128. See G. In Focus: Mark's Relational *Pistis*; moreover, Boring 2006. 71; Rüggemeier 2017. 436.

ened popularity (v. 45) and runs into conflict with those questioning his authority and identity (cf. ch. on Mark 2–3).[313]

3.3.4 Interpretation

The final verses offer some concluding remarks and interpretative guidance. As established, Jesus advises ritual cleansing according to Jewish regulations. It is no contrast that the man is commanded to keep silent and show himself to the priest, who confirms and advises for his reinstatement of *ritual* purity. The audience can be included in the αὐτοῖς due to the statement's position at the end of Mark 1 with its focus on the programmatic introduction of Jesus, his divine yet mysterious identity, powerful healing will, and ἐξουσία in teaching. What they have "witnessed" in the last verses is a "testimony, proof, evidence"[314] *for* Jesus, whoever he is.[315] The command to remain silent then rather refers to Jesus and his ability, to his implied identity, to the "how" and "by whom" the man got healed and not "if."[316] The reasons for this order in the story world are not explicitly explicated. The audience, however, is reminded of the silencing of the demons in Mark 1:25, a motif that occurs frequently in the following narrative (see below). For this primary chapter of Jesus' introduction, the man's "energetical"[317] declaration promotes Jesus' popularity with a surprising twist: it is now Jesus who is hindered (δύνασθαι) from entering social spaces due to his popularity caused by his ability to heal (δύνασαι, v. 40), not anymore the literally stigmatized and probably ostracized skin-diseased man due to his impurity.[318] The ambiguous references of the subjects and personal pro-

---

[313] Cf., e.g., Williams 1994. 96, n. 3; Rüggemeier 2017. 435; Eisen in Eisen; Mader (ed.) 2020; Eisen in Barth; Eisen; Fritz (ed.) 2023.
[314] Cf. μαρτύριον in Montanari, s.v. 1283.
[315] Cf., e.g., Collins 2007. 179–180; Müller in Zimmermann (ed.) 2013. 224. Although grammatically possible, it is unlikely that the dative αὐτοῖς is to be understood adversatively (but 6:11; 13:9; cf. also: Mark 6:48; 10:13, 27; Matt 23:31; Amos 3:13^{LXX} et al.), since its condition of an opposition of Jesus to the priests and/or the system or regulations they represent is not implied by the narrative. Jesus' touching of the impure man might (!) and then only tacitly create an implicit tension between his actions and the purity regulations guarded by the priests which would contradict such a blatant impudence on Jesus' part at this point. Narratively, however, because his healing on the Sabbath in Mark 1:21–31 possibly causes similar implicit frictions and the following chapters explicitly discuss and challenge the Markan Jesus' stance on Jewish law and traditions (2:1–3:6, see ch. 4; and again in 7:1–23), this verse together with the entire chapter might as well serve as a prelude for the following discourses on an adversative note. Cf. Boring 2006. 72; Rüggemeier 2017. 437.
[316] Cf. Haenchen 1968. 95; Grundmann 1980. 67.
[317] Cf. Boring 2006. 70; Collins 2007. 179.
[318] Cf. Williams 1994. 98.

nouns underline precisely this punchline. It is knowledge about Jesus that spreads uncontrollably, not *lepra.*

As the last healing narrative of the introductory and programmatic Mark 1, this account adds another common and therefore relatable dis/ability that encompasses a variety of clinical pictures. Similarly to *fever, lepra* is easy to detect as a (white) change of the surface of the skin, yet incumbent upon discursive observation of specialists regarding its source, severity, purification methods, and curative stages. Even the healing must be officially confirmed in the context of purity regulations to which the text alludes. The disease's strong connotation with stigmatizing notions, quite literally, assign the afflicted a (temporary) liminal space in society. The account uses this to portray Jesus' efficacious healing touch that bridges with his outstretched hand, literally and symbolically, the social distance and becomes a characteristic image of Jesus' divine δύναμις imparting healing in the further unraveling gospel narrative. Here, it is memorably and emphatically introduced when Jesus reveals his palpable spatial, material, and physical identity to a man severely "struck" by a *skin* disease, rendering him impure by touch.[319] His healing then heightens Jesus' popularity to an almost hyperbolic extend.

D In Focus: Silencing in Mark's Healing Narratives

Twice in this first chapter, Jesus orders dis/abled characters to be silent. Besides the command to silence for the knowledgeable and vociferous demons (1:25, 34; 3:12), the order to remain silent in Mark 1:44, with the man's following reaction, lingers at the end of this first programmatic introduction. It is the first of many of such instructions addressed to those witnessing Jesus' might: while the healed man here is the only individual responsible for the prohibited promotion after his healing, Jesus strictly orders (διαστέλλω) the different groups of witnesses of the successful healings in Mark 5:43 (the parents of the girl, Simon, James, and John) and in 7:36 (possibly those who brought the man, disciples, and/or the crowd that witnessed the petition in vv. 32–33) not to share what had happened (ἵνα μηδεὶς γνοῖ τοῦτο; ἵνα μηδενὶ λέγωσιν). He moreover commands his disciples to remain silent about events revelatory of his identity (ἐπιτιμάω; διαστέλλω; 8:30: ἵνα μηδενὶ λέγωσιν περὶ αὐτοῦ; 9:9: ἵνα μηδενὶ ἃ εἶδον διηγήσωνται).

Although orders to be silent after healings seem to focus on the curative act rather than the identity of the healer, all the commands share language, structure, and primary function as they underscore the significance of the witnessed event.

---

[319] The etymology of Semitic terms for *lepra* explicitly connote a forceful touch, a "beating" affliction, cf. Heb., ערץ; Babylonian Aramaic, בגג. See also Hasselmann 2023. Esp. 282–300, and her innovative and thorough study on purity as a marker of social identity.

While knowledge of his healing cannot be contained, quite to the contrary (cf. 1:44–45 and 7:36 except for Jaïrus' daughter), demons and disciples (at least as an argument *e silentio*) stick to the order. In both cases of disregarded secrecy, the public acclamation only has a "publicizing" yet not "revealing" effect for Jesus' identity.

Thus, while each command, kept or broken, might have its own function within the scope of the individual narrative, it develops into a common yet dynamic motif within the narrative arc of the gospel: all silenced characters hold accurate knowledge about Jesus but are not allowed to share it—an intriguing tension for the audience.

As such, this element is part of a narrative device, that aims at a gradual revelation of Mark's theological tapestry to characterize the power and passion of Jesus, his message, mission, and its eschatological horizon.[320] This denotes the narrative's treatment of Jesus' *identity* as finally revealed in his passion and promised return.

As the narrative progresses, the group of addressees of Jesus' command narrows down to the inner circle. At first and only until Mark 3:12, those commanded to keep their knowledge to themselves are demons, who underscore the significance of Jesus' power best in their antagonistic nature precisely by following Jesus' order—contrary to the delivered (not silenced) or healed characters. Moreover, their preternatural perception of Jesus stands in contrast to that of other characters at this early point of the plot, yet it alludes to information given by the extradiegetic narrator, which keeps the audience wondering about the further

---

[320] This is part of a broad discussion of what is frequently referred to as "messianic secret." While the term was coined by William Wrede, its meaning has shifted from an explanation of the post-resurrection belief-system regarding the earthly "non-messianic" life of Jesus by the early church (Wrede 1963 [1901]; cf. also the chronological shift to the life of Jesus, in, e. g., Schniewind 1952; Sjöberg 1955; Schweitzer 2001), to *the* literary strategy of textual and theological coherence employed by the evangelist in redaction criticism (cf., e. g., Schweizer 1964; Schweizer in Schweizer (ed.) 1970; Schweizer 1989 [1967]; Gnilka 2010. 167–170), to simply one of many intentional, theological, Christological threads of the gospel text and an important literary device created at some time of textual genesis to guide and engage the audience, mainly regarding the composition and understanding of the passion (cf. each with different nuances and methods, e. g., Ebeling 1939; Luz 1965; Söding; Scholtissek 1995; Guttenberger 2004; also Marcus 2000; Moloney 2002; Schenke 2005; Boring 2006). Cf. also the sociological approach of Theissen in Kippenberg; Stroumsa (ed.) 1995. As a comprehensive, conceptual analysis needs to include other Markan references, such as the debatable parable theory (Mark 4:10–12; cf. Räisänen 1990. 73), the development of the audiences and disciples' understanding of Jesus' identity (e. g., 4:13; 8:14–21, 27–30), and allusions to the complex chronology of his mission (e. g., 9:9, 30) all within their specific traditional and narrative setting, the following solely concentrates on the literary function of the silencing commands with regard to healing accounts according to the scope of this study.

development and revelation of the narrative and its protagonist. Then those healed of sicknesses and their witnesses are introduced as failing secret keepers as they reveal the experience of Jesus' healing power as uncontainable and by that validate the audience's knowledge about him.

Finally, the disciples take up the function of the secret keepers—and that only too well. Their esoteric knowledge is (besides the events in the beginning of the gospel) similar to that of the audience as it also includes the knowledge of experiences with divine provenance (cf., e.g., 9:1–13). In the final prohibition to partake their experience and knowledge of the transfiguration (esp. 9:7) until the Son of Man is resurrected, the built-up tension is slowly released: the audience can apply this timeframe to the previously recounted commands as the entire motif of Jesus' (un)veiled identity gradually unravels when first Jesus himself breaks his silence in 14:62 and then 15:39 reprises Mark 1:1 and 1:11 in the speech of the centurion. The disciples, however, even after the allusion to Jesus' resurrection, remain silent about their Jesus experience (16:8), which is picked up and solved only in Mark's secondary ending in 16:20,[321] hence a complex issue brought to bear for the audience.

Here in 1:45, the dis/abled man breaks this command, not as a display of "disrespect,"[322] but due to the uncontainable character of the encounter that is underscored in the following verses, his intention is completely disregarded:[323] while κηρύσσω is used to designate speech acts of John the Baptist (1:4, 7), Jesus (1:14, 38–39), and the disciples (3:14; 6:12; 13:10; 14:9; 16:15, 20), and the always unqualified ὁ λόγος seems to generate a specific meaning with regard to Jesus' message

---

[321] Cf. Koch in Oyen (ed.) 2019. 589–592.
[322] Cf. Müller in Zimmermann (ed.) 2013. 223; Kiffiak 2017. 137.
[323] It is more likely, although not unequivocal, that ἤρξατο refers to the healed man, since ὁ δὲ often indicates a change of subject in Mark and Jesus is the subject of the preceding λέγει in v. 44 (cf., e.g., Mark 3:4; 5:34; 6:24, 37, 38, 49; 7:6, 28), even if a) it is stylistically clumsy that Jesus becomes the subject again in v. 45b by the ambiguous pronoun, yet otherwise redundant αὐτὸν (cf., e.g., Kazmierski 1992. 38–39; Elliott (ed.) 2010. 342; Focant 2012. 82) and b) there is a strong connection of Jesus and his teaching of ὁ λόγος with the often-recounted effect of a (pestering) crowd drawing in (cf. 1:28, 39; 2:1–2, 13, 15; 3:7–10, 20; 4:1; 6:31–32, 54–55; 7:24; and κηρύσσω in 1:14, 39; 3:14; 5:20; 13:10; 14:9 and διαφημίζειν τὸν λόγον in 2:2, 8:32; 4:13; 16:33). Rather, it would be highly unusual, that the gospel would focus such extended attention on a healed person (Focant 2012. 84). However, when reading Jesus as the implied subject, v. 45 serves a similar function as the summaric passages (cf. ch. 2) in reflecting the progress and growing radius of his teaching and healing ministry and his heightened popularity. It thereby connects preceding and succeeding narratives and anchors the progressing plot. This would fit its position here, at the end of Mark 1 and the programmatic introduction of Jesus and his ministry, which will cause conflict and commotion, rejoicing and riot and is by that in its narrative function not so different to the variant reading. For evidence of the textual genesis of this ambiguous passage cf., e.g., Elliott (ed.) 2010.

throughout the gospel narrative,³²⁴ the meaning here, when implying the man as the subject, is unparalleled and first and foremost charged by the immediate context as the more detailed and parallel phrasing in Mark 5:20 spells out: καὶ ἤρξατο κηρύσσειν [...] ὅσα ἐποίησεν αὐτῷ ὁ Ἰησοῦς (also similar to Mark 7:36). These healed men, and in case of Mark 7:36 the witnesses, proclaim Jesus and his just-experienced curative capability, although all of them have been asked to contain the message, in case of Mark 5:19–20 within a certain circle (see ch. 5.1.4).³²⁵ However, Mark 5:19–20 and 7:36–37 do not speak of ὁ λόγος, which might be explained by the programmatic function of Mark 1: here, Jesus' ministry in *word* and deed is powerfully established to be unraveled.

E In Focus: Healing Spaces in Mark—Synagogues, Houses, and In-Betweens
The first chapter of Mark's gospel witnesses to Jesus' "dislodging" actions in sacred, domestic, and liminal spaces—another programmatic feature that recurs in the following healing narratives.

Only in the beginning of Jesus' ministry, synagogues (συναγωγή) as spatial structures constituted for or by gatherings in Galilee³²⁶ serve as a setting for his healing yet are always connected to or preceded by his teaching (1:21, 23, 29, 39; 3:1). To this "pedagogical" connotation in the gospel context, a sacred notion is added by the timeframe: the Sabbath (with exception of 1:39). While the first deeds in Mark 1 go unquestioned, the synagogue, as a literary motif, turns into a place of skepticism, confrontation, and rejection in 3:1–6 and finally in 6:1–5. The healings in each of those contexts are portrayed as validation for Jesus' "new teaching" that is attributed to his ἐξουσία (Mark 1:27), his ability to "do good" and "save a life" on the Sabbath (ψυχὴν σῶσαι, Mark 3:4), and his σοφία (and δύναμις; Mark 6:2).

Domestic (healing) encounters between the Markan Jesus and mainly female characters³²⁷ must be regarded in light of literary, archaeological, and architectural evidence on life and housing in Galilee in the early centuries CE. These findings suggest houses were rarely closed but rather dynamic structures that changed according to the time of day and the seasons, the activities and relationships of the

---

324 Cf., e.g., 2:2; 4:14–20, 33; 8:32; furthermore, Kilpatrick in Kilpatrick (ed.) 1993.
325 Differently to Mark 1:34; 3:12 (demons) or 5:43 and 8:26, where no infringement of the command for silence is recounted.
326 For the complex discussion on the meaning and function of places termed συναγωγή cf., e.g., Runesson; Binder; Olsson 2010; Eberhart et al. 2020. For the Markan texts on healing in connection with συναγωγή, the prepositional terminology used in the focal texts (εἰσέρχομαι, ἐν, ἐξέρχομαι, εἰς) suffices for a glance at its use as a spatial setting.
327 Cf. Mark 1:28–31; 5:21–24, 35–43; 7:24–30; but: 2:1–12 and 5:25–34.

inhabitants, and economic factors.³²⁸ A separation between public domesticity and the often claimed distinction between male and female sphere cannot be derived from spatial structures.³²⁹ This also applies to literary representations of women in various spatial situations.³³⁰ To be distinguished from this, but by no means isolated, is the house as a literary motif. In the Gospel of Mark, the terms οἰκία/οἶκος³³¹ imply kinship and familiarity as well as belonging,³³² illustrate social (re)integration, and demonstrate successful healing, when those who are healed are sent home by Jesus.³³³ Certain houses are defined more precisely by their owner (Simon and Andrew in 1:29–32; Jaïrus in 5:35–43)³³⁴ or by their geographical location (e. g., Tyre).³³⁵ Furthermore, unspecific houses are visited for teaching units of Jesus.³³⁶ In each of these cases, the house often serves as a shielding retreat from the tumultuous crowd that keeps harassing the increasingly famous Jesus.³³⁷ On a literary level, then, it is clear that the domestic setting of the healings is intended to emphasize seclusion and intimacy (Mark 2:1–12 by inversion): Simon's mother-in-law and the daughter of Jaïrus are healed under the eyes of only a few witnesses. The healing of the daughter of the Syrophoenician woman is even imparted from a distance.³³⁸ The "domestic" healings are thus not based in a "gendered space" but rather fulfill a literary function.

---

328 Cf. for the following, Osiek; Balch 1997. 54–55; Trainor 2001. 19; Baker 2002. 35–42, esp. 38; Meyers in Balch; Osiek (ed.) 2003; Freyne in Navarro Puerto; Perroni (ed.) 2012. 43–44.
329 Cf. Trainor 2001. 91.
330 Cf. Meyers in Balch; Osiek (ed.) 2003. 66.
331 Cf. Malbon 1991. 107–108.
332 Cf. οἰκία in 3:25–27; 6:4; 10:29–30; 12:40; 13:15, 34–35; οἶκος in 2:26; 11:17. Cf. Collins 1993.
333 Cf. 2:11; 5:19; 8:26; furthermore, 7:30.
334 Cf. also Mark 2:14–17 and 14:3–9.
335 Cf. as well 2:1–12 and 9:33–50, perhaps in the context of Mark 3:20.
336 Cf. Mark 7:17–23; 9:28–29; 10:10–12.
337 Cf. 1:45–2:4; 5:38; 7:17, 24. For a detailed analysis on literary, narratological, architectural, and archeological aspects, see Bosenius 2014. Esp. 134–169; furthermore, 443–450, 451–460; Malbon 1991. 118–119, on domestic teachings, cf. ibid. 115–116.
338 However, no gender-related contrast is established. Thus, Jesus' intimate and personal healing comes to all sexes far from or in the midst of the crowd with explicitly few or no witnesses at all (including the woman in Mark 5:25–34; and two men in 7:31–37; 8:22–26). Likewise, healings of both sexes (see p. 76, n. 161) are reported as a result of "failed" retreats in domestic structures (2:1–12; 7:24–30) and attention-generating healings often take place in the context of disputes and conflicts between Jesus and the Pharisees and scribes regardless of location (synagogues, public places, and houses, see 2:1–12; 3:1–6; 9:14–29). This applies not only to healings but also to other encounters with female protagonists (cf. 14:1–9). Therefore, it can be concluded that although all healing stories with female patients have the motif of retreat and intimate attention (which is often, but as in the case of blood fluids not always, expressed in the form of domesticity), this is not a proprium of female healings. Cf. Malbon 1991; Collins 1993.

Lastly, the majority of healings take place in places in- or explicitly outside of architecturally defined structures,[339] with the addition of vague generalizing and summarizing locality determinations that "function periphrastically for 'everywhere'."[340] Jesus encounters the sick and tormented on the agora in (unspecified) towns (e.g., esp. 6:56); around the "lake" (e.g., esp. 5:1–21), on and around mountains, in the wilderness (e.g., 1:45; 5:5, 11; 9:9, 14–29); and on the open road (esp. 10:46, 52; also 8:23). While each description or allusion to geographical, social, and ideological space is charged with meaning and has its own function within the gospels' journey to Jerusalem,[341] these localities serve four main functions regarding the healing narratives:

They witness to a) a pathological setting, the need for healing is great and encountered basically everywhere, leading to b) the rapid spreading of Jesus' fame, reflected in the uncontainable notice of his power met with c) a countermovement into less inhabited, more intimate spaces for his d) transgressional healing ministry. While the first two are particularly emphasized in the summaric notes and concluding remarks of individual accounts, the latter two are aimed at by nuanced characterizations of Jesus in the individual accounts. This brief overview already shows that the Markan Jesus shares liminal spaces with those forced to occupy them on account of their dis/abilities (e.g., Mark 1:40–45, esp. 1:45; 5:1–20, esp. 5:14), he seeks intimate encounters with few witnesses for particular healings (e.g., 8:22–26), and his healing ministry expands in place and time so he even feels the need to withdraw (cf., e.g., 1:45; 6:31, 32, 35; 8:4).

The settings of Markan healings seem far from accidental when deviating characters are encountered in particular places that not only relate to their specific images of dis/ability but illustrate its narrative function as they correspond with teachings and debates, community and belonging, development of mission and plot.

3.4 Conclusion and Interpretation of Dis/ability in Mark 1

Mark 1 closes its programmatic onset by giving "testimony" to Jesus' teaching and healing ability and will, as witnessed throughout the chapter with an ever-increasing and now also challenging popularity. The images of dis/ability employed aid this aim in the following ways:

---

339 Cf. 1:40–45; 5:1–20; 5:25–34; 7:31–37; 8:22–26; 9:14–29; 10:46–52.
340 Malbon 1991. 101. Cf. 1:28, 45; 5:14; 6:55–56.
341 For conceptional approaches towards Markan space, see, e.g., Malbon 1991. Esp. 18–106; Bosenius 2014. Esp. 101–272; Rüggemeier in Bartsch; Bode (ed.) 2019.

First, they showcase Jesus as an authoritative teacher and a helpful and powerful healer on the grounds of general and therefore relatable images of dis/ability he encounters everywhere. His ability encompasses sovereignty over unclean spirits, pulling a radically passive woman back into active life and removing the source of impurity from a *leprous* man.

Moreover, all three images of deviating physicality depict severe social conditions, characters forced into socially deviating and aggressive conduct, passivity to the extent of utter non-participation (not only with regard to social expectations), and a liminal and marginalized existence. Jesus' healing by authoritative words and touch reflects participation in verbal and tactile communication and provides a return into the community. Jesus is depicted as mobile, approachable, and tangible to these characters. This is underscored by the fact that they reflect personal problems by being pinned to concrete places and/or persons. The common motif of Jesus adjusting his healing touch according to the dis/ability of the person is emphatically introduced in two instances: one where he heals an ailment that is observable by touching but not clearly visible, and another where he heals a clearly visible condition that might be better left untouched.

He overcomes physical distance when he meets the secluded mother-in-law and bridges the social distance of the stigmatized man with his stretched-out healing hands. At the same time, a growing crowd continuously draws in on him, by the end of the chapter too close for comfort. Thereby, the healing narratives emphatically confirm and illustrate the introductory characterization by the narrator (1:1), in line with the heralding of Isaiah (1:2–3) and John (1:7–8), verified by God (1:9–11).[342]

Moreover, throughout the depiction of his rising popularity, the chapter already scatters narrative seeds that sprout in the following chapters with regard to questions of authority and status, all negotiated by these concrete deviating bodies: Jesus' teaching—intrinsically connected to his healing (cf. ch. 2)—as being in conflict with demonic and religious opponents (cf. exorcism in light of Mark 3:20–30, healing on the Sabbath, and questionable treatment of impurity), a physical transformation that implicitly transpires an entirely new existence (as the bodies rise and raise in 1:31; 2:9, 11; 3:3; 5:41; 9:27; 10:49; and drastically change to activities in, e. g., 1:31, 45; 2:12; 5:19, 34, 42–43; 10:52), and the continuous tension about the disclosure of his embodied identity (knowing demons and commands to silence, mysterious ἐξουσία, and efficacious healing touches).

The images of dis/ability in all three narratives also share a striking commonality in their spatiality. Not only are the settings where Jesus encounters those ail-

---

[342] Cf. Rüggemeier 2021. 341.

ing programmatic for the gospel's staging (until Jesus reaches Jerusalem; see E. In Focus: Healing Spaces in Mark), but Jesus questions the dis/abilities' appropriation of space: while each transformation comes in its common terminology, all three dis/abilities *depart* from the patients. Obviously, in the case of possession, with its spatial clinical picture (i.e., shared speech, knowledge, body) and etiological onset as a cosmic battle, the demon is expelled and leaves its host. However, the *fever* also leaves the body of the mother-in-law, and the source of the man's impurity, *lepra*, departs from him. While Mark does not comment on a common etiology of possession and sickness, but quite to the contrary depicts their symptoms and healing differently (see 3.1.2), this feature rather alludes to a general exposure and universal susceptibility of humanity to dis/abling influences, even if only affected temporarily. These common and constantly threatening "weakening" conditions (see 2.1) yield when Jesus and his message quite literally reach out. It seems as when the maverick healer Jesus embarks on his journey through the gospel narrative from Galilee to Jerusalem, spaces shift. He heals wherever he encounters those in need in sacred, domestic, and liminal spaces in an ever-growing radius with a crowd closing in on him, heightened by the need to retreat and inaccessible areas for his mission. His powerful yet sensitive "extricating" actions reveal him to be spatially tangible in a dis/abled world.

4 Mark 2:1–3:6: A Plot in Motion

After Mark's programmatic introduction of the powerful teacher and approachable and increasingly popular healer of common yet socially effective dis/abilities in religious, domestic, and open spaces, the successive sequence presents a growing resistance to Jesus, his mission, and his progressively differentiated teachings. Accordingly, the following two healing narratives are embedded in a new, concentrically structured complex regarding Jesus and his opponents. While there can be many interesting observations and connections made from various vantage points concerning this dense section in the Gospel of Mark, only a few regarding the following analysis of dis/ability will need to suffice.[1]

The first two narratives, Mark 2:1–12 and 2:13–17, continue the opposition between Jesus and the scribes (see Mark 1:22) and fill it thematically with Jesus' controversial approach toward sin and sinners. The latter two, Mark 2:23–28 and 3:1–6, introduce the Pharisees to the gospel narrative as taking offense at Jesus' conception of the Sabbath. The flanked section, Mark 2:18–22, describes an impersonal group conflicted by Jesus' disciples' lack of fasting; hence, it connects to the frame through the thematic intersection of "eating/not eating" (eating with sinners and tax collectors, fasting, plucking grains on the Sabbath).

The narratives' concentric structure visualizes the development of the conflict theme: while the two framing healing narratives depict silent protest against only Jesus by representations of consciousness (the disciples are not explicitly active), the opponents in the intercalated narratives openly voice their disagreement with Jesus once to the disciples (2:13–17) and once directly to Jesus but regarding his disciples' behavior (2:18–22, 23–28). Disagreement with Jesus and his ministry then escalates at the end of the entire section, with the decision to kill Jesus in 3:6, which is already anticipated at midpoint of the central narrative in Mark 2:20. After Mark 3:6, there is no reference to the conspiracy against Jesus until the beginning of its culmination in Jerusalem. The entire complex is framed by the healing of the *leper* (1:40–45, see 3.3) and the summaric statement in 3:7–12 (see 2.3), which both speak of Jesus' fame and unchallenged popularity.

The two healing narratives in question are at the beginning and end of the chiastic section. This position and their shared setting in Capernaum put them in direct comparison with each other, which is enforced by their similar content and several formal commonalities: Firstly, they both feature a controversy apoph-

---

[1] See, e.g., the pertinent dissertation on the structure of Mark 2:1–3:6 and the function of its literary technique of Dewey 1980. For the following structure, cf. esp. Dewey 1980. 23, 42, 109–16; Iersel in Focant; Neirynck (ed.) 1993; Williams 1994. 43; Collins 2007. 182; Focant 2012. 85–87.

thegm embedded in a healing narrative, placing Jesus in conflict with authorities due to his teachings and deeds. Furthermore, both narratives are similarly structured:[2] Jesus enters a place (εἰσελθών/ εἰσῆλθεν πάλιν εἰς, 2:1 and 3:1, hence the healings are effected indoors) and is confronted with a (partially) paralyzed person whom he has to address twice (2:5, 11 and 3:3, 5, λέγει τῷ ἀνθρώπῳ/ παραλυτικῷ) since the healing is interrupted by silent and motionless accusations of surrounding opponents (2:6; 3:2; cf. καρδία in 2:6; 3:2), which Jesus nevertheless discerns and contests with questions (2:9; 3:4). After Jesus' rhetoric, including counter- and alternative questions on authoritative possibilities of certain conduct (2:9; 3:4),[3] the paralyzed bodies are finally healed by Jesus' word alone (2:11–12; 3:5). The similar character groups are correspondingly arranged: Jesus and the (partially) paralyzed men are staged at the center of space and attention, surrounded by scholarly opponents and a witnessing crowd. Moreover, the pericopes are similarly narrated regarding semantical accordance (cf. ἐγείρω in 2:9, 11, 12 and 3:3), point of view, and representations of consciousness.[4]

4.1 Mark 2:1–12: The Forgiven (Im-)Mobile Man

4.1.1 Introduction to the Narrative

Mark 2:1–12 is not only mirrored in the closing narrative of the structural conflict-and-authority compound, but it is also connected to other passages on Jesus' growing popularity and the rising expectations from the crowds. These passages include the summaric statement in Mark 1:32–34 and the narrative of the healing of the *leper* in 1:40–45 (see 2.1 and 3.3): As news of Jesus spreads rapidly (1:45 διαφημίζω; 2:1 ἀκούω), people who are suffering are brought to him (φέρω 1:32; 2:3), causing a crowd to gather that exceeds the spatial capacity of Jesus' location, even blocking the way (ἐπι-/συνάγω 1:33; 2:2; πρὸς τὴν θύραν 1:33; 2:2; ὥστε μηκέτι 1:45; 2:2).[5] Mighty deeds are expected of Jesus: his authoritative teaching is described and contrasted specifically with the teaching of the scribes (cf. 1:14–15, 21–22; cf. 2:2), and his healing ability is emphatically reprised in the praising "testimony" only two verses prior (1:45).[6] Moreover, the foundation of the following

---

2 Cf. Dewey 1980. 111–112; Williams 1994. 43–44.
3 Cf. Dewey 1980. 101, 111–112.
4 See moreover, Rüggemeier 2017. 91, on various narrative criteria to describe connections of narratives.
5 Cf. Dewey 1980. 67; Williams 1994. 99.
6 Cf. Collins 2007. 184.

controversies is laid by Jesus' thus far uncontested healing on the Sabbath in Mark 1:21–31, 32–34 and questionable treatment of impurity in 1:40–45.

The storyline continues with another healing narrative set in Capernaum (2:1), where Jesus, who is not explicitly named, enters a house. This furthermore ties the following episode closely to Mark 1:21–38 (cf. πάλιν; also in Mark 3:1),[7] so ἐν οἴκῳ could refer to the house of Simon and Andrew (cf. 1:29) or, if not to another unspecific house in Capernaum, may even signify "at home."[8] In any case, the setting connotes a teaching environment and Jesus' increasing popularity (see E. In Focus: Healing Spaces in Mark). The introductory sequence is narrated in the aorist and complemented by the imperfect describing Jesus' ongoing teaching when the narrator interrupts the setting of the scene with the historical present by prominently staging four people carrying a *paralytic* (v. 3; cf. also χαλῶσι in v. 4). This is underscored by the shift in perspective to these five characters (2:3–4), which builds on the narrated knowledge of Jesus' teaching and healing ability (1:14–15, 22, 39; 2:2 and 1:21–27, 32–34, 40–44).[9] The audience participates in their pursuit of help.[10] The narrative then continues in "rapid sequences of completed action in the aorist," shedding light every now and then on the (constant) position of the characters with the imperfect or imperfective periphrastic conjugation (cf. Jesus and the paralyzed man in v. 4, the scribes in v. 6).[11] As Jesus is surrounded by a big, unrelenting crowd, the group around the motionless man makes its way to Jesus over the roof. When Jesus, however, speaks a word of forgiveness instead of healing (see below), he incites a partially silent debate with the surrounding scribes about the authority to forgive sins—another shift in perspective. The closed-off space made inaccessible by the crowd is further narrowed by the scribes (cf. esp. 1:22 and 2:16 for this section), who appear in their silence and immobility throughout the narrative as part of the rigid inventory: verses 6–10 only encompass verbs of motionlessness and sedateness, putting the entire focus on Jesus' controversial teaching and word of forgiveness, while verses 3–5 and 11–12 feature verbs of movement and vitality. Jesus, as the center of the narrative, is teaching, lively and enraged, the only one speaking directly, even verbalizing the scribes' *secret* accusations. His direct speech acts are introduced three times with λέγει in the historical present (vv. 5, 8, 11) and thus are featured prominently as delivered di-

---

[7] Other commonalities include Jesus' initial teaching, his ἐξουσία (1:22, 27; 2:10; see below), that is similarly questioned (1:27; 2:7), opposed with γραμματεῖς (1:22; 2:6), and emphatically qualified (1:27; 2:12). Cf. Kiffiak 2017. 138, n. 395.
[8] Cf. Focant 2012. 91.
[9] Cf. Rüggemeier 2017. 41–42.
[10] Cf. ibid. 40.
[11] Cf. Breytenbach in Breytenbach (ed.) 2021a [2019]. 195.

rectly to the audience of the gospel as he claims the divine prerogative to forgive sins, calls out his opponents' silent objection, and proves his authority by the astonishing healing of an im-/mobile man. Again, the enclosed space structures the "transformations performed throughout the narrative [...] at the spatial level in a double opposition: at the beginning, the paralytic had to be gotten in lying down (a horizontal position) through the roof (vertically); at the end, getting up (vertically), he goes out again through the door (horizontally) (2:12)."[12] Jesus' active counterparts, the paralytic and his bearers, are characterized by active πίστις and highly physical movement, although it remains unclear if the paralyzed man is included in the motivating *pistis* of his friends or not (v. 5) and, in case of the latter, whether *pistis* is necessary for the healing and can be transferred from the petitioner to the person in need (see G. In Focus: Mark's Relational *Pistis*).[13] In any case, their active, transboundary behavior is interpreted with their *pistis*,[14] accounting for the healing of their then-moving friend. Their mobility and *pistis* are contrasted by the suspicion and immobility of the scribes.[15]

Grammatically, it remains ambiguous if the opponents are included in the hyperbolic "all" who witness the healing and respond with amazement (ἐξίστημι)[16] and praise (δοξάζω). It seems rather unlikely regarding their opposition in also the subsequent sequences (see below).[17] The ambiguity of the concrete subjects practicing *pistis* and responding positively engages the audience as it demands their positioning in return. The wonder about Jesus and his ἐξουσία is, in response, not questioned anymore (cf. 1:22, 27) but broadened to a positive and certain reflection of God in this unique encounter (cf. furthermore, 7:37)[18] and hence probably encompasses the divine forgiveness demonstrated vividly by the visually perceived healing.[19]

---

12 Focant 2012. 91.
13 Cf. 1:15, and esp. 5:34, 36; 9:23; 10:52; 11:22–24.
14 Cf. Focant 2012. 91.
15 Cf. Williams 1994. 100.
16 Cf. 5:42 or 6:51–52, moreover, Pascut 2017. 193–199.
17 Cum Kiffiak 2017. 139, n. 397; differently, Dwyer 1996. 103; Klumbies in Zimmermann (ed.) 2013. 237–238.
18 Cf. Kiffiak 2017. 138.
19 Cf., e.g., Dschulnigg 2007. 95.

4.1.2 Images of Dis/ability

4.1.2.1 A Man Unable to Walk

The man is introduced as a παραλυτικός. The only symptom implied is his inability to walk. Within the New Testament, this lexeme is used only in the Gospels of Mark and Matthew. Besides the eight occurrences in this narrative and its parallel account in Matt 9:1–8, it can be found twice. In Matt 4:24, the expression is mentioned in a summaric account concluding Jesus' healing activity of those suffering from various νόσοι and βάσανοι, those δαιμονιζομένους καὶ σεληνιαζομένους καὶ παραλυτικούς. Furthermore, in Matt 8:6, it describes the ailment of a centurion's servant, who lies "paralyzed" and severely "tormented"[20] (again βασανίζω). The latter's parallel account in Luke 7:1–10 omits the lexeme altogether and describes the servant as κακῶς ἔχων ἤμελλεν τελευτᾶν, as lying near death. Moreover, a variant reading of John 5:3 uses παραλυτικων instead of ξηρῶν to picture a group of those waiting for healing at the pool of Bethesda, together with those χωλός (and τῶν ἀσθενούντων, τυφλῶν). Especially the Johannine account raises the question of the exact parameters of what is labeled παραλυτικός, in contrast or similarity to those designated as χωλός and ξηρῶν. Overall, in none of the mentioned passages is the designation further described or enriched with details on etiology, diagnosis, severity, or prognosis. The same is true for other occurrences of the term. Interestingly, παραλυτικός is not found in writings prior to the New Testament texts and only seldomly appears elsewhere in first-centuries accounts, from which the majority are early Christian texts inspired by the accounts of Matthew and Mark.[21] There as well, nothing particular is stated about the symptoms or origin of this condition; the focus lies rather on its medical treatments. In Dioscorides' *De Materia Medica*, for example, παραλυτικός occurs in a series of ailments, such as febrile, pulmonic, nervous, or menstrual conditions or headaches, that have in common that they can be relieved by certain herbal remedies.[22] Similarly, the very

---

20 This lexeme is used to designate a variety of (physical) pain: birth pain (Rev 12:2), inner turmoil (2Pet 2:7), apocalyptical torture (e.g., Luke 16:23, 28; Rev 14:10; 20:10), and demons when being in Jesus' exorcising presence (Mark 5:7par.).
21 Cf., e.g., Dioscorides, *Mat. Med.* 1.16.2; 3.78.2; 4.176.2; 4.183.2; 5.18.3; *Cyranides* 1.1.110; 3.9.12; Galen, *Comp. Med.* 13.1045. Cf. moreover, von Bendemann in Labahn; Lietaert Peerbolte (ed.) 2006. 116, n. 55; Peterson 2006. 265; Schiefer Ferrari in Kollmann; Zimmermann (ed.) 2014. 640; Solevåg 2018. 34, who all give profound overviews over the ancient etiological, diagnostic, and prognostic meanings.
22 Cf., e.g., *Mat. med.* 1.16.2.

mutilated lines 1.16–17 of the first-century medical text *P.Mon.Gr.* inv. 123 mentions παραλυτικός alongside "epilepsy."[23]

However, the perfect passive participle of παραλύω is prevalent: It is found in the Lukan parallel account of Mark 2:1–12 (Luke 5:17–26). In Acts, it describes people healed by Philip or Peter, in the first instance in the form of a summaric note in Acts 8:7, here again together with χωλός; in the case of the latter in Acts 9:33, within the personal healing narrative of Aeneas, who is described as having been bedridden (κατακείμενον ἐπὶ κραβάττου) for eight years. Finally, in Heb 12:12, it figuratively designates "weak knees" (παραλελυμένα γόνατα), which are again parallelized with τὸ χωλὸν in need of healing (ἰάομαι) in the following verse. Moreover, παραλελυμένος can be found in the Corpus Hippocraticum and writings of Aristotle and Galen designating weakened and paralyzed limbs and elsewhere with a variety of other meanings, such as "to be undone/untied/separated/liberated/exempted."[24]

Neither does the closely related παράλυσις indicate a more specific meaning but implies an even greater range of physical conditions—including a loss of physical and/or nervous sensory control in context of drunkenness, a form of water and food poisoning, emotional distress (e.g., the παράλυσις τῆς ψυχῆς), and childbirth (wombs are "paralyzed")[25]—meaning quite generally a "lack of proper function of the human skeletomuscular system or a metaphorical extension thereof."[26] After the rather vague and uncharacteristic descriptions in the Corpus Hippocraticum, later texts show a more explicit clinical picture with regard to content and terminology.[27] For example, Aretaeus differentiates among various forms of mobility impairment such as "paralysis," anaisthesia, paresis, and paraplegia but concludes that they "are all of the same kind, and denote a defect of motion or of sense, or of both, sometimes of the mind, and at other times of the other senses."[28] However, he distinguishes more thoroughly concerning the etiology, yet it still all remains vague in the quantity of possible causes.[29] Furthermore, the severity of the ailment and its physical consequences for daily life vary in their arduous-

---

[23] Cf. παθῶν οἷον ἐπιληπτικ[ῶν] | [-----παρ]αλυτικῶν καὶ τῶν περὶ τὰ | [κτλ., as reconstructed by Horsley 1983. 79.
[24] Cf., e.g., CH, *Epid.* 1.26.13; *Morb.* 3.3 L 7.120; 1.4 L 6.146; *Coac.* 193.2; Aristotle, *Eth. Nic.* 18/1102b; Galen, *Morb. caus.* 7.30.7–31; Polybius, *Hist.* 8.4.2; 11.14.6; 20.10.9; 32.8.1; Philo, *Spec.* 2.193. Cf. also LN, *s.v.* 23.170, 25.152, also 23.171; LSJ, *s.v.*; Montanari, *s.v.*; Rissi, *παραλυτικός*; Balz; Schneider, *παραλύομαι*.
[25] Cf., e.g., Athenaeus, *Deipn.* 2.36; Diodorus, *Bib. hist.* 4.3; Polybius, *Hist.* 30.32; Strabo, *Geogr.* 16.4.24; Soranus, *Gyn.* 4.2.
[26] Peterson 2006. 268.
[27] Cf., e.g., Caelius, *Chron.* 2.1; Paulus Aegineta, 3.18.1–6, and generally, Karenberg, *Lähmung.* 550.
[28] Aretaeus, *Sign. diut.* 1.7 (ed. Moffat, p. 131); cf. also, Peterson 2006. 268.
[29] Cf. Aretaeus, *Sign. Diut.* 1.7.

ness.³⁰ Therapies include rather invasive forms of orthopedic and manual treatments.³¹

Taking these exemplary occurrences into account, it becomes difficult and probably futile to differentiate among the semantically so closely related lexemes παραλυτικός, παραλύω, and παράλυσις. They all describe a variety of clinical pictures that result in some sort of (partial or limited) physical motionlessness. Therefore, it is best to follow Louw and Nida in their nontechnical and vague translation of παραλυτικός as "one who cannot walk,"³² which fits the descriptions of the man's entrance as carried on a stretcher and by inversion the demonstrative autonomous exit after the healing. The precise anatomical location of this motionlessness, or if it corresponds with a lack of sensation, cannot be concluded from the Markan text.

4.1.2.2 Physical Motionlessness

Such descriptions of impaired physical mobility also occur with other terms and labels in ancient texts. Some New Testament narratives envisage a partial paralysis of body parts as chronical or congenital conditions³³ or describe the immobility of legs as part of a full-body motionlessness.³⁴ None of them accounts clearly for a reason for the impairment; rather, New Testament narratives reflect social marginalization and/or diminished quality of life.³⁵ Only Luke 13:10–17 might faintly hint at a demonological etiology behind the πνεῦμα ἀσθένεια, and Mark 2:1–12 might imply a causal connection to sin (see below).

Similarly, the more common and at times even interchangeable label χωλός mostly refers to an immobility of the leg(s) with a range in severity from motionlessness to limping.³⁶ The lexeme is also applied solely to feet, legs, and hands and

---

30 Cf., e.g., CH, *Coac.* 307; *Prorrh.* 1.118; Caelius Aurelianus, *Chron.* 2.15; Celsus, *Med.* 3.27; cf. von Bendemann in Labahn; Lietaert Peerbolte (ed.) 2006. 116.
31 Cf., e.g., Caelius Aurelianus, *Chron.* 2.59; von Bendemann in Labahn; Lietaert Peerbolte (ed.) 2006. 116.
32 LN, *s.v.* 23.171. Cf. also, Peterson 2006. 272.
33 Cf., e.g., *paralysis* of a hand in Mark 3:1; in Acts 14:8 of the feet (from birth); maybe in Luke 13:11 with a spinal distortion (for eighteen years); or in Heb 12:12 of knees; furthermore, Acts 9:33 accounts for a mobility impairment of eight years and 3:2 for a congenital dis/ability.
34 Cf. Mark 2:1–12par.; Acts 3:2; 9:33.
35 Cf., e.g., Luke 14:13, 21; Matt 15:30; Acts 3:2; John 5:3 etc. Cf. von Bendemann in Labahn; Lietaert Peerbolte (ed.) 2006. 115.
36 Cf., e.g., Matt 11:5; 15:30–31; Mark 9:45; Luke 7:22; Acts 3:2; 14:8. Cf. also Rose 2003. 13; von Bendemann in Labahn; Lietaert Peerbolte (ed.) 2006. 116, n. 56.

figuratively describes a "limping" nature, courage, kingship, and so forth.[37] In the New Testament, it can be found thirteen times in the Gospels and Acts,[38] once in Heb 12:13; at times, it specifically characterizes impaired feet and is often mentioned together with blindness.[39] Interestingly, it is only twice used in narratives to designate the ailment of an individual, who is then healed by Peter or Paul (Acts 3:2; 14:8). Besides these occurrences and the one in Heb 12:13, the expression is either used in summaric statements of Jesus' (or, in Acts 8:7, Philippus') healing ministry and teaching, together with other ailments such as blindness (τυφλός), lepra (λεπρός), deafness (κωφός), and mutilation (κυλλός, ἀνάπειρος) or with overcoming death (νεκρός) and poverty (πτωχός),[40] and/or has a clear eschatological nuance to it (Mark 9:45par. Matt 18:8; see below).[41] Due to its frequent and customary use, it is plausible that "whereas χωλός is a more generic, colloquial term, παραλύω and παράλυσις are medical terms, frequently used in the medical corpus" and that the man's ailment in Mark 2 "may point toward an impairment that was recently acquired, painful, and perhaps more serious than the general designation χωλός would imply."[42] The listing of παραλυτικός/παραλύειν and χωλός together in enumerations in Acts 8:7 and the variant reading of John 5:3 could then suggest different nuances in that regard but could also likewise be a hyperbolic device in narrating Jesus' healing ability with the drastic picture of cured motionlessness (cf. Heb 12:12–13). The vagueness of both terms regarding the conditions they designate, their etiological, diagnostic, and prognostic implications at this point in medical history, and their overlap in meaning make a clear distinction for the Markan text difficult to prove.[43]

Moreover, a sudden inability to move the entire body or single body parts was also described with ἀποπληξία, παραπληξία, or ἀπόπλεκτος.[44] Mostly elderly people are witnessed to be fatally affected by this immobilization basically caused by an accumulation of black bile or phlegm leading to a cooling down and consol-

---

[37] Cf., e.g., Homer, Il. 2.217; Aristophanes, Thesm. 24; Lucian, Tim. 20; Plutarch, Quest. conv. 739b; Plato, Leg. 794e; Eup. 264; CH, Prorrh. 2.1. Cf. BDAG, s.v.; LN, s.v. 23.175; LSJ, s.v.; Montanari, s.v.; Sänger, χωλός.
[38] Cf. Matt 11:5 par. Luke 7:22; 15:30–31; 21:14; Mark 9:45 par. Matt 18:8; Luke 14:13, 21; John 5:3; Acts 3:2; 8:7; 14:8.
[39] Cf., e.g., 2Sam 5:6–8; Job 29:15; Jer 31:8; Matt 11:5/Luke 7:22; Matt 15:30, 31; 21:14; Joh 5:3; also Luke 14:13, 21.
[40] Cf., e.g., Matt 11:5 par. Luke 7:22; 15:30–31; 21:14; John 5:3; Acts 8:7.
[41] Cf. also, e.g., Isa 33:23; 35:5–6; Jer 31:8.
[42] Solevåg 2018. 35.
[43] Cf. Peterson 2006. Esp. 272.
[44] Cf., e.g., CH, Morb. 3.3 L 7.120; 1.4 L 6.146; Coac. 18.353 and 26.467 L 5.658; 688. Cf. Karenberg, Apoplexie. 72; Karenberg, Lähmung. 550.

idation of blood, and its suddenness is explained and/or visualized by a divine "stroke."⁴⁵ In general, dietic, pharmacological, and chirurgic measures were taken.⁴⁶ The numerous inscriptions in Epidauros furthermore illustrate a high demand for healing measures for paralyzed body parts.⁴⁷ In later texts, these etiologies were further developed and different types of motoric, partial, and sensible paralysis differentiated (e.g., πάρεσις, ἀναισθησία, παραπλέγια).⁴⁸ Mobility impairment, however termed, seems to have been a very common dis/ability in antiquity.

4.1.2.3 Socio-Anthropological Implications

Besides the vague designation as παραλυτικός, there are only scarce hints in the Markan text on the condition's implications. The man is described as being carried on a pallet (κράββατος), which seems to designate a form of mat or bed to transport a sick person (cf. Mark 6:55) and is compact enough to be picked up and carried by one person (cf. v. 12).⁴⁹ Furthermore, he is depicted to be integrated in a form of social network since he is brought to Jesus by people with *pistis* who are wishing for his healing. Moreover, he is ordered by Jesus to return to his house (ὕπαγε εἰς τὸν οἶκόν σου, v. 11), which indicates a certain social status. Possibly but not necessarily, his impaired mobility affects his ability to partake in social life and work, which could have led to social and economic descent as implied by texts describing denied or reduced juridical sanity and restricted access to priesthood, Jerusalem and the Temple, military service, and gatherings of the community for people with a mobility impairment (who are often grouped together with those affected by blindness, deafness, muteness, and visible "defects").⁵⁰ As subsequent rabbinic discussion reveals, there also could be a social stigma attached to those classified as "lame" as (congenital) paralysis was regarded as God's punishment, connected to "deviation from sexual norms of rabbinic society [...],

---

45 Cf., e.g., CH, *Morb.* 2.6. L 7.14; 2.8 L 7.16; *Aph.* 6.56 and 7.40 L 4.576; 588. Cf. also Karenberg, *Apoplexie*. 72.
46 Karenberg, *Lähmung*. 550. CH, *Morb.* 3.3 L 7.120; 1.4 L 6.146.
47 Cf. A 3 (fingers); 15; 16; B 15(35)–17(37); 18 (38) (knees); C 14 (57); 17 (60); 21 (64); D4 (70); Herzog 1931. 32.138; LiDonnici 1995. 126; also Cotter 1999. 20–22; von Bendemann in Labahn; Lietaert Peerbolte (ed.) 2006. 114, n. 50.
48 Cf., e.g., Ps. Aristotle, *Probl.* 1.9/860a; 30/954a; Celsus, *Med.* 3.26–27; Caelius, *Acut.* 3.5; Galen, *Loc. aff.* 3.11 and 4.3 K 8.193–201 and 299–234; *Cur. rat. sect.* 5. K 11.262–267.
49 Cf. also, κλίνη in 4:21; 7:4, 30. Cf. Focant 2012. 89, n. 24.
50 Cf., e.g., the begging man with a form of congenital "paralysis" in Acts 3:2. Moreover, Lev 21:16–24; 2Sam 5:8 (cf. also lame and blind sacrificial animals in Deut 15:21; Lev 22:19–25; Mal 1:8, 13); 1Q28ᵃ 2.3–9; CD 15.16; 1QM 7.4; *Sifra, Emor* 3:7 regarding Lev 21:18; *SifBem* 75; 11Q19 45.12–18; moreover, *mSan* 8:4; *SifDev* 219; *ySan* 8:5, 26b; *bSot* 27a–b. Cf. Schwartz, Lame, Lameness III. Judaism.

bastardy or illegitimacy,"[51] and as an openly discussed stigma in marriage policies.[52] Nevertheless, there are accounts of "paralyzed" professionals and a noticeable decrease of its mention in comparison to otherwise common descriptions of mocked and discriminated dis/abilities.[53] For the man here, nothing certain can be put on record other than that his friends wish for his healing, hence regard his condition as undesirable.

4.1.3 The Healing

4.1.3.1 Mere Word Alone

The healing in this narrative is conducted by Jesus ordering the man to rise up, take up his bedding, and go home. It is not uncommon for the Markan healing narratives to put emphasis on Jesus' powerful commands (cf. besides the exorcism accounts, e. g., Mark 1:41; 3:5; 5:41; 7:34, 10:52), yet it is the first time after the paradigmatic introduction of the tangible healer and his curative touch (see ch. 3) that there is no physical connection recounted. Furthermore, no summarizing, generic designations are used to describe his actions or their effect as healing, "saving," or cleansing (cf., e. g., 1:40–42; 3:2 and 5; 5:29 and 34; 8:25; 10:25). The entire mobilization hinges only on this emphatic command.

The authoritative order is intercalated in the anticipation of what is going to happen as part of Jesus' argument for forgiveness (v. 9) and the final evidentiary statement of Jesus' authority (v. 12; cf. εὐθύς). All three sentences are repetitively structured and only grammatically adapted.[54] The reiteration of λέγει τῷ παραλυτικῷ from v. 5 in v. 10 frames Jesus' arguments for the audience, emphasizing the equivalence of the utterances and verifying Jesus' authority to heal *and* forgive,[55] although the use of the passive in v. 5 and the imperative in v. 11 disguise the accountable subject for the decisive forgiving and healing action. However, this stylistic dance around the esoteric identity of the Markan Jesus becomes a common feature by means of healings narrated in the passive.[56] Already in the account of the man with *lepra*, he is "made clean" (ἐκαθαρίσθη; 1:42 cf. also v. 41), yet

---

51 Cf. ibid. 662.
52 Cf., e. g., *tBer* 6:3; *bNed* 20a; *bTaan* 4a–b; *bKet* 17a, 77a; *tKet* 7:10; *mKet* 3:5; *bKet* 39a.
53 Cf., e. g., *tBQ* 6:2; 9:2; *bSan* 90 a–b. Cf. Schwartz, Lame, Lameness III. Judaism. 662; also *PesR* 36; *ShirZ* 1:15.
54 Cf. v. 9: ἔγειρε καὶ ἆρον τὸν κράβαττόν σου καὶ περιπάτει; v. 11: ἔγειρε ἆρον τὸν κράβαττόν σου καὶ ὕπαγε εἰς τὸν οἶκόν σου; v. 12: καὶ ἠγέρθη καὶ εὐθὺς ἄρας τὸν κράβαττον ἐξῆλθεν.
55 Cf. Dewey 1980. 69.
56 See Pascut 2017. 160–163, for an extensive analyis of the following.

the entire narrative focuses on Jesus' wish and command to make him clean (see 3.3). Furthermore, in the following account, the withered hand "is restored" (3:5, ἀπεκατεστάθη), yet the narrative aims at Jesus' healing activity on the Sabbath as a central element in the gospel's plot, and again the cure directly succeeds his command (see below). Thirdly, Jesus heals the woman with the issue of blood somewhat "passively," yet it is his physical δύναμις held responsible for her healing (5:30; see 5.2.3). Lastly, in Jesus' very actively depicted healing of the deaf-mute man, the passively formulated command (7:34, διανοίχθητι) and following implementation (7:35, ἠνοίγησαν and ἐλύθη) are in the end credited to Jesus in the chorus: καλῶς πάντα πεποίηκεν (7:37). Similarly, the passive voice in Jesus' forgiving statement here in Mark 2:5 causes offense directed at *Jesus'* authority. Although it also could imply that God is the source of forgiveness and Jesus "only" the enacting personnel,[57] as the power to forgive sin is commonly assigned to only divine beings or humans with divine authority such as prophets, priests, and characters related to the messiah,[58] the entire conflict and thereby narrative hinges on the understanding that by his "passive" utterances, *Jesus* heals and claims to forgive.[59] Furthermore, a human declaration of God's forgiveness is highly unusual in the Jewish tradition; only a few accounts witness to prophets and holy men who by prayer attain YHWH's forgiveness or publicly declare it was granted.[60] Only YHWH, the one God (εἷς ὁ θεός), has the power to forgive as the scribes formulate their reason for accusing Jesus of blasphemy:[61] with his spoken word of forgiveness, Jesus aligns himself, the Son of Man, with the authority of this one God.[62]

Excursus: The Markan "Son of Man"
The unusual Greek Semitism "Son of Man" is ambiguous in its concrete meaning[63] as it occurs here for the first time in the Gospel of Mark, heightening the audience's mystification about this new designation.[64] Beforehand, Jesus was named the "Son of God" (1:1, 11, 24). The two epithets reflect and there-

---

57 Cf., e.g., Bratcher; Nida 1961. 76; Malbon 2009. 184–185; Pascut 2012; Pascut 2017. 159.
58 Cf. Pascut 2017. 3–9.
59 Cf. ibid. 168, also, Focant 2012. 95.
60 Cf. Exod 32:32; Num 14:19; Job 42:10^{LXX}; but 2Sam 12:13; Ps 85:1–3; moreover, Collins 2007. 185.
61 Which counts as a fatal offense according to Exod 34:6–7; Isa 43:25; 44:22, and Mark 14:64; moreover, Pascut 2017. 127.
62 Cf. Deut 6:4–5. Cf. Boring 2006. 77; Collins 2007. 185.
63 Cf. fundamentally, e.g., Vermès in Black (ed.) 1967; Casey 1987; Robinson in Elsas; Colpe; Haffke (ed.) 1994; Casey 1995. The complex linguistic analysis of the development of the Aramaic root provoked a long research history on the redaction, tradition, and socio-historical development of this epithet of Jesus. As the Aramaic origin *bar-('æ)näsch/bar-('æ)näschā'* has a more generic and generalizing meaning in the sense of "everyone"/"everyman," often used self-reflectively by the speak-

fore contrast each other due to semantical similarity and "linguistic assonance and affinity."[65] However, the "Son of Man" title advances to the fundamental and characteristic designation of the Markan Jesus as it is always given self-referentially by Jesus himself and explicated with concrete predications that encompass all stages of the narrative development of Jesus' character—namely and firstly, his powerful earthly mission (cf. esp. 2:1–3:6), which prepares, secondly, his suffering and renunciation (cf. esp. 8:31) and is, thirdly, connected to his current and eschatological authority (cf. esp. 8:38) all tied together in Mark 14:62–64.[66] Foremost, in the two occurrences here in Mark 2, Jesus uses the epithet to refer to himself and explicate its meaning by the two divine "prerogatives he [then] has assumed": to forgive sins, which, "as the rhetorical question in 2:7 correctly anticipates (εἰ μὴ εἷς ὁ θεός), [belongs] only to God,"[67] and to govern Sabbath regulations (2:28). Hence, particularly together with ἐπὶ τῆς γῆς (v. 10), the "Son of Man" claims a divine authority that is explicitly linked with his earthly deeds and expressed in the ensuing fatal βλασφημία-conspiracy (3:6 and 14:62–64).[68] Later in the gospel narrative, the designation describes the suffering, death, and resurrection of the Son of Man,[69] the eschatological and judicial return of Jesus as an eschatological authority.[70] Since it characterizes more than Jesus' concrete authoritative deeds and suffering but also interprets it as a divine and eschatological scheme, it marks a characteristic self-designation of the Markan Jesus' identity and his singular, exclusive authority, which reveals to be the interpretative foundation for his χριστός and υἱὸς θεοῦ denominations.[71] It turns out irrelevant whether or not the audience of the gospel was familiar with such an eschatological typology since its ambiguous basis becomes somewhat self-explanatory when traced through the entire gospel narrative of Jesus' life, death, resurrection, and promised return. At this point, however, the authority of the Son of Man is effective "on earth."[72]

---

er (e. g., "someone like me") it contrasts the determined forms in the Synoptics ("[*the*] son of [*the*] man") particularly in the reprised passages of Dan 7 in Mark 13:26 and 14:62. In any case, the Markan text uses the title precisely to express Jesus' exclusivity.
64 Cf. Chronis 2005. 464.
65 Ibid. 463.
66 Cf. Schröter 2001. 161–168.
67 Chronis 2005. 475.
68 Cf. ibid. 477. Cf. also Luke 7:33–34/Matt 11:18–19; Luke 9:58/Matt 8:20; Luke 12:10/Matt 12:32; Luke 19:10.
69 Cf. Mark 8:31; 9:9, 31; 10:33–34, 45; 14:21, 41. Cf. the parallel accounts in Matthew and Luke.
70 Cf. Mark 8:38; 13:26; 14:62. Cf. also Luke 17:24, 26–27, 30/Matt 24:27, 37–39; Matt 10:23; 13:41; 16:27; 19:28; 25:31–46; Luke 6:22; 12:8–9; 17:22. While the tradition behind the epithet *"the* son of man" remains largely unclear, an intertextual relation to Dan 7:13–14 together with occurrences of the title in the book of Enoch (37–71, esp. 62, 70–71) refer to an interpretation as an (individual!) eschatological judge, cf. Mark 8:38; 13:26; 14:62; 4Esr 13:2; Focant 2012. 94; du Toit in Schröter; Jacobi (ed.) 2022 [2017]. However, it is doubtful that this relates to a fixed and concrete concept or typology of eschatological authority. Mainly it is assumed, that the occurrences regarding an eschatological meaning in the Synoptics and the book of Enoch are parallel developments, cf. ibid. 523. Within the different occurrences in the NT (the gospels and Acts) the Son of Man is always found with a double determination (except for John 5:27) and is always spoken of by Jesus (except John 9:35 and Acts 7:56).
71 Cf., e.g., Schröter 1997. 451–457; Schröter 2001. Esp. 174–176; du Toit in Schröter; Jacobi (ed.) 2022 [2017]. 525.
72 Cf., e.g., Focant 2012. 99; Dewey 1980. 125.

In summary, the passive in Jesus' speech act emphasizes the action, with the actor intriguingly implied by the context,[73] in the case of Mark 2:5, 10–11, alluding to the Son of Man's agency and authority in forgiveness and healing by mere word alone.[74] Jesus even highlights his "method" in his argumentative question: is it easier to *say* one or the other? This not only refers to v. 2 and his teaching but shows that "in both cases it is a matter of powerful, effective, authoritative speech."[75]

Finally, his command with its three actions proves the man's ability to walk, pick up, and carry—all motions requiring the entire musculoskeletal system.

4.1.3.2 A Body in Motion

As established in the analysis of the healing of the mother-in-law in Mark 1:29–31 (see 3.2), ἤγειρεν is a common lexeme in Markan healing narratives (cf. 1:31; 2:9, 11; 3:3; 5:41; 10:49) and is often connected with a physical "hand-seizing" of Jesus to help or "raise" the formerly bedridden patients to their feet (1:31; 5:41; 9:27).[76] In each narrative, it serves to drastically visualize and powerfully demonstrate the effected healing from passive and weak patients to an active, physically autonomous existence, here furthermore underscored by the actions αἴρω τὸν κράβαττον and ἐξέρχομαι (v. 11; cf. διακονέω in 1:31; περιπατέω in 5:42).[77] The man needs no additional assistance in getting from his bedding, which emphasizes his transformation to physical mobility. In Mark's following narratives, the term unfolds a heightened and, in context, eschatological nuance by describing the resurrection of the dead (together with ἀνίστημι).[78] While in its first instance, the lexeme here refers to its basic meaning (the man gets up), the framing theological debate, however, quite literally widens the scope of the risen man to a bigger picture.

F In Focus: Markan Healing and Forgiveness (with Consideration of 9:42–48)
Considering the parallel structure of this episode with previous healing narratives and the prior emphasis on the highly successful and exorbitant healing ministry of Jesus (cf. 1:25–26, 34, 41–42; see above), he acts contrary to the expectations of the audience when he does not immediately heal the man with the inability to walk

---

73 Cf. Pascut 2017. 160.
74 Cf. ibid. 162.
75 Collins 2007. 186.
76 Cf. also Acts 9:40–41, but Acts 9:34 (without a helping hand).
77 Cf. Boring 2006. 77–78; Focant 2012. 89, n. 26.
78 Cf. Mark 6:14, 16; 12:26; 14:28; 16:6, 14. Cf. esp. Matt 10:8 and ch. 5.2 and 7 on the narratives of the un/animated children in Mark 5:41–42 and 9:25–27. Cf. BDAG, s.v.; Klaiber, ἐγείρω; Kremer, ἐγείρω. 899–901; LN, s.v.; LSJ, s.v.; Montanari, s.v.; Oepke, ἀνίστημι/ἐξανίστημι; Oepke, ἐγείρω.

but declares the forgiveness of his sins. This startling speech act of Jesus discloses the lack of an explicitly described intention or petition of the man and/or his friends and is emphasized by Jesus' intimate and endearing address of the man as τέκνον, which stands in contrast to his harsh tone toward the *leper* only a few verses prior.[79] Precisely this emphasized element of surprise suggests a connection of healing and forgiveness.

However, the passage does not make a causal connection explicit. Due to the narrative's lack of an anamnesis, diagnosis, or any explanation of the concrete dis/ability and its potential causes whatsoever, it moreover eludes any punchline regarding (parental) sin as a cause for the man's condition. Any nuance of such an implicit assumption is refuted in the following: First, Jesus speaks the word of forgiveness (v. 5) and then heals the man (vv. 10–11) in two separate acts;[80] the man does not walk after his sins are forgiven. Moreover, the connection between healing and forgiveness is merely made by a spoken argument of Jesus in v. 9 that focuses entirely on his authority and ability to heal.[81] This is enforced by the disrupted sentence in v. 10 and the shift in addressees from the scribes to the man—grammatically and narratively, the acts are separated and literally only contrasted to illustrate Jesus' authority (ἵνα δὲ …). In addition, no other Markan healing narrative features a forgiving act prior or connected to physical transformation.[82]

While the Hebrew Bible/Old Testament[83] and Greco-Roman conceptions,[84] as well as later attested rabbinic discourses,[85] feature—throughout their various gen-

---

[79] Cf. also 10:24, and, e.g., Williams 1994. 100; Collins 2007. 185.
[80] Different to Klumbies in Zimmermann (ed.) 2013. 236.
[81] Cf. Boring 2006. 76.
[82] Cf. Focant 2012. 95.
[83] Here, dis/ability can express individual and collective behavioral consequences in diverse forms, yet there is also a strong negation of a physical "acts-consequences-construct" in the sapiential literature, cf., e.g., Exod 15:26; Lev 26:25; Deut 7:15; 28:20–22, 27–28; 32:39; 2Chr 7:13; Ezek 14:19–20; Ps 91:10; Sir 38:15; 28:23; also Exod 20:5/Deut 5:9; 2Sam 24:10–17; Job 22:1–11; 34:11; Sir 27:25–27; Jub 4:32; 2Macc 9:5–6; 13:7–8. Cf. Gosbell 2018. 11–12, 124–126. Especially in the book of Psalms, sin and ailments are often vital parts of the lamented suffering, as both are placed in a spatial realm of experienced distance from God (e.g., Ps 103:2–5; 41:4–5; 53:4–5, 11–12; 107[106]:17–20; Isa 33:24; 41[40]:2; 38:16–17; 2Sam 12:13), and are at times even consequentially intertwined (cf., e.g., Ps 38; 107:17–18), yet are also connected to portray anger about non-disabled sinners (cf., e.g., Ps 73:2–5; Gosbell 2018. 125). A concrete conception of the interplay of sin and dis/ability, as well as healing and forgiveness remains difficult to distinguish and narrow down for each individual passage, let alone summarize for this complex and literary and culturally diverse corpus.
[84] Cf., e.g., Aelian, *Var. hist.* 3.43; *Nat. an.* 11.31; Hesiod, *Op.* 281–284; Plutarch, *Mor.* 561c; furthermore, Solevåg 2018. 65–66; Collins 2007. 192; Kelley 2007. 80–81.

res—interpretations of dis/ability as a manifestation, consequence, condition, association, or even social or metaphorical interpretation of sin, the New Testament seldomly broaches this subject.[86] Only the Gospel of John explicitly explores it in 5:14 and 9:1–38, while Jas 5:15–16 stays ambiguous on the direct consequential connection of the two but describes healing and then forgiveness as two separate acts of salvation of the "faithful." In any case, as it is here in Mark 2:1–12, dis/ability is literally or metaphorically connected to sin in contexts that convey God(s) as the governing principle, as the explanation of human experience, or as a mighty agent(s) by forgiving individual or corporal sins as well as by healing every ailment.[87] However, an explicit consequential connection between the man's condition and sin, respectively healing and forgiveness, is not made and in no other passage within in the Gospel of Mark explained or implied.

Rather, the narrative enforces that forgiveness is unlike healing by implementing Jesus' proclamation of forgiveness as an element of surprise since healing is anticipated and actively, although not verbally, requested. When Jesus then explicitly compares the two acts, he prioritizes, by his prior powerful statement, forgiveness over healing.

This priority is also reflected in the only other Markan passage that features a connection of sinful behavior with dis/ability. Although the so-called word of autoamputation in 9:42–48 is embedded in an entirely different context, it reflects similar conceptions: after every healing narrative, apart from the exceptional story of blind Bartimaeus in 10:46–52, has been told (see 7.1.3), Jesus—once again and for the last time in Capernaum[88]—sternly explains to his disciples the consequence of σκανδαλίζω behavior. Embedded in a context of teaching and interpretation of his deeds (especially his exorcising power) to his disciples (9:33) and the group of the Twelve (9:35), Jesus explicates that body parts (hand, foot, eye) that cause one to "stumble" or "fall into sin" (σκανδαλίζω) would, within his eschatological horizon, better be forcefully removed (ἀποκόπτω for the extremities, ἐκβάλλω for the eye). An impaired earthly life, namely being κυλλός (with a cut-off

---

[85] Cf. for rabbinic writings, e.g., "leprosy" as punishment in Num 12:10–11; Deut 24:9; SifDev 275.1; WayR 16:1–7; DevR 6:8; impairments of the eyes for (metaphorically) visual transgressions in bBQ 93a; Judg 16:21 and bSot 9b; Gen 27:1; 1Kgs 14:4 and BerR 65. Cf. also Num 14:18; Jer 31:29–30; Ezek 18:1–5 regarding congenital punishment. See furthermore, Marx 1992. 315–316; Gosbell 2018. 125–126, n. 70. Cf. also Josephus, B.J. 3.375; Tob 3:3–4. Although the simple equation found in bNed 41a is often consulted in this regard it presents just one conviction amongst many others.
[86] Cf. esp. Zimmermann in Thomas; Karle (ed.) 2009.
[87] Cf., e.g., Ps 103:2–5; 41:4–5; 53:4–5, 11–12; 107[106]:17–20; Isa 33:24; 41[40]:2; 38:16–17; 2Sam 12:13.
[88] Cf. Mark 1:21; 2:1, and finally 9:33.

hand), χωλός (with a cut-off foot), or μονόφθαλμος (one-eyed), can prevent one from an unimpaired yet "sinful" life. While the latter leads to an afterlife in "Gehenna" (a common *chiffre* for eschatological punishment),[89] the former leads to a more promising, rewarding "life" (ζωή; see also positively μισθός in v. 42).[90] As other Markan passages with σκανδαλίζω convey the meaning of an emotional outrage and offense (4:17; 6:3; 14:27, 29), the strong, common, and comprehensive eschatological consequence here envisages an understanding in line with sinful and offensive behavior. Furthermore, from the macro context, it seems reasonable to assume the offense concerns Jesus and his message (cf. esp. the use of πιστεύω in v. 42), perhaps from a community perspective (v. 42).[91] This is underscored by the setting in a group instruction and the very personal phrasing (cf. the pronouns in second-person singular) that addresses the audience directly. Then the general σκανδαλίζω (illustrated by hand, foot, and eye) visualizes *pars pro toto* disruptive human behavior with eschatological consequences,[92] yet not a physical punishment or penalty. Jesus pictures an afterlife that can be reached impaired but not "having done harm." Of course, the enigmatic wording (especially vv. 48–50 but also the mention of Gehenna) points more toward a metaphorical or rhetorical, even hyperbolic, comparison for emphasis.[93] Nevertheless, this notion hinges on the comparison of impaired but fulfilled, even eternal, life and unimpaired damnation[94] and is thus based on the undesirability of dis/ability.[95] This dis/ability invective passage places amputated physicality in a list of precedence before sin, hence opposing an equation or direct succession of sin and dis/ability. Rather, deformity can prevent sin. While this does not necessarily shed light on notions of eschatological physicality, the passage clearly disagrees with the stigma of sin on the dis/abled body when Jesus places lived corporality in the service of the *basileia*

---

[89] Literally it designates a valley south of Jerusalem, which is used to describe eschatological torments especially by fire, cf. 1Kgs 16:3; 21:6; 23:10; Jer 7:30–8:3; 19:6; *1En.* 54:1–7; 91:9; 100:9; 103:8; *2Bar.* 44:15; 59:2; further, Isa 66:24.
[90] Together with "the kingdom of God" in v. 47, this suggests eternal life. Cf. 2Macc 7:14; *Pss. Sol.* 14:10; *T.Jud.* 25:4.
[91] Cf. Focant 2012. 389, 391.
[92] Therefore, the rather detailed and specific interpretation that the saying has a sexual connotation referring to pedophilia (v. 42), masturbation (hand), adultery (foot as a euphemism for the penis), and lustful desires (eye) cannot be supported. Cf., e.g., Collins 2007. 452.
[93] Cf. Focant 2012. 390.
[94] Cf. Moss in Melcher; Parsons; Yong (ed.) 2018. 292. However, the topic of eschatological healing, i.e., a healed resurrection or resurrected deformity is not discussed. Cf., e.g., *2Bar.* 50:2; *QohR.* 1:6; Isa 29:18; 35:5–7; moreover, *bSan* 91a; *QohR* 1:4.
[95] Cf. Moss; Schipper (ed.) 2011. 1.

with an eschatological horizon and ideal.[96] Again, dis/ability is used as a narrative prosthesis for the message of the gospel, here the importance of *basileia* behavior.

Thus, Jesus' word of *forgiveness* in Mark 2:5 when *healing* is expected reflects his priorities as specified in 9:42–48. In both passages, deviating physicality is used to convey a nuanced image of Jesus' mission. While Mark 9 focuses on his teachings with a general, eschatological significance, in Mark 2, his authority and identity are at the forefront as the narrative aims at confirming Jesus' authority to forgive sins as the Son of Man in close unity with God (see below),[97] which is difficult to prove, let alone narrate. The dis/ability then functions as a narrative prosthesis to account for the effect of the nonvisible, more difficult act of declaring forgiveness.

4.1.4 Interpretation

The dis/ability of the man in Mark 2:1–12 is presented as an inability to walk. No more details on the etiology, diagnosis, prognosis, or social implications are given, which is common for the ancient presentations of "paralysis" (παραλυτικός, παραλύω and παράλυσις). Impaired mobility is, however, a frequently mentioned dis/ability in antiquity. Its inherent physical dependence is reflected in the man's supportive friends and his healed physicality that enables him to independently leave the scene. The change is drastic and dramatic, visible for all to see, which serves as a contrasting illustration of the ensuing conflict with Jesus' opponents and, secondly, as a clear demonstration of Jesus' declaration of forgiveness and ministry.

Firstly, the man's motionlessness serves to display the opponent's response toward Jesus. Not only do the narrative's staging and structure depict (opened) barriers and (un)confined spaces, but the characters are also (un)barred and (in)accessible:[98] the (healed) impaired mobility of the man that is presented by his active *pistis* practicing and brave friends invertedly corresponds with the spiritual and physical posture of the scribes, who are sitting, silently thinking, and persistently judging in their hearts.[99] Even as the formerly motionless, vertical man leaves horizontally (see 4.1.1), they remain motionless and rigid.

Secondly and more importantly, the audience is startled when Jesus first forgives the man instead of healing him. After all, the dependent dis/ability of the

---

[96] Cf. ibid. 2; Moss in Melcher; Parsons; Yong (ed.) 2018. 294.
[97] Cf. Williams 1994. 100.
[98] Cf. Focant 2012. 94.
[99] Cf. Klumbies in Zimmermann (ed.) 2013. 236–237.

man was dramatically introduced right after the gospel extensively established the successful healing ministry of Jesus. While sin often serves to explain physical deviance,[100] this is not the aim here nor in any other passage of Mark's gospel (see F. In Focus: Markan Healing and Forgiveness). Rather, dis/ability is reevaluated within an eschatological context, promoting Jesus' teaching of forgiveness as even more desirable than healing with regard to his eschatological horizon (cf. 9:42–48). Jesus forgives first and then heals. Both acts are performed by mere word alone, which puts the entire focus on his authority and renders the healing to an "empirical" verification for the parallel but separate and not attestable act of divine forgiveness.[101]

The reality of this speech act is underscored by the fact that Jesus is described to perceive the scribes' silent and interior accusation "in his spirit" (ἐπιγνοὺς ὁ Ἰησοῦς τῷ πνεύματι αὐτοῦ, 2:8), an ability that is often credited to only divine characters, respectively God alone,[102] specifically with reference to the heart of the interlocuter (cf. also Mark 3).[103] The reference to Jesus' discerning πνεῦμα furthermore corresponds with the Markan characterization of him from the beginning of the gospel, where he is bestowed with *holy* pneuma (1:8, 10, 12) in opposition to the sphere of evil (1:21–28, cf. 3:28–30 and B. In Focus: Mark's Jesus and Opposing Forces). To the audience, Jesus' word of forgiveness, proven successful by the impressive healing, is yet another demonstration of his divinity in close unity with God,[104] summarized in the self-given epithet ὁ υἱὸς τοῦ ἀνθρώπου (2:10). This links the account strongly to the gospel's previous characterization of Jesus, where his ἐξουσία is revealed in his teaching, exorcising, and curing deeds (see 3.1 on Mark 1:22, 27), now with the addition of his declaration of forgiveness of sins. In the following, it furthermore relates to his interpretative power with regard to the Sabbath and law regulations (2:27–28; 3:4) and his exorcising ability (3:15), which he then passes on to his disciples (6:7; cf. 13:34). Lastly, in 11:27–33, Jesus has to justify the *legitimatization* of all of the above—his earthly life, teachings, and deeds—in front of the accusing high priests, scribes, and elders

---

100 Cf. Solevåg 2018. 41.
101 Cf. Boring 2006. 77; Focant 2012. 93; furthermore, Dewey 1980. 77; Hentrich in Breitwieser (ed.) 2012. 116.
102 Cf. 1Sam 16:7; 1Kgs 8:39; 1Chr 28:9; Ps 7:10; 94:11; 43/44:22; 139:2–4; Prov 15:11; Jer 11:20; 17:9–10; Sir 42:18–20; Job 7:20; Josephus, *C. Ap.* 2.181; and Collins 2007. 185; Pascut 2017. 61.
103 Cf., e.g., Luke 16:15; Acts 1:24; 15:8; Rom 8:27; 1Thess 2:4; Rev 2:23; also Klumbies in Zimmermann (ed.) 2013. 240.
104 To the same result comes Pascut 2017, in his thorough analysis and comparison of concepts of "Forgiveness and Divine Identity in Ancient Judaism and Mark 2:1–12" by applying social scientific models of identity.

in Jerusalem.¹⁰⁵ Hence, his claim to forgive spins the narrative thread on his intriguing identity and authority further and is even explicitly issued by Jesus' argumentative yet esoteric statements.¹⁰⁶ This is met with growing malevolence and skepticism by his opponents and astonishing praise (of God) by the large crowds: "Jesus neither denies nor asserts that others have such authority, but points to his healing as evidence that at any rate one man, himself, does have it. Thus he claims more than his deed demonstrates, and the obliqueness of the self-reference serves to make his authority not so much a claim as an inference which his hearers may draw for themselves from what they see"¹⁰⁷ and will learn in the storyline to come —hinging all on the visually impressive dis/ability.

Moreover, after the healing, the man leaves the scene with the use of his entirely transformed skeleton-muscular system. The lexeme ἐγείρω describes his rise from the horizontal to the vertical, which can imply an additional eschatological nuance.¹⁰⁸ Within the narrative's context of forgiveness and divine authority, as well as in the entire complex of Mark 2:1–3:6, this eschatological potential is enforced. Especially as the center of the entire section, Jesus' general saying in Mark 2:20 reprises the divine identity and eschatological claim attached to the Son of Man epithet and develops it further by the use of the bridegroom imagery. Thereby, the presence of Jesus is equated with God's within an eschatological timeframe that is connected to Jesus' mission.¹⁰⁹ All of this immerses this narrative in an eschatological light as the use of the lexeme ἐγείρω also alludes to a resurrection from the dead.¹¹⁰ This passage envisages a piece of the gospel narrative's eschatological puzzle.

Overall, the narrative employs this dis/ability in the context of sin and forgiveness and of restoration and even resurrection (see below) to convey an intriguing image of Jesus' authority, identity, and mission that is attractive and enabling to those willing to "faithfully" and actively follow but outranging to those "paralyzed" in the judgment of their hearts. Jesus' message is put in a dis/ability invective, visually engaging, and memorable nutshell and serves as an important step in the

---

105 Cf. Mark 1:22, 27; 2:10; 3:15; 6:7; 11:28, 29, 33; 13:34.
106 To Zimmermann 2007. 564–572, it is important to differentiate between the ἐξουσία of the Son of Man and the δύναμις of εἷς ὁ θεός (v. 7), similar to other εἷς θεός-texts of the gospel; different to Hofius in Hofius (ed.) 2000. 41–42.
107 Bauckham in Bauckham (ed.) 2008. 101.
108 See ch. 3.2.3.2.
109 Cf. YHWH's and Israel's relationship in, e.g., Isa 49:14–26; 54:5–8; 61:10; 62:4–5; Jer 2:2; Ezek 16:8; Hos 2:1–3:5; moreover, Collins 2007. 199.
110 This is taken up as such in the narrative's early reception art on sarcophagus and catacombs, cf. Dresken-Weiland 2010. 20–21, 259–266.

gospel narrative away from the unchallenged popularity of the first chapter toward the presupposed passion (and return) of Jesus.[111]

It is precisely this deployment of contrasting deviating bodies that establishes a physical norm that illustrates—nevertheless by drawing on dis/ability invective imagery—a priority of an active response to Jesus' message (παραλυτικός and opponents), forgiveness of sins (forgiveness and healing), and an eschatological standard (restoration and resurrection) over immobile, earthly limbs.

4.2 Mark 3:1–6: A Withered Hand and Petrified Hearts

4.2.1 Introduction to the Narrative

The ensuing healing narrative starts with an introduction of the setting in the aorist as a completed action: Again, πάλιν, Jesus entered a synagogue,[112] which (quite literally) refers to the episode in Capernaum right in the beginning of the gospel in 1:21–28 and 1:39 (see 3.1; 2.2; cf. 2:1). In Mark, Jesus only enters a synagogue for teaching purposes again in 6:2, where skepticism about and suspiciousness of him and his authority leave him seemingly powerless. Afterward, the synagogue is replaced by the temple as a setting for his teachings, while the synagogue becomes a narrative place *in* his teachings (12:39; 13:9).[113] The setting is further complemented by two descriptions in (periphrastic) imperfect, casting light on the ongoing presence of the man with the impaired hand and the watching witnesses.

The time specification is then given one verse later: The following narrative unfolds on the Sabbath, which is problematized in the same breath. Healing in this context seems to be classified as a misdemeanor worthy of some sort of accusation (κατηγορέω, v. 2). Thereby, the lexeme παρατηρέω hints at knowledge about Jesus' healing ability and his disputable—and, just a few verses before, disputed—understanding of Sabbath regulations (Mark 2:23–28; see above).[114] Whether or not it is regarded as public knowledge that Jesus healed on a Sabbath before cannot be concluded from this text. However, the parallel setting of time and place in Mark 1:29 reminds the audience of Jesus' exorcism that, to the contrary, was not composed to depict a problematic action. Rather, Jesus' authoritative deeds cause amazement and popularity (see 2.6.2). However, the setting here in Mark 3, just

---

111 Cf. Grünstäudl; Schiefer Ferrari 2012. 645.
112 Cf. Breytenbach in Breytenbach (ed.) 2021a [2019]. 197.
113 Cf. Malbon 1991. 122. See also E. In Focus: Healing Spaces in Mark.
114 Cf. esp., Haacker; Schütz, *τηρέω*. 170–172; Balz; Schneider, *παρατηρέω*. 81.

as the macro context prepared, is already introduced with an atmosphere of skepticism and malevolence (παρατηρέω, κατηγορέω). Interestingly, in the opponents' pensive and hostile intrigue, the term θεραπεύω is used, which only occurs in the Markan summaric accounts to generalize Jesus' and his disciples' healing activity with emphasis on the effect for the patients from the narrator's point of view (see 2.1.1).[115] Thereby, knowledge about the efficacious healing actions of Jesus has spread. By then the audience must also already expect a healing to unfold (the way has been paved by the previous narratives), even if it is—or, rather, especially because it is—embedded in a context of controversy over Jesus' authority, as in Mark 2:1–12 and in the preceding debate over the Sabbath (Mark 2:23–28; cf. ἔξεστιν in 2:24, 26; 3:4 and τοῖς σάββασιν in 2:23, 24; 3:4; see below).[116]

After this initial staging, the storyline unfolds in two narratological circles, structured by space, alternating groups of people, and three speech acts with λέγει: In the inner circle, Jesus converses with the man (ἄνθρωπος) who has a "withered" hand and is introduced together with the setting in v. 1 (periphrastic imperfect). Just like time and place, he is part of the story's initial inventory. This changes promptly when Jesus, the only one who speaks explicitly in this narrative, calls him to the center (v. 3). Here, he remains ostentatious to the end of the account, for all to see in direct and personal interaction with Jesus. This inner circle is surrounded with hostile spectators who are only in the end (v. 6), at least partially, defined as οἱ Φαρισαῖοι.[117]

To them, Jesus raises his voice from the center, asking them a double question regarding their nonverbalized, secret, animus intentions of finding an allegation against him. He opens with a rabbinic question formula and then formulates an antithetical question that is climactic in its second part:[118] ἔξεστιν τοῖς σάββασιν ἀγαθὸν ποιῆσαι ἢ κακοποιῆσαι, ψυχὴν σῶσαι ἢ ἀποκτεῖναι; Due to the rabbinic style of this parallelism membrorum, to "do good" and "save lives" probably stand in direct connection with doing God's will, the Tora.[119] Within the context of the narrative, however, it is tied to the anticipated and scorned healing on a Sabbath, heightening Jesus' question to a controversial thesis on Tora interpretation and to a critique of his opponents' opinion via the rhetorical dichotomy of options: Not committing to the positive action means facilitating a negative deed. No actual

---

115 Cf. Mark 1:34; 3:10; 6:5, 13; and Rüegger 2002. 88–91.
116 Cf. Dewey 1980. 100; Williams 1994. 102–103.
117 Already in Mark 2:24 the Pharisees are implemented as Jesus' opposing interlocutors regarding this first Sabbath controversy, almost framing these two Sabbath narratives with the ultimate identification as Jesus' adversaries in 3:6.
118 Cf. Doering in Doering; Waubke; Wilk (ed.) 2008. 231.
119 Cf. Doering 1999. 450.

substitute action to doing good/healing is pointed to, but, rather, doing evil equals not healing. The second part of Jesus' question heightens the conflict and suspense even more: He parallelizes doing good—what the Tora commands and healing— with saving a life; "not doing good is doing evil, and, indeed, not saving a 'soul' is killing it."[120] Here again there is no "neutral" failure in rendering assistance within Jesus' interpretation of what is allowed on the Sabbath; there is only killing (see below).[121] With the reaction of Jesus' opponents to this question, the narrative breaks with its simple paratactic καὶ structure, inserting οἱ δὲ ἐσιώπων and thereby marking the narrative's central passage with this δὲ-cesura: The listeners remain continuously (imperfect) silent. Only Jesus' reaction, narrated again (v. 1) in the aorist as completed and quick action, reflects their thinking:[122] He looks *around* with anger (ὀργῃ) and grief (συλλυπέω) at them and their "hardened hearts" before ordering the man next to him to stretch out his healed hand. The usual amazement about Jesus' authority displayed in Mark's healing narratives is this time replaced with the immediate decision of his (finally defined) opponents: the Pharisees who, due to their heart condition (see below), leave the synagogue to continuously take council (inceptive imperfect) with the so-called Herodians (probably referring to a local court or council)[123] and decide to "destroy" (ἀπόλλυμι) Jesus. As Jesus entered the synagogue in the beginning of the narrative, they leave it now as the narrative fades out.[124]

The characters in this narrative oppose one another the same way they are facing each other within the spatial structure of the narrative: The man with the withered hand, who is introduced and identified with his dis/ability two times (vv. 1, 3), stands with Jesus (who was lastly explicitly named in 2:19) in the center and is together with him the only one who moves and changes. Jesus is the only one talking. As in Mark 2:1–12, his speech acts are emphatically introduced at three points in the narrative with the use of λέγει in historical present (vv. 3, 4, 5). This is followed by two imperatives and the double question, which further engages the audience. Jesus is also the only one showing emotions (v. 5) when looking at his adversaries. They, however, silently spy on him, remain unmoved spectators surrounding the two, and only in the end react vigorously when leaving the scene. The only two subclauses in the narrative reveal their (secret) intentions (ἵνα in v. 2, ὅπως in v. 6). These harsh opposites are also featured in the direct

---

120 Back 1995. 112.
121 Cf., e.g., Klumbies in Volp; Horn; Zimmermann (ed.) 2016.
122 Cf. Rüegger 2002. 106.
123 The mention of this historically obscure group gives the accusation an additional political connotation. Cf. Doering 1999. 441–442; Collins 2007. 210, esp. n. 175; Focant 2012. 124.
124 Cf. Focant 2012. 119.

speech of the narrative: good/evil, save life/kill.¹²⁵ As Jesus saves a life (v. 4), they plot to destroy one, also on the Sabbath (εὐθὺς).¹²⁶

4.2.2 Images of Dis/ability

4.2.2.1 A Withered Hand

Right in v. 1, the deviating appendage is described—and by that, the man introduced—with the term ξηραίνω, which can be translated as "to dry, dry out, desiccate, wither."¹²⁷ In the New Testament, this lexeme is most often used to designate the perishing of vegetation and plants due to a lack of access to life-sustaining irrigation;¹²⁸ in Rev 16:12, it designates the ebbing of the river Euphrates. Interestingly, only the Gospel of Mark uses it three times to describe physical conditions: the issue of blood *subsides* in Mark 5:29, the entire body of the boy in Mark 9:18 becomes *stiff*, and, here, the hand is *dried out* (3:1). Similarly, in 3Kgdms 13:4–6, Jerobeam stretched out his hand, which was instantly withered by God as a punishment and left him unable to draw it back. Both lexemes, ξηραίνω and its Hebrew counterpart יבשׁ, share a similar spectrum of meaning and are mainly used to describe parched vegetation and water streams but also body parts to convey despair and hopelessness and, in the case of Jerobeam, a hand with atrophy or paralysis.¹²⁹ However, the LXX and other ancient sources use κατερρύηκεν to describe cases of vegetation dieback, not the New Testament term ξηραίνω. Hence, when assuming a precise, nuanced, and intentional choice of words for the entire Markan narrative, the figurative passages of the *dried* seeds in the parable of the sower (4:6) and the *dried* fig tree (11:20–21; in both instances ξηραίνω) can be read in line with the other physical references as representations of humanity. This in turn can thereby heighten the ailment of the man with the withered hand and the symptom of the possessed boy to a spiritual level.¹³⁰ However, this disregards the positive connotation of the subsided issue of blood. Rather, ξηραίνω in Mark implies a very basic absence of an operative fluid with regard to organic substances when relating to the human body, maybe even in reference to the doctrines of the humors.¹³¹ In

---

125 Cf. ibid. 119.
126 Cf. Broadhead 1992b. 262–263.
127 Cf., e.g., BDAG, s.v.; Kuhn, ξηραίνω; LN, s.v. 23.173, 76.80–82; LSJ, s.v.; Montanari, s.v.
128 Cf. Jas 1:11 and Mark 11:20, 21par.; Matt 13:6/Luke 8:6; John 15:6; 1Pet 1:24; Rev 14:15.
129 Cf. the heart in Ps 102:5; limbs/bones in Ezek 37:11; and the dried-up arm in Zech 11:17.
130 Cf. Weissenrieder in Zimmermann (ed.) 2013. 505.
131 Cf. Collins 2007. 206.

the Corpus Hippocraticum and some of Galen's writings, the term is used to describe temporarily and at times intentionally dried-out organs or body parts due to an imbalance of corporal liquids.[132] However, the term itself is too general and broad to prove that the gospel draws upon this medical concept.

In any case, for the three deviating human bodies in Mark, the label vividly and visually depicts the notion of dynamic physicality dependent on the right amount and distribution of life-sustaining factors (heavy, continuous flow of blood; partial withering of only one hand; temporary stiff episodes), everyday imagery that is easily adaptable for rhetoric purposes (as in Mark 4:1–9; 11:20–25). For the man, this then entails the loss of life in his hand in a rather chronic nature, a partial immobility.[133]

The clinical picture of a (sudden) inability to move the entire body or single body parts is, in antiquity, more commonly designated with other terms, such as ἀποπληξία, παραπληξία, ἀποπλέκτος, or ἀρθρῖτις, which encompasses diverse joint conditions.[134] A serious and very common chronical gout is designated with ποδάγρα for the feet and χειράγρα for the hands. In the Corpus Hippocraticum, similar to ἀποπληξία, it is described as being caused by deteriorated blood due to an imbalance of bile or phlegm.[135] In analogy to the New Testament imagery, here as well, mainly fluid imbalances caused by genetics or a dissolute lifestyle (i.e., an exorbitance of food, alcohol, and sexual contact) were made responsible for the painful and distorted limbs; dietary measures, blood-letting, clysters and cauterization of veins, compresses, and band-aids promised aid.[136] Mainly men between 35 and 65, but also women, children, and Eunuchs, as named by Galen, were diagnosed.[137] In other literary genres, gout is compared to torture, given as a reason for suicide, and described with years of agony.[138]

Such a motionlessness could, but did not necessarily have to, entail economical setbacks and was not specifically known for being stigmatizing or ostracizing. Only the heightening of the man's (economical) suffering in parallel accounts and early

---

132 Cf., e.g., CH, *Vict.* 21.7; Galen, *Loc. aff.* 8.172; *Meth. med.* K 10.410; *Simpl. med. temp.* K 12.146–147, 12.294; moreover, Epidauros A 3, 15, B 15 (35); C 14 (57), 17 (60), 21 (64); Lucian, *Tox.* 24; Galen, *Marc.* 7.666.1; *T.Sim.* 2.12; and Weissenrieder in Weissenrieder; Coote (ed.) 2010. 280.
133 Cf. Aretaeus, *Sign. diut.* 1.7; and "the dried up," i.e., partially paralyzed and infertile body of Peter's daughter in BG 8502.4 and Acts Pet. 135:6–9. Cf. Henning 2015. 311–318; Solevåg 2018. 60.
134 Cf. Stamatu, *Arthritis.* 95.
135 Cf. CH, *Aff.* 31 L 6.242–243; *Morb.* 1.3. L 6.144; AP 50.1.
136 Cf., e.g., AP 50.3.1–20; CH, *Aff.* 31 L 6.242–243; *Morb.* 1.3 L 6.144; Galen, *Comp. Med.* K 13.336–340; Caelius, *Chron.* 5.27–51; Anth. Gr. 12.243; Pliny, *Ep.* 1.12.4–6; Suetonius, *Galb.* 21; and Stamatu, *Gicht.* 357.
137 Cf. Celsus, *Med.* 4.31; CH, *Aph.* 6.28.
138 Cf. Seneca, *Ep.* 67.3; Pliny, *Ep.* 1.12.4–6; and Stamatu, *Gicht.* 356–358.

receptions of the Markan narrative[139] depict possible consequences of the clinical picture that nonetheless are explicitly mentioned. The account in the Gospel of Mark, however, says nothing in this regard nor insinuates further implications for the man's life due to his *paralyzed* appendage.

4.2.2.2 Petrified Hearts

The second representation of deviating physicality in this narrative is the description of the opponents as a collective yet physical body. Jesus is described to be angry and grieved over the hardening of their hearts (v. 5: πωρώσει τῆς καρδίας). He concludes this "diagnosis" from their silence as a response to his controversial question, and indeed, this silence is "eloquent."[140] The terminology of their condition is phenomenologically close to the described dis/ability of the man with the withered hand, as πωρόω refers to the process of hardening or petrification and, as a result and figuratively, insensitivity, numbness, or blindness;[141] πώρωσις itself signifies the "formation of a callus (at the end of a broken bone)" and figuratively "hardening, obtuseness (mental), insensitivity (spiritual)."[142] The figurative translation thrives on the image of petrification, calcification, ossification, or coagulation of organic substances, as i.e., found in processes of bone healing by the formation of a callus.

In the New Testament, both lexemes are without exception used figuratively. In the Gospel of Mark, this condition of the heart occurs again regarding the disciples and their incomprehension after the feeding of the multitudes (cf. Mark 6:52 and 8:17; cf. also Mark 10:5). In other writings, the motif of the hardened hearts is

---

139 The Gospel of Luke extends the controversial debate on the interpretation of Sabbath regulations to several healing narratives and explicates that the man's *right* hand was withered to accentuate his dis/ability, probably with regard to his incapacity to work (Luke 6:6; cf. 13:10–17; 14:1–6). This motif is also reflected in the commentary of Jerome on Matt 12:13, assigned to the Aramaic apocryphal Gos. Naz. 4, where the man's occupation, caementarius, and thereby his social location and the (economical) urgency of his situation are clearly expressed.
140 Focant 2012. 121.
141 Cf. also the variant reading πήρωσις which designates the impairment of limbs yet also sensory organs in reference to cognitive and spiritual perception in, e.g., Philo, *Spec.* 1.117 and 3.181; as well as in Josephus, *B.J.* 5.288 and *A.J* 1.267.
142 Cf., e.g., BDAG, s.v; LN, s.v. 27.51–52; LSJ, s.v; Montanari, s.v; Schenk, πωρόω. Cf. also Vegge in Spencer (ed.) 2017. 244; and fundamentally, Robinson 1901. Cf. also, e.g., CH, *Fract.* 23.10; *Artic.* 15.6; 37.37; *Mochl.* 36.8; *Mul.* 217.7; *Superf.* 19.7; Galen, *Ars med.* 1.387.18; *Loc. aff.* 8.322.17; *Meth. med.* 10.161, 438–40, 442; Theophilius, *Autol.* 2.35; moreover, Passow 1970. 1311; Rüegger 2002. 110; von Bendemann in Labahn; Lietaert Peerbolte (ed.) 2006. 118; Weissenrieder; Dolle 2019. 801.

reflected as a part of Israel's eschatological salvation narrative.¹⁴³ Most prominently, the motif plays a vital role throughout the entire Exodus narrative: it occurs twenty times in Exod 4:21–14:17. While the terminology differs in the Greek and Hebrew, the motif stays the same.¹⁴⁴ Throughout the narrative, (mostly) YHWH is signified as the cause of the Pharaoh's hardened heart—the organ and symbol of perception, will, and decision making.¹⁴⁵ Incomprehension and a decisive refusal to act upon something significant are the characteristics of a hardened heart in many instances of the Hebrew Bible tradition (here, often ascribed to antagonistic characters),¹⁴⁶ which is reprised in the New Testament as in Mark 3:5 in succession of 2:6, 8 (see below).¹⁴⁷

In the context of this narrative, the hardened hearts resonate with the withered hand. In both cases, hardened body parts display a dis/ability to move—physically or mentally/spiritually. In one case, however, the dis/ability is healed by Jesus.

---

143 Cf., e.g., John 12:40; Isa 6:9–11; and Rom 11:7–8, cf. Isa 29:10; moreover, Schenk, πωρόω. 487–488.
144 According to Wilson 1979. 19–20, this is due to the influence of different sources (P, J, and E; σκληρύνω/חזק in, e.g., Exod 4:2; 11:10; 14:4, 8, 17, Deut 31:6–7; 2Sam 10:12; Ezek 2:3–4; σκληρύνω/קשה in Exod 7:3; Ps 95:10; βαρύνω/כבד in, e.g., Exod 8:11, 28; 9:7, 34; 14:4, 17; also Exod 4:10; Gen 48:10; Isa 6:9–10; 59:1; Zech 7:11; cf. Cox 2006. 304–307; McAffee 2010. 333–340).
145 Cf., e.g., 2Sam 7:3; 1Kgs 8:17; Jer 22:17; Prov 6:25; cf. also 1Sam 2:35 and Krüger in Wagner (ed.) 2009; Higgins, *Heart I. ANE and HB/OT*. 523. Wilson 1979. 26, concludes his assessment of this motif throughout the Exodus narrative by stating that the idea of rigidification is "used in connection with the heart to refer to an organ of perception that is malfunctioning and is not receiving outside stimuli." Cox 2006. 298–299, summarizes a few important descriptions of the Pharaohs behavior: "They [the Lord and Moses] warned Pharaoh that he had 'not listened' (7:16); that he should not refuse to let the Israelites go (8:2); that he should not again deal deceitfully by preventing the Israelites from going to worship (8:29); that he should not continue to hold the Israelites (9:2); that he was guilty of exalting himself at the expense of the Lord's people, even though his continued existence was allowed by the Lord (9:16–17); that he did not fear the Lord God (9:30); and that he was refusing to humble himself before the Lord (10:3)." Cf. also the very detailed and nuanced analysis of the hardening of Pharaoh's heart motif in its lexical, grammatical, contextual, and most of all narrative development in McAffee 2010. Cf. also the extended and nuanced surveys of Wagner in Wagner (ed.) 2008. Esp. 291; Janowski in Janowski; Schwöbel (ed.) 2015.
146 YHWH's agency is also found in two other important instances, where the hearts of Israel's enemies are hardened which will ultimately lead to their annihilation and the chosen people's salvation (cf. Josh 11:20 and Deut 2:30, but here with different terminology). However, cf. also Isa 6:10 and the "fat" heart of the people of Israel (שמן/παχύνω).
147 Cf. Rom 11:7, 25. For the connection of hardened hearts with sin and viciousness, cf., e.g., 1QM 14.7 (לבב קושי), and 1QS 4.11 (כיבוד לב) or as God's punishment in *T.Sim.* 2:11–14. On Pauline anthropology, see, e.g., Tieleman 2014. Regarding ancient philosophical and medical discussions on the function of the heart, see, e.g., Harris 1973; Duminil 1983.

4.2.3 The Healing

Jesus' body serves as an active and emotional "contrast medium" to his rigid counterparts, not only with regard to his passionate and empathetical teaching and understanding of Sabbath regulations but in his function as the "mediating" actor of dis- and ability in word and action.

4.2.3.1 Expected Treatment

The first mention of healing in this account is in v. 2, where Jesus' opponents silently anticipate and observe him closely to see if he would heal on the Sabbath. As established above, θεραπεύω is elsewhere only used in the summaric accounts of Mark's gospel, always designating Jesus' public and efficacious healing ministry in a teaching environment as in the synagogue and/or a surrounding crowd.[148] With its more general meaning of "to take care of something" or "to treat medically," the emphasis here lies on its alleged incompatibility with halakhic Sabbath regulations, thereby carrying the sentiment of "work" in the sense of giving medical "treatment."[149] In contrast to the other occurrences, where the effect of Jesus' θεραπεύω actions is emphasized to summarize his power and popularity (1:34, his disciples' in 6:13) or his constraint success due to ἀπιστία (6:5), here in v. 2, the result of the treatment remains irrelevant for the opponents.[150] While they simply anticipate the action itself (which, ironically, is not accounted to be visible), the narrator might, by using θεραπεύω, already implicitly hint at Jesus' powerful accomplishment tied to the accusation's effect for the gospel plot: Jesus' effectual achievement is diverted to his personal misfortune.

4.2.3.2 Compared Treatment: Markan Sabbath Savings (with Consideration of 2:23–28)

Secondly, healing is compared with the lexemes ψυχή and σῴζω in Jesus' provocative answer to his adversaries' silent accusation. It is striking that such an argument with these two terms occurs again in later rabbinic texts in the discussion, that the principle of *saving* endangered *life—piqquah nefesh* (*piqqûach nœfœš*; פקוח נפש)—overrides strict Sabbath observance and is not regarded as an infringe-

---

[148] Cf. Mark 1:34; 3:10; 6:5, 13.
[149] Cf., e.g., BDAG, s.v.; Beyer, θεραπεύω; Grimm, θεραπεύω; LN, s.v. 23.139, 46.6 ; LSJ, s.v.; Montanari, s.v.; Rupprecht, θεραπεύω; Wells 1998. 150–152, 154.
[150] Differently, Rüegger 2002. 90–91.

ment of Sabbath regulations.[151] As this argument is spoken in direct reference to the healing of the man's withered hand, it is essential to regard the Markan conceptions of Sabbath regulations in order to grasp how and why this image of dis/ability is employed.

It is nearly impossible to assign a specific belief about the rules and prohibitions surrounding the Sabbath to Jesus, his opponents, or the Markan audience, and thus determine the exact nature of the dispute. Not only do most of the relevant sources predate the Gospel of Mark, but the texts themselves cannot be fully trusted to hand down historically accurate depictions of the viewpoints and aspects of the first-century discourse without a certain bias.[152]

Therefore, with greatest caution regarding the historical backdrop, it is generally assumed that there was no binding, generally agreed-upon (Jewish) position toward the Sabbath law in the first century CE (that forbids healing).[153] While there are halakhic texts that suggest a stricter and more rigorous position, other

---

[151] Cf., e. g., *tShab* 9[10]:22; 15[16]:11, 16–17; *mYom* 8:6; *mShab* 2:5; 14:3–4; 18:3; 19:1, 5; 22:6; *MekhY, Ki tissa* 1 to Exod 31:13. The (shortened) Matthean parallel account includes in Jesus' closing argument the animal-in-the-pit-tradition as featured in passages from rabbinic and Qumran literature (Matt 12:11; cf. Luke 13:10–17; 14:1–6; CD 11.13–14, 16–17; 4Q265 6.5–7; *tShab* 14:3; *bShab* 128b; Doering 1999. 457–462). Kazen in Schröter; Jacobi (ed.) 2022 [2017]. 407, situates this motif in a sort of (early?) *piqquah-nefesh*-principle debate (*tShab* 16[17]:22). See also Frey in Zimmermann (ed.) 2013, regarding EvNaz 4 and the emphasis on the economic necessity of functioning mobility, however, without any reference to a (Sabbath) conflict. For an interesting analysis of intertextual references with Exod 14:16^{LXX} and Deut 30, see Queller 2010.

[152] Cf. the methodologically precise summary of Doering in Kraus; Rösel (ed.) 2019.

[153] Cf. Doering 1999. 449–450, 566–578, esp. 575; Doering in Doering; Waubke; Wilk (ed.) 2008. 232–233; Mayer-Haas 2003. 212–213. The gospels' Sabbath controversies have brought forward conflictive opinions on Jesus' attitude toward the Sabbath: Some argue Jesus abolished the Sabbath and its regulations altogether, others concede Jesus only softened rigorous implementations, a third group thinks he reestablished the original Sabbath meaning, and lastly it is debated, that Jesus never offended any Sabbath rules but remained within the framework of Judaism and "only" took part in the regulations' (re-)interpretation. Behind these argumentations lie various methods, approaches, and different attitudes on the relation of Judaism and (early) Christianity —all to be understood within the research history of their time—that simply cannot be analyzed here to the extend they deserve. Furthermore, an entire analysis of Jesus' attitude toward the Sabbath taken from all relevant NT passages or even only healing narratives, would not be constructive for the objective of this study. Interested readers shall be relegated to the most recent and extensive research of, e.g., Back 1995; Back in Holmén; Porter (ed.) 2011; Doering 1999; Doering in Doering; Waubke; Wilk (ed.) 2008; Doering in Bieringer; et al. (ed.) 2010; Mayer-Haas 2003; Meier 2009, and Kazen 2013; Kazen in Schröter; Jacobi (ed.) 2022 [2017]. See also Kahl 1998; Tuckett in Holmén (ed.) 2012.

4.2 Mark 3:1–6: A Withered Hand and Petrified Hearts — 137

groups in early Judaism seem to have had a more pragmatic approach.[154] Moreover, it must be borne in mind that (chosen) controversial aspects are simply (more) present in texts, unlike more common understandings,[155] and attest to developments in Jewish halakhic discussions.[156]

Since these texts that feature a discussion on "saving a life" on the Sabbath show a well-developed and accurate pattern of argumentation including exceptions, it seems likely that they reflect a longer process of development as early as the Book of Jubilees and the *Damascus Document*.[157] The latter already shows signs of casuistic exceptions as, e.g., only implements or cloth, not tools, were allowed to be used to help humans (but not animals; flock was not allowed to be carried) out of a pit to underscore the prohibition to work on a Sabbath.[158]

Furthermore, while a list of the thirty-nine main prohibited actions on the Sabbath does *not* explicitly mention healing (*mShab* 7:2), other texts provide more detailed cases that differentiate the severity of the condition and the intention of the treatment. In all cases, deliberate healing is considered prohibited work.[159] Even "minor" diseases and their cure by massages or medicine are forbidden, but if the healing comes as a "by-product" of other actions with other intentions (washing, eating, etc.), it is not a matter for prosecution.[160] This purposeful intention is clearly attested to in the Gospel of Mark with Jesus' argumentation in v. 4. He does not heal by accident (cf. Mark 5:28–30). Moreover, he substantiates his actions by arguing, in a rabbinic question formula, that not doing so would equal doing evil and even killing.

Therefore, in the Markan text, the man's dis/ability does not indicate an unusually severe condition, and the primary focus of the narrative—Jesus being accused of breaking the Sabbath—does not imply that he is acting within the boundaries of any recognized concession, such as intentional healing by mere word, as discussed in later sources. Rather, the Markan account is laid out to show that Jesus' actions were in fact regarded as controversial, which implies a somewhat

---

154 As the Markan text states this clearly, Jesus' opponents are characterized with a Pharisaic background, not as the renowned hardliners on Sabbath regulations, Sadducees and Essenes, which fits the attested prominent presence of Pharisees in Galilee, cf. Mark 2:24; Doering 1999. 447–448; Doering in Doering; Waubke; Wilk (ed.) 2008. 232.
155 Cf. Doering in Doering; Waubke; Wilk (ed.) 2008. 229.
156 Cf. ibid. 229, where Doering suggests the gospel's Sabbath healings are part of the first written sources.
157 Cf. Kazen in Schröter; Jacobi (ed.) 2022 [2017]. 407, regarding Jub 2:29–30; 50:6–13; CD 10.14–11.18, esp. 11:13–14, 16–17; see also, 4Q265 6.4–8. Cf. also 1Macc 2:40–41.
158 Cf. Doering in Doering; Waubke; Wilk (ed.) 2008. 230.
159 Cf. Collins 2007. 207.
160 Cf., e.g., *mShab* 14:3–4, 22:6; *tShab* 12[13]:8–14; 16[17]:16, 19.

basic common understanding of healing as a violation of the Sabbath.¹⁶¹ However, it is ambiguous if the controversy lies in Jesus' healing, the application of an "endangered-life" exception, and/or its expansion to include the "harmless" condition of a withered hand.¹⁶²

In any case, the Markan Jesus is depicted to have and to teach a new perspective on Sabbath regulations contrasted by Pharisaic opposition. This is closely tied to the controversy in Mark 2:23–28, which preludes this logion directly, not only in composition but also thematically. When Jesus' disciples are accused by the Pharisees of breaking the Sabbath by picking grains, Jesus defends their actions with a reference to 1Sam 21:1–7 and David's and his soldiers' eating of sanctified bread of the Presence in a time of need. Jesus supports this by establishing a principle for his understanding of the Sabbath: τὸ σάββατον διὰ τὸν ἄνθρωπον ἐγένετο καὶ οὐχ ὁ ἄνθρωπος διὰ τὸ σάββατον.¹⁶³ By using creation (ἐγένετο) as a fundamental argument for the Sabbath—which is in itself a very common reference point in rabbinic Sabbath discourse—it becomes clear that Mark's Jesus is not only stating a casuistic exception, as his reference to David and the bread of the Presence might have suggested, but manifesting a basic principle of his Sabbath interpretation. While Jesus confirms the Tora and its laws here by accepting the Sabbath as a God-given order,¹⁶⁴ he prioritizes humankind *before* the Sabbath, putting emphasis on its service to humankind.¹⁶⁵ In the context of the preceding verses, it seems plausible to understand the following "Son of Man" epithet in v. 28 as a general reference to humankind.¹⁶⁶ However, seen in its macro context, it is a clear repetition of the title and addition to its definition given in 2:10 (see above). Both verses (2:10 and 2:28) show a very similar structure: first, there is a claim of authority, followed by the verb, the subject, and finally the intriguing object of the authority, namely sin forgiving on earth and the Sabbath.¹⁶⁷ Therefore, the use of the "Son of Man" epithet is not only a play on words regarding Jesus' stand on Sabbath regulations *for* humanity, but it defines more closely what has been analyzed as a characteristic self-designation of Jesus' identity and authority: he claims divine forgiveness of sins and defines the Sabbath within the parameters of creation and divine history (see 4.1).¹⁶⁸

---

161 Cf. Back 1995. 47–48; Doering in Doering; Waubke; Wilk (ed.) 2008. 232.
162 Cf. Doering in Doering; Waubke; Wilk (ed.) 2008. 232.
163 For the objective of this study, it is not relevant if this logion is authentic or not.
164 Cf. Becker in Zimmermann (ed.) 2013. 249.
165 Cf. Doering 1999. 423.
166 Cf. ibid. 419–423.
167 Cf. Dewey 1980. 99.
168 Cf. Pascut 2017. 73–74; Gundry 1993. 144.

The parallelismus membrorum of 2:27 (although here with a chiasm instead of a climactic comparison) is quite clearly stylistically reprised in Jesus' antithetical argumentation in Mark 3:4.[169] Moreover, the use of ἄνθρωπος in Mark 3:1, 3, 5 to designate the man with the withered hand insinuates by this close reference to the previous logion a generic restoration behind the following singular healing.[170]

Both passages, Mark 2:23–28 and 3:1–6, work only with the precondition of an at least controversial activity on the Sabbath according to a general, supposedly Pharisaic Sabbath understanding that can be assumed behind the discussed exemptions. Neither the dis/ability nor Jesus' deliberate healing treatment qualifies as exceptions, as discussed in later sources. Rather, they are constructed to raise the claim of a conceptionally and generally different Sabbath understanding.

Therefore, within the context of Sabbath controversy, the two lexemes ψυχή and σῴζω of Jesus' argumentative statement in Mark 3:4 also aim at a generic and broader, even absolute, objective behind the individual healing of a single body part. While they only occur together once more in a semantically different construction in 8:35,[171] and thereby make a direct connection to a religious salvation as explicated in Mark 8:35 unlikely at this point,[172] they have a proprietary function with the gospel narrative, especially regarding representations of dis/ability.

Notably, σῴζω is found in several Markan healing narratives.[173] In all instances, it designates characters with dis/abilities and their advocates, who, according to their πίστις, reach out to Jesus (at times quite literally) for a healing touch and are *saved*.[174] While a comprehensive interpretation of this lexeme for the Markan healing context warrants a closer analysis of each narrative, Mark 3 suggests a rather theological understanding due to its proximity to the creation theme in Mark 2:27 (see below). Furthermore, ψυχή is usually used in all Markan contexts together with a possessive pronoun or an article.[175] Here in Mark 3:4, however, in its absolute application, it seems to refer to a universal, not-possessed ψυχή, in accordance with the generic use of ἄνθρωπος, reprising the logion of Mark 2:27. This underscores that the Markan Jesus establishes an absolute principle with regard to his understanding of Sabbath regulations, which is echoed in rab-

---

169 Cf. also *MekhY, Ki tissa* 1 to Exod 31:12, 14 par. *bYom* 85b; comprehensively, Doering 1999. 417; also Dietzfelbinger 1978. 295–296.
170 Cf. Rüegger 2002. 72–80, quote on 80.
171 Cf. Doering in Doering; Waubke; Wilk (ed.) 2008. 232; also Dautzenberg 1966. 156–157.
172 Differently, Back 1995. 114.
173 Cf. Mark 5:21–24, 35–43; 5:25–34; and 6:53–56.
174 Cf. Wells 1998. 222.
175 Cf. Mark 8:35–37; 10:45; 12:30; 14:34; Doering 1999. 452.

binic Sabbath discourses of *piqquah nefesh* and thereby seems to represent a current issue within halakhic discussions.[176] First and foremost, however, the gospel context promotes the motif of ψυχὴν σῶσαι as a theological punchline within its narrative development.

4.2.3.3 Actual Treatment: Mere Word Alone

Against the extensive preceding discussion, the healing itself is depicted rather subtly. As in Mark 2:1–12 (see above), Jesus does not physically engage in healing actions but simply asks the man to stretch out his restored hand. It has been argued already early in New Testament reception history[177] that Jesus did not transgress the (Pharisaic) contemporary purity halakha since he was not healing physically but by mere word,[178] which is permitted on the Sabbath in a few (subsequent) rabbinic writings.[179] However, Mark 3:1–6 is a conflict narrative. As established, like the ultimately preceding Sabbath controversy in 2:23–28, it relies on the precondition that generally working or healing on the Sabbath was considered at least controversial. In Mark 2:23–28, the disciple's action causes conflict; Mark 6:2 speaks of the δυνάμεις performed by τῶν χειρῶν αὐτοῦ in direct context with Jesus' Sabbath teachings (cf. also 6:5). Moreover, while the rabbinic exceptions speak of singular cases, Jesus argues for a general ruling and/or interpretation.

Mark's Jesus also heals on other occasions by mere word,[180] which does not necessarily reflect magical connotations that are possibly insinuated by the rabbinic exception.[181] Instead of specific healing words, Jesus speaks with the man in a similar manner as to the opponents (λέγει; vv. 3, 4, 5; the only difference being that he speaks in imperatives to the man and asks the spectators a question). The narrative clearly depicts Jesus as healing on a Sabbath and *thereby* causing controversy.[182] All the arguments defending Jesus' healing as not breaking the Sabbath—a) since he only healed by permissible word, not accusable action; b) because his words only meant to demonstrate the healing, not effect it; or c) by re-

---

[176] Cf. Matt 12:11 and Luke 13:10–17; 14:1–6; CD 11.13–14, 16–17; 4Q265 6.5–7; *tShab* 14:3; *bShab* 128b; and Doering 1999. 455; Doering in Doering; Waubke; Wilk (ed.) 2008. 232.
[177] Cf. Ps.-Athanasius, *Homilia de Semente* (PG 28:144–168); Slavonic Jewish War 2:9:3 (addition to Josephus, *B.J.* 2.174).
[178] Cf. Doering in Schröter; Jacobi (ed.) 2022 [2017]. 222–223.
[179] Cf. "whispering over a wound" in *tShab* 7[8]:23; *yShab* 14.3 [14c]; *bShab* 101a.
[180] Cf. Mark 2:11; 10:51–52; in 7:29 maybe due to the spatial distance or within the context of exorcising unclean spirits/demons as in 1:25 (also on a Sabbath in a synagogue); 5:8, 13; 9:25, etc. Cf. also Luke 17:14.
[181] Cf. Doering in Doering; Waubke; Wilk (ed.) 2008. 224.
[182] Cf. ibid. 229.

ferring the healing agency to God instead of Jesus—do not comply with the narrative's aim. Still, the text did not fail to irritate and cause controversy on the literary level, as in its (early) reception history.

4.2.3.4 Normative Restoration

Finally, v. 5 describes the actual healed physicality with the lexeme ἀποκαθίστημι. Its meaning designates the establishing of a previous condition, a renewal, a recomposition, a reinstatement.[183] With regard to physical conditions, it is in the New Testament only used here and in its parallel accounts (cf. Matt 12:13; Luke 6:10) as well as in the narrative of the healing of the blind man in Bethsaida in Mark 8:25 (see ch. 7). It is also found in Job 5:18^{LXX} and frequently designates the healing of λέπρα, as in, e.g., Lev 13:16^{LXX}, T.Sim. 2:12–13, and Exod 4:7^{LXX}. In the latter two, hands are healed with reference to non-scaly flesh, the ideal behind the "restoration to health,"[184] a non-withered condition.

However, in other New Testament occurrences, the lexeme carries an eschatological nuance: In Mark 9:12 (cf. Matt 17:11) Jesus speaks of eschatological restoration Elia will bring, in Acts 1:6 of the restoration of the kingdom of Israel (cf. Mal 3:23^{LXX}). This follows the use of ἀποκαθίστημι in the LXX, where the eschatological restoration of the people of Israel is prophesied.[185] Taking these notions into account, ἀποκαθίστημι could either denote that the man's hand was restored to its previous condition before the "withering," constructing a norm of everyday-life health, or, read with a creational aspect as the setting and the directly connected account in Mark 2:23–28 implies, it could signify that with Jesus' healing, a norm of perfected pre-fall health, possibly within the context of an eschatological restoration, is made visible. In any case, the man's hand is visibly transformed to a non-withered condition. The audience, however, might suspect that by this imagery and its denomination, this healing narrates a "re-storation" beyond a common, visible health ideal.

The descriptions of Jesus' healing the man with the chronic and non-life-threatening disease reveal his controversial stance on halakhic debates by emphasizing its notion of labor (esp. θεραπεύω), which is seen as problematic effort, and is further connected to his successful ministry. Moreover, the narrative displays

---

[183] For the following, cf., e.g., BDAG, s.v.; Link; Breytenbach, ἀποκαθίστημι; LN, s.v. 13.65, 15.74; LSJ, s.v.; Montanari, s.v.; Müller, ἀποκαθίστημι, ἀποκαθιστάνω; Oepke, ἀποκαθίστημι, ἀποκατάστασις.
[184] Montanari, s.v. 251, lists only Mark 3:5 in this regard. Cf. Dioscorides, Mat. Med. 1.64.4 for "cure" in ἀποκαθίστημι, ἀποκαθίστημι. 200, which von Bendemann in Zimmermann (ed.) 2013. 342, classes without any other source as a "medical *terminus technicus*."
[185] Cf., e.g., Jer 16:15; 23:8; 24:6; Hos 2:3; 6:11; 11:11; Ps 14:7; 85:2.

Jesus' power in argumentative and authoritative speech within the thickening plot of growing (fatal) enmity and, by embedding his curative treatment in halachic discourse, connects it to a grander scheme unfolding among creation, restoration, and salvation.

4.2.4 Interpretation

In a primary, basic reading, the narrative and its characters demonstrate—in line with other healing narratives—Jesus' authority in word and action, which, along with Mark 2:1–12, at this point in the plot not only causes popularity and amazement but growing hostility. Again, characters with deviating physicality are employed to unfold Jesus' (controversial) mission and spur the narrative forward.

The contrasting composition of the narrative's space and characters (Jesus and the man in the inner circle surrounded by opponents), the resonating dis/abilities, and Jesus' antithetical argumentation lead to the conclusion that the opposite cases drawn out by Jesus are applicable to the characters: he heals the withered hand, he does good and saves a life, while his hard-hearted opponents disagree with his healing, do evil, and decide to kill him.

The Markan description of Jesus' healing of the man with the rather chronic, not particularly severe in any regard, and non-life-threatening disease grounds Jesus' argumentative explication of his Sabbath understanding and actions. In connection with Mark 2, this explicates that his teaching and healing aim at a generic and absolute interpretation of the Sabbath as a service to humankind, not only in extreme, exceptional circumstances. He underlines this with a recourse to the order of creation, which heightens his arguments beyond a halakhic discussion to a principal theological level.[186] Hence, the deviating bodies in this narrative point toward a deeper theological plot that is already hinted at by the use of some lexemes with meaningful references and implications within the gospel narrative: For one, ψυχὴν σῶσαι is not only reprised in halakhic terminology but expresses a Markan understanding of healing that, although it is yet to be explicated more closely, points toward a grander salvation than a physical healing. In addition, ἀποκαθίστημι carries an eschatological-creational nuance with it, which implies a more comprehensive understanding of reinstated health than on a mere everyday physical level.

Moreover, the echo of ξηραίνω and its phenomenological parallel clinical picture of πωρώσει τῆς καρδίας explicates the dis/abilities to a dis/ability invective

---

186 Cf. Doering 1999. 424.

and almost physiognomic understanding. Whoever accepts Jesus and his message is healed, softened, and "restored," unlike those who (deliberately) harden their hearts in incomprehension and misapprehension.

Therefore, when taking Jesus' teachings and healings as characteristics of his transformational movement, the recourse to Sabbath and creation is given a corresponding status to his eschatological perspective, an "Urzeit-Endzeit-Entsprechung":

> In the context of Jesus' eschatological mission human beings are refocused in a way that corresponds to primordial creation [...] one could claim that attention to chronically sick on the Sabbath in view of the kingdom of God is in agreement with, and recovery of, the serving role of the Sabbath with respect to humankind in primordial creation.[187]

The narrative (re)constructs the dis/ability of the man's ailment beyond the obvious. On the one hand, Jesus extends the definition of live-saving to the healing of the withered hand, which does not necessarily imply severe (social) implications of this condition[188] but rather that dis/ability is taken "deadly seriously" within Jesus' eschatological horizon.[189] Moreover, the direct connection of this healing to the Sabbath within this context of creation and eschatological mission then puts the dis/ability of the man into direct comparison to the physicality expected from both of those ends of the spectrum: an ideal spanning from the "and behold it was very good" of Gen 1:31 to the coming *basileia* to which Jesus is depicted to raise expectations (Mark 1:15).

In this narrative, the representations of dis/ability do not display Jesus merely as a powerful "mediator" between dis- and ability and promote the narrative's function and claims within the gospel storyline[190] (here, inter alia the thickening plot) but also set a contrast to an idealistic physical normativism of (re)-creation within an eschatological horizon. Whoever does not understand this and believes in Jesus and the *basileia* is left hart-hearted.[191]

---

187 Doering in Doering; Waubke; Wilk (ed.) 2008. 240. Cf. Doering 1999. 477.
188 Cf. Collins 2007. 208–209.
189 Cf. Doering in Doering; Waubke; Wilk (ed.) 2008. 238.
190 Cf. Solevåg 2018. 155.
191 Cf. Doering in Doering; Waubke; Wilk (ed.) 2008; Doering in Bieringer; et al. (ed.) 2010; Becker in Zimmermann (ed.) 2013.

4.3 Conclusion and Interpretation of Dis/ability in Mark 2:1–3:6

Mark 2:1–12 and 3:1–6 share many commonalities. Besides the already mentioned mutuality of structural elements (see above), they both assemble three deviating physicalities that reflect and deflect one another. Firstly, in the settings of rather confined spatial structures, Jesus is surrounded by his rigid opponents, who in both accounts are portrayed as quiet and motionless, doubting and offended, reproachful and literally "hardened" in their judgment and malevolence.[192] As controversy over Jesus' ministry develops over the course of this section (2:16, 18, 24), the first "set-in-stone" judgment (2:6–7) is concluded by the final, yet still silently scheming, disclosure of their destructive intentions (3:2, 6).[193] In correspondence to the paralyzed limbs, rigid perception and unmovable comprehension is depicted as the unfavorable antagonism. With this frequent focus on the opponents' in-/direct representations of consciousness in the entire section, the audience learns to anticipate the fixed and formed response of these authorities as Jesus' antagonists for the following plot, which stands in harsh contrast to the admiration and astonishment of other witnesses (2:12) or previous healings, especially of the first uncontested exorcism on the Sabbath in a synagogue (1:27–28).[194]

Contrarily and secondly, Jesus' opponents are specifically contrasted with characters with (partial) mobility impairments, who are spectacularly moved and then move themselves, restored, through the narrative setting toward an eschatological horizon. As the Markan descriptions of paralyzed body (parts) envisage everyday imagery of lacking life-sustaining fluid, its vivid restorations allude to a physicality beyond any strict binary when contextualized in normative discourse on forgiveness and (re-)creation. Within the gospel context, the dis/abilities of Mark 2:1–3:6 sketch an ideal corporality as the Markan Jesus prioritizes impaired yet forgiven communal life over unimpaired damnation (cf. Mark 9:42–48), extends salvation to the absolute here and now and "minor" ailment (cf. 2:23–28), and alludes to a resurrection of an ideal and primordial physicality.[195]

Moreover and in succession of Mark 1, the drastic visuality of healed paralysis functions as empirical evidence par excellence for the authority of the third body that claims the non-verifiable and divine prerogatives of forgiving sins and interpreting and defining the Sabbath. Only verbally, Jesus negotiates in the center of it

---

192 Cf. also Luke 13:10–17.
193 Cf. Focant 2012. 121.
194 Cf. Rüggemeier 2017. 35; Kiffiak 2017. 139.
195 Cf. von Bendemann in Labahn; Lietaert Peerbolte (ed.) 2006. 119.

all, not only the dis/abled bodies around him but his own ability and authority in teaching, forgiving sins, and (re)claiming halakhic norms and creational intentions. As his divine identity is further unraveled against the dis/abled bodies, the plot against him thickens over the course of the entire section of Mark 2:1–3:6 and already alludes to his subsequent death, resurrection, and the eschatological return of the Son of Man.[196]

Again, representations of deviating bodies facilitate as narrative prosthesis for the gospel's plot, wait "hand and foot" on the depiction of Jesus' identity, and—based on an implied understanding of their undesirability—function as symbols for salvation and resurrection.[197]

While Mark 1 depicts humanity exposed to and (temporarily) affected by dis/abling influences, Mark 2:1–3:6 broadens and reframes this earthly existence with creational and eschatological idealism. Although the gospel's rhetoric remains dis/ability invective, the binary ideal of (un)impaired corporality is explicitly reevaluated in light of undesirable hard-heartedness, recontextualized regarding *basileia* behavior, and reprioritized within an eschatological horizon.

---

[196] Cf. Dewey 1980. 121–122.
[197] Cf. von Bendemann in Labahn; Lietaert Peerbolte (ed.) 2006. 119.

5 Mark 5: The Physical Protagonist between Pathologization and *Pistis*

In Mark 3:7, a new section of the gospel narrative starts with a summary of Jesus' ministry (see ch. 2) and a broadening of its reach—geographically (3:7–8) and regarding personnel by the appointment of the Twelve (3:13–19). Moreover, the themes of conflict and misunderstandings of Jesus' identity and his authoritative ministry are continued after being firmly established in 2:1–3:6, also by use of dis/abled characters (see ch. 4). While these disputations mainly focused on theological themes, the debates ensue to include Jesus' family as critics and increasingly focus on the source of Jesus' identity and authority (see B: In Focus: Mark's Jesus and Opposing Forces). In particular, the rhetorical dismissal of Jesus as mentally deranged and authorized by Beelzebul with the wish to restrain him (3:20–22) is reprised and dismantled in the following section (5:1–20) according to Jesus' cosmic layout given in 3:23–30 (see extensively B. In Focus: Mark's Jesus and Opposing Forces), as is the topic of familial belonging (5:21–43). The opposition of Jesus' message in contrast to a satanic sphere is also expounded by teaching passages in 4:1–34 (esp. 4:15) before his authority is vividly and impressively displayed in a storm of cosmic extent, culminating in questions on πίστις and authoritative identity by Jesus (οὔπω ἔχετε πίστιν) and his disciples (τίς ἄρα οὗτός ἐστιν; 4:40–41). Mark 5 expands on both questions by introducing three characters with deviating physical conditions and providing detailed accounts of their histories and interactions with Jesus, all of which take place in and around the Sea of Galilee.

5.1 Mark 5:1–20: Possessive Spirits

5.1.1 Introduction to the Narrative

The longest Markan healing narrative starts with a change of place. As the account unfolds and emphasizes a particularly detailed narratological landscape,[1] the setting deserves utmost attention: Framed with two "administrative-geographical" references (v. 1: τὴν χώραν τῶν Γερασηνῶν and v. 20: Δεκαπόλει),[2] it is the first time Jesus crosses the lake to the other side (τὸ πέραν τῆς θαλάσσης; i.e., the east-

---

[1] Cf. the detailed topographical lexemes and the locale description εἰς τὸ πέραν, v. 1; ἀπὸ μακρόθεν, v. 6; ἐκεῖ, v. 11.
[2] Cf. Bosenius 2014. 202.

ern shore)³ to the region of the "Gerasenes" (v. 1), as he suggested in 4:35. Since it cannot be assumed that the audience or author possess detailed geographical knowledge, this ambiguous local reference⁴ continues the gospel's narrative of Jesus' expanding sphere of influence as he reaches the eastern shore of the Sea of Galilee, a predominantly Hellenistic region that historically allowed for the coexistence of Semitic religion and culture.⁵ The narratological Gentile character of the region is ultimately hinted at through the mention of the nearby herd of swine and their herdsmen, which also emphasizes the notion of impurity invoked by the impure spirit. However, this does not provide any information about the man's ethnical provenance.⁶ Hence, the narrative's setting first and foremost broadens Jesus' reach yet seems in its further depiction determined by the condition of the dis/abled character (see below).

There, Jesus is encountered by an ἄνθρωπος ἐν πνεύματι ἀκαθάρτῳ, which recalls the narrative of Jesus' initial healing in the rather confined space of the Synagogue of Capernaum (see 3.1). Here as well, the man is introduced without a name and is referred to only by this pneumatic impurity throughout the first half of the narrative (vv. 2, 8, 13). After his healing, he is identified as a (formerly) δαιμονιζόμενος (vv. 15, 16, 18). The following verses concentrate on an exceptionally extensive description of the accompanying implications of his condition. After a dense and chaotic conversation with Jesus, the demonic force is cast into a herd of pigs, who drown themselves in nearby waters, which causes further agitated reactions as word spreads via several reports (see below).

The entire setting of the encounter is characterized by the gradually revealed topographical liminality of the χώρα/ὅριον (vv. 1, 10, 17) close to the looming lake with its steep bank (θάλασσα; vv. 1, 13; cf. 4:35–41; κρημνός, v. 13) between city and country (πόλις and ἀγρός; v. 14). This is heightened in the descriptions of the demoniac's liminal place of residence in tombs (μνημεῖον and μνῆμα; vv. 2, 3, 5) and around mountains (ὅρος; v. 5). As he moves constantly and frenzied throughout this widespread setting, so do the other minor characters, but Jesus ap-

---

3 Cf. Zwiep 2019. 46. Cf. also 6:45; 8:13; 10:1.
4 It might a) refer to present-day Jerash, which, however, by its 60 km distance to the Sea of Galilee challenges the pigs' fall into close-by waters; or b) mean Gergesa due to previous redactional changes; or c) emphasize according to χώρα a broader geographical realm, i.e., "a piece of land, farm or estate," (as proposed by Breytenbach in Meyers (ed.) 1999. 78–79; cf. also Iersel 1998. 196–197, n. 8; Bosenius 2014. 202–203); or d) imply a symbolic reading regarding the Hebrew root גרש, that often occurs in exorcism narratives and anticipates the following (cf. Derrett 1979. 287; Marcus 2000. 342).
5 Cf., e.g., Josephus, B.J. 2.480; Collins 2007. 267.
6 Cf. on the impurity of pigs Lev 11:7; Deut 14:8. Insightful on this matter is moreover Ruane 2015.

pears to firmly face the multitudes of demons, the group of herders, and people from the district alone.⁷ This constant motion is also reflected in the conversation's change from direct to indirect speech (vv. 9–10), the confusing chronology of events (esp. v. 8), veiled intentions, and shifts of perspectives (see below).⁸ The narrator presents the first action from the perspective of the spirit-ridden man (v. 6), then allows the audience to witness the conversation with occasional references to the surroundings (vv. 7–13). In v. 14, the perspective widens to show the movement of the herdsmen throughout the region, before narrowing down again in vv. 15–17 to capture the reaction towards Jesus up close. Finally, the narrative fades out with a satellite perspective to convey the broad scope of the ex-demoniac's proclamation.⁹ The brief survey of the setting already outlines central aspects of the man's dis/ability as his socially deviant and frenzied transgressive behavior forces him to occupy liminal yet widespread space, which conveniently concurs with this impressive and capturing prelude of Jesus' ministry as he broadens his reach to other shores and further territories.

5.1.2 Images of Dis/ability

The man is introduced as ἄνθρωπος ἐν πνεύματι ἀκαθάρτῳ. As established broadly in 3.1, the designation of pneumatic impurity reflects by its qualifier first and foremost the Markan opposition of holy and impure within the context of his hierarchical demonology of Jewish provenance. After the man is introduced by the narrator as ἐν πνεύματι ἀκαθάρτῳ (5:2, 13), Jesus reprises this attribute in his first address of the man-spirit in 5:8, which emphasizes his holy opposition.¹⁰ The allusion to the sphere of impurity with its possible cultic consequences is furthermore explicated by the setting (see below). *After* the successful exorcism, the man's former deviating condition is described with δαιμονίζομαι (always as a participle; vv. 15, 16, 18).¹¹ Remarkably, this description is attributed in present tense by the witnesses (contrasting the aorist participle of v. 18). Possibly this indicates the profound social stigmatization of this dis/ability: to them, he remains the demoniac

---

7 Jesus is the only one explicitly leaving the boat, his disciples are only mentioned again in v. 31; cf. Iersel 1998. 198.
8 Cf. ibid. 198.
9 Cf. Bosenius 2014. 201.
10 Cf. 1:23, 26; 3:11, 30; 6:7; 7:25; 9:25, where the designation is given by the narrator, while in 1:27 the witnesses of Jesus' first exorcism use this label.
11 On Mark's demonology, including a survey of its terminology, see A. In Focus: Markan Images of Sickness and Possession and 3.1.2.

(see below). In any case, the lexeme echoes the summaric account of Jesus' healings and exorcisms in Mark 1:32–34 and its focus on the enhanced insight and knowledge of Jesus' identity of those possessed. Moreover, the described symptoms concur with those of the demonic dis/ability depicted in Mark 1:21–28 (see 3.1.2.1):

5.1.2.1 Disparate Corporality

As in Mark 1:21–28, the disparate corporality of the possessed man, who is portrayed without any social affiliation or name, is expressed with prepositional terminology: The designation ἄνθρωπος ἐν πνεύματι ἀκαθάρτῳ in 5:2, 13 and the spirits' "exit *out* of the man" (ἐξέρχομαι in 5:8, 13; ἐκ τοῦ ἀνθρώπου, 5:8) *into* the pigs (εἰσέρχομαι, 5:12) emphasize the fusion of demon and host.[12] With the ambiguous nuances of these prepositions,[13] they serve to explicate the physically penetrable disposition of humans (and pigs) for spiritual entities that wield power over their seemingly defenseless hosts. The fusion of the man-spirit is moreover explicated in the descriptions of auto-aggression (v. 5) that, based on the undesirability of pain, imply an irreconcilability of physical sensation and determining will. This is underscored by the use of the passive διεσπάσθαι in v. 4, which ascribes the astonishing force not to the decisive action of the man as the subject but to the hidden force within him, similar to the verbal interaction with Jesus (esp. 5:6–7).[14] As the demon makes use of the speech apparatus of the Gerasene, his language and social norms also adapt to this hybridity: The spiritual entity constantly violates sociolinguistic rules by alternating between the first-person singular and plural in his direct speech, which the narrator follows (vv. 9–12). Moreover, as the entity uses its own name, it deprives the man of his position as the physical speaker within the linguistic practices and social and narrative order. The content of the utterances also reveals knowledge that, to the audience, reflects extraordinary and unanticipated status for such a new and nameless character (see below).

5.1.2.2 Socially Transgressive and Deviating Behavior

The disparate corporality of the man is reflected in his boisterous and (self-)destructive behavior, which renders him a deviating, socially transgressive character who is, contrary to the man in Mark 1:23–28, explicitly socially marginalized.

---

12 Cf. also ἐξέρχομαι in 1:25–28; 7:29–30; ἐκβάλλω in 1:34, 39; 3:15, 22; 6:13; 7:26; 9:18, 28; 9:38; 16:9, 17; cf. also 1:12; δέω in 3:27.
13 The preposition can be translated with a locative or instrumental aspect or refer to a description of a certain condition or state. Cf. Mark 5:2 and 5:26; 1:7–8; Luke 22:49; cf. also Mark 7:25 and 9:17, where the children *have* [ἔχω] a spirit. See 3.1.
14 Cf. 1:22–28, 9:18–27.

The man is chronically affected by the hostile entity, as the accompanying symptoms are described to have created a permanent asocial lifestyle: He *resides* at tombs and hills (v. 3), acts out his torments διὰ παντὸς νυκτὸς καὶ ἡμέρας (v. 5), and (by inversion) is characterized by members of his community as constantly moving around irrationally and naked (καθήμενον ἱματισμένον καὶ σωφρονοῦντα, v. 15). The demoniac's characteristically loud, intense, and uncontrollable screaming (κράζω; vv. 5, 7)[15] together with his auto-aggression (κατακόπτω ἑαυτὸν λίθοις) also contribute to this audiovisual scene of his deviating behavior. While v. 5 describes the possessive power of the spirit presumably without specific communicative content, the pleonastic composition φωνῇ μεγάλῃ λέγει in v. 7 depicts the uncontrollable intensity with which the demon uses the man's voice against societal norms. Moreover, his ungovernable force is vividly depicted by the frequent and futile attempts to contain him by fixation as he is not only able to escape chains and fetters but deconstructs and destroys the bonds. The failure of the binding and thereby the man-spirit's strength (and, in succession, Jesus' power) is enforced by negatives (v. 3b: οὐδὲ, οὐκέτι, οὐδεὶς), temporal adjectives (v. 3: οὐκέτι; 4: πολλάκις), and destructive verbs (v. 4: διασπάω, συντρίβω; in contrast: δαμάζω). The demoniac transgresses physical and social boundaries.[16] The reasons for socially isolating and restraining this individual can be attributed to several factors, including fear of his strength, uncontrollable destructiveness, and (inexplicable) self-expression; the need to protect the man's life and/or the community; the desire to avoid him due to his association with impurity; and the disruptive effect he has on social life. Even if futile in its effect, the man is not only bound internally but externally by social marginalization.[17]

This is also reflected in the liminal space he is described to occupy, as the text mentions the tomb(s) he inhabits three times (v. 2: μνημεῖον; vv. 3, 5: μνῆμα, in Plural; τὴν κατοίκησιν εἶχεν).[18] They not only explicate his distance to society but, as places of the dead, commonly convey notions of a spiritual realm in context of impurity.[19] Additionally, unhabitable mountains function as narrative markers of liminality in the Gospel of Mark according to Greek and Jewish practice.[20] For

---

[15] Cf. also ἀνακράζω in 1:24; 3:11; 9:26. In Mark's Gospel also those with other dis/abilities voice their distress and imploring plea loudly (cf. 9:24; 10:47–48). Cf. also 11:9 and 15:13–14.
[16] Cf. Feldt in Verheyden; Kloppenborg (ed.) 2018. 40–41.
[17] Cf. Marcus 2000. 343.
[18] Both lexemes are employed in Mark synonymously, cf. 5:2, 3, 5; 15:46. Cf. also Mark 6:29; 16:2–8.
[19] Cf. esp. Isa 65:1–7, also *bSan* 65b; *mNid* 7a; *bBer* 18b; moreover, Böcher 1972. 74–76; Smith (ed.) 1978. 428; Marcus 2000. 342; Frey-Anthes 2007. 23–25; Gnilka 2010. 203.
[20] Cf., e.g., Bremmer in Feldt (ed.) 2012; Feldt in Feldt (ed.) 2012a; Feldt in Feldt (ed.) 2012b; Feldt in Verheyden; Kloppenborg (ed.) 2018.

one, mountains accommodate retreat in a horizontal axis as a more or less isolated landscape beyond or outside social structures. Moreover, since they also introduce a vertical spatiality beyond the topographical story world, they refer as a literal, "archetypical" motive to a nearness of heaven and are often employed when the divine and earthly realm meet.[21] Most prominently, the Markan Jesus retreats to a mountain for prayer and his transfiguration.[22] Hence, the rocky residence of the Gerasene demoniac possibly refers to rock-cut tombs[23] that emphatically convey the image of an ambiguous boundary region. As he moves around mountains, "high point[s] above the general surface of the earth," and tombs, "low point[s] (or within) the surface of the earth,"[24] he trespasses places connected to unearthly spheres, where death and the divine linger, taking apart any architectural context self-destructively.[25] He is not confined to architecturally defined structures as his reputation causes commotion around an entire neighborhood around the lake.[26] As in the other healing narratives outside of specific civil structures, the place of the encounter is connected to the clinical picture of the patient and accounts for Jesus' transgressional healing ministry that now reaches new shores and is spread from thereon. The extent of the man's tormenting and afflicting symptoms bears witness to the common explanatory and rhetoric connection of mental imbalance with pneumatic possession,[27] as his healed corporality is recounted to be perceived by his community as καθήμενον ἱματισμένον καὶ σωφρονοῦντα (v. 15).[28] However, in Mark, the etiology is clearly attributed to the demonic force; the symptoms cease with the demon's exit.

In comparison to the other Markan demoniacs, it is striking that the man's identity is neither affiliated within a Jewish community (the synagogue, Mark

---

21 Cf. Malbon 1991. 84–85, 88–89, 102. Cf. also Gen 22; Exod 3:12; 24:16; 1Kgs 19.
22 Cf., e.g., Mark 6:46 and 9:2–8; moreover, 3:13; 11:1; 13:3; 14:26.
23 Cf. Mark 15:46; Bosenius 2014. 200.
24 Malbon 1991. 162–163.
25 Cf. the reference to λίθος (v. 5) in architectural contexts in Mark 13:1, 2; 15:46; 16:3, 4.
26 Cf. 1:28, 45; 5:14; 6:55–56, also 1:40–45; 5:25–34; 7:31–37; 8:22–26; 9:14–29; 10:46–52; Malbon 1991. 101–103.
27 See 3.1; cf. Toensing in Avalos; Melcher; Schipper (ed.) 2007.
28 See B. In Focus: Mark's Jesus and Opposing Forces; cf. Mark 3:20–30, also 1:27–28 and 9:14–29. Cf. the descriptions of the socially deviating behavior of a שׁוֹטֶה, who runs around at night (v. 5), sleeps around gravesides (vv. 2, 3, 5), tears his garments, and destroys everything given to him (vv. 4, 5; conversely v. 13) in tTer 1.3; yTer 1.1/40b; bHag 3b; yGit 7.1/48c; cf. Aus 2004. 3–4. Cf. also Saul in 1Sam 16:14–16; 21:13–15; and Olyan 2008. 62–77, esp. 70–71, 76. Moreover, Plutarch reports of Nicias, who to avert being captured, pretends to be mentally unstable by throwing himself to the ground mid-speech, playing with his voice, running around (partly) undressed (Plutarch, Marc. 20.5).

1:21–28), nor explicitly defined by his ethnical or cultural provenance or family ties (cf. differently to Mark 7:24–30; 9:14–29). His constantly moving existence in the area outside social structures literally renders him an outcast. It is only after his healing that he is ordered to return εἰς τὸν οἶκόν σου πρὸς τοὺς σοὺς, which underscores his social rehabilitation. The man is marginalized and socially dis/abled, regarded as dead despite his "vivacious" outbursts.

5.1.2.3 Competing Spheres

As in the other accounts on demonic dis/ability, Jesus and the demoniac are portrayed as antagonists of two opposing spheres. Already the designation as ἄνθρωπος ἐν πνεύματι ἀκαθάρτῳ and δαιμονίζομαι pit the spiritual entities against Jesus.

When the spirit in the body sees and recognizes Jesus from afar, he reacts impetuously by running toward him and falling before him (προσκυνέω). This determined reaction after his visual perception conveys his immediate understanding of Jesus' identity, an indication of his supernatural knowledge often attributed to those possessed (cf. esp. 3:11).[29] With the physical extent of the proskynesis unqualified, the motivation behind it is conjecturably a gesture of concession as it is connected to the then explicitly voiced antagonistic concern to be "tormented" by Jesus, υἱός τοῦ θεοῦ τοῦ ὑψίστου (5:7).[30] Notwithstanding, if this implies a rhetoric device of a cunning and mocking (cf. Mark 15:19), adoring and obeisant,[31] or fearing and capitulating[32] notion, the following address proves that the spiritual entity recognizes Jesus not only as Jesus of Nazareth but also as a powerful, possibly divine superior. As in Mark 1:24, the spirit-man addresses Jesus with an unusual yet, to the audience, accurate name that continues the Markan characterization of knowledgeable demons.[33] Again, the name reflects the Markan hierarchical concept of competing spheres that is tied to Jesus' baptism and his permanent struggle with his foes as witnessed in his commands to silence[34] and in their fear of being destroyed (1:24), bound (3:27), plundered (3:27), and now tormented (βασανίζω, 5:7) by him. Embedded in the direct and highly personal question (τί ἐμοὶ καὶ σοί),[35] he calls Jesus υἱός τοῦ θεοῦ τοῦ ὑψίστου—an unusual title for the Gospel of Mark that

---

[29] See p. 183, n. 182, on the gesture of prostration.
[30] Due to the just precedent lengthily depiction of his captivating loss of control, it is unlikely that the proskynesis is an action of the erupting will of *the human host* to be freed from the tormenting spirit, cf., e.g., Derrett 1979. 290.
[31] Cf., e.g., Marcus 2000. 350.
[32] Cf., e.g., Theissen 1974. 66.
[33] See ch. 3; cf. Rüggemeier 2017. 241–242.
[34] Cf. 1:34; 3:11–12; not, however, in Mark 7:24–30 and 9:14–29.
[35] Cf. 1Kgs 17:18^{LXX}; Judg 11:12^{LXX}.

foremost designates Jesus' relationship to God.[36] Moreover, the hierarchical part of the title can be related to the Jewish designation and LXX translation of the Hebrew עליון to designate the God of Israel, "the most high," which is frequently uttered by non-Israelites.[37] However, Greek literature of non-Jewish provenance also uses this epithet to refer to Zeus.[38] Hence, the name conveys, in accordance with Mark's cosmology, an image of a spatial and hierarchical arrangement of powers that furthermore concurs with the clinical picture of pneumatic knowledge (see 3.1.2).

Following this cosmological order, the demon answers Jesus' direct question and reveals his name to be legion: he is many spirits. While the main emphasis lies on the outrageous force this Latin loanword connotes, namely a 5,000- to 6,000-men strong troop with rather large cavalry,[39] it furthermore associates, with regard to the clinical picture of antagonistic demonic dis/ability, a territorial opposition to Jesus and his growing sphere of influence.[40] As the widespread operational force of legions as *the* conquest device of Roman imperialism that secured conquered territories, the payment of taxes, and the *pax Romana* was widely attested,[41] the rather common term can be read as an illustration of the severity of the possession. This matches the large pig herd into which the demons are cast (vv. 12–13).[42] The possibilities of an allegorical or metaphorical anti-Roman inter-

---

[36] Cf. Schröter 2001. 170–173.
[37] Cf., e.g., Deut 32:8; 1Q20 21.2; Gen 14:18–22; Num 24:16; *3Esr* 2:2–3; Dan 3:93^{LXX}; 4:24^{LXX}; Isa 14:14. Cf. also the fragmentary 4Q246 2.1 and Ps 91/90^{LXX}; also Sanders in Charlesworth (ed.) 1997; Naveh 1998; Eshel in Lange; Lichtenberger; Römheld (ed.) 2003, for more insight on the connection of Psalms, Qumran, and the NT. Cf. furthermore, Luke 1:32, 35, 76; 6:35; Acts 7:48; Philo, *Legat*. 278; SIG ^{3}1181; *Sib.* 3,519; Wis 5:15; 6:3; *3Macc* 6:2; *JosAs* 8:9; *T.Ab.* 15:12; *Flacc.* 46; and Marcus 2000. 343–344.
[38] Cf. the temple inscription from around 22/23 BCE that bears witness to a Zeus Olympius Kult in Gerasa, in, e.g., Pindar, *Nem.* 1.60; 11.2; cf. Breytenbach, *Hypsistos*; Collins 2007. 268.
[39] Cf. Marcus 2000. 344–345; Burdon 2004; Collins 2007. 268–270.
[40] See B. In Focus: Mark's Jesus and Opposing Forces.
[41] As, e.g., first-century inscriptions prove, cf. Klinghardt 2007. 31–35; Collins 2007. 269, n. 71; Ebner in Zimmermann (ed.) 2013. 270; Lau 2007; Lau 2020.
[42] Cf. also the plural of αὐτὰ in v. 10; contra the interpretation as a ῥῆσις βαρβαρική similar to Mark 5:21–24, 35–43, and 7:24–30 in, e.g., Theissen 1974. 252. The employed imagery, including the additional military connotations of, e.g., ἀποστέλλω, ἐπιτρέπω, ἀγέλη, ὁρμάω, can also be read as a political comment against Roman foreign rule as, e.g., "demonic imperialism," cf. Marcus 2000. 351. This, however, must be evaluated regarding other historical and political comments and overtones in the gospel text. Specifically the pig herd could point towards the occupation of Caesar's Legion X. Fretensis that had boars as its emblem on shields and flags. Under Vespasian this legion was part of the intervention against the Jewish revolt and was successful at sea (cf. Josephus, *B.J.* 3.8, 64–65; 5.69–70, 135; 7.5, 17). Then, the concept of demon possession can also be regarded

pretation underscores the fundamental ambiguity of spiritual dis/ability as it is adaptable for any kind of (rhetorical) sensemaking of overwhelming, victimizing, and disparate circumstances, as already witnessed in Mark 3:21–30 (see B. In Focus: Mark's Jesus and Opposing Forces). First, however, the quantitative and qualitative power of the demons, hence severity of the possession, is visualized, as is the independence of the demonic entity: with their appropriate name, they illustrate a unit with controlling and forceful occupational and territorial nature. Tension is running high as Jesus, υἱὸς τοῦ θεοῦ τοῦ ὑψίστου, and Legion oppose another.

5.1.3 The Healing: Embodied Sovereignty

The entire confusing and dense verbal encounter between Jesus and the demoniac depicts a hostile argument, with elements ambiguous in their concrete intention: The fearful demoniac is approaching Jesus instead of fleeing (v. 6),[43] he mockingly or reverently prostrates and adjures Jesus (vv. 5–7), he implores his antagonist with exorcistic terminology not to be exorcised (v. 7),[44] he answers his questions submissively or threateningly, in any case, revealingly (v. 9), repeats his pleas in singular and plural (vv. 10, 12), and deceitfully or blatantly inferiorly negotiates his operative realm (vv. 12–13). The conversation, with its extensive public backlash, focuses on the two interlocuters by the back and forth in direct speech, which draws the audience into this suspenseful conflict.

Casting aside the variety of interpretative tones of their statements and gestures that the narrative accommodates, it becomes clear that the demons recognize Jesus as a divine, opposing agent when they plead with him, υἱός τοῦ θεοῦ τοῦ ὑψίστου, not to torture them (ὁρκίζω σε τὸν θεόν; see 5.1.2.3). The agony the demons fear is explicated in the following verse: Jesus orders the unclean spirits to leave

---

psychologically from this historic perspective, as occupational situations foster the believe in demons due to political and economic pressure, anticipation of liberation, and mental and physical degradation. Moreover, social behavioral patterns of possession offer a strategy to cope and protest the occupying power. Cf. esp. van der Loos 1965. 362; Derrett 1979; Myers 1988. 190–194; Horsley 2001. 140–148; Moore in Moore (ed.) 2006. 24–44; Kollmann 2007. 70; Leander 2013. 201–219; Poplutz in Zimmermann (ed.) 2013. 100. On the performance and possession, see Strecker in Stegemann; Malina; Theissen (ed.) 2002.

[43] Cf. Focant 2012. 198.
[44] Cf. Gundry 1993. 250. The term ὁρκίζω is often used in exorcistic contexts, such as the synonym ὁρκόω, to describe a demon cast out of a possessed person. Here however, it is *not* used by the exorcist. Cf. Acts 19:13; Josephus, *A.J.* 8.46–49, and the Hebrew equivalent ‎ש.ב.ע. in 8Q5; 11Q11 1.7; 4.1; moreover, Collins 2007. 268.

the man (ἐξέρχομαι); he pursues separating the demons and host and frees the disparate body. The use of imperatives is common for exorcistic statements and often found in the Gospel of Mark within these contexts;[45] the imperfect signals the anticipated reply or reaction. The prompt and revealing answer, when Jesus acquires the name of the demonic entity, reflects his power over the possessive force as it already obeys him in his speech act. Due to the dramaturgy of the text and similar structures found in other written sources of exorcistic conversations, it seems unlikely that this verse is only applied as a bridge to the information that many demons live in the man's body. Only the mutual revelation of identity renders the following exorcism possible and reveals the implied cosmological hierarchy "as a method of 'diagnosis' to determine the agent of affliction."[46] Moreover, the knowledge and accurate use of a name implies superiority and power over those named.[47]

The following attempt of the demonic legion to negotiate its range of operation[48] reflects its occupational and territorial nature. As the demons do not want to give up their conquest without a fight, they plea to stay in charge of a region and what supports it, which concurs with the Markan dualistic cosmology. Moreover, the locative aspect of their conflict is emphasized with territorial terminology (cf. πέμπτω 5:12, only here; ἀποστέλλω 5:10, only here; βασανίζομαι 5:7).[49] The four-time occurring παρεκάλει (vv. 10, 12, 17, 18) underscores again the powerful status of Jesus and shows in the imperfect form in v. 10 the iterative and durative imploring, in v. 12 in the aorist a sign of concession: Jesus finally allows the demons to enter the herd of pigs, apparently an unclean alternative to the man's dwelling in the tombs.[50] The separation of host and demon is underscored as the legion is assigned and captures a more suitable residence (εἰσέρχομαι,

---

[45] Cf. Mark 7:29, 30; 9:25, 26, 29; furthermore, PGM 4.1242–1243; 4.2258, 4.2265; 4.3007; 4.3013; 5.158.
[46] Sorensen 2002. 120, n. 4. Cf., e.g., Gen 32:29; Judg 13:17; T.Levi 5.5; 4QVisAmram b–e; Josephus, A.J. 8.48; Philostratus, Vit. Apoll. 4.20; T.Sol. 2:1; 3:6; 5:2–3; 11Q11 5.5–6; 4Q511 35.6–7; PGM 4.2251–53; 2343–45; 4.3037–3045; furthermore, Thraede, Exorzismus. 51; Bird in Blackwell; Goodrich; Maston (ed.) 2018.
[47] Cf. Iersel 1998. 199.
[48] Cf., e.g., PGM 4.3037–39.3041.3045; 4,3007–86.3033f.; T.Sol. 2:1 and 2:6; 5:2–3; 4:3–7; 11:1–7; bPes 112b–113a; Jub 10:1–11; Lucian, Abdic. 6. Cf. Bultmann 1967. 239; Koch 1975. 56, n. 7; Pesch 1972. 34–35. Cf. furthermore, Wiedemann 1905. 20; Maspero 1905. 159; Thraede, Exorzismus. 48.
[49] Cf. also φιμόω in 1:23–28; ἀπόλλυμι 1:24; ἐπιτιμάω in 9:14–29; with regard to authority: οὐκ ἀφίημι, "by no means permit" in 1:34; [ἔχειν] ἐξουσίαν, "to have authority" in 1:27; cf. Sorensen 2002. 133.
[50] There are many texts witnessing that ailments and demons can be transmitted to animals, in Babylonic and Hethitic contexts pigs in particular. Cf., e.g., Weinreich 1929. 176–177; Pesch 1971. 366; Stol 1993. 101; Collins 2007. 270, n. 81, 83.

ἐξέρχομαι).⁵¹ Consequently, the swine rush and disappear into the sea, which is not just a geographical marker but a location symbolically associated with demons, chaos monsters, and the satanic realm.⁵² As Jesus was just witnessed to impressively control raging waters (4:35–41; furthermore, 6:47–52), their ultimate defeat by the "tormenting" antagonist and master of spiritual and natural forces is certain. Then the man adapts to social standards as he is depicted dressed, acting mentally balanced, calm, and poised (v. 15). His request to follow Jesus reveals that he is the undivided "subject of his own words"⁵³ and wishes. He is re-socialized and reintegrated as he is sent to εἰς τὸν οἶκόν σου πρὸς τοὺς σούς.

As the evaluation of the more dominant interlocuter varies depending on the interpretation of the individual gestures and words used in this skirmish, the narrative is unambiguous that Jesus frees the man effortlessly from a violent legion of demonic entities by a powerful command (v. 8) and simple permission (v. 13).⁵⁴ The dramatic panic of the pigs underlines the successful healing of the Gerasene, an important feature in exorcism narratives⁵⁵ since it visually displays the triumph of the exorcist over the disembodied entities. Jesus' embodied identity, divine representation, and resulting power are vividly staged.⁵⁶

---

51 For this typical exorcistic feature, see, e.g., Collins 2007. 271; Ebner in Zimmermann (ed.) 2013. 273. For a sexual interpretation of these terms, see Carter 2015.
52 Cf., e.g., Isa 27:1; 51:9–11; Job 11:8–9; 26:12; Ps 93:3–4; 104:25; *1En*. 10:13; 54:5; 88:1, 3; 11Q11 4.4–9; 5.8–9; *T.Sol*. 5:11; 6:3, 5. Cf. also Rev 13:1. Cf. Malbon 1991. 58–59, 76–79; Thimmes 1992; Stolz, *Sea*; Zwiep 2019. 239.
53 Focant 2012. 200.
54 That the demons anticipated and planned Jesus' rejection in this region by the drowning of the pigs (until the successful mission of the healed man), is unlikely regarding Jesus' superiority (cf. Mark 3:21–30).
55 Cf. Josephus, *A.J.* 8.45–49, where the success of an exorcism officiated by Eleazar in the name of Salomon, is demonstrated by a falling water container. In Philostratus, *Vit. Apoll.* 4.20, Apollonius reports the exorcism of a man, whose previous possession is reflected in uncontrollable emotional outbursts, monologues, and great fear when encountering Philostratus, attesting to the successful exorcistic command by visibly shattering a column. Cf. Collins 2007. 271.
56 For comparisons of Jesus' exorcisms within the complex ancient notions of similarly effective men embedded in rather contingent concepts of magic, shamanism, prophecy, or charismatic, folk healing, see, e.g., Smith 1978. 471–476; Aune (ed.) 1980. 1523–1539; Drewermann 1992; Vermès; Hampel 1993. 45–68; Crossan 1994. 402–468; Kollmann 1996. 310; Stanton in Stanton (ed.) 2004. 129–144; Stegemann in Crüsemann; Schottroff (ed.) 2004. 84–88; Twelftree in Labahn; Lietaert Peerbolte (ed.) 2007. 81–86; Craffert 2008. 245–308; Meier 2009. 537–552; Gemeinhardt in Frey; Schröter (ed.) 2010; Kollmann in Holmén; Porter (ed.) 2011.

5.1.4 Interpretation

The reactions to this powerful exorcism are diverse. While the liberated man wishes to follow Jesus (μετά αὐτοῦ εἰμί), the fearful residents ask him to leave. Although the prior reprises and inverts Jesus' own call to discipleship (cf. Mark 1:16–20; 3:13–19; 6:7–13), Jesus denies the healed man his request, again with inexplicit reasons. However, the ex-demoniac complies with Jesus' command, at least regarding his actions. In particular contrast to the other liminal, dis/abled character in Mark 1:45, the ex-demoniac not only follows Jesus' instructions but strays from their extent—as the account heightens his reporting from ἀπαγγέλλω to κηρύσσω, a lexeme charged with meaning—and its addressees from those in close relationship to him to the entire Decapolis (v. 19).[57] While his dis/ability, as that of previously encountered characters, portrays a healed norm of re-socialization, it also reflects a novelty of his existence that is connected to the proclamation of Jesus. As κηρύσσω was used to designate the report of the man healed from *lepra*, who goes out (ἐξέρχομαι) and spreads (διαφημίζω) ὁ λόγος, it explicitly refers here and in Mark 7:36 to the experienced and witnessed healing: καὶ ἤρξατο κηρύσσειν [...] ὅσα ἐποίησεν αὐτῷ ὁ Ἰησοῦς.[58]

It completes the triad of word-of-mouth reports that structures the final part of the account as word spreads geographically with different results: In Mark 5:14, the pig herders flea and account (φεύγω; ἀπαγγέλλω) for what they have seen (i.e., ἐγένετο τῷ δαιμονιζομένῳ καὶ περὶ τῶν χοίρων) in the polis and on the fields (εἰς τὴν πόλιν καὶ εἰς τοὺς ἀγρούς) to the inhabitants of the region, who come to see for themselves and are frightened (φοβέω) at the sight of the now sound-minded and socially conformed man. Firsthand witnesses then contribute their version of events (διηγέομαι), resulting in the rejection of Jesus. Only when the man himself goes out and proclaims (ἀπέρχομαι; κηρύσσω) in the Decapolis all are amazed (θαυμάζω). This conclusion of the narrative stands in contrast to the negative, fearful rejection of the Gerasene community yet also to the more vigorous astonishment described in preceding and succeeding passages (cf., e. g., 1:27–28; 2:12; 5:42).[59] The inner contrast of the pericope puts emphasis on the proclamation of the personal experience that the redeemed ex-demoniac had with the "merciful" Jesus in contrast to the pieced-together account of a community de-

---

57 Moreover, the Markan motif of house and use of the term κηρύσσω connote discipleship (cf. Mark 5:38–43; 7:17, 24; 8:26; 9:28, 33?; 10:10 and 3:14; 6:12; 13:10; 14:9; 16:15, 20), at times specifically in context of exorcisms (3:15; 6:13), and the fact that Jesus is later on welcomed in this area (Mark 7:31–32) can be explained by the successful previous proclamation of the Gerasene. See 3.3.3.
58 Cf. also 1:4, 7, 14–15, 38–39, moreover, 3:14; 6:12; 13:10; 14:9; and 1:45; 5:20 and 7:36.
59 Cf. Kiffiak 2017. 84.

prived of their income. In its succession of previous healing narratives, the rather diminished astonishment, narrated briefly without further reaction, reflects implicitly the continuous build-up of criticism and hesitant reservation against Jesus, something only a particularly drastic and ambiguous representation of dis/ability could accomplish. Moreover, this is the final time the Gospel accounts for reports of Jesus' healing until the culminating and climaxing verse 7:36.[60] Again, yet on two levels, a dis/abled character is deployed to depict Jesus' astounding authority, on one hand to the characters of the narrative and, on the other, to the audience of the narrative.

Moreover, the dis/ability of the man and its emotional responses reflect upon *Jesus'* ambiguous (physical) nature.[61] During the entire verbal exchange until the demon's final demise, the audience must wonder about the intentions and positions of the two protagonists: who exorcises, adores, deceives, and averts whom. In this deliberate ambiguity, the focus shifts entirely to Jesus' superior yet similarly hybrid spiritual identity. "The charismatic power of Jesus is constructed as functioning authoritatively among other ambiguous, intermediate superhuman beings,"[62] as the narrative recalls the Markan cosmological imagery as outlined in Mark 3:22–30 (see ch. 3). Jesus frees the possessed demoniac, whom previously no one else was strong enough to bind (5:3, οὐκέτι οὐδεὶς ἐδύνατο αὐτὸν δῆσαι; 5:4, καὶ οὐδεὶς ἴσχυεν αὐτὸν δαμάσαι; cf. 3:23–27; see B. In Focus: Mark's Jesus and Opposing Forces), and thereby emphatically depicts his powerful restraint of hostile forces and, by extension, their master, as he already rhetorically announced. By picking up these representations of demonic dis/ability, Mark 5:1–20 continues the storyline of Jesus' divine and opposing cosmic conflict from Mark 1–3 with emphasizing effect on his identity and mission. As immanent mediators of transcendent (holy or impure) pneumatic powers,[63] Jesus and the demoniac encounter each other and negotiate physically within the context of their hierarchical cosmic order. Both accommodate liminal identities and occupy liminal spheres as they embody the inexplicable and socially transgressive origin of their "symptoms." Jesus also experiences rejection from a society in fear of his inexplicable authority; he reveals preternatural, veiled knowledge and is appointed by an elusive spiritual sphere. Wherever he goes, he causes (at times, undesirable) commotion and diverse reactions. The man, however, is freed from his liminal, fright-

---

60 Cf. also 1:28: ἐξῆλθεν ἡ ἀκοὴ αὐτοῦ and 1:45: διαφημίζω. Cf. Kiffiak 2017. 88.
61 Cf. Feldt in Verheyden; Kloppenborg (ed.) 2018. 51.
62 Ibid. 50.
63 See ch. 3; furthermore, Sorensen 2002. 142; Söding in Lange; Lichtenberger; Römheld (ed.) 2003. 528–531.

ening, and marginalized condition. Hence, it is the realm of influence, holy or impure, that seems to determine the desirable norm of (physical) existence.

In this narrative, the gospel plot deviates from its common short, comprised, astonishing accounts of healing to introduce a very unpredictable and intimate healing with diverse reactions in an entire area, "challenging the reader to realize that much of what he or she thinks of as normal might have turned out differently."[64]

While the question of 4:41 still lingers, τίς ἄρα οὗτός ἐστιν, Mark wastes no time in emphatically illustrating the core of Jesus' identity: his divinely bestowed pneumatic power over severe spiritual forces that oppose him. This image of dis/ability is unique in its ability to depict a) the spiritual foes' extradiegetic "disclosure" of Jesus' superior identity, as they raise additional direct questions (even if rhetorical) about Jesus and his relation to them,[65] which are subsequently answered by their demise; b) the demonic preternatural knowledge in contrast to the diverse reactions of witnesses, who are affected by the elusive and frightening nature of the dis/ability and its healing;[66] and c) "the narratively-mediated charisma of Jesus, which is tied to the verbalization of his ambiguity as an intermediate [...] agent,"[67] here in an intimate encounter with a similarly liminal character. The audience is not only directly asked but also answered about Jesus' identity in the cosmic scheme of things, as well as also given several possible reactions to consider as they get to share in a very personal experience of his liberative power.

5.2 Mark 5:21–43: Intercalated Healings of Two Daughters

5.2.1 Introduction to the Narrative

This section features two healing narratives interwoven with one another. When Jesus is on the way to help a girl with a life-threatening condition, he is delayed by the approach of a woman with irregular bleeding before continuing his journey to pull the girl back into life. This stylistic device of framing one narrative with another is common in the Gospel of Mark and provides coherence by similar and/or

---

64 Iersel 1998. 202–203.
65 Cf. 1:24: τί ἡμῖν καὶ σοί, Ἰησοῦ Ναζαρηνέ; 5:7; τί ἐμοὶ καὶ σοί, Ἰησοῦ υἱὲ τοῦ θεοῦ τοῦ ὑψίστου;
66 Cf. 1:27: τί ἐστιν τοῦτο; 5:15, 17: καὶ ἐφοβήθησαν; 5:20: καὶ πάντες ἐθαύμαζον, cf. also 5:18: παρεκάλει αὐτὸν ὁ δαιμονισθεὶς ἵνα μετ' αὐτοῦ ᾖ.
67 Feldt in Verheyden; Kloppenborg (ed.) 2018. 52.

contrasting features.⁶⁸ To the audience, the comparison of the two episodes is simply by their current presentation inevitable.⁶⁹ As the narratives are "connected, but yet separate enough to comment one on the other," they inform the audience with dramatic effect of "a new sense of direction in the Gospel"⁷⁰ revolving around key themes of the plot. As the dis/abled characters are deployed hinging between the two narratives, a closer look at this stylistic feature must be taken.

The mutual setting of the two narratives is implied by the disruption of the chronological sequence and geographical move of Jesus with Jaïrus in a crowd, as it heightens suspense.⁷¹ After Jesus set over to the western shore of the Sea of Galilee, he is encountered by a large crowd, among them Jaïrus, the petitioner of the first character with deviating physicality. Hence, the following sequence unfolds chronologically close to the exorcism of the Gerasene (πάλιν) yet opposes it by its location εἰς τὸ πέραν. As geographical and symbolical marker, the sea (θάλασσα) looms in between⁷² when Jesus finds himself in an undefined area with a large crowd drawing in because of his popularity. As the previous account depicts movement in an entire region around Jesus as a result of his healing actions (see above 5.1.1), on this side, the narrator follows Jesus as *he* moves away from the lake with an increasing local and social densification as his healing

---

68 While the different styles of the two stories (e.g., length of the sentences, tenses, and frequency of verbs) and rather sudden changes in setting and characters suggest that they were joined together at some point. Central motifs and structural connections speak for an intended insertion or original affiliation. Although the number of such "intercalations" in the Gospel of Mark varies according to different definitions, most scholars agree upon six occurrences: Mark 3:20–21(22–30)34–35; 5:21–24(25–34) 35–43; 6:7–13(14–29)30–32; 11:12–14(15–19)20–25; 14:1–2(3–9)10–11; 14:53–54(55–65)66–72. Shepherd 1993. 388–392, for a list of more possible passages. As it is not conducive for the current aim to recall the entire discussion on this Markan phenomenon, see for important stages of the redactional analysis of these "Verschachtelungen," e.g., Weiss 1872; Wendling 1905; Wellhausen 1905; Klostermann 1907; Rawlinson 1925. Esp. 67, 79; Dobschütz 1928; Nineham 1963; Kee 1977; Rhoads 1982; Neirynck 1972; Neirynck; Segbroeck 1982. Esp. 514–515, 517; Neirynck; Segbroeck 1991. 354–355. Cf. also Dibelius 1933. 225, n. 1; Bultmann 1931. 365; and for notions emphasizing the creative, theological, and most of all intentional character of the gospel narrative regarding these framing stories, e.g., Achtemeier 1975; Gnilka 1978; Schmithals 1979; Hurtado 1983; Lührmann 1987; Guelich 1989.
69 For extensive analyses of intercalations and reader-response criticism, see Fowler 1981; Fowler 1991; Shepherd 1991; moreover, van Oyen in Segbroeck (ed.) 1992; Hatton 2015; Proctor 2017, who include paradigms of (Greek) irony, absurdity, and comedy to explain the various ambiguities of the text.
70 Shepherd 1991. 387, quoted in van Oyen in Segbroeck (ed.) 1992. 973.
71 Cf. also other Markan intercalations that provide cohesion of time (and place) by contrast (e.g., 4:1–11; 14:53–72) or parallelism (e.g., 3:20–35; 11:11–25).
72 See above for notions associated with the place (cf. Mark 4:35–41; 5:13; 6:47–52).

power literally emanates to his surroundings.⁷³ This underscores the plot pattern that describes Jesus' movement towards the bedside of Jaïrus' daughter and a stalling, opposing motion through the narrative by flexions of the verb (εἰσ)ἔρχομαι (vv. 22, 27, 33, 35, 38, 39; cf. also ἐξέρχομαι in v. 30), respectively ἐπιστρέφω (v. 30), ὑπάγω (v. 34), ἐκβάλλω, and εἰσπορεύεται (v. 40).⁷⁴

First, Jaïrus *comes* to Jesus at the lake (v. 22), recounts his situation, and publicly, passionately, and successfully pleads Jesus to follow him to his daughter. Then, on the *way* to his house, the narrative is slowed down with a major cliffhanger when the inner story is initiated and the outer story faded out as the group around Jesus is stalled by a woman (ἐλθοῦσα ἐν τῷ ὄχλῳ, v. 27) with a long and arduous history of a hemorrhage, the second character with deviating physicality. Amid this pushing throng, the woman is healed by Jesus' moving δύναμις (ἐξέρχομαι, v. 30), causing a commotion about her secretive encounter (Jesus: ἐπιστρέφω ἐν τῷ ὄχλῳ, v. 30; περιβλέπω, v. 32). When she then *approaches* Jesus again openly (v. 33), she is sent away in peace (ὑπάγω εἰς εἰρήνην v. 34), implicitly leaving the scene.⁷⁵ Subsequently, messengers *arrive* (v. 35) and abruptly notify Jaïrus of his daughter's putative death. At this point, the messengers declare Jesus' coming as useless and involve the audience in their doubts with their open question: τί ἔτι σκύλλεις τὸν διδάσκαλον, which Jesus "overhears."⁷⁶ Whether or not Jesus will arrive in time to save the girl remains open, creating "an ellipsis of the outer story across the inner story" when the audience connects his overflowing δύναμις and the power of πίστις (esp. v. 34) with his emphatical encouragement to Jaïrus to μὴ φοβοῦ, μόνον πίστευε!⁷⁷ From this point on, the thus far rather reserved Jesus determines the plot by decisive actions and words.⁷⁸

On *entering* the house of Jaïrus (v. 38), the group and Jesus are greeted and held by the clamorous cries of a congregation of mourners who challenge the possibility of Jesus' endeavor. As he *enters* (v. 39), he replies to these cries of hopelessness with a remote "diagnosis": the girl hasn't died but is just sleeping. The mourners reply with ridicule and laughter and are involuntarily, maybe even forcefully,

---

73 Cf. Schiffer 2001. 141.
74 For a more detailed description of the effects of opening and closing of narrative gaps for intercalations, see Shepherd 1995. For the following outline of the narrative, see Focant 2012. 209–215; furthermore, Fischbach 1992. 157–160.
75 Cf. Zwiep 2019. 240.
76 The lexeme παρακούω can mean (accidentally/incidentally) listening to something when one is not addressed, not listening, ignoring, being disobedient, cf. Balz; Schneider, *παρακούω*; LSJ, *s.v*; Montanari, *s.v.* In any case, Jesus "was not deterred by the message," Taylor 1957. 294. Cf. Hooker 1991. 149.
77 See below on σῴζω (Mark 5:23, 28) and πίστις/πιστεύω (5:34, 36).
78 Cf. Oppel 1995. 151.

sent away (ἐκβάλλω, v. 40).⁷⁹ Finally, the nameless mother and Jaïrus *enter* (εἰσπορεύεται, v. 40) the room of the girl with Jesus and three of his disciples (cf. Mark 1:29–31). The eagerly anticipated happens: Jesus touches the girl, speaks ταλιθα κουμ, and the body of the daughter (re)awakens to life.

Hence, the setting and the temporal pattern of the two stories draw them close together. While the framing narrative is mainly written in historical present and parataxis, with frequent use of connective καις to portray the rapid succession of events in this pressing situation,⁸⁰ it also restricts the temporal development of the framed narrative. The woman with the hemorrhage is introduced by a long line of participles, an analepsis of her character defining life story. With the first indicative of the inner story, the story time of the outer story continues simultaneously in "historical sequence," mainly in aorist and imperfect with further chronological and spatial elapses for explanatory background information. With the ending of the framed narrative, only scattered and implicit references to the healing of the woman are made, and "synchrony" takes place, "that is, two events occurring at the same time, [...] at the stories' junction in Mark 5:34–36 where Jesus' words of peace to the woman occur at the same time as Jaïrus receives the message of the death of his daughter."⁸¹

Jesus and the two petitioners are the central characters of the narrative (see below). Although Jaïrus' daughter remains an inactive and passive point of reference in the background, her urgent physical condition is not static but dynamic as it worsens.⁸² The surrounding and accompanying amorphous crowd(s) (vv. 21, 24, 27, 31) with the disciples (v. 31; particularly Peter, James, and John, v. 38), messengers (v. 35), and mourners (v. 38), as well as the contrasting physicians (v. 26) and the nameless mother of the girl (v. 38), all serve as continuous witnesses of Jesus' popularity and overcoming healing ability, especially when they oppose, hinder, and question his healing movement. The tight chronological plot with its flashbacks ends abruptly in Mark 5:43, without any fadeout or conclusion, when Jesus and his disciples leave the geographical setting to go to his hometown.⁸³

An important feature of both narratives is contrasting focalization. In the framed account, matching its form, the omniscient narrator grants the audience insight into the woman's intentions, physical sensations, and emotional reactions (vv. 25–29, 33), as well as into Jesus' ambiguity and palpable yet subconscious heal-

---

79 Cf. Zwiep 2019. 68–69.
80 The urgency of the situation is only depicted in the rapid succession of events. There are very few intensifiers (πολλά, vv. 23, 43; εὐθύς, v. 42) or visual descriptions employed.
81 Shepherd 1995. 526, n. 12.
82 Cf. Zwiep 2019. 243.
83 Cf. ibid. 235–236.

ing (vv. 30–32). By contrast, neither Jaïrus nor his daughter is characterized internally; rather, the account is externally focalized.[84] Therefore, the audience identifies with and relates to the hemorrhaging woman and Jesus, while being challenged to comprehend and align Jaïrus' and Jesus' interactions. Moreover, contrary to previous passages, Jesus is depicted oblivious to the intentions and identity of the woman; he neither knows who touched him nor why (vv. 31–32; cf. esp. 2:8; 3:1–6).[85] Hence, the audience must still be irritated when Jesus establishes the condition of the girl without even having looked at her, conflicting with popular and vociferous opinion (v. 39). Contrary to the sandwiched narrative, the narrator refrains from informing the audience of the character's (i.e., the girl's) current state and Jesus' internal conviction, which after his oblivious search for the woman casts doubt on his diagnosis of the girl. Within this increasing suspense, the audience must wonder if this actually is the reliable and omniscient protagonist they have encountered before.[86]

5.2.2 Images of Dis/ability

5.2.2.1 The Daughter of Jaïrus

Firstly, the girl's physical deviance is depicted by implicit descriptions of her passivity in contrast to the described vivid movements of her surroundings, by the physical and outspoken petition of her father, and by the expressive physicalness of Jesus (especially in the framed story), who overcomes obstacles to heal her. Moreover, the spatial and temporal course of the stories does not only develop suspense but emphasizes the girl's dis/ability, the time constraints of her fatal condition, and her unanimated body, lying silently and unmovable in her father's house, locally and socially isolated.

Her social status is emphatically determined by and dependent on her father, who is introduced and mainly referred to by his prestigious office and name (vv. 22, 35, 36, 38). This accounts for historical legitimacy and juxtaposes his nameless daughter and wife along with the other named male characters in the final scene.[87] The ἀρχισυνάγωγος represents his daughter,[88] who is confined to her

---

[84] Cf. Rüggemeier 2017. 38–39.
[85] Cf. Iersel 1998. 205–206. Due to his active search, it is unlikely that his question is rhetorical.
[86] Cf. Bosenius in Du Toit; Gerber; Zimmermann (ed.) 2019. 178–179, n. 56.
[87] Cf. Schiffer 2001. 163. Cf. also the fitting etymology of the Graecized name in Hebrew where it translates to "he who enlightens/is enlightened," cf. also Num 32:41; Judg 10:3–4; Est 2:5; Deut 3:14; Josh 13:30; 1Chr 20:5; and Ilan; Ziem; Hünefeld 2002. Ad loc. in each volume; Wolter 2008. 325; Stare

bed due to her condition. Opposing her physical passivity, her father actively falls to Jesus' feet and appeals intensely (πολλὰ) and with great urgency (cf. the elliptical ἵνα)[89] for his famous healing touch. This recalls the contrast between the passivity of Peter's mother-in-law and the man who could not walk, and their active petitioners who were encouraged by Jesus' popularity and reputation for healing (cf., e. g., 1:28, 33, 37, 39, 45, 3:7–11). The girl's body creates by its immobility a spatial and social distance and isolation, which must be bridged by her active father. Moreover, the text emphatically describes Jaïrus' daughter as κοράσιον (vv. 41, 42), παιδίον (vv. 39, 40, 41), and little θυγάτηρ/ θυγάτριον (vv. 23, 35). The possessive pronouns and diminutives show her dependency and the relationship to her father and define her childish-female body. However, the subsequent mention of her age (v. 42) limits her childishness against the backdrop of cultural stages of coming of age, as she is on the verge of womanhood.[90]

5.2.2.1.1 Between Life and Death, Death and Sleep, Rising and Raising

Her father then describes her to be ἐσχάτως ἔχω (vv. 22–23), pleading Jesus for his healing touch so that she σωθῇ καὶ ζήσῃ. The description ἐσχάτως ἔχω is found only here in the New Testament but is a customary, idiomatic syntagma, frequently encountered in the context of medical texts.[91] It designates a grave and deadly physical condition, "to be at the last extremity."[92] The audience is given no explanation nor indication of the cause, duration, or process of her dis/ability and if

---

in Zimmermann (ed.) 2013. 585. For an interesting intertextual approach regarding Judg 11:34–40[LXX], see Beavis 2010.
88 An ἀρχισυναγώγος supervises, plans, and oversees synagogue gatherings (Schürer et al. 1979. 434–435), as well as the affairs and administration of the Jewish community (Boring 2006. 158; Collins 2007. 279; Focant 2012. 217), or denominates a synagogue donor (Kahl in Zimmermann [ed.] 2013. 285). In any case, it is the title of a person of distinction.
89 Cf. Zwiep 2019. 52.
90 Cf. the transition of נַעֲרָה to בּוֹגֶרֶת in the dialectical texts of bKet 39a.98a.10b; bSan 66b; also Zimmermann 2001. 240–241; Urban in Erlemann; et al. (ed.) 2005. 26; Stare in Zimmermann (ed.) 2013. 588, and the Hellenistic-medical distinctions around the age of fourteen in, e.g., Soranus, Gyn. 1.33. Cf. comprehensively Rogge; Seidler, Kinderkrankheiten; Deissmann, Kind. Esp. 491. Regarding the literary depiction of children in Mark, see Gundry in Bunge; Fretheim; Gaventa (ed.) 2008.
91 Cf. Rochais 1981. 58; von Bendemann in Janssen; Jones; Wehnert (ed.) 2011. 42, n. 10, who lists Galen, Comm. CH Aph. 7.18, 116; vict. att. 71.3; Alexander Med., lumbr. 2.589; Meletius Med., nat. hom. 75.4. See also the usage of the adjective in an inscription from Kos (ca. 200 BCE), honoring the physician Anaxippos, who saved many citizens form "μεγ(ά)λας ἀρωστίας" and "κινδύνους τοὺς ἐσχάτους." Cf. Benedum 1977. 270; Collins 2007. 279; moreover, Josephus, A.J. 9.179; Diodorus, Bib. hist. 10.3.4; Artemidorus, Onir. 3.60.
92 Cf., e.g., Montanari, s.v; LN, s.v 23.151; LSJ, s.v; Schnabel, ἔσχατος. 28.

there were measures taken previously and, if so, which ones. The dire situation is furthermore outlined by the hoped for outcome: σωθῇ καὶ ζήσῃ. Both terms underscore the urgency and illustrate that she "must be saved from imminent death *and* pursue a life that is only beginning."[93] However, the term ζάω (ζῶν and ζωή) is subsequently also employed to designate a fullness of life in context of an eschatological existence.[94] Moreover, it remains unclear why Jesus trusts the passionate plea of Jaïrus and follows him. The lack of information foregrounds the suffering of the father, the girl's dis/ability, and the desperate hope in Jesus. The focus does not lie on a medical diagnosis or advised therapy but on Jesus' prompt intervention. Any questions regarding the girl's physical state get lost in the pressing danger and required haste of the situation.

Indeed, her condition does worsen, as the messengers inform Jaïrus of her death with a lexeme that leaves no doubt about her fatal physical state (ἀπέθανεν, v. 35). However, as they reach the house filled with mourning, Jesus establishes that she is not dead but asleep (οὐκ ἀπέθανεν, ἀλλὰ καθεύδει, v. 39). As in v. 35, the subject (here, the girl) is placed before the predicate, which is an unusual sentence structure for the Gospel of Mark. Jesus' statement is therefore emphatically parallelized and surpassed with that from the mouth of the messengers.[95] Both states share physical similarities, such as unconsciousness, corporal repose, and calm recumbency. However, as in Mark, καθεύδω usually describes, together with ἐγείρω, the daily human physical state of rest, and ἀποθνῄσκω clearly depicts the divinely guarded (physical) cessation of earthly life and its physical states.[96] Both cannot be correct at the same time on the story level, if taken literally. The audience must wonder if Jesus is indeed wrong or, more likely, if his statement figuratively refers to the following demonstration of his *power over death* or to a common ancient *euphemism* for the state of being deceased: to him, death is temporary, not ultimate, just like sleep and his effortless "saving" can be compared to waking some-

---

93 Focant 2012. 210; following Rochais 1981. 59, emphasis added.
94 Cf. esp. Mark 9:43–47, see ch. 4; cf. moreover, 8:34–38; 10:30; 12:27; also 10:45 and 16:11; and Oppel 1995. 163–164.
95 Cf. Gundry 1993. 274.
96 The two states were often featured as related conditions in poetic, philosophical, and medical texts and HB/OT and rabbinic literature account for a euphemistic and eschatological understanding of death as sleep. Cf. comprehensively with numerous sources: Bultmann, θάνατος and cogn; Coenen, καθεύδω; Klein, θάνατος; LN, s.v. 23.66, 23.104, 23.99; LSJ, s.v. Esp. 967–968; Oepke, καθεύδω. 333, 435; Stamatu, *Schlaf*; van Hooff, *Tod.* 868; Völkel, καθεύδω. Cf. also Mark 4:27, 38; 13:36; with metaphorical nuances only in 14:37, 40, 41. For ἀποθνῄσκω cf. 7:10; 8:31; 9:26, 31; 12:19–21; 14:31; 15:44; θάνατος: 9:1; 10:33; 14:34; 14:55; νεκρός: 12:27; ἀποκτείνω and ἀπόλλυμι: 3:4, 6, see ch. 4.

one who is sleeping.[97] It could also be, as suspense is at its height, that the amorphous crowd is proven wrong: the girl is only *believed* to be dead since she is in a sleeplike state, and Jesus indeed knows the truth, or she is only *pronounced* to be dead since her ailment has processed to "the point of death,"[98] where she belongs to the "dynamic" realm of the dead, which can already be experienced in life.[99] Neither a concrete phrasing with regard to a figure of speech or euphemism nor a concrete allusion to a religious or cultural notion of stages of death or eschatological passing can be made explicit for the Markan style and the narratives' conceptions for this pericope and its position in particular. Rather, "the narrator allows the contradiction to stand with no resolution: at the conclusion the girl 'got up' [...]. Hence the ambiguity does appear to be part of the strategy of the narrative [...] the narrator is deliberately contrasting the popular notion in the story that the girl is dead with Jesus' assertion that the girl is sleeping."[100]

Consequently, the narrative also only implicitly recalls notions of corpse impurity, even if the composition with accounts on pneumatic impurity (5:1–20, see above) and irregular, hence impure, bleeding (see below) underscores any allusions thereof. As a prominent and prevalent concept in antiquity, it cannot be negated as an undercurrent notion here as well.[101] However, the seeming indifference of the text toward the inevitable (but to be avoided) proximity to corpses adds another layer to the ambiguity of the text. If the girl really has died, why does Jesus not dread such close contact with her?

5.2.2.1.2 Beyond Pathologization

As the state of the girl remains undefined by an extradiegetic voice, her healed physicality also eludes concrete paradigms by the use of the polysemes ἐγείρω and ἀνίστημι (vv. 41–42). Both can be and are used to depict the waking from

---

97 In correspondence with the ancient concept of sleep and death, the use of κοιμάω would have been unequivocal—a word not once mentioned in the Gospel of Mark (cf., e. g., John 11 for a similar narrative of a raising with a euphemistical remote diagnosis of an explicitly knowledgeable Jesus, v. 11; furthermore, Acts 7:60; 13:36; 1Cor 7:39; 1Thess 4:13 (κοιμώμενοι); 1Cor 15:20 (κεκοιμημένοι). Cf. Boring 2006. 162; Focant 2012. 214.
98 Collins 2007. 279.
99 Cf. the intriguing yet unbalanced analysis of Fischbach 1992. 98–110, on a dynamic aspect of death as accounted for in a selection of (cultic) Psalms. Cf. also Schiffer 2001. 142–143.
100 Hedrick 1993. 230.
101 Cf. Num 5:1–4; 9:6; 19:11–22; 31:19–24; furthermore, Ezek 9:7; Hag 2:13; particularly for priests and Nazarites Lev 21:1–4, 11; Ezek 44:25; Num 6:6–12. For other prevalent cultural notions of the time on impurity of the dead, often regarding cultic spheres, see Choksy 1989; Wächter 1910; Schiffman in Schiffman (ed.) 1990; Assmann; Lorton 2005; Berlejung 2009. Cf. also Kazen 2002. 196; Thiessen 2020. 97–122.

sleep, rising from a lying position, and raising from the dead.¹⁰² Similarly ambiguous, Mark 9:26–27 reprises the tactile healing of an ailment-struck child, stated (λέγω) to have died by several bystanders (Mark 5:35, ἔρχονται ἀπὸ τοῦ ἀρχισυναγώγου and 9:26, τοὺς πολλοὺς).¹⁰³ The social death of both children is certified by their surroundings.¹⁰⁴ By stating that Jaïrus' daughter did not die, Jesus reintegrates her body in the discourse, hence already initiates the overcoming of her "social" death. The change to a standing position proves the successful healing, as does the walking around and Jesus' command to give her something to eat. Similar to the accounts of the other formerly recumbent patients, her healed physical state, after being dead or asleep, alludes to everyday social behavior and live-sustaining measures.¹⁰⁵ Moreover, over the discourse on the girl's passive physical condition, the narrative implicitly constructs a successive emancipation of her body by a) a reversal of dependent familial ties (5:40) and omitted diminutives and possessive pronouns (5:23, 35, 39, 40, 41, 42; 41, το τὸ κοράσιον in 5:42); by b) Jesus' withdrawal of her body from pathologization (5:39); and lastly by c) her now active and, mobility-wise, independent existence, risen, walking around, and eating. Within the standards of ancient everyday life, this might simply allude

---

102 See 3.2; cf. also Bosenius in Du Toit; Gerber; Zimmermann (ed.) 2019. 178–179, n. 56.
103 κρατήσας τῆς χειρός [...] ἤγειρεν [...] ἀνέστη, see 7.1; 7.2.2; 7.3.2.
104 While this contrast of popular or medical opinion with the correct insight and help administered by more powerful men might allude to a prominent feature in similar ancient healing narratives, the Markan text remains too implicit and vague on the matter. Cf., e.g., Philostratus, *Vit. Apoll.* 4.45, who recounts a narrative from the life of Apollonius of Tyana, where he encounters the procession of a congregation mourning the death of a young woman on her wedding day. In the epilogue, Philostratus discusses, if the girl was actually raised from the dead or if she was falsely pronounced dead by the doctors. He closes with the skeptical remark, that this will remain inexplicable to him and the witnesses. Cf. also two accounts about the virtuous doctor Asclepiades, who also encounters funeral processions, where he declares the supposedly dead for alive, pronounced dead by medical mistake. He then uses his pharmacological knowledge to bring the hidden life forth again, cf. Apuleius, *Flor.* 19; on Asclepiades: Pliny, *Nat.* 7.37.124 and furthermore, Celsus, *Med.* 2.6.16–18. Likewise, Jambliochs tells of an old Chaldäer, that noticed a breath of air from the lungs of a girl carried to be buried and saves her from her funeral (cf. Iamblichus, *Bab.*); Talmudic and rabbinic accounts witness to "revifications" performed by Honi the Circle-Drawer and Hanina ben Dosa (cf. *bBer* 34b; *yBer* 9d; comprehensively: Vermès; Hampel 1993). From ancient perspective, raisings of the dead were regarded as supernatural and were used as rhetorical examples for the impossible or inexplicable deeds of mighty men, e.g., in legends of philosophers or magical papyri (cf. more examples in Weinreich 1909. 172; Oepke, ἀνίστημι/ἐξανίστημι. 369). Cf. also the accounts on Asclepius where he is paid to heal those moribund with the magical powers of Medusa's blood and consequently gets killed by Zeus for exceeding his competence. Cf. Weinreich 1909. 142; Blackburn 1991. 24; Edelstein; Edelstein 1998. I. 7–10; 13–16; 33–34; 37–38; 42–43; 49–50; 54; 58–59; 112.
105 Cf. "serving" in 1:31; walking around and returning home in 2:9–12.

to a previous status quo, but considering the ambiguous "resurrection" and the intercalation with the other narrative, a new norm of existence transpires (see below 5.2.3).

5.2.2.2 The Woman with the Hemorrhage

The dis/ability of the woman who secretly draws close to Jesus for his healing touch is mainly reflected in the participles that introduce her. She is not identified by name, status within her family or society, or ethnographic affiliation.[106] She *is* the woman with the hemorrhage with a long clinical history: for twelve years, she has been suffering from an issue of blood (ἐν ῥύσει αἵματος, v. 25), failed therapies, many doctors, and economic deficit.[107] Instead of any improvement, she experienced aggravation of her suffering (vv. 25–26), driving her to Jesus with the wish for healing.

5.2.2.2.1 Flowing Transitions and Incorporated Suffering: Physical Ir-/regular Bleeding and Social Im-/purity

In the New Testament, the substantive ῥύσις occurs in composition with αἵματος only here and in this narrative's parallel accounts.[108] In its wording, it is reminiscent of irregular genital bleeding as accounted for in Lev 15^{LXX} and 12:7^{LXX}. Embedded in the great thematical context of priestly purity regulations, along with λέπρα, childbirth, and corpse contact,[109] Lev 13–15 differentiates between abnormal and normal, male and female genital discharge, its cleansing periods, cultic regulations, and communicability. Here, irregular *and* regular bleedings are also labeled by numerous other, similar terms; hence, the transition between the two is "fluid,"

---

[106] This is different to the other female patients, namely Peter's mother-in-law, Jaïrus' daughter, and the daughter of the Syrophoenician woman.
[107] For the topos of failing medical personnel, cf., e.g., 2Chr 16:12; Tob 2:10; 1Q20 20.20; Sir 10:10, 38:1–15; Philo, *Sacr.* 70; Weinreich 1909. 195–196; Kollmann 1996. 230, n. 34.
[108] Cf. v. 25; Luke 8:43–44; (Matt 9:20: αἱμορροοῦσα).
[109] Cf. the interpretation of the Priestly categorization of dis/ability of man and beast in four categories, embedded between the binary poles of *tahor* and *tame* (im-/pure), *mum* and *not-mum* (un-/maimed) in Stewart in Moss; Schipper (ed.) 2011. 74. On the following, see Cohen in Pomeroy (ed.) 1991; Harrington 1993; D'Angelo in Cavadini (ed.) 1999; Poorthuis; Schwartz 2000; Haber 2003; Wassen in Voitila; Jokiranta (ed.) 2008; Kazen in Ehrlich; Runesson; Schuller (ed.) 2013; Wassen in Kalimi (ed.) 2016, and with great emphasis regarding anti-Judaistic interpretations of this narrative, e.g., Kellenbach 1994; Kahl in Schottroff; Wacker (ed.) 1996; Fonrobert in Evans; Sanders (ed.) 1997; Kraemer; D'Angelo 1999; Levine in Levine; Blickenstaff (ed.) 2001 [1996].

which renders her ailment as specifically uteral.¹¹⁰ According to Lev 15:25–30^LXX, a woman with irregular bleeding, following the regular time of menstruation, is for the entire time of her bleeding and the seven-day cleansing period (including her immersion and offering) regarded as ritually impure, as is her seating and bedding, which can also convey an abbreviated time of impurity to the ones touching it. This temporary yet, from the onset, not limited status as *zabah*¹¹¹ does not hinder normal everyday life but has certain cultic restrictions, demands, and precautions regarding its communicability to others.¹¹² The exact conditions of the latter, however, are not explicitly unequivocal on a textual basis.¹¹³

Similar yet stricter cultic implementations can be found in the somewhat "utopian" or idealized text of Num 5:1–3^LXX for those suffering from abnormal discharge among other cases of impurity.¹¹⁴ The undesirability of permanent genital bleeding is reflected in the demand for sexual abstinence during irregular or regular bleeding in many passages of the Hebrew Bible/Old Testament. This demand implies infertility and may also be connected with social stigma.¹¹⁵ Moreover, Da-

---

110 Cf. Weissenrieder in Stegemann; Malina; Theissen (ed.) 2002. 75–76: ῥύσις αἵματος (Lev 15:25); ἣ ῥέουσα αἵματι (Lev 15:19); ἡ ῥύσις (Lev 15:2, 19, 25–33); ῥέω (Lev 15:33); πηγὴ τοῦ αἵματος (Lev 12:7); αἱμορροῦσῃ (Lev 15:33); cf. also Lev 18:19 und 20:18. Cf. also Weissenrieder 2003. 237. The accounts Preuss 1989. 437, lists to prove that πηγή signifies uterus in several Hebrew texts are not unambiguous.
111 This is in one category with abnormal male discharge, *zab*, cf. Kazen 2002. 128–129; Thiessen 2020. 71–72.
112 Cf. Milgrom 1991. 936, 943; Harrington 1993. 255–259; Kazen 2002. 146–147.
113 For once, in the very detailed and accurately determined regulations, corresponding with those for regular bleeding, the addition πᾶς ὁ ἁπτόμενος αὐτῆς ἀκάθαρτος ἔσται ἕως ἑσπέρας (15:19) is absent, hence explicitly describes only a communicability over objects for irregular bleeding, cf. Weissenrieder in Stegemann; Malina; Theissen (ed.) 2002. 77. This concurs with the Hebrew text of Lev 15:27 in the MT and the Samaritan Pentateuch. However, the LXX and several medieval Hebrew manuscripts also regard those touching a *zabah* as impure. Moreover, the notion that a *zabah* communicates impurity by touching can only be inferred by the usually analogue preceding regulations concerning the *zab* (irregular male dischargers), who convey impurity by touching someone with unwashed hands; cf. Lev 15:1–18^LXX, especially v. 11; cf., e.g., Kazen 2002. 141–143; Haber 2003. 143; Thiessen 2020. 73, moreover, Wenham 1979. 219; Gerstenberger 1993. 184–185; Metternich 2000. 80–83; Kahl in Zimmermann (ed.) 2013. 286. About both discrepancies can be speculated in both directions as they can be explained by different sources, rhetoric, harmonization, redactional changes, or simply practicability, cf. Trummer 1991. 112–113; Gerstenberger 1993. 187; Fonrobert in Evans; Sanders (ed.) 1997. 130–131. Cf. also the subsequent "equalizing tendency […] in both rabbinic and Qumran material" of male and female discharge in, e.g., *mZab* 5:1, 6, 10; Lev 15:24, 33; *mZab* 5:11; *Sifra* to Lev 15:24, Lev 15:25; *bNid* 33a; cf. Kazen 2002. 156.
114 Cf. Cohen in Pomeroy (ed.) 1991.
115 Cf., e.g., Lev 18:19 and 20:18; Ezek 18:6; 22:10; Lam 1:17; also Gen 1:28; 9:1; 11:30; 25:21; 29:31; 30:1–2; Ruth 4:11; Judg 13:2–3; 1Sam 1:6–11; 2:5; Isa 54:1; furthermore, Hos 9:14; Num 5:11–31;

vid's curse in 2Sam 3:29^{LXX} conveys that male and female discharge of semen and blood (here, γονορρυής) count among *lepra*, death in war, and hunger as execrable and severe conditions. This is also reflected in texts of Second Temple Judaism. The successive Mishna tractates interpret the Levitical conceptions with a detailed focus on the materiality, temporality, and communicability of ir-/regular bleeding in a state of impurity—the implications mainly regard cultic participation.[116] Josephus and the Temple Scroll also describe an (idealized) spatial quarantine for those affected by exceptional cases of transmissible impurity (such as *lepra*, *zab*, childbirth) with particular focus on sacred spaces.[117]

As none of the texts reflects authentic descriptions of (common) social reality in any given Jewish community of the time, it is again only the stigmatizing notion of prescriptive, not descriptive,[118] ritual impurity with distancing implementations (at least for cultic realms) and sexual abstinence that can account for this label of the woman's condition.[119] While it is true that the ethnic-religious provenance of the woman is not specified by Mark, as is common for the gospel text unless it is of central relevance for the narrative (cf. Mark 7:27), this does not reflect on the projected notions carried by the audience.

However, the complexity of the alluded notions in these diverse texts with various intentions and sources describing particular circumstances and bodies cannot be stressed enough (see 3.3). Based on the strong terminological link to the conditions described in Leviticus[120] and its reprised yet ambiguous notions in Second Temple literature, those suffering from an irregular ῥύσις αἵματος, must carry some form of social stigma just due to its undesirability, *indefinite* state of cultic unavailability, and caution regarding (sexual) contact. Similar descriptions and evaluations of (genital) ir-/regular bleeding can be found in Greco-Roman texts, where they are among other terms also designated with ῥύσις αἵματος (respective-

---

Exod 23:26; Isa 49:20–21; *bNed* 64b; *ShemR* 1.34; cf. Boyarin 1993. 204–205; Wassen in Voitila; Jokiranta (ed.) 2008. 644; Stewart in Moss; Schipper (ed.) 2011. 76–77.

116 Cf. *mKel* 1.1–5; *mNid* 7.4a and b; *mZab* 2.1, 5.1, 5.6, 5.11; cf. also *bBer* 22a; *bKet* 61a but *bBMes* 83b–85a. For a contextual analysis, see Cohen in Pomeroy (ed.) 1991. Esp. 278–279, 283–284; Milgrom 1991. 948–953.

117 Cf. Josephus, *A.J.* 3.261–262; 9.74; 9.225–226; 11Q19 46.16–18; 48.13–17; also 4Q274 frg. 1, 1.2–3; furthermore, Harrington 1993; Kazen 2002. 133, 113–114; Wassen in Voitila; Jokiranta (ed.) 2008. 133, 113–114; Stewart in Schwartz; et al. (ed.) 2008. See 3.3.

118 Cf. Fonrobert in Evans; Sanders (ed.) 1997. 129.

119 Cf. ibid. 134, n. 34; Kazen 2002. 150, refering to Milgrom 1991. 952–953; Wright; Jones, *Discharge*. 205.

120 Cf. Fonrobert in Evans; Sanders (ed.) 1997. 129.

ly, *flux sanguinis*).[121] These accounts furthermore underscore the ambiguity of such a discharge since the evaluation of any bleeding depends on qualitative descriptions of the fluid and its accompanying symptoms; both are nondisclosed in the Markan text. Issues of blood can be understood as constitutional, cleansing, and balancing measures or as evidence of deadly sicknesses as they indicate a possible etiology of an ailment via consistency and color.[122] Explicit gynecological bleedings are documented in the context of (aborted) pregnancies and menstruation, where the blood can find its way through the various physical openings (e. g., nose, mouth, ear, skin).[123] Usually, they were neither precisely explained nor distinguished as irregular and regular bleedings.[124] The descriptions of chronic issues of the uterus might also include other liquids, and alleviation was promised from showers and bandages, thermal regiments, dietetics and exercise, or vaginal suppositories to "strengthen" the body.[125] There are also accounts that witness to restrictions with regard to sacred sites after giving birth—as sexual abstinence and infertility were discussed—and to a notion of disgust.[126]

While the normal, regular, and regulating blood flow is here positively valued as it cleanses and balances the body when in disequilibrium, it is again the duration of the bleeding that renders the Markan woman as dis/abled: Her body is de-

---

121 Cf. ῥοῦς γυναικείω (CH, *Aph.* 5.56), καταμήνια (CH, *Mul.* 1.2; *Aph.* 5.33, 36, 50); κάθαρσις (CH, *Mul.* 1.4), γυναικείων ἀγωγόν (CH, *Aph.* 5.61; Soranus, *Gyn.* 1.19); menses (Pliny, *Nat.* 26.151–152); mulierum menses (*Nat.* 29.44); fluctiones mulierum (*Nat.* 21.123), purgationes feminarum/ mulierum (*Nat.* 20.21); cf. Weissenrieder 2003. 240–241.
122 Cf., e. g., Caelius, *Chron.* 2.9.117, 126–127.
123 Cf., e. g., Soranus, *Gyn.* 1.46; 2.43; CH, *Coac.* 2.522, 163; *Aph.* 5.32–33 (αἵματος ῥύσις ῥινῶν); Pliny, *Nat.* 26.131 (sanguis profluctio); CH, *Mul.* 1.1; 2.110.; *Morb. mul.* 1.62; Caelius, *Chron.* 9.128–132; Clement of Alexandria, *Paed.* 3.3. An ailing and weak body fails to protect itself from harmful substances. Even warm air and too much liquidness when taking a bath can soften and sicken the body, cf., e. g., Galen, *San. tu.* 5.2. K 6.316. Especially the female body was contrary to the male body regarded as soft, porous, and moist, hence weak. See for the following extensively and with more references, Temkin 1991; Dean-Jones 1994; King 1998; Flemming 2000; Weissenrieder in Stegemann; Malina; Theissen (ed.) 2002. 80; Distelrath, *Menstruation*. 606–607; Hanson; Flemming, *Frau*. 307; Föllinger, *Geschlecht*. 340.
124 Cf. ῥοῦς γυναικείου, ῥυσέως, ῥύσις (CH, *Aph.* 5.56); Soranus for both: ῥοῦς γυναικείου; Pliny uses equivalently: profluvium (Pliny, *Nat.* 26.160), sanguinem et undecumque fluentem (*Nat.* 27.18), sanguis profluvia (*Nat.* 26,131.133), fluctiones mulierum, profluvia feminarum (*Nat.* 27.103; 29.9); cf. Weissenrieder 2003. 241.
125 Cf., e. g., Soranus, *Gyn.* 2.40–44 in Soranus 1894. 124–126. Cf. also, Dean-Jones 1994. 142; D'Angelo in Cavadini (ed.) 1999. 93; Collins 2007. 280.
126 Cf., e. g., Theophrastus, *Characters* 16.9; Censorinus, *The Birthday Book* 11.7; Isidore, *Ethym.* 11.1.141; CH, *Mul.* 1.25; 2.127; 3.213; *Genit.* 4; *Virg.* 1; Pliny, *Nat.* 7.15.64–67; and Thiessen 2020. 76–77; Hanson; Flemming, *Frauenheilkunde*. 311; Hanson; Flemming, *Frau*. 308.

scribed to be porous, soft, and "leaky," not dry, well-regulated, and well-tempered but permeable to harmful substances and "dripping" for twelve years.[127] Accordingly, her healing is depicted as a hardening of the body, as "drying up" the source, and stopping the blood flow.[128]

Hence, the anamnesis of the woman with the issue of blood in Mark 5, the duration of her suffering, and the costly and failed therapies can be regarded as defining determinations of her gynecological bleeding. As is common for the gospel, the text neither alludes to the etiology or reasons for her ailment. The focus lies entirely on the duration, severity, and incurability of her dis/ability: she is "situated" in her blood flow; it has been an inseparable part of the past twelve years of her life.[129] The duration of her ailment, however, also implies a rather steady, not urgent, call for help, contrary to the daughter of Jaïrus. Besides, this physical deviance connotes ritual impurity, with possible relational, familial, and sexual consequences, demands for cultic unavailability, cautious social contact, and stigmatization by narrative associations. However, the Markan text is particularly silent on the "issue" of the woman's impurity, unlike Mark 1:40–45. The woman is not encountered in liminal space but ἐν τῷ ὄχλῳ (v. 27); neither are measures of purification prescribed, nor is her healing termed καθαρίζω or καθαρισμός (see 3.3.2–3.3.3). Rather, "her illness is [made] explicit; her impurity is implicit."[130] Like with the dead-sleeping girl (see 5.2), it seems as if the Markan text intentionally alludes to a popular yet broad spectrum of notions of impurity that leave the audience and, for that matter, the woman in this ambiguous and open state of negotiable pathologization and dis/ability.

This is underscored by the double description of her impairment with the lexeme μάστιξ (vv. 29, 34), "a condition of great distress, torment, suffering" alluding to the "scourging" character of the ailments that Jesus heals (see 2.3).[131] In other contexts it carries the notion of divine punishment or, as in Ps 37:18^{LXX}, designates in particular the individual distress of social scorn and distancing as well as physical, sensuous, and religious constraints within the context of im-/purity.[132] Here, however, nothing can be claimed with certainty. In Mark, it seems to depict a some-

---

[127] Cf. Benthien 2001. 49–56; Weissenrieder 2003. 213–221, esp. 220, n. 357; Moss 2010.
[128] See 4.2; ἐξηράνθη (cf. Mark 3:1; 4:6; 9:18; 11:20–21). Cf. also Montanari, s.v; BDAG, s.v; LSJ, s.v; Thiessen 2020. 76–80.
[129] Cf. Kahl in Zimmermann (ed.) 2013. 288.
[130] Haber 2003. 173.
[131] Cf., e.g., Balz; Schneider, μάστιξ. 975; BDAG, s.v; LN, s.v 19.9, 23.153; LSJ, s.v; Montanari, s.v; Schneider, μάστιξ. 524; Spicq, 2.539–542.
[132] Cf. Ps 38; 37:18^{LXX}; 38:11^{LXX}; 2Macc 7:37; 9:11; 1Q20 20.16–17. Cf. also Weissenrieder in Stegemann; Malina; Theissen (ed.) 2002. 82.

what generic term for any affliction caused by the ailment that is acknowledged by Jesus (v. 34) and is emphatically confirmed to be cured after the discharge has dried up (ἴαται and ὑγιής, vv. 29 and 34, see below). This concurs with the extensive yet ambiguous implications described by a constant gynecological bleeding as well as the particular distress caused *by* her medical history, recounted with an emphatical alliteration in v. 26: πολλὰ παθοῦσα ὑπὸ πολλῶν ἰατρῶν.[133] The woman is not only physically suffering but severely emotionally, socially, and financially scourged; both terms are also recounted within the context of Jesus' passion (cf., e.g., 8:31, 9:31, esp. 10:34). After having been failed by physicians, her approach of Jesus reflects on his reputation.

5.2.2.2.2 Beyond Expectations

The term ἰάομαι is only used here in Mark, and dramatically so, as the perfect tense interrupts and foregrounds the more or less continuous string of completed actions in the aorist to recount what "the woman is experiencing [as] a present state."[134] Thereby, it corresponds with the resultative perfect of Jesus' affirmative statement of the woman's self-perception: ἡ πίστις σου σέσωκέν σε […] καὶ ἴσθι ὑγιὴς ἀπὸ τῆς μάστιγός σου (v. 34, see below). Frequently, the term occurs in contexts of physical healings, often by divine intervention.[135] Here as well, it serves as a counterpart for the failing physicians (v. 26) who could not accomplish what she has just witnessed.[136] However, as it refers to μάστιξ as its defining opposition, it also carries the notion of a more holistic transformation than mere physical wellbeing. She is well regarding *all* the suffering caused by her bleeding. This corresponds with the exclusive occurrence of ὑγιής here. Although this term is typically used in a physical sense elsewhere,[137] in this context it links the woman's healed state with μάστιξ and εἰρήνη, thereby referring to a holistic sense of "health" that encompasses emotional, mental, spiritual, and even economic well-being, in addition to her physical state.[138] Its use in Jesus' conclusive sendoff might even reprise the formulae of Greek inscriptions with ὑγιαίνω, as both are termed in the present

---

[133] Cf. Zwiep 2019. 56.
[134] Wells 1998. 156.
[135] Cf. Tob 12:14; Ps 6:3; 30:2; 41:4; Wis 16:10; Sir 38:9; LiDonnici 1995. 84–131; BDAG, *s.v*; LSJ, *s.v*; LN, *s.v* 23.136, also 13.66; Montanari, *s.v*; Oepke, ἰάομαι; Rupprecht, ἰάομαι. Moreover, Wainwright in Alkier; Weissenrieder (ed.) 2013. 58.
[136] Cf. Oppel 1995. 110–111.
[137] Cf. Matt 12:13; 15:31; John 5:4, 6, 9, 11, 14, 15; 7:23; Acts 4:10; also 1Tim 1:10; 6:3; 2Tim 1:13; 4:3; Tit 1:9; 13; 2:8; Luke 5:31, 7:10, 15:27; and Wells 1998. 208–209.
[138] Cf. ibid. 203; Zwiep 2019. 64; Foerster; von Rad, εἰρήνη.

imperative and reflect a continuous healed existence[139] in εἰρήνη, possibly with an eschatological notion.[140] These terms then also encompass an implicit impurity, although the text does not allude to anything regarding "cleansing," immersion, or offering (unlike Mark 1:40–45, see 3.3).

As her concrete medical symptoms, the precise pathogenesis, and social implications remain uncertain, her healed condition reflects an eradication of any symptom, even if only remotely implied: the continuous blood flow and weak and leaky body are dried up; her hopelessness after many failed medical therapies is restored by πίστις; social, familial, cultic, and religious destitutions are repealed by the intimate encounter with Jesus. The anonymous "hemorrhaging woman," walks away "a daughter," ἴαται, ὑγιὴς, and in εἰρήνη. Together with the implicit nuances of a new existence transpiring the healed condition of the daughter of Jaïrus, the intercalation with the healed woman explicitly illustrates a holistic healing beyond physical integrity. This is examined more closely in the combination of the two healings.

5.2.3 The Healings

The contact between Jesus and the dis/abled character is established in unique ways in both narratives: On the one hand, Jesus is stealthily being touched and obliviously tapped for his healing power, and on the other, he is arduously being brought to the girl's location. Both encounters are linked with the commended and encouraged *pistis* of the supplicants in Jesus' healing touch.

5.2.3.1 Intimate Touches
As analyzed in C. In Focus: Mark's Healing Touches, physical contact is a, if not *the*, central aspect of Jesus' healings. Here as well, the emphasis on his embodied healing runs like a thread throughout the narrative tapestry: Firstly, both supplicants know of his healing power transmitted by physical contact and approach him because of it, Jaïrus regarding Jesus' tactile treatment and the anonymous woman with expectations of his tangible curative authority.[141] Moreover, the four-time occurrence of ἅπτομαι (5:27, 28, 30, 31) marks the woman as the active initiator, not Jesus. This is underscored as ἅπτομαι in v. 27 is the first indicative to break the long

---

139 Cf. extensively Wells 1998. 31–33.
140 Cf. the Semitic expression of departure in Exod 4:18; 1Sam 1:17; 20:42; 29:7; Jdt 8:35; 2Sam 3:21; 15:9; 2Kgs 5:19; Judg 18:6; Acts 16:36; also 2Kgs 4:7; 1Kgs 17:23; 2Kgs 4:36.
141 Cf. also Mark 3:10; 6:56; 7:31; 8:22–23.

line of participles of the woman's introduction, positioned emphatically at the end.¹⁴² In contrast to Jesus' tactile treatments that resonate with the dis/ability (see C. In Focus: Mark's Healing Touches), here the deliberate hand-seizing of the severely passive daughter of Jaïrus, whom Jesus drastically pulls back into active life,¹⁴³ it is difficult to assume the same for the inverted touch *by* the petitioners since this account is the only elaborate narrative for the Markan text besides the general summaric notes. However, if such a customary and/or *compositional* connection of dis/ability and tactile healing can be made here as well, the clandestine touch of the woman corresponds with the implicit impurity of her blood flow. As neither the referential texts of Leviticus and thereafter nor Mark explicate the communicative power of the touch of an impure woman,¹⁴⁴ the ambiguity of the social implications of her condition increases to the audience, and the mystery of the two communicating bodies is suspensefully heightened. Her gesture is executed ὄπισθεν, from behind and secretly, and grasps not the healer himself nor any particular body parts but only his garments. Instead of clarifying the mysterious implications of her touch, the narrator uses the irritating uncertainty and suspense to explicate another emanating, perceivable, physical force: Jesus' curative δύναμις (see below).¹⁴⁵ Although the narrator grants in-depth insights into the intentions, emotions, thoughts, and sensations of the two protagonists and their intimate communication, he leaves the exact parameters of the most pressing exchange veiled. Only the woman and Jesus witness the healing.

Similarly intimate is the setting of the girl's raising as Jesus only takes a small group of witnesses (the parents, three disciples)¹⁴⁶ into her room. While Jaïrus asked Jesus to lay his hands on his daughter, the worsened state of the girl now demands his intentional, immediate, and forceful hand-seizing (see 3.2.3.1). Like Peter's bed-struck and fever-ridden mother-in-law and the boy pronounced dead in the process of his exorcism, Jesus pulls the girl from her lying position, here with a confirmative ἐγείρω in Aramaic (see below).¹⁴⁷ Regarding parallel accounts of fatal dis/abilities, the simplicity of Jesus' "helping-up" stands out together with

---

142 Cf. Marcus 2000. 367; Boring 2006. 156; Zwiep 2019. 54.
143 See 5.2.3.1.
144 Cf. Fonrobert in Evans; Sanders (ed.) 1997. 133; Maccoby 1999. 162–163; Kazen 2002. 139.
145 This is accounted for in the rich and diverse reception history as compiled and surveyed in Baert; Schalley 2014.
146 Cf. 3:16–17; 9:2 and 14:33, also 13:3.
147 See 3.2.3.1.

his verbal encouragement as he never physically expands the touch, schematizes it by an exact number of touches, nor enriches it with prayers.[148]

5.2.3.2 Relational *Pistis*, Holistic *Salvation*, and Jesus' *Dynamic* Identity

As the audience wonders about the healing touch of the woman, Jesus attributes her σῴζω healing to her πίστις and enforces its function when emphatically encouraging Jaïrus (imperative present) a few verses later (v. 36) to continue practicing πίστις unconditionally and absolutely[149] in face of the fatal delay of their journey to σῴζω his daughter (v. 23). The Markan text interweaves the themes of πίστις and σῴζω here in this central transition of the two narratives, which not only ties them closely together and establishes a smooth transition from one to the other but emphasizes the importance of the undercurrent conceptions behind these two ambiguous polysemes as the paramount theme of both extensive narratives. Hence, the use and function of πίστις and σῴζω here and in other passages must be investigated together with the combined notion of Jesus' mysterious and efficacious δύναμις.

G In Focus: Mark's Relational Pistis

Pistis language[150] occurs in the majority of Mark's healing narratives, referring to "a relationship and a praxis, rather than primarily a state of the heart and mind with an object."[151] For one, the relationship of *pistis* and (effective) healing of dis/ability is alluded to throughout the gospel narrative (e.g., Mark 5:34; 6:5–6;

---

[148] Differently: Acts 20:9–12; 1Kgs 17:17–24, esp. 20–23 and 2Kgs 4:18–37, esp. 33–35; John 11:38–44; Josephus, *A.J.* 8.325–27; but: Luke 7:11–17. Cf. esp. 1Kgs 17:8–24 and 2Kgs 4:18–37, as the texts recount the social and local situation of the supplicant, representative parent, an extreme (fatal) physical condition of children, a retreat into more private rooms with bedding where the healing evidently takes place. Additionally, 2Kgs 4:25–34 also depicts a detailed approach of the supplicant and a delayed arrival of the healer. Although a literal dependency is not veritable, a likeness according to history of tradition appears indubitable. Cf., e.g., Kertelge 1970. 117–118; Pesch 1976. 298, 313; Fischbach 1992. 184; Wolter 2008. 324; Gnilka 2010. 212, 219.

[149] Cf. du Toit in Du Toit; Gerber; Zimmermann (ed.) 2019. 193; also Marcus 2000. 362.

[150] Namely, ἀπιστία (Mark 6:6; 9:24; cf. 16:14), ἄπιστος (9:19), πιστεύω (5:36; 9:23, 24; 9:42; cf. 1:15; 11:23–24; 11:31; 13:21; 15:32; 16:13, 14; 16, 17), and πίστις (2:5; 5:34; 10:52; cf. 4:40; 11:22). Cf. also ἀπιστέω in Mark 16:11, 16. In the following, *pistis* remains untranslated to avoid an interpretation fraught with meaning in the attempt of grasping what *pistis* language means in Mark. Since *pistis* is here regarded in narratives, *pistis* practice refers to the attitudes, actions, and activities expressed in or connected to *pistis* language. Cf. the extensive studies and collections of sources in, e.g., Söding 1985; Marshall 1989; Schunack in Stegemann; et al. (ed.) 1999; Morgan 2015; Frey; Schliesser; Kessler 2017; Watson 2018.

[151] Morgan 2015. 348.

9:23–24; 10:52) and *a-pistia* is narrated by using images of deviating bodies (e.g., hardness of hearts).¹⁵²

Mark always depicts Jesus evaluating and valuing the *pistis* of other characters as he encourages to practice *pistis*,¹⁵³ or criticizes¹⁵⁴ or commends¹⁵⁵ others for their practice of *pistis*. In Mark 2:5; 5:34, and 10:52, Jesus implicitly or explicitly commends characters for their *pistis* practice: all characters have in common that they actively pursue Jesus against outer or inner obstacles (roof, opposition of crowd, scribes, disciples, clandestine approach) because they have heard of him and hope to encounter him in their physical need.¹⁵⁶ All three are contrasted with characters who voice a form of uncertainty regarding Jesus' practice of healing (scribes in Mark 2:6–9; disciples in 5:30–31 who wonder about Jesus' awareness of his healing δύναμις; a crowd in 10:48). Those characters whom Jesus encourages or criticizes for their *pistis* practice are characterized by "fear" (5:36: φοβέω, Jaïrus; 4:40: δειλός, disciples) that seems to oppose, but not hinder *pistis* and their request for help (see esp. 4:39–40).¹⁵⁷

In Mark, pistis is almost always used without an object, which makes its concrete point of reference grammatically ambiguous. However, it is always spoken of in relation to Jesus' actions, which seem to develop along with the gospel storyline. The first uses of *pistis* language show characters who know of and believe in Jesus' healing ability: Mark 2:1–12 follows upon the programmatic first chapter on Jesus' effective healing and exorcising ability that is promoted again just before the narrative starts in 1:45. Mark 5:27–28 picks up on this motif and implicitly suggests

---

152 Cf. ch. 4 on Mark 2–3, where *pistis* is practiced by actively and bravely trusting in Jesus' abilities *in contrast* to a spiritual paralysis. For a comparison of other healing narratives that employ *pistis*, cf., e.g., the Iamata of Epidauros, where faithlessness and especially ridicule against supernatural healing are broached but not described as obstacles to healing, but as a literary motif displaying astounding healing powers (cf. IG 4.951.22–33; 4.951.33–41.72–78; 4.951.78–89). Furthermore, the motif of "disbelief" in narratives of powerful divine deeds can be found in Jewish sources where it often refers to certain promises of God (cf., e.g., Gen 17:15–17; 18:10–15; 2Kgs 4:16; 2Chr 16:12; 2Kgs 5:10–12). In medical contexts, πίστις/πιστεύω refers to "trusting" a "convincing" doctor, method, diagnosis, recovery, or "confiding" in the art of medicine. Cf., e.g., CH, *Arte* 4.4; 12.6; *Flat.* 15.2; *Aph.* 2.27; *Prog.* 1; 7; *Epid.* 1.24–26; also Weinreich 1909. 87–88; Fischbach 1992. 11; Müri 2001. 40–41, 94–95.
153 Cf. 1:15; 5:36; 11:22–24; cf. 11:31.
154 Cf. 4:40; 9:19, 23–24; cf. 6:6; 11:31.
155 Cf. 2:5; 5:34; 10:52; cf. 9:42.
156 Cf. moreover, 5:27; 6:55; 7:25; 10:47; cf. also 3:7–8, 21; 5:6, 22; 9:15; 12:28, 37; and 2:6–10.
157 Cf. for an interesting twist on an emotional survey of *pistis* and its counterparts Spencer in Spencer (ed.) 2017. Many thanks also to May-Britt Melzer for the frequent discussions of her work on φοβος-emotions in Mark ("Die Angst der Jünger*innen im Markusevangelium. Eine semantische und narratologische Studie").

that the woman's *pistis* distinguishes her touch from that of the others around Jesus—as shown by the disciples' objection and Jesus' answer in vv. 30–31—and effects the healing without Jesus' conscious doing. All of this takes place amid a crowd that has come together because of the charismatic Jesus, with each person likely having their own expectations. Admittedly, this argument remains quite speculative and hinges on the interpretation that her *pistis* refers to her brave and active approach. However, it proves that when the definition of *pistis* is to include her respectful fear and trembling, her prostration, her "telling him the whole truth"[158] in face of his (divine) δύναμις, her only-then commended *pistis* alludes to a broader understanding of Jesus according to the advanced point of the plot. In any case, Mark 2:1–12 and 5:21–43 refer to knowledge of and trust in Jesus the healer in connection to *pistis* yet already push this characterization when heightening his deed to the forgiveness of sin as the Son of Man and referring to the restoration as σώζω of the woman's entire being (see below). This concurs with other Markan healing narratives where there is no explicit mention of *pistis* as a precondition to or practice of healing but of gestures and motifs that could be interpreted as part of this basic *pistis* practice in relation to Jesus, the healer: In all Markan healing narratives, whether they mention *pistis* or not, the supplicants come to Jesus with their physical request. If this is all the *pistis* practice it takes, it is essential for healing and could explain the very few deeds Jesus was able to do in his hometown in Mark 6:5–6, where he might not have been sought out by many as a healer. However, as the narrative unfolds more and more of Jesus' divine identity, its characters and their *pistis* are measured by this standard, which is explicitly discussed in Mark 9:14–29: Right after the transfiguration, in the middle of a chapter that constantly alludes to the passion and the disciples' relative understanding of Jesus' identity, the question of enough or rather adequate *pistis* for effective healing is raised. It is answered with hints to Jesus' divine identity and the insight that *pistis* is a spectrum according to an understanding of Jesus, his call to discipleship,[159] and his ongoing mission in line with the omnipotent God and the heavenly realm within a historical and cosmological frame. Mark 10:52 then reprises Jesus' saying ἡ πίστις σου σέσωκέν σε after he is accurately and with deep insight identified to be ἔλεος, Ιησοῦς ὁ Ναζαρηνός, υἱὲ Δαυίδ, and ῥαββουνί (see 7.3.3) by blind Bartimaeus. Finally, Mark 11:22–24, 31 dissolve the uncertain vacancy by *explicitly* entering God in the *pistis* equation (here, contrasted with διακρίνω). The connection to prayer refers directly back to the dialogue Jesus has with the father of the tormented boy in Mark 9:19, 23–24 and confirms what was

---

[158] Cf. vv. 25–27 with another sequence of participles; also Zwiep 2019. 62.
[159] Cf. Mark 4:38; 9:38; 10:35; 13:1; 14:14; but 5:35; 10:17, 20; 12:14, 19, 32.

suggested to the audience all along: that Jesus and God are in it together, inviting disciples and the audience to participate in *pistis* practice according to their understanding of Jesus (see 7.3.2.3). Adding to Mark 6:13, 9:19, and 9:37–41, Mark 11:22–24 and secondary 16:16–18 make it undoubtedly clear that after having reached an understanding of the divine Jesus, *pistis* is effective in healing given by God and to those who call on him and his name (ἐπὶ τῷ ὀνόματί μου): "Repeated use of *pistis* language without an object, however, turns it into a concept and relationship […], and enables human beings' relationship with Jesus to evolve as their understanding of him grows."[160]

H In Focus: Mark's Holistic Salvation

Similarly ambiguous and evolving is the Markan use of the lexeme σῴζω. As a polyseme, the variety of meanings is highly dependent on the context. In the Synoptics, it generally conveys the preservation of life in face of distress (e.g., from distress at sea, guilt and sin, agony and sickness).[161] In the first half of the Gospel of Mark, it occurs within healing narratives (3:4; 5:23, 28, 34; 6:56; 10:52),[162] then it evolves to carry eschatological and soteriological associations in the second half.[163] As Jesus is featured as the only person to use σῴζω in the active voice in direct speech, it appears as a central aspect of his message.

As established in the analysis on Mark 3:4, Jesus references with this term a halakhic principle in his argument on Sabbath healing opposing killing/death that contrasts and heightens his cure of the withered hand to a more comprehen-

---

160 Morgan 2015. 364.
161 Cf. for the following Best 1965; Backhaus in Söding (ed.) 1995; Combrink in Van der Watt (ed.) 2005; du Toit, *Salvation*; Frey in Schliesser (ed.) 2016; du Toit in Du Toit; Gerber; Zimmermann (ed.) 2019; Bosenius in Du Toit; Gerber; Zimmermann (ed.) 2019; Schröter in Du Toit; Gerber; Zimmermann (ed.) 2019, and the comprehensive listing of relevant passages in, e.g., BDAG, *s.v.*; Foerster, σῴζω. 990; LSJ, *s.v*; LN, *s.v* 21.18, 21.27, 23.136; Montanari, *s.v.*; Moulton/Miligan, *s.v.*; Radl, σῴζω; Schneider, σῴζω; Spicq, 1.629–643. Cf. also Wells 1998. 180–181. This is also reflected in the use of σῴζω in ancient Greek literature, especially respective physical contexts where σῴζειν can signify an iatrogenic, ritual, or medicinal treatment, the "salvation" from a sickness, as well as a state of holistic well-being, to keep and be fit and healthy. Cf., e.g., SIG ³620; Philo, *Decal.* 12; *Ios.* 76; *Deus* 66; *Sacr.* 123; *Ebr.* 140; *Agr.* 98; *Spec.* 1.197; and Foerster, σῴζω. 967–970, 988. For similar use in OT/early Jewish apocalyptic texts, but with explicit reference to YHWH as more powerful than death, also with an eschatological nuance, cf., e.g., Isa 49:6; Frey in Schliesser (ed.) 2016. 546.
162 In Synoptic accounts on Jesus' healing, σῴζω occurs sixteen times (twice διασῴζω): Mark 3:4par.; 5:23, 28, 34par.; 6:56; 10:52; Matt 14:36; Luke 7:3, 50; 8:36, 50. Cf. also John 11:12; Acts 4:9, 12; 14:9; Jas 5:15.
163 Cf. 8:35; 10:17, 25, 26; 13:13, 20; also 15:30–31, where it mainly discusses deliverance form immanent life dangers paralleled with eternal and kingdom existence.

sive meaning along the lines of an eschatological understanding and primordial ideal of physicality (see 4.2.3). Followed by Mark 5:23, 28, and 34, not only does the number of occurrences emphasize the lexeme but also its central positions within the intercalation of the two narratives. While σῴζω initially simply corresponds with the fatal condition of the daughter laid out by her desperate father in a for Mark customary approach of Jesus as a healer (ἐσχάτως ἔχει),[164] it is contrasted first by the woman's inner monologue and wish for healing of her severe but not necessarily life-threatening ailment and, secondly, by her emphatically recorded cure with ἰάομαι (v. 30). This use of the same lexeme must irritate the audience. Although the verb initially conveys a meaning of pressing physical and literal life-sustaining healing, the steady but not necessarily urgent blood flow of the woman tones it down to a sorely needed but not indispensable-to-life cure, which is referred to as such (ἰάομαι). Then Jesus heightens this "cured" scourge to the resultative and dramatically timeless[165] "salvation" of the woman's entire being (σε),[166] notably after her healing, connects it to her active πίστις and dismisses her in peace.[167] This in turn transpires to the subsequent ambiguous raising of the dead-asleep daughter, who is set to be "saved" and whose physical raising is then surpassed by an eschatological resurrection, even if it is narrated in terms of physical healing (v. 43).

As Mark powerfully displays the possibilities of using a polyseme in an intercalated narrative, the audience must wonder about the exact parameters of the displayed σῴζω for different and in themselves highly ambiguous physical conditions. Mark 5:21–43 unfolds a panorama beyond the binary of *physical* suffering and integrity of a healed existence, which also alludes to social aspects (i.e., reinstated cultic participation, incautious physical communication, belonging in terms of kinship and communal meals) and transpires an eschatological salvation.[168] The general and summaric note in Mark 6:56 then reprises this holistic (including eschatological) understanding by concrete allusions to this narrative, namely the curative touch of Jesus' garments by the supplicants. Finally, the showpiece supplicant, named, blind, and knowing Bartimaeus (10:52), leaves everything behind to follow Jesus on his (soteriological and Christological) path after his πίστις is com-

---

[164] Cf. esp. the request for his healing touch in C. In Focus: Mark's Healing Touches.
[165] "The perfect [...] indicates the state of salvation without specifying the moment of its realization. It does not allow us to locate the precise moment in the past, when the faith saved, as if it were a matter of one action among others in the succession of the narrative; this salvation thus escapes from chronometry," cf. Focant 2012. 212.
[166] Cf. Mark 5:34par.; 10:52par.; Luke 7:50; 17:19.
[167] Cf. von Bendemann in Thomas; Karle (ed.) 2009. 165; Frey in Schliesser (ed.) 2016. 545.
[168] Cf. Marshall 1989. 96.

mended with the same resultative sentence as the hemorrhaging woman's approach, and his restored sight is subsequently recorded. This connection to discipleship henceforth evolves the meaning of σῴζω in line with eschatological judgment and the death of Jesus as foreshadowed in 8:34–35.[169]

In Mark, as established in the healing narratives, salvation does not involve a reinstatement of the previous physical state before suffering, but rather a liberation from human suffering as *visualized* in physical torments that carry social implications and dangers of death. Secondly, it encompasses a reinforcement of social belonging, including the relationship to Jesus and his ministry.[170]

I In Focus: The Markan Jesus' Dynamic Identity

As established, the "chronological and causal connection"[171] of healing when touching a person or object charged with divine or sacred power is a common notion in antiquity.[172] By the woman's touch, a connection is made, through which physical and material thresholds (his garments) are crossed "flowingly." Jesus reveals by his δύναμις to be a spatially, sensually approachable, and experienceable healing body. His δύναμις emanates εὐθύς,[173] without a deliberate act, seemingly uncontrollably but perceivably out of him (ἐξ αὐτοῦ δύναμιν ἐξελθοῦσαν), and effects the healing of the woman (vv. 29–30). It stands in direct nexus with the salvific *pistis* that distinguishes the woman from the pushing crowd, as the disciples' objection and Jesus' answer show (vv. 30–31). Then the ambiguous term relates to what has been established as the essence of Markan *pistis* practice: the growing knowledge of and relationship with Jesus of those in need. This is consistent with the subsequent events in Mark 6:2, 5 and 9:1, 39, where Jesus' deeds and actions from 4:35–5:43 are summarized as δυνάμεις and questioned (in direct connection to his hands); *a-pistia* hinders their effects, and they are connected to

---

[169] Cf. 10:26 with 10:17, 9:43, 45, 47; 13:13, 20 and 10:45 and 14:22–25. Cf. also 10:23–24, 28–31. Cf. du Toit in Du Toit; Gerber; Zimmermann (ed.) 2019. 194–197, 201–205; and regarding Mark 8:35–38, Frey in Schliesser (ed.) 2016. 558–561.
[170] A quite distinguished example for physical recovery and holistic well-being conveyed with the term σῴζω is the eulogy on Asclepius by Aelius Aristides (cf. Aristides, *Or.* 42): The σωτὴρ τῶν ὅλων is equipped with δυνάμεις μεγάλαι τε καὶ πολλαί (Aristides, *Or.* 42.2; 48.37) for supernatural, medical healing, that Aristides experienced himself and that enabled him to give glorious speeches. Aimed to promote the outstanding rhetoric of Aristides, the text reflects notions of holistic well-being when being "saved" by divine δύναμις. Cf. extensively Israelowich 2012.
[171] Kahl in Zimmermann (ed.) 2013. 283.
[172] See C. In Focus: Mark's Healing Touches.
[173] This signals, as often in Mark, a turn of events, cf. Kahl in Zimmermann (ed.) 2013. 282.

the evolving kingdom of God (cf. also 6:14). Thereafter, Mark only uses this term to refer to God (12:24) but also to his opposing forces (13:26) and twice to the Son of Man (13:26; 14:62). Hence, the exact parameters of Jesus' δύναμις then depend on the understanding of his identity, as he "ontologically" emanates this astonishing power.[174] It is literally a force that can be charged itself with meaning along the narrative process. Here, Jesus "oozes" a "restorative life-force."[175]

5.2.3.3 Public Privacy

The woman's physical reaction to her healing (not prior) reflects all of this. Because the woman εἰδυῖα ὃ γέγονεν αὐτῇ, she φοβηθεῖσα καὶ τρέμουσα. She is surprised and overwhelmed by Jesus' δύναμις and his apprehension of her stealthily action. Since she subsequently προσέπεσεν αὐτῷ καὶ εἶπεν αὐτῷ πᾶσαν τὴν ἀλήθειαν, it is likely that she is simply deeply stirred by his might, by a profound revelation of Jesus' supernatural identity.[176] Mutually, Jesus calls her θυγάτηρ, which in this intercalated narrative of Jaïrus and his *daughter* expresses a deep sense of belonging, endearment, and care. Her truth refers the audience, at a minimum, to her previous clandestine actions; at a maximum to the "publication of the painful secret of her serious medical condition, and the disclosure of both her treatment history and her financial woes."[177] In any case, the corresponding physical attention, the intentional touches, and deep corporal communication of δύναμις lead to a profound apprehension of the other, to a new level of intimacy.

Besides the remote setting of the other daughter's healing, the few witnesses, the command to silence, and Jesus' unusual uttering in Aramaic enforce the allusion of a private, intimate, and esoteric event. The last foremost has a dramatic effect as it breaks with the surrounding language pattern. As Aramaic phrases are

---

[174] Thiessen 2020. 93. Cf. also Mark 1:22, 27; 2:10; 3:15; 6:7; 11:28, 29; 13:34, for the similar if not interchangeable term ἐξουσία.
[175] Rosenblatt in Kitzberger (ed.) 2000. 141; Thiessen 2020. 93.
[176] Maybe even with allusions to epi-/theophanies as depicted in esp. Mark 9:2–8; yet also 4Macc 4:10; Phil 2:12; Exod 15:16; Deut 2:25; 11:25; Jdt 15:2; cf. Lohmeyer 1967. 130; Fonrobert in Evans; Sanders (ed.) 1997. 132–133, n. 30, with reference to Trummer 1991. 98. An interpretation of the woman's physical reaction as shame or fear regarding transferred impurity is unlikely due to the only implied notion of im/purity but expressive staging of growing *pistis* and intrinsic *dynamis* as paradigms for Jesus' identity. Neither plausible is an interpretation as fear to have her (former) impurity and secret action exposed to the crowd, because her communication with Jesus stays intimate and private, no other reactions are recounted.
[177] Rosenblatt in Kitzberger (ed.) 2000. 142. Cf. her intriguing comparison of the woman's characterization with that of women's legal status in documents from the Oxyrhynchus Papyri, ibid. 142–145.

not uncommon for the Gospel of Mark,[178] in its emphasis here, it indeed conveys a "performative power,"[179] yet due to its translation, not as a secretive, unintelligible ῥῆσιν βαρβαρικὴν, which is common in ancient incantations.[180] Although it may echo a widespread, traditional Jewish healing formula with κουμ/ קום,[181] the main narrative effect is again a stark contrast between the intimate scene on the story level and the explicative translation of the narrator as a direct address to the audience, who witnesses among the few despite the order to keep it a secret. As with the hemorrhaging woman, the communication between Jesus' and the daughter' body is intimate and confidential, yet the audience gets to participate.

5.2.4 Interpretation

Due to the intercalated structure of Mark 5:21–43, the primary characters of the two stories, the woman with the issue of blood and Jaïrus with his daughter, contrast and comment on one another. While the male supplicant is introduced by name, kinship, and his prestigious religious position, possibly with wealth, the woman's anonymity, poverty, and implicit ritual and social restrictions characterize her. In addition, his open vs. her secretive petition for healing serves as a juxtaposition. Due to their differences, their mutual recognition of Jesus as a powerful healer (manifested in their gestures, approach, and active *pistis* practice)[182] stands out, quite literally at the junction of both narratives, where Jesus encourages Jaïrus to practice *pistis* so his daughter can be saved as the distinguishing *pistis* of the woman has saved her.[183] Because of this, both experience the requested curative force.

However, the two dis/abilities also correspond with each other as both physical conditions are explicitly outlined with the experience of affliction they bring to the person(s) affected and the hopelessness of their cases (see above). This is under-

---

[178] Cf. 3:17; 7:11, 34; 11:9–10; 14:36; 15:22, 34, of which healing: 7:34.
[179] Iersel 1998. 209.
[180] Cf. prominently, Meier 1994. 759, n. 159, in critique of Horton 1986. Cf. also, Bultmann 1967. 238; Böcher 1970. 175–176.
[181] Cf. also the similar phrasing Ταβιθά, ἀνάστηθι in Acts 9:36–43, and Kollmann 1996. 263–265.
[182] As gestures of prostration in context of Markan healing narratives can have several nuances, it here mainly serves as a gesture of recognition of the powerful man encountered (esp. 3:11; 5:6 and 6:33; cf. also 1:7 and ironically 15:19–20), either underscoring the hopeful supplication (1:40; 5:22; 7:25; cf. also 10:17; 14:35), or as a movement of thankfulness and submission (5:33), cf. Glancy 2010b. 353.
[183] Cf. Bomford 2010. 45–47.

scored by the general normality of both conditions as part of life; it is the girl's young age and the long duration of the woman's sickness, both of twelve years, that make their cases hopeless and severe. Furthermore, their femininity and identification as daughters rather than by their names (θυγάτηρ, vv. 23, 34, 35) are reinforced in their healings through intimate tactile communication with Jesus, which provides them with a sense of belonging and care (v. 34). In case of the girl, this communication also grants her a degree of independence, as her previous affiliation with her father, Jaïrus, is reversed (5:40), and diminutives and possessive pronouns are relinquished (5:23, 35, 39, 40, 41, 42; 41, to τὸ κοράσιον in 5:42).[184]

Most importantly, however, both are depicted with great diligence as ambiguously dis/abled, as the exact parameters of their conditions and healings between impurity and peace, as well as death and life, elude the audience. By that, suspense is heightened and the audience engaged as the daughters' physical restorations allude to an all-encompassing, holistic wholesomeness with eschatological nuances that transpire a pre-ailment status quo.

The intercalated narrative depicts Jesus as the only character who "crosses over" between the two stories and moves through the narrative as the traveling spotlight.[185] In his active hurtling to the passive daughter's bedside, he negotiates her physical state as her ambiguity translates to the questionable accuracy of *his* diagnosis and *his* power to help. Additionally, the intimate physical communication of Jesus and the woman with the hemorrhage reveals that Jesus meets the woman in a central aspect of her dis/ability: his body similarly appears as porous when δύναμις leaves it just as uncontrollably and unwillingly, yet physically palpable, as the blood flow from the body of the woman. Both substances imply life-giving and life-sustaining powers; both are bearers of identity.[186] It seems like the narrative macerates a presupposed "binary between 'disability' and 'ability', for all bodies occupy a continuum of control and uncontrollability, boundaries and outflows,"[187] when it depicts a disputable spectrum of physical stances and most of all witnesses to a healing that surpasses physical restoration. Indeed, "the inner/inward sandwiched story depicts tactile inwardness: flows of blood, liquid inner power, the expelling to power, the inward bodily feeling/'knowing' of Jesus and

---

[184] All however within the realm of ancient social locations of females, cf., e.g., D'Angelo in Kraemer; D'Angelo (ed.) 1999; Nogossek-Raithel in El Maaroufi; Strube; Williger (ed.) 2020.
[185] Jaïrus, although implicitly present throughout the inner story, is only directly referred to again in v. 35.
[186] Cf. Schiffer 2001. 206.
[187] Lawrence 2013. 128–129.

the woman, and the whole truth."¹⁸⁸ Likewise, the frame depicts the—literally—outward discourses on the dis/ability of the daughter *and* ability of Jesus. The healing is publicly anticipated, culminating in Jesus' only direct utterance to Jaïrus to μὴ φοβοῦ, μόνον πίστευε, and is directly explicated to the audience.

Although the intercalated narratives focus entirely on the severe suffering and holistic healing of the two female characters, neither depicts a concluding response of astonishment, recognition, rejection, or criticism.¹⁸⁹ While the woman is "complex" and unique in the characterization of her brave and clandestine yet honest and fearful approach and reaction, the emphatic "great amazement" of only selected witnesses of the daughter's rising is moreover extinguished by the following abrupt commands for silence and care as the narrative fades out.¹⁹⁰ The audience is left to respond—in the face of ambiguous dis/abilities and a Jesus who oscillates between confidently knowledgeable and astonishing oblivious.¹⁹¹ Just like the supplicants, the audience has heard of Jesus, the increasingly prominent healer. As they follow him through the "ambiguous abyss"¹⁹² of this intercalation, they learn about relational *pistis* causing holistic *salvation* and his *dynamic* identity and are encouraged to respond, as the texts do not only "present and promote *pistis*" but also are "themselves *pisteis:* arguments or proofs of the validity of *pistis*,"¹⁹³ as summarized in the first mention of *pistis* in the gospel: μετανοεῖτε καὶ πιστεύετε ἐν τῷ εὐαγγελίῳ (1:15).

5.3 Conclusion and Interpretation of Dis/ability in Mark 5

The three healing accounts in Mark 5 disclose, unusually rich in detail, the experiences and clinical histories of three characters with deviating physicalities. They depict three hopeless cases that are written off by restraining society, medical professionals, and their own community and illustrate at great length the suffering and social dimensions of these extraordinary dis/abilities, especially by the more or less explicit allusions to impurity. The three characters embody and occupy liminal stances, between home and otherworld(s), purity and impurity, life and death. In their ambiguous depictions, the three bodies are potentials for the notions of

---

188 On the "narratomimetic" nature of the intercalation in Mark 5:21–43, cf. Hatton 2015. 97, 113–114.
189 Cf. Bomford 2010. 45–47.
190 Cf. Kiffiak 2017. 146–147.
191 For more ambiguities, cf. Hatton 2015. 101.
192 Ibid. 114.
193 Morgan 2015. 393.

the audience as they embody relatable issues of mundane forces—a surrounding spiritual world, discharges, death—that here, however, unleash their powers fiercely and uncontrollably as too strong, too long, and too soon. The gospel composes these images of dis/ability here in an increasing social densification from the public commotion of an entire region around Jesus, to the intimate physical communication amid a crowd, to the private and silent treatment of the girl. Hence, these representations of deviating physicalities are employed to portray an unconditionally powerful Jesus who, unlike others, is able to tame these forces and liberate from any implementations thereof. More so, he acknowledges their suffering and shares aspects of their symptoms as he himself contains a pneumatic force that renders him a mediator between the spiritual worlds, uncontrollably and unwillingly leaks his healing δύναμις, and is exposed to social impediments. Healed conditions then first and foremost constitute a liberation from suffering and an emancipation from social pathologization in a re-socialization that surpasses a prior existence in its recognition of and belonging to Jesus—a new norm of being. His healing is portrayed as effortless and literally intrinsic, as his curative communication with the dis/abled is very intimate and personal. Especially since there are diverse or no responses of the witnesses, the focus is solely on the healings of the severely scourged humans. These transformations go beyond mere physical well-being and allude to a more holistic and even eschatological re-vivification (see more in ch. 7 on Mark 8–10).

As the narrator focuses on these relatable, personal, and impressive encounters, the audience is also personally engaged. The diverging and missing responses and a selective external focalization, combined with unusual and ambiguous behavior of Jesus, ask for a positioning of the audience, different to the unequivocal programmatic or controversial healing ministry of Mark 1 and 2–3.

Mark 4:41 asks τίς ἄρα οὗτός ἐστιν, and Mark 5 gives answers as it uses specific images of dis/ability to vividly and extensively depict Jesus' divine yet corporal identity (cf. 5:7, τί ἐμοὶ καὶ σοί) and his significantly *intrinsic* healing power that conquers strong opposing forces and is tangible even for those moribund. Then it is not surprising that Mark places his first didactic play on the meaning of relational πίστις causing holistic *salvation* and Jesus' *dynamic* identity in between Mark 4:35–42 (esp. v. 38 and v. 40) and 6:45–52 (esp. vv. 48–49 and v. 50), where Jesus displays his salvific power over life-threatening forces to his fearful disciples. Between the τίς ἄρα οὗτός ἐστιν of 4:41, he encourages his followers—and the audience—to practice this relational, salvific πίστις to understand the ἐγώ εἰμι of 6:50 in preparation for Mark 8:31; 9:32; 10:32, and finally 16:8.[194] After this impressive

---

[194] See ch. 7.

initiation, Mark 6:1–6 continues with questioning Jesus' identity, here, however, with a contrasting conclusion of negative reactions when his own kin doubt and reject him after his opponents plot his death (3:6) and he is asked to leave the region of the Gerasenes (5:17), sandwiched between the *pistis*-practicing characters of Mark 5 and the continuing ministry of his disciples (6:6–34).

6 Mark 7:24–37: Transitional Dis/ability

The entire sequence between Mark 5 and 7 heralds the end of Jesus' ministry in Galilee as established up to this point. After the intense focus on Jesus' intrinsic healing abilities in Mark 5, which effectuate a salvific new existence, the summaric notes in Mark 6:5 and 6:13 witness to the limits of Jesus' healing ministry and to its transmission to and commission of the disciples. Quite to the point, the death of John the Baptist (6:14–29; cf. 1:2–14) furthermore foreruns the change of pace as the narrative focuses on an increasingly elusive protagonist. Moreover, 6:53–56 summarizes major characteristics of Jesus' healing ministry as if to remind the audience of his inherent power and authority claims established in Mark 1, 2:1–3:6, and 5.[1]

With 7:1–23, a new thematical set of discussions is introduced, and the conflict between Jesus and his opponents (cf. Mark 2:1–3:6) is further developed. Jesus' interlocuters in this scene are identified with the Pharisees and scribes from Jerusalem (cf. 3:22); in v. 14, "the crowd" is also established as his addressees. Finally, in v. 17, Jesus retires with his disciples into a house for a more private teaching, but after v. 23, they are not mentioned again until 8:1. Instead, another minor character is introduced as his interlocutor for a private and intimate theological debate (see below).

The entire section is thematically held together by its focus on purity and impurity, culminating in Jesus' declaration that nothing entering a person can "defile" (κοινόω) him or her (vv. 15, 18).

6.1 Mark 7:24–30: Syrophoenician Negotiations

6.1.1 Introduction to the Narrative

Within this setting, the following narrative features a discussion by the occasion of an absent deviating body: while Jesus tries to stay hidden in a house (λανθάνω), a Syrophoenician woman encounters him, requesting relief for her daughter who has an unclean spirit (πνεῦμα ἀκάθαρτον). Besides the narrative function of this common Markan motif of Jesus failing to retreat to privacy,[2] the wish to stay hidden here serves as an illustration of growing opposition to and misunderstanding of his previous teaching (cf., e.g., 7:5–6, 18) and healing ministry (cf. in this region,

---
1 See ch. 2.
2 Cf., e.g., 1:35, 45; 2:1; 6:31–34. See also E. In Focus: Healing Spaces in Mark.

esp. 5:17; furthermore, 6:5), which henceforth grow in importance (see below). It moreover implies that Jesus did not intend to travel to this area to continue his public Galilean ministry.[3] However, his hiding was unsuccessful; the woman heard of him (cf. Mark 3:8; 5:27; 10:47) and petitions for her daughter.

The narrative is set in Tyre, a wealthy Phoenician trading city in the north of Galilee.[4] While there is archaeological and narrative evidence for economic trade between Tyre and Galilee, and a minority of Jews were reportedly settling there, its geographical and cultural difference to predominantly Jewish regions remains clearly defined.[5] The summaric account in Mark 3:7–8 already mentions Tyre together with Sidon as a place to where Jesus' popularity had spread.[6] As both cities are in the Hebrew Bible/Old Testament used as general terms for non-Jewish places,[7] its mention here and in 7:31 connote, beyond the geographical or historically correct demographic designation, a stereotypical ethnographical notion.

Besides Jesus, the woman is the only other character present. Although she is introduced anonymously and without a name, she is emphatically defined, analogous to the setting, by her ethnical and religious heritage, which also applies to her daughter. She is Ἑλληνίς, a "culturally privileged class of Greek-speaking city-dwellers in Tyre,"[8] a Gentile by religion in contrast to a Jewish background,[9] and by her geographical provenance (Συροφοινίκισσα τῷ γένει).

Her daughter remains a referential point offstage. She, too, is anonymous and nameless, defined by her ailment, the possession of an unclean spirit. In addition to the geographical and ethnographical setting of the scene with the socioreligious characterization of the women, a domestic structure frames the scene by the mention of the house of the failed retreat. It is mirrored by the house where the daughter remains as an external point of reference. Moreover, as is common for Markan accounts of possession, the spatial aspects of the daughter's disparate corporality and its cosmological, territorial frame transpire the text, explicitly when the moth-

---

3 Cf. Wainwright 2006. 124.
4 Cf. Freyne 1998. 114–121. For a detailed analysis of the cultural, ethnical, political, and socioeconomic status of Tyre and the Galilee region, see Theissen 1984.
5 Cf. Hanson 1980; Rappaport 1992; Horsley 1995a; Meyers 1995; Horsley 1995b.
6 See ch. 2.
7 Cf. Jer 25:15–26; 27:3; 47:1–7; Joel 3:1–8; Zech 9:2; 1Macc 5:15; Judg 2:28; also Rüggemeier in Bartsch; Bode (ed.) 2019. 361, n. 51.
8 Solevåg 2018. 43.
9 Cf., e.g., Ringe in Levine; Blickenstaff (ed.) 2004. 86; Collins 2007. 364, 366; Glancy 2010b. 351–352; Focant 2012. 299, 301.

er asks Jesus to "throw" the demon "out" of her daughter (ἐκβάλλω).[10] Hence, the entire narrative is nested with spatial structures on several layers, dividing various elements of the narrative between in (side-rs) and out (side-rs), while framed by verbs of movement (composita of ἔρχεσθαι in vv. 24–25; 29–30).[11]

The spatial setting is furthermore reflected in the conduct of the two main characters: while Jesus retreats to a defensive argumentation, trying to hold his theological ground, the woman intrudes on his hiding place with courage and determination, challenging Jesus to ignore the "social, political, economic, and symbolic" barriers between their two backgrounds.[12]

The request for expulsion of the unclean spirit and its eventual fulfillment frame a highly elaborate, chiastic argument of Jesus and the Syrophoenician woman in direct speech. This exchange is the focal point of the narrative, as the woman persuades Jesus to help her and heal her daughter despite their outsider status. The entire rhetoric of the account hinges on the opposition of Gentile "dogs" and Jewish "children." As opposed to her ethnic body, the dis/abled body of the daughter is not explicitly depicted and only mentioned as an external point of reference in the narrative, as is her healing, which takes place at a distance without any actions described. The focus lies entirely on the dialogue of Jesus and the Syrophoenician; the dis/ability of her daughter is only its contextual frame. Nevertheless, the described dis/ability offers a few key observations important for the overall scope of dis/ability in the Gospel of Mark.

6.1.2 Images of Dis/ability: Spatial Presence

The label of the daughter's dis/ability refers directly to the previous Markan accounts on pneumatic impurity (see 3.1; cf. also 5:1–20 and 9:14–29). Interestingly, the possessive spirit is here first defined as πνεῦμα ἀκάθαρτον (7:25), later as δαιμόνιον (vv. 26, 29, 30), which proves again the interchangeability of the two terms

---

[10] This is narrated in the imperfect to underline the quest for completion by Jesus' answer. For a closer analysis of the terminology of unclean spirits and/or demons, see A. In Focus: Markan Images of Sickness and Possession. Cf. also Focant 2012. 295–296.
[11] Cf. Gerber in Zimmermann (ed.) 2013. 313.
[12] Ringe in Levine; Blickenstaff (ed.) 2004. Cf. also comprehensively, Strube 2000. One the one hand commentators argue the mother's behavior is extraordinary and contrary to ancient female "role" conceptions: She is intrusive, not modest, not discouraged, but brave, tenacious, and "quick-witted," cf., e.g., Fander 1989. Others as, e.g., Dixon 1988. 210–232, point to her function as a caring mother and argue in favor of a role compliance in this regard, underscored by ancient texts applauding female boldness as shown in her witty riposte.

in Mark for the same demonic etiology. The initial designation may also be closely linked to the previously debated rules on purity (cf. 7:1–23). However, a connection between the dis/ability and the girl's religious and ethnic background cannot be made, as also Jewish characters in explicitly Jewish settings are portrayed as being possessed with verbatim impure spirits (cf. esp. Mark 1:21–28; cf. 3:7–12). Her ailment is neither determined by her femininity or age, as elsewhere in the text only male characters are affected by such spirits, and only one other child is similarly afflicted.[13] As in the other accounts, the characteristic disparate corporality of pneumatic impurity is reprised by spatial prepositions placing the hostile entity within the body of the host (cf., e.g., v. 26 ἐκβάλλω; vv. 29 and 30 ἐξέρχομαι [ἐκ]). However, in this pericope, no other concrete symptoms are mentioned, neither prior to nor after the exorcism. Only the use of βάλλω in v. 30, which describes that the girl is found by her mother "thrown" on the bed, reprises the common Markan terminology of demon possession. This physical abandonment is also reflected in the description of the formerly possessed body in Mark 9:26.[14] Nonetheless, since the girl lies there after the demon has left her without any further specification, it cannot be unequivocally related to the possession. There are no other characteristic symptoms explicitly recounted, neither screaming (cf. 1:26; 5:6–10) nor violent outbursts (cf. with need for containment in 5:4–5; 9:26). However, as the dog metaphor, even if culturally ambiguous, is (also) applied to mirror the (ethnic and religious) body of the daughter (v. 27), it transpires specific characteristics that echo Markan notions of demonic dis/ability, namely the "nonverbal orality on either side of the spectrum of socially accepted speech, that is either irrational screaming or mute silence; the erratic behavior; and the possible need for chaining all link the demon-possessed with animal characteristics."[15] Furthermore, the girl's physicality reflects the framed discussion as it also describes spatial intrusion (of the demon in her body) and exclusion (of her body from the scene) of in- and outsiders.

---

[13] Cf. Mark 1:23–27; 5:1–20; 7:24–30; 9:14–27.
[14] Here κλίνη is used in contrast to the more common κράβαττος in Mark 2:9, 11–12; 6:55, which hints at a higher economic standard. Cf., e.g., Theissen 1984. 212; Focant 2012. 303.
[15] Solevåg 2018. 48–49. See 3.1.2; 5.1; 7.2.2; cf. also the frequent use of βάλλω in reference to the girl's body in vv. 26, 30 and the food thrown to the dogs in v. 27.

6.1.3 The Healing: Remote Negotiations

The exorcism deviates from the other Markan exorcism accounts despite its verbatim designation[16] with focus on the success of Jesus' prediction (v. 29) by its verbal repetition (v. 30).[17] In addition to the absence of a powerful expulsion command, there is no fierce argument between the demon and his exorcist, nor is there a clear revelation of Jesus' divine identity reported. Furthermore, there is no personal and physical encounter between the two contesting bodies witnessed.

One could argue that the argumentative dispute between the divine and demonic entities witnessed in Mark 1:24–25 and 5:1–20 is depicted in the mother's discussion with Jesus,[18] yet the content and tone vary. Instead of harsh arguments on the concealment and revelation of Jesus' identity and his threatening power, we find a well-developed argument about the reach of Jesus' ministry. While demons and spirits refer to Jesus' divine, yet concealed, identity (e.g., 1:24, ὁ ἅγιος τοῦ θεοῦ; 5:7, υἱός τοῦ θεοῦ τοῦ ὑψίστου), the mother addresses Jesus as κύριε, which in the Gospel of Mark rather connotes respect than a distinct legitimating (divine) sovereign title.[19] Therefore, the motif of tension between disclosure and concealment of Jesus' identity that is often found in narratives of demon possession can only be applied to the narrative's beginning and Jesus' failed retreat, where it denotes his powerful reputation that cannot stay hidden, here, however, without a cosmological punchline. Only the territorial negotiations found in Mark 5:10–13 could be defined as slight commonality when regarding this narrative's described focus on spatial allusions. After all, the woman challenges and shifts Jesus' standpoint of separation and exclusion to a message of inclusion, where children and dogs can be fed at the same time.[20] The possessed body does not directly interact with Jesus neither, and the daughter remains unseen and unresponsive. As this distant "treatment" is not required by the dis/ability as the Markan Jesus mainly heals of demon possession by personal encounter (cf. Mark 1:21–28; cf. also 5:1–20 and then 9:14–29), the lack of any concrete action is astonishing for the otherwise characteristically tangible Markan healer and might imply that its reason lies in the women's Gentile provenance. This would concur with the presentation of non-Jewish healings in other gospel accounts where all remotely healed supplicants

---

[16] Cf. v. 26 [ἐκ];βάλλω cf. 1:34, 39; 3:15, 22–23; 6:13; 9:18, 28, 38; 16:9, 17; v. 29 and v. 30 ἐξέρχομαι [ἐκ]; cf. 1:25–26; 5:8, 13; 9:25–26, 29.
[17] Cf. Gerber in Zimmermann (ed.) 2013. 315.
[18] Cf. ibid. 314.
[19] Cf. 1:3; 2:28; 5:19; 7:28; 11:3, 9; 12:9, 11, 29–30, 36–37; 13:20, 35; also secondary 16:19–20; and Gerber in Zimmermann (ed.) 2013. 318, different to Wainwright in Alkier; Weissenrieder (ed.) 2013. 62.
[20] Cf. Wainwright 2006. 128–129.

and/or (socially dependent) patients (e. g., children or slaves) relate to an ethnic or religious outsiders' position: the centurion and his son/slave; the Syrophoenician/ Canaanite woman, her daughter, and the Samaritans with *lepra*. Only the provenance of the royal official and his patient is ambiguous in that regard.[21] However, each narrative must be analyzed within its gospel context, presupposed healthcare system, and characterization of the healing Jesus and must be regarded together with possible historical and redactional interrelations. For the Markan text, a causal connection between the distant treatment and the women's provenance aligns with the narrative's onset and focuses on their outsider identification. A theological convention, however, cannot be firmly established for this singular occurrence.[22]

The narrative scope of this account reveals a rather faint image of dis/ability and healing, particularly in contrast to Markan habits. The main objective of the narrative lies in the argument, as there is no physically present patient and therefore no forceful exorcistic negotiations between the divine and demonic entities, nor is there a final exorcistic order.

6.1.4 Interpretation

This narrative does not explicitly discuss deviating physicalities but *embodies* the debate on cultural identity and the reach of Jesus' ministry by employing distinct images of dis/ability.[23] Instead of an exorcism, it centers on a well-developed argument; instead of the common personal care given to those in need, Jesus only states the transformation from afar.

This is further contrasted by the similar yet very different narrative of Jaïrus and his daughter in Mark 5:21–24, 35–43 (see 5.2; cf. also Mark 9:14–29): here, too, a parent supplicates for the cure of his bedridden daughter, falling to Jesus' feet

---

[21] This is proposed by Harrocks in Taylor (ed.) 2014, who analyzed the NT narratives on the Gerasene demoniac (cf. Mark 5:1–20/Matt 8:28–34/Luke 8:26–37), the Syrophoenician's/Canaanite's daughter (Mark 7:24–30/Matt 15:21–28), the ten *lepers* (Luke 17:11–19), and the centurion's παῖς/ δοῦλος (Matt 8:5–13; Luke 7:1–10; cf. John 4:46–54) with regard to the non-Jewish provenance of the patients. Cf. esp. Harrocks in Taylor (ed.) 2014. 98–99. Whether or not her reasoning proves viable for the Gospels of Matthew and Luke must be considered for each gospel individually and its portrayal of (Jesus') mission to the Gentiles. Cf. also Nicklas in Busse; et al. (ed.) 2008. 97–98.
[22] This is also due to the fact, that the Markan text lacks the strong and explicit emphasis on πίστις as established in the Synoptic parallels, but the Markan Jesus speaks the daughter free from the demon because of her mother's argument, 7:29. Cf. Gerber in Zimmermann (ed.) 2013. 315.
[23] See Glancy 2010b, for an innovative reflection of the intersectional dynamics of cultural representations in this narrative.

with his request (πίπτω; cf. προσπίπτω in 7:25), while the dis/abled child remains in hidden quarters.²⁴ The main difference between the two narratives is Jesus' response to the very distinct supplicant: while the anonymous Gentile mother intrudes on Jesus in a moment of privacy in an area set up to convey disparity and exclusion, the well-established member of the Jewish community, Jaïrus, petitions for his daughter in the middle of a crowd on the emphasized other, Jewish side of the Lake of Galilee. While Jesus reluctantly argues with the one parent about the healing, becoming an obstacle himself and moving only with regard to his opinion, he physically follows the other over the course of a variety of obstacles until he encounters and heals the daughter personally in her room.²⁵ One parent is solely described by her ethnic and religious context; the other is embedded in his social circle of messengers, mourners, and family members. The healing of Jaïrus' daughter is described as a movement of emancipation and even witnessed by a circle of disciples, unlike the simply stated discovery of the daughter, healed from the distance, after the Syrophoenician woman returned home.

Neither status nor gender seems to be crucial for these differences because both supplicants are connected to an established social status, and both patients are female; moreover, the other "intrusive" female supplicant in Mark 5:25–34 is met with understanding and care. Rather, the entire setup of this narrative, also within its gospel context, suggests the woman's religious and ethnic background as the reason for the distinct treatment.

Both children's bodies are negotiated by their parents and their cultural identity. Their physical childishness underscores some of the main points of each narrative. Regarding the main argument of Mark 7:24–30, the entire pericope is set off by the introduction of a daughter in relationship to her mother (v. 25: θυγάτριον; v. 26: θυγάτηρ). In the argument between Jesus and the woman, the semantic field "child" is picked up again first in the form of τέκνα (v. 27) and then as παιδία (v. 28), both in contrast to the dogs. Finally, Jesus tells the woman about her healed θυγάτηρ (v. 29), and the narrator closes the narrative by recounting the unclean spirit had left τὸ παιδίον, the child.²⁶ While both terms, τέκνα and παιδία, designate size and/or age of a human body, τέκνα moreover carries the meaning of "offspring" (cf. τίκτω), of belonging to and dependence on physical and social family ties.²⁷

---

24 Cf. Mark 5:21–24, 35–43 in 5.2. On the narrative where the man seeks help for his dis/abled son, see ch. 7.
25 Cf. Wainwright 2006. 127; Glancy 2010b. 357–358 Cf. also the obstacles overcome by the supplicants/patients in 2:4 and 10:48.
26 Cf. Pokorný 1995. 337.
27 Cf. Focant 2012. 297; Gerber in Zimmermann (ed.) 2013. 316.

The body of the daughter encompasses and frames both—the relationship and the physical development of her description. Her physicality incorporates paradigmatically an "entire ethnic group."²⁸ Furthermore, the corporeal childishness underscores the diminutives of her mother's argument (v. 28: κυνάριον; ψιχίον, παιδίον). While the narrative of the daughter of Jaïrus depicts an individual emancipation, the dis/ability of the daughter of the Syrophoenician functions as an external point of reference and a visualization of the debated problem. The dis/ability of possession with its concept of territorial physical occupation exemplifies the narrative's focus on *in*trusion, *ex*clusion, and *in*tegration. The girl's dis/ability and its healing frame and reflect the narrative's argumentative tension between inside (-rs) and outside (-rs), animals and humans, dogs and children, offspring and adolescents.

6.2 Mark 7:31–37: Intelligible Communication

6.2.1 Introduction to the Narrative

The chapter continues by tracing Jesus' rather "crisscross" itinerary before setting the stage, quite vaguely, in the Decapolis, at the Sea of Galilee (v. 31). The initial πάλιν and mention of Tyre refer to v. 24 and the healing of the Syrophoenician's daughter while indicating a new onset at the same time. The other places have also been named settings for Jesus' healing ministry (e.g., Tyre and Sidon in 3:8; the Sea of Galilee, verbatim, in 1:16; the Decapolis in 5:20),²⁹ which illustrates the fast pace and far geographical reach of Jesus' popularity.³⁰

Jesus is the first character mentioned, although he is not explicitly named throughout the entire narrative and only referred to by verbs and personal pronomina. The indistinctness of characterizations is resumed when an undefined group (φέρουσιν, παρακαλοῦσιν) brings a man, κωφὸν καὶ μογιλάλον, to Jesus and asks him to lay his hands on him. There is no indication given that the disciples are present. The dis/abilities of the man are simply stated and not further explicated. Syntactically, they do not seem to be connected symptoms since they are individually and paratactically noted. No further information is given on the man's identity or ailment.

---

[28] Solevåg 2018. 49.
[29] Cf. Collins 2007. 369.
[30] Cf. Rüggemeier in Bartsch; Bode (ed.) 2019. Esp. 359–361.

The brief exposition is followed by a very detailed description of the succeeding healing, which takes place after a locational shift away from the crowd to an intimate communication between Jesus and the man. The lexemes κατ' ἰδίαν, ἀναβλέψας, and ἐστέναξεν connote a close proximity of the two characters, a local deixis.[31] Connected with numerous καί, Jesus' very corporal and sensualized actions are reported, painting an audiovisual scene for the audience (see below). The immediate success of this series of healing actions is briefly stated. The man's dis/abled organs are "opened" (ἀνοίγω) and "loosened" (λύω); he is able(d) to ἐλάλει ὀρθῶς, although this is not attested by his own direct speech. However, the changes in focalization reflect the dis/ability and healing of the man: while vv. 31–34 are externally focalized, narrating the active sequence for the audience, v. 35 draws into the sensations of the dis/abled man. The healing is recounted traceably and tangibly for the audience, which is just as important for the verification of the healing as the closing and again externally focalized part of the sentence: καὶ ἐλάλει ὀρθῶς.[32] The narrator simply states the healing and continues to explicate Jesus' injunction to silence. Again, the addressees remain ambiguous αὐτά (v. 36), yet (δέ) Jesus' command is broken, and the public consequence of the healing is recapitulated by the narrator.

Interestingly, the epilogue (again briefly internally focalized on αὐτά: ἐξεπλήσσοντο) is set in perfect (πεποίηκεν) and present tense (ποιει), which on the one hand refers back to the ultimately preceding detailed healing of the sensory impaired man (cf. the captivating present tense in vv. 32 and 34) and on the other hand interprets the healing with regard to πάντες, the overall plot of Jesus' precedented deeds and teaching.[33] This matches the change in focalization throughout the narrative: the audience follows Jesus' healing actions closely through the narrator's eyes, listens intently to the healer's direct speech (cf. vv. 34, 37), and directly participates in the dis/abled man's sensations of his released sensory organs and in the amazement of "them" about (all of) the preceding deed(s).[34]

6.2.2 Images of Dis/ability

6.2.2.1 Disturbed Communication

The dis/abled man is introduced as κωφός and μογιλάλος. No other symptoms are directly recounted. The lexeme κωφός can designate being deaf and/or mute yet

---

31 Cf. Willebrand 2017. 74.
32 Cf. ibid. 111, 113.
33 Cf. Pramann 2008. 147; Willebrand 2017. 78–79, 84–85, 109.
34 Cf. Willebrand 2017. 109–110, 113.

often denotes a complete inability to communicate.[35] While muteness as a singular dis/ability is more commonly labeled ἄλαλος and ἄφωνος,[36] "deaf-mutes" are rarely discussed in ancient literature, and if they are, it is usually in the context of congenital deafness and a form of imbecility in the sense of an intellectual deviance (ἐνεός).[37] As such impaired hearing is depicted with direct influence on the communicative abilities that reflect mental clarity, it is often connected to unreasonableness, egocentricity, lack of self-control, distrust, stupidity, imbecility, and "insanity."[38] According to Aristotle, "all who are deaf from birth [κωφοὶ ἐκ γενετῆς] are dumb [ἐνεοί] as well: though they can utter a sort of voice, they cannot talk."[39] Like the ambiguous label κωφός, this reflects the interrelated function of auditory and verbal communication but also alludes to the importance of hearing and speech for an oral culture. Prominently, one of Croesus' sons is described as "ruined/destroyed completely" (διαφθείρω)[40] because of his κωφός condition, which is in Herodotus' text interpreted as a hearing impairment but shifts to muteness in subsequent reception.[41] In addition, the Gospels of Matthew and Luke link κωφός directly to speech impairment (Matt 9:33 and 15:31), connect κωφός with λαλέω (cf. Luke 11:14; Matt 12:22), or indicate that Zacharias stays κωφός and needs gestures and writing to communicate (Luke 1:22, 63). Here in Mark, however, the man's inability to articulate is paratactically and therefore equally defined as μογιλάλος, which makes it more likely that κωφός refers here only to his inability to hear. Furthermore, in vv. 33, 35, and 37, the narrative seems to clearly differentiate between muteness and deafness, when Jesus first touches the man's ears (οὖς) and then his tongue (γλῶσσα). Both organs are treated and liberated individually, and the eventual healing is described by pairing κωφός with ἀκούω and ἄλαλος with λαλέω.[42]

After Jesus' healing actions, the man's ἀκοαί are "opened" according to Jesus' imperative (ἀνοίγω/ἀνοίγνυμι, vv. 34–35). The change from the previously used οὖς

---

[35] Cf. Spittler, *Deafness II. NT.*; Balz; Schneider, κωφός; BDAG, *s.v*; LN, *s.v* 33.106; LSJ, *s.v*; Montanari, *s.v*

[36] In the NT cf., e.g., Mark 9:17, 25; Acts 8:32; 1Cor 12:2; 2Pet 2:16. For ἄλαλος see ch. 7.2.2 and comprehensively von Bendemann in Härle; Preul (ed.) 2005. 61.

[37] Cf. Laes 2011. Esp. 460–465, for an extensive survey of ancient (literary, papyri, inscriptions, juridic) sources from 600 BCE–800 CE. Cf. also, e.g., BDAG, *s.v*; LN, *s.v* 33.108; LSJ, *s.v*; Montanari, *s.v*

[38] von Bendemann in Härle; Preul (ed.) 2005. 56.

[39] Cf. *Hist. An.* 4.9.536.b3–5; Pliny, *Nat.* 10.192; Plato, *Phaedr.* 253c; and Laes 2011. 460.

[40] Cf., e.g., LN, *s.v* 20.40, 88.266; LSJ, *s.v*; Montanari, *s.v*

[41] Cf. Herodotus, *Hist.* 1.34; and Rose in Davis (ed.) 2006; Laes 2011. 455.

[42] Cf. also 7.2.2, where Jesus addresses the tormenting spirit with τὸ ἄλαλον καὶ κωφὸν πνεῦμα (9:25).

denotes first of all the physical organ for hearing yet also shifts the sensory act of perceiving sound[43] to the ability to discern precisely *what* is heard.[44] The description of "opened" organs for a physical change regarding the faculty of sensory perception is frequently applied in the New Testament and ancient literature, although it most often refers to the mouth and tongue, not the ears.[45] Therefore, Jesus' command seems to address both organs, only the effect on the speech apparatus is put in different terms.

The label μογιλάλος defines the parameters of the dis/abled man's ailment more clearly and follows what was already insinuated by the connection of κωφός to speech impediments: he has difficulty with verbal articulation. The term is a hapax legomenon in the New Testament and is in biblical writings only used again in Isa 35:6^{LXX} (see 6.2.4, for an analysis of the associated dis/ability of this passage). The scarce occurrences in other literary sources confirm its rarity and its unequivocal meaning regarding oral communication.[46] Its healing is described as a loosening of the tongue (v. 35: ἐλύθη ὁ δεσμὸς τῆς γλώσσης αὐτοῦ) with the resulting ability to ἐλάλει ὀρθῶς. Due to the abovementioned Markan distinction between deaf- and muteness and the rare yet somewhat more detailed description of the oral dis/ability here, the man's speech impairment seems to fall somewhere on the spectrum of disrupted verbal articulation yet does not seem to affect his general ability to produce oral sounds. Moreover, the healed body reflects the wide and ambiguous spectrum of attested "speech impairment" in Greco-Roman antiquity that also includes "temporary events such as drunkenness and bouts of shyness and embarrassment" and also permanent "lisping along with other peculiarities in pronunciation, ... [and] stuttering."[47] On the one hand, he is said to λαλέω ὀρθῶς, which could refer to any minor to major speech impairment; on the other hand, the account closes by praising Jesus' ability to make the mute (ἄλαλος) speak (λαλέω), paralleled by making the deaf hear, which alludes to a more severe inability to produce coherent speech. In any case, as neither the duration of his ailment is discussed nor any cognitive deviations connected to

---

43 Cf., e.g., Aelian, *Var. hist.* 3.1 p. 39,21; Josephus, *A.J.* 8.172; Plato, *Theaet.* 142 D; also Matt 13:14; Acts 28:26.
44 Cf., e.g., Mark 1:28; 13:7; 1Thess 2:13; Rom 10:16–17; Gal 3:2, 5; Heb 4:2; and von Bendemann in Härle; Preul (ed.) 2005. 67; BDAG, s.v.; Montanari, s.v.; LSJ, s.v.
45 Cf., e.g., Matt 5:2; 9:30; 13:35; 20:33; Luke 1:64; John 9:10, 14, 17, 21, 26, 30, 32; Acts 9:8, 40; 26:18; 2Cor 6:11; Rev 13:6; and CH, *Loc. hom.* 27; *Mul.* 2.133; 1.11; CH, *EDMHi* 23.14–17; furthermore, Weissenrieder 2003. 117–118.
46 Cf. Isa 35:6^{LXX}; and Vettius, *Anth.* 2.17; Ptolemy, *Tetrabibl.* 150; Aëtius, *Tetrabibl.* 8.38 (ed. Aldina); and Laes in Laes; Goodey; Rose (ed.) 2013. 151, esp. n. 21.
47 Ibid. 167, and on a detailed survey of certain lexemes, see ibid. 150–152.

it, the ambiguity of the used labels aims to transport an inability to communicate coherently, which—in a predominantly oral culture that values speech in public affairs and teachings and relies on everyday verbal communication—might have extensive socio-anthropological implications: while a reduced economic and educational capacity seems inevitable with such sensory impairments, its implied intellectual limitations rendered the deaf legally and politically incapacitated and therefore marginalized. Similar to those with mental dis/abilities, they could not hold office, act as guardians or judges, or make a legal will.[48] All of this was more strictly enforced on those with complete or congenital deaf-/muteness.[49] Rabbinic sources successively developed categorizations of different degrees of deaf-/muteness with according patterns of socioeconomic integration (e.g., via sign language).[50] The motif of interrupted communication is also often found in the biblical texts and linked to isolation and poverty.[51] Since the Markan man is brought to Jesus, a certain degree of helplessness can be assumed; whether it concerns an (associated) intellectual incoherence connected to his speech condition or just the help he needs to articulate his wish for healing remains open to speculation. In Mark 7:31–37, neither the duration of his ailment is discussed, nor any mental incapability connected to it.

6.2.2.2 Etiology and Therapy

The vagueness of the exact meaning of the term κωφός regarding deaf-/muteness is reflected in its possible origins. In the Corpus Hippocraticum, it is used in reference to *fever*, restricted control of the tongue (and its connection to throat, palate, and teeth), and temporal states of anxiety and is mainly classified as a symptom or "diagnostic tool" of severe sicknesses. Generally, it is traced back to an accumulation of blood or bile in the brain, which has consequences on the intellectual comprehension of the patient.[52] As a therapy, methods for balancing the liquids are discussed, such as blood-letting. Furthermore, general hearing conditions can be traced back to climatic conditions; injuries of the head, the ears, and nerves; or blockages of the outer auditory canal that can be improved by rinses.

In the Hebrew Bible and Jewish sources, deafness is often mentioned together with blindness.[53] The focus mainly lies on the (lack of) auditory perception and

---

48 Cf. ibid. 153–155; Kollmann in Zimmermann (ed.) 2013. 92; Lawrence 2013. 61–62.
49 Cf. von Bendemann in Härle; Preul (ed.) 2005. 59; Laes 2011. 466–467.
50 Cf. *mTer* 1:2; *tTer* 1:2; *mGit* 5:7; and Abrams, *Deafness III. Judaism.*
51 Cf. Luke 1:22; Prov 31:8–9; Isa 53:7, Ezek 3:26; 24:27; 33:22, but Ps 31:19; 39:3, 10.
52 For the following, cf., e.g., CH, *Coac.* 178; 192–194; *Iudic.* 49; *Carn.* 18 (L 8.608); *Acut.* 2.6; and Weissenrieder 2003. 114–119, 121; von Bendemann in Härle; Preul (ed.) 2005. 57; Laes 2011. 460–465.
53 Cf. Lev 19:14; Isa 6:10; 29:18; 35:5; 42:18–19.

discernment of God's commandments and laws.⁵⁴ Especially in the Book of Isaiah, the cures of both blindness and deafness are motifs promising revelation of YHWH and his words as redemption and restoration from exile.⁵⁵ Another common motif is the auditory capacity of God when it comes to hearing prayer in the Book of Psalms.⁵⁶ Of course, as with any already analyzed ancient dis/ability, divine causes and cures are also recounted for (temporal) deaf- and muteness.⁵⁷

Specific muteness or an impaired faculty of speech is often linked to problems with breath as a vehicle of language or disfigurements of the speech apparatus (e. g., tongue, larynx, tubes, teeth, lips, etc.). The causes could be as diverse as "accidents, injuries and/or maltreatment, and physical violence"⁵⁸ of lips, tongue or palate, dental problems, old age, other severe diseases, or dementia. Narrowed down to the anatomy of the speech apparatus, this could mean a change of conformation, number, magnitude, arrangement, or continuity (partial disfigurement) of the individual parts.⁵⁹ Paradigmatic of the physical complexity behind coherent speech, Galen's *De lociis affectis* 4.9 summarizes:

> Expiration is produced by the contraction of all muscles of the chest. Exsufflation, being a forceful expiration, results mainly from the action of the intercostal muscles. If it is noisy, the pharyngeal muscles are participating. But the sound is produced by the laryngeal muscles. The tongue, however, which articulates the sound, is needed to produce speech. This is accomplished by the aid of teeth and lips, the nasal communications, the palate, the uvula and, in addition, by the median ligament of the tongue itself [τοῦ συμμέτρου δεσμοῦ τῆς γλώττης αὐτῆς]. Those who speak in a lisping, inarticulate manner and those who have a related disturbance of the speech, suffer from a damage of the instruments of speech, either during their natural formation or at a later stage.⁶⁰

The Markan text describes a particular impediment of the tongue, which fits ancient notions that ascribe it a key function in the process of translating thought

---

54 Cf. Isa 42:19; 43:8; Exod 4:11; Lev 19:14; Ps 38:14; 58:5; Isa 29:18; 35:5; 42:18–19 and 43:8/Mic 7:16; Ps 28:1; 35:22; 39:13; 50:3; 83:2; 109:1; von Bendemann in Härle; Preul (ed.) 2005. 57.
55 Cf., e. g., Isa 35; 6:9–10; 29:18; 42:18–19; 48:8–13.
56 Cf., e. g., Ps 35:22; 39:13; 50:3; 83:2; and 109:1.
57 Cf. IG IV 951 1.41–47 = IG IV² 1.121–122.1.41–48; IG IV² 1.123.1.1–3; Herzog 1931. No. 44, and 5, 51; von Bendemann in Härle; Preul (ed.) 2005. 58.
58 Laes in Laes; Goodey; Rose (ed.) 2013. 147.
59 Cf., e. g., Galen, *Diff. Morb.* 6 (K 6.857; 6.861; 6.864; 6.868); *Comm. CH Epid.* 1.2.78 (K 17.1.187); *Loc. aff.* 4.9 (K 8.272); *Meth. med.* 14.8 and 14.12 (K 10.971 and 10.984–986); *Galen, Comm. CH Aph.* 6.32 (18.1.51 K); *Usu part.* 11,10 (K 3.884); Pliny, *Nat.* 7.70; Lactantius, *Opif.* 10; Orbasius, *Collectiones Medicae* 45,16 (169–170 Raeder); Celsus, *Med.* 7.12.6; and Laes in Laes; Goodey; Rose (ed.) 2013. 159–160. For a comprehensive overview of speech impairment in Greek sources from third cent. BCE to late antiquity (sixth cent.) and earlier Greek literature, see ibid.
60 Cf. K 8.271–72; translation by Collins 2007. 373.

into speech.⁶¹ Within the concept of humoral theory, its impairment (i. e., "loss of control and malarticulation, [...] stupor or violent, quick movements"⁶²) can be caused by an excess or lack of moisture or temperature that affects the nerves, brain, or muscle of the tongue.⁶³ There are even reports of surgical measures taken to aid the tongue's proper function and also accounts given on applied speech therapy for the wealthy and those obliged to oratory performances.⁶⁴ A "loosened" (λύω) δεσμός of the tongue (v. 35) could in this context refer to its rehabilitation in flexibility and controllability as the major organ of clear speech production. It could, however, also hint at another line of etiological explanation: As κατάδεσμός is often found in the context of curses and (judicial) "binding spells," for example, of the tongue,⁶⁵ an impairment caused by numinous entities might be implied.⁶⁶ This concurs with the understanding that demons/evil entities can enter the body through its openings and to the apotropaic use of saliva in this context.⁶⁷ Even if not used concerning a binding spell, "loosening" can suggest the unwinding of a forceful personal entity, maybe as part of an exorcism. However, within the Gospel of Mark, such an interpretation is rather unlikely since the differences between possession and sickness, exorcism and therapy are marked clearly throughout the gospel narrative.⁶⁸ The only exception that could be discussed in this regard, also in context with sensory impairments, is Mark 9:14–29 (see 7.1.2; 7.2.2; 7.3.2). Nevertheless, the symptoms of undefined speech and its connection to mental impediments might relate to those described of possessed characters but are in Mark more of an erratic, not silent, nature (cf., e. g., Matt 9:32–33; Luke 11:14).

---

61 Cf., e. g., Euripides, *Suppl.* 203–204; cf. Laes in Laes; Goodey; Rose (ed.) 2013. 158.
62 Ibid. 158–159.
63 Cf. CH, *Epid.* 2.5.2; 2.6.3; 7.43; Galen, *San. tu.* 6.2 (K 6.390); *Comm. CH Aph.* 6.32 (18.1.51); and Laes in Laes; Goodey; Rose (ed.) 2013. 158–159.
64 Cf., e. g., Cicero, *Div.* 2.46; Celsus, *Med.* 7.12.4; Quintilian, *Inst.* 1.1.37; 1.11.1–8; Caelius, *Chron.* 2.41; and Laes 2011. 471–472; Laes in Laes; Goodey; Rose (ed.) 2013. 161–163, 168.
65 Cf. Collins 2007. 372–374, although her following interpretation within the context of "bonds" in Isa 42:6–7 and 49:8–9 is very unlikely due to the lack of more connective terms and/or motifs.
66 Cf., e. g., Matt 9:32–33; 12:22; Luke 11:14; Plutarch, *Mor.* 438B, 121; Zauberpapyrus PGM 13.242–244; also von Bendemann in Härle; Preul (ed.) 2005. 60; Boring 2006. 217; Kollmann in Zimmermann (ed.) 2013. 90.
67 See below; cf. also Ueberschaer in Zimmermann (ed.) 2013. 324–325, 327.
68 See chs. 2, 3, and 5. Cf. Guttenberger 2004. 249–255; von Bendemann in Härle; Preul (ed.) 2005. 58.

6.2.3 The Healing: Sensory Participation

When Jesus encounters the man, he is simply asked to lay his hands onto him (v. 32, ἵνα ἐπιθῇ αὐτῷ τὴν χεῖρα), a phrase that is also used in the plea of Jaïrus in Mark 5:23 and in the summaric account of Mark 6:5. Both times the (anticipated) direct consequence is healing, which must be implied in the request in Mark 7:32 (cf. also 6:2; see C. In Focus: Mark's Healing Touches). The following tactile healing, however, is here, part of a sevenfold curative exercise (a.–f.), which is recounted in only two verses, strung together with connecting καί and participia coniuncta, mainly in aorist (the only exception is the λέγει in v. 34) until culminating in the healing's effect set in a durative imperfect in v. 35.[69]

a. Distance from crowd: At first, Jesus takes the man away from the crowd (ἀπολαμβάνω), which establishes intimacy between the healing body and the dis/abled body and emphasizes the following emphatically sensuous actions "away from hearing culture and a context in which hearing and meaning are perceived as unified."[70] In the gospel context, it moreover hints at the motif of unwarranted disclosure of Jesus' identity[71] or alludes to a "magical connotation," which, however, has no indication in the text or another point of reference in the gospel narrative.[72]

b. The touches: As established in C. In Focus on healing touches, the contact between healer and patient is established in agreement with the dis/ability. In this case, Jesus places his *fingers* on the man's ears and touches his tongue, which is a unique occurrence in the Synoptic Gospels,[73] and is based on the size and number of the organs involved (on the succession of spit and touch, see below). His two hands touch the two organs according to their measurements and reach the vulnerable source of the man's dis/ability. Due to the anatomy of the dis/abled organ, it seems likely that also his fingers touch the tongue, although the text does not narrate this explicitly.

c. Saliva: Jesus spits (πτύω); however, it remains unclear where he spits and why. The confusion about this sequence is reflected in the different versions of the textual witnesses: The focus lies either on connecting or separating Jesus' acts of spitting and touching the man's ears with his fingers.[74] According to the suc-

---

[69] Cf. von Bendemann in Härle; Preul (ed.) 2005. 61.
[70] Lawrence 2013. 68.
[71] Cf. Boring 2006. 216.
[72] Cf. Ueberschaer in Zimmermann (ed.) 2013. 326–327. Cf. Ovid, *Met.* 7.255–256; Lucian, *Philops.* 16; PGM 3.616–617. Cf. von Bendemann in Härle; Preul (ed.) 2005. 61.
[73] Cf. Luke 11:20; but Matt 12:28 and von Bendemann in Härle; Preul (ed.) 2005. 62–62.
[74] Cf. Aland 1996. 221; Collins 2007. 368–369.

cessive Mark 8:23, it is likely that Jesus spits directly on or into the dis/abled organs, which is here nevertheless difficult to imagine due to their narrow and inaccessible physical constitution. More conceivably, Jesus spits onto his hands and then touches ears and/or tongue.[75] Regarding the textual evidence, however, the aorist participle πτύσας ambiguously lingers in between the two flexed verbs ἔβαλεν and ἥψατο, and the possibility remains that Jesus spits on no organ at all but, e.g., on the ground, and there is no contact established between the man and Jesus' saliva. Only when taking the connective καί into account does it seem syntactically more reasonable to link the spitting closer to the touch of the tongue. Then the entire section can be divided into four sequences: the separation from the crowd and the touch of the ears; the spitting and touch of the tongue; the heavenly gaze and the sigh; and, finally, the opening command.

While there is no further indication on the curative properties of Jesus' saliva here, the subsequent use in Mark 8:23 then might recall a common ancient notion of therapeutic qualities of salvia, particularly for visual impairments.[76] Even if less frequent, there are also accounts of healing of muteness with "charged" spittle,[77] which if presupposed here would furthermore indicate a physical connection of Jesus' spit with either or both dis/abled organs.

> The belief in the alleviating force of saliva can be traced back to Aristotle, who attested to its repellant force against snakes.[78] Pliny the Elder also recognized it among other agents as a protection against epilepsy, anxiety disorders, demons/harm, as a means (*precatione*) against blindness and witchcraft, and as a (pharmacological) aid with skin problems when applied regularly.[79] Its force is heightened when spat out under triple worship proclamation of God. The numinously chargeable power of saliva in context with incantations is also reflected in Jewish literature, such as *T.Sol.* 7:3, the rabbinic treaties *bSan* 101a and *bBB* 126b, or in reports of healing by the oral touch of (sacred) animals.[80]
>
> The most prominent "medical practitioner," however, is Galen. He is said to have used saliva together with feces, urine, and so on as parts of the so-called dirty remedies, "Drecksapotheke."[81] In his medical philosophy, Galen describes the mouth to be a place where

---

75 Cf. von Bendemann in Härle; Preul (ed.) 2005. 62.
76 Cf. for the following, Cotter 1999; von Bendemann in Zimmermann (ed.) 2013. 345; moreover, e.g., Pliny, *Nat.* 26.93, 28.7, 35–39; Tob 11:11–13; Tacitus, *Hist.* 4.81.1–3; Suetonius, *Vesp.* 445; *bBB* 126b; *jSot* 16b.
77 Cf. IG 10.51, and Ueberschaer in Zimmermann (ed.) 2013. 327.
78 Cf. Aristotle, *Hist. an.* 8.206–209; Pliny, *Nat.* 7.2.13–15; 26.93; 28.4–28.7, 36–38; Aelian, *Nat. an.* 9.4; and Collins 2007. 370; Ueberschaer in Zimmermann (ed.) 2013. 327–328; Weissenrieder in Schröter; Jacobi (ed.) 2022 [2017]. 299.
79 Cf. esp. Pliny, *Nat.* 28.7.35–39.
80 Cf. also Philostratus, *Vit. Apoll.*6.43; Pliny, *Nat.* 28.7.36; Edelstein; Edelstein 1998. 423.26 (1.226, 234); 423.20; 423.17; and Ueberschaer in Zimmermann (ed.) 2013. 327–328.
81 Cf. Weissenrieder in Schröter; Jacobi (ed.) 2022 [2017]. 298.

food, liquids, and recess of the brain via the palatine and saliva under the tongue are mixed by different forces.[82] Moreover, the theory of humorism explains the effect of saliva with regard to its origin in the human body. Here, it is not only relatable to blood, both carriers of spiritual entities, but also to exhalation and breathing as a dispersion of the mouth, distinguishing saliva as a powerful remedy.[83] This strong connection of saliva to its carrier could explain the belief in its powerful effect when coming from a powerful person.[84]

However, in the Hebrew Bible, it is also regarded as a carrier of impurity, sign for degradation, and in uncontrollable flow, as a symptom of (demonic) possession.[85] Any theories on ritual impurity in this regard, even in connection with Mark 7:1–23, must be dismissed since the narrator would have made this emphasis and connection clear if important, especially since the saliva comes from Jesus with a healing effect cum other actions.[86]

While saliva evidently plays a healing role as a substance "chargeable" with (numinous) powers by spells, deities, and its (human) carriers, it is difficult to establish solid ground to evaluate its function here in Mark 7:33 and later in 8:23 (see 7.3.1). Although an apotropaic purpose in context of a possible demonic interpretation of the δεσμός of the tongue cannot be ruled out, the medical connotations (that also appear in Mark 8:23 without any demonic context) and, above all, the vivid impression of Jesus' intimate "sensory-gustatory" and "sensory-tactile" healing technique[87] are explicitly evident in the text. These serve as markers of his intrinsic healing power and corporality, as suggested by the text's syntax and content.

d. Look up: As ambiguous as the appliance of saliva is the following gesture of Jesus' raised gaze (ἀναβλέπω). The direction and the visual act of the gesture in itself are not uncommon for New Testament narratives and convey a communicative act with God: in Mark 6:41, Jesus thankfully gazes upward before feeding the 5,000 with five loaves of bread and two fish; in Luke 18:13, a tax collector is too ashamed to raise his eyes toward heaven when asking God for forgiveness; in John 17:1, Jesus commits himself into God's hands for the following passion; and in Acts 7:55, Stephanus preaches with God and Jesus as heavenly confirmation in clear sight.[88] Celestial motifs in the Gospel of Mark are furthermore connected to (visionary) divine encounters (cf. 1:10; 9:2–7), and the use of gestures or notions

---

82 Cf., e.g., Galen, *Fac. nat.*, 3.7 § 163; and Collins 2007. 370; von Bendemann in Zimmermann (ed.) 2013. 345; Weissenrieder in Schröter; Jacobi (ed.) 2022 [2017]. 299.
83 Cf. Böcher 1970. 218–220.
84 Cf. Weissenrieder in Schröter; Jacobi (ed.) 2022 [2017]. 299.
85 Cf. 1Sam 21:14–15; Lev 15:8; Deut 25:9; Isa 50:6.
86 Cf. differently, Boring 2006. 217.
87 Cf. Stimpfle in Grünstäudl; Schiefer Ferrari (ed.) 2012. 121.
88 Cf. furthermore, e.g., Ps 121:1; 123:1; Philo, *Mos.* 1.190; 1Kgs 17:21.

of prayer—even if not necessarily in connection to the eyes—occur frequently in New Testament healing narratives (cf., e.g., Mark 9:29; John 11:41–42; Acts 9:40; 28:8; James 5:13–18).[89] Whether the action was employed to underscore Jesus' constant contact and/or his legitimization by God, his divine identity, or the source of his power that he needs to "draw further upon,"[90] remain undistinguishable nuances of this motif. Due to the syntactical placement of the aorist participle with the following flexed aorist within a connective καί structure, it must be regarded together with the following suspiration.

e. Sigh: On its own, the sigh joins this sequence of ambiguous actions. Within the Synoptic Gospels, it is the only occurrence of the term στενάζω; only in Mark 8:12, ἀναστενάζω is used to convey Jesus' frustration regarding the Pharisaic request for a "sign." Other occurrences in the NT all denote an auditory expression of emotion, mostly regarding enduring hardship, injustice, and/or a longing for redemption.[91] Such an emotional and, by its expression, embodied sign of compassion or anger would also concur with the characterization of the Markan Jesus when confronted with dis/ability in the broadest sense (cf. esp. σπλαγχνίζομαι in 1:41, also 9:22; ὀργή in 3:5; also: 6:34 when teaching; 8:2 before feeding). However, due to the previous gaze to heaven and the entire syntactical sequence (see above), it can also be interpreted as an (emotional) expression of prayer, an "appeal to the divine force at the moment in which he [Jesus] is confronted by an opposition difficult to conquer":[92] as in this pericope, retreat from the public, employed to create an intimate setting for a personal encounter with God, and an emotional intercessor are also characteristics of personal and un-liturgical prayers of the Markan Jesus (cf. 1:35; 6:46; 14:32–41; 15:34; mainly: προσεύχομαι). Mark 6:41 even witnesses a glance to heaven before Jesus thankfully praises God for the food feeding the 5,000.[93] Therefore, the gesture can transpire both an expression of passion *and* prayer as it aligns with the depiction of the Markan Jesus as engaging in compassionate dialogue with God on several occasions.[94] On the contrary, a sigh within the context of an exorcistic struggle or in relation to spiritual and "magical" techniques seems unlikely, as there is no precedent or indication of such an audible breath or look above in the gospel text. Furthermore, nothing else in the text suggests such an interpretation. Considering that a sigh also conveys the notion of ex-

---

[89] Cf. von Bendemann in Härle; Preul (ed.) 2005. 63.
[90] Collins 2007. 371.
[91] Cf., e.g., Rom 8:23; 2Cor 5:2, 4; Heb 13:17; Jas 5:9.
[92] Focant 2012. 306.
[93] Cf. however, 8:6–7 and 14:22–23.
[94] Cf. esp. 6:41; also 1:35–38; 6:46; also 8:1–9; 14:12–25.

halation, the interpretation of this gesture as a "drawing-in" (divine) energy for the healing is unapt.⁹⁵

f. ἐφφαθά: After his soundful breathing, Jesus says to the man "Ephphatha," the Greek transliteration of the Aramaic verb פתח in Itpa'al imperative with slight sound assimilations. The narrator immediately translates this term:⁹⁶ ὅ ἐστιν διανοίχθητι. The motif of an unfamiliar lexeme in the context of a healing narrative has occurred already in Mark 5:41. Here again, the immediate translation disenchants a potential ῥῆσις βαρβαρική,⁹⁷ at least for the audience, and serves an intradiegetic function, namely to connect the command over the narrator's translation with the immediate execution by the use of the same verbal root, just as in 5:41.⁹⁸ The powerful effect of Jesus' command is not diminished by the translation, yet an esoteric "magical formula or an incantation" is unlikely, even if the change from the singular to the effected opening in the plural is peculiar.⁹⁹

After this succession of healing actions, the effect is immediately stated in v. 35. Throughout Jesus' touches, gestures, and sounds, the dis/abled man has remained silent and passive until the final statement of this verse: καὶ ἐλάλει ὀρθῶς. Then he vanishes from the narrative altogether, the intimate healing sequence is opened again to "them," and the man is not mentioned again.

Verses 33–35 give the audience an impression of an enclosed space, where "Jesus' tactile actions, inaudible sounds, and use of foreign terms, coupled with the 'deaf-mute's' resistant silence, initiate a space where meaning does not equate solely to verbal language"¹⁰⁰ but is moreover conveyed and perceivable by varied forms of sensuous communication. While this extraordinary physical healing might only emphasize the difficulty of the healing task,¹⁰¹ it also clearly displays Jesus' engaging physicality and a communication framework beyond the "hearing/speaking binary" embodied by the dis/ability of the man:¹⁰² Jesus uses his locomotor system in moving away from the crowd, his tactile hands and fingers when touching the man, his salivary glands to produce the spittle, his eyes when looking up, his entire respirational system when sighing, his speech appara-

---

[95] Cf. however, PGM 4.249–93; 8.942–946; and 4.1406; 7.766–779; also Bonner 1927. 171–181; Hull 1974. 84; Blackburn 1991. 216–218; Kollmann 1996. 233; Boring 2006. 217; Collins 2007. 371–372.
[96] Cf. Willebrand 2017. 77.
[97] Cf. Lucian, *Philops.* 9; 31; Origen, *Cels.* 6.40; Pliny, *Nat.* 28.20; PGM 13.150–152.458–459; Lucian, *Alex.* 13; and Ueberschaer in Zimmermann (ed.) 2013. 328. Cf. also p. 183, n. 180.
[98] Cf. von Bendemann in Härle; Preul (ed.) 2005. 63.
[99] Collins 2007. 372. Cf. Mark 15:22, 34.
[100] Lawrence 2013. 74.
[101] Cf. Focant 2012. 306.
[102] Cf. Lawrence 2013. 75.

tus and language competence when uttering the opening command. This focus on a "potency to communicate" is not only captured by the statement of the man's healing (his faculty to hear is not further explicated) but by the following order to silence.

6.2.4 The Epilogue: Solicited Silence and Prophetic Praise?

After the healing, Jesus issues a command to silence. To whom Jesus gives this command is not explicated. That the ambiguous αὐτά refers to the disciples is unlikely since they have not been mentioned after 7:17–23. Rather, it relates to the previously mentioned group who brought the man to Jesus and/or to the surrounding crowd, although none has reportedly witnessed the healing. Hence, it likely includes the formerly intestable man, who now broadcasts Jesus' healing power with rapid, far-reaching, and contagious enthusiasm. Here, it reflects the transformation of his dis/ability in particular since he thereafter is physically and culturally able to bear witness.[103] The violation of the order is immediately recounted, like in Mark 1:44–45, where the man healed of *lepra* impermissibly recounts his healing, causing an increase of popularity programmatic and summaric for Jesus' healing ministry (see 3.3.4). The only other two commands to silence after healings are not explicitly broken (5:43; 8:26). The use of the imperfect in v. 36 underscores the ongoing transgression *and* injunction[104] and focuses together with the "alliterating double-sigma"[105] in vv. 36–37 (περισσότερον, ἐκήρυσσον, ὑπερπερισσῶς, ἐξεπλήσσοντο) on the distinct and intense verbal disclosure of Jesus' deed. The healing of the man mirrors this development and vice versa: the silenced speak loudly and clearly, or "Jesus has the power to loosen tongues, but not to stop them from wagging."[106] The use of κηρύσσω then refers back to Jesus' appointed mission and growing ministry, which is intrinsically connected to his teachings,[107] as is the emotional dimension of such a proclamation and acclamation.[108]

---

103 Cf. von Bendemann in Härle; Preul (ed.) 2005. 66–69.
104 Cf. Focant 2012. 306.
105 von Bendemann in Härle; Preul (ed.) 2005. 67.
106 Spittler, *Deafness II. NT.* 351.
107 Cf. esp. 1:4, 7, 14–15, 38–39; 3:14; 6:12; 13:10; 14:9; and 1:45; 5:20 and 7:36, and its connection with διδάσκω in Mark 1:21 with 1:39 and 6:12, or 1:14–15; and its content in 4:1–20; 8:31; 9:31; 12:14. Cf. France in France; Wenham (ed.) 1980; Broadhead 1992a. 69; Marcus 2000. 1871.
108 Cf. Mark 1:22; 6:2; 10:26; 11:18; and 6:51.

The following praise emphasizes the difficulty of the cure with the double καί in v. 37: "even" the deaf and "even" the mute are healed. The plural shows that this statement has an exemplary appeal and does not only refer to this one, so far singular, incident in Mark's gospel.

This generic notion in the final direct speech then might also include the previous exorcism with no response recounted and, as it is the final acclamation to Jesus' healing ministry,[109] even serves an overall summaric function. Moreover, it terminologically directly relates to a passage in Isa 35:5–6^LXX (καὶ ὦτα κωφῶν ἀκούσονται [...] καὶ τρανὴ ἔσται γλῶσσα μογιλάλων) that, however, additionally depicts impaired mobility and sight. As the Hebrew version of the poem is highly cohesive,[110] its reference in Mark may as well include by implication the previously narrated healings of paralyzed conditions in Mark 2–3 (see ch. 4) and foreshadow the upcoming cures of blindness in Mark 8:22–26 and 10:46–52. This concrete association of, at a first glance, selective individual images of dis/ability, however, disregards representations of dis/ability that Mark went to great lengths to illustrate (i.e., febrile, skin, hemorrhaging, and fatal conditions, as well as demon possession). Rather, the reprise of the Isaianic passage has two particular functions that align with the context in Mark: For one, as the poem also depicts the strengthening of "weak hands" and "stumbling knees" and encouragement of "faint-hearted minds" and describes the transformation of arid landscapes with similar sensuous imagery,[111] it alludes to the powerful divine transformation as a redemptive force in dire circumstances with eschatological nuances (i.e., exile and transferred states of oppression, desperation, and dependence on salvation).[112] This concurs with Mark, where the eulogistic statement not only witnesses to the uncontainable astonishment about Jesus' powerful deeds but additionally echoes not only Isa 35:5–6 ^LXX but Gen 1:31^LXX—καὶ εἶδεν ὁ θεὸς τὰ πάντα, ὅσα ἐποίησεν, καὶ ἰδοὺ καλὰ λίαν. It thereby enhances Jesus' might to divine causality aligned with creational, redemptive, and, by that, eschatological purpose.[113]

---

[109] This reaction is henceforth mainly applied to his teachings, cf. 9:15; 11:18; 12:17; and Kiffiak 2017. 153.
[110] Cf. the chiastic structure, rhyming, and alliterating verbs in 35:5.
[111] For the comparison of environment with dis/ability in this passage, cf. Olyan 2008. 87–88; Raphael 2008. 127.
[112] Regarding the context of this passage and its representations of dis/ability, cf. concretely Clements in Tucker; et al. (ed.) 1988. 192, 198; Blenkinsopp 2000. 409, 456; Olyan 2008. 86; Raphael 2008. 127; Couey in Melcher; Parsons; Yong (ed.) 2018. 230–231. Cf. also Isa 29:18; 32:4.
[113] Cf. Collins 2007. 374, 376. Cf. also Sir 39:16^LXX.

Secondly, the Isaianic poem concentrates on *sensory* dis/ability when including kinaesthesia as a sensory faculty.[114] While it might be true that this simply reflects the "prevalence of the most common physical disabilities" as also accounted for by, e.g., the sheer amount of "anatomical votives in the shape of eyes, ears, and feet"[115] in popular healing sites of Greco-Roman antiquity, the concrete reference here is striking. Particularly the sensory aspect of spiritual perception has a rhetoric function in prophetic texts but is highly dependent on its concrete placement, even if also regarded as an interconnective motif,[116] and on the precise context and points of reference.[117] In general, however, particularly dis/abled sight[118] and hearing[119] are related to interrupted communication and thereby comprehension between a deity and its people (also polemically regarding idols and their worshipers) due to their collective sensory impairment by punishment and/or oppressive and violent circumstances.[120] Often, the prophetic figure mediates by use of the same faculties, and/or (eschatological) restoration is promised, often through highly idealized bodies.[121] Hence, the Markan application of such an allusion after its first healing of sensory organs seems premeditated, especially when paired with a reference to creation that transpires an ideal physicality, which is paralleled in eschatological anticipation (see ch. 4). Moreover, the following chapters of the Markan gospel depict spiritual incomprehension with similar dis/ability invective sensory imagery, especially regarding visionary and auditory perception. The Gospels of Luke and Matthew then make these prophetic references explicitly and completely.[122] Here, by the epilogue of Mark 7:37, the audience is prepared for the subsequent demonstrative compilation of sensory dis/abilities that Jesus heals at the end of his ministry. As the following section is also scattered with passion predictions, references to Jesus' divine identity, and remarks on the disciples' incomprehension in somatic terms, the fragmentary but distinct allusions in this section and

---

114 Which is established convincingly by Avrahami 2012. Esp. 75–83, 109–112.
115 Trentin in Laes; Goodey; Rose (ed.) 2013. 97.
116 Cf., e.g., Clements 1985. 101–104; Clements in Tucker; et al. (ed.) 1988. 189–200; Williamson 1994. 47–50; Couey in Melcher; Parsons; Yong (ed.) 2018. 219.
117 Cf. Raphael 2008. 122–124; Couey in Melcher; Parsons; Yong (ed.) 2018. 235, 267.
118 Cf., e.g., Isa 40:5; Jer 2:10; Amos 6:2; Zech 10:7; Mal 1:5.
119 Cf., e.g., Isa 40:21, 28; Jer 28:7; Hos 5:1; Hab 3:2; Zech 8:23.
120 Cf., e.g., Isa 5:13; 6:9–10; 42:7; 44:9; 46:7; Zeph 1:17; 3:19; Zech 11:17; 12:4; Mic 4:6; 2:4; Jer 5:21; 29:1, 4, 14; Ezek 39:28; Amos 5:5, 27; cf. also Ps 115:5; 135:16. Cf. esp. Carroll in Broyles; Evans (ed.) 1997. 87; Olyan 2008. 7, 35; Raphael 2008. 120–128; Chavel 2014. For a precise and concise survey, cf. Couey in Melcher; Parsons; Yong (ed.) 2018.
121 Cf., e.g., Ezek 8:3–4; Hos 12:11/12:10; Joel 3:1/2:28; Hab 2:1–3; Zech 2:1 [1:18]; 5:1; Isa 28:14; Jer 2:4; Hos 4:1; Amos 7:16; 8:11; Mic 6:1; Isa 29:18; Hab 2:2; and Olyan 2008. 86; Schipper 2015. 319–333.
122 Cf. Luke 7:22; 4:18–19; Matt 11:5–6; 15:29–31.

in Mark 8:18—which echo Jer 5:21 and its critique of spiritual obtuseness using sensory language—undoubtedly recall the redemptive eschatological, and perhaps even messianic, contexts of these prophetic pretexts.[123]

6.2.5 Interpretation

The very sensuously narrated account of the healing of the man with the inability to hear and difficulty speaking focuses on an extraordinary sequence of Jesus' healing actions. The intimacy, intense physicality, and numinously charged substances and methods illustrate the man's dis/ability in participating in verbal communication and define Jesus' corporality as divinely legitimized and his healing ability as astonishingly conspicuous and literally noteworthy: "Both Jesus and the 'deaf-mute' embody an alternative charged performance in which other sensory dimensions beyond hearing and words become all important [...] They [the audience] encounter a vivid visual scene in which hearing and words seem peripheral and to a certain extent, redundant."[124]

As such, this narrative enhances and summarizes Jesus' sensuous healing ministry. This ministry was established by preceding healing narratives, which become increasingly important as the gospel unfolds a distinct and extensive sensory rhetoric that aims concretely at the comprehension and perception of Jesus, the gospel, and its message.[125]

---

[123] Cf. also, e.g., Isa 29:18; 35:3–6; 42:6–7, 16–19; 61:1; Jer 5:21; Ezek 12:12 (LXX); and du Toit in Du Toit; Gerber; Zimmermann (ed.) 2019. 190. See moreover, du Toit 2015, and his convincing recurs to Isa 61:1^{LXX} to explicate the Markan outline, as Jesus' endowment and mission can be aligned with the first part of the verse (cf. esp. Mark 1:9–11, 14–15), the subsequently described healing and redemptive power are depicted in Mark 1–7 and 9:14–29 (cf. also esp. 1:32–34; 3:10–12 and 1:39, 6:56), as is the healing of blindness as in Mark 8:22–26 and 10:46–52.
[124] Lawrence 2013. 68.
[125] Beyond the purview of this study, it nevertheless remains relevant to embed the discussed pericopes and findings in a comprehensive study on the Markan text dedicated to sensory criticism as it would "(1) provide systematic examination of the different valuation and interaction of the senses in the Bible; (2) furnish a methodological tool to examine texts comparatively inside and outside the biblical corpus; (3) examine how the valuation of the senses is intimately related to the differential valuation of the persons that lies at the core of defining disabilities," Avalos in Avalos; Melcher; Schipper (ed.) 2007a. 47. This then includes, e.g., "(1) contrasting expressions of valuation ('hearing is better than seeing'); (2) expressions of antipathy toward particular senses; and (3) narratives about the performance of valued tasks and functions in the absence or diminution of certain senses," (ibid. 50) in order "to plot ways in which biblical texts evaluate different senses and how these may contribute to various ideological standpoints forwarded by them," Lawrence

Presupposing the Western count of five senses, only sight, hearing, and touch seem to be of particular interest for the Markan text.[126] As established, touch is characteristic for Markan healing narratives, but its tangible sensations are not depicted as significant for any supplicant besides perhaps the skin-sensitive man in Mark 1:40–45. As his ailment connotes a communicative aspect of his impurity by touch, the tangible healing must have influenced the quarantined man. In any case, throughout Markan healing narratives, Jesus is depicted as an experienceable body who emanates healing by physical contact (cf. esp. Mark 5:29–30).

Besides Jesus' curative touch, he is witnessed to heal by powerful verbal commands (cf. for exorcisms 1:25; 5:8, 13; also 9:25, and emphatically in 2:9, 11; 3:5; 5:41 and here in 7:34; cf. also 4:39), hence also engages the auditory capacities of the patients (that are in case of demoniacs occupied by the spiritual entities), of the witnesses, and of course of the audience.[127] Moreover, his reputation to heal (physically) is linked to specific hearsay,[128] and his teachings are also delivered to be heard even if no concrete response is given (but cf., e.g., 1:22 and 6:2);[129] his divine identity is moreover pronounced by heavenly voices in 1:11 and 9:7. Of great importance is then the primacy of auditory perception for spiritual comprehension of the message, as ascribed in the parable of the sower (4:10–20) and heightened, probably in reference to the *shema* as reprised in Mark 2:29, by Jesus' imperative command to use the given ears in 4:9, 23, and 8:18.[130] Both passages additionally attribute spiritual cognition to visual perception (cf. 4:12; also v. 24; 8:18).

Quite similarly to the audible witnessing of Jesus' healing and divine identity, the Gospel of Mark recounts visual recognition when spirits or supplicants see and recognize him, the effects of his healing are visually perceived, and his divinity is underscored by visionary encounters.[131] Invertedly, Jesus can see inner *pistis* (ὁράω, 2:5). Jesus' healing is not only tangible and audible but visible. Prominently, the eyes are the only sensory organ named in the word of autoamputation in Mark 9:47 (see F. In Focus: Markan Healing and Forgiveness) as they are used rhetorically *pars pro toto* and connote moral implications.[132] Likewise, visual language is used to convey caution and attention.[133]

The healing in Mark 7:32–34 emphatically showcases Jesus' characteristic embodied and sensually communicated healing power to an unprecedented extent by nothing less than the transformation of the first of four sensory dis/abilities, which are, moreover, the final healings recounted in Mark. The subsequent epi-

---

2011. 389. For pioneer investigations of biblical texts in that regard cf. Avalos in Avalos; Melcher; Schipper (ed.) 2007a; Lawrence 2011; Lawrence 2013.
126 Cf. Lawrence 2011. 389.
127 Cf. also 2:9; 4:39; 11:23; and Lawrence 2011. 391.
128 Cf. 2:1; 3:8, 21; 5:27; 6:14, 55; 7:25; 10:47.
129 Cf., e.g., 4:3, 9, 20, 23, 24; 6:2; 7:14, 16; 8:17–18; 12:29 also 13:37 and esp. 4:12, 15–20; 6:11; 9:7; and Lawrence 2011. 392.
130 Cf. Collins 2007. 246; Lawrence 2011. 392; Lawrence 2013. 146–147, n. 3. Cf. also Matt 11:15; 13:10–15, 43; Luke 8:9–10, 16–18; 14:35; John 8:38–51; Rev 2:7, 11, 17, 29; 3:6, 13, 22.
131 Cf., e.g., θεωρέω in 3:11; 5:15; ὁράω in 5:6; 9:4; 13:14; 14:26.
132 Cf. 7:22; also Matt 6:23; 20:15.
133 Cf. 8:15; 12:38; 13:5, 9, 23, 33, mainly with βλέπω.

logue of Mark 7:36–37 then interprets this and by implication all the precedented healings in an intriguing interplay of message and medium.

Firstly, the accounts, like the patients and witnesses, *testify* to Jesus' powerful, uncontainable, and increasingly obvious divine healing ability and identity. This is directly linked to the employed image of dis/ability as the acclamation includes the formerly intestable man and references to unhindered spiritual cognition and clear spiritual communication (cf. the prophetic pretexts, see above).[134] As the narrative aims to let the audience sensuously participate in the transformation of the sensory impairment, the final acclamation in direct speech is directed at them. By that, the gospel follows its message as it is, as any ancient text, reliant on auditory performances (due to limited literacy and text production)[135] and *speaks rightly* of Jesus' *astonishing* deeds to be *heard crystal clear.*

Secondly, this summarizes the function of deviating bodies as already seen in previous accounts: The dis/abled characters are foremost employed to illustrate and witness to Jesus' divine healing power. Moreover, however, they embody a transformation that is holistic as it encompasses physical and social healing and is embedded in a divine scheme that unfolds between creational claims and eschatological promise. The final eulogistic statement of Mark 7:32–34 puts this succinctly as it alludes to a creational horizon (Gen 1:31^{LXX}) with an eschatological nuance (Isa 35:5–6^{LXX}).[136] Whether or not this is to be understood literally, as an erasure of (sensory) dis/ability in Jesus' eschatological mission or as an easily adaptable yet dis/ability invective imagery for the reversal of impaired communication between God and his people, for liberation from suffering, and for societal reintegration is explored in the following (see ch. 7).

6.3 Conclusion and Interpretation of Dis/ability in Mark 7

As the locational moves already suggest, Mark 7 is a chapter in transition. Jesus' programmatic healings and teachings have been told and recapitulated in the last of the gospel's summaric statement (cf. 6:53–56), peaking in the final declaration of this chapter with its creational and eschatological connotations. Both narratives in this chapter bear witness to Jesus' known und unconcealable healing identity, and both reprise characteristic features of previous accounts.[137] While Jesus' mission shifts to new places and foreign people, both deviating bodies

---

134 Cf. von Bendemann in Härle; Preul (ed.) 2005. 61.
135 Cf. Couey in Melcher; Parsons; Yong (ed.) 2018. 225.
136 Cf. von Bendemann in Härle; Preul (ed.) 2005. 67.
137 Cf. Marcus 2000. 467.

also *embody* the transition to a new storyline and its theological debates: while one character depicts the struggle with cultural identity and participation in Jesus' mission, the other visualizes sensory participation and thereby spiritual comprehension of his message. While Jesus is witnessed to heal while being physically remote, his intrinsic healing divinity is sensuously perceivable. While the stage is set for the plot's final round of healing and teaching before the passion, the audience is sensuously engaged yet prepared for the withdrawal of the protagonist. While the images of dis/ability are still deployed as narrative prostheses to witness to the powerful healing ability of Jesus, their depiction moreover reflects nuances of the message and most importantly transpires a creational and eschatological transformation beyond any binary of dis/ability that seems to be characteristic for the transitional time that the healing Jesus embodies.

7 Mark 8–10: Beyond Dis/ability

As prepared by the transitional Mark 7, the following section of Mark 8–10 continues the narrative's development regarding the locational shift toward Jerusalem (from the Decapolis, Bethsaida, Caesarea Philippi, to Jerusalem) with an increasingly elusive protagonist. Jesus' teaching and mission concentrate on discipleship and imply his withdrawal (e. g., 8:27–30, 8:31–38; 9:31–37; 10:32–45) as the conflict with his opponents is prepared to come to a head (e. g., 8:10–13, 15; cf. also the passion predictions). Embedded are the final three healing narratives in the gospel that, as in the healing accounts of Mark 7, also employ images of dis/ability to *embody* certain aspects of the storyline and theological debates as they elude a certain binary (see below). Since the three narratives build on one another but are placed in distinct chapters with intermediary accounts, the following analysis first illustrates comparative features and general contextual connections before regarding their interplay according to their images of dis/ability and healing and their common and conclusive message and function in the Markan plot.

To begin, all three narratives introduce and emphasize characters with deviating sensual capacities: Unusually enough, *two* of the three accounts feature the healing of blindness. No other dis/ability is healed twice in the gospel besides demon possession. Moreover, these two healing accounts flank Jesus' journey to Jerusalem thereby accentuate the last events and teachings before the passion and terminate his healing ministry (8:22–26 and 10:46–52). The framed healing account (9:14–29) climactically displays the exorcism of an impure spirit with drastic and dramatic dis/abling effects on his host's auditory and verbal communicative abilities. These images of sensory dis/ability then underscore and illuminate the entire section: It is not only scattered with remarks on the perception of Jesus' message and identity in sensory terminology, but after Mark 7 has already prepared the correlation of sensory dis/abilities with spiritual (in)cognition (see 6.2. on 7:31–37, also 7:18), Mark 8:17–21 explicitly guides the audience to interpret the following (and retrospectively previous) healings of sensory impairments along these lines. Implicitly, the ancient convention of a symbolic understanding of "deaf-muteness" and blindness underscores this effect, especially with regard to the range of im-/possible sensory perception these images of dis/ability encompass (see below).[1]

This interpretative address of the audience is moreover expressed by mutual stylistic devices in all three narratives (see below). Firstly, they are set in liminal

---

[1] Cf., e.g., Plato, *Phraed.* 270e; *Tim.* 88b; *Leg.* 932a; Plutarch, *Fort.* 98C; *Tu. san.* 136F; *Alex. fort.* 336B; and von Bendemann in Härle; Preul (ed.) 2005. 66–69; esp. 68, n. 47.

space around a vague but fixed geographical marker important for the journey to Jerusalem. This concurs with the vague geographical descriptions of the entire section that focuses on encounters ἐν τῇ ὁδῷ (cf. 8:27; 9:33; 10:32, 52).² Moreover, both descriptions of healings of blindness explicitly occur outside of mentioned cities, as if the Markan Jesus wants to steer clear of these towns³ and thereby promote a universal, adaptable interpretation of the healings yet reference to concrete events and teachings. Furthermore, each account features a play on privacy and publicity that continuously increases over the course of the three narratives. Also in this respect, the three narratives blend into the entire section with vague public settings and sudden, concrete private teachings in "the house."⁴

Secondly, each of the three narratives features a central dialogue that engages the audience not only by its direct speech but by rather unusual use of the tenses.

Thirdly, and common to Markan healing narratives, all three accounts introduce supplicants who have heard of and trust in Jesus the healer. In stark contrast to Mark 7:37, however, the final narratives recount no acclamation or reaction toward Jesus' healing ability from the crowd or other witnesses and thereby invite the audience to partake in an interpretative conclusion based on this initial recognition of the healer. This is furthermore challenged by the immediate interposition of suggestive passion predictions (8:31; 9:30–32; 10:32–34; cf. also 8:34–9:1) and the ultimate, emphatic, and provocative illustration of gradual and salvific *pistis*.

Fourthly, the three accounts not only depict sensory dis/ability but narrate the healing encounters in unusually focused sensuous language and thereby become vivid and comprehensible reports of a tangible (Mark 8:22–26), visible (9:14–29), and audible (10:46–52) Jesus (see below).

---

2 Cf., e.g., 8:27; 9:30; 10:1; 10:32. Cf. Bosenius 2014. 251–256. For surveys on the narratological and theological function of the term ὁδός in Mark's gospel see, e.g., Kelber 1974. 67–71; Rhoads; Michie 1982. 63–64; Malbon 1991. 154, 165; Iersel 1998. 276, 297, 299; Marcus 2004; Studenovský in Frey; Schnelle (ed.) 2004; Winter 2005. For the relevant section here, however, only the immediate references to the journey to Jerusalem and the passion are taken into account without excluding the possibility of other additional nuances, esp. with regard to Mark 1:2–3; 4:3–9; 10:33; 12:14; 16:7.
3 Cf. Bosenius 2014. 265.
4 Cf. ibid. 249–250.

7.1 Introductions: Sensory and Spiritual Comprehension

7.1.1 Mark 8:22–26: Introduction to the Narrative

Jesus, although not named explicitly, enters Bethsaida along with his disciples as the unspecified ἔρχονται implies (cf. 6:45; 8:14–21). There, a blind man is brought to him by an unidentified group of people—maybe the blind man's family, neighbors, friends, or simply people of Bethsaida (cf. vv. 23, 26)—[5] with the request for Jesus' touch (ἅπτω). At this point of the narrative, this clearly alludes to Jesus' well-known ability to perform successful tactile treatments (see C. In Focus: Mark's Healing Touches). With an emphatic aorist, Jesus then takes the man, who remains characterized solely by his imperfect sight (see below on τυφλός), and leads him out of the village,[6] an action that reflects that the blind man "needs guidance [...], [or] that Jesus is taking charge of the situation, or both."[7] In any instance, the unspecific territory connotes an unfamiliarity, maybe even danger, as the sightless man must trust Jesus.[8] The change into liminal space remains unexplained and stands in contrast with the initial explicit setting of Bethsaida.[9] The faintly depicted surroundings of who and where then reflect a limited perception associated with sightlessness and contrast and thereby emphasize the following precise physical communication. The vagueness in characterization and retreat for the curative touch also reprise the previous healing of the deaf-mute man (7:31–37); hence, the audience is well prepared when Jesus not only administers the requested touch but first spits directly into the dis/abled organs (see below). Then however, in an uncommon move for the Markan Jesus, he asks the man about the effect of his treatment in an anamnestic manner,[10] using the imperfect tense to highlight the incompleteness of the healing and the need for an answer. This draws the audience in and emphasizes the spectrum of sight that still needs to be acquired, as the answer is also introduced with the imperfect tense.[11] Differently to all the other healing narratives in the gospel, the man is not reported to be immediately healed (εὐθέως/εὐθύς) but instead said to see people walking around like trees. The state

---

[5] Cf. von Bendemann in Zimmermann (ed.) 2013. 341.
[6] On κώμη cf. Collins 2007. 390, esp. n. 94–95.
[7] Ibid. 393.
[8] Cf. von Bendemann in Zimmermann (ed.) 2013. 341.
[9] This, however, concurs with the previously deflected healing ministry of the disciples, cf. Mark 6:45 in contrast to 6:53. Cf. Bosenius 2014. 238–248, on possible historical reasons that might have influenced Mark's rather neglective treatment of Bethsaida.
[10] Cf., e.g., CH, *Epid.* 1.11, also von Bendemann in Zimmermann (ed.) 2013. 341.
[11] See *Excursus: Tenses in the Gospel of Mark*, p. 22–24, and below.

of his transformed vision is reflected in his grammatically abstruse answer that, as direct speech, lets the audience participate directly in the man's indistinct and gradual visual perception.[12]

Finally, after Jesus laid hands on the eyes again, the man reports clear vision and constates his healing (v. 25). The internal perception of the blind man is shared by the narrator as the man's sight can only be evaluated by himself. Hence, with moreover no other characters around, the focus and identification lie entirely on and with the blind man.[13] The two touches then frame the dialogue as center of the narrative. The beginning of the account emphasizes tactile communication and perception, as the man is brought, likely led, to be touched and Jesus leads him by his hands and treats him sensibly with moisture and twice by laying on of hands (see below). The healing itself, however, emphatically highlights the eye's faculty to see. The man is sent to his οἶκος by Jesus, presumptively now independent, and asked in direct speech not to go back into the village (v. 26).[14] Moreover, no acclamation or recognition of the healing is accounted for, which disregards completely those who brought the man initially to Jesus. Although Jesus' command is odd regarding the fact that the text insinuates that Bethsaida is the man's hometown, it concurs with previous explications of restored social community after the healing (cf. esp. 2:11; 5:19 but also 1:44; 5:34; 5:43), with preceding notions of secrecy (cf., e.g., 1:44; 7:36; also 7:24),[15] and with the section's geographical outline.

7.1.2 Mark 9:14–29: Introduction to the Narrative

The following healing narrative is a very dense and populated scene with a variety of different character groups. The focus on visual perception is taken up by "rapid shifts in point of view from one character to the other,"[16] all emphatically intro-

---

[12] Cf. Derrett 1981, on theories of the symbolic, eschatological function of the tree-motif. Cf. also Focant 2012. 330; Lawrence 2013. 53. Cf. furthermore, the Epidauran Inscriptions where the blind supplicant is touched in incubation by the finger of God, sees trees at first, but when awake has completely restored sight. Contrary to Mark 8:22–26, the blind man is not healed in stages but dreams of the accomplished healing. Cf. Herzog 1931. No. 18; Edelstein; Edelstein 1998. 423 (1.224–225, 233).
[13] Cf. Willebrand 2017. 129–131.
[14] Bosenius 2014. 140–145, 242, suggests, to take *Jesus*' house in Capernaum as commanded destination, which resonates with the literary function of the motif οἶκος (see E. In Focus: Healing Spaces in Mark) but bears no further substantial indication for a concrete localization in Capernaum.
[15] Cf., e.g., Guelich 1989. 434; Boring 2006. 234.
[16] Marcus 2009. 657.

duced by ὁράω, which separates the account into four sequences with the addition of an epilogue after a change of scenery.

a. 9:14: The first sentence sets the scene. No precise time and place are given, yet the sequence is firmly integrated into the succession of events on the journey to Jerusalem as it follows the perspective of Jesus, Peter, James, and John when they are returning from the mount of the transfiguration.[17] Only this change of location separates what follows from the previously recounted visionary experience (Mark 9:2–8) and the concluding conversation during the descent (9:9–13). Together with the setting, the greater groups of characters are introduced from the perspective of the intimate circle around Jesus as they see (the rest of) his disciples surrounded by a crowd in dispute (συζητέω)[18] with the scribes.[19]

b. 9:15–20: The narrative shifts to the view of this great crowd, who react amazed (ἐκθαμβέω) at the sight of Jesus and greet him.[20] In this context, their response reflects his reputation that has been built up and is commonly alluded to in previous (healing) accounts. To the audience, however, this extreme astonishment also transcends an idea of Jesus' identity as previously recounted in the transfiguration.[21] Amid the rushing movement of the crowd, Jesus explicitly and directly raises the implied question from the beginning of the sequence that has kept the tension high and now aligns his perspective with that of the guessing audience:[22] what is the reason for the dispute?

This is the first of several (at times rhetorical) questions of this pericope that drive the plot forward (cf. vv. 16, 19, 21, [23], 28). As in this case, the narrative often remains vague on the specific addressees of Jesus' inquiries in the crowded scene, which further opens the question to let the audience participate.

Jesus' question is implicitly answered by "one of the multitude," who by his inquiry shifts the focus from the dispute to a greater problem: His son is, as he

---

[17] For a detailed analysis of the described region, cf. also Bosenius 2014. 256–261.
[18] Cf., e.g., Mark 1:27; 8:11; 12:28.
[19] Despite different provenance, the character group of the γραμματεῖς functions, from 1:22 onwards, as a contrast foil for Jesus' teaching in authority. Additionally, they become his fierce opponents in 2:6, cf. also 3:22; 7:1, 5.
[20] The imperfect sets the scene in the background for the following direct speech.
[21] It is unlikely that the people react to the previously recounted transfiguration witnessed only by the most inner circle of Jesus' disciples or that this form of emotional astonishment can be read negatively (how the lexeme is used later in the gospel), since the crowd is drawn to Jesus rather than frightened and repelled by him, cf. 14:33; 16:5–6; and Exod 34:29–30. Due to its use in Mark 1:27 (together with συζητέω) in connection to Jesus' teaching with ἐξουσία right after the first reported exorcism in vv. 25–26, it rather reflects and echoes Jesus' astonishing authority in word and deed, here in contrast to the failing disciples. Cf. Hofius 2004. 118–120; Collins 2007. 437.
[22] Cf. Nicklas 2001. 508, n. 41.

vividly describes, severely tormented by a mute spirit, and the disciples were unable to cast it out by his request. Jesus answers with an outcry of "impatience and lassitude,"²³ lamenting ἀπιστία and his indispensability by casting a desirable timeframe where he is no longer needed and can withdraw from them.²⁴ Again, the narrative leaves room for speculation about who precisely is addressed in this densely populated scene. In any case, his answer continues to unfold a historical and cosmological frame (Mark 8:11–12; 8:31–38; 9:1–13), placing Jesus with his call to discipleship and his ongoing unraveling mission with the foreshadowed passion (8:31) in line with God and the heavenly realm. Fittingly, what follows is the healing (vv. 25–27) of a dis/ability (vv. 20–24) that precisely portrays this cosmological opposition (see B. In Focus: Mark's Jesus and Opposing Forces) and is instantly initiated by Jesus' call to bring the boy to him.

c. 9:20–24: Accordingly, the demon is described to see Jesus and to immediately illustrate his severe possessing force over the boy's body as an auditory and visual scene (see below).²⁵ While the father is depicted more as an "authoritative requester" in the beginning confronted with the disciples, he exposes now in the ensuing dialogue with Jesus his desperation and hopelessness and "appeals to Jesus' feelings, to his compassion"²⁶ with the urgent, empathetic request: "if it is at all possible for you."²⁷ Jesus answers directly to this by repeating the conditional phrase but generalizes in his terminology his ability from the basic context of healing (everyone from anything) to a divine omnipotence for those practicing *pistis* (v. 23; see below).²⁸ The father responds immediately, confirming his *pistis* yet asking for help as one practicing ἀπιστία.²⁹ The introduction of his direct speech is put in imperfect, which in Mark foremost implies an open question or statement completed by an answer, which sets the scene for the following.³⁰ Moreover, it under-

---

23 Cf. Focant 2012. 369.
24 Cf. Hofius 2004. 120–121.
25 This *constructio ad sensum* of a masculine participle with neuter reference is not accidental but underscores disparate corporality of this clinical picture (see below).
26 Focant 2012. 370. Cf. also the similar use of κράζω in lamenting Psalms, e.g., Ps 3:5; 4:4; 16:6; 17:7; 21:3, 6, 25; 26:7; 27:1; 30:23^LXX; cf. Hofius 2004. 129, n. 69.
27 Cf. ἀλλ' εἴ τι δύνῃ: Reading the conditional τι in v. 22 as an adverbial accusative concurs with the context better than regarding it as an accusative object to δύνῃ—then it associates doubt with regard to Jesus' healing ability and/or the previously failed exorcism ("if you can do something"). Cf. parallel occurrences of such phrasing interpreted by Hofius 2004. 124–126.
28 Cf. 10:27; 14:36; and Hofius 2004. 127; Collins 2007. 438.
29 Cf. the convincing interpretation as a metonymic reading of this phrase in Hofius 2004. 131–132, regarding the rather unusual combination of βοηθέω with an abstract term (not a person) as similarly used in Rom 8:26 and Jdt 6:19.
30 See *Excursus: Tenses in the Gospel of Mark*, p. 22–24, and below.

scores the conative and/or iterative aspects of the plea, as also the request for help (βοήθει, imperative present) echoes his appeal for healing (v. 22, imperative aorist). The condition of his son remains the point of reference, which aligns with the generation's lamented ἀπιστία following the failed healing of the disciples. Additionally, the father's calls for help sandwich Jesus' generalized utterance, positioning him as a paradigmatic character for both the a-*pistis* generation and the struggling disciples. He is henceforth not mentioned again (see below).[31]

d. 9:25–27: While the conversation gave the impression of privacy by focusing entirely and extensively on the dialogue between the father and Jesus (with only side references to the disciples), v. 25 heightens the publicity of this event when Jesus sees a (maybe even bigger)[32] crowd gathering. Immediately and definitely, Jesus exorcises the mute spirit (see below).

e. 9:28–29: Without any conclusive response to the healing, the narrative closes with an epilogue initiated by a sudden change of location. After the crowded setting earlier (as indicated by the mention of ὄχλος in vv. 14, 15, 17, 25), Jesus is alone again with his disciples (κατ' ἰδίαν). They approach him with a question about their inability to cast out the spirit.[33] Again, the use of the imperfect tense conveys the openness, repetitive, important, and possibly desperate nature of their request and sets the scene for the impactful answer in the perfective aspect of the aorist (v. 29). Jesus answers this final question, this time not asked by him and not in the aorist, by naming prayer as the only remedy against this kind of spirit (τοῦτο τὸ γένος; see below). The multiangled episode is conclusively interpreted with Jesus' teaching.[34]

7.1.3 Mark 10:46–52: Introduction to the Narrative

The last healing narrative in Mark and the second one to feature a healing of blindness starts like the prior one: Jesus and his entourage are entering a city, this time Jericho (cf. 8:22).[35] However, instead of the noteworthy encounter, the narrator immediately recounts their exit again (*genitivus absolutus*), which puts emphasis on

---

[31] Grammatically possible but highly unlikely in the gospel context is to interpret Jesus as the one practicing *pistis*.
[32] Cf. Schmithals 1975/1976. 211; Gundry 1993. 493.
[33] Cf. 4:10–13; 7:17–23; 10:10–2; 13:3–37, where the disciples' questioning initiates Jesus' teaching. Cf. Collins 2007. 439.
[34] Cf. Marcus 2009. 657.
[35] For the importance of the location, cf. also Matt 20:29–34 and Luke 18:35–43; moreover, Bosenius 2014. 264–267.

the actual destination: Jerusalem. Jesus, his disciples, and a large crowd continue their journey, when they encounter the son of Timaeus, Bartimaeus, a blind man begging παρὰ τὴν ὁδόν.

Similar to the previous two narratives in this section, the story takes place in a liminal space, but it is anchored to a geographical marker that is embedded in the chronology of the current plot and of importance for its development.

The introduction of the character with a name and patronym[36] is unlikely and reminiscent of the introductions of Peter's mother-in-law (1:30) and Jaïrus' daughter (5:22). However, in those cases, the relation to the supplicant was depicted, whereas in this case, the person with the dis/ability is defined and highlighted. Similar to one of the earliest healing narratives, the cure of Peter's mother-in-law in Capernaum, the concrete mention of a name and place serve as benchmarks for the historical, biographical, and/or narratological verisimilitude of the account and thereby frame Jesus' ministry from there to here and charge the following with great importance.[37] Moreover, the blind and begging Bartimaeus is singled out by his detailed introduction from the other characters of the account, namely the initially implicit Jesus (αὐτός), the subordinate disciples (μαθηταὶ αὐτοῦ), and the indefinite and anonymous large crowd (ὄχλος ἱκανός),[38] who move along with Jesus while the beggar is immobile, seated at the margins. However, neither characteristic is mentioned again in the following verses; begging Bartimaeus is only referred to as "the blind man," while Jesus is extraordinarily often referred to by his name (twice in vv. 47, 49, 50, 51, 52). Nevertheless, the blind man remains the main subject of the text, with very active movements (sitting, standing, jumping up, following, etc.) in the central section, underscored by three initial and distinctive δέ (cf. vv. 48b, 50, 51).[39] After this long and explicit exposition, the stage is set and its characters introduced, and the account continues with a clear composition of three *action-response-consequence* sequences with a conclusive aftereffect in

---

[36] The Greek-Aramaic compound is not followed by a translation or explanation in accordance to similar occurrences in Mark (cf. 3:17; 5:41; 7:11, 34; 12:42; 15:22, 34) and, untypically for the gospel, the name of the actual character, Bartimaeus, follows that of his father (cf. 1:19; 2:14; 3:17, 18; 10:35), cf. Iersel 1998. 339–340. The etymology and accentuation of this unusual composition remain unclear and speculative (cf. also Matt 8:5–6; Luke 7:2).

[37] Often in Mark, the (male as well as female) named characters are political office holders and/or their relatives (e.g., Herodias, 6:17–28), important figures in the history of Jesus such as apostles, disciples, and figures with a certain degree of familiarity (e.g., Mary, the mother of Jesus, 6:3; Mary Magdalene, Mary and Salome, who testify to the death of Jesus, his burial, and the empty tomb in 15:40–41, 47 and 16:1–8).

[38] Cf. Eckstein 1996. 34; Focant 2012. 440.

[39] Cf. vv. 46a, 47a, 48b, 50, 51b, 52b, Jesus is the subject in vv. 49a, 51a, 52a; the crowd is in vv. 48a, 49b, always with καί, cf. Eckstein 1996. 38.

v. 52b.⁴⁰ As the preceding two healing narratives featured the tactile healing of a blind man and the multi-perspective visual experience of the healing of a deaf-mute possessed boy, the following hinges on the only narrated actual sensual perception of the narrative: blind Bartimaeus *hears* that Jesus, ὁ Ναζαρηνός, causes the commotion (ἀκούω, v. 47) and subsequently verbalized his request.⁴¹

a. Mark 10:47–48 depicts Bartimaeus' discussion with the crowd. The emphasis on its size not only reflects Jesus' popularity on this part of his journey (cf., e.g., 8:34; 9:14–17; 10:1), as does the knowledge and call of the blind man, but "its audible presence tells the blind man that something unusual is going on."⁴² He then *solitarily* calls (κράζω) out to the "Son of David, Jesus" asking (λέγω) to have mercy on him (ἐλεάω; action), only to be immediately rebuked (ἐπιτιμάω) by *many* (response). Their intended silencing (σιωπάω) in indirect speech, introduced in the imperfect tense, heightens the tension and underscores Bartimaeus' second, even louder, conative cry (again κράζω but in imperfect) in direct speech, repeating his request verbatim, only omitting "Jesus" (consequence).

b. 10:49–50: When Jesus stops and asks (λέγω) to call (φωνέω) him (action), the attitude of the crowd shifts swiftly, and they animate (φωνέω, λέγω) the blind man to θάρσει, ἔγειρε, φωνεῖ σε! (response), words of encouragement usually said by the Markan Jesus.⁴³ The surprising change of heart is prominently featured in the present tense in the center of the narrative. The frequent repetition and therefore emphasis on calling (φωνέω) bridges the distance between Jesus and Bartimaeus in the middle of the crowd, conveys Jesus' authority, and sets the stage for the blind man's immediate allegiance after the obstacle of the impeding crowd has been removed: he leaps up, casts away his garment, and meets Jesus (consequence). The beggar's cloak marks his social status and occupation, as it may be used to collect charity,⁴⁴ yet regarding his dis/ability, its abandonment is also "a move to assimilate to sighted norms and distance himself from the trappings of his condition."⁴⁵ Mainly, it reflects the swiftness and enthusiasm of the pleading man.⁴⁶

---

40 Cf. ibid. 39–40.
41 Cf. λέγειν (v. 47, twice in v. 49, twice in vv. 51, 52); φωνεῖν (tree times in v. 49); ἀποκρίνεσθαι (v. 51). Cf. also Lohmeyer 1967. 224; Kertelge 1970. 179; Eckstein 1996. 38–39.
42 Iersel 1998. 339.
43 Cf. 6:50 and 2:9, 11; 5:41; also Matt 9:2, 22; 4:27; 3Kgdms 17:13^LXX; Philostratus, *Vit. Apoll.* 3.38; 4.10, 34.
44 Cf. Focant 2012. 437; Moss in Melcher; Parsons; Yong (ed.) 2018. 295.
45 Lawrence 2013. 46.
46 Cf. Culpepper 1982. 131. On allusions to Jesus' call to discipleship, see below.

c. 10:51–52: Finally, Jesus asks (ἀποκρίνομαι, λέγω) Bartimaeus what he desires him to do (action) and thereby reprises a question he asked his disciples a few verses prior (10:36). The question in this context, if not understood rhetorically, may come as a surprise to the audience as the introduction of the blind man already insinuated a healing narrative to ensue.⁴⁷ As established in the gospel text, characters with physical deviance or their supplicants seek out Jesus for healing, as exemplified by the memorable cure of blindness (8:22–26). The answering plea (λέγω; response) enforces this connection by echoing the term ἀναβλέπω, here, however, employed to express his wish for "restored" sight (cf. 8:24, to "look up," see below). Surprisingly for the Markan Jesus, he neither touches the man nor administers any other treatment, which is particularly astonishing after the two ultimately preceding healing narratives on, likewise, sensory impediments focused extensively on Jesus' healing methods (cf. Mark 7:31–37 and 8:22–26). Neither does Jesus utter a specific healing command (cf. 9:14–29) but simply encourages the man (λέγω) to "go" as his *"pistis* saved him" (see below). With his desire immediately fulfilled, as the literal reprise of ἀναβλέπω emphatically states, Bartimaeus begins to follow Jesus "on the way" (conclusion). As in Mark 8:26 and 9:27, no recognition or response of the crowd is recorded. The undisputed publicity of the event is striking with regard to the preceding narratives and, as the final healing narrative, somehow terminates Jesus' hassle with unwarranted disclosure.⁴⁸

7.2 Images of Dis/ability

7.2.1 Mark 8:22–26 and 10:46–52

The blind man in Mark 8:22–26 is characterized solely by his dis/ability. In vv. 22 and 23, he is simply designated as τυφλός, afterward only by personal pronouns. The text insinuates a social integration by the people who bring him to Jesus and by the send-off to his "house." The man's visual impairment, as described in the stages of his recovery after each touch and the treatment of both eyes, suggests that he was likely completely blind or had very limited vision, at least more so than the indistinct state described in verse 24.

In addition, in Mark 10:46–52, strong emphasis is put on the man's characterization as τυφλός. Despite the unusually detailed introduction by name, status, and

---

47 Cf. also allusions to royal audience scenes in, e.g., 2Sam 14:5; 2Kgs 6:28; Est 5:3, 6.
48 Cf. 1:44; 5:43; 7:36; 8:26, and also 1:24–25, 34; 3:11–12; 8:29–30; Focant 2012. 438–439.

patronym, the narrative continues to reference him by his dis/ability. Contrary to the man in Mark 8:22–26, his socioeconomic status is explicitly labeled and thereby associated with his impaired sight (see below). Although implied by the designation, there is no specific mention of the affected organs as in the healing in Mark 8:23, 25.

7.2.1.1 Ranges of Impaired In-/Sight

It is only in these two accounts that the lexeme τυφλός occurs in the Gospel of Mark. Generally, it describes impaired eyesight or a lack of sight, both at varying degrees. The restriction or inability to see is, however, often broached with other terminology and descriptions in the gospel in narrative and rhetoric contexts, also in a transferred sense (cf., e.g., 4:11–12; 8:18).[49]

Likewise, visual impairments receive widespread attention in literary sources of Jewish and Greco-Roman provenance, and the anatomy and function of the eye and the fragility of sight are frequently discussed.[50] Hence, the occurrence of impaired sight with its implications must have been of interest, quite common, and well known.[51] Since eye defects were not classified within a canonized categorical framework, it is difficult to establish criteria to define varying degrees according to the terminology used in different contexts.[52] Generally, many sources account for an awareness of a spectrum of visual perception,[53] and impaired eyesight was valued rather negatively. It could be ascribed to hereditary causes;[54] regarded as a

---

[49] Cf. Mark 7:22; also Matt 6:22–23; 9:27–31; 11:5 (cf. Isa 29:18; 35:5); 12:22–32; 13:13, 16); 15:11–15 (cf. Mark 7:15, 17); 20:15, 29–33; 21:14; 23:16–17, 24; 23:19, 26; and Culpepper, *Blindness III. NT*.
[50] Cf. exemplary and prominently for the HB/OT, e.g., Lev 19:14; 21:17–23; 22:11; Deut 15:21; 27:18; 28:28–29; 1Sam 3:2; 2Sam 5:8; Isa 59:10; Judg 16; 1Kgs 14:4; 2Kgs 25; Ps 146:8; and Mayfield, *Blindness I. HB/OT*; Olyan 1998. For Greco-Roman antiquity, cf., e.g., Homer, Oedipus, Teiesias; Celsus, *Med.* 6.6; Aelius Galen 12.535.4–5 and 12.696–803; Aristotle, *Hist. an.* 7.55 p 585b 30; Plutarch, *Tim.* 37.6–7; Dioscorides, *Mat. Med.*; Herzog 1931. No. 4, 9, 32, 40; P.Oxy. 11.1446.1; and Lesky, *Blindheit*; Esser 1961; Bernidaki-Aldous 1990; Marganne 1994; Vlahogiannis in Montserrat (ed.) 1998; Rose 2003. 79–94; Kelley in Avalos; Melcher; Schipper (ed.) 2007; Laes 2008. 103–105; Christopoulos; Karakantza; Levaniouk 2010; Thompson, *Blindness II. GRA*; Trentin in Laes; Goodey; Rose (ed.) 2013. 18–20. For Second Temple and Hellenistic Judaism, cf., e.g., Tob 1–3; 11; 1Q28ᵃ 2.3–9; 4QMMT B49–51; 11Q19 45.11–14; Philo, *Leg.* 3.108–109; *Somn.* 1.164; *Fug.* 123; *T.Sim.* 2:7; *T.Jud.* 11:1; *mMen* 9:8; *mHag* 1:1; *bHag* 4b; *tHag* 1:1; *mMeg* 4:6; and Preuss 1989. 300–324; Fishbane 2007. 103–120; Tigay, *Blindness*; Stemberger, *Blindness IV. Judaism*.
[51] Cf. Trentin in Laes; Goodey; Rose (ed.) 2013. 91.
[52] Cf. ibid. 93–94.
[53] Cf., e.g., Gen 27:1^{LXX} and 2Kgs 12:24^{LXX}; Plutarch, *Adul. amic.* 53; Thompson, *Blindness II. GRA*. Cf. also Weissenrieder 2003. 318.
[54] Cf. Rose 2003. 84–85.

symptom or consequence of diseases, of humor imbalance or distribution, of (eye) infections and inflammations, of rather general physical and mental ailments;[55] and be acquired by poisoning, punishing or accidental injuries, climatic conditions, or simply old age.[56] Furthermore, many accounts describe blinding as (judicial) punishment of divine or human "institutions" for different transgressions or as a cause of sin and attribute its healing solely to divine ability.[57] In that regard, and probably with reference to various degrees of impaired sight, some accounts vouch for its general incurability, while others ascribe remedy from "eye specialists" (ὁ ὀφθαλμικός/ *medicus ocularius*) with "a wide range of dietary measures, baths, fomentations, purging and clystering, often in combination with the administration of drugs," at times also by surgical intervention.[58] While there are not many narrative accounts on spontaneous cures, there is a large number of archeological evidence in form of votives depicting eyes in many (of the Asclepeian) sanctuaries.[59]

On that basis, Hellenistic, Jewish, and early-Christian literature features a variety of literary topoi of blindness, drawing on notions of helplessness, vulnerability, and dependence such as the "insecure, tentative walk,"[60] pity, disgust, and fear as a reaction to their "empty gaze,"[61] the poor and blind beggar, or a lack of discernment, understanding, and clarity of mind regarding the divine realm, moral and legal regulations, and salvific insights.[62] Especially the last was frequently applied in rhetorical contexts and heightened in ancient physiognomic texts that

---

55 Cf., e.g., Celsus, *Med.* 6.6; Diodorus, *Bib. hist.* 1.59.2; CH, *Epid.* 1.12; *Visu* 9.9; Thuc. 2.49.8; Aelian, *Nat. an.* 4.57; Herzog 1931. No. 11, 32; Anth. Gr. 7.241, 389; Schrage, τυφλός. 271; Rose 2003. 86.
56 Cf., e.g., Caesar, *Bell. civ.* 3.53; Homer, *Il.* 9.375–400; Plutarch, *Exil.* 606B; *Tim.* 37; Lucian, *Tox.* 40–41; Xenophon, *Mem.* 4.7.8.
57 Cf., e.g., Gen 19:11; Exod 4:10–11; Deut 19:21; 28:28–29; Judg 16:21; Jer 39:7, 52:11; also Tob 2:10; bShab 108b; 109a; bTaan 21a; Homer, *Il.* 2.594–600; Plutarch, *Alex.* 3; moreover, Acts 9:1–19; 22:6–16; 26:12–18; John 9:34; and Schrage, τυφλός; Mayfield, *Blindness I. HB/OT*; Thompson, *Blindness II. GRA*; Culpepper, *Blindness III. NT*; Stemberger, *Blindness IV. Judaism*; Tigay, *Blindness*.
58 Trentin in Laes; Goodey; Rose (ed.) 2013. 96–97. Cf. P.Berol. inv. 1944; Pliny, *Nat.* 29.117–31; *CIL* 7:1313; "The Mithras Liturgy" at PGM 4.770–80; Pliny, *Ep.* 7.21.2; Celsus, *Med.* 6.6.1–39; 7.7.14; CH, *Visu* 9.7; also von Bendemann in Zimmermann (ed.) 2013. 342.
59 Cf. Herzog 1931. No. 4, 9, 11, 18, 20, 22, 32, 40, 55, 65, 69, 74; Aleshire 1989. 95–97; Rose 2003. 83–85; Trentin in Laes; Goodey; Rose (ed.) 2013. 97.
60 Schrage, τυφλός. 272.
61 von Bendemann in Zimmermann (ed.) 2013. 343.
62 Cf., e.g., Exod 23:8 and Deut 16:19; Isa 6:9–10; 9:1; 29:18; 35:5; 42:18–20; 43:8; 44:18; 56:10; 59:10; Epictetus, *Diatr.* 2.23.22; 3.22.26; Josephus, *C. Ap.* 2.142; MidTeh 146.5, 146.8; CD 1.8–10; 16.2–4; 1QS 4.11; also T.Sim. 2:7; T.Jud. 11:1; T.Dan 2:2–4; also Matt 15:4; 23:16–26; Luke 6:39; John 9; and von Bendemann in Zimmermann (ed.) 2013. 342–343; Schrage, τυφλός.

show particular interest in the eyes as they exceptionally reveal character.[63] Based on the medical and philosophically extended connection of light and sight, such symbolical conceptions even rose to an ancient epistemology, as applicated, e.g., in Plato's cave allegory, in the importance of eyesight for the development of humanity in Ovid's metamorphosis, and in Aristotle's hierarchy of senses that is headed with vision.[64] However, vice versa, there are also Greek sources who prescribed the blind a heightened sense of extensive perception, with foresight, superior, and esoteric knowledge; comprehensive memory; and particular philosophical and divine understanding because of the diminished faculty of their eyes ascribed to respected and honored artists, teachers, philosophers, jurists, statesmen, heads of state, and seers.[65] There are many sources that account for social dependence of those with impaired eyesight, for financial poverty and unemployment (also due to high medical expenditure), as well as distinctive caritative commitment (of relatives and friends, children, slaves, or guides), and juridical protection.[66] Within ancient Judaism, there are further accounts on cultic and social implications for the blind (and the deaf/mute) with additional observations for or restricted access to the temple and temple service, witness stand, and judgeship.[67] This ambiguous social picture is confirmed by papyrical evidence[68] and

---

[63] Cf. Cicero, *Leg.* 1.9.27; Quintilian, *Inst.* 2.3.75; Pliny, *Nat.* 11.145. Cf. Trentin in Laes; Goodey; Rose (ed.) 2013. 107; Solevåg 2018. 124.

[64] Cf., e.g., Plato, *Resp.* 514a-520e, *Tim.* 47a-b; Ovid, *Met.*; Aristotle, *Metaph.* 1.1/980a, *Eth. Nic.* 1114b; Sophocles, *Oed. tyr.* 1368; furthermore, Schrage, τυφλός; von Bendemann in Zimmermann (ed.) 2013. 342, 346–347. 284–286.

[65] Cf., e.g., Heraklit, Demetrios of Phaleron, Antipatros of Kyrene, Asklepiades of Eritrea, Teiresias. Cf. Lawrence 2011. 391; von Bendemann in Zimmermann (ed.) 2013. 342–343; Kollmann in Zimmermann (ed.) 2013. 91–92; Glenney; Noble 2014. 79; Moss in Melcher; Parsons; Yong (ed.) 2018. 295.

[66] Cf., e.g., Judg 16:26; Deut 27:18; Job 29:15; Lev 19:4; Jer 31:8; Prov 31:8; Num 35:23; Homer, *Od.* 8.106–107; Sophocles, *Ant.* 910–11, 989; *Oed. tyr.* 1321–1322; Seneca the Elder, *Contr.* 10.4.2; Aristotle, *Eth. Nic.* 3.3/4a; *Ant. Gr.* 9.298; CH, *Morb. sacr.* 1.32; Lucian, *Philops.* 16; mMak 2:3; yMeg 4:7, 75b; ySheq 5:6, 49b; Luke 8:43; also Esser 1961. 114–155; Rose 2003. 88; Trentin in Laes; Goodey; Rose (ed.) 2013. 111; von Bendemann in Zimmermann (ed.) 2013. 342–343; Kollmann in Zimmermann (ed.) 2013. 92.

[67] Cf., e.g., Lev 21:16–23; 1Q28ª 2.3–9; 4QMMT B49–51; 11Q19 45.11–14; also 1QM 7.4–5. Great care, however, must be applied in the analysis of rhetoric passages such as 2Sam 5:8. Cf. also the physical imperfection of blind animals unsuitable for sacrifice in Lev 22:22; Deut 15:21; Mal 1:8. Cf. also mMen 9:8; mHag 1:1; bHag 4b; tHag 1:1; mMeg 4:6.

[68] Opatrný 2010, analyzed twenty-two occurrences of τυφλός referring to people in various text forms found on papyri, ostraca, and on one parchment dated from first cent. BC–seventh/eighth cent. CE with regard to the depicted social status of those labeled "blind." Deliberately excluding narratological reasons, he finds that, "in several cases blind people are mentioned without a name, even in lists of names. Such anonymity can be associated with social exclusion [...] But the blind who owned property, governed their own house [...], which provided for them and by

the two men here in Mark, one integrated in a social network, the other named yet begging. The latter, however, by his commended behavior and somewhat insightful addresses of Jesus, additionally alludes to ascribed notions of spiritual wisdom, comprehensive perception, maybe even prophetic knowledge, especially regarding symbolic allusions of his dis/ability (see below).

7.2.1.2 Active Gazing and Perceptive Eyes

By inversion, cognates of βλέπω describe the healed physicality in both narratives. In Mark 8:23–24, the man's ability to see partially after Jesus' first touch is evaluated in their dialogue. Quite generally, the lexeme refers to the act and faculty of the eyes to visually perceive and often denotes the opposite of what the term τυφλός describes.[69] As with other descriptions of visual perception, it also connotes cognitive insight.[70]

Moreover, its compound ἀναβλέπω is in both accounts used to describe the (desired) ability to see: In Mark 8:24, the man with impaired sight is narrated to ἀναβλέπω after Jesus' first touch and subsequently answers Jesus' inquiry by recording only blurry sight. While this can already denote the (gradual) transformation of his sight, it also carries the meaning of "raising" or "opening" one's eyes for simple optical detection and/or as an expressive gesture (cf., e.g., 6:41, 7:34, and 16:4).[71] In any case, the man's eyes are used to attempt visual cognition. In Mark 10:51 and 52, Bartimaeus asks for and is granted the ability to ἀναβλέπω.[72] As the preposition insinuates a return or recovery of sight, the term might imply a norm of abled sight that is being established or that the men were able to see before. However, as the lexeme is also used to refer to the astounding ability to see of those congenitally blind,[73] the prior is more likely and fits with ἀποκαθίστημι (see below).

---

which they continued their business, were known by name in their neighbourhood. [...] The situation of those blind people who were poor was worse, but there was still the possibility for them to perform simple manual work. [...] Definitely it is not true, that every blind man had to be a beggar," ibid. 593.

69 Cf., e.g., 8:15. Cf. also Bayer, ὁράω; BDAG, s.v.; LSJ, s.v.; Michaelis, ὁράω and cogn. Esp. 343–344; Montanari, s.v.; Müller, βλέπω. In opposition to blindness cf., e.g., Exod 4:11; 23:8; 1Kgs 3:2; Ps 68:24; Aelian, Var. hist. 6.12; Dit. Syll.³ 1168, 78; P.Oxy 39.9; Rom 11:8; Luke 7:21; Matt 12:22; 15:31; John 9:7, 15, 25; 11:9; Acts 9:9; Rev 3:18.
70 Cf., e.g., Rom 7:23; 2Cor 4:18; Heb 11:1, 3, 7.
71 Cf. also Luke 4:18; 9:16; 18:41–43; 19:5; 21:1; Matt 14:19; 20:34; Acts 22:13; Herodotus, Hist. 2.111.2, Plato, Phaedr. 243b; Plato, Resp. 621b; Xenophon, Cyr. 8.3.2; and von Bendemann in Zimmermann (ed.) 2013. 342; BDAG, s.v.; LSJ, s.v.; Montanari, s.v.; Müller, ἀναβλέπω.
72 Cf. also Matt 11:5par. Luke 7:22; Acts 9:12, 17–18.
73 Cf. John 9:11, 15, 18, and Pausanias, Descr. 4.12.[7].10.

Furthermore, in Mark 8:25, the man's healed physicality is then emphatically narrated by three lexemes, of which two refer to his ability to see. Firstly, the ingressive or inceptive aorist of διαβλέπω marks the distinction of his vision in contrast to the formerly cloudy perception; fitting to the only other occurrences in the Synoptics in Matt 7:5 and Luke 6:42, the term insinuates "the removal of a visual impediment"[74] (he can quite literally "see through" and "discern well").[75] Additionally, the lexeme carries the notion of an intensity and intentionality of gaze, as in "staring,"[76] similar to the more common ἐμβλέπω,[77] which is subsequently used. Here, however, the evaluation of his vision is quite general, and a distinct object to fixate upon is not mentioned.[78] Rather, he is now able to direct his gaze intentionally and actively without hinderance. Accordingly, after the man's recovery has been once more stated, the eye's faculty is heightened with the durative imperfect ἐνέβλεπεν together with the qualifiers τηλαυγῶς ἅπαντα. This time, the text explicitly generalizes the man's ability to "fix his gaze" at everything and anything henceforth. As in the other Markan occurrences, where the verb implies an accurate observation of the interlocuter, it also insinuates cognitive recognition beyond the obviously observable (10:21, 27; 14:67).[79] Together with the adverb, this nuance heightens the man's recovery from the previously stated διαβλέπω, as already the change of tenses indicates, because it refers to clearness and distinction of (far-)sightedness in particular.[80] The term's cognates are frequently employed in "poetic descriptions of the radiance of the sun or of gods, people, and things that are like it in brightness or splendour".[81] As such, it not only pertains to the ancient extramission theory of vision, which posits that the eyes emit beams that enable sight by illuminating objects,[82] but also highlights the man's newfound ability to see, as *everything* is to him now as conspicuous. Accordingly, it is also used for spiritual ap-

---

74 Marcus 1999. 255. Cf. also Acts 9:18.
75 Cf. Philodemus, *Rhet.* 1.252; Lucian, *Merc. Cond.* 22; also Balz; Schneider, διαβλέπω. 714; von Bendemann in Zimmermann (ed.) 2013. 342; BDAG, *s.v*; LSJ, *s.v*; Montanari, *s.v*
76 Cf. Plato, *Phaedr.* 86d; Aristotle, *Ins.* 462a 13; Plutarch, *Alex.* 14.2; *Sera* 548; *Mor.* 973–4; Johnson 1978–79. 377.
77 Cf., e.g., Mark 10:21, 27; 14:67; Matt 19:26; Luke 20:17; 22:61; John 1:36, 42.
78 Cf. Johnson 1978–79. 378, and his observations on ἐμβλέπω in the sense of "seeing into."
79 Cf. VT Isa 5:12; Matt 6:26; Luke 20:17; John 1:36, 41; Balz; Schneider, ἐμβλέπω. 1079–1080; BDAG, *s.v*; LSJ, *s.v*; Montanari, *s.v*
80 Cf. also Diodorus, *Bib. hist.* 1.50.1; Vettius, *Anth.* 54.7–8; Philo, *Post.* 65; *Cher.* 61; *Congr.* 24.25; also BDAG, *s.v*; LSJ, *s.v*; Montanari, *s.v*
81 Marcus 1999. 252.
82 As shown for NT texts by Betz in Best; Wilson (ed.) 1979; Allison in Allison (ed.) 1997; Marcus 1999, with reference to Matt 6:22–23; Luke 6:34–36; and Wis 11:18; *4Bar.* 7.3; *1En.* 106.2, 5, 10; *bBMes* 59b; Plato, *Tim.* 45c-d; Philo, *Abr.* 150–157; *Cher.* 96–97. Cf. also Glenney; Noble 2014. 71, 78.

prehension and cognitive perception.[83] This underlying concept of beaming vision underscores the faculty of the affected organ, the eyes that Jesus deliberately touched (ὄμμα/ὀφθαλμός, 8:23, 25). The compounds of βλέπω are not simply tautological but denote an increase of visual sharpness, from the man's first hopeful attempt to use his eyes in 8:24 to his clear-sightedness and henceforth emphatically pin-sharp and penetrating insight in 8:25.[84] In contrast to other, rather synonymous verbs, the repetitive use of the compounds stresses the faculty of the eyes.[85]

7.2.1.3 Holistic Healing

As in Mark 3:5, the healing in Mark 8:25 is termed ἀποκαθίστημι[86] (v. 25), which refers to the restoration of an original condition. While parallel accounts explicitly denote the healing of the affected body part (i.e., the hand in Mark 3:5, see 4.2), here the sensory *faculty* of the eyes is accentuated by the framing terms (see above) after the organs have been notably treated. As the creational-eschatological context of Mark 3:1–6 and successive use of the term in, i.e., Mark 9:12 insinuate, the original condition referenced by this term is ambiguous, especially with regard to the gradual spectrum of sight displayed here: either the man's vision is *restored* to the condition before his blinding, which implies that he was not congenitally blind, or—and probably not exclusively—the lexeme also suggests a *restoration* of perfected creational value and/or eschatological promise. Especially with regard to a cognitive perception and understanding implied by the context, this "restoration" points beyond a mere everyday visual capacity.

Such an ambiguous transformation is also reflected in the polyseme σῴζω, which is used to describe the healed condition of formerly blind Bartimaeus in Mark 10:52. By the verbatim reprise of Jesus' performative confirmation of the healing from Mark 5:34, the text recalls the ambivalence of the term established in the intercalation of Mark 5:21–43 as it signifies a physical cure and transpires an eschatological salvation of the entire being (σε) in connection to *pistis* practice (see 5.2.3.2; cf. 3:4 and 6:56). Again, the perfect tense underscores the resultative and timeless aspect as it eludes an exact point of realization[87] and is vocalized before the healed eyesight, and—paratactically—the also consequential fellowship of

---

[83] Cf. Marcus 1999. 253–254, who lists Philo, *Deus* 29; *Plant.* 22; *Leg.* 3.171; *Migr.* 39; *Post.* 57; *Decal.* 101; *Conf.* 63; Josephus, *A.J.* 1.35; 6.169; cf. also Michaelis, ὁράω *and cogn.* 335–338.
[84] Cf. Focant 2012. 330; von Bendemann in Zimmermann (ed.) 2013. 342.
[85] Cf. also Michaelis, ὁράω *and cogn.* 317, 327, 343–344.
[86] Cf. ch. 4.1, also, e.g., BDAG, s.v; Link; Breytenbach, ἀποκαθίστημι; LN, s.v 13.65, 15.74; LSJ, s.v; Montanari, s.v; Müller, ἀποκαθίστημι, ἀποκαθιστάνω; Oepke, ἀποκαθίστημι, ἀποκατάστασις.
[87] Cf. Focant 2012. 212.

Bartimaeus is stated. Again, a holistic aspect of the healing is enforced, which is here not only based on *pistis* practice but relates to discipleship and the subsequent journey of Jesus to his death (as announced in 8:34–35 and the passion predictions in 8:31; 9:32; 10:32–34; see below). From then on, the polyseme σῴζω continuously conveys a more explicit eschatological and soteriological meaning.[88]

In both narratives, the healed condition is not simply described by the ability to see, but also by terms that connote a holistic and even eschatological restoration that is at this point of the plot inherently linked to an understanding of Jesus' identity in the context of the anticipated passion.

7.2.1.4 Summary

By utilizing the image of impaired eyesight, Mark employs a common yet ambiguous dis/ability and refrains from providing further clarification regarding the precise parameters or etiologies of the men's dis/abilities. Instead, the terms and descriptions used serve to heighten the already inherent degrees of visual perception and reinforce the range of cultural implications through depictions of social integration (even if "only" caritative, as seen with the guiding supplicants in 8:22) and financial and social decline (as exemplified by the begging Bartimaeus in 10:46). In both cases, the cured clear-sightedness of the eyes is not only emphatically stated but also heightened by descriptions that focus on social and eschatological integrity and insight, which is additionally accentuated by the philosophical and epistemological understanding of visual perception that transpires any image of (imperfect) sight (see below, 7.3.3).

7.2.2 Mark 9:14–29

Contrary to the rather short and straightforward introductions of the blind men with the desire to see in Mark 8:22–26 and 10:46–52, the dis/ability of the boy in Mark 9:14–29 is described in unusual detail for a Markan narration, including a description of his state by his father (vv. 17–18, 21–22) and a live "performance" (v. 20). All of it is framed by three general qualifications in the vv. 17–18 and 25: firstly, the spirit is characterized as ἄλαλος (vv. 17, 25) and κωφός (v. 25) by characters of this narrative (the father, Jesus); secondly, the narrator classes it as ἀκάθαρτος (v. 25); and, thirdly, common for the Markan conception of possession, the boy's inhabitable physicality is explained in relational terms (here, having a spirit that seizes/occupies, enters and leaves, and needs to be thrown out; see below). In be-

---

[88] Cf. p. 181, n. 170.

tween these verses, the father (v. 18 and vv. 21–22) and the narrator (v. 20) vividly depict the influence the spirit has on the boy. Before addressing these three explicit descriptions of the boy's dis/abling spirit and the concrete and dramatically depicted symptoms (see 7.2.2.2), three rather implicit qualifications of the boy's dis/ability given throughout the text are regarded.

7.2.2.1 Implicit Qualifications: Varying Degrees, Permanent Possession, and a Dependent Body

Firstly, the effect the spirit has on the boy seems to be of varying degrees: For one, the father's descriptions of the boy's physical condition and the disciples' unsuccessful attempt at exorcism suggest that the son is in close proximity but not currently exhibiting the full extent of his symptoms, as he is able to be brought to Jesus. However, his symptoms are still apparent enough to make the crowd and the disciples aware that he is still possessed.[89] It is only this small detail that accounts for an interpretation of a permanent possession contra a continuous coming and leaving of the same spirit cum his dramatic effects on the boy's body. Arguments for the latter interpretation are, to begin, that the described symptoms also fit ancient descriptions of *temporary* seizures and that the Markan text only *suggests* that muteness as a permanent characteristic of the spirit is a chronic symptom (see below). Jesus also commands the spirit not to return (v. 25: καὶ μηκέτι εἰσέλθῃς εἰς αὐτόν), which is, however, also accounted for as a general exorcism practice in other first-century exorcism accounts[90] and concurs with the (Markan) demonological conception of moving demons.[91] Hence, a permanent possession, even if only hinging on this one implication, is more likely. Moreover, the dramatic seizures occur at selective times and places, ὅπου (v. 18), εὐθύς (v. 20), and πολλάκις (v. 22), and can escalate to an almost fatal extent (v. 20 in contrast to v. 22). Thus, the spirit inhabits and influences the boy permanently (ἐκ παιδιόθεν) and shows its violent nature only occasionally in the boy's dramatic fits.[92]

Secondly, and again common for the Markan conception of possession, the text depicts the disparate corporality of demon and host, here reflected in grammatical incongruence (esp. v. 20), changing subjects along with socially deviating behavior:[93] At times the spirit explicitly gains control of the physical capacities of the

---

[89] Cf. Lindemann in Lindemann (ed.) 2009. 94.
[90] Cf., e.g., Matt 12:43–45 par. Luke 11:24–26; Josephus, *A.J.* 8.46–47; Acts Thom. 77; and Kollmann 1996. 214; Wolter 2008. 420–422.
[91] See 5.1.
[92] See also μηκέτι in the description of the exorcism.
[93] See 3.1.

boy, αὐτόν (v. 18: it "seizes" and "strikes him [to the ground]"; v. 20: "convulses" the boy; v. 22: "throws" him to "destroy" him), followed directly by actions relating to the boy as at least the implied subject (e. g., καὶ ἀφρίζει καὶ τρίζει τοὺς ὀδόντας καὶ ξηραίνεται; καὶ πεσὼν ἐπὶ τῆς γῆς ἐκυλίετο ἀφρίζων). His body's actions always depend on an activity explicitly caused by the spirit. In v. 20, the spirit reacts violently when seeing Jesus, implicitly through the boy's eyes (cf. Mark 5:6). While in Mark 1:21–28 and 5:1–20, the demons also gain control of their host's speech apparatus when engaging in aggressive and/or quite frenzied conversation with Jesus, the spirit here remains silent, which underscores another deviance to "socially accepted speech."[94] Nevertheless, the actions following the visual recognition of Jesus transcend a recognition of his identity, similar to those in the other narratives made explicit by speech. Through all this, the boy remains passive; his physical movement seems not intended by him, ὡς τοῦτο γέγονεν αὐτῷ (v. 21).

Thirdly, the boy is passive in the plea for healing. Due to his ailment (esp. his speech impairment, see below) and age, he is dependent on his father, he needs to be brought (φέρω, vv. 17, 19, 20), and his parent supplicates for him and explicates his physical state (cf. Mark 5:21–24, 35–43 and 7:24–30). Hence, the patient is a child in age and size, although it is implied that he is not an infant anymore when the beginning of his ailment is dated back to early childhood in v. 21 (cf. Mark 5:42). More importantly, however, the father-son relationship serves to explicate the suffering of the father and the passivity and dependence of the boy.[95] Moreover, unlike the Gerasene demoniac, he is introduced as part of a family and not excluded by society, although he is encountered in the periphery of a mountain (see 5.1).

While there are some minor differences to previous Markan accounts with dis/abled children (e. g., the bedridden children remaining in their quarters with their supplicants falling to Jesus' feet), the main difference lies in the fact that the parent is not more closely defined by his social or her cultural-religious identity. The supplicating man is simply designated as "one from the crowd" (v. 15) and "father" (vv. 21, 24, and by inversion v. 17). This makes it easier to identify with him; anyone could be him. Furthermore, the unity and relationship of father and son is emphasized since, after his introduction (v. 15), the *parent* is only mentioned in dependence to his offspring (v. 17: τὸν υἱόν μου; v. 21: τὸν πατέρα αὐτοῦ; v. 24: ὁ πατὴρ τοῦ παιδίου; also v. 21: ὁ δὲ εἶπεν· ἐκ παιδιόθεν), culminating in the desperate plea:

---

[94] Solevåg 2018. 48–49.
[95] Cf. also 9:36–37 and 10:16. Luke 9:38 even renders the boy to be his only son.

"Help *us* and have pity on *us!*" (v. 22).⁹⁶ In this narrative, the childish body is only important with regard to his belonging to the father and his dependence on the parent's supplication. No further information is given on his development after the healing. This strong bond, however, is opposed by his close tie to the demon (see above).

Interestingly, two of the four Markan exorcism accounts focus on childish bodies, which underscores the innocence and susceptibility presumed in the Markan etiology of possession; explicates the negotiability of physicality, especially with regard to an underaged body; heightens the severity of the suffering; and, most of all, serves as a more or less "blank space" (they stay in the background)⁹⁷ for visualizing a problem debated around them: here, the necessity of *pistis* and Jesus' mission against the evil sphere.

7.2.2.2 General Qualifications
7.2.2.2.1 The Inhabitable Body

The locative terminology Mark uses to depict demonic dis/ability is in its introduction, differently to Mark 1:23 and 5:2, not expressed with prepositions (e.g., ἄνθρωπος ἐν πνεύματι ἀκαθάρτῳ)⁹⁸ but similar to that of Markan descriptions of other ailments expressed with ἔχω (cf. Mark 1:32; 3:1, 10; 6:55). Nevertheless, this terminology also occurs in the context of spiritual influence in Mark 3:22 and 7:25,⁹⁹ and the explication of the expulsion take up the customary prepositional language to describe the fused corporality of spirit and boy (ἐκβάλλω; ἐξέρχομαι ἐξ; εἰσέρχομαι) that is also expressed in the depiction of the spirit's own movement in vv. 18, 25–26, 28–29. Consistent with the Markan concept of demonic opposition, the term καταλαμβάνω reflects the locative aspects of the competing spheres with its notion of occupation and seizure, yet with a more dynamic, not static, facet (cf. ὅπου). Accordingly, the introduction and termination of the dis/ability characterize the spirit as a separate and movable entity and the human body as a permeable yet habitable and very susceptible place. The latter suggests that a change of this spirit's place is possible, which is also reflected in Jesus' command to the spirit not to return (v. 25).

---

96 Since his plea follows the description of need, he refers, on a primary level, to himself and his son. Thereby the duo "spirit-child" is contrasted with the often-encountered Markan duo "parent-child" (cf. Mark 5:25–34, 7:24–30), the "silencing spirit vs. speaking father." Cf. Focant 2012. 370. However, it is also conceivable that "us" includes himself and the other ἄπιστοι (cf. vv. 19 and 24), the crowd and/or disciples (see below).
97 Cf. also Luke 7:11–17; δοῦλος in Luke 7:1–10/Matt 8:5–13 but υἱός in John 4:46–53.
98 Cf. also εἰσέρομαι Mark 5:12–13.
99 Cf. Matt 11:18; Luke 4:33; 7:33; 8:27; 13:11; Acts 8:7; 16:16; 19:13; John 7:19; 8:48–49, 52; 10:20.

7.2.2.2.2 Spiritual Opposition with Sensory and Cognitive Effects

As a first designation, the possessive spirit is specified as ἄλαλος by the father of the boy (Mark 9:17), then used without any qualifier by the narrator when depicting the dramatic seizure on account of Jesus' presence (9:20), and, finally, in the exorcising sentence, characterized as the opposing πνεῦμα ἀκαθάρτον and addressed by Jesus as τὸ ἄλαλον καὶ κωφὸν πνεῦμα (9:25).

As analyzed in 6.2, the lexeme ἄλαλος (and ἄφωνος) frequently defines the singular dis/ability muteness, while κωφός describes an inability to hear and/or speak or communicate altogether, often in connection with congenital deafness and cognitive deviance of some sort (ἐνεός).[100] The boy's inability to verbally communicate is heightened to the Markan audience as his demon is the first and only one that does not speak to Jesus (cf. 1:23–24, 34; 3:11; 5:7–12). The fact that Jesus characterizes the spirit additionally as κωφός after the consultation indicates that he has then been witnessed to affect the boy's entire communicative abilities. In accordance with the use of κωφός in Mark 7:35, where, as pointed out, the additional designation μογιλάλος, the separate healing touches of ears and tongue, and their separately narrated healing effects indicate an auditory dis/ability expressed by κωφός. The boy can be regarded as deaf-mute due to the spirit's possession. However, since the focus of the preceding verses rather lies on the boy's lack of self-control and savage behavior, the definition of κωφός at this point of the narrative can be expanded to its broader meaning to describe cognitive incomprehension with socially deviating behavior.[101] In contrast to Mark 5:1–20 (esp. v. 15), the boy's intellectual capacities are not explicitly addressed, although ancient medical treatises make note of the brain's disrupted function to make *sense* when affected by similar symptoms (see *Excursus: Epileptic Phenomena*, p. 239–240).[102] In any case, his inability to communicate coherently (i.e., his insensibility) narrates also limited cognitive comprehension in ancient contexts.

While the father and Jesus, as the exorcist, describe the spirit as ἄλαλος and κωφός in its framing designations (vv. 17, 25) and thereby highlight the dis/abling effects the spirit has on the boy, the narrator once again emphasizes its opposing

---

100 See 6.2.2.1 and comprehensively Laes 2011. 460–465.
101 The focus on the boy's cognitive faculties is also witnessed in the parallel accounts of this narrative. Matt 17:14–18 and Luke 9:37–42 don't mention any muting/deafening effect of the spirit but concentrate on its uncontrollable force on the entire childish body although or maybe because these accounts also don't distinguish carefully between deafness and muteness when using κωφός, as the analysis in 6.2 on Mark 7:31–37 has shown; cf. κωφός in connection with λαλέω in Luke 11:14; Matt 12:22; and Zacharias' dis/ability (κωφός) and communication via gestures and writing in Luke 1:22, 63.
102 Cf., e.g., *Morb. sacr.* 17.

nature to Jesus, particularly by placing it right before the exorcism. This reference recalls the competing spheres associated with pneumatic impurity (cf. 1:23, 26; 3:11, 30; 5:2, 13; 6:7; 7:25).[103] Due to the characteristic embodied fusion of spirit and host, a separation of the nature of the spirit and its effect on the boy is futile. Moreover, considering Mark's *narrative* convention to depict human bodies as mediums for the hostile realm to see and communicate with Jesus (except implicitly Mark 1:12–13), a physical muteness or deafness is presupposed when regarding a "host-less" demon, which explicates Jesus' verbal exorcising command as performative and not as a simple auditory statement (see below). The spirit's qualifiers as ἄλαλος and κωφός then aim to narrate the permanent effect the pneumatic force has on the boy for the time he is possessed. The spirit, by its very *nature*, causes muteness and deafness (see below) and, in relation to ἀκάθαρτος, affects the boy physically to oppose Jesus (cf. v. 20). Additionally, this may also reveal (albeit implicitly) social implications related to impurity, such as communicability and cultic restrictions (see 3.1.2.1; 6.2.2).

Then, based on the analysis above that the boy is permanently possessed (see 7.2.2.1), the aforementioned characteristic qualifications illustrate permanent and not "accessory" symptoms in the temporary and varying seizures.[104] Accordingly, the boy's continuous sensory incapability may be the evidence for the previously failed exorcism before the extent of the spirit's violence is displayed in one of the occasional seizures. This concurs with similar depictions of pneumatic dis/ability in the Synoptics, where possession and sensory dis/ability cannot be separated from one another.[105] Here as well, no physical cure for the sensory impediments is demonstrated; the exit of the mute and deaf and impure spirit implies to have ended it all.[106]

---

103 See 3.1.2.1.
104 Cf. Bornkamm in Bornkamm (ed.) 1971. 24, different to Kollmann 1996. 211, who takes the spirit-muteness reference as an opposite to the Matthean occurrences and therefore classes the speech impairment as a temporary epiphenomenon of the seizures.
105 Cf. Luke 11:14–15, where speech demonstrates the successful exorcism of a mute (κωφός) spirit. Similarly, Matt 9:32–33 depicts a mute man being "demonized" (δαιμονίζομαι) and able to speak after the exorcism. Matthew 12:22 reports a demonized man who was blind and mute as *healed* (θεραπεύω) from his sensory impairment without the need to additionally explicate his liberation from the demon. Cf. also Mark 7:31–37 on binding and loosening of the tongue in connection with spiritual influence. Here however, neither tongue nor binding is specifically mentioned.
106 That the boy/spirit screams (κράζω) after the exorcising command is not important for the evaluation of his speech impairment, since ἄλαλος reflects the inability to speak coherently and not to produce oral sounds.

7.2.2.3.3 Seizing Behavior

Besides the deaf-mute spirit's effect on the boy's sensory abilities and his defiling nature, the possession is described in occasional dramatic fits of varying degrees. These seizures encompass a variety of physical actions.

7.2.2.1.3.1 Violent Deviance

The violent nature of the spirit when "seizing" (καταλαμβάνω) the boy is introduced with the term ῥήσσει (v. 18; cf. Luke 9:42). This lexeme can either derive from ῥήσσω, the later form of ῥήγνυμι ("burst, tear," cf. 2:22), or "be taken as an Ionic form of ῥάσσω"[107] ("to beat the ground [dancing], to strike, knock down, fell" or "to dash, overthrow, turn upside down, throw to the ground").[108] From a historical-linguistic perspective, both may be regarded as viable roots that may even be coalesced in Koine Greek.[109]

In this context, the former may be taken as a reflection of convulsive sudden body movements, "tearing" and "dragging" the child's body without clear direction but with the connotation of destruction, similar to (συ)σπαράσσω (vv. 20, 26), which already occurred in Mark 1:26. The latter, however, which is witnessed by the variant reading of D 565, specifies the downward direction of the abrupt beating that is described again when the spirit sees Jesus by πίπτω ἐπὶ τῆς γῆς (v. 20).[110] However, both possible origins fit the following actions of sudden movements ([συ]σπαράσσω, vv. 20, 26; κυλίω, v. 20) on the ground (πίπτω ἐπὶ τῆς γῆς, v. 20; even in fire or water, v. 22; cf. also ὡσεὶ νεκρός and by inversion ἀνίστημι, vv. 26–27) in a violent and destructive manner (ἀπόλλυμι, v. 22).

As established, the falling downward is mentioned (again) in v. 20, πίπτω ἐπὶ τῆς γῆς. It is not to be taken as a form of proskynesis, as witnessed in Mark 5:6 by the Gerasene demoniac (προσκυνέω) or by supplicants asking for healing (cf., e.g., Mark 5:22), but in light of the other, directly following symptoms, it rather signifies the loss of physical control by involuntarily dropping to the ground, out of communicative and social eye level, with the possible cause of injuries. Consequently, Jesus is reported to raise him up (ἀνίστημι, v. 27, see below). This is also reflected in the impressively narrated self-destruction of the Gerasene demoniac and taken up in this narrative's Matthean parallel, where the boy *falls* into fire and water

---

107 Collins 2007. 433.
108 Cf., e.g., Balz; Schneider, *ῥήγνυμι*; BDAG, s.v; LN, s.v 23.168; LSJ, s.v; Montanari, s.v; Collins 2007. 433; Focant 2012. 373.
109 Cf. Blass; Debrunner; Rehkopf 1976. § 101, n. 72.
110 Luke seems to follow the derivation of ῥάσσω, when he differentiates between the demon's movement of "tearing [the boy] to the ground" and causing the body to "convulse" (Luke 9:42, αὐτοῦ *ἔρρηξεν* αὐτὸν τὸ δαιμόνιον καὶ *συνεσπάραξεν*; cf. 9:39).

(πίπτω, Matt 17:15). Fitting to these descriptions of convulsion and falling, the boy's body then "rolls around" (κυλίω, v. 20) in front of Jesus.

The lexeme (συ)σπαράσσω, "shake violently," even "lacerate,"[111] is the only term describing a symptom in this account that occurs in another Synoptic description of the effect of possession, in Mark 1:26.[112] Here, it occurs twice with intensity markers (εὐθύς συ- in 9:20 and πολλά in 9:26) and in prominent positions: it marks the *first* physical utilization of the spirit—and only here quite explicitly in this relation as named subject and object (τὸ πνεῦμα εὐθὺς συνεσπάραξεν αὐτόν, as in Mark 1:26)—and its *last* manipulation in Jesus' presence before it leaves the body. Thereby, the narrator enforces his (v. 25), the father's (v. 17), and Jesus' (v. 25) proposed etiology of all the symptoms framed by this lexeme and those constructed by the father's previous account: The boy is possessed by a spiritual entity that forces him to sudden, involuntary, violent, and destructive movements. The account graphically depicts a severely symbiotic body. These movements are differentiated in the following verses.

7.2.2.1.3.2 Sensuous Symbiosis

The confusion regarding the acting entity responsible for the actions, and thus the evidence of the symbiotic relationship between the spirit and the boy, becomes particularly evident when tracing the lexemes ἀφρίζω (vv. 18 and 20), τρίζω τοὺς ὀδόντας (v. 18), and κράζω (v. 26) and their implied or grammatical subjects throughout the narrative. Especially the use of κράξας (and σπαράξας) in masculine, versus the neuter form of the addressed πνεῦμα in vv. 25–26, enforces the idea that the spirit is a separate entity inhabiting the boy's body while being ambiguous about the acting entity (then: ἐξῆλθεν).[113]

Emphatically, ἀφρίζω is the only lexeme that occurs once in the father's description of the ailment and once in its sudden display before Jesus, therefore vividly visualizing the hindered and uncontrollable oral dis/ability. In v. 18, its subject seems to be the demon, while v. 20 stays vague. The use of τρίζω and also κράζω adds a specific audiovisual effect to the display of dis/ability. Interestingly, the three lexemes all focus on actions of the mouth in contrast to its controllable, socially accepted, and valued function of speech that the spirit denies the boy. Instead, the child's body displays these untypical, even animalistic features: ἀφρίζω is also used for horse muzzles; τρίζω often occurs in context of creaking animal

---

111 Cf., e.g., BDAG, s.v.; LN, s.v. 23.167; LSJ, s.v.; Montanari, s.v.
112 Cf. very rare, συσπαράσσω, in Maximus Tyrius, *Diss.* 7, 5 line 23 on equality of suffering of body and soul.
113 Cf. Focant 2012. 374. See also ἰδών in v. 20.

sounds.¹¹⁴ The more common κράζω is a Markan favorite to describe the violent sounds of demon possession (3:11; 5:5, 7; cf. ἀνακράζω in 1:23).¹¹⁵

7.2.2.1.3.3 Sudden and Dangerous Im-/mobility

Moreover, the seizures are described to stop as dramatically and completely as they have started. In accordance with its use in Mark 3:1 (see ch. 4), the lexeme ξηραίνω, "to dry, dry out, desiccate, wither,"¹¹⁶ is used to describe a (partial) paralysis.¹¹⁷ Here it seems not only to refer to a single immobile body part but to the entire physical being of the boy in contrast to the previous uncontrollable movements (ῥήσσει). Again, this term reflects first and foremost in intelligible imagery the dynamic process of the boy's seizures.¹¹⁸ As established, it is too universal to explicitly refer to a distinct medical notion of im-/balanced corporal liquids, which also makes it unlikely that Mark offers one of the earliest and rare depictions of a hybrid version of what will only be *later* categorized as two types of "epileptic phenomena"¹¹⁹ (see below).¹²⁰ As immobility is also just one of many accompanying symptom and only occurs in the father's description, its comparison with the mobility impairment in Mark 3:1 should not be overemphasized. Although both are embedded in a setting of controversy about healing ability, in this case, it is the disciples who are involved. In this section, the image of stiff and immobile physicality after uncontrollable and boisterous movement depicts the continuous threat of the boy's seizures to recur at any moment and add to the sensory "paralysis" a paralysis of mobility.

In light of these sudden and violent falls, it is only consequential that the boy was prone to be affected by such a seizure in dangerous places (e.g., close to water or fire; for similar phenomena, see below).¹²¹ Here, the father describes the action with the lexeme βάλλω, which additionally implies an intentional threat of the demon.¹²² The demon *wants* the boy to perish (ἀπολέσῃ αὐτόν), which renders

---

114 Cf., e.g., BDAG, s.v.; LN, s.v. 23.41; LSJ, s.v.; Montanari, s.v.
115 Cf. also ἀνακράζειν in CH, *Epid.* 7.25.
116 Cf., e.g., BDAG, s.v.; Kuhn, ξηραίνω; LN, s.v. 23.173, 76.80–82; LSJ, s.v.; Montanari, s.v.
117 Cf. also Mark 5:29 where the issue of blood dries up.
118 See ch. 4.
119 This term encompasses ancient (!) descriptions of similar phenomena that can be grouped around sudden physical seizures (cf. ἐπιληψία).
120 Different to Weissenrieder 2003. 274, 279–280, 282, esp. n. 242, based on Caelius, *Chron.* 1.4.61–64, who furthermore regards v. 26 as indication for this combination of epileptic phenomena, although this refers to the exorcised body that is not afflicted anymore.
121 Cf. Focant 2012. 373, also Caelius, *Chron.* 1.4.68.
122 Cf. Lindemann in Lindemann (ed.) 2009. 97.

the dis/ability a threat to his life. Moreover, the loss of control depicted in this sudden, unintended drop alludes to a break with social conventions, an embarrassing stigmatization to be avoided.[123] As such, involuntary falling is a (eponymous) symptom of similarly described physical phenomena.

Excursus: Epileptic Phenomena
While the terminology used to describe the boy's ailment and its narrated symptoms is quite general, it concurs in conjunction with very common ancient descriptions of phenomena associated with (temporary) seizures termed ἐπιληψία/epilepsia, morbus comitialis,[124] or "sacred disease," ἱερὰ νόσος (or morbus sacer).[125] The latter name derives from the idea that divine intervention was the reason for this ailment.[126] This etiology is already discussed in antiquity[127] and attributed to the ignorance, severity, unexpectedness, and complexity of the affliction: As famously argued in the treatise De morbo Sacro of the Hippocratic Corpus, this ailment is not to be regarded as more sacred than others.[128] Those in favor of a *fundamental* religious etiology and *exclusive* religious treatment, e. g., with simple "purifications and incantations" (καθαρμοῖσί [...] καὶ ἐπαοιδῇσιν) in contrast to its complex etiology are polemically dismissed due to their helplessness, ignorance, and charlatanry.[129] Rather, other etiologies of a more "rational-mechanistic"[130] nature against the backdrop of humoral theory were proposed here and elsewhere,[131] including heredity and a phlegmatic predisposition;[132] blocked passages due to an excess of phlegm, blood, bile, or air (e. g., in the brain);[133] physiological disruptions of, e. g., the nerves, sinews, or meninges;[134] envi-

---

123 Cf., e. g., CH, *Morb. sacr.* 15.1–14; Temkin 1994. 37–40; Collins 2007. 438.
124 The term reflects the notion that seizures of the "morbus comitialis" cancelled the *comitia* due to divine intervention. Cf., e. g., Celsus, *Med.* 3.23.1–2; Tacitus, *Ann.* 13.16; and Leven, *Epilepsie.* 261; Collins 2007. 435.
125 Cf. Temkin 1994. 91, also Wohlers 1999a. 19–20.
126 Cf. in greater detail, Temkin 1994. 6–10; Wohlers 1999a. 122–126; Rose 2003. 6.
127 Cf. comprehensively, Temkin 1994. 31–51. For discussions on ancient Babylonian descriptions, see, e. g., Kinnier Wilson; Reynolds 1990; Daras; Papakostas; Tuchman 1994; Temkin 1994; York 2005. On parallels in the HB/OT, see discussions on, e. g., Num 24:4, 16; 22:31; 1Sam 18:10; 19:24; 28:20, as in Rosner 2000. 115–116; Nissan; Shemesh 2010.
128 Cf., e. g., CH, *Morb. sacr.* 1; 5.1–6. For a discussion of this treatise's key terms (e. g., "divine," "human," "nature"), a reconstruction of its author's "theology," and references to more recent and extensive research on this treatise, see van der Eijk in van der Eijk (ed.) 2005b.
129 Cf., e. g., CH, *Morb. sacr.* 1.10, 2.1–10; and Wohlers 1999a. 121–139.
130 However, differing ancient constructs of diseases, their etiologies, and treatments should not necessarily be understood exclusively, i. e., with regard to "secular medicine and temple medicine," Temkin; Temkin 1987. 239; Krug 1993. 120–121, 159–163; Edelstein; Edelstein 1998. 2.139–141; van der Eijk in van der Eijk (ed.) 2005b. 63–64, 71; Leven, *Epilepsie.*
131 Cf., e. g., Caelius, *Chron.* 1.60–143; Galen, *Loc. aff.* 3.9 K 8.173–179; *Puer. epil.* K. 11.357–378; Celsus, *Med.* 3.23.1–2; and Weissenrieder 2003. 269–272; Leutzsch in Zimmermann (ed.) 2013. 354.
132 Cf. esp. CH, *Morb. sacr.* 5; 8.1–2.
133 Cf., e. g., *Morb. sacr.* 7; CH, *Flat.* 14; Galen, *Ven. sect. Er.* 8; Galen, *Loc. aff.* 3.9; and Temkin 1994. 62–63.
134 Cf. Caelius, *Chron.* 1.4.72–73.

ronmental factors (such as temperature, exposure to sun, humidity, etc.); lifestyle; and diet.[135] The conflict between more profane diagnoses and the divine is also reflected in the proposition that the moon and its phases and/or its goddess Selene can be regarded as source for the seizures.[136] Treatments then include dietetic measures and those that equilibrate the balance of the fluids (e.g., phlebotomies), rest, and even pharmacological and surgical interventions (e.g., trepanations).[137]

The symptoms common to the boy's seizures recounted in ancient medical literature encompass the characteristic convulsion and involuntary falling yet also speechlessness, foaming of the mouth, teeth grinding, loud sounds, and stiffness of the body.[138] Children are also reportedly more prone to such ailments.[139] The boy's lack of intention behind his sudden and dangerous movements that are attributed to the demon's agency and his deaf-/muteness match the descriptions of disrupted (sensual) perception and consciousness.[140] A specifically demonic etiology in contrast to a divine influence with distinct notions of physical possession, however, is only seldomly witnessed in the Synoptics and subsequent (commenting) literature.[141] Here, cathartic rituals and sympathetic cures (often with blood or animals) in connection with amulets and charms, prayer, and powerful commandments promise alleviation.[142]

---

135 Cf., e.g., *Morb. sacr.* 1.1–2; 10.8; 13.2, 11–13; 18.1; Galen, *Comm. CH Aph.* 4.28 K 18.41; *San. tu.* 1.8.17–18 K 6.41; *Comm. CH Epid.* 6, comm. 1.5 K 17.827–828; and Temkin 1994. 31–37; Wohlers 1999a. 96–104; Weissenrieder 2003. 272–273; Kelley in Schipper; Moss (ed.) 2011. 207.
136 Cf., e.g., Aretaeus, *Sign. diut.* 1.1–1.4; Galen, *Die. Decr.* 9.903; Lucian, *Tox.* 24; Lucian, *Philops.* 16; and Temkin 1994. 31–51, 94–95; Wohlers 1999a. 105–121.
137 Cf. Nutton, *Epilepsie*; Wohlers 1999a. 230–234; Solevåg 2018. 106.
138 Cf., e.g., Galen, *Loc. aff.* 3.9 K 8.173; *Def. Med.* 240 K 19.414; Caelius, *Chron.* 1, 4, 61 and 136; Celsus, *Med.* 3.23, 1; CH, *Morb. sacr.* 10.1–7; 4.21–32; 7.1; *Epid.* 7.46; 10.6; and Temkin 1994. 40–42; Collins 2007. 436.
139 Cf. Caelius, *Chron.* 1.4.60, 71; Celsus, *Med.* 3.23.1; and Temkin 1994. 43, 115–116; Weissenrieder 2003. 268, 274; Marcus 2009. 654.
140 Cf., e.g., Galen, *Loc. aff.* 3.9; *Def. Med.* 240.
141 Cf. also Matt 9:32–33; 12:22; Luke 13:11–13, and Wohlers 1999a. 126–127, 131–136, 202–203, who rightfully dismisses sources due to their hypothetical references to potentially apotropaic fingerings or saliva or their early-Christian influence (cf. Notes in Pliny, *Nat.* 28.35 and Apuleius, *Apol.* 43–48; the fragmented writing on an Epidauran Iamata in Herzog 1931. 32–33; Lucian, *Philops.* 16). However, the idea of a "divine indwelling power" with symptomatic epileptic phenomena is attested in Apuleius, *Apol.* 42–48; cf. also *bGit* 70a; *T.Sol.* 18:21[88]; 18.4; Wohlers 1999a. 129–130; Collins 2007. 436. Due to the prominence and similarity to the descriptions found in the Synoptic tradition, Christian authors "used the epileptic boy's body as a site for constructing a communal identity and a rhetorical tool for policing the community's boundaries" since its "unacceptable practices, behaviors, and conditions" was considered of being "representative of what which does not belong in the Christian community" (Kelley in Schipper; Moss [ed.] 2011. 211, 213, 215). On more on this line of reception in writings of Origen, Jerome, John Chrysostom, and others, see ibid. esp. 211–219. On the common motif on Christian Sarkophagi, see Lawrence 2013. 36.
142 Cf., e.g., Celsus, *Med.* 3.23.7; *Morb. sacr.* 1.12, 39; Caelius, *Chron.* 1.4.119; 1.4.130; *T.Sol.* 18:21; Pliny, *Nat.* 28–32; Kollmann 1996. 64–65; Wohlers 1999a. 216–222, 225–228, 232–233.

7.2.2.3 Summary

To conclude, this Markan account uniquely connects two previously established images of dis/ability. On the one hand, the account reprises symptoms and features of demon possession: the boy is described to be physically occupied by the spirit, who severely torments him, displayed in socially deviating behavior with a threat to the boy's life and a disparate corporality that opposes Jesus, according to Markan demonology. By drawing once again on this image, again in the body of an innocent, susceptible, and only faintly characterized child, the gospel text reprises the established cosmological dualism, at this point of the plot, however, connected to the emphatically explained divine identity of Jesus *and* his foreshadowed passion.

On the other hand, the boy shows symptoms of a "falling sicknesses" and displays a permanently disrupted ability to communicate coherently. The everyday need for verbal communication in a predominantly oral culture, especially regarding his education, puts him at a social disadvantage as he faces an incapacitated and economically limited adulthood (see 6.2), which adds to his father's desperate supplication for him.

The etiology of the boy's sensory dis/ability is made clear: he is possessed by a spirit. Muteness and deaf-/dumbness are regarded as severe but permanent symptoms of this possession and expected to be healed with an exorcism.[143]

By combining a sensory dis/ability with the etiology and extent of demon possession, Mark ironically employs a numinous force that, characteristically for the gospel, is dependent on human bodies to *sensually perceive* Jesus and *communicate* with him. While the demons in Mark 1:24 and 5:7 moreover correctly discern his divine identity as opposing and superior, the impure spirit here remains silent and even appears to be deaf to the exorcistic action of Jesus' disciples. As this common image of dis/ability is—literally—turned upside down here, the audience is like the father, demanded to *voice* their understanding of Jesus' identity (see below).

---

[143] Cf. Weissenrieder 2003. 121. See also p. 199, n. 52.

7.3 The Healings

7.3.1 Mark 8:22–26: Embodied Healing—Curative Saliva, Tactile Treatments, and an Engaging Dialogue

Jesus' healing in this narrative is characterized by three successive, tactile actions: he spits in the eyes and lays his hands on the man, specifically his eyes, and shortly converses with the patient in between the healing touches. The very tactile and sensuous treatments in the secluded setting shift the focus to the intimate and, for the blind man in particular, intelligible communication of patient and healer who is again by his sheer embodied presence able to cure the man.

    a. As Jesus' reputation precedes him, he is again approached with a request for his touch (ἅπτω), with the healing effect implied (cf. 7:32; see also 5:23; 6:5). Jesus touches the man in the following three times: Firstly, Jesus takes the man's hand and leads him out of the village. Then he applies his curative "laying-on-of-hands" twice (vv. 23, 25). While the first instance disguises which body part is touched, πάλιν in v. 25 insinuates that Jesus treats the dis/abled organs, which also aligns with the method of Mark 7:33 (see 6.2.3; C. In Focus: Mark's Healing Touches). The terminological repetition of the action reveals that Jesus does not change his "technique" after the initial, only partial, success, even if there is no saliva therapy recounted the second time around. Besides the established effect of Jesus' healing touch, his tactile healing of blindness has an additional notion for the visually impaired patient as it corresponds to his tactile sense of orientation (specifically by guiding touches, as that of Jesus) only a few verses prior.

    b. As established in the chapter on Mark 7:31–37, the use of Jesus' saliva in both accounts recalls the widely recognized curative qualities of spittle.[144] Its application here directly *in* the eyes underscores again the diminished faculty of the dis/abled organs, portrays the intimacy of the sensory treatment, and heightens the surprise when the expected healing is not immediately affected after this "charged" encounter, as in Mark 7:35. Rather, the desired result is achieved after another touch, yet without any spittle. The particular use of saliva to treat visual impairment is also attested in accounts of Tacitus, Sueton, and Dio Cassius in a narrative of Vespasian healing a blind man by the very use of his saliva.[145] Especially the account by Sueton stresses the legitimizing function of this healing for the emperor's rise to power as a result of Serapis' divine appointment. Although the Mar-

---

[144] See 6.2.3.
[145] Cf. Tacitus, *Hist.* 4.81; Suetonius, *Vesp.* 7.2–3; Philostratus, *Vit. Apoll.* 3.39; and Collins 2007. 392; von Bendemann in Zimmermann (ed.) 2013. 345–346.

kan healing is not staged as publicly, quite to the contrary, the employed notion of healing salvia in connection to touches that partake of curative power has a similar purpose as in the narratives on Vespasian as it locates the (divinely) appointed curative authority in the body of the healer. This is underscored by the fact that, unlike Mark 7:34, this account features no additional powerful command and focuses entirely on the embodied curative force of Jesus.[146]

c. Another difference to the otherwise similar and just previously recounted healing of Mark 7:31–37, which the audience will pick up on as it is not featured in other healing accounts, is the short dialogue in between the two touches. Its direct speech, which is introduced in imperfect twice, not only sets the scene for the eventually following healing but underscores the fragmentary and incomplete state of his sight as the audience is drawn into the encounter and gets to partake in this sensuous experience (see below). Moreover, it echoes common Hellenistic patient-doctor dialogues as accounted for in, e.g., Hippocratic treatise,[147] and thereby witnesses to Jesus' care and competence although the healing is not immediately effective.

7.3.2 Mark 9:14–29: Exorcistic Superiority, a Performative Passion Prediction, Prayer and *Pistis* Practice

The emphasis on Jesus' divine legitimization is picked up again in the following healing account and uniquely accentuated: while the rather common exorcistic commands echo his established superiority over the opposing, demonic realm, the treatment of the boy after the demon has left and the desperate conversation on *pistis* with the successive explanation of prayer further unravel the facete of Jesus' identity alluded to by the passion predictions.

7.3.2.1 Exorcistic Superiority

After the illustration and discussion of the boy's dis/ability and the dialogue on the necessity of *pistis* and Jesus' healing ability, Jesus successfully expels the spirit with an efficacious instruction, described with ἐπιτιμάω and ἐπιτάσσω. While both connote an order with some sort of hierarchal legitimization,[148] enforced by the strong ἐγώ – σοι opposition, ἐπιτιμάω (as already pointed out in 3.1), carries the meaning of very forceful subordination in accordance with the Markan conception

---

146 Cf. Willebrand 2017. 117–119.
147 Cf., e.g., CH, *Epid.* 1.11; von Bendemann in Zimmermann (ed.) 2013. 341.
148 For ἐπιτάσσω, cf., e.g., 1:27; 6:27.

of opposing spheres (see B. In Focus: Mark's Jesus and Opposing Forces).[149] This time, however, ἐπιτιμάω is not connected to the spirits' full-throated acknowledgment of Jesus' identity (cf. 1:25; 3:12; cf. 1:34). On the contrary, the text highlights by Jesus' extensive address that Jesus *speaks* to the *mute-muting* and *deaf-deafening* spirit, which underscores the disparate corporality and the performative power of his word: while the boy is unable to hear Jesus' words, the spirit follows them (cf. v. 26). The boy remains an unresponsive canvas physically, socially, and narratologically. He has lost his (physical) standing in the sociolinguistic practices (cf. 5.1). His body is negotiated by the narrator but also on the story level by the father, the spirit, and Jesus. Moreover, the fact that Jesus embodies his powerful ability to exorcise is heightened in comparison to the exorcisms of Mark 1:23–28 and 5:1–20: while he neither there nor here relies on additional treatments, the narrative here features no explicit reference to a cosmological hierarchy as alluded to by the ascribed sovereign titles, nor does Jesus converse with the opposing force. Rather than an executing mediator, he is depicted as sovereign exorcist in his own right.[150]

7.3.2.2 Performative Passion Prediction

After the exorcism, the boy is depicted to lose consciousness; he is regarded as dead.[151] Here, the terminology is explicitly drastic, although the audience is instructed by the narrator that the boy only appears to the crowd to be dead (ὡσεί). This sets the scene for the following "raising."

The terminology now shifts to Mark's very typical language of healing: Jesus takes the boy's hand and raises him (κρατέω τῆς χειρὸς; ἐγείρω; cf. 1:31 and 5:41). As established and also applicable here,[152] this action is used to describe Jesus' helping or calling of healed patients from their lying position.[153] In each narrative, the vertical position served as proof for the healing and encouraged re-socializing behavior,[154] in Mark 5:35 and here conversely for the *socially* stated deaths of the children.[155] Here, however, no explicit following action is named; the narrative leaves the boy standing (ἀνίστημι) with no other witnessing actions

---

[149] Cf. Wells 1998. 145–146.
[150] Cf. Strecker in Stegemann; Malina; Theissen (ed.) 2002. 61.
[151] Cf. Josephus, *A.J.* 8.47–48; Philostratus, *Vit. Apoll.* 4.20; cf. also Acts Thom. 77; Kollmann 1996. 214, n. 50.
[152] See 3.2; ch. 4 and 5.
[153] Cf. also Acts 9:40–41, but Acts 9:34 (without a helping hand).
[154] Cf. "serving" in 1:31; walking around and returning home in 2:9–12, walking around and eating in 5:41–43.
[155] Cf. literally: κρατήσας τῆς χειρός ... ἤγειρεν ... ἀνέστη.

and not even an acclamation explicated. His standing itself, in contrast to the convulsions on the ground, implies he is back in control of his body and able to conform to socially conventional postures and communication with his community. As established in ch. 4, both lexemes, ἐγείρω and ἀνίστημι, are also used to designate the resurrection from the dead.[156] An interpretation in this regard is already insinuated by the previous verse, where spectators (λέγειν ὅτι ἀπέθανεν) and the narrator (ἐγένετο ὡσεὶ νεκρός) witness different physical states. The language of the healing in v. 27 meets both conditions.[157] At this stage of the gospel plot, however, with the entire focus of the healed body hinging on ἀνίστημι concluding this dramatic ending, the connection to the surrounding passion predictions is not unreasonable (cf. esp. 8:31; 9:31; 10:34). Furthermore, within this pericope's frame of instructions to the disciples, the connection to Mark 9:9–10 is striking and shifts the meaning of the boy's raising toward a general eschatological (physical) restoration (9:12; cf. 3:5; 8:25) and a performative passion prediction. With the question τί ἐστιν τὸ ἐκ νεκρῶν ἀναστῆναι of 9:10 still lingering, the description of the boy's recovery in v. 27 serves as a rough explanatory blueprint and narratological herald for the disciples and audience, advancing the plot and raising expectation.

7.3.2.3 Prayer and *Pistis* Practice

Instead of an acclamation, the account features a unique discussion on exorcising ability between Jesus and the disciples. While their failure heightens the protagonist's healing ability,[158] it is nevertheless surprising in light of their calling, Mark 3:14–15, and 6:7, 12–13, 30. Jesus' answer, however, turns the tables again as he defers the subject from the *disciples*' not "being able to *cast out*" to the *demons*' "being able to *come out*."[159] This concurs with the fact that by the combination of a negation and εἰ μή, a strict exception in a general sense with regard to the demonic forces is expressed and not the particular treatment of the disciples referenced.[160] Astonishingly, Jesus then names προσευχή as precondition for this kind

---

156 Cf. ἐγείρω of Jesus: 14:28; 16:6; and of others: 6:14, 16; 12:26. Cf. BDAG, s.v.; Klaiber, *ἐγείρω*; Kremer, *ἐγείρω*; Kremer, *ἀνάστασις and cogn*; Kuhn, *ἀνάστασις and cogn*; LN, s.v. 17.10, 17.9, 23.77, 13.83, 23.94, 13.65, 23.140; LSJ, s.v.; Montanari, s.v.; Oepke, *ἐγείρω*; Oepke, *ἀνίστημι/ἐξανίστημι*.
157 See also 5.2.3.
158 See this common motif in ancient healing narratives in, e.g., 2Kgs 4:29–31; Lucian, *Philops.* 35–36; Aelian, *Nat. An.* 9.33; Tob 2:10; Philostratus, *Vit. Apoll.* 4.45; Weinreich 1909. 81–87, 195–196; Kollmann 1996. 213, n. 45.; Edelstein; Edelstein 1998. No. 422 (1.220–21).
159 Hofius 2004. 134.
160 Cf. ibid. 134; cf. 2:26; 5:37; 6:4, 8; 10:18; 11:13.

of demon to come out,[161] which as the final word of the narrative has a lasting effect on the audience. As Jesus himself did not explicitly pray but called the spirit to *come out* (also ἐξέρχομαι, v. 26) by his embodied forceful command,[162] the effective praying action must refer to the emphatic dialogue with the father as the only passage of the narrative that depicts a turning point and alludes to a precondition for the following healing.[163] Hence, the text does not contrast the failing disciples and the non-praying, yet effective, Jesus. If anything, it connects this general statement in v. 29 with the other central and universal utterance on the omnipotence of those who practice *pistis*. This interweaves the motifs of powerful possibilities with *pistis* practice (ἰσχύω in v. 18 and ὦ γενεὰ ἄπιστος in v. 19; δύναμαι in v. 22, twice in v. 23 with πιστεύω/ ἀπιστία in v. 23 and twice in v. 24; cf. also 2:5 and 2:7; cf. also Mark 3:20–35) and prayer (δύναμαι in vv. 28, 29, and προσευχή in v. 29). Accordingly, the text insinuates that the *supplicant*'s call for help in vv. 22 and 24 can be regarded as the all-changing prayer and necessity for the spirit to leave. As *pistis* practice was established to be relative according to an understanding of Jesus' identity (G. In Focus: Mark's Relational *Pistis*), it does not have to be an either v. 22 or v. 24. Rather, in the gospel context, his primary approach of Jesus already establishes *pistis* in his healing ability *and* mercy,[164] which is then enforced and heightened in the father's positive and *pistis*-practicing reply to the generalizing extension of Jesus' πάντα. Quite literally, the father is *pistis* practicing in the sense of exercising and rehearsing; the successive healing in v. 25 then shows that precisely this is "adequate."[165] Jesus is not the subject but the object of the prayer, which concurs with his divine, superior opposition to the unclean spirit (cf. then 11:22–25), with his characteristic mercy (cf. 1:40–45; 5:19),[166] and with the use of commended and requested *pistis* practice in other Markan healing narratives that always refers to the supplicant and never to Jesus.[167] Thereof, a potential specification of demonic entities as suggested by τοῦτο τὸ γένος (v. 29) eludes the generality of Jesus' statement, which concurs with the not particularly defined or organized Markan demonology. Rather, Jesus' conclusive definition refers to the nature of those enti-

---

161 Some textual witnesses add και νηστεια and thereby a possibly "later ecclesiastical emphasis," Marcus 2009. 655; cf. also Mark 2:19–20.
162 Cf. also his solitary and non-specific prayer in Mark 1:35; 6:46; also 14:32–42; and quite differently, 1Kgs 17:21; 2Kgs 4:33; *bHag* 3a; *bBer* 34b.
163 Cf. Lindemann in Lindemann (ed.) 2009. 107.
164 Cf. Mark 1:41, see 3.3; and Mark 6:34 and 8:2, and ἔλεος in Mark 10:47–48.
165 Nicklas 2001. 511.
166 Cf. similar calls for divine mercy in, e. g., Ps 44:26; 60:11; 108:12; 123:2–3; Sir 36:1; 2Chr 14:11; Add Est 14:14. Cf. also Marcus 2009. 660–661.
167 Cf. esp., Mark 2:5; 5:34; 6:5–6; 9:23–24; 10:52.

ties opposed to him, the only superior force and recipient of such relational *pistis* prayer. The previously lamented ἄπιστος generation[168] (v. 19) then encompasses the father by his admitted ἀπιστία and the disciples since v. 19 can be read as a direct retort to their incapability to help the father and their lack of *pistis* has been called out before (cf. Mark 4:40 and 8:17–18). The Markan Jesus might also include the scribes with reference to Mark 8:12 and/or the crowd with reference to 8:38.[169] According to the Markan syntactical style, αὐτοῖς refers to those αὐτούς, whom Jesus addresses in the beginning of the dialogue, namely the crowd, including the father (v. 16).[170] This underscores again the father's representative position as "one of the crowd," which then powerfully concludes the fundamental character of Jesus' central claim (v. 23) and interpretative teaching (v. 29). Together with Jesus' introductory lament of his indispensability at this point of his ministry (v. 19), the focus on another demonic defeat and the insinuation of his healing divine embodiment—also regarding the connection of prayer and omnipotence—heightens the relevance and adequacy of *pistis* practice to a historical and even cosmological event, which fits the setting and position in the gospel plot.

Following on the transfiguration, in a section in constant anticipation of the subsequent passion, filled with debate and teaching over Jesus' identity, the audience has witnessed another, and insofar the most extensive, teaching on the omnipotent power of relational *pistis* practice also available to them. This is underscored by the successive treatment of successful exorcisms in Jesus' name in 9:38–39, the commended *pistis*-practicing approach of blind Bartimaeus in 10:52, and the final conclusive teachings on *pistis* in 11:20–25 and 14:36, with finally and explicitly God as the central object of all possible power and salvific will.

7.3.3 Mark 10:46–52: Salvific *Pistis* Practice, Inspiring Insight, and Discipleship

As established, Mark 10:46–52 then exhibits another *pistis*-practicing character. In accordance with Mark 2:5 and 5:34, the knowledge of Jesus and an active and obstinate pursuit of him against opposing crowds (or as in the case of Mark 9:22–24,

---

168 Cf. Matt 17:17/Luke 9:41, that also add διεστραμμένη as a designation to generation. Cf. Deut 32:5, 30^{LXX} and Num 14:27.
169 Cf. Nicklas 2001. 509–510, n. 48. For the interpretation that Jesus calls on all who are present, cf. Leutzsch in Zimmermann (ed.) 2013. 352, or on all questioners (disciples, crowd, and/or father), cf. Marcus 2009. 653; Focant 2012. 369.
170 As Hofius 2004. 122, n. 27, analyzed precisely: The dative object always refers to the direct counterpart(s) of those responding not surrounding characters (cf., e.g., 3:33; 10:51; 11:33; 15:2; furthermore, 6:37; 7:28; 8:4, 29; 10:3, 24; 11:22; 12:34; 15:9, 12).

against initial failure) illustrate this *pistis* practice. Particularly, the phrase ἡ πίστις σου σέσωκέν σε of v. 52 echoes verbatim the healing of the woman with the issue of blood when Jesus now commends persistent blind Bartimaeus. Here, however, the utterance is made *prior* to the healing and due to the lack of any other curative treatment, takes on a performative meaning along with the preceding ὕπαγε (cf. εὐθύς). The first part of Jesus' utterance and send-off also recalls elements of previous narratives, namely the similarly succinct healing of Mark 2:11 (cf. also 7:29) and Jesus' commands *after* the healings regarding the social reintegration of the healed characters and the dis- or encouraged proclamation of him and his healing ability (cf. 1:44; 5:19, 34; 8:26).

Moreover, Bartimaeus' *pistis* practice is illustrated not only in its tenacity but also in the trust he has in Jesus, to be ἔλεος, Ιησοῦς ὁ Ναζαρηνός, υἱὲ Δαυίδ, and ῥαββουνί. The first designation of Jesus' name with reference to his hometown (v. 47) not only unequivocally identifies him but also signifies his reputation[171] and refers to the first healing narrative in the gospel, where he is recognized as such by the unclean spirit (1:24; cf. also 5:7; 14:67; 16:6). In addition, the plea for Jesus' mercy (ἔλεος, vv. 47, 48) recalls one of the first programmatic encounters where his benevolence is emotionally discussed and established in his cure of *lepra* (1:40–45, see 3.3). Moreover, Jesus himself characterizes his healing of the Gerasene demoniac as an expression of ἔλεος in Mark 5:19 (see 5.1). By connecting name, hometown, and the ability to be merciful, Bartimaeus' recognition proves to be in accordance with what the audience knows and has witnessed from the first healings on.

Then, however, Bartimaeus tries to get Jesus' attention by calling him twice "Son of David" (vv. 47, 48). As these are the first occurrences of this designation in the gospel, a concrete Markan contextualization is limited to allusions to similar addresses, its traditional connotations, and most of all its narrative function here. Regarding the last, it is difficult to evaluate the accuracy of Bartimaeus' utterance. It is striking that neither the narrator, nor the Markan Jesus, nor God or a heavenly voice confirms, encourages, or rejects this title.[172] The fact that Jesus does not silence the loud address could be explained by its faultiness in contrast to the accurate designations of the demonic entities (cf. 1:24–25, 34; 5:7 and 5:13), or as a silent acceptance since it is *not* spoken by an opposing force but a character in need, and/or because it is accurate and fits the increasing revelation of Jesus' identity at this point in the plot. Moreover, Jesus listens and answers the man's request because of

---

[171] Cf. 1:9, 24; moreover, Broadhead 1993; Collins 2007. 509.
[172] Cf. Malbon 2009. 147, 167.

or—compassionately—despite this designation, *or* because Bartimaeus promptly changes his approach to "rabbouni."[173] Due to the ambiguity of the man's dis/ability, also his blindness, status, and position, παρὰ τὴν ὁδόν, can either be taken as a criterium to discredit his address (cf. 4:4, 15)[174] or as a contrasting, even prophetic, insight in accordance with a generous interpretation of his *pistis* practice (see below).[175] Therefore, it is not out of the question that by this designation, the healing account (also) alludes to Salomon, "Son of David," a great exorcist and healer.[176] In any case, Bartimaeus' recognition of Jesus "of Nazareth" as reprised in his call is undisputable, and his own introduction by patronym and name in the same unusual succession, υἱὸς Τιμαίου Βαρτιμαῖος, parallels and therefore highlights the designation υἱὲ Δαυίδ Ἰησοῦ, which the narrative otherwise leaves unexplained.[177] Neither prior (2:23–28) nor successive (11:1–11; 12:35–37) passages unequivocally clarify the gospel's stance on Jesus' representation in Davidic lineage; neither does contextual literature of the time.[178] Again, the audience is left to confirm and interpret the connection of the ὁ υἱὸς τοῦ ἀνθρώπου,[179] ὁ υἱὸς τοῦ θεοῦ (τοῦ ὑψίστου; 3:11; 5:7; cf. also 1:24) with the confirmed ὁ υἱός μου ὁ ἀγαπητός (1:11; 9:7), which will moreover be complemented by ὁ χριστὸς ὁ υἱὸς τοῦ εὐλογητοῦ in 14:61 and ὁ ἄνθρωπος υἱὸς θεοῦ ἦν in 15:39.

Thirdly, Bartimaeus addresses Jesus in his final request with the rare Aramaic lexeme "rabbouni," which, like the more frequently employed "rabbi" (cf. 9:5; 11:21; 14:45) and the numerous mentions of διδάσκαλος (4:38; 5:35; 9:17, 38; 10:17, 20, 35; 12:14, 19, 32; 13:1; 14:14), reflects the respected position of a teacher. In its untranslated Aramaic form here, it carries an additionally intimate note, especially after all the rather dramatic yelling.[180] This address also shifts the focus from Jesus' be-

---

173 Cf. also the continuation of this idea as "anti-kingship" or "anti-imperialistic" in Horsley 2001. 23, 236–253, esp. 251.
174 Cf. esp. Boring 2006. 305.
175 Cf., e.g., Beavis 1998. 27; Lawrence 2011. 391; Focant 2012. 437.
176 Cf. also *T.Sol.* 20:1, 22:2–3, *4Esr* 6:25–26; 7:26–29; 13:49–50.
177 Cf. 1:1, 24; 5:7; 10:47a; 16:6; but 14:67. Maybe the blind man's name is also employed as an un-/intended allusion to Plato's encomium *Timaeus*, another story on eyesight and insight which would imply a symbolic function of the name, similar to that of the named demon "Legion" in Mark 5:9, cf. Iersel; Nuchelmans 1995; Hilgert in Mack; Castelli; Taussig (ed.) 1996. 191; Iersel 1998. 340–341.
178 See Botner 2017b, on the rich history of research of the so-called "Davidssohnfrage" and his promising suggestion to not only include references to David but search the gospel text more broadly for allusions to a Davidic tradition.
179 See *Excursus: The Markan "Son of Man"*, p. 119–120, and 2:10, 28; 8:31, 38; 9:9, 12, 31; 10:33, 45; 13:26.
180 Iersel 1998. 343, furthermore suggests, that "if, for the reader, the son of Timaeus [as allusion to Plato's dialogue] represents Greek culture, the title rabbouni points to the story's affinity with the Jewish world."

nevolent power to his teachings, especially regarding the increasing frequency of these designations in the end of the gospel narrative. This aligns well with the narrative's other allusions to discipleship. For one, the text recalls elements of narratives that depict Jesus' call to discipleship, namely a passing-by Jesus who encounters named characters in their everyday tasks and encourages them to leave their life behind (here, the cloak as image for his livelihood, similar to boats, nets, tollhouse, and κτήματα πολλά/χρήματα; by contrast, 10:17–22) and "follow" him (Mark 1:16–18; 1:19–20; 2:14).[181] Moreover, by employing the term ἀκολουθέω, the account echoes the teaching on discipleship of 8:34–38, especially v. 34, and by the multilayered term ὁδός, calls on surrounding debates of the disciples about Jesus' identity, teachings, and passion (cf. 8:27; 9:33, 34; 10:17, 32; cf. 10:46, 52). While the Gerasene demoniac was not allowed to follow Jesus (cf. 5:18–19; cf. also 3:14), now, as Jesus' identity is continuously revealed (cf. esp. the transfiguration) and connected to his ministry, teaching, and passion, "the audience know that 'to follow Jesus on the way' means to follow him to suffering and death."[182]

As powerfully established in the narrative of Mark 5:21–43 and according to the (particularly in 9:14–29) established relational and ranging *pistis*, here as well the *pistis*-practicing character is employed to encourage the disciples and thus the audience to participate in *pistis* practice according to their understanding of Jesus and his identity, here with increasing importance of the incipient passion (9:32; 10:32 and finally 16:8). This finds corroboration in the image of dis/ability as a spectrum of insight—ambiguously ranging from auditory hearsay to prophetic wisdom—and the threefold address of Jesus according to the advanced point in the plot: Jesus of Nazareth is pursued as a renowned healer, but he is also recognized for his historical and possibly cosmological significance due to his mighty heritage, which may include messianic allusions. In any case, he is a personal and intimate helper and teacher who is worthy of continuous following (imperfect) on a path that is predicted and will be revealed in due course to be arduous yet soteriological. Particularly Mark 11:22–24, 31 further enforces the soteriological and Christological notions already alluded to by Bartimaeus' *pistis* plea and *salvific* transformation as Jesus and his mission are explicitly recognized to be aligned with God.[183]

---

[181] Cf. Culpepper 1982; Focant 2012. 437; Moss in Melcher; Parsons; Yong (ed.) 2018. 295.
[182] Collins 2007. 511. Cf. Achtemeier 1978; Menken 2005, who interpret Bartimaeus as an ideal disciple.
[183] Mark 11 reprises several motifs: reference to David (10:47–48 and 11:10); "cry" of blind man and crowd (10:47–48 and 11:9); large crowds (10:48; 11:8); cloaks (10:50; 11:7–8); "go" (10:52; 11:2).

7.3.4 Summary

All three healing narratives focus on the embodied and communicable healing force of Jesus. Building on the previously established characteristic of his curative touch and mighty command, his intrinsic healing is heightened when Mark 8:22–26 elaborates on his healing by bodily saliva, when Mark 9:14–29 discusses his divinity via omnipotence, prayer, and exorcistic verbal superiority, and when Mark 10:46–52 employs the *pistis*-practicing attributions of Bartimaeus and a healing without any curative treatments whatsoever. The sensuous language of the texts underscores the motif of the experienceable healer Jesus.

Furthermore, it is striking that neither account portrays an acclamation, response, or reaction to the successful treatments. Rather, they display the events from ranging perspectives and focus at length on engaging dialogues in direct speech between Jesus and the patient or supplicant. Particularly the latter is enforced by three imperfects that introduce direct speech as markers of open and incomplete utterances until answered with great rhetoric effect and also, similar to the use of the present tense, reduce the perceived distance to the narrated world and thereby set the scene for the following responsive actions and each narrative's characteristic twist (see *Excursus: Tenses in the Gospel of Mark*, p. 22–24).[184] Moreover, in these accounts on ranges of (sensory) perception and gradual healing, the dialogues underscore precisely the fragmentary states in between until powerfully resolved: In Mark 8:23–24, Jesus *asks* what the man sees, and he *answers* by stating his partial healing; then he is effectively made able to see. In Mark 9:24, the man *states* his *pistis* with a plea for help with his incomplete *pistis*, and his son is healed. Then in 9:28, the disciples *inquire* about their inadequate ability to exorcise that Jesus answers with the need for prayer; and in Mark 10:48, the conative debate between the clamorous Bartimaeus and the silencing crowd is dramatically disrupted by their change of heart (present tense) and Bartimaeus' henceforth durative following (imperfect, v. 52 in contrast to ἐκάθητο in v. 46).

---

[184] Cf. Willebrand 2017. 125; different to Zerwick 1937. 62, who interprets the imperfect in Mark 8:24 and 9:24 as implications of hesitation, which then, however, would imply an also hesitant Jesus in the same section (8:23; cf. also the unfitting characterization of the frustrated disciples in 9:28) as Zerwick does not seem to differentiate interrogative verbs (ἐπηρώτα/ἐπηρώτων; 8:23; also 9:28) from more general verbs of saying (ἔλεγεν in 8:24; 9:24). Moreover, the interpretation of the temporal shift in both instances as indications of something "permanently valid" put forward by Willebrand 2017. 125, only works if extended beyond the utterances because they depict *temporary* descriptions that are, however, about to change permanently (cf. esp. the imperfect in 8:25).

In accordance with the vivid and sensuously dense style of the accounts, the narrator seems to create a void after the all the more exuberant and guiding acclamation of 7:37 and let the audience participate and establish an opinion on Jesus' identity, especially in light of the looming passion.

7.4 Conclusion and Interpretation of Dis/ability in Mark 8–10

7.4.1 Summaric Healing

As the gospel plot prepares for its final sequence, so do the three narratives by drawing connecting and thereby summarizing lines to many of the previously recounted healing narratives. Beginning with Mark 1:23–31 and its focus on both possession and sickness, Mark 9:14–29 manages to broach both by using its typical language to describe the boy's recovery: not only is the boy possessed by an unclean spirit (1:23, 26, 27), with a variety of symptoms relatable to other dis/abilities, but the spirit is expelled (1:25) *and* the boy is risen from his state of impairment (1:30–31). Moreover, Mark 9:22 and 10:47–48 reprise the programmatic introduction of Jesus as a benevolent healer from Mark 1:40–45, when the supplicants call on Jesus' mercy (cf. also Mark 5:19).

Moreover, the holistic and eschatological nuance of physical integrity is reprised in accordance with Mark 2–3 and Mark 5:21–43. In the prior Jesus is similarly depicted to help paralyzed limbs to rise in order to contrast incomprehensive hardened hearts, elaborate on redemptive *pistis* (esp. 2:5), and unfold an eschatological horizon. In the latter Jesus also raises a helpless bedridden child believed to be dead and the healings challenge salvific *pistis*.

Furthermore, the intrinsic healing body of Jesus is accentuated, similar to Mark 5, with its vivid accounts on contrasting body-encompassing possession and divine superiority, emanating astonishing power, and intimate communication.

Additionally, the narration on the disciples' healing ministry established in Mark 6:7, 12–13, 30 is continued in Mark 9:14–29, and the final three healing narratives take up and diligently elaborate on the transition of Jesus' ministry (introduced in Mark 7) with conclusive elements that emphasize spiritual comprehension of Jesus and his message with images of spiritual and sensory dis/ability.

By these (exemplary listed) references to previous accounts, the audience is able to connect Mark's narrative conception of Jesus' identity and mission, his teachings of discipleship and *pistis*, and his struggle with the evil sphere, as witnessed in his astonishing embodied healing power, with the following and frequently foreshadowed suffering and death.

7.4.2 Beyond Binary

It is striking that the Markan gospel compiles three images of deviating sensual perception together at the end of the section on Jesus' active ministry. While each dis/abled body reveals unique characteristics important for the individual storyline, they share three commonalities that are of particular importance for the development of the Markan plot:

a. They are ambiguous. The degrees of visual perception and the effect the deaf-mute demon has on the boy range, as do the socio-anthropological implications attached to the images of dis/abilities—either implicitly by Markan standards and/or cultural convention or explicitly by narrative invention. The characters and (by that) the audience navigate between silent possession and raucous sickness, disparate corporality and disparate a-*pistis*, solicitous supplication and societal silencing, pitied poverty and honored enlightenment, hazy trees and precise *pistis*. Despite the intimate encounters and concretely anchored settings, the gospel text generalizes the healings by peripheral locations and, particularly in combination, indistinct ailments of paradigmatic characters. On the one hand, the images of dis/ability are easily applicable to a range of experiences and serve as facile identification with the dis/abled characters; on the other hand, they demand sensuous attention.

b. More than in any other account, the three narratives focus on the sensory perception of Jesus by the characters of the narratives and the audience. As sensory faculty can only be evaluated by its perceiving subject; the point of view of the characters with the impaired organs becomes of central importance for the audience and is, however, emphatically witnessed when Jesus' omnipotent power is displayed with the cognitive- and sensory-impaired body of the boy. Since these representations of sensory impairment are moreover depicted in concentrated narratives on tactile, visionary, and auditory cures and perception, the audience is led to a sensuous experience of the embodied healing power of Jesus. By additionally reprising established motifs of previously recounted healing narratives (see above), Jesus' embodied healing power is concentrated in comprehensive and holistic cures only to be contrasted by annunciations of his suffering and dematerialization.[185]

c. In this ambiguity, these images of dis/ability and their healing furthermore transcend any binary of sickness and health.

Firstly, the inherent and described degrees of sensory impairment already establish a range of deviance that eludes such a strict binary.

---

[185] Cf. Moss in Melcher; Parsons; Yong (ed.) 2018. 299.

Secondly, the text continues to insinuate through the employed images of healed physical integrity, cognitive insight beyond the visually perceivable, eschatological restoration, resurrection, and salvation (see above).

Thirdly, the sensory engagement of the audience and focus on the perception of Jesus' identity in the entire section indicate an (additional) symbolic understanding of the described dis/abilities: as established, blindness and deafness are often in ancient texts and the gospel narrative employed in a transferred sense of ignorance, poor discernment, weak comprehension, diminished apprehension, and resulting misconduct.[186] As briefly outlined in the introduction, in this section's ultimately preceding passage after the impressive feeding of the 4,000, Jesus calls out his opponents' (8:10–13) and his disciples' (8:14–21) obtuseness when the prior demand a legitimizing sign of his identity and the latter disregard his powerful provision. With three dis/ability invective images, Jesus calls out their ignorance: As the hardened heart was first introduced as a characteristic of Jesus' opponents (3:5), 6:52 diagnoses the disciples with a hardened heart in light of their lack of insight (συνίημι) into Jesus' mighty identity (cf. esp. 6:48, ἡ καρδία πεπωρωμένη). This is reprised in Jesus' rant in 8:17 and complemented by an echo of Jer 5:21, which adds the inability to see and hear despite the possession of necessary organs (8:18) to describe the disciples' incapability to still not (οὔπω, vv. 17, 21) understand (νοέω, 17), comprehend (συνίημι, vv. 17, 21), and remember (μνημονεύω, v. 18)—imagery already applied earlier to those not able to understand Jesus' esoteric teachings (4:10–13; cf. also 7:17–18).[187] The frequent use of direct speech, the harshness of Jesus' language, and these concrete references to previously narrated events must engage the audience.[188] Then the succeeding passages reveal that the disciples' incomprehension concerns their imperfect understanding of Jesus' identity,[189] which is frequently, and also explicitly sensuously, revealed and affirmed (Peter's confession in 8:27–30; the transfiguration in 9:2–8 and 9:12–13[190]; and insinuations in 9:37; 10:18, 27), complemented with explicit references to Jesus' passion (8:31; 9:31–32; 10:33–34), and disclosed with the meaning of true discipleship (8:33–9:1; 9:33–50; 10:41–45). Precisely in this dense and some-

---

[186] A subordination of one or the other is futile here as the narratives explicitly focus on a protagonist that engages with several senses. Additionally, it needs to be emphasized that after all, the Markan text is a non-visual, literary medium mainly to be heard. Cf. Mitchell; Snyder 2001. 53; Weissenrieder 2003. 117, n. 204; von Bendemann in Härle; Preul (ed.) 2005. 55–56.
[187] Cf. Glenney; Noble 2014. 81.
[188] Cf. also Johnson 1978–79. 379.
[189] Cf. also Jesus' family and hometown in 3:21, 31–35; 6:1–6.
[190] Cf. von Bendemann in Zimmermann (ed.) 2013. 346. See also the elaborate, yet maybe far-fetched analysis of Hilgert in Mack; Castelli; Taussig (ed.) 1996.

what summaric section of Jesus' entire ministry, the three final healing narratives feature an intriguing interplay of *relational* and *imperfect pistis* with ranging sensory dis/ability and powerful encounters with Jesus' intrinsic healing divinity contrasted by passion predictions. When reading the three narratives together, this then shifts the entire debate from a binary opposition of "incomprehension" vs. "full illumination"[191] to a correspondence of ranges of (in)sight and *pistis* practice that indeed is "synchronic and dialectic rather than diachronic and quantitative."[192] Even if the gospel casts a timeframe or "evolution"[193] of the disciples' comprehension on a story level (cf. maybe 13:9–13), perhaps with regard to the resurrection,[194] the audience is left with a dematerialized protagonist at the end of the narrative. Without any sensuously perceivable incarnation of the healing, suffering, or even resurrected Jesus, the audience is directed to start again at the beginning in corresponding, relative, and ranging *pistis* practice.[195]

Fourthly and conclusively, the final healing narrative of the Gospel unhinges all presupposed notions of normed able-bodiedness when Jesus, against all established Markan conventions, asks blind Bartimaeus: τί σοι θέλεις ποιήσω. The Markan Jesus swiftly disregards the supposed deviating physicality of the man and thereby shifts the focus of the gospel's stance on dis/ability to a simple message of self-determination, recognition, and relationship (i.e., *pistis* practice; cf. 10:36), notwithstanding the narratively evident dis/ability.

Consequently, the gospel's final encounter negates notions regarding a striving for an erasure of dis/ability in Jesus' ministry, discipleship, or eschatological teaching. Rather, together with the two preceding narratives, it continues to employ dis/ability invective imagery to illustrate Jesus' identity, ministry, and message and here, quite literally, also their precise comprehension. In the process, however, the section also enforces already established Markan conceptions, namely that healing encompasses a liberation from affliction, a societal reintegration, and a transformation of spiritual cognition and communication, literally or as powerful imagery for Jesus' ministry.

---

[191] Collins 2007. 394.
[192] Boring 2006. 234.
[193] Focant 2012. 328.
[194] Cf. Collins 2007. 395.
[195] Cf. von Bendemann in Härle; Preul (ed.) 2005. 68–69.

8 Conclusion: This Is (Not) the End ...

This investigation started with the claim that the Gospel of Mark relies on dis/ability to establish the divine identity of its protagonist and his appointed εὐαγγέλιον. However, the analysis of these representations of physical deviances in each narrative setting, against their cultural backdrop and along the narrative arc, revealed an even greater function in three regards: Firstly, the representations of dis/ability not only correspond in their *distinct* depiction with the message of their individual healing narratives but trace and enforce the gospel plot. Moreover, the dis/abled characters in particular engage the audience to reflect and respond to the gospel message. Mark is a gospel of dis/ability (8.1). Secondly, it has proven correct that the gospel text hinges Jesus' authority in large on his healing ability. More so, the investigation has shown that the images of dis/ability employed refine the characterization of the very physical protagonist Jesus in distinct ways (8.2). Thirdly, the analysis of dis/ability has revealed central paradigms of the Markan normalizing body scheme and by its ambiguous allusions shed light on his concept of salvation. Upon exposing this rhetoric as almost exclusively dis/ability invective, the close historical reading of deviating bodies revealed another dimension that focuses on critiquing dis/abling factors, such as social pathologization, on re-evaluating them against creational and eschatological standards, and on interlacing them with suffering as a *self-acclaimed* criterion yet elusive trajectory regarding Jesus' ministry and mission. In this regard, Markan dis/ability eludes a binary (8.3).

8.1 Mark as a Gospel of Dis/ability and Relational *Pistis*

The comprehensive investigation of images of dis/ability in each Markan healing narrative has proven that these accounts and their distinct depictions of bodies not only reflect but structure and develop the gospel's plot.

As already established, Mark's final three healing narratives share common descriptions with the initial accounts of Mark 1, namely Jesus' benevolence,[1] his superiority over unclean spirits,[2] and his ability to raise patients from their horizontal passivity.[3] These then frame the intermediary accounts as fixed characteristics of this gospel section before the passion narrative unfolds. Moreover, the healing narratives and their elected images of dis/ability are significantly involved

---

[1] Cf. 1:40–41; 9:22; 10:47–48; also 5:19.
[2] Cf. 1:23–27; 9:14–29; also 5:1–20; 7:24–30.
[3] Cf. 1:30–31; 9:27; also 5:41–42.

in the development of the plot as they are employed to a) introduce Jesus and define his mission and message (Mark 1, Mark 2–3, Summaric accounts); b) characterize his opponents and inaugurate the conspiracy against him (Mark 2–3); c) refine his intriguing divine identity (Mark 5) and illustrate his message and ministry (Mark 7) while d) purposefully engaging the audience to participate in his call for *pistis* practice and for comprehension of his dynamic identity and holistic salvation (Mark 8–10). Of course, this attribution to individual chapters is not selective as each narrative more or less contributes to these individual points. However, the listed sections by chapters particularly enforce these themes and thereby structure the plot accordingly: Jesus' identity and programmatic healing ministry (see below) is established in Mark 1 in accordance with his teaching and appointment. Already the first healing, the exorcism in the Synagogue in Capernaum explicitly connects these threads. Along with the primary summaric accounts, the first Markan chapters focus on general and universal images of dis/ability that depict acute conditions with possibly permanent effects. Relatable as they are, they inaugurate the benevolent and astonishingly powerful protagonist as an approachable and tangible healer and become reason for his far- and fast-spreading public ministry.[4] They then introduce and contrast the opposing hardened front to his stirring movement by vivid visualization of his teachings,[5] which initiates the conspiracy against Jesus and thereby the suspenseful and fatal storyline. Moreover, the images of dis/ability give a continuous and literally "in-depth" characterization of Jesus' divine identity as he engages and physically corresponds with progressively more complex and detailed clinical pictures by increasingly elaborate healings. While Mark 1–3 mainly labeled the dis/abilities and established more or less generally the opposing demonic influences (i.e., πυρετός, λεπρός, παραλυτικός, man with a withered—ξηραίνω—hand, and ἄνθρωπος ἐν πνεύματι ἀκαθάρτῳ with a few minor characteristic symptoms), Mark 5 depicts descriptive deviating symptoms and implications of its representations of dis/ability that particularly reflect and unravel more of Jesus' dynamic identity (see below 8.2). His intrinsic healing power is then transferred to his disciples and those ministering in his name,[6] as the narrative legitimizes his ministry and its reach in preparation of the protagonist's death.[7] As such, the deviating bodies foreshadow the passion narrative as they account for Jesus' withdrawal, stage his passion predictions, and exemplify spiritual comprehension and a continuous intelligible communication of his message (see

---

[4] Cf. esp. 1:33; 1:45; 2:12; 3:7–12.
[5] Cf. 2:1–12 and 3:1–6; see below.
[6] Cf. 6:7, 12–13, 30; 9:14–29, 38–39.
[7] Cf., e.g., 7:24–30, and 9:19.

below 8.3).⁸ Paradigmatic for this is the account of the boy with the deafening and muting, impure, and violent spirit and his *pistis*-practicing (also in the sense of rehearsing), petitioning father. Right after the transfiguration and embedded in debates over Jesus' identity and predications of his passion, allusions to an elusive timeframe of Jesus' ministry are underscored by another demonic defeat according to his divine, omnipotent superiority as he moreover raises the boy from his rumored death. Thereby, the hopeless and helpless case refines the Markan paradigms of *pistis* practice to an event with historical and cosmic importance and audience participation considering the setting.

If strung together without the intermediary sections, the Markan healing narratives would give a sufficient account of the basic gospel plot until its climax: the protagonist, his entourage, and his message are engagingly characterized, as are his opponents who scheme against him and his ever-growing ministry as something suspenseful is announced.

Even more so, the images of dis/ability color in these rough sketches by conveying central aspects of Jesus' εὐαγγέλιον: For one, the healings are intrinsically connected to Jesus' teachings as witnesses of his authority, legitimacy, and dynamic identity (see below 8.2). Secondly, in their programmatic onset in Mark 1, the images of dis/ability depict a spatiality that alludes to a (cosmic) retreat of suffering and of the demonic realm as Jesus, quite literally, reaches out. This territorial shift is then repeatedly displayed in the accounted exorcisms. Thirdly, the dis/abled characters embody theological debates and are deployed to define Jesus' authoritative teachings as also superior of the demonic realm,⁹ as deviating from common religious legal issues,¹⁰ as an inclusive and personal aspect of his ministry.¹¹ In this, the dis/abled bodies are not only empty display dummies but witnesses in their distinct clinical pictures and literary setting to concrete motifs and characteristics.

Most importantly and, for that matter, continuously and without many side references needed, the dis/abled characters *embody* the gospel's messages of relational *pistis* practice and holistic salvation. The term *embody* thereby reflects that the narratives use the deviating characters and witnesses of the healings as examples and "promoters" of *pistis* practice as they testify to Jesus' uncontainable and increasingly revealed divine healing ability and identity on the story level, as the

---

8 Cf. 7:31–37; 8:22–26; 10:46–52.
9 Cf. the possessed and liberated bodies in 1:21–28, 32–34, 39; 3:7–12, 20–30; 5:1–20; 9:14–29.
10 Which is portrayed in his questionable treatment of an impure condition (1:40–45) and his controversial Sabbath healings (3:1–6, cf. also 1:21–31, 32–34).
11 As indicated by the transmission of his ministry to his disciples in 6:7, 12–13 and 9:14–29, 38–39; personal negotiations of its reach in 7:24–30; and comprehension and consequential discipleship in 10:46–52.

accounts are at the same time themselves demonstrations of the validity of this *pistis* practice promoting to μετανοεῖτε καὶ πιστεύετε ἐν τῷ εὐαγγελίῳ (1:15) to the audience. The characters' understanding of Jesus and his identity is, according to that of the audience, measured by the position of their encounter in the plot: Due to his reputation, Jesus is actively pursued as a renowned healer against outer or inner obstacles and against miscomprehending characters who voice uncertainty regarding his abilities. The carriers of the man who cannot walk make their way through the roof of a house; the woman with the issue of blood touches Jesus in a pushing throng, with doubting disciples and in emotional turmoil; and Bartimaeus persistently drowns the hushing voices.[12] At the same time, Jesus' characterization is continuously refined as his deeds are connected to, for instance, the declaration of forgiveness of sins as the Son of Man (2:1–12), notions of eschatological transformations (5:21–43, see below 8.3), his transfiguration, and passion predictions (9:14–29). In the gospel's final healing narrative, Bartimaeus' addresses sum this up as Jesus is approached as a personal and benevolent helper and teacher (ἔλεος, Ιησοῦς ὁ Ναζαρηνός, ῥαββουνί), as well as someone of historical and cosmic, perhaps even messianic, importance (υἱὲ Δαυίδ) in midst of the gospel's display of relative and relational *pistis* practice as visualized by ranging sensory dis/abilities.[13] As such, the gospel prompts and engagingly explicates the powerful possibilities of *pistis* practice also as a response to the gospel itself,[14] and the deviating characters function as points of reference for the audience: their personal and relatable conditions of suffering, liberation, and healing are disclosed to identify, participate, comprehend, experience, and finally witness to the tangible healer in contrast to hardened incomprehension or rejections of certain character groups and entire areas.[15] As the gospel transitions to the passion narrative, the final healings involve the audience in a captivating testimony of degrees of comprehension and abilities to testify, as the accounts on tactile, visionary, and auditory perception demand sensuous attention themselves and are narrated from multiple perspectives with particularly engaging features to be concluded and acclaimed by the audience. Jesus' intrinsic healing is illustrated in contrast to the annunciations of his suffering and dematerialization.

Images of dis/ability structure the Gospel of Mark in its basic plot development, define central characters and messages, and serve as vivid reference points for the audience. As such, deviating bodies create a basis that the following passion

---

12 Cf. explicitly Mark 2:5–9; 5:30–34, and 10:48–52; cf. also 6:5–6.
13 Cf. finally, Mark 11:22–24, 31.
14 Cf. esp. 2:1–12; 5:21–43; 9:14–29.
15 Cf., e.g., 3:5; 5:17; 8:17–18.

narrative draws upon regarding its soteriological and Christological significance for characters and audience alike.[16]

8.2 The Physical Protagonist and His Dynamic Identity

The deviating characters indeed "prop up the divine healer's authority and power and support the narrative's truth claims"[17] over the course of the Markan storyline. Nevertheless, this basic function is nuanced again by the distinct pictures of dis/ability, which reveal a *dynamic* characterization of the protagonist.

a) Generally, Jesus is introduced and validated as the benevolent, (pre-)disposed, and approachable healer (1:40–45; 5:19) who heals by his intrinsic force anywhere and everywhere in sacred, domestic, and liminal spaces yet is pinned to concrete encounters in an ever-expanding radius with dangerously growing, unrelenting crowds (see E. Healing Spaces in Mark, and ch. 2). Characteristic for his healing is his intimate and sensuously tangible communication that he, however, adjusts according to the condition quite literally "at hand." He drastically and intentionally seizes hands to raise bedridden patients back into (social) life;[18] holistically bridges the marginalization of stigmatized men or remotely heals included outsiders;[19] proficiently, sensitively, inclusively, and intelligibly touches impaired sensuous organs;[20] fiercely opposes the demonic realm with simultaneous care for the possessed host;[21] acknowledges the suffering of the petitioners;[22] and determinately and unrelentingly overcomes physical and spatial seclusion.[23] Jesus' approach is universal yet personal, intrinsic yet transferrable.[24]

b) Successively, other characteristics are also attached to this intrinsic authority, transpiring an intriguing play on the revelation of Jesus' identity. The employed dis/abilities confirm and demonstrate empirical evidence for Jesus' ἐξουσία in teaching; for his divine authority as he claims the non-verifiable, divine prerogatives of forgiving sins and interpreting and defining the Sabbath; and for his discerning πνεῦμα, all within a cosmic setting and eschatological timeframe connect-

---

16 Cf. esp. 11:22–24, 31.
17 Solevåg 2018. 155.
18 Cf. Mark 1:31; 5:41; 9:27.
19 Cf. 1:40–45; 5:1–20; see below 1.3; 7:24–30.
20 Cf. 7:31–37; 8:22–26.
21 Cf. esp. 5:1–20; 9:14–29.
22 Cf. esp. 5:34; 7:33.
23 Cf. 1:29–31; esp. 5:21–43.
24 Cf., e.g., 6:7, 12–13, 30; 9:14–29, 38–39.

ed to his mission (see below). This is particularly enforced in the exorcisms which not only establish his cosmic sovereignty and reflect a continuous tension about a preternatural disclosure of his embodied identity, as explained in the silencing commands,[25] but also nuance this, as the final demonic encounter portrays him as a sovereign exorcist in his own right, without any reference to his role as a mediator of the divine sphere.[26]

c) Contrarily or accordingly, some dis/abilities demonstrate Jesus exposed to social and physical repercussions. This is particularly staged in his encounters with stigmatized and marginalized men, where Jesus similarly accommodates liminal identities and occupies liminal spheres, depicts socially transgressive behavior, and is rejected and labeled with the dis/ability invective stigma of mental disorder and pneumatic possession.[27] Rightfully so, as he reflects a similarly hybrid identity as demoniacs when he meets them in an arena of hierarchical order as another mediator of a transcendent, (however holy) pneumatic power. He also embodies an inexplicable and socially transgressive, frightening force; reveals esoteric knowledge; and is appointed by an elusive spiritual sphere. Moreover, Jesus similarly experiences physical liabilities when his body is confronted with social barriers and leaks uncontrollably and unwillingly healing δύναμις.[28]

Precisely the latter image of a physically intrinsic healing force that is transmitted by touch and motivated by *pistis* (as it distinguishes the woman from the pushing crowd; cf. 5:30–31) intertwines the two thematic storylines established by the Markan healing narratives and their deviating bodies: Jesus' tactile *dynamic* treatments correspond with the supplicant's growing knowledge of him.[29] This relative force can literally be charged itself with meaning along the narrative process and guides the audience accordingly, as indicated above, from the astonishing healer and liberator from occupational forces (esp. Mark 1, Summaric Accounts), to a fascinating teacher who argumentatively embodies divine prerogatives (Mark 2–3), to a determined and at times oblivious carrier with physical liabilities of a highly effective, divine power (esp. Mark 5:21–43), to the founding leader of a growing ministry (Mark 7:24–37), to an intimately communicating and intriguingly elusive protagonist with multiple attributed ambiguous identities (Mark 7:31–37; 8–10). As such, Jesus' characterization is mutually dependent on the dis/abilities he encounters, from the acute and general labels of harmful and weakening expo-

---

25 Cf. 1:25, 34; 3:12; see D. In Focus: Silencing in Mark's Healing Narratives.
26 Cf. esp. the contrast between Mark 5:1–20 and 9:14–29.
27 Cf. 1:40–45; 3:20–35; 5:1–20; cf. also 9:14–29.
28 Cf., e.g., 1:45; 2:2; 7:24; and 5:29–30.
29 Cf. the description of Jesus' deeds and actions of 4:35–5:43 as δυνάμεις in Mark 6:2, 5, and 9:1, 39 in direct connection to his hands, hindered by *a-pistia*; cf. moreover, 12:24; 13:26, and 14:62.

sures of humanity with rhetoric conventions (Mark 1–3), to more complex and ambiguous but severe and hopeless cases (Mark 5), to those conceptually and spiritually sensuous experiences that stage his ministry and (fatal) assignment (Mark 7–10). As the narrative continuously asks the audience τί ἐστιν τοῦτο (1:27), τί οὗτος οὕτως λαλεῖ (2:7), τίς ἄρα οὗτός ἐστιν (4:41), πόθεν τούτῳ ταῦτα, καὶ τίς ἡ σοφία ἡ δοθεῖσα τούτῳ, καὶ αἱ δυνάμεις τοιαῦται διὰ τῶν χειρῶν αὐτοῦ γινόμεναι (6:2), and οὐχ οὗτός ἐστιν ὁ τέκτων, ὁ υἱὸς τῆς Μαρίας καὶ ἀδελφὸς Ἰακώβου καὶ Ἰωσῆτος καὶ Ἰούδα καὶ Σίμωνος; καὶ οὐκ εἰσὶν αἱ ἀδελφαὶ αὐτοῦ ὧδε πρὸς ἡμᾶς (6:3), it is always dis/abilities that either evoke these questions or deploy the dynamic answers as the protagonist prepares to physically suffer himself.[30] Then the passion and crucifixion reveal the most detailed physical deviance of the entire gospel narrative as, over two chapters, the powerful protagonist is weakened, beaten, socially scorned, severely suffering, ineffectively and desperately praying for relief, and killed—τίς ἄρα οὗτός ἐστιν;

8.3 Beyond Binaries: Holistic Salvation

Jesus' dynamic identity is reflected in his encounters that accordingly portray and encourage *pistis* practice. The analysis of cultural taxonomies and literary inventions reveals that the transformed bodies and Jesus' transversal body create an ambiguous play on normalizing body schemes, alluding to the concept of holistic salvation.

a) The healing narratives establish the first differentiated physical categories as sickness and possession. The early encounters and programmatic passages witness to distinct clinical pictures and necessary treatments: the etiology and therapy of demonic dis/ability is explicitly referenced as a fusion, respectively separation of spirit and host. The symptoms always explicate disparate embodiment expressed by locative terminology and socially transgressive and (auto-) aggressive behavior.[31] Contrarily, the Markan text never insinuates, however, neither refutes, that the demonic realm is likewise responsible for other physical ailments. In Mark, this bifurcation serves most of all a narrative function: exorcisms are employed to witness to Jesus' divine superiority and ongoing intrinsic opposition to the knowledgeable demons as an additional function compared to other healings (cf. paradigmatic Mark 1:32–34, and for the Markan demonic and cosmic concep-

---

[30] Cf. 8:31; 9:31; 10:33, and then, e.g., 14:35–36; 15:25, 34.
[31] Cf. 1:21–28, 32–34, 39; 3:7–12; 5:1–20, moreover, 9:14–29 with additional symptoms; see A. In Focus: Markan Images of Sickness and Possession and B. In Focus: Mark's Jesus and Opposing Forces.

tualization 3:20–35). Regarding the dis/abled bodies, both sickness and possession witness to—and as two distinct phenomena, emphatically so—a general human exposure and universal susceptibility to (temporarily) dis/abling influences that Jesus spatially separates as his ministry and message spread (cf. programmatically Mark 1). As such, the gospel *relies* on common ancient frameworks.

This is particularly heightened as severe suffering is also portrayed as a consequence of acute conditions, as in the case of the febrile and skin conditions in Mark 1, and as an affliction of mundane forces that simply strike too strong, too long, and too soon, as in the case of the three dis/abled characters in Mark 5 affected by strong spirits, extending discharge, and early death. As such, physical deviance is not an exclusive and singular occurrence but is displayed as a general and "normal" undercurrent of life.

This aligns with the sheer quantity of healing encounters emphatically demonstrated by the summaric accounts. Although the help-seekers are characterized by a deviance, the implied norm does not have to be embodied by a majority. Rather, it appears that the protagonist encounters a large and vulnerable group of individuals with a range of afflictions. The images used to describe these afflictions are ambiguous and relatable, but they are also accompanied by personal clinical histories and tied to specific places and characters for the sake of narrative coherence, historical accuracy, and verification. The Markan dis/abled characters seem to have been singled out *pars pro toto* from an implied larger dis/abled setting. On this premise, Jesus' healing ministry is aimed at those who want to be liberated and petition for healing due to their suffering as a first act of *pistis* practice. Hence, Jesus' ministry and message do not account for an erasure of the deviance of a minority or singular cases but for an erasure of *suffering* as a general and universal human condition.

b) Despite the individuality of the characters and their stories, they all bear witness to a disruption of societal integration caused by their dis/abilities. Jesus' healing hence eludes an exclusive *physical* integrity and sets a norm of holistic transformation: Jesus sends the healed bodies home,[32] enables them to serve, independently walk around, eat,[33] and literally return from marginalized and liminal space.[34] While all post-healing actions are employed to emphatically visualize the healed body, this re-socialization also often surpasses any prior existence: the continuously serving mother-in-law, the beginning-to-proclaim liberated men, the timelessly saved and at-peace daughter with the dried issue of blood, and the per-

---

[32] Cf., e.g., 2:11; 5:19; 8:26.
[33] Cf., e.g., 1:29–31; 2:12; 5:42–43.
[34] Cf., e.g., 1:45; 5:19.

manently following Bartimaeus all set a *new* standard of social existence that is embedded in Jesus' ministry and mission.

Additionally, the assumed binary of re-socialization is challenged in several instances when Jesus questions and exposes the social setting and pathologization prior to or during the healing process: he treats conditions related to impurity in a questionable manner, evaluates the withered hand as a Sabbath exception, and shares the symptomatic hybrid and frightening identity of possessed bodies, as well as the uncontrollability of physical borders (see above 8.2). Most prominently, the Markan Jesus reevaluates the proclaimed condition of the patient when he dispossesses Jaïrus' daughter from social pathologization (5:39)—which the narrator follows by attributing her a subtle social emancipation—and unhinges the implied necessity for healing blind Bartimaeus by asking him, also against all established Markan conventions, what he wants (τί σοι θέλεις ποιήσω). The Markan Jesus thereby shifts the focus to a message of self-determination, recognition, and relationship (i.e., *pistis* practice; cf. esp. 5:34, 36; 10:36), notwithstanding the supposed evidence of the dis/ability.

Jesus' healing not only aims at a transformation of disrupted community as a byproduct of physical deviance but progresses to a new existence that encompasses a newfound peace and community. Moreover and more importantly, the Markan Jesus *rejects* and delegitimizes social pathologization, however acknowledges and emancipates the patients from social and physical suffering they have acclaimed for themselves.

c) Thereby, the universal suffering, the polyphone diagnoses, and the expanding notion of holistic transformation already elude any strict binary of dis/ability. Moreover, and fitting to the Markan ambiguous style, the narratives not only stay vague on the exact parameters of the (healed) conditions but draw on images with a range of severity and implications. While this can be attributed to the function of the accounts as not devoted to conceptual explorations of the human body, their overall brevity, and the lack of any popular and canonized sociology of knowledge of the human body, the Markan accounts witness to an additional intentional ambiguity.

As established, the primary and summaric passages deploy applicable and relatable images as a programmatic benchmark for facile identification and concise narration. However, as the plot unfolds, the Markan text continuously transcends the concrete parameters of restoration, σῴζω, rising, and raising.[35] Naturally, these polysemes and descriptions can always refer to a simple physical transformation;

---

35 Cf. esp. 2:12 and 3:5; 5:39, 41; 9:26–27 with 8:31; 9:31 and 10:34; moreover, 9:9–10, 12; 8:25.

8.3 Beyond Binaries: Holistic Salvation — 265

however, their contexts and continuity shift the perspective to a creational-eschatological ideal as well as a ministry priority.

As Mark 2:1–12 implies, 5:21–43 enforces, and 9:14–29 substantiates, the raisings of bedridden patients (in two narratives, accounted to be dead) function in their context of *pistis* teachings[36] not only as verifications of the healings but in their communication with the powerful protagonist as performative passion predictions of his resurrection and in their application to holistic transformations beyond physical integrity as allusions to an eschatological existence (see above). This is moreover confirmed by similar developments of notions attached to σῴζω, from physical transformations[37] to eschatological and soteriological associations in Jesus' teachings.[38] Firstly, this concurs with the term's contextualization in the halakhic Sabbath discussions as an expression of an eschatological understanding and primordial ideal of physicality together with ἀποκαθίστημι and its eschatological nuances.[39] It is, secondly, displayed in the comparative treatments of life-threatening *and* chronic, not necessarily urgent, conditions of, for example, the withered hand, the daughter on her death bed, the continuous blood flow, and blind Bartimaeus and its resultative display of dramatically timeless *salvation* in *peace* of the *entire being*: ἡ πίστις σου σέσωκέν σε (5:34; also 10:52). Thirdly, it is reflected in the use of this term regarding the soteriological and Christological scheme of discipleship and spiritual comprehension.[40]

Impressively, this frame of creational idealism and eschatological promise is reprised at the central eulogistic statement of Mark 7:36–37, which echoes Gen 1:31[LXX] and Isa 35:5–6[LXX]. Correspondingly, the Markan Jesus continuously fills this frame of the "and behold it was *and will be* very good" with references to his ministry and message as he prioritizes a) forgiveness of sins over healing immobile, earthly limbs (2:1–12; cf. 2:23–28); b) forgiven communal life over unimpaired damnation (9:42–48); c) salvation from suffering to the here and now and minor (esp. 3:1–6; 5:25–34); d) an active yet relative *pistis* response to him and his message (2:5; 5:34, 36; 9:23–24); and e) a spectrum of cognitive insight against hardened hearts and spiritual incomprehension of characters and of the audience (esp. 2–3; 8–10).

However, the grandest priority is revealed after the healing narratives have been told. After Jesus' ministry focused on this transformation of suffering into holistic salvation, he suffers himself. This interlacing of a self-acclaimed criterion for

---

36 Cf. esp. 2:5; 5:34, 36; 9:23–24.
37 Cf. 3:4; 5:23, 28, 34; 6:56; and 10:52.
38 Cf. 8:35; 10:17, 25, 26; 13:13, 20; also 15:30–31.
39 Cf. 3:4; see 4.2; for the latter, cf. Mark 9:12.
40 Cf. 10:52; moreover, 8:34–35.

what can be labeled a Markan dis/ability that Jesus heals is transpired when he announces and undergoes his own physical suffering as the climax of his ministry and mission. Without much explanation and a resurrection and return only announced, the gospel text leaves the audience with a physically suffering protagonist, the powerful healer of all. It is a tension that surpasses the text to an existence of suffering in all its forms and yet a promise of its possible transformation.

8.4 Future Prospects

Through this careful analysis of representations of dis/ability, it becomes evident that the gospel text challenges physical binaries when the Markan Jesus heals many who are suffering and wish to be transformed, while also acknowledging their suffering. However, at times he rejects cultural taxonomies by prioritizing other trajectories, reclaiming their pathologization, and deconstructing and reconstructing the ideal of "health" as a communal and eschatological existence. The gospel text thereby also relies on a dis/ability invective rhetoric when physically deviating bodies are used to demonstrate all of the above, Jesus' theological teachings and the narrative's propositions. The prominent staging of dis/abled characters in need of physical transformation implies an understanding of the undesirability of their physical condition. Only as such can it be compared to sin, be important enough for Sabbath healing, and be used to visualize spiritual incomprehension and disrupted communication, salvation, and resurrection. This precondition must be noted and carefully extracted when reading, interpreting, preaching, and teaching the Markan healing narratives. Only on such a firm historic, hermeneutical investigation can the texts be (re)appropriated, (re)evaluated, and (re)interpreted according to their sociopolitical power in the spirit of dis/ability studies. In this regard lies the hope that this historical investigation is not the end but inspires those struggling for an accurate and inclusive application.

This study has not only provided significant insights into the composition of the Markan text, its characterization of Jesus, and its illustration of salvation, but it has also established a solid foundation for its modern interpretation and application. As a result, it has demonstrated the fruitfulness of analyzing biblical texts through the hermeneutical framework of dis/ability. Again, this is hopefully not the end of such research as there are many more texts to be regarded.

On a story level, the dis/abled characters are confined to their episodes and "dispensable in the end."[41] However, it is clear that the gospel text uses nuanced,

---

[41] Solevåg 2018. 155.

ambiguous, and polyphonic depictions of deviating bodies to encourage the audience to identify with their physical and/or social suffering. Thereby, the text invites the audience to experience the hopeful encounter with the sensuously tangible healer, be intrigued and inspired by the exemplary relational *pistis* practice, comprehend the dynamic identity of Jesus, and witness the transformed holistic existence of those who encounter him. Ultimately, the text engages the audience to find out how the story of this passionate divine protagonist ends. As such, these narrative prostheses stay with the audience as heralds of the plot and embodied blueprints of its message—at least until the narrative has ended and is read again.

Indeed, this is not their end.

Bibliography

Primary Sources

Accordance Bible Software Version 13.0.2 (Nov 2019).
Aland, Kurt. 1996. *Synopsis Quattuor Evangeliorum: Locis Parallelis Evangeliorum Apocryphorum et Patrum Adhibitis*. 15th ed. Stuttgart: Deutsche Bibelgesellschaft.
Atzpodien, Jens. 1986. *Galens "Subfiguratio emperica"*. Abhandlungen zur Geschichte der Medizin und der Naturwissenschaften 52. Husum: Matthiesen.
Bauer, Walter (ed.). 1963. *Griechisch-deutsches Wörterbuch: Zu den Schriften des Neuen Testaments und der frühchristlichen Literatur*. 5th ed. Berlin: Verlag Alfred Töpelmann.
Blass, Friedrich; Albert Debrunner; Friedrich Rehkopf. 1976. *Grammatik des neutestamentlichen Griechisch*. 14th ed. Göttingen: Vandenhoeck & Ruprecht.
Bratcher, Robert G.; Eugene Albert Nida. 1961. *A Translator's Handbook on the Gospel of Mark*. Helps for Translators 2. Leiden: Brill.
Caelius, Aurelianus; Gerhard Bendz. 1990ff. *Akute Krankheiten, I – III. Chronische Krankheiten I–V*. Corpus Medicorum Latinorum. Berlin: Akademie-Verlag.
Celsus; W. G. Spencer. 1960. *De Medicina*. 3 vols. LCL 292. London: Heinemann.
Danker, Frederick W.; Walter Bauer (eds.). 2000. *A Greek-English Lexicon of the New Testament and Other Early Christian Literature: Based on Walter Bauer's Griechisch-Deutsches Wörterbuch zu den Schriften des Neuen Testaments*. 3rd ed. Chicago, IL: University of Chicago Press.
Dittenberger, Wilhelm. 1917. *Sylloge Inscriptionum Graecarum*. 3rd ed., 2 vols. Leipzig: Apud S.Hirzelium.
Durling, R. J. 1993. *A Dictionary of Medical Terms in Galen*. Studies in Ancient Medicine 5. Leiden: Brill.
Edelstein, Emma Jeannette Levy; Ludwig Edelstein. 1998. *Asclepius: Collection and Interpretation of the Testimonies*. 2 vols. Baltimore, MD: Johns Hopkins University Press.
Elliger, Karl; Wilhelm Rudolph. 1997. *Biblia Hebraica Stuttgartensia*. Stuttgart: Deutsche Bibelgesellschaft.
Elliott, J. Keith. 1993. *The Apocryphal New Testament: A Collection of Apocryphal Christian Literature in an English Translation*. Oxford: Clarendon Press.
Fichtner, Gerhard; Berlin-Brandenburgische Akademie der Wissenschaften. 2012. *Corpus Galenicum: Verzeichnis der galenischen und pseudogalenischen Schriften*. Berlin: Berlin-Brandenburgische Akademie der Wissenschaften.
Flavius Josephus Online (https://scholarlyeditions.brill.com/fjo/).
Flavius Josephus, Henry St J. Thackeray; Ralph Marcus; et al. 1933ff. *Josephus: In Nine Volumes*. LCL. Cambridge, MA: Harvard University Press.
Flavius Josephus; S. A. Naber; Immanuel Bekker. 1856. *Flavii Iosephi Opera omnia*. Leipzig: Teubner.
Gaius Plinius Caecilius, Secundus. 1938–1962. *Natural History: In Ten Volumes*. LCL. Cambridge, MA: Harvard University Press.
Galen; Carl Wolfram Brunschön. 2021. *De locis affectis V–VI*. Corpus Medicorum Graecorum Band 5/6,1,3. Berlin: de Gruyter.
Galen; Florian Gärtner. 2015. *De locis affectis I–II*. Corpus Medicorum Graecorum Band 5/6,1,1. [Dt.: *Über das Erkennen erkrankter Körperteile I–II*]. Berlin: de Gruyter.
Gesenius, Wilhelm; Rudolf Meyer; Herbert Donner. 2013. *Hebräisches und aramäisches Handwörterbuch über das Alte Testament*. 18th ed. Heidelberg: Springer.

Hippocrates; Emile Littré. 1844–1861. *Oeuvres complètes d'Hippocrate: Traduction nouvelle avec le texte grec en regard, collationné sur les manuscrits et toutes les éditions; accompagnée d'une introduction, de commentaires médicaux, de variantes et de notes philologiques; suivie d'une table générale des matières*. 10 vols. Paris/ London: Libraire de l'Académie Royale de Médecine.

Iamblichus; Elmar Habrich. 1960. *Babyloniaca. Iamblichi Babyloniacorum reliquiae*. Lipsiae: Teubner.

Ilan, Tal; Thomas Ziem; Kerstin Hünefeld. 2002. *Lexicon of Jewish Names in Late Antiquity*. 4 vols. TSAJ 91, 126, 141, 148. Tübingen: Mohr Siebeck.

Kinnier Wilson, James; E. H. Reynolds. 1990. "Translation and Analysis of a Cuneiform Text Forming Part of a Babylonian Treatise on Epilepsy." *Medical History* 34.2: 185–198.

Kraus, Wolfgang; Martin Karrer. 2009. *Septuaginta Deutsch. Das griechische Alte Testament in deutscher Übersetzung*. Stuttgart: Deutsche Bibelgesellschaft.

Kropp, Angelicus. 1930–31. *Ausgewählte koptische Zaubertexte*. 3 vols. Bruxelles: Éd. de la Fondation Égyptologique.

Kühn, Carl Gottlob. 1821–1833. *Claudii Galeni Opera omnia. Editionem curavit D. Carolus Gottlob Kühn*. 20 vols. Cambridge Library Collection. Hildesheim: Olms.

Liddell, Henry George; Robert Scott; Henry Stuart Jones (eds.). 1965. *A Greek-English Lexicon*. Oxford: Clarendon Press.

LiDonnici, Lynn R. 1995. *The Epidaurian Miracle Inscriptions*. Texts and Translations 36. Atlanta, GA: Scholars Press.

Louw, Johannes P.; Eugene A. Nida (eds.). 1989. *Greek-English Lexicon of the New Testament based on Semantic Domains*. New York: United Bible Societies.

Maloney, G.; W. Frohn. 1986–1989. *Concordantia in Corpus Hippocraticum. Concordance des Oeuvres Hippocratiques. Avec la collaboration du Dr. Paul Potter*. 6 vols. Hildesheim: Olms-Weidmann.

Metzger, Bruce Manning. 1994. *A Textual Commentary on the Greek New Testament*. 2nd ed. Stuttgart: Deutsche Bibelgesellschaft.

Montanari, Franco et al. (eds.). 2015. *The Brill Dictionary of Ancient Greek*. Leiden/ Boston, MA: Brill.

Moulton, James Hope; George Milligan (eds.). 1972. *The Vocabulary of the Greek Testament*. London: Hodder and Stoughton.

Naveh, Joseph; Shaul Shaked. 1987. *Amulets and Magic Bowls: Aramaic Incantations of Late Antiquity*. 2nd ed. Jerusalem: Magnes Press, Hebrew University.

Naveh, Joseph; Shaul Shaked. 1993. *Magic Spells and Formulae: Aramaic Incantations of Late Antiquity*. Jerusalem: Magnes Press, Hebrew University.

Naveh, Joseph. 1998. "Fragments of an Aramaic Magic Book from Qumran." *IEJ* 48: 252–261.

Nestle, Eberhard; Barbara Aland; Aland Nestle; et al. 2012. *Novum Testamentum Graece 28*. Stuttgart: Deutsche Bibelgesellschaft.

Passow, Franz. 1970. *Handwörterbuch der griechischen Sprache*. 5th ed., 4 vols. Darmstadt: Wissenschaftliche Buchgesellschaft.

Philo, Alexandrinus. 1994. *Philo: In Ten Volumes (and two supplementary volumes)*. LCL. Cambridge, MA: Harvard University Press.

Philostratus, Flavius. 1999. *Heroicus. Helden und Heroen, Homer und Caracalla*. Bari: Levante Editori.

Philostratus, Flavius. 2014 [1983]. *Vita Apollonii. Philostratos: Das Leben des Apollonios von Tyana*. Berlin: de Gruyter.

Preisendanz, Karl (ed.). 1931. *Papyri Graecae Magicae. Die griechischen Zauberpapyri*. Leipzig: Teubner.

Rahlfs, Alfred; Robert Hanhart (eds.). 2006. *Septuaginta. Editio Altera*. Stuttgart: Deutsche Bibelgesellschaft.

Reed, Stephen A.; Marilyn J. Lundberg; Michael B. Phelps. 1994. *The Dead Sea Scrolls Catalogue: Documents, Photographs, and Museum Inventory Numbers.* SBLRBS 32. Atlanta, GA: SBL Press.
Rosner, Fred. 2000. *Encyclopedia of Medicine in the Bible and the Talmud.* Northvale, NJ: Jason Aronson.
Sefaria. A Living Library of Torah (https://www.sefaria.org/texts).
Spicq, Ceslas (ed.). 1978–1982. *Notes de Lexicographie Néo-Testamentaire.* 3 vols. Göttingen: Vandenhoeck & Ruprecht.
Temkin, Owsei; C. Lilian Temkin (eds.). 1987. *Ancient Medicine: Selected Papers of Ludwig Edelstein.* Baltimore, MD: Johns Hopkins University Press.
Temkin, Owsei. 1991. *Soranus' Gynecology.* Baltimore, MD: Johns Hopkins University Press.
Thesaurus Linguae Graecae (http://stephanus.tlg.uci.edu/).
Thesaurus Linguae Latinae (http://emedia.bibliothek.uni-halle.de).

Secondary Sources

Abrams, Judith Z. 1998. *Judaism and Disability: Portrayals in Ancient Texts from the Tanach through the Bavli.* Washington, DC: Gallaudet University Press.
Abrams, Judith Z. 2013. Deafness III. Judaism. In: *Encyclopedia of the Bible and Its Reception* 6, Berlin: de Gruyter, 352–354.
Achtemeier, Paul J. 1975. *Mark.* Philadelphia, PA: Fortress Press.
Achtemeier, Paul J. 1978. "'And he followed him': Miracles and Discipleship in Mark 10.46–52." *Semeia 11:* 115–145.
Albrecht, Gary L.; Katherine D. Seelman; Michael Bury. 2001. Introduction: The Formation of Disability Studies. In: Albrecht, Gary L./ Katherine D. Seelman/ Michael Bury (eds.), *Handbook of Disability Studies.* Thousand Oaks, CA: Sage, 1–8.
Aleshire, Sara B. 1989. *The Athenian Asklepieion: The People, Their Dedications, and the Inventories.* Amsterdam: J.C. Gieben.
Allison, Dale C. Jr. 1997. The Eye As A Lamp: Finding the Sense. In: Allison, Dale C. Jr. (ed.), *The Jesus Tradition in Q.* Harrisburg, PA: Trinity Press International, 133–167.
Allison, Dale C. Jr. 2014. Fever II. NT. In: *Encyclopedia of the Bible and Its Reception* 8, Berlin: de Gruyter, 1195.
Altman, Barbara M. 2001. Disability Definitions, Models, Classification Schemes, and Applications. In: Albrecht, Gary L./ Katherine D. Seelman/ Michael Bury (eds.), *Handbook of Disability Studies.* Thousand Oaks, CA: Sage, 97–122.
Anderson, Herbert; Edward Foley. 1994. *Developmental Disabilities and Sacramental Access: New Paradigms for Sacramental Encounters.* Collegeville, MI: Liturgical Press.
Annen, Franz. 2010. ἐκβάλλω. In: *Exegetisches Wörterbuch zum Neuen Testament* 1, Stuttgart: Kohlhammer, 984–987.
Arnold, Gerhard. 1977. "Mk 1,1 und Eröffnungswendungen in griechischen und lateinischen Schriften." *ZNW* 68: 123–127.
Assmann, Jan; David Lorton. 2005. *Death and Salvation in Ancient Egypt.* Ithaca, NY: Cornell University Press.
Auffarth, Christoph; Loren T. Stuckenbruck (eds.). 2003. *Fall of the Angels.* Themes in Biblical Narrative 6. Leiden: Brill.

Aune, David Edward. 1980. Magic in Early Christianity. In: *ANRW 2.23.2*. Berlin: de Gruyter, 1507–1558.

Aus, Roger David. 2004. *My name is "Legion": Palestinian Judaic Traditions in Mark 5, 1–20 and Other Gospel Texts*. Studies in Judaism. Lanham, MD: University Press of America.

Avalos, Hector. 1999. *Health Care and the Rise of Christianity*. Peabody, MA: Hendrickson.

Avalos, Hector. 2007a. Introducing Sensory Criticism in Biblical Studies. Audiocentricity and Visiocentricity. In: Avalos, Hector/ Sarah J. Melcher/ Jeremy Schipper (eds.), *This Abled Body: Rethinking Disabilities in Biblical Studies*. SBL SemeiaSt 55. Leiden: Brill, 47–59.

Avalos, Hector. 2007b. "Redemptionism, Rejectionism, and Historicism as Emerging Approaches in Disability Studies." *PRSt* 34.1: 91–100.

Avalos, Hector; Sarah J. Melcher; Jeremy Schipper. 2007. Introduction. In: Avalos, Hector/ Sarah J. Melcher/ Jeremy Schipper (eds.), *This Abled Body: Rethinking Disabilities in Biblical Studies*. SBL SemeiaSt 55. Leiden: Brill, 1–9.

Avalos, Hector; Sarah J. Melcher; Jeremy Schipper. 2007. *This Abled Body: Rethinking Disabilities in Biblical Studies*. SBL SemeiaSt 55. Leiden: Brill.

Avemarie, Friedrich. 1996. *Tora und Leben: Untersuchungen zur Heilsbedeutung der Tora in der frühen rabbinischen Literatur*. TSAJ 55. Tübingen: J.C.B. Mohr (Paul Siebeck).

Avemarie, Friedrich. 2010. Jesus and Purity. In: Bieringer, Reimund/ Florentino García Martínez/ Didier Pollefeyt; et al. (eds.), *The New Testament and Rabbinic Literature*. Supplements to the Journal for the Study of Judaism 136. Leiden/ Boston, MA: Brill, 255–279.

Avrahami, Yael. 2012. *The Senses of Scripture: Sensory Perception in the Hebrew Bible*. Library of Hebrew Bible/Old Testament Studies 545. London/ New York: T&T Clark.

Baarda, Tjitze. 2012. "Mk 1:41: ὀργισθείς: A Reading Attested for Mar Ephraem, the Diatessaron, or Tatian." *ZNW* 103.2: 291–295.

Bach, Ulrich. 2006. *Ohne die Schwächsten ist die Kirche nicht ganz. Bausteine einer Theologie nach Hadamar*. Neukirchen-Vluyn: Neukirchner.

Back, Sven-Olav. 1995. *Jesus of Nazareth and the Sabbath Commandment*. Turku/Åbo: Åbo Akademi University Press.

Back, Sven-Olav. 2011. Jesus and The Sabbath. In: Holmén, Tom/ Stanley E. Porter (eds.), *Handbook for the Study of the Historical Jesus 4*. Leiden/ Boston, MA: Brill, 2597–2633.

Backhaus, Knut. 1995. ,Lösepreis für viele' (Mk 10,45): Zur Heilsbedeutung des Todes Jesu bei Markus. In: Söding, Thomas (ed.), *Der Evangelist als Theologe: Studien zum Markusevangelium*. Stuttgarter Bibelstudien 163. Stuttgart: Verlag Katholisches Bibelwerk, 91–118.

Baden, Joel S.; Candida R. Moss. 2011. "The Origin and Interpretation of ṣāraʻat in Leviticus 13–14." *JBL* 130.4: 643–662.

Baert, Barbara; Niels Schalley. 2014. *The Woman with the Blood Flow (Mark 5:24–34): Narrative, Iconic, and Anthropological Spaces*. Art & Religion 2. Leuven: Peeters.

Baker, Cynthia M. 2002. *Rebuilding the House of Israel: Architectures of Gender in Jewish Antiquity*. Stanford, CA: Stanford University Press.

Balz, Horst; Gerhard Schneider. 2010. ἄρρωστος. In: *Exegetisches Wörterbuch zum Neuen Testament* 1, Stuttgart: Kohlhammer, 380.

Balz, Horst; Gerhard Schneider. 2010. διαβλέπω. In: *Exegetisches Wörterbuch zum Neuen Testament* 1, Stuttgart: Kohlhammer, 714.

Balz, Horst; Gerhard Schneider. 2010. ἐμβλέπω. In: *Exegetisches Wörterbuch zum Neuen Testament* 1, Stuttgart: Kohlhammer, 1079–1080.

Balz, Horst; Gerhard Schneider. 2010. κωφός. In: *Exegetisches Wörterbuch zum Neuen Testament* 2, Stuttgart: Kohlhammer, 826.
Balz, Horst; Gerhard Schneider. 2010. μάστιξ. In: *Exegetisches Wörterbuch zum Neuen Testament* 2, Stuttgart: Kohlhammer, 975.
Balz, Horst; Gerhard Schneider. 2010. παρακούω. In: *Exegetisches Wörterbuch zum Neuen Testament* 3, Stuttgart: Kohlhammer, 67–68.
Balz, Horst; Gerhard Schneider. 2010. παραλύομαι. In: *Exegetisches Wörterbuch zum Neuen Testament* 3, Stuttgart: Kohlhammer, 72.
Balz, Horst; Gerhard Schneider. 2010. παρατηρέω. In: *Exegetisches Wörterbuch zum Neuen Testament* 3, Stuttgart: Kohlhammer, 80–81.
Balz, Horst; Gerhard Schneider. 2010. ῥήγνυμι In: *Exegetisches Wörterbuch zum Neuen Testament* 3, Stuttgart: Kohlhammer, 504.
Barclay, John M. G. 2007. "There is Neither Old nor Young? Early Christianity and Ancient Ideologies of Age." *NTS* 53: 225–241.
Barton, George A. 1922. "The Use of ἐπιτιμᾶν in Mark 8:30 and 3:12." *JBL* 41.3/4: 233–236.
Barton, Stephen. 2011. "Eschatology and the Emotions in Early Christianity." *JBL* 130: 571–591.
Bauckham, Richard. 2008. The Son of Man: 'A Man in my Position' or 'Someone'? In: Bauckham, Richard (ed.), *The Jewish World Around the New Testament: Collected Essays*. WUNT 233. Tübingen: Mohr Siebeck, 93–101.
Baumgarten, Joseph M. 1990. "The 4Q Zadokite Fragments on Skin Disease." *JJS* 41.2: 153–165.
Bayer, Hans F. 2014. ὁράω. In: *Theologisches Begriffslexikon zum Neuen Testament*, Wuppertal: Brockhaus, 1648–1652.
Bazzana, Giovanni B. 2018. Beelzebul vs Satan: Exorcist Subjectivity and Spirit Possession in the Historical Jesus. In: Verheyden, Joseph/ John S. Kloppenborg (eds.), *The Gospels and Their Stories in Anthropological Perspective*. WUNT 409. Tübingen: Mohr Siebeck, 7–27.
Beardslee, William A. 1970. *Literary Criticism of the New Testament*. New Testament Series. Philadelphia, PA: Fortress Press.
Beavis, Mary Ann. 1998. "From the Margin to the Way: A Feminist Reading of the Story of Bartimaeus." *JFSR* 14: 19–39.
Beavis, Mary Ann. 2010. "The Resurrection of Jephthah's Daughter: Judges 11:34–40 and Mark 5:21–24, 35–43." *CBQ* 72.1: 46–62.
Becker, Eve-Marie. 2009. "Mark 1:1 and the Debate on a "Markan Prologue"." *Filología Neotestamentaria* 22.42: 91–105.
Becker, Eve-Marie. 2010. "Die markinischen Summarien – ein literarischer und theologischer Schlüssel zu Markus 1–6." *NTS* 56: 452–474.
Becker, Michael. 2013. Feiertagsarbeit? (Der Kranke mit der ‚verdorrten' Hand). In: Zimmermann, Ruben (ed.), *Kompendium der frühchristlichen Wundererzählungen: Die Wunder Jesu*. Gütersloh: Gütersloher Verlags-Haus, 248–256.
Behm, Johannes. 1957. καινός. In: *Theologisches Wörterbuch zum Neuen Testament* 3, Stuttgart: Kohlhammer, 450–452.
Behm, Johannes. 1968. *Die Handauflegung im Urchristentum. Nach Verwendung, Herkunft und Bedeutung in religionsgeschichtlichem Zusammenhang untersucht*. 2nd ed. Darmstadt: Wissenschaftliche Buchgesellschaft.
Belser, Julia Watts. 2018. *Rabbinic Tales of Destruction: Sex, Gender, and Disability in the Ruins of Jerusalem*. Oxford: Oxford University Press.

Belser, Julia Watts; Melanie S. Morrison. 2011. "What No Longer Serves Us: Resisting Ableism and Anti-Judaism in New Testament Healing Narratives." *JFSR* 27.2: 153–170.

Ben Zvi, Ehud; Diana Vikander Edelman. 2014. *Imagining the Other and Constructing Israelite Identity in the Early Second Temple Period*. Library of Hebrew Bible/Old Testament Studies 456. London/ New York: T&T Clark.

Benedum, Jost. 1977. "Griechische Arztinschriften aus Kos." *ZPE* 25: 270.

Bengtsson, Staffan. 2016. "The two-sided Coin – Disability, Normalcy and Social Categorization in the New Testament." *Scandinavian Journal of Disability Research* 18: 269–279.

Bennett, Simon. 1978. *Mind and Madness in Ancient Greece: The Classical Roots of Modern Psychiatry*. Ithaca, NY: Cornell University Press.

Benthien, Claudia. 1998. *Im Leibe Wohnen: Literarische Imagologie und Historische Anthropologie der Haut*. Berlin: Berlin-Verlag Spitz.

Benthien, Claudia. 2001. *Haut: Literaturgeschichte, Körperbilder, Grenzdiskurse*. 2nd ed. Reinbek bei Hamburg: Rowohlt-Taschenbuch-Verlag.

Berger, Klaus. 1984a. Hellenistische Gattungen im Neuen Testament. In: *ANRW 2.25.2*. Berlin: de Gruyter, 1031–1432.

Berger, Klaus. 1984b. *Formgeschichte des Neuen Testaments*. Heidelberg: Quelle & Meyer.

Berger, Klaus. 1988. "Jesus als Pharisäer und frühe Christen als Pharisäer." *NovT* 30: 231–262.

Berlejung, Angelika. 2009. "Variabilität und Konstanz eines Reinigungsrituals nach der Berührung eines Toten in Num 19 und Qumran. Überlegungen zur Dynamik der Ritualtransformation." *TZ* 65.4: 289–331.

Bernidaki-Aldous, Eleftheria A. 1990. *Blindness in a Culture of Light: Especially the Case of Oedipus at Colonus of Sophocles*. American University Studies Series XVII, Classical Languages and Literature 8. New York: Peter Lang.

Berthelot, Katell. 2006. "La place des infirmes et des 'lépreux' dans les texts de Qumrân et les Évangiles." *RB* 113: 211–241.

Best, Ernest. 1965. *The Temptation and The Passion: The Markan Soteriology*. SNTSMS 2. Cambridge: University Press.

Best, Ernest. 1983. *Mark: The Gospel as Story*. Studies of the New Testament and Its World. Edinburgh: T&T Clark.

Betcher, Sharon V. 2007. *Spirit and the Politics of Disablement*. Minneapolis, MN: Fortress Press.

Betcher, Sharon V. 2013. Disability and the Terror of the Miracle Tradition. In: Alkier, Stefan/ Annette Weissenrieder (eds.), *Miracles Revisited: New Testament Miracle Stories and their Concepts of Reality*. Studies of the Bible and its Reception 2. Berlin: de Gruyter, 161–181.

Betz, Hans Dieter. 1979. Matthew 6.22 f. and Ancient Greek Theories of Vision. In: Best, Ernest/ R. McLachlan Wilson (eds.), *Text and Interpretation: Studies in the New Testament Presented to Matthew Black*. Cambridge/ New York: Cambridge University Press, 43–56.

Beyer, H. W. 1957. θεραπεύω. In: *Theologisches Wörterbuch zum Neuen Testament* 3, Stuttgart: Kohlhammer, 128–132.

Beyer, H. W. 1960. διακονέω. In: *Theologisches Wörterbuch zum Neuen Testament* 2, Stuttgart: Kohlhammer, 81–93.

Bieder, Werner. 1960. πνεῦμα. In: *Theologisches Wörterbuch zum Neuen Testament* 6, Stuttgart: Kohlhammer, 366–373.

Bietenhard, Hans; Klaus Heß. 2014. διακονέω. In: *Theologisches Begriffslexikon zum Neuen Testament*, Wuppertal: Brockhaus, 941–944.

Bird, Michael F. 2018. The Testament of Solomon and Mark 5:1–20: Exorcism and Power over Evil Spirits. In: Blackwell, Ben C./ John Goodrich/ Jason Maston (eds.), *Reading Mark in Context: Jesus and Second Temple Judaism*. Grand Rapids, MI: Zondervan, 77–83.

Blackburn, Barry. 1991. *Theios Anēr and the Markan Miracle Traditions: A Citique of the Theios Anēr Concept as an Interpretative Background of the Miracle Traditions used by Mark*. Das Markus-Evangelium im Rahmen antiker Historiographie 2.40. Tübingen: J.C.B. Mohr (Paul Siebeck).

Blenkinsopp, Joseph. 2000. *Isaiah 1–39: A New Translation with Introduction and Commentary*. AB 19. New York: Doubleday.

Böcher, Otto. 1970. *Dämonenfurcht und Dämonenabwehr. Ein Beitrag zur Vorgeschichte der christlichen Taufe*. BWA(N)T 5.10 (90). Stuttgart: Kohlhammer.

Böcher, Otto. 1972. *Christus Exorcista. Dämonismus und Taufe im Neuen Testament*. BWA(N)T 5.16 (96). Stuttgart: Kohlhammer.

Böcher, Otto. 1981. Dämonen. In: *Theologische Realenzyklopädie* 8, Berlin: de Gruyter, 270–274.

Böcher, Otto. 2010. δαίμων. In: *Exegetisches Wörterbuch zum Neuen Testament* 1, Stuttgart: Kohlhammer, 649–657.

Bohak, Gideon. 2012. Demons, Demonology V. Judaism A. and B. In: *Encyclopedia of the Bible and Its Reception* 6, Berlin: de Gruyter, 546–553.

Bolt, Peter. 2003. *Jesus' Defeat of Death: Persuading Mark's Early Readers*. SNTSMS 125. Cambridge: Cambridge University Press.

Bomford, Rodney. 2010. "Jairus, His Daughter, the Woman and the Saviour: The Communication of Symmetric Thinking in the Gospel of Mark." *Practical Theology* 3: 41–50.

Bonner, Champbell. 1927. "Traces of Thaumaturgic Technique in the Miracles." *HTR* 20.3: 171–181.

Boring, M. Eugene. 1990. "Mark 1:1–15 and The Beginning of the Gospel." *Semeia* 52: 43–81.

Boring, M. Eugene. 2006. *Mark: A Commentary*. The New Testament Library. Louisville, KY: Westminster John Knox Press.

Bornkamm, Günther. 1971. Πνεῦμα ἄλαλον. In: Bornkamm, Günther (ed.), *Geschichte und Glaube*. Beiträge zur Evangelischen Theologie 48. München: Kaiser, 21–36.

Bosenius, Bärbel. 2014. *Der literarische Raum des Markusevangeliums*. Wissenschaftliche Monographien zum Alten und Neuen Testament 140. Neukirchen-Vluyn: Neukirchener Theologie.

Bosenius, Bärbel. 2019. "Retten" oder "heilen" – welchen frame aktiviert σῴζειν in Mk 5,21–43? Überlegungen zur "Bedeutung" eines Wortes aus der Perspektive der Kognitiven Semantik. In: Du Toit, David S./ Christine Gerber/ Christiane Zimmermann (eds.), *Sōtēria: Salvation in Early Christianity and Antiquity. FS in Honour of Cilliers Breytenbach on the Occasion of his 65th Birthday*. NovTSup 175. Leiden/ Boston, MA: Brill, 166–185.

Bosenius, Bärbel. 2019. Satan oder Jesus? Wer wohnt im Haus des Starken? In: Oyen, Geert van (ed.), *Reading the Gospel of Mark in the twenty-first century: Method and Meaning*. BETL 301. Leuven: Peeters, 443–454.

Bösl, Elsbeth. 2009. "Dis/ability History: Grundlagen und Forschungsstand." *H-Soz-Kult*: 1–37.

Bösl, Elsbeth. 2010. Was ist Disability History? Zur Geschichte und Historiografie von Behinderung. In: Bösl, Elsbeth/ Anne Klein/ Anne Waldschmidt (eds.), *Disability History: Konstruktionen von Behinderung in der Geschichte. Eine Einführung*. Disability Studies. Bielefeld: transcript, 29–43.

Bösl, Elsbeth; Anne Klein; Anne Waldschmidt (eds.). 2010. *Disability History: Konstruktionen von Behinderung in der Geschichte. Eine Einführung*. Disability Studies. Bielefeld: transcript.

Botner, Max. 2017a. "The Messiah Is "the Holy One": ὁ ἅγιος τοῦ θεοῦ as a Messianic Title in Mark 1:24." *JBL* 136.2: 417–433.

Botner, Max. 2017b. "What Has Mark's Christ to Do with David's Son? A History of Interpretation." *Currents in Biblical Research* 16.1: 50–70.

Bourquin, Yvan. 2005. *Marc, une théologie de la fragilité: Obscure clarté d'une narration.* Geneva: Labor et Fides.

Boyarin, Daniel. 1993. *Carnal Israel: Reading Sex in Talmudic Culture.* The New Historicism. Berkeley, CA: University of California Press.

Braumann, Georg. 2014. κράτος. In: *Theologisches Begriffslexikon zum Neuen Testament*, Wuppertal: Brockhaus, 1191–1193.

Bremmer, Jan N. 2012. Greek Demons of the Wilderness: The Case of the Centaurs. In: Feldt, Laura (ed.), *Wilderness in Mythology and Religion: Approaching Religious Spatialities, Cosmologies, and Ideas of Wild Nature.* Religion and Society. Berlin: de Gruyter, 25–53.

Brenk, Frederick E. 1986. In the Light of the Moon. Demonology in the Early Imperial Period. In: *ANRW 2.16.3.* Berlin: de Gruyter, 1283–1299.

Breytenbach, Cilliers. 1995. Hypsistos. In: *DDD*, Leiden: Brill, 439–443.

Breytenbach, Cilliers. 1999. Mark and Galilee. In: Meyers, Eric M. (ed.), *Galilee Through the Centuries: Confluence of Cultures.* Duke Judaic Studies Series 1. Winona Lake, IN: Eisenbrauns, 75–85.

Breytenbach, Cilliers. 2011. Current Research on the Gospel according to Mark: A Report on Monographs Published from 2000–2009. In: Becker, Eve-Marie/ Anders Runesson (eds.), *Mark and Matthew I. Comparative Readings: Understanding the Earliest Gospels in their First Century Settings.* WUNT 271. Tübingen: Mohr Siebeck, 13–32.

Breytenbach, Cilliers. 2021. "Mark's Tense Future." *Early Christianity* 12.3: 287–321.

Breytenbach, Cilliers. 2021 [1985]. The Gospel of Mark as "Episodic Narrative". In: Breytenbach, Cilliers (ed.), *The Gospel according to Mark as Episodic Narrative.* NovTSup 182. Leiden/ Boston, MA: Brill, 11–40.

Breytenbach, Cilliers. 2021a [2019]. Alternation between Aorist, Historical Present and Imperfect: Aspects of Markan Narrative Style. In: Breytenbach, Cilliers (ed.), *The Gospel according to Mark as Episodic Narrative.* NovTSup 182. Leiden/ Boston, MA: Brill, 179–219.

Breytenbach, Cilliers. 2021b [2019]. Metaphor in Argument: The Beelzebul Controversy in the Gospel according to Mark. In: Breytenbach, Cilliers (ed.), *The Gospel according to Mark as Episodic Narrative.* NovTSup 182. Leiden/ Boston, MA: Brill, 220–232.

Broadhead, Edwin Keith. 1992a. *Teaching with Authority: Miracles and Christology in the Gospel of Mark.* JSNTSup 74. Sheffield: JSOT Press.

Broadhead, Edwin Keith. 1992b. "Mk 1,44: The Witness of the Leper." *ZNW* 83: 257–265.

Broadhead, Edwin Keith. 1993. "Jesus the Nazarene: Narrative Strategy and Christological Imagery in the Gospel of Mark." *JSNT* 52: 3–18.

Brock, Brian. 2011. "Theologizing Inclusion: 1 Corinthians 12 and the Politics of the Body of Christ." *Journal of Religion, Disability & Health* 15: 351–376.

Brock, Brian; John Swinton. 2012. *Disability in the Christian Tradition: A Reader.* Grand Rapids, MI: William B. Eerdmans Publishing.

Brockmann, Christian. 2013. "Galen und Asklepios." *ZAC* 17.1: 51–67.

Browne, Stanley G. 1989. The History of Leprosy. In: Hastings, R. C. (ed.), *Leprosy.* Medicine in the Tropics Series. Edinburgh: Churchill Livingstone, 1–14.

Bultmann, Rudolf. 1921. *Die Geschichte der synoptischen Tradition.* Göttingen: Vandenhoeck & Ruprecht.

Bultmann, Rudolf. 1931. *Die Geschichte der synoptischen Tradition.* 2nd ed. Göttingen: Vandenhoeck & Ruprecht.

Bultmann, Rudolf. 1957. θάνατος and cogn. In: *Theologisches Wörterbuch zum Neuen Testament* 3, Stuttgart: Kohlhammer, 7–25.

Bultmann, Rudolf. 1967. *Die Geschichte der synoptischen Tradition*. FRLANT 29. Göttingen: Vandenhoeck & Ruprecht.

Burdon, Christopher. 2004. "'To the Other Side': Construction of Evil and Fear of Liberation in Mark 5.1–20." *JSNT* 27.2: 149–167.

Burke, Paul F. 1996. Malaria in the Greco-Roman World: A Historical and Epidemiological Survey. In: *ANRW 2.37.3*. Berlin: de Gruyter, 2252–2281.

Camery-Hoggatt, Jerry. 1992. *Irony in Mark's Gospel: Text and Subtext*. SNTSMS 72. Cambridge/ New York, NY: Cambridge University Press.

Campbell, Constantine R. 2007. *Verbal aspect, the Indicative Mood, and Narrative: Soundings in the Greek of the New Testament*. Studies in Biblical Greek 13. New York: Peter Lang.

Campbell, Constantine R. 2008. *Basics of Verbal Aspect in Biblical Greek*. Grand Rapids, MI: Zondervan.

Carroll, Robert P. 1997. Blindsight and the Vision Thing: Blindness and Insight in the Book of Isaiah. In: Broyles, Craig C./ Craig A. Evans (eds.), *Writing and Reading the Scroll of Isaiah: Studies of an Interpretive Tradition 1*. VTSup 70. Leiden/ New York: Brill, 79–93.

Carson, D. A.; Stanley E. Porter. 1993. *Biblical Greek Language and Linguistics: Open Questions in Current Research*. JSNTSup 80. Sheffield: JSOT Press.

Carter, Warren. 2011. "The blind, lame and paralyzed" (John 5:3): John's Gospel, Disability Studies, and Postcolonial Perspectives. In: Moss, Candida R./ Jeremy Schipper (eds.), *Disability Studies and Biblical Literature*. New York: Palgrave Macmillan, 129–150.

Carter, Warren. 2015. "Cross-Gendered Romans and Mark's Jesus: Legion Enters the Pigs (Mark 5:1–20)." *JBL* 134.1: 139–155.

Casey, P. Maurice. 1987. "General, Generic and Indefinite: The Use of the Term 'Sof of Man' in Aramaic Sources and in the Teaching of Jesus." *JSNT* 29: 21–56.

Casey, P. Maurice. 1995. "Idiom and Translation: Some Aspects of the Son of Man Problem." *NTS* 41: 164–182.

Cave, C. H. 1978/79. "The Leper: Mark 1.40–45." *NTS* 25: 245–250.

Chavel, Simeon. 2014. "Prophetic Imagination in the Light of Narratology and Disability Studies in Isaiah 40–48." *Journal of Hebrew Scriptures* 14: 40–48.

Choksy, Jamsheed K. 1989. *Purity and Pollution in Zoroastrianism: Triumph Over Evil*. Austin, TX: University of Texas Press.

Christopoulos, Menelaos; E. D. Karakantza; Olga Levaniouk (eds.). 2010. *Light and Darkness in Ancient Greek Myth and Religion. Part III: Eye-Sight/In-Sight*. Greek Studies: Interdisciplinary Approaches. Lanham, MD: Lexington Books.

Chronis, Harry L. 2005. "To Reveal and to Conceal: A Literary-Critical Perspective on 'the Son of Man' in Mark." *NTS* 51.4: 459–481.

Cizek, Paul. 2018. Leper, Leprosy IV. Judaism. In: *Encyclopedia of the Bible and Its Reception* 16, 150–152.

Clark-Soles, Jaime. 2016. "Mark and Disability." *Interpretation: A Journal of Bible and Theology* 70.2: 159–171.

Clements, Ronald E. 1985. "Beyond Tradition History: Deutero-Isaianic Developments of First Isaiah's Themes." *JSOT* 31: 95–113.

Clements, Ronald E. 1988. Patterns in the Prophetic Canon: Healing the Blind and Lame. In: Tucker, Gene M./ David L. Petersen/ Robert R. Wilson; et al. (eds.), *Canon, Theology, and Old Testament Interpretation: Essays in Honor of Brevard S. Childs*. Philadelphia, PA: Fortress Press, 189–200.

Coenen, Lothar. 2014. καθεύδω. In: *Theologisches Begriffslexikon zum Neuen Testament*, Wuppertal: Brockhaus, 1246–1248.

Coenen, Lothar; Klaus Haacker. 2014. Krankheit/Heilung. In: *Theologisches Begriffslexikon zum Neuen Testament*, Wuppertal: Brockhaus, 1197.

Cohen, Shaye J. D. 1991. Menstruants and the Sacred in Judaism and Christianity. In: Pomeroy, Sarah B. (ed.), *Women's History and Ancient History*. Chapel Hill, NC: University of North Carolina Press, 273–299.

Collins, Adela Yarbro. 2007. *Mark: A Commentary*. Hermeneia – a Critical and Historical Commentary on the Bible. Minneapolis, MN: Fortress Press.

Collins, Adela Yarbro; John J. Collins. 2008. *King and Messiah as Son of God: Divine, Human, and Angelic Messianic Figures in Biblical and Related Literature*. Grand Rapids, MI: William B. Eerdmans Publishing.

Collins, Raymond F. 1993. "The Transformation of a Motif: 'They Entered the House of Simon and Andrew' (Mark 1,29)." *SNTSU* 18: 5–40.

Colston, Lowell G. 1978. *Pastoral Care with Handicapped Persons*. Creative Pastoral Care and Counseling Series. Philadelphia, PA: Fortress.

Combrink, H. J. Bernard. 2005. Salvation in Mark. In: Van der Watt, J. G. (ed.), *Salvation in the New Testament: Perspectives on Soteriology*. NovTSup 121. Atlanta, GA: SBL Press, 33–66.

Cook, John Granger. 1997. "In Defence of Ambiguity: Is there a hidden Demon in Mark 1.29–31?" *NTS* 43: 184–208.

Corley, Kathleen E. 1993. *Private Women, Public Meals: Social Conflict in the Synoptic Tradition*. Peabody, MA: Hendrickson Publishers.

Cotter, Wendy. 1999. *Miracles in Greco-Roman Antiquity: A Sourcebook*. London/ New York: Routledge.

Cotter, Wendy. 2010. *The Christ of the Miracle Stories: Portrait through Encounter*. Grand Rapids, MI: Baker Academic.

Couey, J. Blake. 2018. Isaiah, Jeremiah, Ezekiel, Daniel, and the Twelve. In: Melcher, Sarah J./ Mikeal C. Parsons/ Amos Yong (eds.), *The Bible and Disability: A Commentary*. London: SCM Press, 215–273.

Cox, Dorian G. Coover. 2006. "The Hardening of Pharaoh's Heart in Its Literary and Cultural Contexts." *Bibliotheca Sacra* 163: 292–311.

Craffert, Pieter F. 2008. *The Life of a Galilean Shaman: Jesus of Nazareth in Anthropological-Historical Perspective*. Matrix: The Bible in Mediterranean Context 3. Eugene, OR: Cascade Books.

Creamer, Deborah Beth. 2009. *Disability and Christian Theology: Embodied Limits and Constructive Possibilities*. Academy Series. Oxford/ New York: Oxford University Press.

Crossan, John Dominic. 1994. *Der historische Jesus*. München: Beck.

Crossan, John Dominic. 1996. *Jesus. Ein revolutionäres Leben*. München: Beck.

Croy, N. Clayton. 2001. "Where the Gospel Text Begins: A Non-Theological Interpretation of Mark 1:1." *NovT* 43: 105–127.

Culpepper, R. Alan. 1982. "Mark 10:52: Why Mention The Garment?" *JBL* 101.1: 131–132.

Culpepper, R. Alan. 1983. *Anatomy of the Fourth Gospel: A Study in Literary Design*. Foundations and Facets: New Testament. Philadelphia, PA: Fortress Press.

Culpepper, R. Alan. 2007. *Mark*. Smyth & Helwys Bible Commentary. Macon, GA: Smyth & Helwys Publishing.

Culpepper, R. Alan. 2012. Blindness III. NT. In: *Encyclopedia of the Bible and Its Reception* 4, Berlin: de Gruyter, 178–182.

D'Angelo, Mary Rose. 1999. Gender and Power in the Gospel of Mark: The Daughter of Jairus and the Woman with the Flow of Blood. In: Cavadini, John C. (ed.), *Miracles in Jewish and Christian Antiquity: Imagining Truth*. Notre Dame Studies in Theology 3. Notre Dame, IN: University of Notre Dame Press, 83–109.

D'Angelo, Mary Rose. 1999. (Re) Presentations of Women in the Gospels John and Mark. In: Kraemer, Ross Shepard/ Mary Rose D'Angelo (eds.), *Women and Christian Origins*. New York: Oxford University Press, 129–149.

Danove, Paul L. 2005. *The Rhetoric of the Characterization of God, Jesus, and Jesus' Disciples in the Gospel of Mark*. JSNTSup 290. New York: T&T Clark.

Daras, Michael; George Papakostas; Alan J. Tuchman. 1994. "Epilepsy and the Ancient World: From the Magic Beliefs of the Babylonians to the Hippocratic Scientific Thinking." *Journal of the History of Neuroscience* 3.4: 233–236.

Dautzenberg, Gerhard. 1966. *Sein Leben bewahren. Ψυχή in den Herrenworten der Evangelien*. München: Kösel.

Davidsen, Ole. 1993. *The Narrative Jesus: A Semiotic Reading of Mark's Gospel*. Aarhus: Aarhus University Press.

Davies, Stevan L. 1995. *Jesus the Healer: Possession, Trance, and the Origins of Christianity*. London: SCM Press.

Dean-Jones, Lesley. 1994. *Women's Bodies in Classical Greek Science*. Oxford/ New York: Oxford University Press.

Decker, Rodney J. 2013. The Function of the Imperfect Tense in Mark's Gospel. In: Porter, Stanley E./ Andrew W. Pitts (eds.), *The Language of the New Testament: Context, History, and Development*. Linguistic Biblical Studies. Leiden: Brill, 347–364.

Decker, Rodney J. 2014. *Mark 1–8: A Handbook on the Greek Text*. Baylor Handbook on the Greek New Testament. Waco, TX: Baylor University Press.

Dederich, Markus. 2007. *Körper, Kultur und Behinderung: Eine Einführung in die Disability Studies*. Disability Studies. Körper – Macht – Differenz 2. Bielefeld: transcript.

Dederich, Markus. 2007. Textkörper und Körpertexte: Behinderung in der Literatur. In: Dederich, Markus (ed.), *Körper, Kultur und Behinderung: Eine Einführung in die Disability Studies*. Disability Studies. Körper – Macht – Differenz 2. Bielefeld: transcript, 107–123.

Deines, Roland. 2003. Josephus, Salomo und die von Gott verliehene τέχνη gegen die Dämonen. In: Lange, Armin/ Hermann Lichtenberger/ Diethard Römheld (eds.), *Die Dämonen – Demons: die Dämonologie der israelitisch-jüdischen und frühchristlichen Literatur im Kontext ihrer Umwelt*. Tübingen: Mohr Siebeck, 365–394.

Deissmann, Marie-Luise. 2005. Kind. In: *Antike Medizin. Ein Lexikon*, München: C.H. Beck, 491–493.

Derrett, J. Duncan M. 1979. "Spirit-Possession and the Gerasene Demoniac." *Man* 14.2: 286–293.

Derrett, J. Duncan M. 1981. "Trees Walking, Prophecy, and Christology." *Studia Theologica* 35.1: 33–54.

Devlieger, Patrick; Beatriz Mairanda-Galarza; Steven E. Brown; et al. 2016. *Rethinking Disability: World Perspectives in Culture and Society*. 2nd ed. Antwerp: Garant Uitgevers.

Dewey, Joanna. 1980. *Markan Public Debate: Literary Technique, Concentric Structure, and Theology in Mark 2:1–3:6*. SBLDS 48. Chico, CA: Scholars Press.

Dewey, Joanna. 1993. Mark. In: Schüssler Fiorenza, Elisabeth/ Shelly Matthews/ Ann Brock (eds.), *Searching the Scriptures: A Feminist Introduction and Commentary 1*. 2 vols. New York: Crossroad, 450–509.

Dibelius, Martin. 1933. *Die Formgeschichte des Evangeliums*. 2nd ed. Tübingen: J.C.B. Mohr (Paul Siebeck).

Dietzfelbinger, Christian. 1978. "Vom Sinn der Sabbatheilungen Jesu." *EvT* 38: 281–298.

Distelrath, Götz. 2005. Menstruation. In: *Antike Medizin. Ein Lexikon*, München: C.H. Beck, 606–607.

Dixon, Suzanne. 1988. *The Roman Mother*. London: Croom Helm.

Dobschütz, Ernst von. 1928. "Zur Erzählerkunst des Markus." *ZNW* 27: 193–198.

Dodd, Charles Herold. 1953. The Framework of the Gospel Narrative (1932). In: Dodd, Charles Herold (ed.), *New Testament Studies*. Manchester: Manchester U.P., 1–11.

Dodd, Charles Herold. 1970. *The Apostolic Preaching and Its Developments: Three Lectures, with an Appendix on Eschatology and History*. 4th ed. London: Hodder and Stoughton.

Doering, Lutz. 1999. *Schabbat: Sabbathalacha und -praxis im antiken Judentum und Urchristentum*. TSAJ 78. Tübingen: J.C.B. Mohr (Paul Siebeck).

Doering, Lutz. 2008. Much Ado Nothing? Jesus' Sabbath Healings and their Halakhic Implications Revisited. In: Doering, Lutz/ Hans-Günther Waubke/ Florian Wilk (eds.), *Judaistik und neutestamentliche Wissenschaft: Standorte – Grenzen – Beziehungen*. FRLANT 226. Göttingen: Vandenhoeck & Ruprecht, 213–241.

Doering, Lutz. 2010. Sabbath Laws in the New Testament Gospels. In: Bieringer, Reimun/ Florentino García Martínez/ Didier Pollefeyt; et al. (eds.), *The New Testament and Rabbinic Literature*. Supplements to the Journal for the Study of Judaism 136. Leiden/ Boston, MA: Brill, 207–253.

Doering, Lutz. 2019. Rabbinische Belege und Neues Testament. In: Kraus, Wolfgang/ Martin Rösel (eds.), *Update-Exegese 2.2: Ergebnisse gegenwärtiger Bibelwissenschaft*. Leipzig: Evangelische Verlagsanstalt, 301–310.

Doering, Lutz. 2022 [2017]. Jesus in the Judaism of His Time (Jewish Influence on Jesus). In: Schröter, Jens/ Christine Jacobi (eds.), *The Jesus Handbook*. Grand Rapids, MI: William B. Eerdmans Publishing, 222–224.

Donahue, John R.; Daniel J. Harrington. 2002. *The Gospel of Mark*. Sacra Pagina Series v 2. Collegeville, MI: Liturgical Press.

Dorman, Anke. 2014. The Other Others: A Qumran Perspective on Disability. In: Ben Zvi, Ehud/ Diana Vikander Edelman (eds.), *Imagining the Other and Constructing Israelite Identity in the Early Second Temple Period*. Library of Hebrew Bible / Old Testament Studies 456. London/ New York: T&T Clark, 297–316.

Dorman, Johanna H.W. 2007. *The Blemished Body: Deformity and Disability in the Qumran Scrolls*. University Library Groningen.

Dormeyer, Detlev. 1987. „Die Kompositionsmetapher ‚Evangelium Jesu Christi, des Sohnes Gottes' Mk 1,1: Ihre theologische und literarische Aufgabe in der Jesus-Biographie des Markus." *NTS* 33: 452–468.

Dormeyer, Detlev. 1999. *Das Markusevangelium als Idealbiographie von Jesus Christus, dem Nazarener*. Stuttgarter biblische Beiträge. Stuttgart: Verlag Katholisches Bibelwerk.

Dormeyer, Detlev. 2005. *Das Markusevangelium*. Darmstadt: Wissenschaftliche Buchgesellschaft.

Dormeyer, Detlev. 2013. Hinführung. In: Zimmermann, Ruben (ed.), *Kompendium der frühchristlichen Wundererzählungen: Die Wunder Jesu*. Gütersloh: 193–201.

Doudna, John Charles. 1961. *The Greek of the Gospel of Mark*. JBL Monograph Series 12. Philadelphia, PA: Society of Biblical Literature and Exegesis.

Dresken-Weiland, Jutta. 2010. *Bild, Grab und Wort: Untersuchungen zu Jenseitsvorstellungen von Christen des 3. und 4. Jahrhunderts*. Regensburg: Schnell & Steiner.
Drewermann, Eugen. 1992. *Tiefenpsychologie und Exegese Bd. II, Wunder, Vision, Weissagung, Apokalypse, Geschichte*. 3rd ed. Olten: Walter-Verlag.
Dschulnigg, Peter. 1984. *Sprache, Redaktion und Intention des Markus-Evangeliums: Eigentümlichkeiten der Sprache des Markus-Evangeliums und ihre Bedeutung für die Redaktionskritik*. Stuttgarter biblische Beiträge. Stuttgart: Verlag Katholisches Bibelwerk.
Dschulnigg, Peter. 2007. *Das Markusevangelium*. Theologischer Kommentar zum Neuen Testament. Stuttgart: Kohlhammer.
du Toit, David. 2013. Salvation. In: *Dictionary of Jesus and the Gospels: A Compendium of Temporary Biblical Scholarship*, Downers Grove, IL: 826–832.
du Toit, David. 2015. "Treasuring Memory: Narrative Christology in and beyond Mark's Gospel." *Early Christianity* 6: 334–353.
du Toit, David. 2022 [2017]. Christological Titles. In: Schröter, Jens/ Christine Jacobi (eds.), *The Jesus Handbook*. Grand Rapids, MI: William B. Eerdmans Publishing, 515–526.
du Toit, David S. 1997. *Theios Anthropos: Zur Verwendung von "Theios Anthrōpos" und sinnverwandten Ausdrücken in der Literatur der Kaiserzeit*. WUNT 2.91. Tübingen: J.C.B. Mohr (Paul Siebeck).
du Toit, David S. 2019. Heil und Unheil: Die Soteriologie des Markusevangeliums. In: Du Toit, David S./ Christine Gerber/ Christiane Zimmermann (eds.), *Sōtēria: Salvation in Early Christianity and Antiquity. FS in Honour of Cilliers Breytenbach on the Occasion of his 65th Birthday*. NovTSup 175. Leiden/ Boston, MA: Brill, 186–208.
Duden, Barbara. 1987. *Geschichte unter der Haut: Ein Eisenacher Arzt und seine Patientinnen um 1730*. Stuttgart: Klett-Cotta.
Duminil, Marie-Paule. 1983. *Le sang, les vaisseaux, le cœur dans la collection hippocratique: anatomie et physiologie*. Collection d'études anciennes. Paris: Société d'édition "Les Belles Lettres".
Dupont-Sommer, André. 1960. "Exorcismes et guérisons dans les récits de Koumrân." *Vetus Testamentum Supplements* 7: 246–261.
Dwyer, Timothy. 1996. *The Motif of Wonder in the Gospel of Mark*. JSNTSup 128. Sheffield: Sheffield Academic Press.
Ebeling, Hans Jürgen. 1939. *Das Messiasgeheimnis und die Botschaft des Marcus-Evangelisten*. BZNW 19. Berlin: A. Töpelmann.
Eberhart, Christian; Martin Karrer; Siegfried Kreuzer; et al. (eds.). 2020. *Tempel, Lehrhaus, Synagoge: Orte jüdischen Lernens und Lebens. FS für Wolfgang Kraus*. Paderborn: Ferdinand Schöningh.
Ebner, Martin. 2013. Wessen Medium willst du sein? (Die Heilung des Besessenen von Gerasa). In: Zimmermann, Ruben (ed.), *Kompendium der frühchristlichen Wundererzählungen: Die Wunder Jesu*. Gütersloh: Gütersloher Verlags-Haus, 266–277.
Eckstein, Hans-Joachim. 1996. "Markus 10,46–52 als Schlüsseltext des Markusevangeliums." *ZNW* 87: 33–50.
Edwards, Martha L. 1996. "The Cultural Context of Deformity in the Ancient Greek World: Let There Be a Law That No Deformed Child Shall Be Reared." *The Ancient History Bulletin* 10: 79–91.
Edwards, Martha L. 1997a. Constructions of Physical Disability in the Ancient Greek World: The Community Concept. In: Mitchell, David T./ Sharon L. Snyder (eds.), *The Body and Physical Difference: Discourses of Disability*. The Body, in Theory. Histories of Cultural Materialism. Ann Arbor, MI: University of Michigan Press, 35–50.
Edwards, Martha L. 1997b. Deaf and Dumb in Ancient Greece. In: Davis, Lennard J. (ed.), *The Disability Studies Reader 1*. New York: Routledge, 29–51.

Egger, Wilhelm. 1969. "Die Verborgenheit Jesu in Mk 3,7–12." *Biblica* 50: 466–490.

Egger, Wilhelm. 1976. *Frohbotschaft und Lehre: Die Sammelberichte des Wirkens Jesu im Markusevangelium*. Frankfurt a. M.: Knecht.

Ehrman, Bart D. 2006. "A Leper in the Hands of an Angry Jesus." *Studies in the Textual Criticism of the New Testament* 33: 120–141.

Eibisch, Frank. 2009. *Dein Glaube hat dir geholfen. Heilungsgeschichten des Markusevangeliums als paradigmatische Erzählungen und ihre Bedeutung für diakonisches Handeln*. Reutlingen: Reutlinger Theologische Studien.

Eiesland, Nancy L. 1994. *The Disabled God: Toward a Liberatory Theology of Disability*. Nashville, TN: Abingdon Press.

Eiesland, Nancy L.; Don E. Saliers. 1998. *Human Disability and the Service of God: Reassessing Religious Practice*. Nashville, TN: Abingdon Press.

Eisen, Ute E. 2020. Mitleid (splagchnizomai) in den synoptischen Evangelien. In: Eisen, Ute E./ Heidrun E. Mader (eds.), *Talking God in Society: Multidisciplinary (Re)constructions of Ancient (Con)texts, vol. 1: Theories and Applications, FS für Peter Lampe*. NTOA 120.1. Göttingen: Vandenhoeck & Ruprecht, 425–450.

Eisen, Ute E. 2023. Barmherzigkeitsdiskurse in der Evangelienüberlieferung. In: Barth, Roderich/ Ute E. Eisen/ Martin Fritz (eds.), *Barmherzigkeit. Das Mitgefühl im Brennpunkt zwischen Religion und Ethik*. Tübingen: Mohr Siebeck.

Elliott, J. Keith. 1993. *The Language and Style of the Gospel of Mark: An Edition of C.H. Turner's "Notes on Marcan Usage" together with Other Comparable Studies*. NovTSup 71. Leiden: Brill.

Elliott, J. Keith. 2010. The Conclusion of the Pericope of the Healing of the Leper in Mark 1:45. Is ὁ ἐξελθών a Title for Jesus in Mark 1:45? The Healing of the Leper in the Synoptic Parallels. In: *New Testament Textual Criticism: The Application of Thoroughgoing Principles. Essays on Manuscripts and Textual Variation*. NovTSup 137. Leiden/ Boston, MA: Brill, 341–352.

Elliott, Matthew. 2005. *Faithful Feelings: Emotion in the New Testament*. Leicester: Inter-Varsity Press.

Emden, Cecil S. 1953/54. "St. Mark's Use of the Imperfect Tense." *ExpTim* 65.5: 146–149.

Ernst, Josef. 1981. *Das Evangelium nach Markus*. Regensburger Neues Testament. Regensburg: Pustet.

Eshel, Esther. 2003. Genres of Magical Texts in the Dead Sea Scrolls. In: Lange, Armin/ Hermann Lichtenberger/ Diethard Römheld (eds.), *Die Dämonen: die Dämonologie der israelitisch-jüdischen und frühchristlichen Literatur im Kontext ihrer Umwelt*. Tübingen: Mohr Siebeck, 395–415.

Esser, Alexander Albert Maria. 1961. *Das Antlitz der Blindheit in der Antike: Die kulturellen und medizinhistorischen Ausstrahlungen des Blindenproblems in den antiken Quellen*. 2nd ed., Janus revue internationale de l'histoire des sciences, de la médecine, de la pharmacie et de la technique Suppléments 4. Leiden: Brill.

Eurich, Johannes. 2008. *Gerechtigkeit für Menschen mit Behinderung: Ethische Reflexionen und sozialpolitische Perspektiven*. Campus Forschung 940. Frankfurt a. M./ New York: Universität Heidelberg.

Fander, Monika. 1989. *Die Stellung der Frau im Markusevangelium: Unter besonderer Berücksichtigung kultur- und religionsgeschichtlicher Hintergründe*. Münsteraner theologische Abhandlungen. Altenberge: Telos-Verlag.

Fanning, B. M. 1990. *Verbal Aspect in New Testament Greek*. Oxford Theological Monographs. Oxford: Clarendon Press.

Feder, Yitzhaq. 2012. "The Polemic Regarding Skin Disease in 4QMMT." *Dead Sea Discoveries* 19.1: 55–70.

Feder, Yitzhaq. 2013. "Contagion and Cognition: Bodily Experience and the Conceptualization of Pollution (ṭum'ah) in the Hebrew Bible." *JNES* 72.2: 151–167.

Feldt, Laura. 2012a. Wilderness in Mythology and Religion. In: Feldt, Laura (ed.), *Wilderness in Mythology and Religion: Approaching Religious Spatialities, Cosmologies, and Ideas of Wild Nature*. Religion and Society. Berlin: de Gruyter, 1–23.

Feldt, Laura. 2012b. Wilderness and Hebrew Bible Religion – Fertility, Apostasy and Religious Transformation in the Pentateuch. In: Feldt, Laura (ed.), *Wilderness in Mythology and Religion: Approaching Religious Spatialities, Cosmologies, and Ideas of Wild Nature*. Berlin: de Gruyter, 55–94.

Feldt, Laura. 2018. Monster Theory and the Gospels: Monstrosities, Ambiguous Power and Emotions in Mark. In: Verheyden, Joseph/ John S. Kloppenborg (eds.), *The Gospels and Their Stories in Anthropological Perspective*. WUNT 409. Tübingen: Mohr Siebeck, 29–52.

Feneberg, Wolfgang. 1974. *Der Markusprolog: Studien zur Formbestimmung des Evangeliums*. SANT 36. München: Kösel-Verlag.

Fink, Renate Maria. 2000. *Die Botschaft des heilenden Handelns Jesu: Untersuchung der dreizehn exemplarischen Berichte von Jesu heilendem Handeln im Markusevangelium*. Salzburger theologische Studien 15. Innsbruck: Tyrolia.

Fischbach, Stephanie M. 1992. *Totenerweckungen: zur Geschichte einer Gattung*. Würzburg: Echter-Verlag.

Fishbane, Simcha. 2007. *Deviancy in Early Rabbinic Literature: A Collection of Socio-Anthropological Essays*. The Brill Reference Library of Judaism 27. Leiden/ Boston, MA: Brill.

Fitzmyer, Joseph A. 2004. *The Gensis Apocryphon of Qumran Cave 1 (1Q20): A Commentary*. 3rd ed., Biblica et Orientalla 18/B. Rome: Biblical Institute Press.

Flemming, Rebecca. 2000. *Medicine and the Making of Roman Women: Gender, Nature, and Authority from Celsus to Galen*. Oxford/ New York: Oxford University Press.

Flusser, David. 1957. "Healing through the Laying-on of Hands in a Dead Sea Scroll." *IEJ* 7.2: 107–108.

Focant, Camille. 2012. *The Gospel according to Mark: A Commentary*. Eugene, OR: Pickwick Publications.

Foerster, Werner. 1960. δαίμων. In: *Theologisches Wörterbuch zum Neuen Testament* 2, Stuttgart: Kohlhammer, 1–21.

Foerster, Werner. 1964. σῴζω. In: *Theologisches Wörterbuch zum Neuen Testament* 7, Stuttgart: Kohlhammer, 981–1012.

Foerster, Werner; Gerhard von Rad. 1960. εἰρήνη. In: *Theologisches Wörterbuch zum Neuen Testament* 2, Stuttgart: Kohlhammer, 298–416.

Föllinger, Sabine. 2005. Geschlecht. In: *Antike Medizin. Ein Lexikon*, München: C.H. Beck, 339–342.

Fonrobert, Charlotte. 1997. The Woman with a Blood-Flow (Mark 5:24–34) Revisited: Menstrual Laws and Jewish Culture in Christian Feminist Hermeneutics. In: Evans, Craig A./ James A. Sanders (eds.), *Early Christian Interpretation of the Scriptures of Israel: Investigations and Proposals*. JSNTSup. Sheffield: Sheffield Academic Press, 121–140.

Fowler, Robert M. 1981. *Loaves and Fishes: The Function of the Feeding Stories in the Gospel of Mark*. SBLDS 54. Chico, CA: Scholars Press.

Fowler, Robert M. 1991. *Let the Reader Understand: Reader-Response Criticism and the Gospel of Mark*. Minneapolis, MN: Fortress Press.

France, R. T. 1980. Mark and the Teaching of Jesus. In: France, R. T./ David Wenham (eds.), *Gospel Perspectives 1: Studies of History and Tradition in the Four Gospels*. 2 vols. Sheffield: JSOT Press, 118–123.

Frey, Jörg. 2013. Hilfe zur Selbstständigkeit (Der Kranke mit der 'verdorrten Hand' als Maurer). In: Zimmermann, Ruben (ed.), *Kompendium der frühchristlichen Wundererzählungen: Die Wunder Jesu*. Gütersloh: Gütersloher Verlags-Haus, 878–882.

Frey, Jörg. 2016. Heil. In: Schliesser, Benjamin (ed.), *Von Jesus zur neutestamentlichen Theologie*. WUNT 2.368. Tübingen: Mohr Siebeck, 539–584.

Frey, Jörg; Benjamin Schliesser; Nadine Kessler (eds.). 2017. *Glaube: Das Verständnis des Glaubens im frühen Christentum und in seiner jüdischen und hellenistisch-römischen Umwelt*. WUNT 373. Tübingen: Mohr Siebeck.

Frey-Anthes, Henrike. 2007. *Unheilsmächte und Schutzgenien, Antiwesen und Grenzgänger*. OBO 227. Göttingen: Vandenhoeck & Ruprecht.

Freyne, Seán. 1998. *Galilee from Alexander the Great to Hadrian, 323 B.C.E. to 135 C.E.: A Study of Second Temple Judaism*. 2nd ed., University of Notre Dame Center for the Study of Judaism and Antiquity 5. Edinburgh: T&T Clark.

Freyne, Seán. 2012. Zwischen römischem Imperium und Synagoge: Die Rolle von Frauen im römischen Palästina durch die Brille des Markusevangeliums. In: Navarro Puerto, Mercedes/ Marinella Perroni (eds.), *Evangelien: Erzählungen und Geschichten. Die Bibel und die Frauen: Eine exegetisch-kulturgeschichtliche Enzyklopädie 2.1*. Stuttgart: Kohlhammer, 39–59.

Fuchs, Albert. 1981/2. "Entwicklungsgeschichtliche Studie zu Mk 1,29–31 par Mt 8,14–15 par Lk 4,38–39. Macht über Fieber und Dämonen." *SNTSU* 6: 21–76.

Fuchs, Ernst. 1960. ἐκτείνω. In: *Theologisches Wörterbuch zum Neuen Testament* 2, Stuttgart: Kohlhammer, 458–463.

Garland, Robert. 1995. *The Eye of the Beholder: Deformity and Disability in the Graeco-Roman World*. London: Duckworth.

Garland-Thomson, Rosemarie. 1997. *Extraordinary Bodies: Figuring Physical Disability in American Culture and Literature*. New York: Columbia University Press.

Garland-Thomson, Rosemarie. 2010 [2002]. Integrating Disability, Transforming Feminist Theory. In: Davis, Lennard J. (ed.), *The Disability Studies Reader 3*. London/ New York: Routledge, 353–373.

Garner, Stephen. 2011. *Theology and the Body: Reflections on Being Flesh and Blood*. Interface: A Forum for Theology in the World 14.2. Hindmarsh: ATF Theology.

Garrison, Daniel H. 2014. *A Cultural History of the Human Body in Antiquity 1*. London/ New York: Bloomsbury.

Gemeinhardt, Peter. 2010. Magier, Weiser, Gott. Das Bild Jesu bei paganen antiken Autoren. In: Frey, Jörg/ Jens Schröter (eds.), *Jesus in apokryphen Evangelienüberlieferungen: Beiträge zu ausserkanonischen Jesusüberlieferungen aus verschiedenen Sprach- und Kulturtraditionen*. WUNT 254. Tübingen: Mohr Siebeck, 467–492.

Gemünden, Petra von. 2009. *Affekt und Glaube: Studien zur Historischen Psychologie des Frühjudentums und Urchristentums*. NTOA 73. Göttingen: Vandenhoeck & Ruprecht.

Gerber, Christine. 2013. Es ist genug für alle da! (Die Heilung der Tochter der Syrophönizierin) Mk 7,24–30. In: Zimmermann, Ruben (ed.), *Kompendium der frühchristlichen Wundererzählungen: Die Wunder Jesu*. Gütersloh: Gütersloher Verlags-Haus, 313–322.

Gerstenberger, Erhard. 1993. *Das dritte Buch Mose: Leviticus*. 6th ed., Das Alte Testament Deutsch (ATD) – Neubearbeitungen 6. Göttingen: Vandenhoeck & Ruprecht.

Gevaert, Bert; Christian Laes. 2013. What's in a Monster? Pliny the Elder, Teratology and Bodily Disability. In: Laes, Christian/ C. F. Goodey/ M. Lynn Rose (eds.), *Disabilities in Roman Antiquity: Disparate Bodies. A Capite ad Calcem*. Leiden: Brill, 211–230.

Giesen, Heinz. 2010. ἐπιτιμάω. In: *Exegetisches Wörterbuch zum Neuen Testament* 2, Stuttgart: Kohlhammer, 106–108.

Glancy, Jennifer A. 2010b. "Jesus, the Syrophoenician Woman, and Other First Century Bodies." *Biblical Interpretation* 18: 342–363.

Glenney, Brian; John T. Noble. 2014. "Perception and Prosopagnosia in Mark 8.22–26." *JSNT* 37.1: 71–85.

Gnilka, Joachim. 1978. *Das Evangelium nach Markus*. 2 vols. Neukirchen-Vluyn: Neukirchener Verlag.

Gnilka, Joachim. 2010. *Das Evangelium nach Markus*. EKKNT. Studienausgabe. Neukirchen-Vluyn: Neukirchner Verlag.

Golder, Werner. 2007. *Hippokrates und das Corpus Hippocraticum: Eine Einführung für Philologen und Mediziner*. Würzburg: Königshausen & Neumann.

Goodey, C. F.; M. Lynn Rose. 2013. Mental States, Bodily Dispositions and Table Manners: A Guide to Reading 'Intellectual' Disability from Homer to Late Antiquity. In: Laes, Christian/ C. F. Goodey/ M. Lynn Rose (eds.), *Disabilities in Roman Antiquity: Disparate Bodies. A Capite ad Calcem*. Leiden: Brill, 17–44.

Goodley, Dan. 2011. *Disability Studies: An Interdisciplinary Introduction*. Los Angeles, CA/ London: Sage.

Goodley, Dan. 2014. *Dis/ability Studies: Theorising Disablism and Ableism*. London/ New York: Routledge.

Gosbell, Louise A. 2018. *"The Poor, the Crippled, the Blind, and the Lame": Physical and Sensory Disability in the Gospels of the New Testament*. WUNT 2.469. Tübingen: Mohr Siebeck.

Graumann, Lutz Alexander. 2013. Monstrous Births and Retrospective Diagnosis: The Case of Hermaphrodites in Antiquity. In: Laes, Christian/ C. F. Goodey/ M. Lynn Rose (eds.), *Disabilities in Roman Antiquity: Disparate Bodies. A Capite ad Calcem*. Mnemosyne: Supplements. Leiden: Brill, 181–209.

Grethlein, Jonas; Antonios Rengakos. 2009. *Narratology and Interpretation: The Content of Narrative Form in Ancient Literature*. Trends in Classics Supplementary Volumes 4. Berlin: de Gruyter.

Grimm, Werner. 2010. θεραπεύω. In: *Exegetisches Wörterbuch zum Neuen Testament* 2, Stuttgart: Kohlhammer, 354–357.

Gross, Karl. 1985. *Menschenhand und Gotteshand in Antike und Christentum*. Stuttgart: Hiersemann.

Grue, Jan. 2017. "Now you see it, now you don't: A Discourse View of Disability and Multidisciplinarity." *Alter. European Journal of Disability Research* 11.3: 168–178.

Grundmann, Walter. 1960. δύναμαι/δύναμις. In: *Theologisches Wörterbuch zum Neuen Testament* 2, Stuttgart: Kohlhammer, 286–318.

Grundmann, Walter. 1980. *Das Evangelium nach Markus*. 8th ed., THKNT. Berlin: Evangelische Verlagsanstalt.

Grünstäudl, Wolfgang. 2011. "An Inclusive Mark? Critical Reflections on Ulrich Bach's Theology After Hadamar." *Journal of Religion, Disability & Health* 15.2: 130–138.

Grünstäudl, Wolfgang; Markus Schiefer Ferrari (eds.). 2012. *Gestörte Lektüre: Disability als hermeneutische Leitkategorie biblischer Exegese*. Behinderung, Theologie, Kirche. Stuttgart: Kohlhammer.

Guelich, Robert A. 1989. *Mark 1–8:26*. Word Biblical Commentary 34 A. Dallas, TX: Word Books.

Guijarro, Santiago. 2002. Die politische Wirkung der Exorzismen Jesu – Gesellschaftliche Reaktionen und Verteidigungsstrategien in der Beelzebul-Kontroverse. In: Stegemann, Wolfgang/ Bruce J. Malina/ Gerd Theissen (eds.), *Jesus in neuen Kontexten*. Stuttgart: Kohlhammer, 64–74.

Gundert, Beate. 2005. Fieber. In: *Antike Medizin. Ein Lexikon*, München: C.H. Beck, 299–301.

Gundry, Judith M. 2008. Children in the Gospel of Mark, with Special Attention to Jesus' Blessing of the Children (Mark 10:13–16) and the Purpose of Mark. In: Bunge, Marcia J./ Terence E. Fretheim/ Beverly Roberts Gaventa (eds.), *The Child in the Bible*. Grand Rapids, MI: William B. Eerdmans Publishing, 143–176.

Gundry, Robert Horton. 1993. *Mark: A Commentary on his Apology for the Cross*. Grand Rapids, MI: William B. Eerdmans Publishing.

Guttenberger, Gudrun. 2004. *Die Gottesvorstellung im Markusevangelium*. BZNW 123. Berlin: de Gruyter.

Haacker, Klaus; Hans-Georg Schütz. 2014. τηρέω. In: *Theologisches Begriffslexikon zum Neuen Testament*, Wuppertal: Brockhaus, 170–172.

Haber, Susan. 2003. "A Woman's Touch: Feminist Encounters with the Hemorrhaging Woman in Mark 5.24–34." *JSNT* 26: 171–192.

Haelewyck, Jean-Claude. 2013. "The Healing of a Leper (Mark 1,40–45): A Textual Commentary." *ETL* 89.1: 15–36.

Haenchen, Ernst. 1968. *Der Weg Jesu. Eine Erklärung des Markus-Evangeliums und der kanonischen Parallelen*. Berlin: Töpelmann.

Hahn, Ferdinand (ed.). 1985. *Der Erzähler des Evangeliums: Methodische Neuansätze in der Markusforschung*. Stuttgarter Bibelstudien 118/119. Stuttgart: Verlag Katholisches Bibelwerk.

Hankey, P. J. 1995. "Promise and Fulfillment: Reader-Response to Mark 1:1–15." *JSNT* 58: 3–18.

Hanson, Ann Ellis; Rebecca Flemming. 2005. Frau. In: *Antike Medizin. Ein Lexikon*, München: C.H. Beck, 307–310.

Hanson, Ann Ellis; Rebecca Flemming. 2005. Frauenheilkunde. In: *Antike Medizin. Ein Lexikon*, München: C.H. Beck, 310–313.

Hanson, Richard S. 1980. *Tyrian influence in the Upper Galilee*. Meiron Excavation Project no 2. Cambridge, MA: American Schools of Oriental Research.

Harnack, Adolf von; J. R. Wilkinson. 1911. *Luke the Physician: The Author of the Third Gospel and the Acts of the Apostles*. London/ New York: Williams & Norgate.

Harrill, J. Albert. 2001. Invective against Paul (2 Cor 10:10), the Physiognomics of the Ancient Slave Body, and the Greco-Roman Rhetoric of Manhood. In: Collins, Adela Yarbro/ Margaret Mary Mitchell (eds.), *Antiquity and Humanity: Essays on Ancient Religion and Philosophy. Presented to Hans Dieter Betz on His 70th Birthday*. Tübingen: Mohr Siebeck, 189–213.

Harrington, Hannah K. 1993. *The Impurity Systems of Qumran and the Rabbis: Biblical Foundations*. SBLDS 143. Atlanta, GA: Scholars Press.

Harris, C. R. S. 1973. *The Heart and the Vascular System in Ancient Greek Medicine: From Alcmaeon to Galen*. Oxford: Clarendon Press.

Harris, William V. 2001. *Restraining Rage: The Ideology of Anger Control in Classical Antiquity*. Cambridge, MA: Harvard University Press.

Harris, William V. 2013. *Mental Disorders in the Classical World*. Columbia Studies in the Classical Tradition 38. Leiden: Brill.

Harrocks, Rebecca. 2014. Jesus' Gentile Healings: The Absence of Bodily Contact and the Requirement of Faith. In: Taylor, Joan E. (ed.), *The Body in Biblical, Christian and Jewish Texts*. Library of Second Temple Studies 85. London: Bloomsbury, 83–101.

Hartsock, Chad. 2008. *Sight and Blindness in Luke-Acts: The Use of Physical Features in Characterization.* Leiden: Brill.

Hasselmann, Milena. 2023. *Konstruktion sozialer Identität: Studien zum Reinheitsverständnis im antiken Judentum und im Neuen Testament.* Ancient Judaism and Early Christianity 115. Leiden: Brill.

Hatton, Stephen B. 2015. "Comic Ambiguity in the Markan Healing Intercalation." *Neot* 49.1: 91–123.

Hauck, Friedrich. 1957. καθαρός and cogn. D. NT. In: *Theologisches Wörterbuch zum Neuen Testament* 3, Stuttgart: Kohlhammer, 427–434.

Heckel, Ulrich. 2014. ἀσθένεια. In: *Theologisches Begriffslexikon zum Neuen Testament*, Wuppertal: Brockhaus, 1199–1203.

Hedrick, Charles W. 1984. "The Role of 'Summary Statements' in the Composition of the Gospel of Mark. A Dialog with Karl Schmidt and Norman Perrin." *NovT* 26.4: 289–311.

Hedrick, Charles W. 1993. "Miracle Stories as Literary Compositions: The Case of Jairus's Daughter." *PRSt* 20.3: 217–233.

Heil, John Paul. 1992. *The Gospel of Mark as Model for Action: A Reader-Response Commentary.* New York: Paulist Press.

Heinen, Sandra; Roy Sommer. 2009. *Narratology in the Age of Cross-Disciplinary Narrative Research.* Narratologia. Berlin: de Gruyter.

Helm, Rudolf. 2005. Hautkrankheiten. In: *Antike Medizin. Ein Lexikon*, München: C.H. Beck, 382–383.

Hengel, Martin; Anna Maria Schwemer. 2007. *Jesus und das Judentum.* Geschichte des frühen Christentums 1. Tübingen: Mohr Siebeck.

Henning, Meghan. 2015. "Paralysis and Sexuality in Medical Literature and the Acts of Peter." *Journal of Late Antiquity* 8.2: 306–321.

Hentrich, Thomas. 2012. The Forgiveness of Sins as Healing Method in the New Testament. In: Breitwieser, Rupert (ed.), *Behinderungen und Beeinträchtigungen / Disability and Impairment in Antiquity.* BAR International Series 2359. Oxford: Archaeopress, 111–116.

Hentschel, Anni. 2007. *Diakonia im Neuen Testament: Studien zur Semantik unter besonderer Berücksichtigung der Rolle von Frauen.* WUNT 2.226. Tübingen: Mohr Siebeck.

Herzog, Rudolf. 1931. *Die Wunderheilungen von Epidauros: ein Beitrag zur Geschichte der Medizin und der Religion.* Iamata Epidauria. Leipzig: Dieterich.

Hester, J. David. 2005. "Queers on Account of the Kingdom of Heaven: Rhetorical Constructions of the Eunuch Body." *Scriptura* 90.3: 809–823.

Hibbitts, Bernard J. 1992. "'Coming to Our Senses': Communication and Legal Expression in Performance Cultures." *Emory Law Journal* 41: 873–960.

Hieke, Thomas. 2014. *Levitikus 1–15.* Herders Theologischer Kommentar zum Alten Testament. Freiburg: Herder.

Hieke, Thomas. 2018. Leper, Leprosy A. ANE and HB/OT. In: *Encyclopedia of the Bible and Its Reception* 16, Berlin: de Gruyter, 144–147.

Higgins, Ryan. 2015. Heart I. ANE and HB/OT. In: *Encyclopedia of the Bible and Its Reception* 11, Berlin/ Boston, MA: de Gruyter, 522–527.

Hilgert, Earle. 1996. The Son of Timaeus. Blindness, Sight, Ascent, Vision in Mark. In: Mack, Burton L./ Elizabeth A. Castelli/ Hal Taussig (eds.), *Reimagining Christian Origins: A Colloquium honoring Burton L. Mack.* Valley Forge, PA: Trinity Press International, 185–198.

Hofius, Otfried. 2000. Jesu Zuspruch der Sündenvergebung. Exegetische Erwägungen zu Mk 2,5b. In: Hofius, Otfried (ed.), *Neutestamentliche Studien.* WUNT 132. Tübingen: Mohr Siebeck, 125–143.

Hofius, Otfried. 2004. "Die Allmacht des Sohn Gottes und das Gebet des Glaubens. Erwägungen zu Thema und Aussage der Wundererzählung in Mk 9,14–29." *ZTK* 101.2: 117–137.

Hogan, Larry P. 1992. *Healing in the Second Temple Period.* NTOA 21. Göttingen: Vandenhoeck & Ruprecht.
Holden, Lynn. 1991. *Forms of Deformity.* JSOTSup 131. Sheffield: JSOT Press.
Holmén, Tom. 2011. Jesus and the Purity Paradigm. In: Holmén, Tom/ Stanley E. Porter (eds.), *Handbook for the Study of the Historical Jesus 3.* Leiden/ Boston, MA: Brill, 2709–2744.
Holmes, Brooke. 2014. Marked Bodies: Gender, Race, Class, Age, Disability, and Disease. In: Garrison, Daniel H. (ed.), *A Cultural History of the Human Body in Antiquity 1.* London/ New York: Bloomsbury, 159–183.
Hooker, Morna Dorothy. 1991. *The Gospel according to Saint Mark.* Black's New Testament Commentaries. Peabody, MA: Hendrickson Publishers.
Horn, Hans-Jürgen. 1969. Fieber. In: *RAC* 7, Stuttgart: Anton Hiersemann, 877–909.
Horsley, Gregory H. R. 1983. *New Documents Illustrating Early Christianity: A Review of the Greek Inscriptions and Papyri published in 1978.* North Ryde: Ancient History Documentary Research Centre, Macquarie University.
Horsley, Richard A. 1995a. "Archaeology and the Villages of Upper Galilee: A Dialogue with the Archaeologists." *BASOR* 297: 5–16.
Horsley, Richard A. 1995b. "Response." *BASOR* 297: 27–28.
Horsley, Richard A. 2001. *Hearing the Whole Story: Politics of Plot in Mark's Gospel.* Louisville, KY: Westminster John Knox Press.
Horton, Fred L. 1986. "Nochmals ἐφφαθά in Mk 7:34." *ZNW* 77: 101–108.
Hull, John M. 1974. *Hellenistic Magic and the Synoptic Tradition.* Studies in Biblical Theology 2.28. London: SCM Press.
Hull, John M. 2001. *In the Beginning there was Darkness: A Blind Person's Conversations with the Bible.* London: SCM Press.
Hulse, E. V. 1975. "The Nature of Biblical 'Leprosy' and the Use of Alternative Medical Terms in Modern Translations of the Bible." *PEQ* 107: 87–105.
Hultgren, Stephen. 2002. *Narrative Elements in the Double Tradition: A Study of Their Place within the Framework of the Gospel Narrative.* BZNW 133. New York/ Berlin: de Gruyter.
Hurtado, Larry W. 1983. *Mark.* San Francisco, CA: Harper & Row.
Iersel, Bas van. 1993. Concentric Structures in Mark 2,1–3,6 and 3,7–4,1: A Case Study. In: Focant, Camille/ Frans Neirynck (eds.), *The Synoptic Gospels: Source Criticism and the New Literary Criticism.* BETL 110. Leuven: Peeters, 75–97.
Iersel, Bas van. 1998. *Mark: A Reader-Response Commentary.* JSNTSup 164. Sheffield: Sheffield Academic Press.
Iersel, Bas van; Johannes C. Nuchelmans. 1995. "De zoon van Timeüs en de zoon van David: Marcus 10,46–52 gelezen door een grieks-romeinse bril." *Tijdschrift voor Theologie* 35: 107–124.
Inselmann, Anke. 2012. *Die Freude im Lukasevangelium: Ein Beitrag zur psychologischen Exegese.* WUNT 2.322. Tübingen: Mohr Siebeck.
Irwin, Brian P. 2008. "The Laying on of Hands in 1 Timothy 5:22: A New Proposal." *BBR* 18.1: 123–129.
Isherwood, Lisa; Elizabeth Stuart. 1998. *Introducing Body Theology.* Sheffield: Sheffield Academic Press.
Israelowich, Ido. 2012. *Society, Medicine and Religion in the Sacred Tales of Aelius Aristides.* Mnemosyne: Supplements 341. Leiden: Brill.
Iverson, Kelly R.; Christopher W. Skinner. 2011. *Mark as Story: Retrospect and Prospect.* SBLRBS 65. Atlanta, GA: SBL Press.

Janowski, Bernd. 2015. Das Herz als Beziehungsorgan. Zum Personverständnis des Alten Testaments. In: Janowski, Bernd/ Christoph Schwöbel (eds.), *Dimensionen der Leiblichkeit: Theologische Zugänge*. Theologie Interdisziplinär Band 16. Neukirchen-Vluyn: Neukirchener Theologie, 1–45.

Jeremias, Jochen. 1959. πολλοί. In: *Theologisches Wörterbuch zum Neuen Testament* 6, Stuttgart: Kohlhammer, 536–545.

Jochum-Bortfeld, Carsten. 2008. *Die Verachteten stehen auf: Widersprüche und Gegenentwürfe des Markusevangeliums zu den Menschenbildern seiner Zeit*. BWA(N)T 9.18 (178). Stuttgart: Kohlhammer.

Johnson, E. J. 1978–79. "Mark VIII. 22–26: The Blind Man from Bethsaida." *NTS* 25.3: 370–383.

Johnson, Nathan C. 2017. "Anger Issues: Mark 1.41 in Ephrem the Syrian, the Old Latin Gospels and Codex Bezae." *NTS* 63: 183–202.

Johnston, S. I. 1997. Dämonen V. Griechenland und Rom. In: *DNP* 3, Stuttgart: Metzler, 261–264.

Jouanna, Jacques. 2013. The Typology and Aetiology of Madness in Ancient Greek Medical and Philosophical Writing. In: Harris, William V. (ed.), *Mental Disorders in the Classical World*. Columbia Studies in the Classical Tradition 38. Leiden: Brill, 97–118.

Juel, Donald. 1994. *A Master of Surprise: Mark Interpreted*. Minneapolis, MN: Fortress Press.

Just, Felix N. W. 1997. *From Tobit to Bartimaeus, from Qumran to Silòam: The Social Role of Blind People and Attitudes toward the Blind in New Testament Times*. [unpublished].

Kahl, Brigitte. 1996. Jairus und die verlorenen Töchter Israels. Sozioliterarische Überlegungen zum Problem der Grenzüberschreitungen in Mk 5,21–43. In: Schottroff, Luise/ Marie-Theres Wacker (eds.), *Von der Wurzel getragen: Christlich-Feministische Exegese in Auseinandersetzung mit Antijudaismus*. Biblical Interpretation Series 17. Leiden/ New York: Brill, 61–78.

Kahl, Werner. 1994. *New Testament Miracle Stories in their Religious Historical Stetting: A Religionsgeschichtliche Comparison from a Structural Perspective*. Göttingen: Vandenhoeck & Ruprecht.

Kahl, Werner. 1998. "Ist es erlaubt, am Sabbat Leben zu retten oder zu töten? (Marc 3:4). Lebensbewahrung am Sabbat im Kontext der Schriften vom Toten Meer und der Mischna." *NovT* 40: 313–335.

Kahl, Werner. 2011. "Neutestamentliche Wunder als Verfahren des In-Ordnung-Bringens." *Interkulturelle Theologie* 37.1: 19–29.

Kahl, Werner. 2013. Glauben lässt Jesu Wunderkraft heilsam überfließen. (Die Tochter des Jaïrus und die blutflüssige Frau) Mk 5,21–43. In: Zimmermann, Ruben (ed.), *Kompendium der frühchristlichen Wundererzählungen: Die Wunder Jesu*. Gütersloh: Gütersloher Verlags-Haus, 278–293.

Kamionkowski, S. Tamar; Wonil Kim. 2010. *Bodies, Embodiment, and Theology of the Hebrew Bible*. Library of Hebrew Bible/Old Testament Studies 465. London/ New York: T&T Clark.

Kamlah, Eberhard; Klaiber, Walter. 2014. πνεῦμα. In: *Theologisches Begriffslexikon zum Neuen Testament*, Wuppertal: Brockhaus, 698–708.

Kaplan, David L. 1993. "Biblical Leprosy: An Anachronism Whose Time Has Come." *Journal of the American Academy of Dermatology* 28.3: 507–510.

Karenberg, Axel. 2005. Apoplexie. In: *Antike Medizin. Ein Lexikon*, München: C.H. Beck, 71–73.

Karenberg, Axel. 2005. Lähmung. In: *Antike Medizin. Ein Lexikon*, München: C.H. Beck, 550.

Kartzow, Marianne Bjelland; Halvor Moxnes. 2010. "Complex Identities: Ethnicity, Gender and Religion in the Story of the Ethiopian Eunuch (Acts 8:26–40)." *Religion and Theology* 17: 184–204.

Kazen, Thomas. 2002. *Jesus and Purity Halakhah: Was Jesus Indifferent to Impurity.* Coniectanea Biblica New Testament Series 38. Stockholm: Almqvist & Wiksell.

Kazen, Thomas. 2010. Jesus, Scripture and Paradosis: Response to Friedrich Avemarie. In: Bieringer, Reimund García Martínez, Florentino/ Didier Pollefeyt/ Peter F. Tomson (eds.), *The New Testament and Rabbinic Literature.* Supplements to the Journal for the Study of Judaism 136. Leiden/ Boston, MA: Brill, 281–288.

Kazen, Thomas. 2011. *Emotions in Biblical Law: A Cognitive Science Approach.* Hebrew Bible Monographs 36. Sheffield: Sheffield Phoenix Press.

Kazen, Thomas. 2013. Jesus and the Zavah. Implications for Interpreting Mark. In: Ehrlich, Carl S./ Anders Runesson/ Eileen M. Schuller (eds.), *Purity, Holiness, and Identity in Judaism and Christianity: Essays in Memory of Susan Haber.* WUNT 305. Tübingen: Mohr Siebeck, 112–143.

Kazen, Thomas. 2013. *Scripture, Interpretation, or Authority? Motives and Arguments in Jesus' Halakic Conflicts.* WUNT 320. Tübingen: Mohr Siebeck.

Kazen, Thomas. 2014. "The Role of Disgust in Priestly Purity Law: Insights from Conceptual Metaphor and Blending Theories." *Journal of Law, Religion and State* 3: 62–92.

Kazen, Thomas. 2017. Disgust in Body, Mind, and Language: The Case of Impurity in the Hebrew Bible. In: Spencer, F. Scott (ed.), *Mixed Feelings and Vexed Passions: Exploring Emotions in Biblical Literature.* SBLRBS 90. Atlanta, GA: SBL Press, 97–115.

Kazen, Thomas. 2022 [2017]. Jesus's Interpretation of the Torah. In: Schröter, Jens/ Christine Jacobi (eds.), *The Jesus Handbook.* Grand Rapids, MI: William B. Eerdmans Publishing, 400–413.

Kazmierski, Carl R. 1992. "Evangelist and Leper: A Socio-Cultural Study of Mark 1.40–45." *NTS* 38: 37–50.

Kee, Howard Clark. 1968. "The Terminology of Mark's Exorcism Stories." *NTS* 14: 231–246.

Kee, Howard Clark. 1977. *Community of the New Age: Studies in Mark's Gospel.* Philadelphia, PA: Westminster Press.

Kee, Howard Clark. 1986. *Medicine, Miracle and Magic in New Testament Times.* SNTSMS 55. Cambridge/ New York: Cambridge University Press.

Kelber, Werner H. 1974. *The Kingdom in Mark: A New Place and A New Time.* Philadelphia, PA: Fortress Press.

Kelber, Werner H. 1979. *Mark's Story of Jesus.* Philadelphia, PA: Fortress Press.

Kellenbach, Katharina von. 1994. *Anti-Judaism in Feminist Religious Writings.* Atlanta, GA: Scholars Press.

Kellenberger, Edgar. 2011. *Der Schutz der Einfältigen: Menschen mit einer geistigen Behinderung in der Bibel und in weiteren Quellen.* Zürich: Theologischer Verlag Zürich.

Kelley, Nicole. 2007. Deformity and Disability in Greece and Rome. In: Avalos, Hector/ Sarah J. Melcher/ Jeremy Schipper (eds.), *This Abled Body: Rethinking Disabilities in Biblical Studies.* SBL SemeiaSt 55. Leiden: Brill, 31–45.

Kelley, Nicole. 2007. "The Theological Significance of Physical Deformity in the Pseudo-Clementine Homilies." *PRSt* 34.1: 78–90.

Kelley, Nicole. 2011. 'The Punishment of the Devil was Aparent in the Torment of the Human Body': Epilepsy in Ancient Christianity. In: Schipper, Jeremy/ Candida R. Moss (eds.), *Disability Studies and Biblical Literature.* New York: Palgrave Macmillan, 205–221.

Kertelge, Karl. 1970. *Die Wunder Jesu im Markusevangelium. Eine redaktionsgeschichtliche Untersuchung.* SANT 33. München: Kösel-Verlag.

Kiffiak, Jordash. 2017. *Responses in the Miracle Stories of the Gospels: Between Artistry and Inherited Tradition.* WUNT 2.429. Tübingen: Mohr Siebeck.

Kilpatrick, G. D. 1993. Mark i 45 and the Meaning of λόγος. In: Kilpatrick, G. D. (ed.), *The Language and Style of the Gospel of Mark*. NovTSup 71. Leiden: Brill, 149–152.
King, Helen. 1998. *Hippocrates' Woman: Reading the Female Body in Ancient Greece*. London/ New York: Routledge.
Kingsbury, Jack Dean. 1983. *The Christology of Mark's Gospel*. Philadelphia, PA: Fortress Press.
Kingsbury, Jack Dean. 1986. *Matthew as Story*. Philadelphia, PA: Fortress Press.
Kingsbury, Jack Dean. 1989. *Conflict in Mark. Jesus, Authorities, Disciples*. Minneapolis, MN: Fortress Press.
Kinnier Wilson, James. 1967. Organic Disease in Ancient Mesopotamia. In: Brothwell, Don R./ A. T. Sandison (eds.), *Diseases in Antiquity: A Survey of the Diseases, Injuries, and Surgery of Early Populations*. Springfield, IL: C. C. Thomas, 281–288.
Kirchenschläger, Walter. 1976. "Exorcismus in Qumran?" *Kairos* 18: 135–153.
Kitz, Anne Marie. 2014. Fever I. HB/OT. In: *Encyclopedia of the Bible and Its Reception* 8, Berlin: de Gruyter, 1194–1195.
Klaiber, Walter. 2014. ἐγείρω. In: *Theologisches Begriffslexikon zum Neuen Testament*, Wuppertal: Brockhaus, 92–102.
Klauck, Hans-Josef. 1981. *Hausgemeinde und Hauskirche im frühen Christentum*. SBS 103. Stuttgart: Katholisches Bibelwerk.
Klauck, Hans-Josef. 1989. Die erzählerische Rolle der Jünger im Markusevangelium. Eine narrative Analyse [1982]. In: Klauck, Hans-Josef (ed.), *Gemeinde – Amt – Sakrament. Neutestamentliche Perspektiven*. Würzburg: 137–159.
Klauck, Hans-Josef. 1997. *Vorspiel im Himmel?: Erzähltechnik und Theologie im Markusprolog*. Biblisch-Theologische Studien 32. Neukirchen-Vluyn: Neukirchener.
Klein, Anne. 2010. Wie betreibt man Disability History? Methoden in Bewegung. In: Bösl, Elsbeth/ Anne Klein/ Anne Waldschmidt (eds.), *Disability History: Konstruktionen von Behinderung in der Geschichte. Eine Einführung*. Disability Studies. Bielefeld: transcript, 45–62.
Klein, Hans. 2014. θάνατος. In: *Theologisches Begriffslexikon zum Neuen Testament*, Wuppertal: Brockhaus, 1236–1246.
Kliesch, Klaus. 2011. Blinde sehen, Lahme gehen. Der heilende Jesus und seine Wirkungsgeschichte In: Eurich, Johannes/ Andreas Lob-Hüdepohl (eds.), *Inklusive Kirche*. Stuttgart: Kohlhammer, 81–100.
Klinghardt, Matthias. 2007. "Legionsschweine in Gerasa. Lokalkolorit und historischer Hintergrund von Mk 5,1–20." *ZNW* 98: 28–48.
Klostermann, Erich. 1907. *Die Evangelien: 1. Markus*. HNT 3. Tübingen: J.C.B. Mohr (Paul Siebeck).
Klumbies, Paul-Gerhard. 2013. Die Heilung eines Gelähmten und vieler Erstarrter (Die Heilung eines Gelähmten). In: Zimmermann, Ruben (ed.), *Kompendium der frühchristlichen Wundererzählungen: Die Wunder Jesu*. Gütersloh: Gütersloher Verlags-Haus, 235–247.
Klumbies, Paul-Gerhard. 2016. Die ätiologisch-narrative Begründung geltender Normen in Mk 2,1–3,6. In: Volp, Ulrich/ Friedrich Wilhelm Horn/ Ruben Zimmermann (eds.), *Metapher – Narratio – Mimesis – Doxologie: Begründungsformen frühchristlicher und antiker Ethik*. WUNT 356. Tübingen: Mohr Siebeck, 169–188.
Koch, Dietrich-Alex. 1975. *Die Bedeutung der Wundererzählungen für die Christologie des Markusevangeliums*. Berlin: de Gruyter.
Koch, Stefan. 2019. Der allwissende Erzähler und das Schweigegbot Jesu im Markusevangelium. In: Oyen, Geert van (ed.), *Reading the Gospel of Mark in the twenty-first century: Method and Meaning*. BETL 301. Leuven: Peeters, 581–593.

Köcher, Franz. 1986. Saḫaršubbû: Zur Frage nach der Lepra im alten Zweistromland. In: Wolf, Jörg Henning (ed.), *Aussatz, Lepra, Hansen-Krankheit: Ein Menschheitsproblem im Wandel: Teil 2 Aufsätze*. Würzburg: Kataloge des Deutschen Medizinhistorischen Museums, 27–34.

Kollmann, Bernd. 1996. *Jesus und die Christen als Wundertäter: Studien zu Magie, Medizin und Schamanismus in Antike und Christentum*. Göttingen: Vandenhoeck & Ruprecht.

Kollmann, Bernd. 2007. *Neutestamentliche Wundergeschichten: Biblisch-Theologische Zugänge und Impulse für die Praxis*. 2nd ed., Urban-Taschenbücher 477. Stuttgart: Kohlhammer.

Kollmann, Bernd. 2011. Jesus and Magic: The Question of the Miracles. In: Holmén, Tom/ Stanley E. Porter (eds.), *Handbook for the Study of the Historical Jesus 4*. Leiden/ Boston, MA: Brill, 3057–3085.

Kollmann, Bernd. 2013. Krankheitsbilder und soziale Folgen. In: Zimmermann, Ruben (ed.), *Kompendium der frühchristlichen Wundererzählungen: Die Wunder Jesu*. Gütersloh: Gütersloher Verlags-Haus, 87–93.

Körting, Corinna. 2015. Hands, Laying on of I. HB/OT. In: *Encyclopedia of the Bible and Its Reception* 11, Berlin: de Gruyter, 202–203.

Kosak, Jennifer. 2015. Interpretations of the Healer's Touch in the Hippocratic Corpus. In: Petridou, Georgia/ Chiara Thumiger (eds.), *Homo Patiens: Approaches to the Patient in the Ancient World*. Studies in Ancient Medicine 45. Leiden: Brill, 247–264.

Kraemer, Ross Shepard; Mary Rose D'Angelo. 1999. *Women and Christian Origins*. New York: Oxford University Press.

Krahe, Susanne. 2002. "Sonderanfertigung oder Montagsmodell. Behinderte Menschen in der Bibel." *INFO. Informationen für Religionslehrerinnen und Religionslehrer Bistum Limburg* 3: 162–171.

Kranemann, Benedikt. 2006. Krankenöl. In: *RAC* 11, Stuttgart: Anton Hiersemann, 915–965.

Krause, Deborah. 2001. Simon Peter's Mother-in-Law – Disciple or Domestic Servant? Feminist Biblical Hermeneutics and the Interpretation of Mark 1:29–31. In: Levine, Amy-Jill/ Marianne Blickenstaff (eds.), *A Feminist Companion to Mark*. Sheffield: Pilgrim Press, 37–53.

Kremer, Jacob. 2010. ἀνάστασις and cogn. In: *Exegetisches Wörterbuch zum Neuen Testament* 1, Stuttgart: Kohlhammer, 210–221.

Kremer, Jacob. 2010. ἐγείρω. In: *Exegetisches Wörterbuch zum Neuen Testament* 1, Stuttgart: Kohlhammer, 899–910.

Kremer, Jacob. 2010. πνεῦμα. In: *Exegetisches Wörterbuch zum Neuen Testament* 1, Stuttgart: Kohlhammer, 279–291.

Krug, Antje. 1993. *Heilkunst und Heilkult: Medizin in der Antike*. 2nd ed., Beck's Archäologische Bibliothek. München: Beck.

Krüger, Thomas. 2009. Das "Herz" in der alttestamentlichen Anthropologie. In: Wagner, Andreas (ed.), *Anthropologische Aufbrüche: Alttestamentliche und interdisziplinäre Zugänge zur historischen Anthropologie*. Göttingen: Vandenhoeck & Ruprecht, 103–118.

Kudlick, Catherine Jean. 2018. Social History of Medicine and Disability History. In: Rembis, Michael A./ Catherine Jean Kudlick/ Kim E. Nielsen (eds.), *The Oxford Handbook of Disability History*. New York, NY: Oxford University Press, 105–124.

Kuemmerlin-McLean, J. K. 1992. Demons. Old Testament. In: *ABD* 2, New York: Doubleday, 138–140.

Kuhn, Heinz-Wolfgang. 2010. ἀνάστασις and cogn. In: *Exegetisches Wörterbuch zum Neuen Testament* 1, Stuttgart: Kohlhammer, 210–221.

Kuhn, Heinz-Wolfgang. 2010. ξηραίνω. In: *Exegetisches Wörterbuch zum Neuen Testament* 2, Stuttgart: Kohlhammer, 1191.

Kuhn, Karl Allen. 2009. *The Heart of Biblical Narrative: Rediscovering Biblical Appeal to the Emotions*. Minneapolis, MN: Fortress.
Külken, Thomas. 1985. *Fieberkonzepte in der Geschichte der Medizin*. Heidelberg: Verlag für Medizin Fischer.
Laes, Christian. 2008. "Learning from Silence: Disabled Children in Roman Antiquity." *Arctos* 42: 85–122.
Laes, Christian. 2011. "Silent Witnesses: Deaf-Mutes in Graeco-Roman Antiquity." *Classical World* 104.4: 451–473.
Laes, Christian. 2013. Silent History? Speech Impairment in Roman Antiquity. In: Laes, Christian/ C. F. Goodey/ M. Lynn Rose (eds.), *Disabilities in Roman Antiquity: Disparate Bodies. A Capite ad Calcem*. Mnemosyne: Supplements. Leiden: Brill, 145–180.
Laes, Christian (ed.). 2017. *Disability in Antiquity*. Rewriting Antiquity. London/ New York: Routledge.
Laes, Christian. 2017. Introduction: Disabilities in the Ancient World: Past, Present and Future. In: Laes, Christian (ed.), *Disability in Antiquity*. Rewriting Antiquity. London/ New York: Routledge, 1–21.
Laes, Christian; C. F. Goodey; M. Lynn Rose (eds.). 2013. *Disabilities in Roman Antiquity: Disparate Bodies. A Capite ad Calcem*. Mnemosyne: Supplements. Leiden: Brill.
Lagrange, Marie-Joseph. 1935. *Évangile selon Saint Marc*. Études bibliques. Paris: J. Gabalda.
Lake, Kirsopp. 1923. "'ΕΜΒΡΙΜΗΣΑΜΕΝΟΣ and 'ΟΡΓΙΣΘΕΙΣ Mark 1,40–43." *HTR* 16.2: 197–198.
Lamarche, Paul. 1996. *Évangile de Marc: Commentaire*. Études Bibliques 33. Paris: J. Gabalda.
Lane, William L. 1974. *The Gospel according to Mark. The English text with Introduction, Exposition, and Notes*. Grand Rapids, MI: William B. Eerdmans Publishing.
Lange, Armin; Hermann Lichtenberger; Diethard Römheld. 2003. *Die Dämonen – Demons: die Dämonologie der israelitisch-jüdischen und frühchristlichen Literatur im Kontext ihrer Umwelt*. Tübingen: Mohr Siebeck.
Lattke, Michael. 2010. κακῶς. In: *Exegetisches Wörterbuch zum Neuen Testament* 2, Stuttgart: Kohlhammer, 590–591.
Lau, Markus. 2007. "Die Legio X Fretensis und der Besessene von Gerasa. Anmerkungen zur Zahlenangabe "ungefähr Zweitausend" (Mk 5,13)." *Biblica* 88: 351–364.
Lau, Markus. 2013. Fieberfrei auf dem Weg zu Jesus: Mk 1,29–31. In: Zimmermann, Ruben (ed.), *Kompendium der frühchristlichen Wundererzählungen: Die Wunder Jesu*. Gütersloh: Gütersloher Verlags-Haus, 214–220.
Lau, Markus. 2020. "Capta et devicta? Eine mk Gegenerzählung zur römischen Judaea-Capta-Münzprägung – Anmerkungen zur literarischen Technik einer narrativen Münzüberprägung in Mk 5,1–20." *RB* 127.1: 35–63.
Lawrence, Louise Joy. 2011. "Exploring the Sense-scape of the Gospel of Mark." *JSNT* 33.4: 387–397.
Lawrence, Louise Joy. 2013. *Sense and Stigma in the Gospels: Depictions of Sensory-Disabled Characters*. Biblical Refigurations. Oxford: Oxford University Press.
Lawrence, Louise Joy. 2018. *Bible and Bedlam: Madness, Sanism and New Testament Interpretation*. Library of New Testament Studies 594. London: T&T Clark.
Leander, Hans. 2013. *Discourses of Empire: The Gospel of Mark from a Postcolonial Perspective*. SBL SemeiaSt 71. Leiden: Brill.
Lesky, Erna. 1954. Blindheit. In: *RAC* 2, Stuttgart: Anton Hiersemann, 433–446.
Leutzsch, Martin. 2013. Vermögen und Vertrauen, Dämonie und Exorzismus (Die Erzählung vom besessenen Jungen) Mk 9,14–29. In: Zimmermann, Ruben (ed.), *Kompendium der*

frühchristlichen Wundererzählungen: Die Wunder Jesu. Gütersloh: Gütersloher Verlags-Haus, 350–358.
Leven, Karl-Heinz. 2004. "At times these ancient facts seem to lie before me like a patient on a hospital bed" – Retrospective Diagnosis and Ancient Medical History. In: Horstmanshoff, H. F. J./ Marten Stol/ C. R. van Tilburg (eds.), *Magic and Rationality in Ancient Near Eastern and Graeco-Roman Medicine*. Studies in Ancient Medicine 27. Leiden/ Boston, MA: Brill, 369–386.
Leven, Karl-Heinz. 2005. Dämonen. In: *Antike Medizin. Ein Lexikon*, München: C.H. Beck, 206–207.
Leven, Karl-Heinz. 2005. Epilepsie. In: *Antike Medizin. Ein Lexikon*, München: C.H. Beck, 260–262.
Leven, Karl-Heinz. 2005. Lepra. In: *Antike Medizin. Ein Lexikon*, München: C.H. Beck, 565–567.
Levin, S. 1988. "Isaac's Blindness: A Medical Diagnosis." *Judaism* 37: 81–83.
Levine, Amy-Jill. 2001 [1996]. Discharging Responsibility: Matthean Jesus, Biblical Law, and Hemorrhaging Woman. In: Levine, Amy-Jill/ Marianne Blickenstaff (eds.), *A Feminist Companion to Matthew*. Symposium Series. Sheffield: Sheffield Academic Press, 70–87.
Lewis, Orly; David Leith; Sean Coughlin (eds.). 2020. *The Concept of Pneuma after Aristotle*. Berlin Studies of the Ancient World 61. Berlin: Edition Topoi.
Lieber, Elinor. 2000. Old Testament 'Leprosy,' Contagion and Sin. In: Conrad, Lawrence I./ D. Wujastyk (eds.), *Contagion: Perspectives from Pre-modern Societies*. Aldershot: Ashgate, 99–136.
Liedke, Ulf. 2009. *Beziehungsreiches Leben: Studien zu einer inklusiven theologischen Anthropologie für Menschen mit und ohne Behinderung*. Arbeiten zur Pastoraltheologie, Liturgik und Hymnologie. Göttingen: Vandenhoeck & Ruprecht.
Lindemann, Andreas. 2009. Jesus und das epilepsiekranke Kind. Zur Auslegung der Wundererzählung Mk 9,14–29. In: Lindemann, Andreas (ed.), *Die Evangelien und die Apostelgeschichte: Studien zu ihrer Theologie und zu ihrer Geschichte*. WUNT 241. Tübingen: Mohr Siebeck, 93–108.
Link, Hans-Georg. 2014. ἀσθένεια. In: *Theologisches Begriffslexikon zum Neuen Testament*, Wuppertal: Brockhaus, 1199.
Link, Hans-Georg; Cilliers Breytenbach. 2014. ἀποκαθίστημι. In: *Theologisches Begriffslexikon zum Neuen Testament*, Wuppertal: Brockhaus, 1774–1776.
Lisboa, Joel E. 2015. "Comparative Narrative Analysis as a Tool in Determining the Lectio Difficilior in Mark 1:40–45." *Neot* 49.1: 75–89.
Lohmeyer, Ernst. 1967. *Das Evangelium des Markus*. 17th ed., Kritisch-exegetischer Kommentar über das Neue Testament. Göttingen: Vandenhoeck & Ruprecht.
Lohse, Eduard. 1973. χείρ and cogn. In: *Theologisches Wörterbuch zum Neuen Testament* 9, Stuttgart: Kohlhammer, 413–427.
Lührmann, Dieter. 1987. *Das Markusevangelium*. HNT 3. Tübingen: J.C.B. Mohr (Paul Siebeck).
Luz, Ulrich. 1965. "Das Geheimnismotiv und die markinische Christologie." *ZNW* 56: 9–30.
Maccoby, Hyam. 1999. *Ritual and Morality: The Ritual Purity System and its Place in Judaism*. Cambridge/ New York: Cambridge University Press.
MacFarlane, Patrick. 2014. Health and Disease. In: Garrison, Daniel H. (ed.), *A Cultural History of the Human Body in Antiquity 1*. London/ New York: Bloomsbury, 45–66.
Machiela, Daniel A. 2015. Luke 13:10–13: 'Woman, You Have Been Set Free from Your Ailment' – Illness, Demon Possession, and Laying on Hands in Light of Second Temple Period Jewish Literature. In: Notley, R. Steven/ Jeffrey Paul Garcia (eds.), *The Gospels in First-Century Judaea*. Jewish and Christian Perspectives Series 29. Leiden: Brill, 122–135.

Mahr, Dominik. 2013. Heilende Macht daheim (Die Heilung der Schwiegermutter des Simon Petrus). In: Zimmermann, Ruben (ed.), *Kompendium der frühchristlichen Wundererzählungen: Die Wunder Jesu.* Gütersloh: Gütersloher Verlags-Haus, 536–542.

Maier, J. 1976. Geister (Dämonen) B.I.c. Israel. In: *RAC* 9, Stuttgart: Anton Hiersemann, 579–585.

Mainwaring, Simon. 2014. *Mark, Mutuality, And Mental Health. Encounters with Jesus.* Atlanta, GA: SBL Press.

Malbon, Elizabeth Struthers. 1991. *Narrative Space and Mythic Meaning in Mark.* The Biblical Seminar 13. Sheffield: JSOT Press.

Malbon, Elizabeth Struthers. 2000. *In the Company of Jesus: Characters in Mark's Gospel.* Louisville, KY: Westminster John Knox Press.

Malbon, Elizabeth Struthers. 2009. *Mark's Jesus: Characterization as Narrative Christology.* Waco, TX: Baylor University Press.

Malina, Bruce J. 1993. *The New Testament World: Insights from Cultural Anthropology.* Louisville, KY: Westminster/John Knox Press.

Manchester, Keith. 1992. Leprosy: The Origin and Development of the Disease in Antiquity. In: Gourevitch, Danielle/ Mirko D. Grmek (eds.), *Maladie et Maladies: Histoire et Conceptualisation: Mélanges en l'honneur de Mirko Grmek.* Genenva: Droz, 31–49.

Marcus, Joel. 1999. "A Note on Markan Optics." *NTS* 45: 250–256.

Marcus, Joel. 2000. *Mark 1–8: A New Translation with Introduction and Commentary.* AB 27. New York: Doubleday.

Marcus, Joel. 2004. *The Way of the Lord: Christological Exegesis of the Old Testament in the Gospel of Mark.* T&T Clark Academic Paperbacks. London/ New York: T&T Clark.

Marcus, Joel. 2009. *Mark 8–16: A New Translation with Introduction and Commentary.* AB 27 A. New Haven, CO: Yale University Press.

Marganne, Marie-Hélène. 1994. *L'ophtalmologie dans l'Égypte gréco-romaine d'après les papyrus littéraires grecs.* Studies in Ancient Medicine 8. Leiden: Brill.

Marguerat, Daniel. 2008. *L'aube du christianisme.* Le Monde de la Bible 60. Paris: Bayard.

Marshall, Christopher D. 1989. *Faith as a Theme in Mark's Narrative.* Cambridge/ New York: Cambridge University Press.

Martin, Dale B. 1995. *The Corinthian Body.* New Haven, CO: Yale University Press.

Martin, Dale B. 2004. *Inventing Superstition: From the Hippocratics to the Christians.* Cambridge, MA: Harvard University Press.

Marx, Tzvi. 1992. *Halakha and Handicap: Jewish Law and Ethics on Disability.* Jerusalem: Katholieke Theologische Universiteit te Utrecht, 1993.

Marx-Wolf, Heidi; Kristi Upson-Saia. 2015. "The State of the Question: Religion, Medicine, Disability and Health in Late Antiquity." *Journal of Late Antiquity* 8.2: 257–272.

Marxsen, Willi. 1959 [1956]. *Der Evangelist Markus: Studien zur Redaktionsgeschichte des Evangeliums.* 2nd ed., FRLANT 67. Göttingen: Vandenhoeck & Ruprecht.

Maspero, Gaston. 1905. *Les contes populaires de l'Egypte ancienne.* 3rd ed. Paris: Guilmoto.

Mayeda, Goro. 1946. *Das Leben-Jesu-Fragment Papyrus Egerton 2 und seine Stellung in der urchristlichen Literaturgeschichte.* Bern: Paul Haupt.

Mayer-Haas, Andrea J. 2003. *"Geschenk aus Gottes Schatzkammer" (bSchab 10b): Jesus und der Sabbat im Spiegel der neutestamentlichen Schriften.* NTAbh 43. Münster: Aschendorff.

Mayfield, Tyler. 2012. Blindness I. HB/OT. In: *Encyclopedia of the Bible and Its Reception* 4, Berlin: de Gruyter, 171–174.

McAffee, Matthew. 2010. "The Heart of Pharaoh in Exodus 4–15." *BBR* 20.3: 331–354.

McCloughry, Roy; Wayne Morris. 2002. *Making a World of Difference: Christian Reflections on Disability*. London: SPCK.

McRuer, Robert. 2006. *Crip Theory: Cultural Signs of Queerness and Disability*. Cultural Front. New York: New York University Press.

Meekosha, Helen; Russell Peter Shuttleworth. 2009. "What's So Critical About Critical Disability Studies?" *Australian Journal of Human Rights* 15.1: 47–75.

Meier, John P. 1994. *A Marginal Jew: Rethinking the Historical Jesus. Vol. 2: Mentor, Message and Miracles*. ABRL. New York: Doubleday.

Meier, John P. 2009. *A Marginal Jew: Rethinking the Historical Jesus. Vol. 4: Law and Love*. ABRL. New York: Doubleday.

Meier, Sam. 1989. "House Fungus: Mesopotamia and Israel (Lev. 14:33–53)." *RB* 96: 184–192.

Melcher, Sarah J. 2017. Introduction. In: Melcher, Sarah J./ Mikeal C. Parsons/ Amos Yong (eds.), *The Bible and Disability: A Commentary*. Studies in Religion, Theology, and Disability. Waco, TX: Baylor University Press, 1–27.

Melcher, Sarah J.; Mikeal C. Parsons; Amos Yong. 2017. *The Bible and Disability: A Commentary*. Studies in Religion, Theology, and Disability. Waco, TX: Baylor University Press.

Menken, Maarten J. J. 2005. "The Call of Blind Bartimaeus (Mark 10:46–52)." *HTS* 61: 273–290.

Metternich, Ulrike. 2000. *‚Sie sagte ihm die ganze Wahrheit': die Erzählung von der ‚Blutflüssigen' – feministisch gedeutet*. Mainz: Matthias-Grünewald-Verlag.

Meyer, Rudolf. 1957. καθαρός and cogn. C. Judentum. In: *Theologisches Wörterbuch zum Neuen Testament* 3, Stuttgart: Kohlhammer, 421–427.

Meyers, Eric M. 1995. "An Archaeological Response to a New Testament Scholar." *BASOR* 297: 17–26.

Meyers, Eric M. 2003. The Problem of Gendered Space in Syro-Palestinian Domestic Architecture: The Case of Roman-Period Galilee. In: Balch, David L./ Carolyn Osiek (eds.), *Early Christian Families in Context: An Interdisciplinary Dialogue*. Religion, Marriage and Family. Grand Rapids, MI: William B. Eerdmans Publishing, 44–69.

Michaelis, Wilhelm. 1935. λέπρα, λεπρός. In: *Theologisches Wörterbuch zum Neuen Testament* 4, 240.

Michaelis, Wilhelm. 1967. ὁράω and cogn. In: *Theologisches Wörterbuch zum Neuen Testament* 5, Stuttgart: Kohlhammer, 315–381.

Milgrom, Jacob. 1991. *Leviticus 1–16: A New Translation with Introduction and Commentary*. AB 3. New York: Doubleday.

Milgrom, Jacob. 2004. *Leviticus: A Book of Ritual and Ethics*. Continental Commentaries. Minneapolis, MN: Fortress Press.

Miller, Susan. 2004. *Women in Mark's Gospel*. JSNTSup 259. London/ New York: T&T Clark.

Mitchell, David T.; Sharon L. Snyder. 1997. *The Body and Physical Difference. Discourses of Disability*. The Body in Theory. Histories of Cultural Materialism. Ann Arbor: University of Michigan Press.

Mitchell, David T.; Sharon L. Snyder. 2001. *Narrative Prosthesis: Disability and the Dependencies of Discourse*. Corporealities. Ann Arbor, MI: University of Michigan Press.

Mitchell, David T.; Sharon L. Snyder. 2013. Narrative Prosthesis. In: Davis, Lennard J. (ed.), *The Disability Studies Reader*. London/ New York: Routledge, 222–235.

Mittmann-Richert, Ulrike. 2003. Die Dämonen und der Tod des Gottessohns im Markusevangelium. In: Lange, Armin/ Hermann Lichtenberger/ Diethard Römheld (eds.), *Die Dämonen – Demons: Die Dämonologie der israelitisch-jüdischen und frühchristlichen Literatur im Kontext ihrer Umwelt*. Tübingen: Mohr Siebeck, 476–504.

Mohr, Lars. 2011. *Schwerste Behinderung und theologische Anthropologie*. Lehren und Lernen mit behinderten Menschen 22. Oberhausen: Athena.

Møller-Christensen, Vilhelm. 1967. Evidence of Leprosy in Earlier Peoples. In: Brothwell, Don R./ A. T. Sandison (eds.), *Diseases in Antiquity: A Survey of the Diseases, Injuries, and Surgery of Early Populations*. Springfield, IL: C. C. Thomas, 295–305.

Moloney, Francis J. 2002. *The Gospel of Mark: A Commentary*. Peabody, MA: Hendrickson Publishers, Inc.

Moltmann-Wendel, Elisabeth. 1995. *I Am My Body: A Theology of Embodiment*. New York: Continuum.

Monot, Marc et al. 2005. "On the Origin of Leprosy." *Science* 308: 1040–1042.

Moore, Stephen D. 2006. 'My Name Is Legion, for We Are Many': Representing Empire in Mark. In: Moore, Stephen D. (ed.), *Empire and Apocalpyse: Postcolonialism and the New Testament*. The Bible in the Modern World 12. Sheffield: Sheffield Phoenix Press, 24–44.

Morgan, Teresa. 2015. *Roman Faith and Christian Faith: Pistis and Fides in the Early Roman Empire and Early Churches*. Oxford: Oxford University Press.

Moss, Candida R. 2010. "The Man with the Flow of Power: Porous Bodies in Mark 5:25–34." *JBL* 129.3: 507–519.

Moss, Candida R. 2011a. "Corporal Knowledge: Early Chrisitan Bodies, Review." *RelSRev* 37.2: 138.

Moss, Candida R. 2018. Mark and Matthew. In: Melcher, Sarah J./ Mikeal C. Parsons/ Amos Yong (eds.), *The Bible and Disability: A Commentary*. London: SCM Press, 275–301.

Moss, Candida R.; Joel S. Baden. 2015. *Reconceiving Infertility: Biblical Perspectives on Procreation and Childlessness*. Princeton, NJ: Princeton University Press.

Moss, Candida R.; Jeremy Schipper (eds.). 2011. *Disability Studies and Biblical Literature*. New York: Palgrave Macmillan.

Moss, Candida R.; Jeremy Schipper. 2011. Introduction. In: *Disability Studies and Biblical Literature*. New York: Palgrave Macmillan, 1–11.

Muhammed, Louwai. 2013. "A Retrospective Diagnosis of Epilepsy in Three Historical Figures: St Paul, Joan of Arc and Socrates." *Journal of Medical Biography* 21.4: 208–211.

Müller, Paul-Gerhard. 2010. ἀναβλέπω. In: *Exegetisches Wörterbuch zum Neuen Testament* 1, Stuttgart: Kohlhammer, 181–182.

Müller, Paul-Gerhard. 2010. ἀποκαθίστημι, ἀποκαθιστάνω. In: *Exegetisches Wörterbuch zum Neuen Testament* 1, Stuttgart: Kohlhammer, 310–312.

Müller, Paul-Gerhard. 2010. βλέπω. In: *Exegetisches Wörterbuch zum Neuen Testament* 1, Stuttgart: Kohlhammer, 532–535.

Müller, Peter. 2013. Nicht nur rein, auch gesund (Heilung eines Aussätzigen). In: Zimmermann, Ruben (ed.), *Kompendium der frühchristlichen Wundererzählungen: Die Wunder Jesu*. Gütersloh: Gütersloher Verlags-Haus, 221–234.

Müller, Peter. 1995. *"Wer ist dieser?" Jesus im Markusevangelium: Markus als Erzähler, Verkündiger und Lehrer*. Biblisch-Theologische Studien 27. Neukirchen-Vluyn: Neukirchener.

Müri, Walter. 2001. *Der Arzt im Altertum: griechische und lateinische Quellenstücke von Hippokrates bis Galen mit der Übertragung ins Deutsche*. 6th ed., Sammlung Tusculum. Düsseldorf: Artemis & Winkler.

Myers, Ched. 1988. *Binding the Strong Man: A Political Reading of Mark's Story of Jesus*. Maryknoll, NY: Orbis Books.

Naluparayil, Jacob Chacko. 2000. *The Identity of Jesus in Mark. An Essay on Narrative Christology*. Studium Biblicum Franciscanum Analecta 49. Jerusalem: Franciscan Printing Press.

Navarro Puerto, Mercedes. 2012. Jüngerinnen bei Markus? Problematisierung eines Begriffs. In: Navarro Puerto, Mercedes/ Marinella Perroni (eds.), *Evangelien: Erzählungen und Geschichten*.

Die Bibel und die Frauen: Eine exegetisch-kulturgeschichtliche Enzyklopädie 2.1. Stuttgart: Kohlhammer.

Neirynck, Frans. 1972. *Duality in Mark: Contributions to the Study of the Markan Redaction.* BETL 31. Leuven: Peeters.

Neirynck, Frans. 1991. Papyrus Egerton 2 and the Healing of the Leper (1985). In: *Evangelica II. 1982–1991: Collected Essays.* BETL 99. Leuven: Peeters, 773–783.

Neirynck, Frans; Frans van Segbroeck. 1982. *Evangelica. Gospel Studies – Études d'évangile. Collected Essays.* BETL 60. Leuven: Peeters.

Neirynck, Frans; Frans van Segbroeck. 1991. *Evangelica II. 1982–1991: Collected Essays.* BETL 99. Leuven: Peeters.

Neumann, Josef N. 2017. *Behinderte Menschen in Antike und Christentum: Zur Geschichte und Ethik der Inklusion.* Standorte in Antike und Christentum 8. Stuttgart: Anton Hiersemann.

Nicklas, Tobias. 2001. "Formkritik und Leserrezeption. Ein Beitrag zur Methodendiskussion am Beispiel Mk 9,14–29." *Biblica* 82.4: 496–514.

Nicklas, Tobias. 2008. Jesu zweites Zeichen (Joh 4,43–45.46–54). Abgründe einer Glaubensgeschichte. In: Busse, Ulrich/ Joseph Verheyden/ Gilbert van Belle; et al. (eds.), *Miracles and Imagery in Luke and John: FS Ulrich Busse.* BETL 218. Leuven: Peeters, 89–104.

Nicklas, Tobias. 2009. The 'Unknown Gospel' on Papyrus Egerton 2. In: Nicklas, Tobias/ Michael J. Kruger/ Thomas J. Kraus (eds.), *Gospel Fragments.* Oxford Early Christian Gospel Texts. Oxford: Oxford University Press, 11–121.

Nicklas, Tobias. 2013. "Werde rein … und sündige nicht mehr!" (Heilung eines Aussätzigen) P.Egerton 2. In: Zimmermann, Ruben (ed.), *Kompendium der frühchristlichen Wundererzählungen: Die Wunder Jesu.* Gütersloh: Gütersloher Verlags-Haus, 869–872.

Nineham, Dennis Eric. 1963. *The Gospel of St. Mark.* Pelican Gospel Commentaries. Baltimore, MD: Penguin Books.

Nissan, Ephraim; Abraham Ofir Shemesh. 2010. "King Saul's 'Evil Spirit' (ruach raʻah): Between Psychology, Medicine and Culture." *La Ricerca Folklorica* 62: 149–156.

Nogossek-Raithel, Lena. 2020. "Gendered Dis/ability" im Markusevangelium. In: El Maaroufi, Asmaa/ Sonja A. Strube/ Deborah Williger (eds.), *Jenseits der Grenzen. Dualistische Denkmuster überwinden.* Jahrbuch Theologische Zoologie 3.2020. Berlin: LIT Verlag, 115–127.

Nolte, Cordula; Bianca Frohne; Uta Halle; et al. 2017. *Dis/ability History der Vormoderne. Ein Handbuch. Premodern Dis/ability History. A Companion.* Affalterbach: Didymos-Verlag.

Nünning, Ansgar. 2000. Towards a Cultural and Historical Narratology: A Survey of Diachronic Approaches, Concepts, and Research Projects. In: Reitz, Bernhard/ Sigrid Rieuwerts (eds.), *Anglistentag 1999 Mainz Proceedings.* Trier: Wissenschaftlicher Verlag Trier, 345–373.

Nünning, Ansgar; Vera Nünning. 2002. Von der strukturalistischen Narratologie zur ‚postklassischen' Erzähltheorie: Ein Überblick über neue Ansätze und Entwicklungstendenzen. In: Nünning, Ansgar/ Vera Nünning (eds.), *Neue Ansätze in der Erzähltheorie.* WVT-Handbücher zum Literaturwissenschaftlichen Studium 4. Trier: Wissenschaftlicher Verlag Trier, 1–34.

Nutton, Vivian. 1998. Epilepsie. In: *DNP* 3, Stuttgart: Metzler, 1141.

Nutton, Vivian. 1998. Fieber. In: *DNP* 4, Stuttgart: Metzler, 510–511.

Nutton, Vivian. 1999. Medizin. In: *DNP* 7, Stuttgart: Metzler, 1103–1117.

Nutton, Vivian. 2004. *Ancient Medicine.* Series of Antiquity. London/ New York: Routledge.

Oegema, Gerbern S. 2003. Jesus' Casting Out of Demons in the Gospel of Mark against Its Greco-Roman Background. In: Lange, Armin/ Hermann Lichtenberger/ Diethard Römheld (eds.), *Die*

Dämonen – Demons: die Dämonologie der israelitisch-jüdischen und frühchristlichen Literatur im Kontext ihrer Umwelt. Tübingen: Mohr Siebeck, 505–518.
Oeming, Manfred. 2011. "Auge wurde ich dem Blinden, und Fuß dem Lahmen war ich!" (Hi 29,15). Zum theologischen Umgang mit Behinderung im Alten Testament. In: Eurich, Johannes/ Andreas Lob-Hüdepohl (eds.), *Inklusive Kirche. Behinderung, Theologie, Kirche.* Stuttgart: Kohlhammer, 81–100.
Oepke, Albrecht. 1957. ἀνίστημι/ἐξανίστημι. In: *Theologisches Wörterbuch zum Neuen Testament* 1, Stuttgart: Kohlhammer, 368–372.
Oepke, Albrecht. 1957. ἀποκαθίστημι, ἀποκατάστασις. In: *Theologisches Wörterbuch zum Neuen Testament* 1, Stuttgart: Kohlhammer, 386–392.
Oepke, Albrecht. 1957. ἰάομαι. In: *Theologisches Wörterbuch zum Neuen Testament* 3, Stuttgart: Kohlhammer, 194–215.
Oepke, Albrecht. 1957. καθεύδω. In: *Theologisches Wörterbuch zum Neuen Testament* 3, Stuttgart: Kohlhammer, 434–440.
Oepke, Albrecht. 1960. ἐγείρω. In: *Theologisches Wörterbuch zum Neuen Testament* 2, Stuttgart: Kohlhammer, 332–337.
Oko, Ohajuobodo I. 2004. *"Who then is this?": A Narrative Study of the Role of the Question of the Identity of Jesus in the Plot of Mark's Gospel.* BBB 148. Berlin: Philo.
Olyan, Saul M. 1998. "'Anyone Blind or Lame Shall Not Enter the House': On the Interpretation of Second Samuel 5:8b." *CBQ* 60.2: 218–227.
Olyan, Saul M. 2008. *Disability in the Hebrew Bible: Interpreting Mental and Physical Differences.* Cambridge/ New York: Cambridge University Press.
Opatrný, Dominik. 2010. "The Figure of a Blind Man in the Light of the Papyrological Evidence." *Biblica* 91: 583–594.
Oppel, Dagmar. 1995. *Heilsam erzählen, erzählend heilen: Die Heilung der Blutflüssigen und die Erweckung der Jairustochter in Mk 5,21–43 als Beispiel markinischer Erzählfertigkeit.* BBB 102. Weinheim: Beltz Athenäum.
Oser-Grote, Carolin. 2005. Pneuma. In: *Antike Medizin. Ein Lexikon*, München: C.H. Beck, 717–718.
Osiek, Carolyn; David L. Balch. 1997. *Families in the New Testament World: Households and House Churches.* The Family, Religion, and Culture. Louisville, KY: Westminster John Knox Press.
Parrat, J. K. 1969. "The Laying on of Hands in the New Testament: A Re-examination in the Light of the Hebrew Terminology." *ExpTim* 80.7: 210–214.
Parsons, Mikeal Carl. 2006. *Body and Character in Luke and Acts: The Subversion of Physiognomy in Early Christianity.* Grand Rapids, MI: Baker Academic.
Pascut, Beniamin. 2012. "The So-Called "Passivum Divinum" in Mark's Gospel." *NovT* 54.4: 313–333.
Pascut, Beniamin. 2017. *Redescribing Jesus' Divinity Through a Social Science Theory: An Interdisciplinary Analysis of Forgiveness and Divine Identity in Ancient Judaism and Mark 2:1–12.* WUNT 2.438. Tübingen: Mohr Siebeck.
Pellegrini, Silvia. 2012. Frauen ohne Namen in den kanonischen Evangelien. In: Navarro Puerto, Mercedes/ Marinella Perroni (eds.), *Evangelien: Erzählungen und Geschichten.* Die Bibel und die Frauen: Eine exegetisch-kulturgeschichtliche Enzyklopädie 2.1. Stuttgart: Kohlhammer, 383–420.
Perrin, Norman. 1974. *The New Testament: An Introduction. Proclamation and Parenesis, Myth and History.* New York: Harcourt Brace Jovanovich.
Pesch, Rudolf. 1968a. "Ein Tag vollmächtigen Wirkens Jesu in Kapharnaum (Mk 1,21–34.35–39): Teil 1–3." *Bibel und Leben* 9: 114–128; 177–195; 261–277.
Pesch, Rudolf. 1968b. *Neuere Exegese – Verlust oder Gewinn?* Freiburg: Herder.

Pesch, Rudolf. 1970. *Jesu ureigene Taten? Ein Beitrag zur Wunderfrage.* Freiburg: Herder.
Pesch, Rudolf. 1971. "The Markan Version of the Healing of the Gerasene Demoniac." *The Ecumenical Review* 23.4: 349–376.
Pesch, Rudolf. 1972. *Der Besessene von Gerasa: Entstehung und Überlieferung einer Wundergeschichte.* Stuttgarter Bibelstudien 56. Stuttgart: Verlag Katholisches Bibelwerk.
Pesch, Rudolf. 1976. *Das Markusevangelium. Erster Teil: Einleitung und Kommentar zu Kap. 1,1–8,26.* 3rd ed., 2 vols. HTKNT. Freiburg: Herder.
Pesch, Rudolf. 1980. *Das Markusevangelium. Zweiter Teil: Kommentar zu Kap. 8,27–16,20.* 3rd ed., 2 vols. HTKNT. Freiburg: Herder.
Peterson, Dwight N. 2006. "Translating παραλυτικός in Mark 2:1–12: A Proposal." *BBR* 16.2: 261–272.
Pier, John. 2017. Von der französischen strukturalistischen Erzähltheorie zur nordamerikanischen postklassischen Narratologie. In: Huber, Martin/ Wolf Schmid (eds.), *Grundthemen der Literaturwissenschaft: Erzählen.* Berlin: de Gruyter, 59–87.
Pilch, John J. 1999. *Healing in the New Testament. Insights from Medical and Mediterranean Anthropology.* Minneapolis, MN: Fortress Press.
Pokorný, Petr. 1977. ‚Anfang des Evangeliums': Zum Problem des Anfangs und des Schlusses des Markusevangeliums. In: Schnackenburg, Rudolf/ Josef Ernst/ Joachim Wanke (eds.), *Die Kirche des Anfangs: FS für Heinz Schürmann zum 65. Geburtstag.* ETS 38. Freiburg: Herder, 115–132.
Pokorný, Petr. 1995. "From a Puppy to the Child. Some Problems of Contemporary Biblical Exegesis Demonstrated From Mark 7.24–30/Matt 15.21–28." *NTS* 41: 321–337.
Poorthuis, Marcel; Joshua Schwartz. 2000. *Purity and Holiness: The Heritage of Leviticus.* Jewish and Christian Perspectives Series 2. Leiden/ Boston, MA: Brill.
Poplutz, Uta. 2013. Dämonen – Besessenheit – Austreibungsrituale. In: Zimmermann, Ruben (ed.), *Kompendium der frühchristlichen Wundererzählungen: Die Wunder Jesu.* Gütersloh: Gütersloher Verlags-Haus, 94–107.
Porter, Stanley E. 1989. *Verbal Aspect in the Greek of the New Testament, with Reference to Tense and Mood.* Studies in Biblical Greek 1. New York: Peter Lang.
Powell, Mark Allan. 2011. Narrative Criticism: The Emergence of a Prominent Reading Strategy. In: Iverson, Kelly R./ Christopher W. Skinner (eds.), *Mark as Story: Retrospect and Prospect.* SBLRBS 65. Atlanta, GA: SBL Press, 19–43.
Pramann, Susanne. 2008. *Point of View im Markusevangelium. Eine Tiefenbohrung.* Europäische Hochschulschriften 23. Frankfurt a.M.: Peter Lang.
Preuss, Julius. 1989. *Biblisch-talmudische Medizin: Beiträge zur Geschichte der Heilkunde und der Kultur überhaupt.* Leipzig: Zentralantiquariat der DDR.
Proctor, Mark A. 2017. "'It was not the Season for Figs': Aesthetic Asburdity in Mark's Intercalations." *Biblica* 98.4: 558–581.
Qimron, Elisha. 1991. "Notes on the 4Q Zadokite Fragment on Skin Disease." *JJS* 42.2: 256–259.
Queller, Kurt. 2010. "'Stretch out your hand!': Echo and Metalepsis in Mark's Sabbath Healing Controversy." *JBL* 129.4: 737–758.
Radl, Walter. 2010. σῴζω. In: *Exegetisches Wörterbuch zum Neuen Testament* 3, Stuttgart: Kohlhammer, 766–770.
Räisänen, Heikki. 1990. *The 'Messianic Secret' in Mark's Gospel.* Edinburgh: T&T Clark.
Ramsay, William Mitchell. 1908. *Luke the Physician and other Studies in the History of Religion.* London: Hodder and Stoughton.

Raphael, Rebecca. 2008. *Biblical Corpora: Representations of Disability in Hebrew Biblical Literature*. Library of Hebrew Bible/Old Testament Studies 445. London/ New York: T&T Clark.

Rappaport, Uriel. 1992. "Phoenicia and Galilee: Economy, Territory and Political Relations." *Studia Phoenicia 9*: 262–268.

Rawlinson, A. E. J. 1925. *St Mark. With Introduction, Commentary and Additional Notes*. Westminster Commentaries. London: Methuen.

Reed, Carlson. 2022. *Unfamiliar Selves in the Hebrew Bible: Possession and Other Spirit Phenomena*. Berlin: de Gruyter.

Reese, David George. 1992. Demons New Testament. In: *ABD* 2, New York: Doubleday, 139–142.

Reinders, Hans S. 2008. *Receiving the Gift of Friendship: Profound Disability, Theological Anthropology, and Ethics*. Grand Rapids, MI: William B. Eerdmans Publishing.

Reinders, Hans S. 2014. *Disability, Providence, and Ethics: Bridging Gaps, Transforming Lives*. Studies in Religion, Theology, and Disability. Waco, TX: Baylor University Press.

Resseguie, James L. 2005. *Narrative Criticism of the New Testament: An Introduction*. Grand Rapids, MI: Baker Academic.

Rhoads, David M. 1982. "Narrative Criticism and the Gospel of Mark." *JAAR* 50.3: 411–434.

Rhoads, David M. 2004. *Reading Mark: Engaging the Gospel*. Minneapolis, MN: Fortress Press.

Rhoads, David M.; Joanna Dewey; Donald Michie. 2012. *Mark as Story: An Introduction to the Narrative of a Gospel*. 3rd ed. Minneapolis, MN: Fortress Press.

Rhoads, David M.; Donald Michie. 1982. *Mark as Story: An Introduction to the Narrative of a Gospel*. Philadelphia, PA: Fortress Press.

Riede, Peter. 2003. Fieber. In: *Calwer Bibellexikon* 1, Stuttgart: Calwer Verlag, 360.

Riley, Greg J. 1999. Demon. In: *DDD*, Leiden: Brill, 445–456.

Ringe, Sharon H. 2004. A Gentile Woman's Story, Revisited: Rereading Mark 7.24–31. In: Levine, Amy-Jill/ Marianne Blickenstaff (eds.), *A Feminist Companion to Mark*. Cleveland, Ohio: Pilgrim Press, 79–100.

Rissi, Mathias. 2010. παραλυτικός. In: *Exegetisches Wörterbuch zum Neuen Testament* 3, Stuttgart: Kohlhammer, 72–74.

Roberts, Charlotte A.; Mary E. Lewis; Keith Manchester. 2002. *Past and Present of Leprosy: Archaeological, Historical, Paleopathological and Clinical Approaches*. BAR International Series 1054. Oxford: Archaeopress.

Robinson, J. Armitage. 1901. "ΠΩΡΩΣΙΣ AND ΠΗΡΩΣΙΣ." *JTS* 3.9: 81–96.

Robinson, James M. 1994. The Son of Man in the Sayings Gospel Q. In: Elsas, Christoph/ Carsten Colpe/ Renate Haffke (eds.), *Tradition und Translation: Zum Problem der Interkulturellen Übersetzbarkeit Religiöser Phänomene (FS Carsten Colpe)*. Berlin: de Gruyter, 315–335.

Rochais, Gérard. 1981. *Les récits de résurrection des morts dans le Nouveau Testament*. SNTSMS. Cambridge: Cambridge University Press.

Rogge, Christine; Eduard Seidler. 2005. Kinderkrankheiten. In: *Antike Medizin. Ein Lexikon*, München: C.H. Beck, 494–495.

Roloff, Jürgen. 1969. "Das Markusevangelium als Geschichtsdarstellung." *EvT* 29: 73–93.

Rose, Christian. 2007. *Theologie als Erzählung im Markusevangelium: Eine narratologisch-rezeptionsästhetische Untersuchung zu Mk 1,1–15*. WUNT 2.236. Tübingen: Mohr Siebeck.

Rose, M. Lynn. 2006. Deaf and Dumb in Ancient Greece. In: Davis, Lennard J. (ed.), *The Disability Studies Reader*. London/ New York: Routledge, 17–31.

Rose, Martha L. 2003. *The Staff of Oedipus: Transforming Disability in Ancient Greece*. Corporealities. Ann Arbor: University of Michigan Press.

Rosenblatt, Marie-Eloise. 2000. Gender, Ethnicity, and Legal Considerations in the Haemorrhaging Woman's Story Mark 5:25–43. In: Kitzberger, Ingrid R. (ed.), *Transformative Encounters: Jesus and Women Re-viewed*. Biblical Interpretation Series 43. Leiden: Brill, 137–161.

Ruane, Nicole J. 2015. "Pigs, Purity, and Patrilineality: The Multiparity of Swine and Its Problems for Biblical Ritual and Gender Construction." *JBL* 134.3: 489–504.

Rüegger, Hans-Ulrich. 2002. *Verstehen, was Markus erzählt: Philologisch-hermeneutische Reflexionen zum Übersetzen von Markus 3,1–6*. WUNT 2.155. Tübingen: Mohr Siebeck.

Rüggemeier, Jan. 2017. *Poetik der markinischen Christologie: eine kognitiv-narratologische Exegese*. WUNT 2.458. Tübingen: Mohr Siebeck.

Rüggemeier, Jan. 2019. Ein See, zwei Ufer. Raum und erzählte Welt im Markusevangelium. In: Bartsch, Christoph/ Frauke Bode (eds.), *Welt(en) erzählen. Paradigmen und Perspektiven*. Narratologia 65. Berlin: de Gruyter, 347–368.

Rüggemeier, Jan. 2021. "Mark's Narrative Christology Following the Cognitive Turn." *Early Christianity* 12.3: 322–345.

Runesson, Anders; Donald D. Binder; Birger Olsson. 2010. *The Ancient Synagogue from its Origins to 200 C.E.: A Source Book*. Leiden: Brill.

Rupprecht, Friederike. 2014. θεραπεύω. In: *Theologisches Begriffslexikon zum Neuen Testament*, Wuppertal: Brockhaus, 1203–1205.

Rupprecht, Friederike. 2014. ἰάομαι. In: *Theologisches Begriffslexikon zum Neuen Testament*, Wuppertal: Brockhaus, 1205–1210.

Samama, Evelyne. 2017. The Greek Vocabulary of Disabilities. In: Laes, Christian (ed.), *Disability in Antiquity*. Rewriting Antiquity. London/ New York: Routledge, 121–138.

Sanders, James A. 1997. A Liturgy for Healing the Stricken (11 QPsApa = 11Q11). In: Charlesworth, James H. (ed.), *The Dead Sea Scrolls: Hebrew, Aramaic, and Greek texts with English translations. 4 A. Pseudepigraphic and Non-Masoretic Psalms and Prayers*. Tübingen: J.C.B. Mohr (Paul Siebeck), 216–233.

Sänger, Dieter. 2010. χωλός. In: *Exegetisches Wörterbuch zum Neuen Testament* 3, Stuttgart: Kohlhammer, 1177–1178.

Schenk, Wolfgang. 2010. πυρετός. In: *Exegetisches Wörterbuch zum Neuen Testament* 3, Stuttgart: Kohlhammer, 484–485.

Schenk, Wolfgang. 2010. πωρόω. In: *Exegetisches Wörterbuch zum Neuen Testament* 3, Stuttgart: Kohlhammer, 487–488.

Schenke, Ludger. 1974. *Die Wundererzählungen des Markusevangeliums*. Stuttgarter biblische Beiträge. Stuttgart: Verlag Katholisches Bibelwerk.

Schenke, Ludger. 2005. *Das Markusevangelium. Literarische Eigenart – Text und Kommentierung*. Stuttgart: Kohlhammer.

Schiefer Ferrari, Markus. 2014. Gestörte Lektüre: Dis/abilitykritische Hermeneutik biblischer Heilungserzählungen am Beispiel von Mk 2,1–12. In: Kollmann, Bernd/ Ruben Zimmermann (eds.), *Hermeneutik der frühchristlichen Wundererzählungen: Geschichtliche, literarische und rezeptionsorientierte Perspektiven*. WUNT 339. Tübingen: Mohr Siebeck, 627–646.

Schiffer, Barbara. 2001. *Fließende Identität: Körper und Geschlechter im Wandel. Symbole von Krankheit und Heilung, feministisch-theologisch gedeutet im Kontext postmoderner Körper- und Geschlechterkonstruktionen*. Europäische Hochschulschriften 23. Frankfurt a.M.: Peter Lang.

Schiffman, Lawrence H. 1990. The Impurity of the Dead in the Temple Scroll. In: Schiffman, Lawrence H. (ed.), *Archaeology and History in the Dead Sea Scrolls: The New York University*

Conference in Memory of Yigael Yadin. Journal for the Study of the Pseudepigrapha Supplement Series 8. Sheffield, England: JSOT Press, 135–156.
Schille, Gottfried. 1957. "Die Topographie des Markusevangeliums, ihre Hintergründe, ihre Einordnung." *ZDPV* 73: 133–166.
Schille, Gottfried. 1966. *Anfänge der Kirche: Erwägungen zur apostolischen Frühgeschichte*. BEvT 43. München: Kaiser.
Schille, Gottfried. 1967. *Die urchristliche Wundertradition: Ein Beitrag zur Frage nach dem irdischen Jesus*. Arbeiten zur Theologie 1.29. Stuttgart: Calwer Verlag.
Schinkel, Dirk. 2003. "Mirjam als Aussätzige? Zwei Bemerkungen zu Num 12." *ZAW* 115: 94–101.
Schipper, Jeremy. 2006. *Disability Studies and the Hebrew Bible: Figuring Mephibosheth in the David Story*. Library of Hebrew Bible/Old Testament Studies 441. London/ New York: T&T Clark.
Schipper, Jeremy. 2011. *Disability and Isaiah's Suffering Servant*. Biblical Refigurations. Oxford/ New York: Oxford University Press.
Schipper, Jeremy. 2015. "Why Does Imagery of Disability Include Healing in Isaiah?" *JSOT* 39: 319–333.
Schipper, Jeremy; Nyasha Junior. 2013. Disability Studies and the Bible. In: McKenzie, Steven L./ John Kaltner (eds.), *New Meanings for Ancient Texts: Recent Approaches to Biblical Criticisms and their Applications*. Louisville, KY: Westminster John Knox Press, 21–38.
Schlier, Heinrich. 1953. ἀλείφω. In: *Theologisches Wörterbuch zum Neuen Testament* 1, Stuttgart: Kohlhammer, 230–232.
Schmidt, Karl Ludwig. 1919. *Der Rahmen der Geschichte Jesu: Literarkritische Untersuchungen zur ältesten Jesusüberlieferung*. Berlin: Trowitzsch.
Schmidt, Karl Matthias. 2010. *Wege des Heils: Erzählstrukturen und Rezeptionskontexte des Markusevangeliums*. NTOA 74. Göttingen: Vandenhoeck & Ruprecht.
Schmithals, Walter. 1975/1976. "Die Heilung des Epileptischen (Mk 9,14–29). Ein Beitrag zur notwendigen Reform der Formgeschichte." *Theologia Viatorum* 8: 211–233.
Schmithals, Walter. 1979. *Das Evangelium nach Markus*. Ökumenischer Taschenbuchkommentar zum Neuen Testament. Gütersloh: Gütersloher Verlags-Haus.
Schmitt, Rüdiger. 2012. Demons, Demonology II. HB/OT. In: *Encyclopedia of the Bible and Its Reception* 6, Berlin: de Gruyter, 536–539.
Schnabel, Eckhard J. 2014. ἔσχατος. In: *Theologisches Begriffslexikon zum Neuen Testament*, Wuppertal: Brockhaus, 28–35.
Schneider, Carl. 1952. μάστιξ. In: *Theologisches Wörterbuch zum Neuen Testament* 4, Stuttgart: Kohlhammer, 524–525.
Schneider, Johannes; Haubeck, Wilfried. 2014. σῴζω. In: *Theologisches Begriffslexikon zum Neuen Testament*, Wuppertal: Brockhaus, 369–374.
Schneider, Werner; Anne Waldschmidt. 2012. Disability Studies: (Nicht-)Behinderung anders denken. In: Moebius, Stephan (ed.), *Kultur. Von den Cultural Studies bis zu den Visual Studies: Eine Einführung*. Edition Kulturwissenschaft 21. Bielefeld: transcript, 128–150.
Schniewind, Julius. 1952. *Nachgelassene Reden und Aufsätze*. Theologische Bibliothek Töpelmann. Berlin: Töpelmann.
Schottroff, Luise. 1993. *Let the Oppressed Go Free: Feminist Perspectives on the New Testament*. Gender and the Biblical Tradition. Louisville, KY: Westminster/John Knox Press.
Schottroff, Luise. 1994. *Lydias ungeduldige Schwestern: Feministische Sozialgeschichte des frühen Christentums*. Gütersloh: Kaiser.

Schrage, Wolfgang. 1969. τυφλός. In: *Theologisches Wörterbuch zum Neuen Testament* 8, Stuttgart: Kohlhammer, 270–294.
Schröter, Jens. 1997. *Erinnerung an Jesu Worte: Studien zur Rezeption der Logienüberlieferung in Markus, Q und Thomas.* Neukirchen-Vluyn: Neukirchener Verlag.
Schröter, Jens. 2001. *Jesus und die Anfänge der Christologie: Methodologische und Exegetische Studien zu den Ursprüngen des christlichen Glaubens.* Biblisch-Theologische Studien 47. Neukirchen-Vluyn: Neukirchener.
Schröter, Jens. 2019. Die Heilungen Jesu und das Heil Gottes: Beobachtungen zu den Heilungserzählungen der Evangelien im Horizont antiker medizinischer und religiöser Traditionen. In: Du Toit, David S./ Christine Gerber/ Christiane Zimmermann (eds.), *Sōtēria: Salvation in Early Christianity and Antiquity. FS in Honour of Cilliers Breytenbach on the Occasion of his 65th Birthday.* NovTSup 175. Leiden/ Boston, MA: Brill, 131–154.
Schulz, Siegfried. 1967. *Die Stunde der Botschaft: Einführung in die Theologie der vier Evangelisten.* Hamburg: Furche.
Schulz, Siegfried. 1976. *Die Mitte der Schrift: Der Frühkatholizismus im Neuen Testament als Herausforderung an den Protestantismus.* Stuttgart/ Berlin: Kreuz-Verlag.
Schumm, Darla Y.; Michael Stoltzfus. 2011. *Disability in Judaism, Christianity, and Islam: Sacred Texts, Historical Traditions, and Social Analysis.* New York: Palgrave Macmillan.
Schumm, Darla Y.; Michael Stoltzfus. 2011. Sacred Texts, Historical Tradition, and Disability. In: Schumm, Darla Y./ Michael Stoltzfus (eds.), *Disability in Judaism, Christianity, and Islam: Sacred Texts, Historical Traditions, and Social Analysis.* New York: Palgrave Macmillan, 1–4.
Schunack, Gerd. 1999. Glaube in griechischer Religiösität. In: Stegemann, Hartmut/ Bernd Kollmann/ Wolfgang Reinbold; et al. (eds.), *Antikes Judentum und frühes Christentum: FS für Hartmut Stegemann zum 65. Geburtstag.* BZNW 97. Berlin: de Gruyter, 296–326.
Schürer, Emil; Géza Vermès; Fergus Millar; et al. 1979. *The History of the Jewish People in the Age of Jesus Christ (175 B.C.-A.D. 135) 2.* 3 vols. Edinburgh: T&T Clark.
Schüssler Fiorenza, Elisabeth. 1983. *In Memory of Her: A Feminist Theological Reconstruction of Christian Origins.* New York: Crossroad.
Schüssler Fiorenza, Elisabeth. 2009. Introduction: Exploring the Intersections of Race, Gender, Status, and Ethnicity in Early Christian Studies. In: Nasrallah, Laura Salah/ Elisabeth Schüssler Fiorenza (eds.), *Prejudice and Christian Beginnings: Investigating Race, Gender, and Ethnicity in Early Christian Studies.* Minneapolis, MN: Fortress Press, 1–23.
Schwartz, Joshua. 2017. Lame, Lameness III. Judaism. In: *Encyclopedia of the Bible and Its Reception* 15, Berlin: de Gruyter, 661–663.
Schweitzer, Albert. 2001. *The Quest of the Historical Jesus.* Minneapolis, MN: Fortress Press.
Schweizer, Eduard. 1964. "Die theologische Leistung des Markus." *EvT* 24: 337–355.
Schweizer, Eduard. 1970. Zur Frage des Messiasgeheimnisses bei Markus. In: Schweizer, Eduard (ed.), *Beiträge zur Theologie des Neuen Testaments. Neutestamentliche Aufsätze 1955–1970.* Zürich: Zwingli-Verlag, 11–20.
Schweizer, Eduard. 1989 [1967]. *Das Evangelium nach Markus.* 7th ed. Göttingen: Vandenhoeck & Ruprecht.
Seifert, Andreas. 2019. *Der Markusschluss: Narratologie und Traditionsgeschichte.* BWA(N)T 220. Stuttgart: Kohlhammer.
Shakespeare, Tom. 2006. The Social Model of Disability. In: Davis, Lennard J. (ed.), *The Disability Studies Reader.* London/ New York: Routledge, 197–204.

Shemesh, Aharon. 1997. "'The Holy Angels are in their Council': The Exclusion of Deformed Persons from Holy Places in Qumranic and Rabbinic Literature." *Dead Sea Discoveries* 4.2: 179–206.
Shepherd, Tom. 1991. *The Definition and Function of Markan Intercalation as Illustrated in a Narrative Analysis of Six Passages.* Berrien Springs, MI: Andrews University.
Shepherd, Tom. 1993. *Markan Sandwich Stories: Narration, Definition, and Function.* Berrien Springs, MI: Andrews University Press.
Shepherd, Tom. 1995. "The Narrative Function of Markan Intercalation." *NTS* 41: 522–540.
Shively, Elizabeth E. 2012. *Apocalyptic Imagination in the Gospel of Mark: The Literary and Theological Role of Mark 3:22–30.* BZNW 189. Berlin: de Gruyter.
Shively, Elizabeth E. 2014. Characterizing the Non-Human: Satan in the Gospel of Mark. In: Skinner, Christopher W./ Matthew Ryan Hauge (eds.), *Character Studies and the Gospel of Mark.* Library of New Testament Studies 483. London/ New York: T&T Clark, 127–151.
Short, A. J. Rendle. 1953. *The Bible and Modern Medicine: A Survey of Health and Healing in the Old and New Testaments.* The Second Thoughts Library 9. London: Paternoster Press.
Sjöberg, Erik. 1955. *Der verborgene Menschensohn in den Evangelien.* Lund: C. W. K. Gleerup.
Sjöberg, Erik. 1960. πνεῦμα. In: *Theologisches Wörterbuch zum Neuen Testament* 6, Stuttgart: Kohlhammer, 373–387.
Smit, Peter-Ben. 2003. "Simon Peter's Mother in Law Revisited. Or Why One Should Be More Careful With Mothers-In-Law." *Lectio Difficilior* 1: 1–12.
Smith, Gregory A. 2008. "How thin is a Demon?" *JECS* 16: 479–512.
Smith, Jonathan Z. 1978. Towards Interpreting Demonic Powers in Hellenistic and Roman Antiquity. In: *ANRW 2.16.1.* Berlin: de Gruyter, 425–439.
Smith, Morton. 1978. *Jesus the Magician.* New York: Harper and Row.
Söding, Thomas. 1985. *Glaube bei Markus: Glaube an das Evangelium, Gebetsglaube und Wunderglaube im Kontext der markinischen Basileiatheologie und Christologie.* Stuttgarter biblische Beiträge 12. Stuttgart: Verlag Katholisches Bibelwerk.
Söding, Thomas. 2003. "Wenn ich mit dem Finger Gottes die Dämonen austreibe ..." (Lk 11,20) – Die Exorzismen im Rahmen der Basileia-Verkündigung Jesu. In: Lange, Armin/ Hermann Lichtenberger/ Diethard Römheld (eds.), *Die Dämonen – Demons: die Dämonologie der israelitisch-jüdischen und frühchristlichen Literatur im Kontext ihrer Umwelt.* Tübingen: Mohr Siebeck, 519–549.
Söding, Thomas; Klaus Scholtissek (eds.). 1995. *Der Evangelist als Theologe: Studien zum Markusevangelium.* Stuttgarter Bibelstudien 163. Stuttgart: Verlag Katholisches Bibelwerk.
Solevåg, Anna Rebecca. 2016. "No Nuts? No Problem! Disability, Stigma, and the Baptized Eunuch in Acts 8,26–40." *Biblical Interpretation* 24.1: 81–99.
Solevåg, Anna Rebecca. 2017. Hysterical Women? Gender and Disability in Early Christian Narrative. In: Laes, Christian (ed.), *Disability in Antiquity.* Rewriting Antiquity. London/ New York: Routledge, 315–327.
Solevåg, Anna Rebecca. 2017. Listening for the Voices of Two Disabled Girls in Early Christian Literature. In: Laes, Christian/ Ville Vuolanto (eds.), *Children and Everyday Life in the Roman and Late Antique World.* London/ New York: Routledge, 287–299.
Solevåg, Anna Rebecca. 2018. *Negotiating the Disabled Body: Representations of Disability in Early Christian Texts.* Early Christianity and Its Literature 23. Atlanta, GA: SBL Press.
Solevåg, Anna Rebecca. 2020. Gender und Disability in den Petrusakten: Die apostolische Macht, Menschen zu lähmen. In: Lehtipuu, Outi/ Silke Petersen (eds.), *Antike christliche Apokryphen:*

Marginalisierte Texte des frühen Christentums. Die Bibel und die Frauen. Stuttgart: Kohlhammer, 161–176.

Solevåg, Anna Rebecca. 2021. "Leap, Ye, Lame for Joy": The Dynamics of Disability in Conversion. In: Nicolet, Valérie/ Marianne Bjelland Kartzow (eds.), *The Complexity of Conversion: Intersectional Perspectives on Religious Change in Antiquity and Beyond*. Studies in Ancient Religion and Culture. Sheffield: Equinox Publishing Ltd, 99–122.

Soranus. 1894. *Die Gynäkologie. Geburtshilfe, Frauen- und Kinder-Krankheiten, Diätetik der Neugeborenen.* Bibliothek medicinischer Klassiker Bd. 1. München: Lehmann.

Sorensen, Eric. 2002. *Possession and Exorcism in the New Testament and Early Christianity.* WUNT 2.157. Tübingen: Mohr Siebeck.

Sorensen, Eric. 2012. Demons, Demonology III. NT. In: *Encyclopedia of the Bible and Its Reception* 6, Berlin: de Gruyter, 539–543.

Spencer, F. Scott. 2014. "Why did the "Leper" Get Under Jesus' Skin? Emotion Theory and Angry Reaction in Mark 1:40–45." *Horizons in Biblical Theology* 36.2: 107–128.

Spencer, F. Scott. 2017. "Your Faith Has Made You Well" (Mark 5:34; 10:52): Emotional Dynamics of Trustful Engagement with Jesus in Marks Gospel. In: Spencer, F. Scott (ed.), *Mixed Feelings and Vexed Passions: Exploring Emotions in Biblical Literature*. SBLRBS 90. Atlanta, GA: SBL Press, 217–241.

Spittler, Janet. 2013. Deafness II. NT. In: *Encyclopedia of the Bible and Its Reception* 6, Berlin: de Gruyter, 350–352.

Stählin, Gustav. 1953. ἀσθενής and cogn. In: *Theologisches Wörterbuch zum Neuen Testament* 1, Stuttgart: Kohlhammer, 488–492.

Stählin, Gustav. 1954. ὀργή E. In: *Theologisches Wörterbuch zum Neuen Testament* 5, Stuttgart: Kohlhammer, 419–448.

Stamatu, Marion. 2005. Arthritis. In: *Antike Medizin. Ein Lexikon*, München: C.H. Beck, 95.

Stamatu, Marion. 2005. Geisteskrankheit. In: *Antike Medizin. Ein Lexikon*, München: C.H. Beck, 334–335.

Stamatu, Marion. 2005. Gicht. In: *Antike Medizin. Ein Lexikon*, München: C.H. Beck, 356–358.

Stamatu, Marion. 2005. Schlaf. In: *Antike Medizin. Ein Lexikon*, München: C.H. Beck, 774–776.

Stanton, Graham N. 2004. Jesus of Nazareth: A Magician and a False Prophet Who Deceived God's People? In: Stanton, Graham N. (ed.), *Jesus and Gospel.* Cambridge: Cambridge University Press, 127–147.

Stare, Mira. 2013. Im Stress Wunder wirken (Die Heilung der blutenden Frau und die Auferweckung der Tochter des Jaïrus). Lk 8,40–56. In: Zimmermann, Ruben (ed.), *Kompendium der frühchristlichen Wundererzählungen: Die Wunder Jesu.* Gütersloh: Gütersloher Verlags-Haus, 583–592.

Staubli, Thomas. 1996. *Die Bücher Levitikus/Numeri.* Neuer Stuttgarter Kommentar Altes Testament 3. Stuttgart: Verlag Katholisches Bibelwerk.

Stegemann, Wolfgang. 2004. Dekonstruktion des rationalistischen Wunderbegriffs. In: Crüsemann, Frank/ Luise Schottroff (eds.), *Dem Tod nicht glauben: Sozialgeschichte der Bibel. FS für Luise Schottroff zum 70. Geburtstag.* Gütersloh: Gütersloher Verlag-Haus, 67–90.

Stemberger, Günter. 2012. Blindness IV. Judaism. In: *Encyclopedia of the Bible and Its Reception* 4, Berlin: de Gruyter, 182–186.

Stewart, David Tabb. 2008. Does the Priestly Purity Code Domesticate Women? In: Schwartz, Baruch J./ David P. Wright/ Jeffrey Stackert; et al. (eds.), *Perspectives on Purity and Purification in the Bible.* Library of Hebrew Bible/Old Testament Studies 474. New York: T&T Clark, 65–73.

Stewart, David Tabb. 2011. Sexual Disabilities in the Hebrew Bible. In: Moss, Candida R./ Jeremy Schipper (eds.), *Disability Studies and Biblical Literature*. New York: Palgrave Macmillan, 67–87.
Stewart, David Tabb. 2018. Leviticus – Deuteronomy. In: Melcher, Sarah J./ Mikeal C. Parsons/ Amos Yong (eds.), *The Bible and Disability: A Commentary*. London: SCM Press, 57–91.
Stewart, Eric Clark. 2009. *Gathered around Jesus: Alternative Spiritual Practices in the Gospel of Mark*. Cambridge: Cambridge James Clarke.
Stiker, Henri-Jacques. 1999. *A History of Disability*. Corporealities. Ann Arbor, MI: University of Michigan Press.
Stimpfle, Alois. 2012. ‚Von Geburt an blind' (Joh 9,1). Disability und Wirklichkeitskonstruktion. In: Grünstäudl, Wolfgang/ Markus Schiefer Ferrari (eds.), *Gestörte Lektüre: Disability als hermeneutische Leitkategorie biblischer Exegese*. Behinderung, Theologie, Kirche. Stuttgart: Kohlhammer, 98–126.
Stol, Marten. 1993. *Epilepsy in Babylonia*. Cuneiform Monographs 2. Groningen: Styx Publications.
Stolz, Fritz. 1995. Sea. In: *DDD*, Leiden: Brill, 737–742.
Strecker, Christian. 2002. Jesus und die Besessenen. In: Stegemann, Wolfgang/ Bruce J. Malina/ Gerd Theissen (eds.), *Jesus in neuen Kontexten*. Stuttgart: Kohlhammer, 53–63.
Strecker, Christian. 2012. Die Wirklichkeit der Dämonen. Böse Geister im Altertum und in den Exorzismen Jesu. In: Frey, Jörg/ Gabrielle Oberhänsli-Widmer (eds.), *Das Böse*. Jahrbuch für Biblische Theologie 26. Neukirchen-Vluyn: 117–150.
Strecker, Christian. 2013. Mächtig in Wort und Tat (Exorzismus in Kafarnaum) Mk 1,21–28. In: Zimmermann, Ruben (ed.), *Kompendium der frühchristlichen Wundererzählungen: Die Wunder Jesu*. Gütersloh: Gütersloher Verlags-Haus, 205–213.
Strube, Sonja A. 2000. *"Wegen dieses Wortes ..." Feministische und nichtfeministische Exegese im Vergleich am Beispiel der Auslegungen zu Mk 7,24–30*. Theologische Frauenforschung in Europa. Münster: LIT Verlag
Studenovský, Zbyněk. 2004. "Dort werdet ihr ihn sehen" (Mk 16,7): Der Weg Jesu nach Galiläa bei Johannes und Markus. In: Frey, Jörg/ Udo Schnelle (eds.), *Kontexte des Johannesevangeliums: Das vierte Evangelium in religions- und traditionsgeschichtlicher Perspektive*. WUNT 175. Tübingen: Mohr Siebeck, 517–558.
Suk, Won Sik. 2002. *Die ‚reale' Welt in den Wundererzählungen des Markusevangeliums: Untersuchungen zu den Heilungen und Exorzismen Jesu*. Bethel: Kirchliche Hochschule Bethel.
Tannehill, Robert C. 1979. "The Gospel of Mark as Narrative Christology." *Semeia* 16: 57–95.
Tannehill, Robert C. 1986, 1990. *The Narrative Unity of Luke-Acts: A Literary Interpretation*. 2 vols. Foundations and Facets. Philadelphia, PA: Fortress Press.
Taylor, Vincent. 1957. *The Gospel according to St. Mark: The Greek Text with Introduction, Notes and Indexes*. 2nd ed. London: Macmillan.
Temkin, Owsei. 1994. *The Falling Sickness: A History of Epilepsy from the Greeks to the Beginnings of Modern Neurology*. Publications of the Institute of the History of Medicine, the Johns Hopkins University 4. Baltimore, MD: Johns Hopkins University Press.
Temmerman, Koen de; Evert van Emde Boas. 2018. *Characterization in Ancient Greek Literature*. Mnemosyne: Supplements 411. Leiden/ Boston, MA: Brill.
Theissen, Gerd. 1974. *Urchristliche Wundergeschichten: Ein Beitrag zur formgeschichtlichen Erforschung der synoptischen Evangelien*. Gütersloh: Mohn.
Theissen, Gerd. 1983. *The Miracle Stories of the Early Christian Tradition*. Studies of the New Testament and its World. Edinburgh: T&T Clark.

Theissen, Gerd. 1984. "Lokal- und Socialkolorit in der Geschichte von der syrophönikischen Frau (Mk 7,24 – 30)." *ZNW* 75: 202 – 225.

Theissen, Gerd. 1995. Die pragmatische Bedeutung der Geheimnismotive im Markusevangelium: Ein wissenssoziologischer Versuch. In: Kippenberg, Hans G./ Guy G. Stroumsa (eds.), *Secrecy and Concealment: Studies in the History of Mediterranean and Near Eastern Religions*. Studies in the History of Religions 65. Leiden/ New York: Brill, 225 – 245.

Theissen, Gerd. 2007. *Erleben und Verhalten der ersten Christen – eine Psychologie des Urchristentums*. Gütersloh: Gütersloher Verlags-Haus.

Thiessen, Matthew. 2020. *Jesus and the Forces of Death: The Gospels' Portrayal of Ritual Impurity within first-century Judaism*. Grand Rapids, MI: Baker Academic.

Thimmes, Pamela Lee. 1992. *Studies in the Biblical Sea-Storm Type-Scene: Convention and Invention*. San Francisco, CA: Mellen Research University Press.

Thomas, Carol. 2004. Theorien der Behinderung. Schlüsselkonzepte, Themen und Personen. In: Weisser, Jan/ Cornelia Renggli (eds.), *Disability Studies: Ein Lesebuch*. Luzern: Ed. SZH/CSPS, 31 – 57.

Thommen, Lukas. 2007. *Antike Körpergeschichte*. Zürich: vdf-Hochschulverlag.

Thompson, Trevor. 2012. Blindness II. GRA. In: *Encyclopedia of the Bible and Its Reception* 4, Berlin: de Gruyter, 174 – 178.

Thompson, Trevor. 2018. Leper, Leprosy III. GRA. In: *Encyclopedia of the Bible and Its Reception* 16, Berlin: de Gruyter, 149 – 150.

Thraede, Klaus. 1969. Exorzismus. In: *RAC* 7, Stuttgart: Anton Hiersemann, 44 – 117.

Thumiger, Chiara. 2013. The Early Greek Medical Vocabulary of Insanity. In: Harris, William V. (ed.), *Mental Disorders in the Classical World*. Columbia Studies in the Classical Tradition 38. Leiden: Brill, 61 – 95.

Thumiger, Chiara. 2017. Mental Disability? Galen on Mental Health. In: Laes, Christian (ed.), *Disability in Antiquity*. London/ New York: Routledge, 267 – 282.

Tieleman, Teun. 2014. "The Pauline Corpus Considered against the Medical and Philosophical Backdrop." *Religion and Theology* 21.1 – 2: 86 – 106.

Tigay, Jeffrey H. et al. 2007. Blindness. In: *Encyclopaedia Judaica* 3, Detroit, MI: 753 – 756.

Tiwald, Markus. 2012. Von gesunden Kranken und kranken Gesunden... Rochierende Rollen im Markusevangelium. In: Grünstäudl, Wolfgang/ Markus Schiefer Ferrari (eds.), *Gestörte Lektüre: Disability als hermeneutische Leitkategorie biblischer Exegese*. Stuttgart: Kohlhammer, 81 – 97.

Toensing, Holly J. 2007. "Living among the Tombs". Society, Mental Illness, and Self-Destruction in Mark 5:1 – 20. In: Avalos, Hector/ Sarah J. Melcher/ Jeremy Schipper (eds.), *This Abled Body: Rethinking Disabilities in Biblical Studies*. SBL SemeiaSt 55. Leiden: Brill, 131 – 143.

Tolbert, Mary Ann. 1989. *Sowing the Gospel: Mark's World in Literary-Historical Perspective*. Minneapolis, MN: Fortress Press.

Tolbert, Mary Ann. 1992. Mark. In: Newsom, Carol A./ Sharon H. Ringe (eds.), *The Women's Bible Commentary*. Louisville, KY: Westminster John Knox Press, 263 – 274.

Trainor, Michael F. 2001. *The Quest for Home: The Household in Mark's Community*. Collegeville, MN: Liturgical Press.

Trentin, Lisa. 2013. Exploring Visual Impairment in Ancient Rome. In: Laes, Christian/ C. F. Goodey/ M. Lynn Rose (eds.), *Disabilities in Roman Antiquity: Disparate Bodies. A Capite ad Calcem*. Mnemosyne: Supplements. Leiden: Brill, 89 – 114.

Trummer, Peter. 1991. *Die blutende Frau: Wunderheilung im Neuen Testament*. Freiburg: Herder.

Tuckett, Christopher. 2012. Jesus and the Sabbath. In: Holmén, Tom (ed.), *Jesus in Continuum*. WUNT 289. Tübingen: Mohr Siebeck, 411–442.

Turner, C. H. 1993. Marcan Usage: Notes, Critical and Exegetical on the Second Gospel. In: Elliott, J. Keith (ed.), *The Language and Style of the Gospel of Mark*. NovTSup 71. Leiden: Brill, 3–139.

Twelftree, Graham H. 1993. *Jesus the Exorcist. A Contribution to the Study of the Historical Jesus*. WUNT 2.54. Tübingen: J.C.B. Mohr (Paul Siebeck).

Twelftree, Graham H. 2007. Jesus the Exorcist and Ancient Magic. In: Labahn, Michael/ L. J. Lietaert Peerbolte (eds.), *A Kind of Magic. Understanding Magic in the New Testament and its Religious Environment*. London/ New York: T&T Clark, 57–86.

Ueberschaer, Nadine. 2013. Mit allen Sinnen leben! Mk 7,31–37. In: Zimmermann, Ruben (ed.), *Kompendium der frühchristlichen Wundererzählungen: Die Wunder Jesu*. Gütersloh: Gütersloher Verlags-Haus, 323–331.

Urban, Christina. 2005. Hochzeit, Ehe und Witwenschaft. In: Erlemann, Kurt/ Karl L. Noethlichs/ Klaus Scherberlich; et al. (eds.), *Neues Testament und Antike Kultur: 2. Familie – Gesellschaft – Wirtschaft*. Neukirchen-Vluyn: Neukirchener Verlag, 25–30.

Valentine, Katy E. 2018. "Reading the Slave Girl of Acts 16:16–18 in Light of Enslavement and Disability." *Biblical Interpretation* 26.3: 352–368.

van der Eijk, Philip; Detlev Ganten; Roman Marek. 2021. *Was ist Gesundheit? Interdisziplinäre Perspektiven aus Medizin, Geschichte und Kultur*. Humanprojekt 18. Berlin: de Gruyter.

van der Eijk, Philip J. 2005a. *Medicine and Philosophy in Classical Antiquity: Doctors and Philosophers on Nature, Soul, Health and Disease*. Cambridge: Cambridge University Press.

van der Eijk, Philip J. 2005b. The 'theology' of the Hippocratic treatise 'On the Sacred Disease'. In: van der Eijk, Philip J. (ed.), *Medicine and Philosophy in Classical Antiquity: Doctors and Philosophers on Nature, Soul, Health and Disease*. Cambridge: Cambridge University Press, 45–73.

van der Eijk, Philip J. 2011. Medicine and Health in the Graeco-Roman World. In: Jackson, Mark (ed.), *The Oxford Handbook of the History of Medicine*. Oxford Handbooks in History. Oxford: Oxford University Press, 21–39.

van der Eijk, Philip J. 2013. Cure and (In)curability of Mental Disorders in Ancient Medical and Philosophical Thought. In: Harris, William V. (ed.), *Mental Disorders in the Classical World*. Columbia Studies in the Classical Tradition 38. Leiden: Brill, 307–338.

van der Eijk, Philip J.; E.F.J. Horstmanshoff; P.H. Schrijvers (eds.). 1995. *Ancient Medicine in its Socio-Cultural Context*. Clio Medica 27. Leiden: Brill.

van der Horst, Pieter W. 1976/77. "Peter's Shadow. The Religio-Historical Background of Acts V 15." *NTS* 23: 204–212.

van der Horst, Pieter W. 2017. Ein kräftiger Tritt von der Märtyrerin – MirThecl 17. In: Zimmermann, Ruben (ed.), *Kompendium der frühchristlichen Wundererzählungen: Die Wunder der Apostel*. Gütersloh: Gütersloher Verlags-Haus, 553–558.

van der Loos, Hendrik. 1965. *The Miracles of Jesus*. NovTSup 9. Leiden: Brill.

van Hooff, Lieve. 2005. Tod. In: *Antike Medizin. Ein Lexikon*, München: C.H. Beck, 868–870.

van Oyen, Geert. 1992. Intercalaltion and Irony in the Gospel of Mark. In: Segbroeck, Frans van et al. (ed.), *The Four Gospels. FS Frans Neirynck 2*. BETL 100. Leuven: Peeters, 949–974.

van Oyen, Geert. 2006. Markan Miracle Stories in Historical Jesus Research. Redaction Critisism and Narrative Analysis. In: Labahn, Michael/ L. J. Lietaert Peerbolte (eds.), *Wonders Never Cease. The Purpose of Narrating Miracle Stories in the New Testament and its Religious Environment*. London/ New York: T&T Clark, 87–99.

Vander Stichele, Caroline; Todd C. Penner. 2009. *Contextualizing Gender in Early Christian Discourse: Thinking Beyond Thecla*. London: T&T Clark.

Vegge, Ivar. 2017. Not "Hardened Hearts" but "Petrified Hearts" (Mark 6:52): The Challenge to Assimilate and Accommodate the Vastness of Jesus in Mark 6:45–52. In: Spencer, F. Scott (ed.), *Mixed Feelings and Vexed Passions: Exploring Emotions in Biblical Literature*. SBLRBS 90. Atlanta, GA: SBL Press, 243–263.

Vermès, Géza. 1967. The Use of *bar nash / bar nasha* in Jewish Aramaic. In: Black, Matthew (ed.), *An Aramaic Approach to the Gospels and Acts*. Oxford: Clarendon Press, 310–330.

Vermès, Géza; Volker Hampel. 1993. *Jesus der Jude: Ein Historiker liest die Evangelien*. Neukirchen-Vluyn: Neukirchener Verlag.

Vlahogiannis, Nicholas. 1998. Disabeling Bodies. In: Montserrat, Dominic (ed.), *Changing Bodies, Changing Meanings: Studies on the Human Body in Antiquity*. London/ New York: Routledge, 13–35.

Voelz, James W. 2013. *Mark 1:1–8:26*. Concordia Commentary Series. Saint Louis, MO: Concordia Publishing.

Völkel, Martin. 2010. καθεύδω. In: *Exegetisches Wörterbuch zum Neuen Testament 2*, Stuttgart: Kohlhammer, 544–545.

von Bendemann, Reinhard. 2005. Auditus et Testamentum – Die Heilung des Tauben/Stummen in der Dekapolis (Mk 7,31–37). In: Härle, Wilfried/ Reiner Preul (eds.), *Systematisch praktisch: FS für Reiner Preul zum 65. Geburtstag*. Marburg: N.G. Elwert, 55–69.

von Bendemann, Reinhard. 2006. "Many-coloured Illnesses" (Mark 1.34) – On the Significance of Illnesses in New Testament Therapy Narratives. In: Labahn, Michael/ L. J. Lietaert Peerbolte (eds.), *Wonders Never Cease. The Purpose of Narrating Miracle Stories in the New Testament and its Religious Environment*. London/ New York: T&T Clark, 100–124.

von Bendemann, Reinhard. 2007. Christus der Arzt. Krankheitskonzeptionen in den Therapieerzählungen des Markusevangeliums. In: Pichler, Josef/ Christoph Heil (eds.), *Heilungen und Wunder: Theologische, historische und medizinische Zugänge*. Darmstadt: Wissenschaftliche Buchgesellschaft, 105–130.

von Bendemann, Reinhard. 2009. Krankheit in neutestamentlicher Sicht: Ansätze – Perspektiven – Aporien. In: Thomas, Günter/ Isolde Karle (eds.), *Krankheitsdeutung in der postsäkularen Gesellschaft: Theologische Ansätze im interdisziplinären Gespräch*. Stuttgart: Kohlhammer, 163–185.

von Bendemann, Reinhard. 2010. "Christus der Arzt. Krankheitskonzeptionen in den Therapieerzählungen des Markusevangeliums (erweiterte Fassung)." *BZ* Teil 1 54/1; Teil 2 54/2: 36–53, 162–178.

von Bendemann, Reinhard. 2011. Die Latinismen im Markusevangelium. In: Janssen, Martina/ F. Stanley Jones/ Jürgen Wehnert (eds.), *Frühes Christentum und Religionsgeschichtliche Schule: FS G. Lüdemann*. NTOA 95. Göttingen: Vandenhoeck & Ruprecht, 37–52.

von Bendemann, Reinhard. 2013. Sehen und Verstehen Mk 8,22–26. In: Zimmermann, Ruben (ed.), *Kompendium der frühchristlichen Wundererzählungen: Die Wunder Jesu*. Gütersloh: Gütersloher Verlags-Haus, 341–349.

von Bendemann, Reinhard. 2014. Elementar feurige Hitze. Krankheitshermeneutik frühjüdischer, hellenistisch-römischer und frühchristlicher Fieberheilungen. In: Kollmann, Bernd/ Ruben Zimmermann (eds.), *Hermeneutik der frühchristlichen Wundererzählungen: Geschichtliche, literarische und rezeptionsorientierte Perspektiven*. WUNT 339. Tübingen: Mohr Siebeck, 231–262.

von der Osten-Sacken, Peter. 2010. κρατέω. In: *Exegetisches Wörterbuch zum Neuen Testament 2*, Stuttgart: Kohlhammer, 776–778.

Voorwinde, Stephen. 2011. *Jesus' Emotions in the Gospels*. London: T&T Clark.
Wächter, Theodor von. 1910. *Reinheitsvorschriften im griechischen Kult*. Religionsgeschichtliche Versuche und Vorarbeiten 9.1. Giessen: A. Töpelmann.
Wagenvoort, Hendrik. 1957. Contactus. In: *RAC* 3, Stuttgart: Hiersemann, 404–421.
Wagner, Andreas. 2008. Körperbegriffe als Stellvertreterausdrücke der Person in den Psalmen. In: Wagner, Andreas (ed.), *Beten und Bekennen. Über Psalmen*. Neukirchen-Vluyn: Neukirchener, 289–317.
Wahlen, Clinton. 2004. *Jesus and the Impurity of Spirits in the Synoptic Gospels*. WUNT 2.185. Tübingen: Mohr Siebeck.
Wainwright, Elaine Mary. 2006. *Women Healing/ Healing Women: The Genderization of Healing in Early Christianity*. BibleWorld. London: Equinox Pub. Ltd.
Wainwright, Elaine Mary. 2013. Of Dogs and Women: Ethology and Gender in Ancient Healing. In: Alkier, Stefan/ Annette Weissenrieder (eds.), *Miracles Revisited: New Testament Miracle Stories and their Concepts of Reality*. Studies of the Bible and Its Reception 2. Berlin: de Gruyter, 55–69.
Waldschmidt, Anne. 2010. Warum und wozu brauchen Disability Studies die Disability History? Programmatische Überlegungen. In: Bösl, Elsbeth/ Anne Klein/ Anne Waldschmidt (eds.), *Disability History: Konstruktionen von Behinderung in der Geschichte. Eine Einführung*. Disability Studies. Bielefeld: transcript, 13–27.
Waldschmidt, Anne. 2018. "Disability – Culture – Society: Strengths and Weaknesses of a Cultural Model of Dis/ability." *Alter. European Journal of Disability Research* 12.2: 65–78.
Wanke, G. 1981. Dämonen (böse Geister) II. Altes Testament. In: *Theologische Realenzyklopädie* 8, Berlin: de Gruyter, 275–277.
Wassen, Cecilia. 2008. Jesus and the Hemorrhaging Woman in Mark 5:24–34: Insights from Purity Laws from the Dead Sea Scrolls. In: Voitila, Anssi/ Jutta Jokiranta (eds.), *Essays on Septuagint, Hebrew Bible, and Dead Sea Scrolls in Honour of Raija Sollamo*. Supplements to the Journal for the Study of Judaism 126. Leiden: Brill, 641–660.
Wassen, Cecilia. 2008. What do Angels Have against the Blind and the Deaf? Rules of Exclusion in the Dead Sea Scrolls. In: McCready, Wayne O./ Adele Reinhartz (eds.), *Common Judaism: Explorations in Second-Temple Judaism*. Minneapolis, MN: Fortress Press, 115–129.
Wassen, Cecilia. 2016. Jesus' Work as a Healer in Light of Jewish Purity Laws. In: Kalimi, Isaac (ed.), *Bridging between Sister Religions: Studies of Jewish and Christian Scriptures Offered in Honor of Prof. John T. Townsend*. The Brill Reference Library of Judaism 51. Leiden/ Boston, MA: Brill, 87–104.
Watson, David F. 2018. "Questiones Disputatae: Roman Faith and Christian Faith." *NTS* 64: 243–261.
Webb, Robert L. 2006. "Jesus Heals a Leper: Mark 1.40–45 and Egerton Gospel 35–47." *Journal for the Study of the Historical Jesus* 4.2: 177–202.
Weeden, Theodore J. 1971. *Mark: Traditions in Conflict*. Philadelphia, PA: Fortress Press.
Weinreich, Otto. 1909. *Antike Heilungswunder: Untersuchungen zum Wunderglauben der Griechen und Römer*. Religionsgeschichtliche Versuche und Vorarbeiten 8.1. Giessen: Töpelmann.
Weinreich, Otto. 1929. *Gebet und Wunder: 2 Abhandlungen zur Religions- und Literaturgeschichte*. Stuttgart: Kohlhammer.
Weiser, Alfons. 1993. *Theologie des Neuen Testaments 2: Die Theologie des Evangelien*. Kohlhammer Studienbücher Theologie 8. Stuttgart: Kohlhammer.
Weiss, Bernhard. 1872. *Das Marcusevangelium und seine synoptischen Parallelen*. Berlin: Wilhelm Hertz.
Weiß, Konrad. 1959. πυρέσσω, πυρετός. In: *Theologisches Wörterbuch zum Neuen Testament* 6, Stuttgart: Kohlhammer, 956–959.

Weissenrieder, Annette. 2002. Die Plage der Unreinheit? – Das antike Krankheitskonstrukt "Blutfluss" in Lk 8,43–48. In: Stegemann, Wolfgang/ Bruce J. Malina/ Gerd Theissen (eds.), *Jesus in neuen Kontexten*. Stuttgart: Kohlhammer, 75–85.

Weissenrieder, Annette. 2003. *Images of Illness in the Gospel of Luke: Insights of Ancient Medical Texts*. WUNT 2.164. Tübingen: Mohr Siebeck.

Weissenrieder, Annette. 2010. The Didactics of Images: The Fig-Tree in Mark 11:12–14, 20–21. In: Weissenrieder, Annette/ Robert B. Coote (eds.), *The Interface of Orality and Writing: Speaking, Seeing, Writing in the Shaping of new Genres*. WUNT 260. Tübingen: Mohr Siebeck, 260–282.

Weissenrieder, Annette. 2013. Der verdorrte Feigenbaum und das Bittgebet (Die Verfluchung eines Feigenbaums). In: Zimmermann, Ruben (ed.), *Kompendium der frühchristlichen Wundererzählungen: Die Wunder Jesu*. Gütersloh: Gütersloher Verlags-Haus, 503–510.

Weissenrieder, Annette. 2013. Stories Just Under the Skin: lepra in the Gospel of Luke. In: Alkier, Stefan/ Annette Weissenrieder (eds.), *Miracles Revisited: New Testament Miracle Stories and their Concepts of Reality*. Studies of the Bible and its Reception 2. Berlin: de Gruyter, 73–100.

Weissenrieder, Annette. 2022 [2017]. Jesus's Healings. In: Schröter, Jens/ Christine Jacobi (eds.), *The Jesus Handbook*. Grand Rapids, MI: William B. Eerdmans Publishing, 294–307.

Weissenrieder, Annette; Katrin Dolle. 2019. *Körper und Verkörperung: Biblische Anthropologie im Kontext antiker Medizin und Philosophie: Ein Quellenbuch für die Septuaginta und das Neue Testament*. Fontes et Subsidia ad Bibliam pertinentes 8. Berlin: de Gruyter.

Wellhausen, Julius. 1905. *Einleitung in die drei ersten Evangelien*. Berlin: G. Reimer.

Wells, Louise. 1998. *The Greek Language of Healing from Homer to New Testament Times*. BZNW 83. Berlin: de Gruyter.

Wendling, Emil. 1905. *Ur-Marcus: Versuch einer Wiederherstellung der Ältesten Mitteilungen über das Leben Jesu*. Tübingen: J.C.B. Mohr (Paul Siebeck).

Wenham, Gordon J. 1979. *The Book of Leviticus*. The New International Commentary on the Old Testament 3. Grand Rapids, MI: William B. Eerdmans Publishing.

Wiedemann, Alfred. 1905. *Magie und Zauberei im alten Ägypten*. Der alte Orient 6.4. Leipzig: Hinrichs.

Wilder, Amos N. 1964. *Early Christians Rhetoric: The Language of the Gospel*. London: SCM Press.

Wilhelm, Dorothee. 1998. "Wer heilt hier wen? Und vor allem: Wovon? Über biblische Heilungsgeschichten und andere Ärgernisse." *Schlangenbrut* 62: 10–12.

Wilkinson, John. 1978. "Leprosy and Leviticus: A Problem of Semantics and Translation." *SJT* 31: 153–166.

Willebrand, Martin. 2017. "Markus mit narratologischer Brille gelesen. Beobachtungen und Deutungsperspektiven zur Erzählerinstanz in Mk 7,31–37 und 8,22–26, Teil 1 und 2." *Biblische Notizen* 172–173: 65–86, 105–138.

Williams, Joel F. 1994. *Other Followers of Jesus: Minor Characters as Major Figures in Mark's Gospel*. Sheffield: Marquette University.

Williams, Joel F. 2018. The Characterization of the Demons in Mark's Gospel. In: Broadhead, Edwin Keith (ed.), *Let the Reader Understand: Essays in Honor of Elizabeth Struthers Malbon*. The Library of New Testament Studies 583. London: Bloomsbury, 103–118.

Williams, Peter J. 2012. "An Examination of Ehrman's Case for ὀργισθείς in Mark 1:41." *NovT* 54.1: 1–12.

Williamson, H. G. M. 1994. *The Book Called Isaiah: Deutero-Isaiah's Role in Composition and Redaction*. Oxford: Clarendon Press.

Wilson, Robert R. 1979. "The Hardening of Pharaoh's Heart." *CBQ* 41.1: 18–36.

Winter, Martin. 2005. "Jesu Weg und der Weg der Jünger: Zur literarischen und theologischen Bedeutung des Weges im Markusevangelium." *Wort und Dienst* 28: 73–88.

Wittern, Renate. 1989. "Die Wechselfieber bei Galen." *History and Philosophy of the Life Sciences* 11: 3–22.

Wohlers, Michael. 1999a. *Heilige Krankheit: Epilepsie in antiker Medizin, Astrologie und Religion.* Marburger theologische Studien 57. Marburg: N.G. Elwert.

Wohlers, Michael. 1999b. "'Aussätzige reinigt' (Mt 10,8): Aussatz in antiker Medizin, Judentum und frühem Christentum. In: Maser, Stefan/ Egbert Schlarb (eds.), *Text und Geschichte: Facetten theologischen Arbeitens aus dem Freundes- und Schülerkreis: Dieter Lührmann zum 60. Geburtstag.* Marburg: N.G. Elwert, 294–304.

Wolter, Michael. 2008. *Das Lukasevangelium.* Handbuch zum Neuen Testament 5. Tübingen: Mohr Siebeck.

Wrede, William. 1963 [1901]. *Das Messiasgeheimnis in den Evangelien. Zugleich ein Beitrag zum Verständnis des Markusevangeliums.* 3rd ed. Göttingen: Vandenhoeck & Ruprecht.

Wright, David P. 1987. *The Disposal of Impurity: Elimination Rites in the Bible and in Hittite and Mesopotamian Literature.* SBLDS 101. Atlanta, GA: Scholars Press.

Wright, David P.; R. N. Jones. 1992. Discharge. In: *ABD* 2, New York: Doubleday, 204–207.

Wynn, Kerry H. 2007. "Johannine Healings and the Otherness of Disability." *PRSt* 34.1: 61–75.

Yong, Amos. 2007. *Theology and Down Syndrome: Reimagining Disability in Late Modernity.* Studies in Religion, Theology, and Disability. Waco, TX: Baylor University Press.

Yong, Amos. 2011. *The Bible, Disability, and the Church: A New Vision of the People of God.* Grand Rapids, MI: William B. Eerdmans Publishing.

York, George. 2005. "The 'Falling-Down Disease' – Epilepsy First Described in Ancient Babylonia." *Neurology Today* 5.10: 33–34, 37.

Zelyck, Lorne R. 2019. *The Egerton Gospel (Egerton Papyrus 2 + Papyrus Köln VI 255): Introduction, Critical Edition, and Commentary.* Texts and Editions for New Testament Study 13. Leiden: Brill.

Zerwick, Max. 1937. *Untersuchungen zum Markus-Stil: Ein Beitrag zur stilistischen Durcharbeitung des Neuen Testaments.* Scripta Pontificii Instituti Biblici. Rome: Romae Pontificio Instituto Biblico.

Zimmermann, Christiane. 2007. *Die Namen des Vaters: Studien zu ausgewählten neutestamentlichen Gottesbezeichnungen vor ihrem frühjüdischen und paganen Sprachhorizont.* Ancient Judaism and Early Christianity. Leiden: Brill.

Zimmermann, Ruben. 2001. *Geschlechtermetaphorik und Gottesverhältnis: Traditionsgeschichte und Theologie eines Bildfelds in Urchristentum und antiker Umwelt.* WUNT 2.122. Tübingen: Mohr Siebeck.

Zimmermann, Ruben. 2009. Krankheit und Sünde im Neuen Testament am Beispiel von Mk 2,1–12. In: Thomas, Günter/ Isolde Karle (eds.), *Krankheitsdeutung in der postsäkularen Gesellschaft: theologische Ansätze im interdisziplinären Gespräch.* Stuttgart: Kohlhammer, 227–246.

Zimmermann, Ruben (ed.). 2013. *Kompendium der frühchristlichen Wundererzählungen: Die Wunder Jesu.* Gütersloh: Gütersloher Verlags-Haus.

Zmijewski, Josef. 2010. ἀσθενής and cogn. In: *Exegetisches Wörterbuch zum Neuen Testament* 1, Stuttgart: Kohlhammer, 408–413.

Zwiep, Arie W. 2019. *Jairus's Daughter and the Haemorrhaging Woman. Tradition and Interpretation of an Early Christian Miracle Story.* WUNT 421. Tübingen: Mohr Siebeck.

Index

Andrew 70, 105, 111
anointment 39f., 42, 83
Aretaeus 83, 114, 132, 240
Aristotle 44, 73, 114, 117, 197, 203, 224, 226, 228
Asclepius 27, 73, 90, 92, 167, 181, 255

baptism 51, 63, 65, 152
Bartimaeus 31, 95, 123, 178, 180, 221–223, 227, 229f., 247–251, 255, 259, 264f.
basileia 31, 33, 51, 61, 124f., 143, 145
Beelzebul 61, 146
behavior / conduct 3, 13, 30, 37, 39, 48, 51, 54, 56, 58, 60, 64–66, 71, 88, 107, 109f., 112, 122–125, 134, 145, 148–151, 154, 167, 186, 190f., 227, 232, 234, 241, 244, 261f.
Bethsaida 42, 141, 214, 216f.
binary 9, 18f., 45, 144f., 168, 180, 184, 206, 213f., 253, 255f., 264
blood 17, 35f., 38, 45, 59, 84, 86, 89, 94, 105, 117, 119, 131f., 167f., 170–172, 174f., 180, 183f., 199, 204, 238, 240, 248, 259, 263, 265
– bleeding 74, 159, 166, 168–173
– hemorrhage 161–163, 168, 174, 181, 183f., 208

Capernaum 21, 27f., 42, 49, 51f., 70, 80f., 109, 111, 123, 128, 147, 217, 221, 257
Celsus 30, 74, 83, 115, 117, 132, 167, 200f., 224f., 239–241
cleansing 39, 59, 63, 82f., 85–89, 95–97, 100, 118, 168f., 171, 174
– καθαίρω 86
– καθαρίζω 83, 86, 88, 95–97, 172
commission 27, 29, 32, 41f., 50, 67, 82, 91, 188
Corpus Hippocraticum 30, 73f., 76, 85f., 114, 132, 199, 239, 243
creation 10, 15, 17f., 92, 138f., 141–145, 208f., 212f., 229, 256, 265
crowd 21, 22, 24f., 27, 33–35, 38, 40, 43f., 48f., 68f., 81, 88, 98, 101, 103, 105, 107f., 110f., 127, 135, 160, 162, 166, 177f., 181f., 186, 188, 194, 196, 202f., 206f., 215, 218, 220–223, 231–233, 244, 247, 250f., 260f.
cult 10, 13, 84, 87, 92, 148, 166, 168–170, 172, 174, 180, 226, 235

Decapolis 20, 157, 195, 214
dis/ability invective 5, 60, 124, 127f., 142, 145, 209, 212, 254–256, 261, 266
discipleship 51f., 72, 157, 178, 181, 214, 219, 222, 230, 247, 250, 252, 254f., 258, 265
– disciples 8, 16, 23, 25, 27–29, 32–35, 38f., 41f., 44, 47–52, 63, 67, 70, 82, 98, 101–103, 109, 123, 126, 129, 133, 135, 138, 146, 148, 162, 175, 177–179, 181, 186–188, 194f., 207, 209, 216, 218–221, 223, 231, 233, 238, 241, 245–247, 250–252, 254f., 257–259

emotion 8, 53, 69, 85, 89, 96–99, 114, 124, 130, 135, 156, 158, 162, 173, 175, 177, 205, 207, 218, 248, 259
Epidauros 90, 117, 132, 177, 217, 240
epithet *see title*
eschatology 10, 15, 17f., 45, 59, 62, 68, 80, 102, 116, 120f., 123–128, 134, 141–145, 165f., 174, 179–181, 184, 186, 208–210, 212f., 217, 229f., 245, 252, 254–256, 259f., 265f.
ethnicity 4, 147, 152, 170, 189–191, 193–195
etiology 2, 10, 30f., 36, 60, 66, 73, 75–77, 81, 84, 87, 95, 108, 113–116, 125, 151, 171f., 191, 199, 201, 233, 237, 239–241, 262

Flavius Josephus *see Josephus*
forgiveness 17, 23, 85, 110–112, 118–123, 125–128, 138, 144, 178, 204, 211, 259, 265

Galen 72, 74, 83, 86, 90, 113f., 117, 132f., 164, 171, 200f., 203f., 224, 240
Galilee 20, 28, 32, 48, 52f., 72, 81, 104, 108, 137, 188f.
Sea of Galilee 17, 33, 35, 42, 49, 146f., 160, 194f.

gender   3f., 71, 74, 76, 105, 194
Gentile   147, 189f., 192–194

Halakha   135–137, 140–142, 145, 179, 265
Hippocratic Corpus   see *Corpus Hippocraticum*
holy spirit   55, 61–63, 91, 98

Jaïrus   23, 35, 50, 71, 78f., 91, 102, 105, 160–165, 167f., 172, 174–177, 182–185, 193–195, 202, 221, 264
Jerusalem   33, 87, 106, 108f., 117, 124, 127, 188, 214f., 218, 221
John the Baptist   31f., 42, 51, 78, 82, 103, 188
Josephus   40, 44, 56, 58f., 61, 75, 84f., 87, 92, 94, 123, 126, 133, 140, 147, 153–156, 164, 170, 176, 198, 225, 229, 231, 244

Leviticus   87, 89, 96f., 170, 175
liminality   101, 104, 106–108, 147f., 150, 157–159, 172, 185, 214, 216, 221, 260f., 263

marginalization   1, 17, 66, 81, 107, 115, 149f., 152, 159, 199, 260f., 263
ministry   5, 16–18, 20f., 24f., 27–29, 31–33, 38, 42, 48, 51f., 60, 63, 66, 69, 72, 81, 90, 98f., 103f., 106, 109, 116, 121, 125f., 135, 141, 144, 146, 148, 151, 181, 186–189, 192f., 195, 207–210, 214, 216, 221, 247, 250, 252f., 255–258, 261–266
Mosaic law   82f., 86, 97
Moses   53, 84f., 92, 134

narrative prosthesis   8, 69, 125, 145
Nazareth   32, 38, 40, 49, 51, 53, 65, 152, 249f.

ostracism   88, 100, 132

passion   12, 18, 38, 64, 80, 99, 102, 128, 173, 178, 204f., 209, 213–215, 219, 230, 241, 243–245, 247, 250, 252, 254, 256–259, 262, 265, 267
pathologization   2, 17, 64, 146, 166f., 172, 186, 256, 264, 266
Pharisees   25, 105, 109, 129f., 137–140, 188, 205
Philo   56, 58–60, 75, 83f., 86, 114, 133, 153, 168, 179, 204, 224, 228f.

prayer   18, 59, 75, 77f., 91f., 119, 151, 176, 178, 200, 205, 220, 240, 243, 245–247, 251
preaching   27–33, 39, 41f., 50, 66, 99, 266
priest   84–86, 90, 100, 117, 119, 126, 166
prophet   25, 59, 90, 94, 119
purity   18, 36, 41, 55, 58–60, 63, 76, 83–90, 95–97, 99–101, 107f., 111, 140, 147f., 150, 158f., 166, 168–170, 172, 174f., 182, 184f., 188, 190f., 204, 211, 214, 235f., 239, 241, 258, 264

Qumran   13, 58f., 87, 136, 153, 169

rabbinic literature   13, 58f., 75, 87f., 117, 122f., 129, 135–138, 140, 165, 167, 169, 199, 203

Sabbath   17, 21, 23, 27, 37, 52, 58, 69f., 81, 100, 104, 107, 109, 111, 119f., 126, 128f., 130f., 133, 135–140, 142–144, 179, 258, 260, 264–266
saliva   86, 201–204, 240, 242, 251
Satan   51, 57, 59–64, 146, 156
– σατανᾶς   57, 61f.
scribes   61, 63, 105, 109–112, 119, 122, 125f., 177, 188, 218, 247
Second Temple Judaism   7, 86, 88f., 92, 170, 224
silence   7, 12, 16, 23, 28, 30, 32f., 37f., 47, 49, 53, 64–69, 81f., 97, 99–104, 107, 109–112, 125f., 130, 133, 135, 144, 152, 163, 172, 182, 185f., 191, 196, 201, 206f., 222, 232f., 241, 248, 251, 253, 261
Simon Peter   21, 70, 72, 76–78, 80f., 101, 105, 111, 114, 116, 132, 162, 164, 168, 175, 218, 221, 254
sin   17, 23, 84, 87f., 91, 109, 111f., 115, 119f., 122–128, 134, 138, 144f., 178f., 225, 259f., 265f.
Son of Man   72, 103, 119–121, 125, 127, 138, 145, 178, 182, 249, 259
speech   23, 37, 52, 54, 56, 65–68, 81f., 98, 103, 108, 111, 121f., 126, 129–131, 142, 148f., 151, 154f., 166, 179, 190f., 196–201, 206, 208, 212, 215, 217–219, 222, 232, 235f., 238, 243, 251, 254
stigma   4f., 7, 15, 60, 85–88, 93, 100f., 107, 117f., 124, 132, 148, 169f., 172, 239, 260f.

synagogue 28, 32, 51f., 54, 69f., 81, 87, 104f., 128, 130, 135, 140, 144, 147, 151, 164, 257
Syrophoenician 17, 20, 23, 33, 105, 168, 188–195

teaching 11, 16, 27–29, 32f., 40f., 44, 50–54, 63, 68f., 100, 103–107, 109–111, 116, 121, 123, 125f., 128, 135, 140, 142f., 145f., 188, 196, 199, 205, 207f., 211–215, 218, 220, 247, 250, 252, 254f., 257f., 260, 265f.

– teacher 50–52, 107, 109, 226, 249f., 259, 261
temptation 44, 51, 60, 62f.
title 37f., 53, 61, 120, 138, 152f., 164, 192, 244, 248f.
– epithet 119f., 126f., 138, 153
Tora 60, 129f., 138
Tosefta 87

Index of Biblical and Ancient Sources

Old Testament/ Hebrew Bible
- Genesis
  - 1:31$^{(LXX)}$ 18, 143, 208, 212, 265
  - 6:1–4 58
  - 12:17 92

- Exodus
  - 4:6–7 90
  - 4:7$^{(LXX)}$ 141
  - 4:21–14:17 134
  - 17:11–12 94

- Leviticus
  - 12:7$^{(LXX)}$ 168
  - 13–14 84
  - 13–15 168
  - 13:16$^{(LXX)}$ 89, 141
  - 14 97
  - 15$^{(LXX)}$ 168
  - 15:25–30$^{(LXX)}$ 169
  - 26:16$^{(LXX)}$ 74

- Numeri
  - 5:1–3$^{(LXX)}$ 169
  - 12 84
  - 12:4–6 90
  - 15:38–39 46

- Deuteronomy
  - 22:12 46
  - 28:22$^{(LXX)}$ 74 f.

- 1 Samuel
  - 21:1–7 138

- 2 Samuel
  - 3:29$^{(LXX)}$ 170

- 1 Kings
  - 13:4–6/3Kgdms 13:4–6 131
  - 17:17–24 94

- 2 Kings
  - 4:18–37 94
  - 5 84
  - 5:8–14 90
  - 5:11/4Kgdms 5:11$^{(LXX)}$ 91
  - 13:20–21 94

- Job
  - 5:18^{LXX} 141

- Psalms
  - 37:18$^{(LXX)}$ 172

- Isaiah
  - 35:5–6$^{(LXX)}$ 18, 208, 212, 265
  - 35:6$^{(LXX)}$ 198

- Jeremiah
  - 5:21 210, 254

- Zechariah
  - 13:2$^{(LXX)}$ 59

- Malachi
  - 3:23$^{(LXX)}$ 141

Dead Sea Scrolls
- 1Q20 / 1QapGen^{ar}
  - 20.28–29 92

Old Testament Pseudepigrapha
- Testament of Simeon
  - 2:12–13 141

- Testament of Solomon
  - 7:3 203

New Testament
- Matthew
  - 4 57
  - 4:24 113
  - 7:5 228
  - 8:2–4 82

- 8:6 113
- 8:14-15 75
- 9:1-8 113
- 9:32-33 201
- 9:33 197
- 9:38 98
- 10:8 83, 88
- 11:5 82
- 12:13 141
- 12:22 197
- 14:14 39
- 15:31 197
- 17:11 141
- 17:15 237
- 18:8 116
- 23:5 46
- 26:6 83

- Mark
  - 1 16, 51-108, 144f., 186, 188, 256-258, 261, 263
  - 1-3 158, 257, 262
  - 1:1 103, 107, 119
  - 1:2-3 107
  - 1:2-14 188
  - 1:4 31f., 103
  - 1:7 31f., 51, 62, 103
  - 1:7-8 107
  - 1:8 57, 62, 126
  - 1:9 51, 53, 65
  - 1:9-11 107
  - 1:10 62, 126, 204
  - 1:10-11 65
  - 1:10-12 57
  - 1:11 37, 67, 103, 119, 211, 249
  - 1:12 62, 98, 126
  - 1:12-13 57, 62, 235
  - 1:13 57
  - 1:14 32, 103
  - 1:14-15 31, 51, 61, 110f.
  - 1:15 143, 185, 259
  - 1:16 52, 195
  - 1:16-18 250
  - 1:16-20 51, 70, 157
  - 1:19-20 250
  - 1:21 21, 52, 104
  - 1:21-22 22, 110
  - 1:21-27 32, 111
  - 1:21-28 28f., 31, 33, 37, 41, 52-69, 126, 128, 149, 152, 191f., 232
  - 1:21-39 52
  - 1:21-31 111
  - 1:21-38 111
  - 1:22 53, 61, 109, 111f., 126, 211
  - 1:23 52, 55, 104, 233, 235, 238, 252
  - 1:23-24 52, 56, 234
  - 1:23-28 16, 99, 244
  - 1:23-31 252
  - 1:24 28, 51, 63, 65, 119, 152, 192, 248f.
  - 1:24-25 32, 192, 248
  - 1:25 100f., 211, 244, 252
  - 1:25-26 52, 121
  - 1:26 55, 65f., 76, 191, 235-237, 252
  - 1:27 52, 55, 58, 61, 68, 104, 112, 126, 252
  - 1:27-28 61, 144, 157
  - 1:28 52, 69, 164
  - 1:29 52, 104, 111, 128
  - 1:29-31 28, 70-81, 121, 162
  - 1:29-32 105
  - 1:30 221
  - 1:30-31 16, 99, 252
  - 1:31 22, 36, 69, 78f., 80, 90, 93, 107, 121, 244
  - 1:32 23, 26, 48, 110, 233
  - 1:32-34 15, 20-31, 33, 37, 42, 44-49, 60, 66, 67, 99, 110f., 149, 262
  - 1:33 110, 164
  - 1:34 12, 20-33, 37, 39, 42, 44, 52, 58, 65, 68, 101, 135, 234, 244
  - 1:35 205
  - 1:35-38 28
  - 1:37 164
  - 1:38 28, 31, 33
  - 1:38-39 31f., 51, 103
  - 1:39 15, 20, 27-33, 39, 47, 49f., 52f., 58, 61, 104, 111, 128, 164
  - 1:40-42 83, 118
  - 1:40-44 83, 96, 111
  - 1:40-45 16, 32f., 81-106, 109-111, 172, 174, 211, 246, 248, 252, 260
  - 1:41 36, 90, 93, 118, 205
  - 1:41-42 121
  - 1:42 118
  - 1:44 32, 67, 83, 96f., 101, 217, 248
  - 1:44-45 102, 207

– 1:45 23, 32, 69, 82, 100, 103, 106 f., 110, 157, 164, 177
– 2 116, 120, 125, 142
– 2–3 100, 186, 208, 252, 257, 261, 265
– 2:1 33, 110 f., 128
– 2:1–12 16 f., 40, 45, 105, 109–130, 140, 142, 144, 177 f., 259, 265
– 2:1–20 95
– 2:1–3:6 16 f., 33, 109–146, 188
– 2:2 22, 110 f.
– 2:3 110
– 2:3–4 111
– 2:3–5 111
– 2:4 44
– 2:5 41, 110 f., 119, 121, 125, 177, 211, 246 f., 252, 265
– 2:6 22, 110, 134
– 2:6–7 144
– 2:6–9 177
– 2:6–10 111
– 2:7 120, 246, 262
– 2:8 111, 126, 134, 163
– 2:9 44, 78 f., 80, 107, 110, 121, 211
– 2:10 126, 138
– 2:10–11 121
– 2:11 44, 78–80, 107, 110 f., 121, 211, 217, 248
– 2:11–12 80, 110 f.
– 2:12 44, 53, 69, 107, 110, 112, 144, 157
– 2:13–17 109
– 2:14 250
– 2:16 111, 144
– 2:17 26, 76
– 2:18 144
– 2:18–22 109
– 2:19 130
– 2:20 109, 127
– 2:21–38 111
– 2:22 236
– 2:23 129
– 2:23–28 109, 128 f., 135–141, 144, 249, 265
– 2:24 129, 144
– 2:26 129
– 2:27 139
– 2:27–28 126
– 2:28 120, 138
– 2:29 211
  3 126, 128, 139
– 3:1 104, 110 f., 131, 139, 233, 238
– 3:1–6 16, 95, 104, 109, 128–145, 163, 229, 265
– 3:2 22, 26 f., 37, 39, 42, 110, 118, 144
– 3:3 78 f., 87, 107, 110, 121, 139
– 3:4 104, 110, 126, 129, 139, 179, 229
– 3:5 98, 110, 118 f., 134, 139, 205, 211, 229, 245, 254
– 3:6 69, 109, 120, 144, 187
– 3:7 44, 146
– 3:7–8 146, 189
– 3:7–10 30
– 3:7–11 164
– 3:7–12 15 f., 20, 28, 33–39, 45, 47–50, 109, 191
– 3:8 22, 189, 195
– 3:10 23, 26 f., 31, 36, 38 f., 42, 93, 110, 233
– 3:10–11 60
– 3:10–12 32, 36, 67
– 3:11 55, 65, 152, 234 f., 238, 249
– 3:11–12 23, 31, 65
– 3:12 68, 101 f., 244
– 3:13–19 146, 157
– 3:14 32, 103, 250
– 3:14–15 29, 32 f., 39, 42, 50, 53, 67, 245
– 3:15 27, 58, 126
– 3:20–22 146
– 3:20–30 61, 107
– 3:20–35 16, 57–64, 67, 246, 263
– 3:21 23
– 3:21–30 63 f., 66, 154
– 3:22 188, 233
– 3:22–23 27
– 3:22–30 158
– 3:23–27 62, 158
– 3:23–30 146
– 3:27 62 f., 152
– 3:28–30 62, 126
– 3:30 23, 55, 235
– 4:1–9 132
– 4:1–34 146
– 4:4 249
– 4:6 131
– 4:9 211
– 4:10–13 254
– 4:10–20 211
– 4:11–12 224

- 4:12 211
- 4:15 63, 146, 249
- 4:17 124
- 4:21 44
- 4:23 211
- 4:24 211
- 4:35 147
- 4:35-41 147, 156
- 4:35-42 186
- 4:35-5:43 181
- 4:38 249
- 4:39 37, 68, 211
- 4:39-40 177
- 4:40 177, 247
- 4:40-41 146
- 4:41 17, 159, 186, 262
- 5 17f., 36, 40, 146-188, 252, 257, 262f.
- 5:1-20 31-33, 57, 61-64, 67f., 89, 106, 146-159, 166, 190, 192, 232, 234, 244
- 5:1-21 106
- 5:2 55, 62, 147-149, 233, 235
- 5:3 62, 158
- 5:3-4 22
- 5:3-5 56
- 5:4 62, 158
- 5:4-5 191
- 5:5 22, 56, 65, 106, 238
- 5:6 232, 236
- 5:6-7 149
- 5:6-10 56, 191
- 5:7 37, 63, 65, 152, 155, 186, 192, 238, 241, 248f.
- 5:7-12 234
- 5:8 23, 55, 68, 147-149, 211
- 5:8-9 23
- 5:9 23
- 5:10 44, 155
- 5:10-13 192
- 5:11 22, 106
- 5:12 149, 155
- 5:13 22, 55, 147-149, 211, 235, 248
- 5:14 106, 123, 157
- 5:14-17 69
- 5:15 232
- 5:17 187, 189
- 5:18 44
- 5:18-19 250
- 5:19 107, 217, 246, 248, 252, 260
- 5:19-20 32, 104
- 5:20 23, 32, 69, 104, 195
- 5:21 162
- 5:21-43 40, 146, 159-185, 229, 250, 252, 259, 261, 265
- 5:21-24, 35-43 50, 89, 193, 232
- 5:22 161, 163, 221, 237
- 5:23 44, 79, 91, 167, 179f., 184, 202, 242
- 5:24 22, 35, 38, 162
- 5:25-29 162
- 5:25-26 168
- 5:25-29 162
- 5:25-34 36, 45f., 89, 194, 265
- 5:26 76, 162, 173
- 5:27 38, 94, 144, 161f., 174, 189
- 5:27-28 93, 177
- 5:27-34 38
- 5:28 23, 38, 94, 174, 179f.
- 5:28-30 137
- 5:29 27, 36, 118, 131, 172f.
- 5:29-30 181, 211
- 5:30 38, 94, 119, 161, 174, 180
- 5:30-31 93, 177f., 181, 261
- 5:30-32 163
- 5:31 35, 38, 94, 174, 162
- 5:32 161
- 5:33 37, 161f.
- 5:34 22, 36, 41, 107, 118, 161, 172f., 176f., 179f., 184, 217, 229, 247f., 264f.
- 5:34-36 162
- 5:35 161-163, 167, 184
- 5:35-43 50, 89, 105, 193, 232
- 5:36 163, 176f., 264f.
- 5:38 161-163
- 5:39 161, 167, 184, 264
- 5:40 22, 98, 161, 167, 184
- 5:41 78f., 93, 107, 118, 121, 167, 184, 206, 211, 244
- 5:41-42 22, 80
- 5:42 78, 80, 121, 157, 167, 184, 232
- 5:42-43 107
- 5:43 32, 67, 101, 162, 180, 207, 217
- 6:1-3 65
- 6:1-5 104
- 6:1-6 27, 40, 187
- 6:2 32, 41, 47, 104, 140, 181, 202, 211, 262

– 6:2–3 41, 69
– 6:3 40, 124, 262
– 6:4 40
– 6:5 15, 20, 26f., 37–42, 46f., 49f., 69, 91, 135, 140, 181, 188, 202, 242
– 6:5–6 23, 38f., 48, 176, 178
– 6:6 33, 40
– 6:6–34 187
– 6:7 29, 55, 126, 235, 245, 252
– 6:7–11 38
– 6:7–12 41
– 6:7–13 157
– 6:12 32, 103
– 6:12–13 29, 32f., 50, 53, 245, 252
– 6:13 15, 20, 23, 26f., 29, 37–42, 46–49, 135, 179, 188
– 6:14 79, 182
– 6:14–15 69
– 6:14–29 188
– 6:16 49
– 6:17 78
– 6:30 245, 252
– 6:31 106
– 6:32 106
– 6:34 98, 205
– 6:35 106
– 6:41 204f., 227
– 6:45 216
– 6:45–52 186
– 6:46 205
– 6:47–52 156
– 6:48 254
– 6:50 186
– 6:52 133, 254
– 6:53–56 15, 17, 20, 42–50, 188f., 212
– 6:54 44
– 6:55 22, 26, 43, 117, 233
– 6:56 23, 38, 48, 93, 106, 179f., 229
– 7 17f., 188–213, 251f., 257
– 7–10 262
– 7:1–23 188, 191, 204
– 7:17–23 207
– 7:4 44
– 7:5–6 188
– 7:14 188
– 7:15 188
– 7:17 188
– 7:17–18 254
– 7:18 188, 214
– 7:23 188
– 7:24 22, 217
– 7:24–30 17, 31, 64f., 67f., 152, 188–195, 232
– 7:24–37 188–213, 261
– 7:25 22, 37, 55, 190, 233, 235
– 7:26 27
– 7:27 170
– 7:27–28 23
– 7:29 248
– 7:29–30 22
– 7:30 44
– 7:31 91, 189
– 7:31–37 18, 32f., 45, 93, 195–212, 214, 216, 223, 242f., 261
– 7:32 44, 196, 202, 242
– 7:32–33 101
– 7:32–34 211f.
– 7:33 93, 197, 204, 242
– 7:33–35 206
– 7:34 118f., 196, 202, 211, 222, 227, 243
– 7:34–35 22, 197
– 7:35 119, 196f., 234, 242
– 7:36 22, 32, 67, 69, 196, 101f., 104, 157f., 207, 217
– 7:36–37 104, 112, 207, 212, 265
– 7:37 23, 53, 69, 119, 196f., 208f., 215, 252
– 8–10 18f., 80, 186, 214f., 252, 257, 261, 265
– 8:1 188
– 8:2 98, 205
– 8:4 106
– 8:10–13 214, 254
– 8:11–12 219
– 8:12 98, 205, 247
– 8:14–21 216, 254
– 8:15 214
– 8:17 133, 254
– 8:17–18 247
– 8:17–21 214
– 8:18 209, 211, 224, 254
– 8:21 254
– 8:22 44, 220, 230
– 8:22–23 91
– 8:22–26 18, 45, 106, 208, 214–217, 223–230, 242f., 251
– 8:23 91, 106, 203f., 224, 229

- 8:23–24 23, 227, 251
- 8:24 23, 223, 227, 229
- 8:25 22, 91, 93, 118, 141, 224, 228f., 245
- 8:26 32, 207, 223, 248
- 8:27 215, 250
- 8:27–30 214, 254
- 8:30 67, 101
- 8:31 120, 173, 186, 215, 219, 230, 245, 254
- 8:31–38 214, 219
- 8:33 37, 57, 63, 68
- 8:33–9:1 254
- 8:34 222, 250
- 8:34–35 181, 229f.
- 8:34–38 250
- 8:34–9:1 215
- 8:35 139
- 8:38 120, 247
- 9 55, 80, 125
- 9:1 181
- 9:1–13 103, 219
- 9:2–8 204, 218, 254
- 9:5 249
- 9:7 37, 103, 211, 249
- 9:9 67, 101, 106
- 9:9–10 245
- 9:9–13 218
- 9:10 245
- 9:12 141, 229, 245
- 9:12–13 254
- 9:14–17 222
- 9:14–29 18, 30f., 40, 45, 47, 57, 61, 64f., 67, 106, 152, 178, 190, 192f., 201, 214f., 217–220, 223, 230–241, 243–247, 251f., 259, 264
- 9:15 22f., 218
- 9:17 33, 55f., 234, 249
- 9:18 27, 131f.
- 9:18–22 56
- 9:19 178f.
- 9:20 55, 65, 218f., 232, 234, 237
- 9:22 56, 98, 205, 232, 252
- 9:22–24 247
- 9:23–24 176, 178, 265
- 9:24 251
- 9:25 37, 55, 68, 80, 211, 220, 234
- 9:26 65, 68, 167, 191, 237
- 9:26–27 167
- 9:27 78, 80, 93, 107, 121, 223
- 9:28 23, 27, 251
- 9:28–29 23, 220
- 9:29 205
- 9:30–32 215
- 9:31 173, 245
- 9:31–32 254
- 9:31–37 214
- 9:32 186, 230, 250
- 9:33 123, 215, 250
- 9:33–50 254
- 9:34 250
- 9:35 123
- 9:37 254
- 9:37–41 179
- 9:38 27, 249
- 9:38–39 247
- 9:38–40 47
- 9:39 181
- 9:42–48 17, 121–126, 144, 265
- 9:48–50 124
- 9:45 116
- 9:47 98, 211
- 10:1 222
- 10:5 133
- 10:14 98
- 10:17 249f.
- 10:17–22 250
- 10:18 254
- 10:20 249
- 10:21 228
- 10:25 118
- 10:27 228, 254
- 10:32 186, 215, 250
- 10:32–34 215, 230
- 10:32–45 214
- 10:33–34 254
 10:34 173, 245
- 10:35 249
- 10:36 223, 255, 264
- 10:41–45 254
- 10:46 22, 106, 230, 250f.
- 10:46–52 18, 31f., 95, 123, 208, 214, 220–224, 230, 247–252
- 10:47 53, 189
- 10:47–48 222, 252
- 10:48 177, 251
- 10:49 78f., 107, 121

- 10:49–50 222
- 10:51 33, 223, 227
- 10:52 22, 69, 106f., 118, 177–180, 215, 223, 227, 229, 247, 250, 265
- 11:1–11 249
- 11:15 98
- 11:20–21 131
- 11:20–25 132, 247
- 11:21 249
- 11:22–24 178f., 250
- 11:22–25 246
- 11:27–28 69
- 11:27–33 126
- 11:31 178, 250
- 12:8 98
- 12:14 249
- 12:19 249
- 12:24 182
- 12:26 79
- 12:32 249
- 12:35–37 249
- 12:39 128
- 13:1 249
- 13:9 128
- 13:9–13 255
- 13:10 32f., 103
- 13:26 182
- 13:34 126
- 14:1 78
- 14:3 83
- 14:5 97
- 14:9 32f., 103
- 14:14 39, 249
- 14:27 124
- 14:28 79
- 14:29 124
- 14:32–41 205
- 14:36 247
- 14:44 78
- 14:45 249
- 14:46 78
- 14:49 78
- 14:61 249
- 14:62 103, 182
- 14:62–64 120
- 14:67 53, 228, 248
- 15:19 152
- 15:39 103, 249
- 15:34 205
- 16:4 227
- 16:6 53, 65, 79, 248
- 16:8 103, 186, 250
- 16:9 16, 27
- 16:15 103
- 16:15–18 33, 50
- 16:16–18 179
- 16:17 27
- 16:20 103

– Luke
- 1:22 197
- 1:63 197
- 4 57
- 4:27 82
- 4:38–39 75
- 5:12–16 82
- 5:17–26 114
- 6:10 141
- 6:42 228
- 7:1–10 113
- 7:21 36
- 7:22 82
- 9:42 236
- 10:2 98
- 11:14 56, 197, 201
- 13:10–17 115
- 13:16 57
- 17:11–19 82f., 88
- 18:13 204
- 22:3 57

– John
- 4:46–54 75f.
- 5:3 113, 116
- 5:14 123
- 9:1–38 123
- 11:41–42 205
- 17:1 204

– Acts
- 1:6 141
- 3:2 116
- 5:12–16 94
- 6:6 94

– 7:55 204
– 8:7 114, 116
– 9:33 114
– 9:40 205
– 14:8 116
– 19:11–12 94
– 28:7–8 75f.
– 28:8 205

– Hebrews
 – 12:12 114
 – 12:12–13 116
 – 12:13 116

– James
 – 5:13–18 205
 – 5:14–15 39
 – 5:15–16 123

 – Revelation
 – 16:12 131

Rabbinic Works
– b. Baba Batra
 – 126b 203

– b. 'Arakin
 – 29a 87

– b. Sanhedrin
 – 101a 203

– m. Nega'im
 – 1–2 87
 – 1:1–2 87
 – 3:1 87, 97
 – 3:3 87
 – 4–8 87
 – 9–13 87
 – 13:12 87
 – 14 87
 – 14:2 87

– m. Šabbat
 – 7:2 137

– m. Kelim
 – 1:7 87

– t. Nega'im
 – 7:3 87

Papyri and Inscriptions
 – Papyrus Egerton 2 88
 – P.Mon.Gr. inv. 123 114

Greco-Roman Literature
 – Galen, De lociis affectis 4.9 200

www.ingramcontent.com/pod-product-compliance
Lightning Source LLC
Chambersburg PA
CBHW020221170426
43201CB00007B/275